The Systematization
of Russian Government

GEORGE L. YANEY

The Systematization of Russian Government

*Social Evolution in
the Domestic Administration
of Imperial Russia, 1711-1905*

University of Illinois Press
Urbana Chicago London

© 1973 by The Board of Trustees of the University of Illinois
Manufactured in the United States of America
Library of Congress Catalog Card No. 72–85613
ISBN 0–252–00248–2

To the Memory of
THURMAN ARNOLD
Comic Prophet

Acknowledgments

A number of people have given me support, guidance, and inspiration during the years this book was in preparation. I owe much to Aubrey Land, Walter Pintner, Richard Pipes, David Ransel, Edward Thaden, the late Nicholas Timasheff, and Theodore Von Laue. I am indebted to the Russian Research Center at Harvard University, the General Research Board of the University of Maryland, and the Inter-university Travel Grant Committee for their financial aid during my research and writing. The Graduate School at the University of Maryland has been generous in helping to meet the costs of publication. Lev Magerovsky of the Russian Archive at Columbia University, Frederick Arnold of the Princeton University Library, Mrs. Frances Woodruff of the University of Maryland Library, Armins Rusis and the late Vladimir Gsovsky of the Library of Congress, and Nina Matveevna Rossinnova of the Central State (Historical) Archive in Leningrad have all been very helpful to me in my research, as have the librarians and archivists in the Saltykov-Shchedrin Library in Leningrad, the Leningrad State University Library, and the Central State Archive of the October Revolution in Moscow. I wish to thank Mrs. Linda Edwards of the history department at the University of Maryland for her kind cooperation in getting the manuscript typed, and I am very grateful to my students Lillian Liu and Mark Steinberg for their aid in preparing and revising the manuscript. Finally, I would like to express my appreciation to Mrs. Bonnie Depp of the University of Illinois Press for her very thorough editorial work.

My wife, Ann, has done more than she knows to make this book possible.

Contents

ILLUSTRATIONS

Preface

When I began writing this book, I intended it to be a history of the agrarian reform that the tsarist government introduced into the peasant villages of European Russia in 1906–1914. This reform has intrigued me for some years, primarily because it represented a government's attempt to impose social change on its own people. The air is quite as filled now as it was then with talk about social change and the problems involved in bringing "modernness" to "backward" societies. Thus the record of an actual attempt to carry out such a change through administrative methods is of interest not only as a historical phenomenon but also as a source of practical wisdom in the present day, especially since the attempt was in many ways successful.[1]

As it turns out, I have written not an account of the agrarian reform but only a background to it. In order to introduce the history of the reform properly, I set out to describe the tsarist administrative organization as it was in 1905 on the eve of the reform, and this description has blossomed into the full-length book that now confronts the reader. Instead of discussing the reform itself, this book describes the government organization that was expected to carry it out.

Why such an elaborate background? Because it seems to me that the social change of 1906–1914 took place in both government administration and peasant society. It was not essentially an effect produced on the peasantry by the government's thinking and acting, as if the peasants were pieces in a game being played by the administrators. The government was not an engine designed to carry out decrees, nor was peasant society a number of parts to be assembled by all-knowing policy-makers and ideologues. Both government and peasantry were in essence societies, and the reform was in essence an interaction between them: a social interaction in which both played active roles and each felt the impact of the other. The reform represented a stage in a long history of interaction, and the government organization that enacted it and carried it out was in part the product

1. For a preliminary investigation of the agrarian reform along these lines, see George L. Yaney, "The Imperial Russian Government and the Stolypin Land Reform" (unpublished Ph.D. dissertation, Princeton University, 1961).

of this history. In order to comprehend the government organization of 1905, therefore, there must be some discussion of its prior inter-action with the peasantry.

There are already many scholarly works that touch on government-peasant interaction before 1905. A multitude of learned men have studied Russian peasant life,[2] and there are whole libraries full of books on the tsarist government's policies with regard to the peasants. Events in which government and peasantry come in contact with one another appear continually in historical descriptions. Despite all this scholarly production, however, government-peasant interaction has never been studied as a subject in itself. To my knowledge, it has never been conceived of as a mutually formative experience.[3]

Students of the peasantry have generally assumed that contact with the tsarist government brought them only oppression and corruption, which is to say that the government played no positive role in the evolution of peasant society. It "enslaved" the peasants, "enserfed" them, "impoverished" them, destroyed their "freedom," and so forth. Government never became an element in the peasant way of life but remained always one of the circumstances surrounding it: an evil force that afflicted the peasants from the outside, not a characteristic feature in their own attitudes and relationships.[4]

Students of government, on the other hand, have been inclined either to ignore peasant society entirely (e.g., N. M. Korkunov and N. I. Lazarevskii) or to see rural "backwardness" and "corruption" as nothing more than discrepancies in proper government operation and obstacles to "progress." In other words, they have viewed the peasantry as an external problem that the government has tried and should go on trying to solve. Typically, they describe peasant society in such terms as "absence of law," "lack of education," "undeveloped

2. A series of annotated bibliographies devoted to peasant custom was compiled in the period 1875–1909 by E. I. Iakushkin: *Obychnoe pravo* (4 vols., Iaroslavl, 1875, 1896; Moscow, 1908, 1909). Iakushkin listed all the books and articles he could find on Slavic peasants in the Russian Empire. They total over 6,000 works, of which about one-third had been published before 1875. He covered the non-Slavic peoples of the empire in two additional volumes that came out in the 1890s, each listing over a thousand works.

3. See, however, K. D. Kavelin, *Krestianskii vopros* (St. Petersburg, 1882), pp. 3–6, 19–30. Kavelin mentions the possibility of such a concept, though he does not see its implications. See, e.g., p. 198.

4. The assumption underlying virtually all anthropological studies of the peasants is that village societies can and should be viewed as if they had been isolated from government influence throughout their development. In all the fifty-five volumes of *Etnograficheskoe obozrenie*, a journal published at Moscow University during the period 1889–1902, government influence is referred to not more than a half-dozen times.

class consciousness," "inability to change," "helpless poverty," and, above all, "unreliability." No student of Russian government has ever suggested that rural society actually played a positive role in the government's evolution or formed an important and vital element in its organization.[5]

It is true that the documentary evidence tends to support the belief that government and peasantry were separate entities, the one active and the other passive. But it is also true that the terms and symbols by which a society defines itself are not a reliable basis for comprehending the evolution of these same terms and symbols. Lack of evidence regarding relationships between a mutually interacting government and peasantry only reflects the government's inability to articulate them, not their absence or insignificance. Despite the "gap" between Russian government and peasant society that the documents reflect, especially after 1700, a description of the development of the government over a period of two centuries must stress mutual influences and relationships between it and its people—thus my need to write this book before embarking on a description of the Stolypin land reform.[6]

We are not yet equipped to write a history of government-peasant interaction. Too many documents need re-examining and too many problems need rethinking. Even if a historian could get through all the documents, he would still have great difficulty using them. Describing a development of which the participants themselves were unaware requires the historian not only to know the documents but also to read meanings into them that their authors never would have understood. His conclusions, therefore, are not likely to be "sound" according to the canons of historical scholarship. They must be derived from acts of imagination as well as inductions from evidence.[7] So be it.

5. Lev Petrazhitskii suggested a theoretical framework for considering such a proposition in the first decade of the twentieth century. His theoretical works— e.g., *Law and Morality*, tr. Hugh W. Babb (Cambridge, Mass., 1955)—were generally ridiculed when he wrote them and continue to be ignored to the present day.

6. For an elaborate discussion of the effects of social evolution on bureaucracy and vice versa, see S. N. Eisenstadt, *The Political Systems of Empires* (Glencoe, Ill., 1963). An excellent case study of the molding of an administration by the society on which it is imposed is Ralph Braibanti, "Public Bureaucracy and Judiciary in Pakistan," in J. G. LaPalombara, ed., *Bureaucracy and Political Development* (Princeton, N.J., 1963), pp. 360–440.

7. Many social scientists would disagree on the ground that the proper aim of the "behavioral" sciences is to find a system (model) into which human behavior will fit. They are loathe to admit that their findings might have less than universal significance. Ralph Braibanti offers a more sophisticated statement

Conventional history is equally presumptuous. Studies based exclusively on "valid" evidence assume that the men who wrote the documents actually understood the connection between what they were doing and what they thought they were doing, and this, too, demands an act of imagination.

This volume, then, does not purport to be a history of tsarist administration. It cannot pretend to be definitive or even thorough; it only provides *some* indications of the extent to which peasant society acted upon the tsarist administration until the year 1905. The purpose is to point to at least *some* of the relationships that had formed between government administration and peasant society by 1905 in order to portray the tsarist administration of that year as a social configuration, i.e., a configuration of attitudes acquired from experience rather than a diagram of formal laws, policies, and ideologies.[8] I have written this book not to prove anything, only to provide a basis for visualizing the tsarist government's achievements in 1905–1914 and, ultimately, the agonizing necessities that confronted and formed the Soviet regime after 1917.

---

in his introduction to *Asian Bureaucratic Systems Emergent from the British Imperial Tradition* (Durham, N.C., 1966), p. 17. He says that in the comparative study of bureaucracy, the accumulation of data is not enough. There must be "two research modes: the one scientific, the other non-scientific and impressionistic."

8. A recent work that calls attention to the importance of studying modern organization as a society is Samuel Huntington, *Political Order in Changing Societies* (New Haven, Conn., 1968), pp. 11–15.

The advance of culture not only does not lessen the dependence of the individual on society but actually strengthens it. We cannot speak of eliminating this dependence, only of minimizing its annoyances.

NIKOLAI MIKHAILOVICH KORKUNOV

Abbreviations

IPS	*Istoriia Pravitelstvuiushchego Senata*
IZO	*Izvestiia zemskogo otdela*
PPSZ	(*Pervoe*) *polnoe sobranie zakonov Rossiiskoi Imperii*
RGP	N. M. Korkunov, *Russkoe gosudarstvennoe pravo*
SIRIO	*Sbornik imperatorskogo russkogo istoricheskogo obshchestva*
TPSZ	(*Trete*) *polnoe sobranie zakonov Rossiiskoi Imperii*
TsGIAL	Tsentralnyi gosudarstvennyi istoricheskii Arkhiv Leningrada
	f. fond
	op. opis
	d. delo
	l. list (page with one number for both sides)
VPSZ	(*Vtoroe*) *polnoe sobranie zakonov Rossiiskoi Imperii*

Introduction

If we are to be happy in a climate of opinion where reason purports to be king, we cannot rest until we have discovered the thread of a rational principle running through the apparent confusion. We succeed in doing this by failing to observe the irrational elements of institutions, or, where such factors cannot be ignored, by refusing them a place in our system.

THURMAN ARNOLD

In 1905 the Imperial Russian *pravitelstvo* (government administration) included a legal order and an administrative organization; that is, it had one set of rules establishing what people could not do and another set establishing what government servitors were obliged to do. In short, the *pravitelstvo* was a legal-administrative order, and since it purported to be systematic,[1] it was to some extent a legal-administrative system: a formal structure of rules and official responsibilities, all of which conform explicitly or implicitly to certain basic principles and no one of which may be inconsistent with any other.

Leaving aside the question of how systematic the tsarist government's formal organization actually was in 1905, it is important to note an essential feature of the ideal legal-administrative system that it affected to be. In the ideal, the legitimacy of any particular rule (command, principle) is established and its force is delimited not solely by its own terms but also—and even chiefly—by its logical relation to other rules. Its "rightness" and its practical effect depend on and derive from its conformity to the system as a whole. No rule is an absolute in itself. It must constantly be tested and interpreted as it is applied to specific cases, and whenever its application to a case makes

---

1. According to the government's own advertisement, "the wide expansion of the functions of the State make a complete system of subordinate institutions unavoidable; these may not, however, be permitted to use their own discretion; while, at the same time, the personal control of the Sovereign, considering the vastness of the territory, is fraught with extreme difficulty. It is therefore indispensable to regulate the functions of subordinate institutions by certain general rules, determined by the law. Only with this condition will they be organs of Sovereign power, and not independent authorities, acting in their own interests" (*Statesman's Handbook for Russia* [2 vols., St. Petersburg, 1896], I, 3–4).

it appear to be inconsistent with other rules, its meaning is likely to change. In a legal-administrative *system,* then, legitimacy ultimately resides not in the rules themselves but in their rational consistency with each other. Administrative orders, judicial decisions, statutes, and the most basic constitutional principles are all susceptible to changes in meaning whenever such changes seem necessary in order to sustain the pretense that the legal-administrative order as a whole is free from any logical inconsistency.[2]

Obviously there is no such thing in any human society as an operational legal-administrative system that is also ideal. There are many organizations, however, whose members affect and/or aspire to operate systematically; that is, they act as if they believe that legitimacy resides in the logical order of their rules, not in the rules themselves. If we regard a legal-administrative order as a social phenomenon rather than a formal structure, we may say that a legal-administrative *system* is a government whose servitors act and think as if they believe that their rules (commands, principles) must mean and can only mean what their logical connections with each other allow.[3] To put it on a more fundamental level, an organization can operate systematically only if its servitors act as if they believe in the supreme power of reason. This is not an explicit theological requirement. The servitors may believe in one supreme God who is assumed to be perfectly reasonable, or they may believe in the power of reason (science, universal harmony) per se. System requires no specific faith, only that the servitors' beliefs lead them to act and think as if they believed in the supreme power of reason.

2. Max Weber, *Max Weber on Law in Economy and Society* (Cambridge, Mass., 1954), pp. 73–76, 233–234.

3. The idea that the substance of law and authority lies in the minds of those who recognize them began to evolve into a legal science with the generation of Lorenz von Stein. See his *Gegenwart und Zukunft der Rechts und Staatswissenschaft Deutschlands* (Stuttgart, 1876), pp. 92–150, 213–236. This evolution reached its culmination in the time of N. M. Korkunov (d. 1904), Lev Petrazhitskii (d. 1931), Max Weber (d. 1920), and Axel Hägerstrom (d. 1939). The most convincing theoretical expressions of it that I have seen are N. M. Korkunov, *Ukaz i zakon* (St. Petersburg, 1894), pp. 132–190, and Petrazhitskii, pp. 7–42, 119–213. For a general discussion of Korkunov's work, see my article "Bureaucracy and Freedom: N. M. Korkunov's Theory of the State," *American Historical Review* LXXI (Jan. 1966), 468–486. Concerning this general approach to legal history, see Weber, *Max Weber on Law,* p. 33, and Axel Hägerstrom, *Inquiries into the Nature of Law and Morals* (Stockholm, 1953), pp. 17–69, 97–192.

Recently, Harold Sprout has called this the "ecological" approach. He says, "Moods, attitudes, values, preferences, choices, decisions, projects and undertakings are relatable to the milieu through the perceptions and other psychological processes of the environed individual—*and in no other way*" (*The Ecological Perspective on Human Affairs* [Princeton, N.J., 1965], p. 140).

We now have two definitions of the term "legal-administrative system." On the one hand, it is a formal structure; on the other, it is an actual group of men who depend on and organize themselves around their common pretense and/or aspiration to operate within this formal structure.

With this dual definition of legal-administrative system in mind, we can begin to speak of systematization. If we take a legal-administrative system to be nothing more than a formal structure, systematization is a process of rewriting rules that are not yet in systematic relation to each other. This process may be nothing more than drawing up a list of the necessary revisions, or it may refer to the thought processes by which some scholar formulates the revisions, or, finally, it may include the whole political process by which a group of men reach some agreement on the revisions that are actually to be put in force. This already makes three definitions of the word "systematization," two of which contain the seeds of unending complexities in themselves, and we have as yet mentioned only one definition of system. Fortunately, none of the three have much to do with the subject of this book (though it is important that they be kept in mind, lest the reader forget that I am *not* talking about them).

The systematization that interests us here pertains to the second definition of legal-administrative system given above: an actual group of men who organize themselves around their common pretense and/or aspiration to operate within a formal legal-administrative system. If system means a group of men possessing certain attitudes and engaged in certain social relationships, then systematization refers to the process or processes by which the group took form or, to be more specific, the process by which the group came to acquire its attitudes toward its legal rules. For our purposes, then, the systematization of Russian government refers to the historical evolution through which the servitors gradually came to organize themselves to some extent around their common pretense and/or aspiration to operate within a formal legal-administrative system—the process by which the servitors came to depend on one another to act and think as if they believed that their laws and authorities had to be in logical order in order to possess legitimacy. This, at last, is our subject.

A few words on what systematization is *not*. It is not equivalent to centralization or to unification. It may happen that under certain circumstances the evolution of system in a government will accompany a conscious program of centralization or unification—as happened in Russia—but this is by no means inevitable. Systematization may equally well be associated with the development of a loose federation, as happened in the United States and some other British colonies. For that matter, systematization may be part of a great variety of governments and ideologies. Autocracy or democracy, Prussian unity or Swiss local autonomy, slavery or wage labor, genocide or universal salvation—all may flourish in a systematic or systematizing society. On the other hand, a centralizing government does not always wish to introduce system to its administration. Russian rule over Polish society, for example, involved a number of attempts to centralize and unify Russian government by forcibly reorganizing Polish institutions, but these reorganizations were not generally intended to systematize the Poles.

To go further, since systematization is defined here as an evolution of attitudes, it cannot be equated directly with any formal policies and programs, *not even when their explicit purpose is to introduce system.* A conscious attempt to set up a system may actually further systematization as we have defined it, but it may also hinder it. A reform may disrupt system in the short run and further it in the long run, or vice versa. All this depends on circumstances. As will be seen (below, ch. III, sec. E), the tsarist government's attempts to survey landed estates in the late seventeenth and eighteenth centuries were designed to introduce system into civil law and revenue collection; yet their actual short-run effect was to disrupt such dependence on system as already existed in gentry society. On the other hand, patently nonsystematic policies and methods, such as those by which the tsars governed the non-Russian steppe peoples, may have contributed to systematization.[4]

In sum, systematization is not the same thing as centralization or unification. Moreover, there is no necessary connection between any conscious policies, even those explicitly designed to further systematization, and the social processes through which systematization goes forward.

Admittedly, the study of systematization as I have defined it opens the door to a host of considerations that do not lend themselves to coherent discussion, let alone scholarly study. In order to achieve coherence, it is necessary to set limits to our study. This is not hard to do if it be kept in mind that this book is not a study of the process of systematization in toto. Such a study would include not only the evolution of domestic administration but also the history of science, education, diplomatic relations, etc. But I shall not venture to take up

---

4. Russian policies in the settlement of the Trans-Volga area are described in A. Donnelly, *The Russian Conquest of Bashkiria: 1552–1740* (New Haven, Conn., 1968), especially pp. 16–20, 51–52, 72–95, 101–102, 149–150.

these matters. All I want to do in this book is to set forth *some* indications that systematization was occurring in the government after about 1700 and to point out *some* of the effects this produced on the attitudes of Russian government servitors in 1905–1914. I do not presume to account for the process of systematization or even to describe it exhaustively but only to recognize it and to ponder its impact.

In brief, the history that interests us goes as follows: in 1711–1722 Peter I established the Ruling Senate (*Pravitelstvuiuschii Senat*) and its subsidiary colleges in St. Petersburg and Moscow. In 1775 Catherine II added a network of partly elective collegial administrations in the provinces. Alexander I set executive ministries at the head of his government in 1802, and Alexander II established a relatively clear separation between local elective institutions and the organs of the central administration in 1861–1864.

It is convenient to divide this evolution into three periods: the rise of formally collegial administration, or "senatorial" government, in 1711–1802; transition to bureaucratic administration in 1802–1861; and the predominance of bureaucratic administration in 1861–1905. The year 1905 does not mark the end of the evolution of bureaucracy, but the transformation it underwent in 1905–1906 introduced such basic changes in law and government that the subsequent period requires a separate study.

As said before, we are concerned not with the whole of the tsarist government but only with how system evolved in it. In the eighteenth century the Senate was the focal point around which the elements of systematic domestic administration took form. After the 1850s the State Council (*Gosudarstvennyi Sovet*) and the Committee of Ministers (*Komitet Ministrov*) formed the constitutional framework under which bureaucracy was supposed to operate. Thus this study focuses on the Senate, the State Council, the Committee of Ministers, and the organizations that emerged under them, though in fact, as will be seen, these bodies did not direct the government.[5]

The limits set forth above allow me to dismiss a number of administrative bodies from consideration. Throughout the period 1711–1905 many centers of "real power" lay outside what passed for the systematic sectors of the government in a confusing array of imperial cabinets, court cliques, military governors, and gentry families. All

5. N. P. Eroshkin, *Ocherki istorii gosudarstvennykh uchrezhdenii dorevoliutsionnoi Rossii* (Moscow, 1960), presents a far more complete and detailed chronicle of the development of the formal administrative apparatus in the tsarist government up to its fall in 1917.

these were very important at one time or another in the management of the domestic administration and even in government-peasant interaction, but they are peripheral to this study. Likewise, the army and the conduct of Russia's foreign relations need not be described in any detail, nor the church. The semi-military organizations that governed the territories and peoples outside European Russia doubtless had much to do with the evolution of Russian attitudes toward system, but for the most part they were formally separate from the sectors of government that ultimately formed Russia's civil administration. Whatever their influence, therefore, they were not the locus of systematization in the tsarist government, and they, too, can be left on the periphery.

One final limit: the book confines itself largely to the government's interaction with rural society. Russia was still basically rural in 1905. An urban society of the Western variety, with its own institutions, only began to emerge in Russia in 1861, and it only began to exert political influence around the end of the century.[6] Consequently, the evolution of legal-administrative system in Russia from 1711 to 1905 took its characteristic features almost wholly from the government's interaction with peasantry and gentry. In 1905 the government's most pressing domestic problems and dilemmas were still either in the countryside or connected with it,[7] and many of the participants in the urban culture of the late nineteenth and early twentieth centuries felt that not only the government's destiny but also their own identities were closely involved in what happened or failed to happen there.[8]

It is true, of course, that the urban society that began to evolve in the nineteenth century did feel itself to be culturally apart from both gentry and peasants. It is also true that by 1905 the government was profoundly involved in the rise of cities and powerfully affected by urban development. Nevertheless, government administrators were

6. Max Weber, *The City* (Glencoe, Ill., 1958), pp. 68–69, 82, 93, 200, notes that until 1861 most of the cities in Russia were primarily government centers and places of residence and consumption for the rural gentry. They lacked any autonomous culture or corporate political order of their own. See also Reinhard Wittram, *Peter I, Czar und Kaiser* (2 vols., Göttingen, 1964), I, 41.

7. Wayne S. Santoni, "P. N. Durnovo as Minister of Internal Affairs in the Witte Cabinet: A Study in Suppression" (unpublished Ph.D. dissertation, University of Kansas, 1968), p. 171, points out that in late 1905 and early 1906 the governors and the then minister of internal affairs, Petr N. Durnovo, considered the peasantry a greater threat to political order than the city workers.

8. See, e.g., Kavelin, *Krestianskii vopros*, pp. 28–32. "Whatever the situation of the peasants is," said Kavelin, "it is also the situation of the educated classes" (p. 32).

only beginning to recognize that urban society represented something fundamentally new. The ministry of internal affairs was still inclined to regard the cities as oversized villages, while the ministry of finance still treated them primarily as a means to national economic development.[9] Only in the 1900s did the government make any serious effort to adjust itself to urban society as a new phenomenon in itself and to treat cities as something more than big villages with factories in them. It may be said, then, that the deepest historical roots of the administration that presumed to govern Russia in 1905 lay in its relationships with rural society. It will not be too great a distortion if we keep these relationships at the center of our attention.

9. A. Ia. Avrekh, *Stolypin i tretia duma* (Moscow, 1968), pp. 153–196, describes the two ministries' arguments over labor policy in 1905–1906, giving therein many illustrations of their attitude (or lack of an attitude) toward urban society.

CHAPTER I

Background: The Dilemmas of Systematization

> Every attempt of the finite subject to form or to define, on the one hand, the concept of religion and of God, and, on the other, of political justice as the ligature of community and of human sociality, must not only fall short of the idea of the one and of the other, but appear in actual contradiction to them.
>
> A. R. CAPONIGRI (paraphrasing
Giambattista Vico)

A. THE CONCEPT OF LEGAL-ADMINISTRATIVE SYSTEM

FORMAL STRUCTURE

The formal structure of any legal order, systematic or nonsystematic, is made up of two elements: 1) rules that limit the behavior of those who live under it, and 2) men who possess the authority to interpret these rules and apply them to specific cases. An administrative order is likewise made up of two elements: 1) rules that determine who has authority over whom, and 2) purposes, deities, and/or sentiments in the name of which the authority may be legitimately exercised.

Most societies require both a legal and an administrative order, especially when these orders pretend to be systematic. By itself, a legal system cannot perform tasks. Its judges and lawyers can do nothing but decide how the principles of law should be applied in particular cases, and they can only do this in cases where all interested parties request and accept their opinions by mutual agreement. No modern political order could hold itself together solely on this basis.[1] At the very least, it

---

1. Pacifistic-democratic religious sects such as the Hutterites and Mennonites are no exception. They have never been purely legal orders and would not be even if they worked ideally. They have relieved themselves of many administrative necessities by paying taxes to a supposedly external government and accepting its protection, but it is not they who keep administration external to themselves. It is, rather, the sufferance of the administration, i.e., the government of the state in which they reside. They enjoy a seeming absence of administrative order only by coincidence, just as armies are sometimes at peace by coincidence. If the social milieu of these religious sects be considered as an unfolding in time, it includes an administrative order as well as a legal order, and the administrative order—that of the "external" state—is as fundamental to it as its legal order.

must provide for defense and enforce the legal rules. If there were such a thing as a perfectly systematic government, therefore, it would derive its authority not only from principles of law but also from principles that set forth its purposes. The principles might apply to many categories of human activity or only a few; in any case, behavior could be pronounced illegal only if it was inconsistent with them. Legality and illegality, authority and freedom from authority, duty and treason, would always be identified by a process of logical deduction, not by the simple exercise of any person's will.

The ideal legal-administrative system is an essential ingredient in the modern ideals of political freedom, equality, justice, and democracy. Not all legal-administrative systems necessarily include these ideals among their basic principles. The administration of a modern prison, for example, is organized around a system whose principles explicitly deny them. Nevertheless, no society can aspire to establish political freedom, equality, justice, or democracy without also aspiring —at least by implication—to establish an operational legal-administrative system. When we speak of the evolution of legal-administrative system, we are speaking of a fundamental and vitally necessary element in the evolution of those social and political ideals that all modern men cherish.

There is a potential contradiction even in an imaginary, perfect legal-administrative system. Commands derived from principles of purpose may conflict with rules derived from principles of law. Ordinarily, any such conflict is resolved by setting the principles of law above those of purpose, but in a case where the observance of principles of law would prevent the government from acting to preserve itself against some threat, then the legal rules might have to be violated. In such an event the government would be violating not only this or that principle of law but the supremacy of principles in general. System would no longer be able to direct action or to define what was legal and illegal. Thus even in a perfect legal-administrative system the degree to which system dominates behavior depends on circumstances.

THE MYTHICAL NATURE OF LAW

It is common knowledge that real organizations of human beings do not work or structure themselves solely or even fundamentally by reasoning from principles. The formal structures of legal-administrative systems that operate or have operated in the real world are not reducible to charts of syllogisms in which all principles, rules, and commands fit together in perfect consistency. The Anglo-American legal order, for example, rests on a number of practices—e.g., trial by jury and judicial decision on the basis of a debate—that explicitly deny the pre-eminence of logic over practical requirements.[2] Political and governmental systems that have pretended to be more rigidly consistent, chiefly those derived from Roman law, have had to make a formal separation between local practice and central system in order to maintain their pretense.[3] And even if formal structures could be perfectly self-consistent, they still would not govern the actual operation of organizations or the conduct of the men in them. Even in the most intricate and closely controlled bureaucracies much of the functioning and the operating organizational structure proceed from the more or less random initiative of subordinates at all levels and from the social relationships that form among them.[4]

The realization that logic does not prevail in legal-administrative systems has not led to the abandonment of the ideal of system. On the contrary, administrators and judges, who know better than anyone the small degree to which logical reasoning dominates administrative and judicial decision-making in practice, are often the most adamant in upholding the formal supremacy of principles.[5] Roscoe Pound has said that the "chief influence" in determining legal rules in American law has been "the quest of jurists and of judges for an ideal of absolute, eternal justice, well or ill conceived."[6] Obviously, then, mere observation and common sense are not enough to sweep away the model of the perfect legal-administrative system and its underlying assumptions. The main reason for this is that the model is not simply a hypothesis, to be weakened by mere evidence or rationalization. It is, rather, the product of a common habit of thought, a set of assumptions that men depend on one another to uphold in order that they might

2. See J. Redlich, *The Common Law and the Case Method in American University Law Schools* (1914), especially pp. 12–13, 41.

3. Separation of local practice from code is fundamental to Roman law. See T. C. Sandars, tr., *The Institutes of Justinian* (7th ed., London, 1952), pp. 8, 12. F. J. Goodnow, *Comparative Administrative Law* (2 vols., New York, 1893), I, 266–268, 283–284, 292, compares local autonomy in continental and Anglo-American legal systems. The classic statement regarding the general need for local autonomy in a highly centralized system is Lorenz von Stein, *Handbuch der Verwaltungslehre* (2nd ed., Stuttgart, 1876), pp. 34–41.

4. See P. M. Blau, *Dynamics of Bureaucracy* (Chicago, 1955); Chester I. Barnard, *Functions of the Executive* (Cambridge, Mass., 1938), pp. 113, 231–235; N. I. Lazarevskii, *Lektsii po russkomu gosudarstvennomu pravu* (2nd ed., 2 vols., St. Petersburg, 1910), II, 158; C. D. Burns, *Government and Industry* (London, 1921), pp. 58–62, 288–298.

5. Thurman Arnold, *The Symbols of Government* (New Haven, Conn., 1935), pp. 10–17, 44–49.

6. Quoted in M. S. Amos, "Roscoe Pound," in *Modern Theories of Law* (London, 1933), p. 95.

identify themselves and communicate with one another. In essence, an operational legal-administrative system is a myth.[7]

A myth gains acceptance in a society because it makes sense of the members' experience. Originally, as Ruth Benedict says, a myth is a "wishful projection of a universe of will and intention."[8] It is conceived, in much the same way as a hypothesis is conceived, in order to support a man's belief or hope that he can manipulate the forces that he senses operating around and within him. Perhaps it would be more accurate to put the matter less positively, to say that a myth is conceived in order to fortify a man against his continuing dread that he is helpless before the forces he senses.[9] In either case, whether it is optimism or desperation that leads men to conceive myths, their effect, when accepted, is to give each member of the society a degree of assurance that he can predict the results of certain of his actions. A fertility myth, for example, may explain why crops grow and thus give a primitive farmer the feeling that he can predict the results of his planting.

Once a myth gains common acceptance in a society, it becomes a force in itself. People grow accustomed to it, develop habitual behavior patterns around it, teach it to their children, and generally put themselves in a position where any explicit denial of it is an affront to themselves and a threat to their way of life. Not only do people believe in the myth; they depend on their fellows to believe in it. Indeed, a man may go on depending on his fellows to act as if they believed in a myth long after he has lost or forgotten his own belief. The customs attached to a myth may go on making sense of experience long after the myth itself has ceased to correspond to observed facts, because they are a vital part of the social relationships through which men conduct their affairs.[10]

7. Arnold, pp. 65–71. See also Hägerstrom, pp. 88–89.

8. Ruth Benedict, "Myth," in *Encyclopedia of the Social Sciences* (15 vols., New York, 1937), XI, 181. Similarly, Giovanni Gentile refers to man's myth-making propensity as a basic inclination to believe that the world he experiences is "something immediately identical" with his own "spiritual activity" (*Theory of Mind as Pure Act* [London, 1922], p. 7).

9. In Erik Erikson's words: "Where man cannot establish himself as the thinking one (who therefore is), he may experience a sense of panic; which is at the bottom of our myth-making . . . and our artificial creation of 'ideal' realities in which we become and remain the central reality" (*Young Man Luther* [New York, 1958], p. 111).

10. On the creation and evolution of myths in society, see Arnold, pp. 44–71, and J. Huizinga, *Homo Ludens* (New York, 1950), pp. 6–48. With regard to Russia in particular, see E. I. Iakushkin, "Zametki o vliianii religioznykh verovanii i predrassudkov na narodnye iuridicheskie obychai i poniatiia," *Etnograficheskoe obozrenie*, IX (1891), 1–19.

A law or body of laws is a special kind of myth.[11] Like all myths, it gives a member of society some basis for manipulating his environment by enabling him to predict the results of some of his own actions. The law myth, however, has to do only with one part of a man's environment, i.e., with the other people in his social group. A man obeys a legal norm not to propitiate a god, or invoke the power of a demon, or stop the rain, or make his arrows fly straighter. Basically, he obeys it and believes in its legitimacy because he consciously depends on his fellows to obey it and to enforce it. If they do not obey the law, he cannot manipulate them. If he does not obey the law, then his own behavior and that of his fellows may become unpredictable, and their mutual dependence—their "power" over themselves and each other—will disappear.

In its earliest stages of development, law is an outgrowth of custom. Custom originates when the members of a society learn to follow certain common behavior patterns and come to expect one another to conform to them. Many such patterns—e.g., language and table manners—are not yet legal norms. They are likely to become norms only when the members of a group (or some members) come not only to *expect* their fellows to conform to them but also to *depend* on their expectation, as the driver of an automobile depends on his expectation that the drivers coming in the opposite direction will stay on their side of the road.

It is only when the members of a society become conscious that they depend on one another to act in a certain way that law emerges. This consciousness is not constant and unceasing, even though the dependence is. Our automobile driver, for example, depends constantly on his expectation that the drivers coming the other way will stay to the right when they pass him, but his awareness of this dependence is not constant. Explicit awareness comes only when circumstances bring it on—when a car coming the other way does not in fact keep to the right, or when he himself veers to the left, or when he simply happens to think about the perils of driving. Whichever experience produces his awareness of dependence, his probable response will be to try to make sense of and to articulate it, which ordinarily means that he will identify a "wrong" action, either his own or someone else's. In the case of our driver, of course, an appropriate norm already exists. Instead of formulating a law, he is reminded of his dependence on the existing

11. The following three paragraphs follow the reasoning of N. M. Korkunov in his article "O nauchnom izuchenii prava," in *Sbornik statei N. M. Korkunova* (St. Petersburg, 1898), pp. 17–64. See also my article "Bureaucracy and Freedom," pp. 473–475.

legal order and, more directly, his dependence on the authorities who enforce it.

In the case of a man who first recognizes his dependence on his associates to behave in a certain way, he will have to articulate his own "wrong." If his formulation gains general acceptance, then it becomes a legal norm. The norm may be legitimized in any appropriate way: a solemn pronouncement by a chief or high priest, a decision reached by a council of elders, an order from an army commander, legislation from a parliament. What all these forms have in common is that they proceed from an authority—a god, a man, or a formal process of decision-making—that the members of the society regard as legitimate.

It may be said, then, that law and authority originate in society out of a common awareness of mutual dependence. A legal-administrative order is, at base, the embodiment and expression of this awareness. As men become aware of their dependence on each other, therefore, they learn to depend on legal-administrative order as such.

These remarks apply to a systematic legal-administrative order as much as they do to any other kind. Men who live within a legal-administrative system believe in it, or at least they regard themselves as believing in it, because its common acceptance allows them to manipulate their fellow men and thereby to cope with their environment. They do not care so much whether the principles that are supposedly basic to their legal-administrative system are true or false; nor is it of basic importance whether or not the principles actually do govern behavior.[12] The members of a modern society accept their system regardless of its flaws and regardless of their own occasional inclinations to violate it, because whenever they are made aware of their dependence on one another, they can usually employ it to articulate and symbolize—to make sense of—this dependence. For a man who lives in a "nonsystematic" society, the image of law that comes to his mind when he senses his dependence is usually a god or some person with authority. In a modern society the most likely image is that of a legal norm that derives its ultimate authority from being part of a legal-administrative system, that is, a norm that has come down from higher principles through a process of logical deduction.

12. According to Arnold, principles of law that have reached the status of myths need not have any actual validity in order to be operational. He points out that "realistic" legal scholars in the United States have gone to considerable pains to prove that American law does not actually derive from principles; nevertheless, they have not changed anyone's mind on the matter. "Realists prove incontrovertibly that there can be no objective reality behind the concept of law as a brooding omnipresence in the skies—only to find their own writings swallowed up and becoming a part of that brooding omnipresence which they are insistently denying" (pp. 37–38).

THE NONSYSTEMATIC MYTH OF LAW

If legal-administrative system is not an absolute truth but a myth, then it is not a goal of historical evolution but an outcome. It is not only a liberation from the past but also an expression of it. What is the nature of this evolution? One obvious feature is that it begins in a society where system is absent. It will be useful, therefore, to discuss the general nature of nonsystematic society, visualizing it not as the antithesis of system but as its point of origin.

If a nonsystematic legal-administrative order ever existed in pure form, it would be one in which the rules of law proceeded entirely from habitual attitudes and/or persons with authority. There would be no formal requirement that habits and commands be logically consistent with each other or with general principles. When a non-systematic man senses that a "wrong" has been done, the image that comes to his mind is a command from some divine or semi-divine personality who is assumed to possess power. The personality may be a father or a chieftain, a god, an ancestor identified by his prowess, or anyone at all who can somehow inspire fear in those who behold him. Whoever he is, it is his power and only his power that gives legitimacy to the rule in question. The members of a nonsystematic society make sense of (articulate, symbolize) their dependence on one another by acting as if they believed in a world organized around a multitude of divine personalities.[13]

Since it is the image of a personality rather than that of a system which sanctifies each legal rule in a nonsystematic society, personal authority can be formally limited not by rules per se but only by other personal authorities. In practice, of course, the legal rules that reside in common habits usually guide the powerful person's decision-making, but *formally* the strength and legitimacy of all rules can only derive from the personality that supposedly stands behind them, not from any rational connection they might have with each other. Nonsystematic man is likely to interpret an action that disappoints his expectations regarding the behavior of his fellows as a challenge to a personal authority, and his consciousness of dependence is likely to give rise to the demand that the authority avenge the wrong. A systematic man may cherish a similar expectation regarding the agencies of law en-

13. A. S. Diamond, *Primitive Law* (London, 1935), pp. 26–35, 188–190, 307–308. On the general nature of primitive law, see also E. A. Hoebel, *The Law of Primitive Man* (Cambridge, Mass., 1954), and Weber, *Max Weber on Law,* p. 147. For a discussion of customary law in Russia, see V. I. Sergeevich, *Lektsii i issledovaniia po drevnei istorii russkogo prava* (4th ed., St. Petersburg, 1910), pp. 5–24. Concerning the dependence of "backward" society on personal power, see O. Mannoni, *Prospero and Caliban* (New York, 1964), pp. 39–81.

forcement, but in the myth of system the personal identity of the agency is not likely to be of primary importance. In a nonsystematic society the divine person is crucial. His will is the very essence of the legal rule in question. He may even change the rule if it pleases him.

The violator of a legal rule in a nonsystematic society may well seek protection against the deity who stands behind it by appealing to some other god, or person, or cult of ancestors. If he does make such an appeal, his violation is likely to become the occasion for a contest between one deity and another—that is, a power struggle between factions, each organized around its chosen deity. The "right" decision will be thought of not as the most reasonable one but, rather, as the one that comes from the most powerful person. The usual result of a contest over the law, then, is to destroy or weaken one divine personality—one faction or clan—and to enhance the power of another. In nonsystematic society, then, the interpretation of legal rules is primarily a matter of deciding which divine personality possesses the greatest power. So far as the mythical structure of nonsystematic society is concerned, the meaning of a legal rule and its logical connection with other rules are of no importance.[14]

The myth of law in a nonsystematic society is likely to be more adaptable to the needs of the moment than it is in a system, especially if the society frequently comes into contact with outside influences that prevent habit from becoming rigid. Since persons of power are not limited by the requirement of consistency, they can set aside specific rules more easily when and if the need arises; that is, they can incorporate new legal rules and deities without disturbing the old ones unduly. Mannoni (see above, n. 13) has pointed out that in nineteenth-century Madagascar, as in many areas affected by European colonization, the natives made sense of the French colonizers' overwhelming

---

14. The members of a nonsystematic society are generally unable to make lasting agreements with one another, mainly because an oath sworn to one god may be legitimately broken either by persuading the god to change his mind or by appealing to another god against him. So long as isolation and a stable natural environment keep the need for social change to a minimum, agreements and customary laws may continue to serve the needs that gave rise to them and thus retain their original meanings over a long period of time. If the social milieu is in any way unstable, however, contracts are likely to become unreliable. An interesting illustration of the difficulties involved in nonsystematic contracts is a treaty made between the Egyptians and the Hittites in about 1280 B.C. The signers found it necessary to prefix the terms of their agreement with the following formula: "As for these words, a thousand gods . . . of the land of Hatti, together with a thousand gods . . . of the land of Egypt, are with me as witnesses." Even this was not enough. The names of some of the gods had to be listed. An English translation of the treaty is printed in J. B. Pritchard, *Ancient Near Eastern Texts* (Princeton, N.J., 1950), pp. 199–201.

power by regarding them as emissaries from the natives' own ancestors—not an ideal adjustment, perhaps, but one that was relatively easy to make. In general, then, nonsystematic orders are better able than systematic ones to accept changes in law and/or morality in response to immediate practical problems. On the other hand, since a nonsystematic society does not conceive of itself as a single framework, its members cannot *conceive* of changing it. Living in a constant flux of deities, they may alter their customs and relationships inadvertently by their responses to immediate situations, but they cannot consciously reform their laws in order to satisfy rationally calculated needs. In short, a nonsystematic legal-administrative order is likely to be *adaptable* but not *changeable*. As individuals, nonsystematic men can calculate and conceive of purposes, but they cannot reorder their relationships around a common sense of purpose.

The peasant villages of nineteenth-century Russia were by no means entirely nonsystematic, but they were typically adaptable rather than changeable. The peasant courts established by the Liberation Statute of 1861 generally made their decisions on the basis of the circumstances in each case and did not strive to stay within the bounds set by laws or precedents, either their own or those of the central government. Rules existed, of course, and earlier decisions were not forgotten, but in the peasants' minds a "just" verdict had above all to fit the practical requirements of the case at hand. For peasant judges, the ideal end of a case was to bring the disputants into agreement with each other and dismiss the whole matter, even in criminal cases. To this end, rules and precedents were infinitely adjustable. This may have been disorderly, but verdicts and decisions acceptable to the community were actually much easier to arrive at in Russian peasant courts than they are in the modern West, where a legal decision has no legitimacy until a number of legal experts make sure it is consistent with all relevant rules. On the other hand, the peasant legal order was unchangeable in that it could not easily reorganize itself on a broad scale around the commercial relationships that were growing up around and within it.[15]

It is not true that men in nonsystematic societies are incapable of

---

15. A. Leontev, "Volostnoi sud i obychnoe pravo," *Zhurnal iuridicheskogo obshchestva pri S-Peterburgskogo Universiteta,* XXIV (Nov. 1894), 26–55. J. D. Kingsley, "Bureaucracy and Political Development with Particular Reference to Nigeria," in LaPalombara, pp. 301–317, describes this phenomenon in British colonial government in Nigeria. W. R. Augustine, "Notes toward a Portrait of the Eighteenth-Century Russian Nobility," *Canadian Slavic Studies,* IV (Fall 1970), 395–402, shows that much the same thing happened in Russian gentry society after the law of 1731 twisted customary rules of land inheritance into statutory form.

reasoning; nor, on the other hand, can it be maintained that modern men are distinguished by any particular inclination to be logical in practice. "Nonsystematic" and "systematic" refer not to personal qualities but to characteristics of social relationships and to the attitudes that express these relationships. Plato, for example, lived in a nonsystematic society, yet he was very good at reasoning and even believed it to be divine. What he did not believe in, however, was *the power of reason to hold society together or to make men act rationally.* Indeed, he explicitly denied the efficacy of reason in the world of sense perception. In *Gorgias* he has Socrates argue that an orator cannot persuade a mob and exercise power over it except by joining it and becoming its tool. From this he concludes that reason possesses no "power" at all in society.[16] In the dialogue with Protagoras he goes even further and. asserts that virtue (reason) cannot be taught. Reason, in other words, not only does not influence the mass of men; it cannot even be communicated to them.[17] Its power comes only as an inherent quality in rare individuals.

Plato's estimate of society indicates that his experience in the social environment of Athens did not teach him to expect his fellow citizens to act according to a law that derived from principles, and we may safely surmise that social relationships in Greece in 400–300 B.C. were essentially nonsystematic. Plato's worship of reason and his idea that philosophers might rule did not stem from any need to make sense out of his dependence on other men. On the contrary, his notions cut him out of Athenian society entirely.[18] Individual men who adopt beliefs that alienate them from their fellows can emerge in any society— primitive, modern, or what have you—and their experience will be much the same. When we speak of societies and legal orders and their characteristics, however, we are speaking of men who depend on their expectations regarding the behavior of their fellows, and we are only interested in the images these men see (or conjure up) in order to make sense of their dependence.

16. *Gorgias,* tr. W. C. Helmbold (New York, 1952), pp. 10–15, 90.
17. *Protagoras,* tr. B. Jowett and rev. M. Ostwald (New York, 1956), pp. 18–21.
18. According to Ernest Barker, the first men to believe that reason was the highest power *in society* were the Stoics. See his introduction to Otto Gierke, *Natural Law and the Theory of Society, 1500 to 1800* (2 vols., Cambridge, 1950), I, xxxv–xxxvi. The fall of Greek society from glory after the Peloponnesian War produced not only Plato's rejection of society but also the Stoics' new awareness of their dependence on it. The Stoics combined a Platonic belief in the divinity of reason with an awareness of dependence on a society that did not and could not organize itself rationally, and it was the need to resolve this dilemma that forced them into social action.

B. The Evolution of Domestic Administration
in Russia in 1711–1905

The evolution of Russian government from 1711 to 1905 was very different from that of other European countries; consequently, the myth of system has played a different role in both government and society. The domestic administration strove mightily to be European, but it always operated within an essentially non-European framework.

To express the difference between Western and Russian myths of system in a very general way, legal system in the modern West does reflect by and large what men expect each other to do and not to do, and men generally depend on these expectations in practice. More specifically, the system reflects what that class or quality of men loosely referred to as the bourgeoisie expect each other to do and not to do under "normal circumstances."[19] In Russia, on the other hand, the legal-administrative system that emerged in the eighteenth and nineteenth centuries reflected the way in which many politically conscious Russians believed they *should* behave, but there was no significant number of them who depended on the expectation that their fellows would actually behave this way. What politically conscious Russians did expect to find in one another—and on this expectation they relied very heavily—was the conviction that a legal system of some sort *should* prevail in Russia. Russians relied on each other not so much to behave consistently according to system as to act zealously in behalf of it.[20]

19. The Anglo-American legal-administrative system has brought theory and practice closer together than any other. Frederick W. Maitland discusses the historical development that brought this about in many of his works. See, e.g., his introduction to Otto Gierke, *Political Theories of the Middle Ages* (2nd ed., Cambridge, 1951), pp. x–xxx. For a description of the more recent evolution of the American legal system and an analysis of its relation to society, see J. R. Commons, *Legal Foundations of Capitalism* (Madison, Wis., 1959), especially pp. 2–17.

20. Marc Raeff, *Origins of the Russian Intelligentsia: The Eighteenth-Century Nobility* (New York, 1966), pp. 35–36, 48–50, 75–80, 102–107. P. P. Mendeleev, an official in the chancellery of the Committee (and Council) of Ministers in 1904–1909, recounts, typically, that he and his fellow servitors were not mere bureaucrats (*chinovniki*) but, rather, a "closely united caste—devoted servitors, proud, esteeming fanatically the responsibilities laid on them" (from bk. 2, p. 51, of his untitled notebooks in the Russian Archive at Columbia University).

It is true that Russians were also hostile to system. Feodor Dostoievskii's *Notes from the Underground*, for example, is explicitly antirational. Such negations, however, only demonstrate how overwhelming the impetus to system was in Russia in the nineteenth century. The same may be said for Alexander I's devotion to Madame Krüdener and Nicholas II's high regard for Rasputin. The blatant, almost self-conscious absurdity of these rebellions is perhaps the clearest indication of the power that the myth of system had over the capital-city imagination.

As Konstantin Leontev put it, "It is easier for a Russian to be holy than to be honorable."[21]

In Imperial Russia the myth of legal system did not allow men to articulate and make sense of their social relationships. On the contrary, it was more like a moral ideal, and its effect on a man who cherished it was to increase the difficulty he experienced in making sense of Russian government as it worked in practice. For this reason a conscientious Russian bureaucrat who thought of himself as part of a system, and sincerely tried to function as such, was likely to find himself playing the crusader. By the same token, a government agency often had not only to perform its official functions and enforce its rules but also to conduct a crusade on behalf of them, a crusade that went on simultaneously within its own organization and in society at large. This is why so many of the statutes of Russian law throughout the period 1711–1905 were not enforceable legal rules but exhortations to behave or work according to this or that ideal.[22] Far from imposing a belief in the power of reason on the administrators, the laws either could be ignored entirely or they could serve a strong-willed official as a basis for compelling people to do his bidding regardless of regulations to the contrary. In short, the principles of law and administration were much the same in Russia and the West on paper, but the role of system in society and its place in the individual's sense of values were very different.

The legal-administrative order that ultimately developed into the Russian Empire began to take recognizable form in the region between the upper Volga and Oka rivers in the 1240s A.D. as a section of the Tatar (Mongol) horde. There was a political order before the Tatars came, but it could not have been a very strong or unified one; otherwise, it would have reacted to the coming of the Tatars in some coherent fashion, by either resisting or negotiating with them.[23] The fact is, however, that if the Russian princes did do anything collec-

21. Quoted in B. A. Kistiakovskii, *Sotsialnyia nauki i pravo* (Moscow, 1916), p. 621.

22. Wittram, II, 125–126, describes Peter's practice of including explanations of his statutes and discussions of their purposes in the statutes themselves. His successors all followed his example until at last, in 1885, Alexander III ordered that the statutes of Russian law (*Svod zakonov*) be purged of explanations and statements of purpose. See the law of 5 Nov. 1885, in (*Trete*) *polnoe sobranie zakonov Rossiiskoi Imperii* (33 vols., St. Petersburg, 1885–1916, hereinafter cited as *TPSZ*), 3261.

23. Concerning the relations among the Russian princes and cities in the 1200s before and after the Tatar conquest, see A. Eck, *Le moyen age russe* (Paris, 1933), pp. 23–114, especially pp. 63–66.

tively to cope with the Tatars who were campaigning and ravaging through their lands in 1237–1240, they have left no record of it. The first sign of organized activity among them was the establishment, under Tatar direction, of a tribute-collecting network to provide recruits and protection money to the Tatars. Schurmann has pointed out that in China and Persia the Mongol khans rapidly abandoned their attempts to organize their own tribute collection because the native administration could do the job better. In the Volga-Oka region, on the other hand, the crude Tatar methods seem to have been the only ones available in the 1200s, which would indicate that however crude the Tatar order was, it was at least as effective as the one that obtained before the horde came.[24]

The chief functions around which the Russian princes of the upper Volga organized themselves during the first two centuries of their existence as a unified political order were the collection of the Tatar horde's tribute and the recruiting of its armed forces.[25] It was more or less natural, therefore, that forced collection and recruiting would continue to be the foundation of Russian political order even after the Tatar horde fell apart. Thus the overriding necessity to force the "Russian people" to furnish tribute and recruits against their will was a vital element in the Russian state from its beginnings. Had the Russian princes and tsars failed to cope with it, all the military successes and cultural roots that legions of patriotic historians have discovered in Russia's history could never have produced a native political organization. The relationship between collectors and payers of forced tribute was the most enduring heritage that came down to the generation of Peter I from five centuries of experience, and it was the attitudes and problems involved in this relationship that first gave birth to the

24. H. F. Schurmann, "Mongolian Tributary Practices of the Thirteenth Century," *Harvard Journal of Asiatic Studies*, XIX (Dec. 1956), 304–389. The relationships between the church and the Tatars in the first decades after the conquest are described in E. Golubinskii, *Istoriia russkoi tserkvi* (2 vols., Moscow, 1880, 1900), II, 16–62. The instructions, or charters (*iarlyki*), from the Tatar khans to the church, which furnish perhaps the best indication of the degree to which the Russians depended on the Tatars for their political order, are printed in *Pamiatniki russkogo prava*, 8 vols., III (Moscow, 1955), 463–470.

Authorities differ about the degree to which the Volga-Oka region was politically unified before the Tatar invasion. A. E. Presniakov, *The Formation of the Great Russian State* (Chicago, 1970), pp. 49–74, assumes that it was unified before the Tatars came and that the Tatars weakened its unity. But Presniakov neglects to mention the princes' utter lack of inclination to unite against the Tatars and the church's willingness to accept Tatar protection against the relatively disorderly princes and boiars of Vladimir.

25. On Alexander Nevskii's pioneering efforts to establish this organization in the 1250s, especially his use of Tatar armies to quell his rebellious subjects, see S. M. Solovev, *Istoriia Rossii* (15 vols., Moscow, 1960–1966), II, 155–160.

Russian variety of legal-administrative system.[26] Peter's original purpose in proclaiming the need for system in his government was not to reform society or even to protect it but to organize the forced collection of tribute and recruits more effectively.[27]

In its simplest form the old government of tribute collectors was a hierarchy of personal agents. The highest authorities were regional collectors, and below them a chain of subordinates extended down to the men who actually collected from the villages, i.e., the men who compelled the peasants to pay or work more than they wanted to.[28] In the absence of legal system, each relationship between superior and subordinate up and down the hierarchy was highly personal, taking its form more from the interaction between the individuals concerned than from any official rules. Without an accurate census or measure of the land, no superior official had any reliable way of knowing how much tribute his subordinate should be bringing in. Consequently, the

26. On the "parasitical" tribute-collecting political order, see W. H. McNeill, *Europe's Steppe Frontier: 1500–1800* (Chicago, 1964), pp. 4–8. Its nature in the period before the emergence of the tsarist government is described in L. V. Cherepnin, *Obrazovanie russkogo tsentralizovannogo gosudarstva v XIV–XV vekakh* (Moscow, 1960), pp. 10, 423–896, especially pp. 530–538. Cherepnin does not wish to see that the Muscovite state arose in the fourteenth and fifteenth centuries as a section of the Tatar horde, but his account indicates that this was the case. After the horde began to fall apart in the 1350s (p. 552), the Muscovite princes had increasingly to make their own way (i.e., to conquer their own territory), and it was only after this process was well underway that opposition to the Tatars began to take the place of tribute collecting on their behalf as a basis for political-social order (pp. 550–606). On this point, see also M. K. Liubavskii, *Lektsii po drevnei russkoi istorii do kontsa XVI veka* (Moscow, 1918), pp. 167–168.

A recent work by an American scholar suggests that as late as the sixteenth century the Muscovite government, far from being hostile to the Tatars, was still engaged with them in a cooperative effort to maintain the steppe-wide political-economic order that the Tatar horde had established and maintained during the 1200s and early 1300s. See Edward L. Keenan, "Muscovy and Kazan, 1445–1552: A Study in Steppe Politics" (unpublished Ph.D. dissertation, Harvard University, 1965), especially pp. 178–180.

According to S. B. Veselovskii, *Soshnoe pismo* (2 vols., Moscow, 1915–1916), I, 141–142, Muscovite taxation was still in essence a primitive tribute collection in the early sixteenth century. On the development of the "administration" for collection in the seventeenth century, see A. Lappo-Danilevskii, *Organizatsiia priamogo oblozheniia v moskovskom gosudarstve so vremen smuty do epokhi preobrazovanii* (St. Petersburg, 1890), and B. Chicherin, *Oblastnyia uchrezhdeniia Rossi v XVII-m veke* (Moscow, 1856), pp. 2–36. It is of interest that the *dan*, the original Tatar tribute collection, continued to exist in name as a part of Muscovite revenue until the late seventeenth century. See Lappo-Danilevskii, pp. 27–29.

27. The early development of Peter's interest in domestic reform is traced in M. M. Bogoslovskii, *Petr I: Materialy dlia biografii: Tom pervyi, Detstvo-iunost, Azovskie pokhody* (Moscow, 1940).

28. Schurmann, pp. 304–312, describes the Tatar methods.

amount of tribute that actually changed hands in each such relationship depended largely on the nature of the relationship.[29] In practice, the tribute-collecting hierarchy was something like a pile of islands, each of them cut off from the others and each likely to operate according to its own special interpersonal arrangements.[30]

Since the hierarchy performed its functions through a series of personal relationships, the nature of which could not be predicted or known in terms of a single framework, the ruler had no reliable way of foretelling the results that his commands would produce. On an open battlefield, where a khan or tsar could see his commanders of thousands and their subordinates, he might be able to tell who was obeying him and who was not at least part of the time, but in a tribute-collecting hierarchy the servitors were no longer visible. No official could tell what would happen to the orders he gave to his immediate subordinates. The orders the tsar's henchmen issued to their subordinates doubtless bore some relation to his initial commands, but the tsar could not know what that relation would be. In short, the tsar possessed great power to act arbitrarily according to his whims but very little control over what his subordinates actually did. When one subordinate accused another of disobedience or treason, the tsar had naught but his knowledge of personalities to tell him whether or not the accusation was true. Likewise, if a collector failed to make his quota, the tsar had no reliable way to find out the reasons for his failure.[31]

29. I. E. German, *Istoriia russkogo mezhevaniia* (2nd ed., Moscow, 1910), pp. 22–32, notes that the Tatars tried to take a census, but with a semi-migratory peasant population, the records, if there were any, must have been no more than facades. According to Michel Roublev, "The Periodicity of the Mongol Tribute as Paid by the Russian Princes during the Fourteenth and Fifteenth Centuries," *Forschungen zur osteuropäischen Geschichte*, XV (Berlin, 1970), 7–13, collections in the fifteenth century were probably based on local registers that had been drawn up long before. There is no indication that the Muscovite princes knew or cared how these registers were made or whether they were made at all, so long as the tribute kept coming in. With regard to the lack of correspondence between tax registers and the property they purported to assess during the sixteenth and seventeenth centuries, see S. B. Veselovskii, especially I, 7–42.

30. Braibanti, "Public Bureaucracy and Judiciary," p. 394, has coined the term "cellular" administration to describe a similar social-administrative structure in modern Pakistan.

31. William Rubruck's description of the "court" of Sartak (one of the sons of Batu Khan) as it was in 1253 A.D. will do for a model of a despot who is all-powerful, yet unable to know in any reliable way what his subordinates are doing. Sartak, it seems, did not even know what the guards in front of his tent were doing. See W. Rockhill, ed., *The Journey of William Rubruck to the Eastern Parts of the World 1253–1255, as Narrated by Himself, with Two Accounts of the Earlier Journey of John of Pian de Carpine* (London, 1900), pp. 105–107. Concerning the practical limitations on the power of the various Tatar khans within

What means were available to the tsar to manipulate the tribute-collecting hierarchy as an organization? What generalizations can be made about it that would offer some basis for comprehending its operation as a whole? The most obvious answer is that in the relationship that obtained between each superior and subordinate, the subordinate's primary motive for carrying out his superior's orders was the awe he felt for the personal power of the superior, whereas the superior's motive for responding to the subordinate's expectations was his need for tribute. In the absence of commonly accepted legal rules, the subordinate attempted to fulfill his superior's demands for tribute and soldiers only because he believed in the superior's power and hoped it would protect him and further his personal interests. The subordinate had no reliable way of knowing the commands and rules his superior was supposed to obey. Therefore, he depended on the power of his superior as such: absolute and unlimited power that would give the superior the freedom of action to respond to the subordinate's needs no matter what they might be. The more powerful the superior, the more valuable he was to the subordinate. This was the practical significance of the subordinate's "awe." As for the superior, he had no reliable way of knowing how the subordinate got his tribute, or what resources were available to him, or how much he actually got. In order to get as much tribute as possible from the subordinate, therefore, the superior had to keep the subordinate in awe of him.

To some extent, awe implied fear, and it behooved the superior to frighten the subordinate in order to make him beware of bringing in too little tribute. It must be emphasized, however, that a fearful subordinate always had the option of running away and finding another powerful superior to protect him. There were laws against this, but they had little real effect in the absence of system. On the lowest level, that of the peasant village, flight involved all the problems and dangers of a move to new lands, but this does not seem to have discouraged the peasants unduly. Their customary way of life included migration, both collective and individual, as a viable method for coping with their environment. Fear, therefore, had a natural limit beyond which a superior could not go, lest he lose his subordinate and with him a significant amount of tribute. After all, the superior had as much to fear from a shortage of tribute as did the lowliest of peasants. It behooved him to instill not only fear in his subordinates but also the

---

their respective hordes in the fifteenth and sixteenth centuries, see Keenan, pp. 84–114. See below, ch. III, secs. D and E, for a description of the Russian tsar's lack of control over his domestic administration in the eighteenth century.

expectation that his, the superior's, power would satisfy the subordinates' needs and serve their purposes. In practice, then, the subordinate's awe implied not only fear but also his expectation that he would be able to use the power of his superior.

Our original question was: what means were available to the tsar to manipulate the tribute-collecting hierarchy? The answer is: when the tsar contemplated his hierarchy as an organization to be used, he could perceive a series of superior-subordinate relationships that were only utilizable if the subordinates stood in awe of their superiors and were able to utilize them. When the tsar desired to manipulate the hierarchy—whenever he needed to increase the tribute, or mobilize a gang of workers to fortify a town, or fight a battle—his most reliable procedure was to overawe his own subordinates and to encourage all his officials to overawe theirs.[32]

The necessary counterpart of awe was bribery. Without bribery, the subordinate could not utilize the power of his superior, and awe, therefore, could not become a basis for the development of practical relationships of mutual dependence between superior and subordinate. Bribery was not only a form of submission but more essentially a method of negotiation and even of self-assertion. It was the most important means by which servitors on all levels were able to elicit predictable responses from their superiors and thereby to manipulate them and come to depend on them. By using bribes, a peasant or a subordinate on any level could construct a relationship of personal interdependence with his superior that gave them both a measure of stability against the sudden or arbitrary exercise of pressure from outside. Bribery formed the little islands of resistance up and down the hierarchy that sealed the tsars off from the lower levels of their "organization," which is why the tsars denounced bribery from the earliest times.[33] But formal denunciations had no lasting effect because,

32. I know of no explicit order to this effect by any tsar, but an example of the state of mind to which I am referring may be seen in the written instructions serf owners gave to the stewards who managed their estates in the late eighteenth century. M. Confino, *Domaines et seigneurs en Russie vers la fin du XVIII siècle* (Paris, 1963), p. 49, notes that these instructions frequently emphasized the primary importance of keeping the serfs in awe. It was often suggested that a steward begin his tour of duty by discovering some offense, however slight, and punishing it severely so as to put the serfs in awe of him from the beginning. The steward was also supposed to care for the serfs, to measure the fields and harvests, and generally to know what was going on. Clearly the most important thing, however, was that he keep the serfs in awe of him.

33. The first recorded Russian law against bribery dates from the reign of Ivan III, although Byzantine strictures doubtless applied in the preceding centuries. Until Peter I's time only bribe takers were punished. Peter was the first ruler to make the giving of bribes a crime, which reflects the unique strength of

without bribery, the hierarchy could not have held together. Indeed, in a hierarchy of despotic tribute collectors, bribery was by far the most important practical means for achieving the equivalent of such modern concepts as political freedom, local autonomy, individual initiative, suffrage, and the protection of traditional institutions against the arbitrary authority of the state.[34]

To sum up, the hierarchy of tribute collectors was an expression not only of the tsar's will but also of the nature of Russian society and the peculiar history of Russian political order. It was the weakest kind of instrument for the consistent execution of policies or for controlled action of any kind, and all the tsars from Ivan III's time on knew it. They all struggled to strengthen their control over their subordinates

---

his determination to introduce system. See "Vziatochnichestvo," in F. A. Brockhaus and I. A. Efron, *Entsiklopedicheskii slovar* (41 vols. plus 2 supplementary vols., St. Petersburg, 1891–1907), VI (1892), 213–216. In the early nineteenth century a new law was enacted, reducing the punishment for giving bribes and distinguishing between poor officials, who took bribes to support themselves, and oppressive bribe takers, who enriched themselves unduly. See Sergei A. Korf, *Dvorianstvo i ego soslovnoe upravlenie za stoletie 1762–1855 godov* (St. Petersburg, 1906), pp. 380–381.

34. On the omnipresence and general acceptance of bribery in the government's practical operations during the eighteenth and early nineteenth centuries, see, e.g., H. Torke, *Das russische Beamtentum in der ersten Hälfte des 19 Jahrhunderts* (*Forschungen zur osteuropäischen Geschichte*, vol. XIII, Berlin, 1967), pp. 224–227, and Korf, p. 443.

In the 1770s–1780s, when A. I. Viazemskii was serving as governor-general of Penza and Tambov gubernias, he felt compelled to put out an order to the new local governing institutions that were being set up under his supervision (see below, ch. II, sec. D) strictly forbidding them to accept gifts from the state peasants. More, he ordered them to take action against peasants who tried to bring gifts. See his *Arkhiv Kniazia Viazemskogo* (St. Petersburg, 1881), pp. 83–85. Alexander Herzen recalled an occasion during his exile in the provinces in the 1830s–1840s when he engaged in bribery in what he considered to be a good cause, acknowledging that "it is only through such irregularity that life is possible in Russia" (*My Past and Thoughts* [6 vols., New York, 1926], I, 322–326). When Vladimir P. Meshcherskii was an uezd-level judicial official in the 1850s, he found that he had to allow his clerks to accept bribes—under his careful supervision—in order to be able to hire and keep competent subordinates. See his *Moi vospominaniia* (3 vols., St. Petersburg, 1897–1912), I, 136.

The vital role of bribery in social organization and development is mentioned very rarely in scholarly literature. Some works on Soviet industrial organization have referred to the utility of illegal procurement methods in the time of Stalin's five-year plans. See, e.g., Joseph Berliner, *Factory and Manager in the USSR* (Cambridge, Mass., 1957), pp. 182–230. The most sophisticated general discussion of bribery that I have seen is in Huntington, pp. 59–71. "Corruption," says Huntington, "may . . . be functional to the maintenance of a political system in the same way that reform is" (p. 64). There is a massive literature on the role of "private enterprise" in the social order, much of which applies quite well to bribery. More recently, studies of "informal organization" in administration, such as Barnard's, pp. 104–120, have come up with insights that suggest the positive aspects of bribery.

by enacting laws and employing a variety of crude administrative devices designed to impose a measure of unity on their domestic administrations. Progress, however, was slow and erratic at best. The tsars had to depend on the hierarchy and use it even as they assaulted it, and their assaults, however vigorous, did not produce enduring results. When Peter came to the throne at the end of the seventeenth century, he faced basically the same sort of tribute-gathering mechanism that his predecessors had, though by his time it had grown somewhat more complex.[35]

The domestic administration that Peter I took over in 1689 rested on a number of territorial chiefs—voevodas, *gubnye starosti*, and others—each of whom held rather vaguely defined powers in his own area and was in turn generally responsible to the central administration for what occurred there.[36] The central administration, however, was divided into more than forty separate offices, all of which possessed varying degrees of authority to order the local chiefs about. Commands from the center came down to the territories in such volume and confusion that the territorial officials were unable to carry them out even when they wanted to.[37] During the course of his reign Peter set up the institutions of senatorial government—chiefly the Senate, the procuracy, and the central colleges—with the general purpose of combining the central offices into a coherent, collegial administration that could cope with the provincial authorities in an orderly and reasonably predictable fashion. In theory, the Senate and its subordinate colleges were to hear *all* appeals and reports from below, receive *all* the tsar's commands from above, and digest the whole into usable procedural formulas. The Senate, in other words, was to develop a legal-administrative system that, hopefully, would enable the tsar to establish orderly communications with his local authorities and allow the people to communicate their needs and desires to him.

But senatorial government did not actually introduce a legal-administrative system. What it did throughout the eighteenth century was to struggle to expand its jurisdiction and introduce a measure of standard form into its procedures. By the end of the century the struggle had produced some results. Many commands from the tsar and appeals to him actually did go through the Senate and its subor-

---

35. See Chicherin, pp. 2–36; German, pp. 33–86; and S. B. Veselovskii, I, 30–49, 342–349, for general descriptions of the tsars' methods of collecting revenue before Peter's time.

36. Chicherin, pp. 75–81, 119, 483–488.

37. *Ibid.*, pp. 104–287, describes the voevodas' duties and the bewildering variety of orders that came down to them from the central offices.

dinate institutions with at least the appearance of good order. But the administrative role of the senatorial institutions remained essentially a passive one. The Senate widened the area it regulated and imparted at least the pretense of systematic operation to most of the domestic administration, but it did not *govern* according to its own prerogatives. It only *functioned* when some person with authority invited it to do so (see below, ch. II, sec. E). It decided and enacted only what it was told to decide and enact. All that can be said of its progress in the eighteenth century is that both the populace and the leading statesmen were more apt to use its agencies at the end of the century than they had been at the beginning.

The basic belief that the Senate's upholders came to cherish was that a uniform law existed naturally in Russian society and, indeed, in all men in all societies. Men were constructed in accordance with this natural law, and if they were properly governed, they would also act in accordance with it. The proper aim of government was to "find" this law, to articulate it, and to live by it.[38]

How was the government to find this law? Senatorial statesmen thought that the best way was for each government to see to it that all transactions between officials and people were conducted by groups (colleges) of officials—thereby insuring their impartiality—and that all legal decisions were recorded according to a uniform procedure. Eventually, so went the assumption, the records thus accumulated would lend themselves to systematic organization, and the government would be able to formulate the law into mutually consistent principles and rules that could be written down and enshrined forever. Then at last the government would be truly systematic ("constitutional").

The hope that proper judicial procedure might someday produce law by itself has never left the Russian imagination, but another kind of government, informed by a different ideal, emerged alongside the senatorial colleges during the course of the eighteenth century. In 1802, with the establishment of the ministries, it acquired institutional expression. There is no general term for it in Russian, except for such

38. G. Telberg, *Pravitelstvuiushchii Senat i samoderzhavnaia vlast v nachale XIX veka* (Moscow, 1914), pp. 10–20, describes the views of the "senatorial" conservative statesmen in the first years of Alexander I's reign. They drew their inspiration chiefly from Montesquieu and Pufendorf. Montesquieu's work *The Spirit of the Laws,* which he first published in 1748, exercised an important (but by no means determining) intellectual influence on enlightened Russians in the late eighteenth and early nineteenth centuries. On the influence of Pufendorf throughout the European world, see L. Krieger, *The Politics of Discretion* (Chicago, 1965), pp. 254–266. Krieger, pp. 39–49, describes Pufendorf's beliefs regarding the unity of all natural law.

limited technical words as *edinolichnoe* (individual) and *ministerskoe* (ministerial), both of which refer to a government organization in which each official has his own definite responsibilities and discharges them on his own precisely delimited authority. A broader and more descriptive term for the new order of 1802 is "bureaucratic" government.

In contrast with senatorial institutions, bureaucratic government was active. Its advocates and officials did not want to wait for law—i.e., legal-administrative system—to emerge by itself from court records; indeed, some of them doubted that it ever would. Instead of functioning only when they were asked to, bureaucrats aspired to identify state "necessities" and to derive plans and programs from them that could be imposed on the population by the government's agencies. The bureaucrats did not abandon the idea of a law residing in the hearts of the people, but they generally harbored the assumption that it would not achieve expression unless the government inaugurated reform programs conceived in accordance with abstract conceptions of necessity and/or the good society. Planned programs, carried out by a bureaucratic administration, would induce social change by the sheer force of their general utility. Government would teach society to accept its aims as society's own by virtue of their logical consistency with the government's necessities. In short, senatorial government developed out of the assumption that the state should embody some sort of established law, whereas bureaucracy emerged along with the growing realization that the state had to usurp (and create) law in accordance with its necessities.[39]

The contrast between senatorial and bureaucratic government was rarely clear in practice. Senatorial institutions did not strive consciously to embody an exclusively passive role, nor did bureaucratic ministries conspire to invade the countryside without any regard for existing custom. Ideally, the Senate was to direct the domestic administration, and the ministries were to base their programs on existing laws and social conditions. In fact, however, the Senate's inherent passivity could not be made to harmonize with the aspirations that the

39. The ascendancy of bureaucratic over senatorial government in Russia corresponds roughly to that of nationalism over national consciousness in Europe. In the early nineteenth century, says Friedrich Meinecke, there was in Germany "an intense longing for national realization" that would not be "satisfied until everything is nationalized that is at all capable of nationalization" (*Cosmopolitanism and the National State* [Princeton, N.J., 1970], p. 14). This longing was often expressed in rhapsodies about freedom and spontaneity, but its less poetic aspect was the transformation of the state from protector of tradition into disruptor, or, as Geoffrey Bruun, *Europe and the French Imperium* (New York, 1963), pp. 1–5, describes it, the evolution from enlightenment to Napoleon.

ministries embodied, and a conflict broke out between the two as soon as the ministries came into being. The result was that the ministries assumed a predominant role in the central government, while the Senate fell to the position of a service organization within the emerging bureaucracy.

As the Senate lost its central position, the dichotomy between the senatorial ideal of government and the bureaucratic did not disappear. On the contrary, it continued to lie at the heart of the government throughout the tsarist period. By the 1850s the ministries had undercut the Senate, but this did not change the fact that they had emerged from senatorial government and that they made no sense whatever in the tsarist government-society apart from the aspirations and pretensions that the old order had imparted to them. When the senatorial "path" to the discovery of law in society lost its concrete institutional expression, it still had to be given a place of honor in the pretensions (ideology) of the bureaucracy. "Finding" the law in the practical relationships between people and government remained one of the basic principles of purpose in Russian legal-administrative system until the Revolution.

In sum, the evolution from 1711 to 1905 involved three kinds of government: personal-hierarchical, senatorial-collegial, and bureaucratic. Each superseded the one before it, but only by adopting its pretenses, taking over its goals, and assuming its responsibilities. Each one, therefore, embodied the contradictions between its own purposes and those of its predecessor. All the institutions of senatorial government were introduced to strengthen and improve the tribute-collecting hierarchy, but they ended by trying to destroy it and replace it. Likewise, all the institutions of the bureaucracy were set up with the intention of rendering the Senate effective and extending its influence, but they ended up by reducing the Senate to an instrument of bureaucratic administration. At last, in 1861, the bureaucracy found itself triumphant, but its triumph burdened it with the very contradictions that had given rise to it. The ministers were obliged simultaneously: 1) to mobilize human and natural resources for purposes the populace did not comprehend, 2) to "discover" and preserve the law within which the people supposedly lived, and 3) to formulate and impose a legal-administrative system that would permit them to discharge their official responsibilities to the state. The ministers had to pursue these conflicting aims within the framework of what purported to be a single, uniform legal-administrative system. At least this was their pretense and/or aspiration.

C. The Dilemmas of Systematization in Russia

It may be said that there was a fundamental contradiction from Peter's time on between the practical purpose of system in Russian government and the way in which it was supposed to operate in theory. When Peter commanded his officials to stop bribing their superiors and overawing their subordinates and instead to begin depending on one another to observe official rules and procedures, he not only was changing rules but was destroying the main basis on which the government officials were able to understand each other. Take, for example, Peter's formal prohibitions against bribery. Had they been enforced, government officials would still have been responsible for carrying out their tribute-collecting missions; yet their practical operations would have exposed them to accusations and punishments for crimes against the state. Had a superior been hamstrung by regulations, he would not have had the power either to inspire awe in his subordinates or to respond to their bribes; yet he was required to enforce new and more exorbitant demands from the center.[40] Fortunately, anti-bribery laws were not enforced consistently, nor was the personal authority of the officials effectively constrained. Thus the government managed, albeit with considerable difficulty, to survive the introduction and slow expansion of system for another two centuries after Peter's time. Even so, rules that were intended to establish system had the effect of forcing operating officials to become outlaws, and this could not help but have a negative influence on the strength of legal-administrative order.

It must be kept in mind, then, that systematization did not eliminate the contradictions between system and the hierarchy of personal relationships. In many respects the growth of organization actually sharpened these contradictions and strengthened the officials' deter-

40. Braibanti describes the situation of an official in present-day Pakistan, caught between a backward society organized around bribery and a would-be bureaucratic government: "The official must not only be physically detached but must exaggerate the drama of his detachment. To be close to the people is to place oneself in a web from which there is no escape. In a society so full of intrigue, of tribal animosity, of vengeance . . . the mere posture of familiarity inevitably creates a reputation for partiality which leads to actual partiality. Overnight the inexorable progression of this syndrome collapses the edifice of bureaucratic equity. This situation is aggravated by the encompassing power of government. In the absence of effective voluntary organization, virtually every group action requires bureaucratic impetus and sanction. There being no escape from bureaucratic power, the total pressures of the entire social realm are brought to bear upon the single person who represents this bureaucratic power in microcosm. . . . The Pakistani official is almost helpless against the web which threatens to strangle him. His aloofness is his instinctive response to the need for self-preservation" ("Public Bureaucracy and Judiciary," p. 394).

mination to oppose system. The government servitors learned to hate
the restraints of system even as they learned the techniques of systematic organization, and—contradiction piled upon contradiction—
they even learned to organize themselves systematically to oppose
systematization (see below, ch. III, sec. E).

Not long after Peter's time, the practical contradictions involved in
the systematization of Russian government began to acquire a moral
dimension. By the 1760s "enlightened" capital-city Russians were coming to believe that system was not only necessary but morally right.[41]
A half-century of native Russian pretense, together with inspiration
derived from European philosophy, taught them to cherish the ideals
of systematic control—associated in some cases with the companion
myths of freedom and justice—as values in themselves, quite apart
from their practical purposes. Armed with, or trapped by, this new
morality, the generations that grew up after Peter's reign found it increasingly difficult to stomach what they actually did in order to
govern Russia. For the enlightened, a tribute-collecting hierarchy was
not only an annoying obstacle to proper operation that had to be
recognized and accepted for the sake of expediency. It was a sin, and
if the government of Russia could not work without it, then the government of Russia was an outrage against humanity. In fact, the Imperial Russian government could not work without relying upon and
utilizing the tribute-collecting hierarchy; therefore, those enlightened
men who continued to serve the government suffered under the burden
of an apparently insoluble moral dilemma.

They resolved the dilemma by repression. In the reign of Catherine
II (1762–1796) the leading statesmen generally found it impossible to
conceive of the basic features and processes of their government as it
actually worked without denouncing them as forms of corruption. No
one conceived of "old ways" of bribery and personal influence as a
tradition that should be upheld against the new pretensions of system;
consequently, very few statesmen defended the existing order as it
really was. As legal-administrative system evolved, therefore, almost
no dialogue developed between traditional practices and new ideals.
No constructive dialectic between practice and theory enabled men to
communicate meaningfully with one another as they became aware
that their collective behavior was changing. Such debate as there was
in Catherine's time came to little more than a contest between those
who pretended to *be* systematic and those who aspired, or affected to
aspire, to *become* systematic. Both sides condemned the actual opera-

41. See Raeff, *Origins*, pp. 48–50, 75–80, 102–107, for a brilliant discussion of
gentry attitudes toward organization in the eighteenth century.

tion of government; therefore, the question of integrating practice with theory never arose. It may be said, then, that one of the effects of systematization on the society in Russian government was to render public discussion of domestic problems and even of morality virtually irrelevant.[42]

This was *collective* repression. An individual represses a personal need or desire that he cannot bear to contemplate by keeping it out of his conscious mind. In the same way a society can repress a common practice among its members by keeping it out of all public and polite communication among them. In order to achieve this end, the members must be compelled to avoid any public mention of the possibility that the practice might have social value. How is this done? Most commonly, the force that compels collective silence derives from the common habit of regarding the practice as inherently immoral. This, at any rate, was how repression worked in enlightened Russian society in the late eighteenth and nineteenth centuries. Enlightened Russians could never speak of bribery without the proper pejorative adjectives, and the tacit assumption that bribery was evil became a prerequisite for any formal discussion of public issues. A capital-city Russian of the late eighteenth and nineteenth centuries who publicly questioned the assumption was a social phenomenon analogous to a police commissioner in a modern American city addressing a meeting of the Americans for Democratic Action and explaining to them how he negotiates with criminal organizations in order to control crime more effectively.

Enlightened Russians were no more consciously dishonest or hypocritical than any other people. They adopted their collective repression because it allowed them to live in a world where no one could maintain moral identity or sense of purpose without denouncing bribery but where no one could function without taking and giving bribes. Denunciation and practical acceptance of bribery fitted them-

---

42. Now and then men spoke more or less frankly about bribery. One of the delegates to Catherine II's Commission of 1767–1768 (see below, ch. II, sec. D) brought an instruction (*nakaz*) asserting that it was unjust to punish givers of bribes. See Vladimir A. Grigorev, *Reforma mestnogo upravleniia pri Ekaterine II: Uchrezhdenie o guberniiakh 7 noiabria 1775* (St. Petersburg, 1910), p. 126. James Hassell, "The Vicissitudes of Russian Administrative Reform, 1762–1801" (unpublished Ph.D. dissertation, Cornell University, 1967), pp. 172–173, mentions a note of 1797 from a governor to the *general-prokuror* in which the governor requested permission to rehire a number of officials he had discharged for taking bribes. The reason, he said, was that he could find no one to take their places. For other examples, see above, n. 34. In general, however, the possibility that bribery constituted a social need was not discussed. That it might be an authentic tradition or a positive good was never considered.

selves together in a single habit of thought that made sense out of a difficult experience and furnished Russians with a myth of sorts. They needed the myth; therefore, they needed the repression as well. There is nothing unusual about this.[43]

Contrast the Russians' relatively sudden assault on bribery with the gradual evolution that took place in western Europe. To be sure, practice and theory conflicted with each other in western Europe just as they did in Russia, but at all stages of its evolution payments of fees that were generally recognized and accepted were distinguished more or less publicly from those denounced as "bribery." In all eras men could usually appeal to authorities and conduct practical negotiations with them without committing a crime.[44] Not so in eighteenth- and nineteenth-century Russia. "Law" manifested itself to the leaders of society as an ideal to be worshipped, not as a means by which men could influence one another and develop mutual confidence. When Russian administrators wanted to influence one another in order to perform practical tasks, they resorted to "crime," not the law. They had to violate the ideal of system in order to systematize, which meant that they suffered not only from a criminal's insecurity but from bad conscience and a sense of futility as well.

Contradictions between morality and reality did not soften the government-society's impetus toward system. On the contrary, they intensified it. From Catherine II's time on, the government-society responded to its internal philosophical and psychological problems by

43. A number of writers have agreed with Freud that repression is indispensable to civilization, but many of them have been inclined to reject (or ignore) the possibility that it plays a positive role. Norman Brown, for example, in *Life against Death* (London, 1959), pp. 3–15, assumes that repression is in all cases an evil. He never considers the obvious fact that creative individual self-expression and the spontaneous evolution of myths in society require acts of repression just as much as they require "exuberance" and "creativity" (as Hoebel, pp. 10–25, has pointed out).

In Russia the vital role of repression in cultural development is spectacularly obvious. The Russian intelligentsia of the nineteenth century could not have written or spoken a line without it. It has been frequently noted that they were unable to face reality, but this is only valid in the sense that what they said did not describe reality objectively. They were responding to reality and coping with it as best they could; if this was not objective, it certainly was realistic. More, their continuing response constituted an affirmation of themselves, their country, and life itself, under unusually difficult circumstances. Their "failure" to recognize realities such as the role of bribery in Russian society was not a result of blindness but a sine qua non of their very existence.

44. Two good descriptions of the gradual evolution that took place in Europe are G. T. Matthews, *The Royal General Farms in Eighteenth-Century France* (New York, 1958), and Frederick W. Maitland, *Township and Borough* (Cambridge, 1898).

embarking on a crusade to systematize not only its own administrative organization but all of Russian society. In the late eighteenth and nineteenth centuries the idea gradually emerged in the capital cities that the Russian people were not only a resource to be used but a society that had to be transformed.

When the repressed-enlightened Russian of the capital cities contemplated peasant villages and the lower reaches of rural administration, he was not likely to see men going about their business in their own way. Instead, he conjured up images of "good" men—good, that is, according to the principles of legal-administrative system. These imaginary good men were not happy and/or productive enough, and they did not always behave well. The reason was that "evil" men— those who engaged in bribery and/or exercised authority on a personal basis—were corrupting and/or oppressing them. This vision, unopposed by any articulate representative from the villages, allowed —indeed, commanded—enlightened Russians to mount an attack on Russian society outside the capital cities in the name of their concept of it. In their own eyes they loved the Russian people—the imaginary "good" peasants—and were saving them. In fact, they abhorred the Russian people as they were. In the nineteenth century both government and "intelligentsia" were intent on destroying the peasant way of life, which is why they both found it not only necessary but also moral to carry out a series of invasions into rural society. It may be said, then, that the systematization of Russian government led it more or less irresistibly into a massive effort to impose social change on the peasantry.

This brings us to the dilemmas involved in government-imposed social change. Perhaps the most basic of these in any country is that of the alienated innovator.[45] It makes itself felt in all reform programs that attempt to deal with individuals rather than whole societies. Typically, the reformers seek out the most "advanced" and give them encouragement, in the hope that these few "leaders" will bridge the gap between backward and modern and bring their people into the light. Many social reforms of the nineteenth and twentieth centuries, in Russia and elsewhere, have taken this form. The Russian agrarian reform of 1905–1914 was originally conceived in this way.[46]

45. The general problem is described at some length in George M. Foster, *Traditional Cultures and the Impact of Technological Change* (New York, 1962), pp. 27–36. Ethel Dunn, "Educating the Small Peoples of the Soviet North: The Limits of Cultural Change," *Arctic Anthropology*, V, no. 1 (1968), 1–31, describes how Soviet sociologists have had to face it in their efforts to modernize some of the peoples in the Far North.

46. See my "Concept of the Stolypin Land Reform," *Slavic Review*, XXIII (June 1964), 275–293.

The trouble is that the advanced individuals, the innovators, do not generally lead their people forward. Most of them become alienated from their associates and either victimize them, leave them, or suffer expulsion. Instead of reforming society, a program that encourages a few individuals to "advance" actually tends to freeze the remaining majority in their backwardness by consistently depriving them of their best leaders. In practice, advanced individuals are as likely to be obstacles to social change as a means to it. The possibility arises, therefore, that an effective program of social change may actually strive to prevent advanced individuals from breaking away from their fellows. This has been a feature of many programs introduced by modern communist regimes, including, most spectacularly, their campaigns to prevent their citizens from going abroad. Government programs of social change do not all have to be so drastic, but a general rule of thumb that emerges from consideration of the alienated innovator is that government-imposed social change must ultimately cope with whole societies.

Unfortunately, our rule of thumb only leads into more dilemmas. All the imperial government's attempts to impose legal-administrative system on peasant society as a whole followed either one or both of two courses of action. One was to declare the existing customary legal order null and void and to try to replace it with a new set of ready-made, properly systematic regulations and agencies. The other was to try to systematize the traditional legal order itself. Both of these approaches were self-defeating.

The first approach presupposes a dictatorial government with large numbers of loyal and highly trained servitors, willing and able to enforce alien regulations on a people who are not inclined to enforce them on themselves. In fact, there was no such corps of servitors available to the imperial government, but even if there had been, they could not have achieved much. The peasants could have been compelled to learn new rules by rote, but they could not have been taught to depend on one another to follow them. The strictest discipline or the most sophisticated incentive plan could have done no more than to teach them to depend on the servitors (instructors, agitators) who were imposing the rules upon them. As a general rule, the forced imposition of alien regulations cannot by itself establish an operational legal-administrative system with its roots in the behavior patterns of the people, not even under the most ideal conditions.[47] Thus the intro-

47. Mannoni describes at some length the psychological reasons why an alien power cannot establish an operational legal system of its own devising in the society of its subjects.

duction of system into peasant society required that the peasants'
social relationships evolve into systematic form through their own
collective action and experience.[48]

The question was: just how was the imperial government to go
about inculcating habits and initiating actions that would cause the
peasants to comprehend their existing relationships—that is, their
customary ways—as elements in a systematic pattern? As we have
seen, peasant law was adaptable enough as long as it remained nonsystematic. Attempts to systematize it, insofar as they were effective,
led to the practical result of rendering it unusable. It was absurd to
try to derive general laws from the polyglot of customs, ad hoc personal agreements, and magical hocus pocus that was thrown together
in the imaginations of the Russian peasants without any thought for
logical order. To the extent that such laws were enacted and enforced, they only made it impossible for peasant judicial institutions
to arrive at verdicts that would make any sense to anyone.

In sum, government-imposed social change must cope with whole
societies, yet it can neither change societies according to the government's own formulas nor modernize custom. It does not follow that
government-imposed change is impossible. What these dilemmas suggest is that such change is not likely to be orderly and that it will not
proceed according to a single, "correct" program drafted in advance
by wise and well-informed men. On the contrary, it is likely and perhaps even preferable that government-imposed change consist of
several mutually contradictory programs directed by men who rely
more on ad hoc judgment than on legal formulas.

So much for the dilemmas involved in the process of systematization
per se. Before leaving the subject of dilemmas, it will be appropriate to
consider some of those that economic development brought to rural
Russia. During the period 1861–1905 a railroad network suddenly
brought towns and world trade routes close to much of the countryside, causing a sharp increase in the demand for grain. Grain consumption increased rapidly in the cities at the same time that the new
railroads were carrying it to the seaports in ever larger quantities for
export.[49] As a result, grain flowed out of the countryside much faster
than before. From about 1887 on the government consciously accel-

48. On this general point, see H. G. Barnett, *Anthropology in Administration*
(Evanston, Ill., 1956), pp. 3–6.
49. Grain export quintupled from the 1850s to the mid-1880s—see *Istoricheskoe obozrenie piatidesiatiletnei deiatelnosti ministerstva gosudarstvennykh imushchestv 1837–1887* (5 vols., St. Petersburg, 1888), IV, 258–259—and in the following two decades grain came to make up more than half of Russia's total export.

erated the flow by adjusting railroad rates to encourage grain export in order to balance the rising imports that industrial development required.[50]

Individual peasants were able to respond to the new Russia-wide market and to profit from it. A few became wealthy, and a substantial number lived in better circumstances than their forefathers of the serf era had. It was in the two or three generations between 1861 and 1905 that the peasants acquired the habit of drinking tea (and putting samovars in their homes), learned to smoke tobacco, took to burning kerosene in their lamps, and began to rely on matches to light their fires. At the same time their love of vodka did not diminish, and their taste for sugar seems to have grown sharper.[51] All these items cost money, especially since the government imposed high taxes on them, and growing peasant demand for them indicated that the peasants had more money to spend in 1861–1905 than they had had before.

On the other hand, peasant society was sadly unprepared for the commercialization of agriculture. Most peasants were unable to conceive of farming as a productive enterprise. They knew a good harvest when they saw one, and they valued it highly. They were quite capable of working harder and farming a greater area of land in order to increase their production. But they generally took what soil and climate gave them in response to traditional usages rather than tampering with new methods of cultivation. They did not calculate the productivity of their agricultural techniques; consequently, they did not seriously attempt to improve them.[52] When they had a good year, they did not accumulate reserves in order to sell later when the price rose or to provide against years of drought and crop failure.[53] In short,

50. Theodore Von Laue, *Sergei Witte and the Industrialization of Russia* (New York, 1963), pp. 18–28, traces the evolution of the government's attitude toward grain export in the 1880s. It was I. A. Vyshnegradskii, minister of finance in 1887–1892, who first began to conceive of and to foster grain export as a major element in economic development.

51. A report of 1891 on a Belorussian village indicated that samovars and kerosene lamps were just beginning to come into use at that time. See A. Gruzinskii, "Iz etnograficheskikh nabliudenii v Rechitskom uezde Minskoi g.," *Etnograficheskoe obozrenie*, XI (1891), 143. A recent Soviet anthropological study of a village in Tambov gubernia points out that kerosene lamps first came into use there in 1879. Baths, brick buildings, curtains, tin roofs, and wooden cradles all appeared and came into general use during the period from about 1860 to 1910. See P. I. Kushner, ed., *The Village of Viriatino*, tr. Sula Benet (New York, 1970), pp. 60–73, 120.

52. A. V. Chayanov, *The Theory of Peasant Economy* (Homewood, Ill., 1966), pp. 5–9. In the early nineteenth century many of the gentry were similarly disinclined to calculate the productivity of their agriculture. See Confino, *Domaines*, pp. 166–180.

53. On peasant attitudes toward grain reserves, see V. S. Prugavin, *Russkaia zemelnaia obshchina v trudakh ee mestnykh issledovatelei* (Moscow, 1888), pp. 237–247.

the peasants had no objection to wealth, but experience within their traditional way of life gave them little reason to associate the acquiring of it with *systematic* effort. Customary attitudes encouraged them to work hard in the old, godly ways but gave them no incentive to engage in economic enterprise on their lands.

It will not do to visualize these peasant attitudes solely within the context of village society. They were, rather, elements in a larger scheme that included the government and its historical relationship with the peasantry. By 1905 the tribute-collecting hierarchy had been operating in the villages for hundreds of years in the absence of effective regulation, and, speaking generally, its methods did not favor the consistent accumulation of wealth. When a harvest was good, collectors would usually take in most of the excess. In years of crop failure they would collect less or none at all, or they might even dispense grain to those who needed it. Under these freewheeling conditions, it was wasted effort for a village (or a peasant) to save grain or money. The collectors would take care of those who needed help in bad years, while those who accumulated wealth would probably have to pay it out whenever the collector discovered they had it. The peasants were not characteristically lazy under this regime, but they had little reason to change their way of life in order to produce more.[54]

The government hoped that this situation would change with the abolition of serfdom and the gradual regularization of the peasants' financial obligations. It seems, however, that the old irregularities persisted, largely because the villages were still held collectively responsible for the taxes and debts of their members and because they generally fell into arrears in these payments. Collectors often followed the traditional practice of allowing the villages to avoid payments in bad times and then collecting excessive amounts in good years without differentiating between those families who had fallen into arrears and those who had not. In effect, then, tax collection continued to be a matter of grabbing money whenever and wherever it could be found, and the newly freed serfs had very little incentive to learn new lessons of fiscal responsibility or to improve their agricultural techniques.[55]

54. The same generalizations apply to the rural gentry before the nineteenth century. Augustine, pp. 412–416, 421–425, notes a general unawareness of market relationships among both gentry and peasants in the 1760s. According to I. I. Ignatovich, *Pomeshchich i krestiane nakanune osvobozhdeniia* (Leningrad, 1925), p. 29, serf owners habitually tried to put off paying taxes, anticipating that the government would ultimately forgive them their arrears. It often happened that the government justified their hopes, but only when they could demonstrate their poverty. Thus in many cases it was not production that brought wealth in rural Russia but the ability to manipulate tax collectors.

55. A report published by the ministry of finance in 1892 gives a graphic de-

The massive economic development that Russia underwent after the 1850s did not bring with it a basis for social change.

Economic development resembles systematization in that it comes as a blessing to societies able to cope with it and as a destructive force to those that cannot. In Russia, in the period from the 1860s to the 1930s, the most striking manifestation of this destructive force was famine, especially the massive famines that occurred in the grain-producing regions in 1891, 1901, 1906, and 1911. Famine, of course, was nothing new in Russia in the late nineteenth century, but these famines were much more extensive than any that had occurred before. Moreover, they were a new and peculiar kind. They struck in a time of rapidly increasing national wealth, and they affected the people who actually produced the greater part of Russia's food. In short, they were not basically a result of food shortage.

When the Russia-wide market struck the countryside, it brought an increasing supply of money and credit.[56] This meant, among other things, that a poor peasant who ran out of food between harvests could borrow in order to support himself instead of going begging or appealing to his owner, as he had done in the past. As security for their loans, the peasants could offer their lands—despite government prohibitions against this—and work animals, in which case they could easily lose everything they had if the forthcoming crop failed. More commonly, they made relatively small loans and offered only their future labor and/or their future crops as security.

The peasants made their loans at a serious disadvantage. Usually their grain supply gave out in the middle of winter, when grain was high in price and labor was cheap; thus they paid high for the grain they had to buy and sold their labor at a low price. When next summer's crops came in, wages went up and grain prices went down, but the debtor-peasants had to go to work at the rate they had agreed to the previous winter. Moreover, they had to turn over the harvest on their own lands to their creditors as soon as they brought it in, that is, at precisely the time of year when grain prices were at their lowest.[57]

scription of this state of affairs. See *Neurozhai i narodnoe bedstvie* (St. Petersburg, 1892), pp. 154–176. According to K. Golovin, *Moi vospominaniia* (2 vols., St. Petersburg, 1908, 1910), II, 239–240, the author of this report was A. S. Ermolov, minister of agriculture from 1894 to 1905. A similar description of the peasants' plight from another point of view is in I. J. Poliakoff, *Die bäuerlichen Loskaufzahlungen in Russland* (Munich, 1916), pp. 36–65.

56. The impact of money is described accurately, if somewhat luridly, in S. Stepniak (S. M. Kravchinskii), *The Russian Peasant* (New York, 1888), pp. 20–59. See also *Neurozhai*, pp. 180–191.

57. Concerning the government's policy to collect revenue precisely at those times when the peasants received their income, see *Neurozhai*, pp. 154–156. Con-

Presumably, the wealthier peasants could avoid seasonal price fluctuations, but even these more fortunate citizens were likely to go into debt in order to expand their lands and stock. In years of crop failure, therefore, they might well have to sell their holdings at a disadvantage, thereby suffering considerable personal loss and at the same time throwing what little grain they had onto the market and contributing to the general shortage in their locales.[58]

Under these circumstances a great deal of grain got into the market, more than the local population in the grain-producing areas could afford.[59] Once sold, the grain could be carried far away by the new railroads, leaving not only individual peasants and villages without sufficient supply but whole areas. A crop failure, therefore, could create far more drastic and widespread shortages than had ever occurred before.[60]

The problem was compounded by the rapid increase in population after the 1860s and the concomitant development of a land shortage.[61] As usable land was taken up, its value and the cost of renting it rose sharply, so sharply, in fact, that in many instances the rental on a piece of land actually came to exceed the income that the peasants could derive from it with their backward agricultural methods. The peasants frequently did not realize that they were farming at a loss, and many of them went right on paying excessive rent in the sincere belief that they were bettering their condition.[62]

---

cerning the landowners' policy in many areas to hire their labor in the winter preceding the working season in order to pay the lowest possible wage, see the testimony of a number of landowners in *Doklad vysochaishe utverzhdennoi* (26 *maia 1872*) *komissii dlia issledovaniia nyneshnego polozheniia selskogo khoziaistva i proizvoditelnosti v Rossii* (7 vols., St. Petersburg, 1873), I, sec. 1, 13 (Simbirsk), 16 (Penza), 33–34 (Kiev).

58. On the general instability that burdened the peasant economy, see *Neurozhai*, pp. 93–108.

59. It has been argued that the outflow of grain was enough to cause a steady decrease in per capita grain consumption after about 1880. See, e.g., George Carson, "The State and Economic Development; Russia, 1890–1939," in H. G. J. Aitken, ed., *The State and Economic Growth* (New York, 1959), pp. 121–122.

60. A. Baykov, "The Economic Development of Russia," *Economic History Review*, VII (Dec. 1954), 137–149, gives a general description of this situation.

61. "Land shortage" was the contemporary term. Actually, it often meant no more or less than Daniel Boone's legendary complaint when he saw smoke from his neighbor's chimney. There was a land shortage of this sort in Russia as long as there was agriculture, because the peasants were continually looking for new lands to replace the ones they had just worn out. In the 1890s land shortage meant simply that there was not enough free land to suit the peasants' tastes within the framework of their culture under the impact of the market. See A. A. Kaufman, *Pereselenie i kolonizatsiia* (St. Petersburg, 1905), pp. 162–183. But if land shortage was more a cultural phenomenon than a geographic one, the fact remains that the peasants starved from it.

62. Chayanov, pp. 5–20, 39–40.

These pressures were at their worst in the grain-producing areas of European Russia—the steppe area bounded roughly by the Caucasus Mountains, the Ural Mountains, the Oka River, and the western border of the empire. Why were conditions so bad in the steppe? Mainly because steppe agriculture was unusually ruinous and wasteful even by Russian standards. The soil there was better than anywhere else, and it required less care. When the peasants settled on it, therefore, they got in the habit of growing crops without taking any measures to preserve the soil. They even neglected to spread manure. When they exhausted one field, they simply left it fallow for a few years and switched to another.[63] The best fields were reduced to minimal productivity, and by the 1890s there were no longer enough even of these to go around. If the peasants continued to live and farm in their "godly" ways, they could not produce enough grain to support themselves and pay their taxes.

The peasants of the northern and central regions of European Russia were already more or less adjusted to "overpopulation" by the 1860s. Well before then, the number of people had come to exceed that which local agriculture could support, and the peasants had long since gotten used to the idea that agriculture could be unprofitable. Many had abandoned it in order to take up industrial and commercial work, and a few had actually improved their farming techniques, especially in the western provinces. The majority had learned at least to manure their fields. In short, the population in the grain-*consuming* regions of Russia was relatively well prepared to live with a Russia-wide market by the late nineteenth century and even stood to benefit from the cheaper grain that came from the steppe. There were crop failures in the central and northern regions in 1861–1905, and large numbers of poor peasants frequently went hungry, but there were no famines on the scale of the ones that occurred in the grain-producing areas.[64]

In the 1880s a few economists began to become aware of the problems of peasant agriculture, but they had trouble finding practical solutions. Obviously, there had to be some sort of economic improvement, but it was precisely economic growth that was causing the famines in the first place. Industrial expansion depended on grain

---

63. *Neurozhai*, p. 93.
64. *Ibid.* In 1916–1920 large-scale famines did occur in the cities and in northern and central Russia, whereas the grain-producing areas were able to feed themselves. This was because the grain market broke down, relieving the pressure on the farmers and at the same time bringing about the collapse of the national economy and of the state itself. See A. M. Anfimov, "Zernovoe khoziaistvo Rossii v gody pervoi mirovoi voiny," in *Materialy po istorii selskogo khoziaistva i krestianstva SSSR*, III (Moscow, 1959), 478–493.

export, and any measures that interrupted it would actually block development. Any interference with the exploitation of steppe agriculture would raise the price of bread in the cities and in the northern and central regions, lowering living standards in these areas and forcing factories to pay higher wages. Peasant suffering, therefore, had to be considered together with the broad requirements of Russia's industrial development. When it was so considered, it appeared that any measures to help the peasants were likely to hinder economic development as a whole, thereby, paradoxically, defeating their own purpose. The government's problem in 1905 was not simply to feed or educate some starving peasants. More fundamentally, it had to reassess its whole relationship to Russian society.

What was the nature of this relationship? With the gradual expansion of commerce in the course of the eighteenth and nineteenth centuries, the government got ever more of its revenue from trade and ever less from its direct taxes on the peasant villages (tribute). In the period 1880–1905 the government was able to cancel direct taxes almost entirely and to let the market "collect the tribute" from the peasants.[65] The heaviest burden on the peasant budget ceased to be governmental tribute and became instead overly high rents and mortgage payments on their lands,[66] together with high prices for the goods they bought in the market, chiefly vodka, tea, sugar, kerosene, and tobacco (see above, n. 51). In short, the government faced an entirely new set of problems in 1905. It had ceased to be a mechanism for extracting tribute and had become instead a structure that rested directly on the flow of goods through a nationwide market. To put it in a broader framework, government, cities, and the population of the grain-*consuming* regions depended on the operation of a process that was reducing the steppe peasants to starvation.[67]

65. See below, ch. VIII, sec. A. The year 1906 marked virtually the end of the central government's exactions of "tribute" from the peasants until the end of the tsarist regime. The peasants continued to pay a small property tax until 1917— see I. F. Gindin, *Gosudarstvennyi bank i ekonomicheskaia politika tsarskogo pravitelstva (1861–1892 gody)* (Moscow, 1960), p. 34—and they also continued to pay direct taxes for the support of their zemstvoes and their own volost and village institutions (see below, ch. IX, sec. D), but these did not constitute a serious economic burden. As for labor obligations (*naturalnye povinnosti*)—road repair, police duty, fighting forest fires—they were irritating and oppressive, but they too were not economically significant.

66. Chayanov, pp. 39–40.

67. The concept of Russia as a monstrosity is well stated in a German document of 1941 that set forth the Nazi plan for the economic arrangements to be established after the conquest of the Soviet Union. According to the Nazis, Russia was monstrous because the food surplus of the steppe was taken from the farmers by force to support the "unnatural" industry that had been constructed in the

In 1905, then, the government found itself faced with the necessity of mediating between opposing socio-economic interests. Instead of simply squeezing the peasants, it had to protect those of the grain-producing regions from the rest of the population. It had to counteract the effects of the very urban economy it had been striving to create, without seriously impeding the development of this economy. This was the dilemma of economic development with which the government-society had to cope in 1905 in order to survive. It was a dilemma that called for a fundamental reordering of the relationships between government and peasantry.

To sum up, systematization plunged the government-society in Russia into a series of dilemmas. In the eighteenth century the forms of system turned out to be irreconcilable with the hierarchy of persons that actually ran the government. Politically conscious Russians resolved this dilemma by dreaming up images of Russian society that were somehow amenable to systematic order, thereby allowing themselves to abhor the reality in the countryside without consciously renouncing their own people. In this way they made sense of what they were doing but found themselves committed to a crusade against the whole population on behalf of their fantasies. From Catherine's time on, they were seeking to destroy that which they professed to love in the name of their love. The resolution of this dilemma required nothing less than the systematization of all Russian society, i.e., its transformation into the mythical images of capital-city society. Work toward this end resolved the moral dilemma of the government-society but involved it in turn in the practical dilemmas of economic development and government-imposed social change.

D. Concluding Remarks on Method

The general point of this chapter is that the imposition of legal-administrative system on a nonsystematic society—the work to which enlightened Russians have consciously devoted themselves since the time of Catherine II—is fundamentally a self-negating, self-defeating

---

northern and central sections, thus plunging the steppe farmers into famine and subjecting them to political oppression. The Nazis proposed to eradicate the "false" civilization in the northern and central regions while joining the southern and western areas to Europe, where they belonged. The plan is printed in Karl Brandt, *Management of Agriculture and Food in the German-Occupied and Other Areas of Fortress Europe* (Stanford, Calif., 1953), pp. 621–639. This statement is often dismissed as Nazi demagoguery, and in part it was, but it also contains a sound analysis of the economic structure of the Russian state. Indeed, it is the most concise prose expression of the tragedy in Russia's development that I have seen.

process that has continually plunged both imposers and imposed upon into dilemmas and absurdities. Systematization demands more of its participants than education and good will. Given all the tact, understanding, loyalty, and high moral quality in the world, the process is still very likely to be a rough and unpredictable one.[68]

The dilemmas described in the foregoing section provide a background for the study of systematization in Russia, not the substance of it. They bring a certain degree of focus to a blurred image by suggesting a relatively concrete definition of systematization: to wit, a long process of creating, recognizing, and coping with dilemmas.

Unfortunately, the sharpening of focus inevitably narrows the view. If we draw a picture of the tsarist government coping with dilemmas, we obscure other pictures—the government committing crimes, making unnecessary errors, holding back "progress," destroying "freedom." It must be acknowledged, therefore, that by focusing on the dilemmas of systematization, I am making a choice among several possible approaches. Moreover, this choice is essentially subjective. The evidence does not prove that the tsarist government was struggling to cope with dilemmas, nor do I know of any theory that irresistibly compels us to take this view. Creating and coping with dilemmas is not what "really happened" in Russia in 1711–1905, in the sense that it was the only thing occurring. In the last analysis it is only a picture, one of many that could be drawn.

What is the purpose of depicting the tsarist government engaged in a struggle with its dilemmas? Primarily to provide some concept of what it did and what it was. Why is this necessary? Because traditional views of the tsarist government, though accurate enough in themselves, show only what it failed to do and be. The conventional pictures do not show the tsarist government undergoing a process of systematization or, indeed, any process at all. They only show that it failed for two hundred years to be a system.

Until recently, legal theory in Russia and Europe insisted almost unanimously that the coming of legal-administrative system was equivalent to a liberation, or that it would be if it were introduced properly, and this ideology has not yet lost its hold on the imaginations of Europeans and Russians in the present day. According to the assumptions underlying this view, the rise of legal-administrative system should bring with it justice, enlightenment, democracy, efficiency, etc., not dilemmas. Systematization should lead more or less smoothly toward a vaguely perfect society. The very nature of man, so goes

68. "Modernity breeds stability," says Huntington, "but modernization does not" (p. 41).

the ideology, compels him to struggle toward the above ideals as soon as he becomes aware of them, and the only conceivable obstacles in his way are poverty, a lack of enlightenment, and perhaps psychological maladjustment. These surrogates for evil have sustained and been sustained by kings, privileged orders, demagogues, mobs, wars, class struggles, conspiracies, totalitarian dictators, and what have you. Legal system, like God, could not possibly be harmful in itself.[69] If anything goes wrong in the steady climb to perfect system, it must be something else that is doing the harm.

All this is simply a culture based on faith in system writing history to suit itself. It is the view of men who live within a systematic legal-administrative order and who do not wish to see anything outside it, least of all its history. In fact, however, tyrants and conquerors have played a vital role in the evolution and preservation of all extant legal systems, and the positive contributions of demagoguery and mob hysteria to the rise of democratic nations and their constitutions during the last one or two centuries can hardly be exaggerated.

In particular, Russian history is full of conquerors like Peter I whose violent whims and ambitions led inadvertently to the creation and development of new and more "progressive" political orders. It is full of progressive economic systems like Witte's that caused famines, successful and humane reforms like Stolypin's that provoked revolts and revolutions, violent and barbaric oppression like Batu Khan's and Peter I's and Stalin's that turned the "oppressed" into loyal and stalwart followers, sound and progressive legal systems like the one established in 1864 that obstructed effective government, enlightened and liberal men like Victor Chernov and Pavel Miliukov whose well-meaning actions helped to render moderate and systematic government impossible, military debacles like that of 1854–1856 and famines like the one of 1891 that led directly to progress and enrichment, and— last but not least—anarchist-demagogues like the Bolsheviks of 1917 who restored order out of chaos and laid the groundwork for the development of a powerful industrial society and a modern legal system.[70] None of this will fit the unwarranted but still flourishing as-

69. The evolution in modern Western civilization of the essentially absurd notion that principles of law hover above society and guarantee individual rights by virtue of their divine (or scientific) truthfulness is described in Gierke, *Natural Law,* I, 96–107. According to Frederick W. Maitland, *The Constitutional History of England* (Cambridge, 1963), pp. 142–143, the English version of this notion began to emerge in the minds of the lawyers at the Inns of Court in the late sixteenth century and came to prevail there by the middle of the eighteenth. For a more detailed discussion of the evolution of the myth of "natural law" (or equity, or system), see below, ch. III, sec. F.

70. Adam Ulam, *The Unfinished Revolution* (New York, 1960), pp. 191–192,

sumption that the process of systematization constitutes a continual betterment of the human condition.

Few scholars have been completely unaware that the imperial government faced unique problems. Indeed, some have carried this approach to the point of implying that these necessities had much to do with the actions the administration took in 1905. This is much better than the assumption that system poses no necessities outside its own framework, but the traditional notion of state necessity still leaves much to be desired as an explanation of the formation of the tsarist government.

According to the traditional way of depicting state necessities, they are concepts in the minds of statesmen on the basis of which these statesmen formulate policies. Alternatively, they are concepts that were not in the minds of some statesmen that should have been there. In either case a necessity is taken to be the basis for a policy, and the policy is in turn a basis on which the government acts and produces effects. In Imperial Russia we see the tsar and his leading henchmen identifying (or failing to identify) what they took to be the Russian state's necessities and then issuing (or failing to issue) appropriate commands to the *pravitelstvo*. A traditional history of Russian government, therefore, is a record of the leading statesmen's commands, along with some discussion of the motives behind them and the results of the *pravitelstvo*'s operations to carry them out. This kind of history shows the government acting while society is acted upon. The recognizable problems of the state—chiefly those involved in foreign relations and military organization—drove the leading statesmen into a continuing effort to mobilize Russia's people and her resources, and as the statesmen labored, the *pravitelstvo* slowly developed into a piece of machinery that could carry out their commands. In essence, then, the imperial legal-administrative system evolved as an instrument of compulsion, acting upon an essentially passive society in the name of alien goals formulated in the imaginations of the leading statesmen.[71]

But the *pravitelstvo* was not simply a machine designed to cope with recognizable, alien necessities. As said before, it was a society made up of men whose main organizing principle was a common belief that they should be parts of a machine. In their conscious efforts to

---

suggests that when the Bolsheviks seized power in Nov. 1917, they were doing so in the name of anarchist principles.

71. My article "War and the Evolution of Russian Government," *South Atlantic Quarterly*, LXVI (Summer 1967), 291–306, sets forth a brief sketch of governmental evolution in Russia from this point of view.

mobilize the population and resources of the countryside, these servitors interacted with peasant society. They encountered obstacles, pitfalls, and dilemmas that were very hard to recognize or conceptualize, and the things they did to cope with these problems were often irreconcilable with the conscious purposes their leaders handed down to them. Faced with this situation, the members of the government-society generally went on reacting in ad hoc fashion to specific difficulties as they arose, and over a long period of time working relationships among themselves and with the peasantry developed out of their experience.

Seen in this light, the government-society of men aspiring to behave collectively like a machine slowly took form, not out of the conscious intentions of leading statesmen but out of the experience of lower-level servitors in dealing with a peasant society they could not comprehend. It was peasant society, then, that imposed necessities upon the government. Far from being only a passive object that had nothing to do but experience results, the peasantry played an active role in forming the *pravitelstvo* and the attitudes of its officials.

Viewed as a part of society, the tsarist government was essentially an expression of the reaction of the Russian people to external forces that threatened both their existence and their collective identity. It embodied a common urge, as it were, to collective self-preservation. To be sure, the people were not explicitly aware of the necessities that confronted their political order. The peasants of Peter's time neither knew nor cared about Turks, or Swedes, or the navy. Insofar as the Russian people constituted a social entity, however, this entity was sensing new impacts and needs and was reacting to them. Interaction between peasants and domestic administration created social forces through which and by which the Russian people as a whole gradually reorganized themselves to produce an army, a bureaucratized administration, an urban culture, and, at last, a modern industrial plant. None of these "modern" phenomena were alien innovations imposed from above. All of them grew up out of the internal dynamics of Russian society as it reacted to its environment.

It must be emphasized that the foregoing is not a historical interpretation contrived to justify tsarism, communism, statism, or Russian nationalism. I am not saying that Peter's reforms or autocracy in general was either beneficial or inevitable. I am only suggesting that the behavior of the men in the *pravitelstvo* was intelligible and meaningful, that their actions and relationships had some significance other than their well-publicized failure to live up to Western standards or achieve Western goals. When I say that the tsarist government evolved fundamentally out of the efforts of the Russian people to cope with their environment, I am not pretending to say that this was how it "really happened"; I am only describing a way of looking at the tsarist government.

CHAPTER II

The Structure of
Senatorial Government: 1711-1796

> If we do not make a bad beginning then we cannot hope for a good
> ending.
>
> PETER I

Senatorial government was the first administrative organization in
Russia that the tsar and his statesmen consciously intended to be systematic. Its institutions came into being during the period 1711–1796,
at the end of which time the Senate itself reached its point of greatest
influence. For a few years more, until 1803, the Senate continued to
be the titular center of what passed for systematic organization in the
tsarist government, but from then on its influence began to decline. As
the Senate lost its central position, the institutions, practices, and purposes of senatorial government gradually faded into the background,
while ministerial bureaucracy, formally established in 1802, rose to
supremacy. It was in 1796, then, that the structure of senatorial government reached its fullest development.

The formal structure of senatorial government was not of itself
a vital element in the systematization of Russia. It is described here
only because it reflects the nature of the "system" that bureaucracy
took over in the nineteenth century. Senatorial government did not
give bureaucracy its form, but it did provide the social milieu from
which bureaucratic government ultimately arose.

A. THE ARMY

Peter I's reforms began with the army. His military organization preceded the Senate and gave birth to it, and senatorial government
evolved as a continuing response to the interaction of the new army
(and navy) with Russian society. The basic purpose of senatorial
institutions never ceased to be the creation and maintenance of a
domestic administration that could furnish a steady, predictable
quantity of men and supplies for the purposes of war. Moreover, almost all men who staffed these institutions learned their first lessons in

administrative work while in military service. Thus the description of senatorial government must begin with the army.

During most of the century before Peter's reign, there had been two armies in Russia, each of them comprising about one-half of Russia's total armed forces. One was a congeries of militia-type units; the other, the so-called "new organization" (*novyi stroi*), consisted of more or less professional units under the command of foreign mercenaries.[1] In the militia units there was little or no separation between military organization and domestic administration. The officials who mobilized recruits also led them into battle. Landholders led their bonded men, and administrators of the crown and church lands led detachments from the villages under their purview. The musketeers (*streltsy*) stayed permanently with their regiments, but when they were not on campaign they engaged in nonmilitary pursuits, mostly handicrafts. In effect, their regiments became civil administrations, with officers functioning as judges and tax collectors. Finally, the frontier guards were mostly farmers who lived near the southern and western borders and did their military service under their peacetime administrators.

The semiprofessional regiments, on the other hand, were somewhat more separated from Russian society and government. They were strictly military organizations that performed no civil functions and had no connections with civil officials, and the peasant-soldiers, recruited by quota from all over Russia, found themselves in a world apart when they entered the ranks. Even in the "new organization," however, the separation from society was not absolute. In time of peace the peasant-soldiers were allowed to go home.[2]

The new recruiting system that Peter introduced in 1699 transformed both armies into a single force, resembling the "new organization" but much more sharply separated from Russian society. In Peter's system, civil government lost its military role. Landholders and/or local administrators continued to deliver quotas of recruits to

1. According to Wittram, I, 50, about 70 percent of Russia's armed forces were in the "new organization" by the 1680s. The majority of its officers above company grade were foreign, but almost all the officers of lower rank were native Russians.

2. Sergeevich, pp. 320–334, presents a brief history of pre-Petrine military organization. N. E. Nosov, *Ocherki po istorii mestnogo upravleniia russkogo gosudarstva pervoi poloviny XVI veka* (Moscow, 1957), pp. 115–119, describes the origins of the pre-Petrine army in the early sixteenth century. On the gentry militia, see Raeff, *Origins,* pp. 23–24. On the professional units, see Richard Hellie, "Muscovite Law and Society: The Ulozhenie of 1649 as a Reflection of the Political and Social Development of Russia since the Sudebnik of 1589" (unpublished Ph.D. dissertation, University of Chicago, 1965), pp. 11–12, 76. I am indebted to Professor Hellie for pointing out to me that the "new organization" sent its soldiers home in peacetime.

the army, but they left them there to be assigned to regiments that had been organized by a separate agency under officers appointed from elsewhere by the central government. Once delivered, Peter's recruits were permanently separated from their villages. They never went home again. The gentry landholders also had to serve for life, though they, unlike the peasants, could occasionally go home on leave.[3] In effect, Peter severed the army organization from the old tribute-collecting hierarchy—from Russian society itself—and freed its officers from responsibility for domestic government. This, at least, was what he tried to do. Ideally, the new army would devote itself solely to military functions. Those officers who had estates would have to find someone else to manage them.[4] After Peter's reform only a few domestic organizations, chiefly those that governed the cossacks, continued to furnish military units directly out of their own hierarchies.[5]

Peter's army quickly became a large one, and it continued to grow throughout the following century. The "draft" of 1699 brought in 23,000 recruits,[6] and the "general levies" of 1705–1709 raised the size of the regular army to well over 100,000.[7] By 1725 a total of 287,000 recruits had been enrolled,[8] and the field army had reached a strength of about 130,000.[9] In 1745 it had grown to somewhat less than 200,000,[10] and by 1796 Catherine had 500,000 men under arms, including both field and garrison units.[11] The Napoleonic Wars brought the army up to one million men.[12] From then until the Crimean War it stayed at

3. V. O. Klyuchevsky, *Peter the First* (New York, 1961), pp. 93–100. The service requirement for the gentry was cut down to twenty-five years in 1736 and shortly thereafter to twenty years. After Peter's death officers on active duty were frequently able to obtain year-long leaves of absence in peacetime, presumably so that they could see to the management of their estates, and from 1762 on their actual terms of service averaged fifteen years. See Raeff, *Origins*, pp. 61–63, 113.

4. "Rekrutskaia povinnost," in Brockhaus and Efron, XXIV (1899), 530–532.

5. A. D. Ferguson, "The Russian Military Settlements, 1810–1866" (unpublished Ph.D. dissertation, Yale University, 1954, hereinafter cited as Ferguson, dissertation), pp. 30–50, gives a brief history of the combined civil-military organization within which the cossacks and border settlers lived.

6. "Rekrutskaia povinnost," in Brockhaus and Efron, XXIV, 530–532.

7. Klyuchevsky, *Peter*, p. 81.

8. V. V. Kafengauz and N. I. Pavlenko, eds., *Ocherki istorii SSSR: Period feodalizma: Rossiia v pervoi chetverti XVIII v.* (Moscow, 1954), p. 347.

9. *Ibid.*, p. 349. According to Wittram, II, 9, garrison troops numbered an additional 130,000.

10. *Istoriia Pravitelstvuiushchego Senata* (5 vols., St. Petersburg, 1911, hereinafter cited as *IPS*), II, 279. In 1756 the total strength was at 330,000, of which 172,500 constituted the field army. See Herbert Kaplan, *Russia and the Outbreak of the Seven-Years War* (Berkeley, Calif., 1968), p. 57.

11. M. V. Klochkov, *Ocherki pravitelstvennoi deiatelnosti vremeni Pavla I* (Petrograd, 1916), pp. 504–505.

12. Ferguson, dissertation, p. 64, says that in 1825 the regular army still amounted to almost a million officers and men.

about 800,000.[13] Needless to say, the cost of the army was also large. In 1701–1709 the army and navy absorbed 70–90 percent of the funds available to the central government,[14] and military expenditures continued to absorb the greater part of the tsarist government's funds from then on.

On the whole, Peter's military organization was a success. By the 1760s the Russian army had become one of the most formidable in Europe, while within Russia the gentry had come to regard their ranks in it as the main basis for social as well as official status.[15] In Peter's time many of the gentry tried to avoid military service by securing civil posts, but their offspring grew up to regard a career in the army as more honorable than one in the "civil" administration.[16]

Such was the effectiveness of the army that Peter and his successors used it not only for military purposes but also to accomplish many of the tasks of domestic administration, although this combining of military and civil functions was inconsistent with the general aim to keep the army separate. In 1708 Peter put it in all but direct charge of a new set of territorial administrations (the gubernias),[17] and toward the end

13. "Istoricheskoe obozrenie voenno-sukhoputnogo upravleniia s 1825 po 1850 goda," *Sbornik imperatorskogo russkogo istoricheskogo obshchestva* (148 vols., St. Petersburg, 1867–1916, hereinafter cited as *SIRIO*), XCVIII, 326.

14. Kafengauz and Pavlenko, p. 384.

15. James Hassell, "Implementation of the Russian Table of Ranks during the Eighteenth Century," *Slavic Review*, XXIX (June 1970), 289–290. It is true that service to the tsar was already the main basis for social status before Peter's time, but until the 1680s service was itself largely bound to and formed by traditional relationships (except in the foreign-commanded "new organization"). The service that the gentry learned to accept as honorable after 1700 had nothing to do with tradition.

16. Klyuchevsky, *Peter*, pp. 92–100; Hassell, "Implementation," pp. 285–286; Paul Dukes, *Catherine the Great and the Russian Nobility* (Cambridge, 1967), p. 23; W. Slany, "Russian Central Government Institutions: 1725–1741" (unpublished Ph.D. dissertation, Cornell University, 1958), pp. 237–238, 535–537.

17. *IPS*, I, 65–67. The *guberniia*, anglicized here to gubernia, was first introduced to Russia in 1708, when Peter divided the country into eight of them. By the end of his reign there were twelve, and from then until 1775 the number gradually increased to twenty-three. Catherine then introduced a relatively drastic reform that produced fifty gubernias. There were many minor changes in the ensuing decades, but in European Russia Catherine's gubernias remained substantially the same until well into the Soviet period.

Before Peter's reforms the fundamental territorial unit of domestic administration was the uezd. In 1719 Peter established the *provintsiia* as a subdivision of his huge gubernias, and in 1727 these new territories were divided in turn into uezds. Authorities disagree about how many *provintsii* and uezds there were at any one time. Suffice it to say here that European Russia was divided originally into about forty *provintsii*, increasing by 1775 to sixty or seventy, at which time they were subdivided into about 250 uezds. The *provintsii* were eliminated by the edict of 7 Nov. 1775, and in the following twenty years they were replaced by Catherine's new-style gubernias, subdivided into a new set of uezds. From

of his reign he sent out his regiments to organize and to collect the new "soul" (*podushnyi*) tax.

Peter had not planned to use his soldiers to collect taxes. From 1700 on he had made repeated attempts to put together a "civil" administration that could take a reasonably accurate census and then collect a tax based on its findings. Only in 1722, after his new institutions had failed repeatedly to take a satisfactory census, did he send his regiments en masse into the countryside and quarter them in the villages. In 1723, under the severe pressure of the military presence, a census of sorts was at long last completed: not an accurate one to be sure, but sufficient to provide a rough basis for assigning tax and recruitment quotas. The soldiers remained in the villages to collect the new tax, withdrawing only in 1727 after a military occupation of five years.[18] With the removal of the army, civil officials resumed control over the territorial administrations, but by this time virtually all of Peter's new domestic agencies had disappeared (if, indeed, they had ever existed).[19] In the absence of sufficient civil organs to replace them, the soldiers continued to help with the soul tax until 1763, though after 1727 they worked under the direction of the civil administration and they no longer lived in the villages.[20]

The role the new army played in domestic administration went far beyond its official functions. Until the 1760s civil administration outside the capital cities was made up almost entirely of retired army officers, who assumed their positions and held them according to their

Catherine's time on, then, domestic administration in European Russia was based on two territorial units: the gubernia and the uezd.

The official title *voevoda* is closely related to these territorial reforms. Before Peter's reign the voevodas were in charge of the old uezds. During the period 1719–1775 some voevodas ran *provintsii* while others ran uezds and larger towns. After 1775 the title no longer existed. Before Peter's time the voevoda was both civil administrator and military leader. After about 1700 he was purely a civil official. The voevodas were the real centers of domestic administration outside the capital cities throughout the time of their existence, which means that the uezds before Peter and the *provintsii* after him were the main centers of domestic administration. After 1775 the gubernias and their governors (*gubernatory*) took over this role.

18. See E. E. Kankrin, "Kratkoe obozrenie rossiiskikh finansov," *SIRIO*, XXXI, 11–12; Kafengauz and Pavlenko, pp. 328–330. The soul tax was collected only from the nonprivileged classes. Up to Catherine II's time the official rate was 70 kopeks per male per year.

19. Iu. V. Gote, *Istoriia oblastnogo upravleniia v Rossii ot Petra I do Ekateriny II* (2 vols., Moscow, 1913, 1941), I, 95–100. Peter's institution of city management, the *ratusha*, lasted on until 1775, but Eroshkin, pp. 143–144, and A. V. Chernov, *Gosudarstvennye uchrezhdeniia Rossii v XVIII veke* (Moscow, 1960), pp. 69–72, tell us that it had no local organs after 1727.

20. Gote, I, 23–42, 52–67, 423–424; Kafengauz and Pavlenko, p. 341.

military rank.[21] Operating alongside this quasi-military "civil" administration were a considerable number of special inspectorates and agents-on-mission, all of whom were army officers, some retired and some still on active duty. These special agents took the census, hunted brigands, inspected local administrations, and brought accusations against the regular officials.[22]

In the capital cities the army's influence was even more pervasive. Throughout the eighteenth century the central organs of military and diplomatic organization were by far the biggest and most influential part of the government. The war college alone had more ranking servitors than the Senate.[23] Moreover, the colleges of war, navy, and foreign affairs operated apart from the other colleges and were not even formally subordinate to the Senate.[24] Most important, the leading statesmen in the government, those who were close to the ruler, concerned themselves almost entirely with military and diplomatic affairs and left domestic administration to lesser men—except, of course, when a case came up that involved their personal interests.[25] The only top-ranking position associated with the institutions of senatorial government was the *general-prokuror,* established by Peter in order to make the Senate function more effectively (see below, ch. V, sec. D). It says much for the predominance of the army in the years immediately after Peter's death that from 1725 to 1740 the *general-prokuror* exercised no influence at all among the highest statesmen. P. I. Iaguzhinskii held the office from 1722 until his death in 1736, but his power—which he held initially only because he was himself one of Peter's personal favorites—evaporated shortly after Peter died. From 1731 to 1735 he was not in Russia, and from his death

21. Gote, I, 40–42, 140–141, 185–188, 205–206.

22. *Ibid.,* pp. 38–39; II, 46–110; *IPS, II,* 304.

23. There are no reliable figures on numbers of personnel in eighteenth-century administration. It is suggestive, however, that in 1725 the chancellery of the war college numbered almost 250 officers (Slany, p. 144), whereas in 1762 that of the Senate still numbered only 100 officials of equivalent rank (Klochkov, p. 102). In all likelihood the Senate chancellery had been even smaller in 1725.

24. The relations between the Senate and the colleges of domestic administration shifted too rapidly during and after Peter's reign to permit easy generalization. It is illustrative of the special status enjoyed by the military colleges that in 1726 they only sent their agents (*sovetniki*) to the Senate meetings, whereas the heads (*prezidenty*) of the civil (*shtatskie*) colleges had to attend in person. See Chernov, p. 22.

25. The Supreme Privy Council, which ruled Russia from 1725 to 1730, included the heads of the war, navy, and foreign affairs colleges but not a single official who had anything to do with domestic administration. See *IPS,* I, 356–357.

in 1736 until 1740 there was no *general-prokuror* at all, not even an absent one.[26]

After 1740 domestic administration seems to have begun slowly to assert itself and to acquire an identity of its own in the capital cities. From that year to 1760 N. Iu. Trubetskoi was *general-prokuror*, which made him, in effect, the manager of senatorial government, and he was also one of the leading statesmen in the government, possessing influence that was at least on a par with that of the military leaders.[27] For the first time since Peter's reign the Senate came close to the center of power. But Trubetskoi was only one among half a dozen favorites. All the others were engaged almost exclusively in military and diplomatic affairs. Through him, senatorial institutions had a place in the highest level of authority, but only a place.

In sum, Peter's army dominated the entire government on all its levels until the 1760s. Army chiefs occupied commanding positions in the central offices, army veterans staffed the civil administration, and army units intervened actively in civil affairs. Peter's new army initiated a basic change in the nature of tsarist government organization, not only in its structure but in the very attitudes of the servitors.

The general nature of this change was that the government acquired a concrete and explicit organizational *separation* between means and end, thereby giving institutional expression to the Russian state as an abstract purpose beyond the person of the tsar. Despite the de facto involvement of the army in domestic administration, the most important feature of its organization was the separation of its hierarchy from the old tribute-collecting apparatus. True, the army became involved in the collection of tribute, but even in its earliest days, when it sometimes resembled the domestic organization in both form and function, its units moved about too much for its officials to become absorbed in local hierarchies. Whenever soldiers participated actively in the tribute-collecting process, they only performed particular functions in particular situations, restoring order or guarding the collectors as circumstances required. In general, the army did not receive its tribute via a hierarchy that extended upward from the villages through its own lowest echelons. Instead, the domestic administration delivered revenue directly to the higher echelons of the

26. P. I. Ivanov, *Opyt biografii general-prokurorov i ministrov iustitsii* (St. Petersburg, 1863), pp. 1–7. According to V. I. Veretennikov, *Ocherki istorii general-prokurory v Rossii do ekaterinskogo vremeni* (Kharkov, 1915), pp. 89–90, 92–94, 144–145, there was no formally appointed *general-prokuror* in the period 1727–1740. See also Gote, II, 5–8; Slany, pp. 238–242; N. V. Muravev, *Prokurorskii nadzor v ego ustroistve i deiatelnosti* (Moscow, 1889), pp. 273–275.

27. P. I. Ivanov, pp. 13–22; *IPS*, II, 11–14.

army in lump sums, at first on the gubernia level, then, after 1732, in the *provintsii*.[28] In the army superior officers did not normally depend on their subordinates to sustain them; quite to the contrary, subordinates generally received their sustenance from their superiors and distributed it downward. This was the main practical difference between the new army and the old tribute-collecting hierarchy.

The army was the end purpose of the *pravitelstvo,* and the hierarchy of domestic administration was a means to achieve this end. From Peter's time on, Russian government would no longer be merely an arrangement of authority in hierarchical order existing largely for its own sake but would become an institutionalized organization with recognizable, regular, and calculable tasks to perform. The sense of abstract purpose had existed before Peter's reforms; otherwise there never would have been a Pozharskii and a Minin.[29] It was Peter, however, who made it the very basis of government organization.

It is true, of course, that the army, like any functioning part of the government, was itself a means to an end. In its relationship with the domestic hierarchy, however, military organization was clearly identified as the end and "civil" administration was the means. The civil hierarchy (which comprised Russian society as a whole) began to find its identity not only qualitatively, in the tsar's personal power over it, but also quantitatively, in the tsar's measurable need for the means to sustain the army. So far as the domestic organization was concerned, the army not only coped with necessities but was itself a necessity—one that could be reduced to annual budgetary requirements and to specific orders based on these requirements. In effect, the army hovered over the domestic regime much as the tsar image itself had always done, and it gradually became an attribute of the tsar image, adding the force of its concrete necessities to the traditional aura of absolute personal power.

By the 1760s the army seems to have done its work in domestic administration. In 1762, when Catherine II came to the throne, she began methodically to sweep it out of the civil administration on all levels.[30]

28. Gote, I, 38–42, 423–424.

29. Prince Dmitri Pozharskii and Kuzma Minin were leaders in the popular movement to drive the Poles out of Moscow in 1611–1612. The government's attempt to introduce a state budget in 1623 (Hellie, p. 11) certainly reflected a sense of abstract purpose; so did the establishment of the *novyi stroi* army (see above, n. 2).

30. Kerry Morrison, "Catherine II's Legislative Commission: An Administrative Interpretation," *Canadian Slavic Studies,* IV (Fall 1970), 467–471, shows that serious attempts to clear the army out of domestic administration began in the latter years of Elizabeth's reign and continued through Peter III's. When the war with Prussia (1756–1761) pulled the army out of Russia for an extended period

Her reign marked the end of an era. From then on, the army continued to be a predominating *consideration* of government, but with the development of a relatively effective domestic administration, its *role* in civil government became more and more circumscribed. Peter had wanted to keep the army out of domestic administration, but he had not been able to fabricate a civil organization that could support a separate military organization. Catherine II did fabricate one after a fashion, and in so doing she completed what Peter had begun; that is, she completed the construction of senatorial government.

What, then, was the historical nature of senatorial government? It was the organization that took form during almost a century of struggle to sustain Peter's army and to relieve it from domestic responsibilities. This process was not yet over at the end of Catherine's reign, but civil government had come a long way. In the process it had begun to change fundamentally from a tribute-collecting hierarchy to a civil administration whose servitors, like those of the army, were aware of general purposes and were at least beginning to believe that they should organize themselves around them.[31]

It is no exaggeration to say that Peter's new army created senatorial government, gave birth to it, and raised it to adulthood. True, the army attacked the civil administration now and then, especially in the 1720s, when it descended on the countryside to collect the "soul tax." Doubtless, its attacks undermined the authority of the "civilian" officials. Nonetheless, the same motives that compelled the army to interfere in domestic administration drove it also to favor and encourage the development of a civil organization that could operate predictably and systematically on its own. Artificial separation rendered the army and the conduct of foreign affairs vitally dependent on the domestic administration, and the military chiefs could not but want it to work effectively. The leading statesmen of the period often evaded the procedures of senatorial administration and set aside its decisions, but their basic aim was to make it workable. Count Ostermann, who came closer than anyone else to being foreign minister in the period 1725–1741, often acted to weaken the Senate and the *general-prokuror* when they got in his way,[32] but he also concerned himself with long-

---

of time, it became vitally necessary to construct a domestic administration that could function on its own. Actual reform, however, did not begin until Catherine II's reign.

31. Raeff, *Origins*, pp. 33–36, points out that the Russian gentry had already come to believe that they should serve the tsar long before Peter's time. It was only in the eighteenth century, however, that they learned to serve the concept of the state.

32. Gote, II, 9; Slany, pp. 293–296, 341–342.

range reform and development of the Senate.[33] Likewise, A. P. Bestuzhev-Riumin alternately attacked and upheld the Senate during the period 1741–1756, when he was playing a key role in making Russian foreign policy.[34] In general, the army only undermined the domestic hierarchy on specific occasions to satisfy immediate needs. Its overall effect and the conscious aim of its leaders were to build up and strengthen a systematic domestic administration.

The experience of running the army transformed at least some of the gentry into an elite of sorts. By Catherine's time they were coming to regard the governing of Russia as their duty and to derive their sense of moral identity from the performance of this duty. For the peasants, on the other hand, the recruiting system tended to increase the government's pressure upon them and at the same time to cut them off more sharply than before from the world outside their villages.

To take up the gentry first, the most important characteristic of the new army from their point of view was its simplicity. War, especially European warfare in the eighteenth century, provided an impetus to identify and to face practical problems and to set all other considerations aside. It organized a man; it told him clearly what was primary and what was secondary. To be sure, Russian officers and soldiers had more than their share of social and psychological problems, such as the humiliation of learning foreign techniques from foreign officers using foreign equipment. But hurts of this sort, deep as they were, lost their sting in the face of military necessity and the overriding purpose of battle, all the more so because soldiers and officers alike had been uprooted from traditional society. The gentry officers did not face their foreign associates from within the haven of their own society, as the boiars and townsmen of Muscovy had always done. Instead, they stepped out of their social framework, so to speak, and met the foreign officers on common ground, sharing with them a common uprootedness and a common subordination to compelling and easily recognizable purposes.[35] The army was a melting pot—somewhat like the immigrant slums of nineteenth-century New York—where men came close to being those *tabulae rasae*, free from "tradition's chains," in whom

33. *IPS*, I, 544–545.
34. *Ibid.*, II, 20–34.
35. Marc Raeff, "Home, School, and Service in the Life of the 18th-Century Russian Nobleman," *Slavonic and East European Review*, XL (June 1962), 295–307, describes the characteristic uprootedness of the eighteenth-century gentry and their attachment to Russia as a whole. See also his *Origins*, pp. 70–73, on the education that the gentry received in the army.

many eighteenth-century idealists placed their hopes for human development. The relationships of mutual dependence that developed in it could be strong enough to override national and traditional barriers.

This is not to suggest that service in the Russian army was essentially a pleasant or ennobling experience. Actually, the status of a Russian soldier was not much better than that of a galley slave. The fact remains, however, that in the army Russian gentry could work with Russian peasants within the framework of a *systematic* organization and learn to identify themselves with relationships of mutual dependence formed within this framework. In any case, the relationship between officer and soldier was not all a matter of whips and knouts and the running of gauntlets. Brutal treatment by itself does not even come close to explaining the performance of Russian soldiers on the battlefields of the eighteenth and nineteenth centuries, and it certainly does not constitute the most important distinction between the military way of life and that of the peasants who remained in the villages. The essential distinction was that the peasant-soldier could be organized effectively to perform functions, whereas the unrecruited Russian peasants and workers did not readily learn to work in new ways. By the 1760s Russian soldiers were already at least as good as any in Europe, whereas Russian peasants and workers were famous only for their appalling backwardness. This was the main lesson the gentry learned about peasants in the army.[36] For them, therefore, the new army was a social development. They were not only exposed to foreign influence, but they learned from their own experience to *be* foreign; yet, since they did learn from their own experience, they were still Russian.[37]

For the peasantry and the lower classes, the impact of the new army was more complex. Military service ceased to be a recognizable part of the peasant way of life. Before Peter's reform men from the same villages and towns had generally served together, many of them under their own local authorities. No one had had to do lifelong service, and therefore most pre-Petrine villages had been full of veterans. This is not to suggest that there had been anything patriotic about the peasants' association with the army before Peter's time. Many of them

36. A number of authors have noted that the gentry of the late eighteenth and early nineteenth centuries were inclined to apply military methods to the management of their estates. See Raeff, *Origins*, pp. 48–50; Confino, *Domaines*, p. 10.

37. Huntington, pp. 23–24, has noted that the qualities required in a modern war organization are equivalent to those necessary for the modernization ("institutionalization") of a society.

had hated it and run from it whenever they could. Nevertheless, *local society had shared the experience of military service.*

Under Peter's system the peasants who went into the army simply disappeared. For those who stayed home, the army ceased to be a part of experience and became instead a sort of human sacrifice that had to be made from time to time—a sacrifice that had no meaning apart from the power of the government to demand it. Of course, the process of deciding who would go to the army had always been a nasty negotiation. The villagers had always been forced to decide for themselves which of them was to do the dirty work. After 1700, however, it was no longer merely a question of unpleasant assignments. Now the peasant elders had to decide which of their sons would leave the village forever. Worse, the elders could see no purpose whatever in their decision, since they themselves had never been in the army and had never seen enemies at first hand. For the peasants, then, Peter's army (and state) represented little more than a series of grotesquely arbitrary acts that they were forced periodically to perpetrate upon each other.[38]

It may be surmised that the recruiting system tended to make the peasants more aware of their dependence on hierarchical relationships and less likely to depend on each other as fellow citizens who would act together in the name of some common cause. When a peasant contemplated the possibility that he or his son or his brother might be recruited, it made him anxious above all to secure the patronage of a powerful man, inside or outside the village: a protector powerful enough to see to it that his relatives and protégés would not be chosen. Each peasant had not only to find such a protector but also to please him, and the general need to do this sort of thing gave new strength to hierarchical relationships both within the villages and families and between the villagers and their overlords (see below, ch. IV, sec. B). Someone had to go when the recruiters called, and a villager was inclined to rejoice when the hierarchy protected him and sent off in his place some orphan or "troublemaker" who had not made himself sufficiently pleasing to a patron (father).

It may be seen, then, that Peter's army produced quite different effects on gentry and peasants. It gradually tied the gentry to a new government organization and rendered them to some extent conscious of themselves as a corporate society the members of which shared a common sense of purpose. For the peasant, on the other hand, the

38. For a discussion of the peasants' attitudes toward Peter I and eighteenth-century government, see Michael Cherniavsky, *Tsar and People* (New Haven, Conn., 1961), pp. 95–99, and Ignatovich, pp. 45–46.

government became less meaningful than it had ever been, and his village became less of a community. The gentry were introduced to system and prepared for it; peasant society was rendered less capable than ever of responding to the demands of systematization and economic development.

B. Peter's Domestic Reforms: 1711–1725

Peter established the Ruling Senate in 1711 and the functional colleges in 1718–1720. At first the Senate was only a small body of nine leading servitors that Peter left in charge of his government while he went off to fight the Turks. It had no detailed instructions and no hint of constitutional definition.[39] The only sign that Peter aspired to do something of more permanent significance was the name he gave to his new institution. *Senat* was an entirely new word to Russian government, implying not only a certain grandeur but also a departure from traditional forms. Not that the new term carried its Western meaning with it. The last thing Peter wanted in 1711 was to establish a body of "elder statesmen" with guaranteed prerogatives. He had only recently laid the boiar duma to rest, and he had no desire to revive it or anything like it.[40] What he needed was a body that would be able to preside over the government organization without losing itself in the traditional oligarchies of Russian society, and the term "'Senate" answered his purposes perfectly. What recommended it was not its meaning but its awesome lack of meaning.[41]

Between 1711 and 1720 Peter used the Senate chiefly as a sometime executive cabinet[42] and as a high court of appeals for legal and administrative disputes.[43] From about 1715 on, his decrees reflected a vague desire to give it the status of a legal institution in order that it might impose systematic regulation on domestic administration.[44] A decree of 1718 suggested explicitly that the Senate was not only an agency of the tsar but also a guardian of legality.[45] In 1718–1720 the colleges (*kollegii*) were set up as functional agencies of the State. Peter established nine of them initially: foreign affairs, war, navy, revenue (*kammer*), justice, auditing (*revizion*), commerce, mines and

39. See the decrees establishing the Senate in *Pamiatniki*, VIII, 42–45.
40. Kafengauz and Pavlenko, pp. 303–305.
41. *IPS*, I, 52.
42. *Ibid.*, pp. 94–106.
43. *Ibid.*, pp. 326–331.
44. For the most important decrees that gave form to the Senate in 1711–1720, see *Pamiatniki*, VIII, 42–47.
45. *IPS*, I, 282–283.

manufacturing, and budget (*shtatskontor*).[46] Each one was supposed to consist of a board of ten to thirteen appointed officials who would decide matters collectively and take collective responsibility for their decisions.[47]

Aside from the procuracy, which will be discussed below (ch. V), the Senate and the central colleges of domestic administration were the only significant institutions of civil government that survived Peter's reign. Even the colleges did not last very long in the form he gave them. Three of them—war, navy, and foreign affairs—changed very little, but these were the ones that had to do with military organization. They operated separately from the others and were virtually independent from the formal organization of senatorial government. The rest of the colleges, however, underwent many changes in form and function, appearing and disappearing so rapidly in the decades following Peter's reign that keeping track of them would be an exercise in itself. A host of other offices, some collegial and some under a single head, emerged alongside them to serve this or that special purpose. Nevertheless, the main structural outlines of Peter's functional divisions remained intact down to the reign of Alexander I. Catherine II virtually eliminated the colleges as such, but she retained Peter's basic principle of functional organization by dividing the Senate into six departments, each having its own functional jurisdiction.[48]

Peter also attempted to set up an elaborate apparatus of locally elected institutions and local agencies of the central colleges. As said before, however, he himself swept most of it away in the last years of his reign, and his successors soon eliminated whatever might have been left intact. After 1727 the institutions of senatorial government were almost entirely confined to the cities of St. Petersburg and Moscow, and there they remained until the reign of Catherine II.

Peter's orders to the Senate do not suggest that he was attempting to establish a constitutional order. He did not assign prerogatives to the Senate but simply used it, ad hoc, to perform tasks. The closest thing to a prerogative may be found in the first clause in the decree of 2 March 1711, which vaguely implied that the Senate was a court of final appeal. It ordered the Senate "to judge without deceit and to punish unrighteous judges by stripping them of their honor and all their possessions."[49] This, however, was simply a command to act in a

---

46. *Pamiatniki*, VIII, 55–57; Kafengauz and Pavlenko, pp. 291–309.
47. *Pamiatniki*, VIII, 77–78.
48. P. I. Ivanov, p. 45; Lazarevskii, I, 451–452; Eroshkin, p. 153.
49. *Pamiatniki*, VIII, 44.

certain way, not a delegation of authority or establishment of jurisdiction. Thus, although the Senate often played the role of supreme
court in the following years, it had no legal claim to do so.

Likewise, the Senate played legislative and executive roles without
possessing any formal powers. Peter never promised that he would
issue all his decrees with the Senate's consultation; he only indicated
(in 1714) that he intended to make this his general practice.[50] If the
Senate played a major lawmaking role in the first half of the eighteenth
century, it was largely because decrees from the rulers and their
special councils came to it in very rough form, and the process of
writing them up in suitable fashion involved much more than merely
clerical activity.[51]

Even the structure of the Senate and its procedural forms had no
firm legal basis. Peter and his successors changed them at will. To
take one example, Peter had difficulty making up his mind whether
the Senate should arrive at its decisions by unanimous vote or by a
simple majority. In 1711 he ordered it to decide unanimously, in 1714
he said a majority vote would be sufficient,[52] and later decrees continued to change back and forth as the statesmen changed their
minds.[53]

The Senate began, then, as a makeshift substitute for the tsar while
he was away, and it continued to exist and develop primarily as an
office that the tsar happened to find useful. A vague desire to transform the Senate into a governing institution only began to emerge
after it had been operating for a few years.

The unplanned, spontaneous development of Peter's institutions
suggests that their introduction was not simply a matter of transplant-
ing Western institutions into Russian government. Peter only utilized
Western models and concepts; he did not emulate them, nor did he
want to. The colleges, for example, were an adaptation from Swedish
government,[54] but they did not resemble Swedish colleges in practice.
In general, it may be said that Peter's new institutions evolved from
a series of experiments with European models under the conditions of
Russian society.[55] What Peter wanted was to set up an organization
that would manage domestic administration without interfering in

50. *IPS*, I, 319.
51. See, e.g., *ibid.*, pp. 276–277; II, 256–262.
52. *Pamiatniki*, VIII, 46–47.
53. See, e.g., the somewhat more complex rules set forth in the decree of 27
Apr. 1722 (*ibid.*, pp. 211–214).
54. *IPS*, I, 209, 277–279.
55. See Veretennikov, pp. 26, 50, regarding the essentially Russian nature of
the procuracy.

military activities or foreign relations.[56] He sought not to westernize his domestic administration but to regularize and unify it so that it would fulfill the needs of the army on a regular and predictable basis.

C. SENATORIAL GOVERNMENT FROM 1725 TO 1762

In the late 1720s Senate membership fell as low as three, the frequency of its sessions diminished, and it all but disappeared.[57] Empress Ann set it up again in 1730, but her high-ranking statesmen virtually ignored it, and at the end of her reign it enjoyed no more prestige or influence than at the beginning. When Elizabeth came to the throne in 1741, she felt called upon to "re-establish" the Senate, and in order to achieve this, she made all her leading statesmen senators.[58] In practice, however, most of her favorites, following the example of their predecessors, avoided taking any active part in the Senate and usurped its procedures whenever it pleased them. Power struggles among the tsar's favorites and the leading gentry continued to roll over and through the Senate and the colleges, disrupting and corrupting official procedures in order to accomplish immediate purposes. Under the circumstances the Senate could go on functioning as a sort of chancellery, but it did not acquire formal status as an institution of government.[59]

In the countryside there was no observable institutional development in domestic administration after Peter's death, not even a haphazard one. Peter's redivision of European Russia into a dozen gubernias and forty or fifty *provintsii* remained in effect until 1775, but within the new boundaries administration still came under the same centrally appointed voevodas who had dominated the countryside throughout the seventeenth century.[60] These local "satraps" were formally subordinate to the Senate, but the Senate's actual control over them was no more effective than that of the pre-Petrine central offices had been, mainly because the Senate and colleges had no agents in the *provintsii* who worked with the voevodas on a regular basis.[61] A few specialized agencies had subordinate officials outside the capital cities—the salt administration, the post, the management of the crown lands, and the office of mines. These, however, operated

56. *IPS*, I, 57.
57. Slany, pp. 111–113. See also A. D. Gradovskii, *Sobranie sochineniia* (9 vols., St. Petersburg, 1899–1904), VIII, 269–270.
58. *IPS*, II, 11–12.
59. *Ibid.*, pp. 311–313.
60. Chicherin, pp. 339–340; Gote, I, 71–74, 170; Slany, pp. 182–184.
61. *IPS*, I, 292–293; Grigorev, pp. 51–55.

independently of the voevodas and, in turn, left the voevodas to collect and disburse revenue more or less arbitrarily, subject only to the army's demands. Ordinarily, the voevodas hired their own subordinates, and they could use as many or as few as they deemed appropriate.[62] The only way the central government could limit the voevodas' power in their territories was to transfer them frequently from one *provintsiia* to another. Under Ann the central government made a practice of transferring them relatively frequently. In Elizabeth's time, on the other hand, they were allowed longer terms, averaging five years.[63] In both reigns territorial administration tended to degenerate into satrapies that were powerful enough to be oppressive but ineffective as administrative agencies (see below, ch. III, sec. D). In short, domestic administration outside the capital cities continued to retain the essential features of a tribute-collecting hierarchy until the end of the century.

Despite the Senate's lack of power in the period 1725–1762, its endurance was by no means without significance for administrative development. It was, after all, the closest thing to a governing institution that the tsarist government had in the eighteenth century. Other bodies held supreme power from time to time, but they did not acquire institutional prerogatives or even roles in the government. The Supreme Privy Council under Catherine I and Peter II, the *Kabinet* under Ann, the *Konferentsiia* under Elizabeth, and the *Sovet* under Peter III and Catherine II all derived their authority solely from the personal influence of their members. This influence was very real, but the bodies themselves never acquired it.

Unlike the "supreme" bodies, the Senate depended not on the personal power of its members but on its capacity to go on functioning. True, it functioned rather ineptly, but the fact that it was able to function at all set it apart from the supreme bodies and ruling favorites. The sheer physical requirements involved in pretending to handle the government's domestic affairs systematically were far too heavy for casual groups of courtiers, no matter how powerful; thus they generally let the Senate handle them. Sooner or later all the little privy councils and cabinets adopted the same policy: dump most of their official business on the Senate.[64] Precisely because they could

62. Gote, I, 30–32, 130–132; *IPS*, I, 457–458; II, 265–268.
63. Gote, I, 149–153.
64. Slany, pp. 68, 111, 118–119; *IPS*, II, 47–69, 245–304. The evolution of Ann's *Kabinet* is typical. It undertook to run the government and quickly found itself buried in a flood of cases and orders demanding action, whereupon the members gave up coming to its meetings. See Slany, pp. 330–338, 340–341; *IPS*, I, 512–547.

use the Senate in this way—that is, precisely because of the Senate's lack of formal power—they came to need it. It was from the rulers' inadvertent but more or less consistent dependence on functional offices that the Senate, along with its colleges and chancelleries, slowly grew into a central position in domestic administration.[65]

D. CATHERINE II's REFORMS: 1762–1796

As we have said, Catherine II extended senatorial institutions from the capital cities into the countryside, thereby completing the edifice that Peter I had begun and effectively separating the military organization from the domestic political order. Her first major reforms along these lines began almost immediately after her accession. In 1763–1764 she substantially increased the administrative staffs in the gubernias, *provintsii*, and uezds, ordering that the new officials be appointed by and subordinated to the Senate, and receive regular salaries from the central government.[66] During the following decade Catherine increased the number of gubernias from eighteen to twenty-three, with corresponding increases in the number of *provintsii* and uezds.[67]

These measures were the first attempts to set up a civil administration in the countryside to replace the army.[68] An additional step, more ambitious than effective, came with an order of 19 December 1774, which called for peasant-elected police forces to act as low-level agencies of the uezd offices. These police were assigned many functions, but the most important was to see to the collection of the soul tax in the villages.[69]

In 1775 Catherine issued a far more ambitious edict calling for a drastic redivision of Russia's territory and a fundamental reorganization of the government's local agencies.[70] It took the remainder of her

65. *IPS*, I, 640; II, 81–83, 256–272; Slany, pp. 561–567.
66. Gote, I, 115–116, 187, 277, 290–291, 297–302, 449, 456; Grigorev, pp. 105–108. The relevant orders are the manifesto of 15 Dec. 1763, in (*Pervoe*) *polnoe sobranie zakonov Rossiiskoi Imperii* (46 vols., St. Petersburg, 1830–1839, hereinafter cited as *PPSZ*), 11988, and the decree of 11 Oct. 1764, in *ibid.*, 12259.
67. Grigorev, pp. 101–102, 310.
68. Peter III had passed a law calling upon the civil administration and the landlords to assume full control over the soul tax collection (decree of 31 Jan. 1762, in *PPSZ*, 11429), but it does not seem to have reached the gubernias before its enactor was swept from the throne. Catherine's laws of 1763–1764 went somewhat further. However, as Robert Jones, "Catherine II and the Provincial Reform of 1775," *Canadian Slavic Studies*, IV (Fall 1970), 506, points out, they did not actually establish salaries but only called for them to be established.
69. Grigorev, pp. 116–118. The *instruktsiia* of 19 Dec. is in *PPSZ*, 14231.
70. This was the "Uchrezhdenie" of 7 Nov. 1775, in *PPSZ*, 14392. For a brief description of it, see Gradovskii, IX, 109–111.

reign to put this edict into effect, but by 1796, the year of her death, Catherine had divided the empire, including its new acquisitions from Poland and the Turks, into fifty gubernias, which were subdivided in turn into about 360 uezds (see above, n. 17). The *provintsii* and their voevodas were entirely eliminated,[71] while the new gubernias and uezds were formed around a nucleus of functionally defined collegial institutions made up partly of centrally appointed officials and partly of elected representatives. In their general outlines these new territorial organizations resembled the local institutions that Peter had tried to set up. Unlike Peter, however, Catherine did not destroy her own institutions.

There is no need to describe all of Catherine's new offices here, but a few remarks regarding the ones that had to do with the rural population will be relevant. Figure 1 presents their main structural outlines.

On the uezd level Catherine set up a college comprised of the police commandant (*ispravnik*), who acted as chairman, two members elected by and from the local gentry, and two members elected by the nongentry population.[72] This "lower land court" (*nizhnii zemskii sud*) managed the uezd police.[73] Other officials in the uezd with executive responsibilities were the treasurer (*kaznachei*), surveyor, and doctor.[74] In addition to these executive agencies, the law called for two elective judicial bodies: a gentry court (*uezdnyi sud*) and a court for other rural inhabitants (*nizhnaia rasprava*).[75] General surveillance over all uezd officials and courts was the responsibility of an agent of the procuracy.[76]

71. See Grigorev, pp. 310–317. The gubernias were supposed to have a population (male) of 300,000–400,000, while the uezds were to have 20,000–30,000 (*ibid.*, p. 317), but these figures were only averages. Actual populations varied widely from one area to another.

72. J. LeDonne, "The Provincial and Local Police under Catherine the Great, 1775–1796," *Canadian Slavic Studies*, IV (Fall 1970), 516.

73. Gradovskii, IX, 119–120; *Ministerstvo vnutrennikh del: 1802–1902* (St. Petersburg, 1902), p. 7; N. M. Korkunov, *Russkoe gosudarstvennoe pravo* (6th ed., 2 vols., St. Petersburg, 1908, 1909, hereinafter cited as Korkunov, *RGP*), II, 436.

74. Gradovskii, IX, 120–121. See also *Ministerstvo finansov, 1802–1902* (2 vols., St. Petersburg, 1902), I, 12–13, 36, 38.

75. Korkunov, *RGP*, II, 431–432. The *raspravy* were only set up in uezds where there were over 10,000 state peasants (males). See *Istoricheskoe obozrenie*, I, pt. 1, 16.

76. I have not mentioned the local urban institutions. The most complete listing of the uezd- and gubernia-level officials I have seen is in D. P. Troshchinskii, "Zapiska ob uchrezhdenii ministerstv," *SIRIO*, III, 24–27. Troshchinskii's list, though ostensibly pertaining to the year 1802, may well be a more reliable record of institutions actually in being during Catherine's reign than the laws themselves. Klochkov, pp. 419–420, 438, who generally assumes that the laws reflected reality, says that Catherine's system called for approximately thirty-seven appointed and seven elected officials in each uezd.

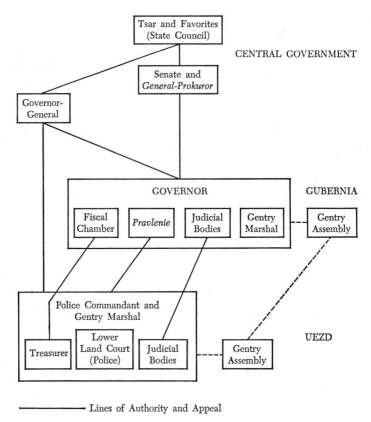

Figure 1. Simplified schematic diagram of Russia's domestic administration after the reforms of 1763–1785.

Elections of nongentry members in the uezd colleges were to be conducted under the supervision of the police. Generally speaking, the law mentioned very few such members, and in practice their elections either were not held at all or were reduced to a formality. Gentry-elected posts, on the other hand, constituted an important part of uezd government.

Ostensibly, the gentry managed their own elections—and all their corporate affairs—in the uezd gentry assembly (*sobranie*). The edict of 1775 did not clearly define this institution, but in 1785 Catherine issued a "charter" to the gentry that described it in some detail. It provided that all gentry who lived in an uezd could attend meetings of the assembly but that the only ones who could vote or hold office were those who were over twenty-five years of age, who held a rank (*chin*) in the government service, and whose lands *in the uezd* produced an annual income of at least 100 rubles.[77] The assembly was to meet every third year to fill the elective posts, which, aside from the above named, included the uezd gentry marshal (*predvoditel dvorianstva*), whose function was to preside over the assembly and, in general, to represent the gentry in the offices of uezd government.[78]

Of all these new agencies on the uezd level, the most important and powerful were the gentry marshal and the police commandant. In a few areas of European Russia, e.g., Archangel gubernia, there were no gentry; hence there could be no uezd assembly, no gentry-elected officials, and no gentry marshal. All officials, including the police commandant, were appointed by the central government. It may be said, however, that in most of European Russia Catherine's legislation gave considerable power to gentry-elected officials in the uezds.

Catherine's gubernia administration was set up so that one man would be the leading authority. At first the law of 21 April 1764 accorded this position to the governor (*gubernator*),[79] but the edict of 1775 established a new, higher office, called either *namestnik* (viceroy) or *general-gubernator* (governor-general).[80] The governor did not lose his central position in the gubernia administration, but the new official, who was supposed to be a personal agent of the tsar, was clearly superior to him.[81]

77. The charter (*zhalovannaia gramota*) of 21 Apr. 1785 is in PPSZ, 16187 (see arts. 62–64). A similar charter was issued to the city merchants on the same day.

According to Arcadius Kahan, "The Costs of Westernization in Russia," *Slavic Review*, XXV (Mar. 1966), 43, the average obrok (annual payment for the use of the land) for a male serf in 1795 came to about 5 rubles. If we take obrok as a rough measure of income, 100 rubles of annual income implied an estate of approximately twenty male serfs. Only about half the gentry had this many serfs in the late eighteenth century; thus only half the gentry could vote in the assemblies. See *ibid.*, p. 47. In 1831 the qualification for voting in the gentry assemblies was changed from money income to the size of the estate, and the minimum was raised to 100 male serfs (or 8,100 acres of unoccupied land). This cut the number of voting gentry to about one-sixth of the total. See Terence Emmons, *The Russian Landed Gentry and the Peasant Emancipation of 1861* (Cambridge, 1968), pp. 3–7.

78. See "Dvorianstvo," in Brockhaus and Efron, X (1893), 206–208. The marshals and assemblies first came into existence in 1766, when the government ordered them to elect the gentry deputies to the Commission of 1767–1768 and to fulfill other demands the government might make upon them. See Grigorev, pp. 110–112.

79. Gradovskii, I, 309; Gote, I, 122; IPS, II, 365.

80. Art. 2 of the edict of 7 Nov. 1775 uses both terms. See PPSZ, 14392. In the nineteenth century the general term that the law used to describe the leading authority in a gubernia was *glavnyi nachalnik*.

81. Korkunov, RGP, II, 439.

As it turned out, however, Catherine appointed no more than twenty governors-general to rule over her (initially) forty gubernias, and this left at least half of her gubernias under governors.[82] By 1796 the number of gubernias had risen to fifty while the number of governors-general had fallen to thirteen, and when Paul came to the throne, he discharged all thirteen.[83] In practice, then, many of the governors possessed supreme authority in their gubernias from the very beginning. To use the more precise terms of nineteenth-century law, the governors were both *grazhdanskie gubernatory* (civil governors) and *glavnye nachalniki* (supreme authorities) in their gubernias (see below, ch. IX, sec. A).

Even where they were not officially supreme, the governors in European Russia gradually emerged as the real administrative heads of their gubernias during the course of Catherine's reign. Many of the governors-general were among her most trusted servitors, and it may be assumed that they played an important role in setting up the new administrations. They also seem to have been involved in the government of larger cities and, in general, the suppression of disorders. None of these matters were insignificant in the late eighteenth century, but they were not of direct importance to the operation and development of regular administration.[84] This, it seems, was left to the governors. It was the governors, then, who actually managed the gubernias once they were set up.

In the decades that followed Catherine's reign, governors-general were re-established in the borderlands, in Moscow and St. Petersburg (primarily the cities themselves rather than the gubernias), and occasionally in this or that internal area, usually for the purpose of suppressing unusually widespread disorders. In general, however, it may be said that the governors of European Russia became the supreme authorities in their territories in 1796 or before and retained this position from then on.[85]

82. Gradovskii, I, 311. See also Grigorev, p. 327.
83. E. Amburger, *Geschichte der Behördenorganisation Russlands von Peter dem Grossen bis 1917* (Leiden, 1966), pp. 369–374, lists the names of thirteen governors-general still holding office when Catherine died. Paul's decree of 12 Dec. 1796 officially eliminated the *namestnichestvo* and replaced it with the gubernia. See Chernov, pp. 444–445; Eroshkin, pp. 150, 172.
84. Gradovskii, I, 308–315.
85. Korkunov, *RGP*, II, 439. Alexander I appointed new governors-general here and there, but he set each of them up according to a particular statute for a particular purpose. The only governors-general in the interior gubernias of European Russia after 1796—except for those of Moscow and St. Petersburg—were temporary expedients or experiments rather than permanent institutions. See Amburger, pp. 374–375.
Authorities differ concerning the fate of the governors-general in the early

Catherine wanted her governors to rule their gubernias, but she also wanted them to serve the central administration. In the law of April 1764 she required them to obey and enforce all orders they received from the Senate and to act in accordance with the Senate's regulations. To assure the governors' compliance, the law demanded that they act only through the *gubernskoe pravlenie*, or governing board (see Figure 1). In Catherine's time the *pravlenie* was comprised of the board itself (*prisutstvie*) and its chancellery. The board consisted of the governor, acting as chairman, and two advisors (*sovetniki*), appointed by the Senate. The *pravlenie* could not act on its own but only carried out the governor's orders. The members, however, could appeal to the Senate whenever they considered one of the governor's orders or decisions to be illegal.[86]

Alongside the *pravlenie* were several other collegial bodies, similarly authorized to appeal to the Senate. The "office of public welfare" (*prikaz obshchestvennogo prizreniia*) and the courts of appeal were made up of elected members, but their chairmen were appointed.[87] The fiscal chamber (*kazennaia palata*) contained only appointed officials.[88] All these bodies were subject to the surveillance of the gubernia *prokuror* and his agents.[89]

---

nineteenth century. Gradovskii, I, 314, seems to have been unaware that Paul abolished them. Amburger is probably more reliable, but even his work seems to have gaps. He fails to mention Richelieu's term of office as governor-general of New Russia in 1805–1814. In any case, the post of governor-general was eliminated from the statute books in 1837 in all the interior gubernias of European Russia except Moscow and St. Petersburg. See Eroshkin, p. 221.

In gubernias where military rule seemed necessary, the tsar could establish military governors (*voennye gubernatory*), and they were superior to the civil governors. But military governors were generally only temporary officials in European Russia, and they were used extensively only in the reign of Nicholas I. See Korkunov, *RGP*, II, 439. In Siberia, Central Asia, and the Caucasus, on the other hand, they continued to exist in a few places up to 1917. When they were used in European Russia, their power generally extended only over the gubernia capitals, leaving the gubernia territory to the civil governor. See "Voennyi gubernator," in Brockhaus and Efron, VI (1892), 859–860; Amburger, pp. 375–376.

86. Korkunov, *RGP*, II, 437. If there was a governor-general, he presided over the board, and the governor attended as a member.

87. The laws regarding the *prikaz obshchestvennogo prizreniia* are described in Chernov, pp. 462–463.

88. The laws regarding the fiscal chambers are described in *ibid.*, pp. 448–451. In addition to these executive bodies, the edict of 1775 called for several law courts: the *verkhnii zemskii sud* for the gentry, the *verkhnaia rasprava* for the state peasants, and the *sovestnyi sud* for both. The highest courts in the gubernia for all classes of the population—the *ugolovnaia* (criminal) and *grazhdanskaia* (civil) *palaty*—were made up entirely of appointed judges. There were other gentry-elected institutions, but the above are the most significant. I have not mentioned the urban institutions.

89. Gradovskii, IX, 120–121. Despite the rise in the significance of the *general-*

Besides the gubernia colleges, there were various officials on the gubernia level with particular technical functions, similar to those in the uezds. Some were subordinate to the governors, and some, like the postal administrator, were relatively free of their supervision.[90] The charter of 1785 established a gubernia-level gentry assembly, made up of delegates elected by the uezd assemblies. It met to elect qualified gentry to the elective posts in the gubernia colleges, just as the uezd assembly did on its level. It also nominated two candidates for the position of gubernia gentry marshal, one of whom was selected by the governor to fill the post (see above, n. 77).

Catherine's uezd and gubernia institutions were to have been only the beginning of a general reform of the entire legal-administrative system of the empire. She had planned to go on to provide the state peasants with a charter of rights, similar to the ones she granted to the gentry and the towns in 1785, and then to carry out a sweeping reorganization of the central administration. At the time of her death, however, her uezd and gubernia administrations were turning out to be less than satisfactory in operation, and the proposed charter for the state peasants remained a rough draft.[91] In the central government the pace of her activity seems only to have intensified the disorder, especially in her last years. Klochkov says that the backlog of undecided cases in the Senate rose from about 8,000 at the beginning of 1790 to over 14,000 at the end of 1796.[92]

What was the significance of Catherine's new local organs? According to one view, still widely accepted, Catherine and her leading statesmen intended their reforms to accomplish the purposes set forth in her famous *Nakaz* (instruction) of 1767. The new institutions neither embodied nor achieved these purposes; ergo, the reforms failed. The elective institutions did not give the local gentry and merchants a "real voice" in government; it follows that the elective institutions did not achieve their purpose.[93]

The *Nakaz*, however, was not a scheme of reform. It was a call to the identifiable institutions of Russian government and society to send

prokuror and his organization in the capital cities during the reigns of Catherine and Paul, the power of the *prokurory* in the gubernias did not increase correspondingly, mainly because the governors themselves became powerful enough to offset them. See Muravev, pp. 313–321; below, ch. V, sec. D.

90. Gradovskii, IX, 137.

91. Klochkov, pp. 99, 408.

92. *Ibid.*, pp. 103–104. Concerning the difficulties of Catherine's last years, see *ibid.*, pp. 95–108, 155–157, and Troshchinskii, pp. 30–31.

93. See, e.g., V. O. Kliuchevsky, *History of Russia* (5 vols., New York, 1960), V, 29–58.

representatives to St. Petersburg to form an assembly—called the Commission—that could make proposals for administrative reorganization. Catherine included philosophical observations in the *Nakaz* not to tell anyone what to do but simply to set forth concepts of state and society that were generally not familiar to her servitors in order to stimulate discussion among them.[94] As to the introduction of representative elements in the government, it is true that elected servitors formed a part of Catherine's local institutions, but they were by no means the most important element, nor were they anything new in Russia. Like the elected servitors called for in the *Sudebnik* of 1497 and other, similar enactments of the sixteenth and seventeenth centuries, they were called into being primarily to serve the government, not to represent anyone.[95] Least of all were they intended to realize Western political ideals.[96]

The significance of Catherine's governmental reforms lies primarily in the direction they gave to domestic administration. Catherine did not ignore the problems of civil administration, as Elizabeth had. Nor did she solve them by quartering the army on the population after the fashion of Peter I. Instead, she attempted to set up effective, systematic agencies *under the Senate* that could collect the requisite revenue and leave the army free to fight. She not only attempted this; she put the government to considerable expense to pay the salaries of a host of new local officials.[97] If, then, Catherine's reforms repre-

94. N. N. Firsov, *Petr III i Ekaterina II* (Petrograd, 1915), pp. 88–89. Catherine did this sort of public-opinion prompting on a number of occasions. Concerning her efforts in the late 1760s to stimulate discussion of the serf problem, see V. I. Semevskii, *Krestianskii vopros v Rossii v XVIII i pervoi polovine XIX veka* (2 vols., St. Petersburg, 1888), I, 46–51.

95. Korkunov, *RGP*, II, 438–439. On earlier uses of elected officials, see Grigorev, pp. 15–31.

96. See Klochkov, pp. 153–154. Catherine's administrative reforms in toto are described as essentially practical measures in Gote, I, 115–134, 277–301. Even Gote overemphasizes the significance of elected servitors (e.g., I, 227), but his account suggests the interpretation I have offered above, i.e., that Catherine's use of elected men was only one part of a program to extend and strengthen the central government's domestic administration. A recent suggestive study—M. P. Pavlova-Silvanskaia, "Sotsialnaia sushchnost oblastnoi reformy Ekateriny II," in N. M. Druzhinin, ed., *Absoliutizm v Rossii (XVII–XVIII vv.)* (Moscow, 1964), pp. 460–491—pays homage to the old notion of the *Nakaz* but then virtually destroys it by describing the practical considerations that went into the legislation of 1775 and thereafter. In the process she also destroys the traditional Soviet myth that Catherine's reforms were a concession to gentry "class interests." The best study I know of concerning the motivations behind Catherine's edict of 1775 is Jones, "Catherine II and the Provincial Reform," pp. 504–511.

97. N. D. Chechulin, *Ocherki po istorii russkikh finansov v tsarstvovanie Ekateriny II* (St. Petersburg, 1906), pp. 282–289. See also Jones, "Catherine II and the Provincial Reform," p. 511; Klochkov, p. 412; Gote, I, 449; Dukes, pp. 236–237.

sented something unprecedented in Russia, it was that the conscious purpose behind them was not merely to extract revenue and recruits from the population but *to extend legal-administrative system into the countryside.*[98] The purpose was not new in itself; it had been Peter I's. What was new about Catherine's institutions was her relative success at getting them set up.

It must be acknowledged that Catherine's new "system" did not operate systematically. Moreover, it did not produce substantially more revenue per capita than the army had, despite the fact that it cost a good deal more to run.[99] Another way to judge Catherine's institutions, however, is to begin with the attitude that the elemental and mercurial Emperor Paul adopted toward them. Paul loved the army even more fanatically than Peter I had,[100] and he was inclined to put his trust in military methods of administration. Nevertheless, he never showed the slightest inclination to use his soldiers to sweep the domestic administration away and collect the revenue on their own, as Peter's soldiers had done. Paul hated Catherine and all her reforms, but the senatorial institutions that Catherine had introduced in the gubernias and uezds had established themselves sufficiently well that although he made some drastic changes—especially in the elective posts—he never thought of eliminating them. Paul's response to the administrative confusion that Catherine left behind was to try to reform the Senate and the local institutions and to make them work— that is, to make them collect enough revenue to support themselves and the army.[101] Separation of military and civil administration had been Catherine's operating principle; Paul made it a commandment[102] —one which he and his successors would violate from time to time but never abandon. This was the most important "success" that Catherine's experiments in local government had wrought.[103]

98. V. Leontovitsch, *Geschichte des Liberalismus in Russland* (Frankfurt am Main, 1957), p. 26, would have it that Catherine was consistently "liberal" throughout her reign. What he means, or what his excellent description of her reforms conveys, is that her innovations were consistently aimed at the development of legal-administrative system in Russian government.

99. The real revenue more than doubled during Catherine's reign, but this was primarily the result of the seizure of church lands, population growth, territorial expansion, and the rise of trade and manufactures. See Firsov, p. 76; Klochkov, p. 100; *IPS*, II, 609. Indeed, this increase loses all its significance when compared to an increase of about 2.5 times in the period 1724–1769, obtained without benefit of any basic administrative reform or significant territorial extension. See S. M. Troitskii, *Finansovaia politika russkogo absoliutizma v XVIII veke* (Moscow, 1966), p. 214.

100. Klochkov, p. 129.

101. *Ibid.*, pp. 144, 157–174, 184–201, 223, 412–431.

102. *Ibid.*, pp. 143–160, 188–189.

103. Catherine's local colleges do compare favorably with the essentially (but

E. The Nature of Senatorial Government

As said before, the government organization that reached its fullest development at the end of the eighteenth century was essentially a passive one, responsive to external stimuli rather than active in its own name in behalf of its own purposes and responsibilities. Peter established the Senate in 1711 to be the active head of government, and for a few years its members were leading statesmen, playing executive, judicial, and legislative roles more or less at random as need arose. In its first decade, then, the Senate was powerful in fact but only very loosely defined as an institution. By the end of Peter's reign, however, the Senate and the colleges had acquired the character or at least the pretensions of a formal system, and in so doing they came to represent what should have been rather than what was. The Senate began to represent the ideals and standards of systematic operation, and the government-society came to depend on it to do so. Consequently, senatorial government lost the capability of coping actively with the problems of domestic administration and responding to its needs as they arose. Instead of being places where things were done, senatorial institutions became places where things should be done if they were to be done properly. As a rule, this meant that the Senate handled only those matters that leading statesmen referred to it when and if they chose to do so, i.e., routine affairs in which no person in power had any particular interest. By 1725 active statesmen had all but ceased to have any formal connection with the Senate, and despite the abortive efforts of Ann and Elizabeth at the beginnings of their respective reigns to channel the operations of government through senatorial administration, the high-level officials continued to stay clear of it.[104]

One cannot say that the Senate ceased to play an executive role shortly after its founding. Such terms as "executive," "judicial," and "legislative" do not describe meaningful categories in eighteenth-century Russian government. What happened, in essence, was simply that the Senate became passive. After about 1720 no one seriously

crudely) collegial staffs of voevodas and clerks (*diaki*) who governed the Russian countryside in the seventeenth century. The voevoda's "college," all of whose members were appointed, had only to countersign his orders and reports. See Chicherin, pp. 75–81. Catherine's *sovetniki*, on the other hand, were supposed to protest against the governor's illegal actions. In practice, Catherine's local officials often operated much as those of the seventeenth century had; even so, her institutions embodied an entirely new aspiration.

104. Concerning Ann's and Elizabeth's efforts, see *IPS*, I, 480–486; II, 11–12, 37–86. A. P. Bestuzhev-Riumin and the Shuvalovs, Elizabeth's highest servitors, actually considered getting rid of the Senate. See *ibid.*, II, 31.

expected the Senate and the colleges to *do* anything on their own but only to inform anyone who asked them what the proper law or action was in a given case. In the absence of a coherent legal-administrative system, any senatorial institution could "legislate" and participate in "executive" action, but the role it played in such actions was that of a referee and/or a glorified chancellery.[105]

Outside the capital cities the situation was much the same. From about 1727 to 1763 the voevodas were the only agencies available to carry out the Senate's orders and enforce its decisions in the country-side, but these local bosses were too independent to be reliable subordinates. Catherine's introduction of salaried officials and local colleges strengthened the Senate's ties with the countryside, but Catherine consciously designed the local colleges to be responsive rather than active on their own. Like the Senate, they decided all manner of disputes, complaints, and appeals, but only when some person or institution called upon them to do so. When the person was an inhabitant of the area, the college's decision was judicial. When the person was the governor himself, the decision took the form of an executive action. But in either case it was not the college that initiated the action; it only responded to someone else's initiative.[106]

At best, then, the institutions of senatorial government worked to maintain a degree of coherence in government and society and to render decisions that would pass for legal rules on those occasions when they were called upon to do so. They lacked the means to "run" the tsarist administration, and by Catherine's time it had become clear that it was not their business to "run" it. Catherine, unlike Peter, wanted the Senate only to "preserve" law and to oversee the govern-ment's operation, not to operate on its own.[107]

A good example of the role that the Senate and colleges played in local government in Catherine's time comes from Semevskii's account of the introduction of land redistribution among the "black-plowing" (*chernososhnye*) peasants in northern Russia.[108] These were officially classed as peasants of the state, which meant that they were not subject to any owner. Their villages paid taxes and filled recruit quotas

---

105. *Ibid.*, I, 455–456; II, 243–251, 311–313; Lazarevskii, I, 457–458.
106. See *Ministerstvo vnutrennikh del*, pp. 4–7, 12–24.
107. *IPS*, II, 271–272, 351–353.
108. The following paragraphs are based on V. I. Semevskii, *Krestiane v tsar-stvovanie Imperatritsy Ekateriny II* (2nd ed., 2 vols., St. Petersburg, 1903), II, 633–646. Semevskii gives many examples of the Senate's interaction with local administrators and the various types of nonserf peasants. See, e.g., II, 81–120, regarding the relationships between the Senate and the peasants of the court (*dvortsovye*) lands in the eighteenth century.

on their own account, and they made their own arrangements for the use and distribution of their land.

In the 1760s–1770s a number of these peasants petitioned the government to redistribute the cultivated fields in their areas in order to take land from those who had more than they needed and give it to those who did not have enough. Land redistribution of some sort was no novelty among the northern peasants in the late eighteenth century, but it was far from being an established custom. The peasants could buy and sell land as they wished, and those who bought it were inclined to oppose any collective arrangement that would deprive them of their purchases. By Catherine's time free trade in land and/or population increase seems to have produced a shortage in some areas. Or perhaps the physical shortage of land was not so important as the simple fact that government agents were now available in increasing numbers to hear complaints. In any case, the government began to receive petitions asking for redistributions. In 1778 Catherine responded by outlawing the sale of land among the northern peasants, and in 1783–1785 she sent orders to the governors-general of the northern gubernias to submit their considerations to the Senate on the possibility of redistributing the black-plowing peasants' cultivated land.

In 1785 the governor-general of Archangel and Olonets gubernias made this mere request for information the basis for a command to the fiscal chamber of Olonets gubernia to the effect that the chamber should allot land to any village that "felt the lack of it."[109] Not to be outdone in the exercise of initiative, the fiscal chamber responded by sending out an order not only to equalize landholdings *between* the villages, as the governor-general had directed, but also *within* each village among the separate households. Families holding an excessive amount of land in relation to the number of members, said the fiscal chamber, should be deprived of the excess.

These measures aroused protests from some of the wealthier peasants in Olonets. When the Senate heard of the matter, it asked the governor of Olonets (Gavril Derzhavin) to investigate. Derzhavin made an investigation and reported that the governor-general and the fiscal chamber had exceeded their authority, which, on the face of it, seems to have been quite correct. Nevertheless, the Senate chose to ignore Derzhavin—he was transferred to Tambov—and to confirm the fiscal chamber's procedures. This was no small affair. From the 1780s on, the practice of government-directed redistribution became

109. *Ibid.,* p. 633.

increasingly common in northern Russia. By 1861 "communal" land-holding had replaced individual possession in most of the northern villages.[110]

The decision regarding the northern peasants might be termed one of the Senate's successes. It decided a dispute, and its decisions became the basis for the further development of legal relationships between government administration and peasants. At the same time it should be noted that the Senate's part in the matter was only that of a referee. It did not itself devise a policy or a law and impose it on local government agencies. The central administration did not initiate or enforce or even guide the redistribution, but only acted at the invitation of its supposed subordinates. Its success lay only in the viability of its decision, which seems to have enabled the northern peasants to find an acceptable solution to one of their problems.

This was the best that senatorial government could do. Such arbitrary, freewheeling activity did not always produce constructive results. Administrators who were free of effective control could easily victimize peasants and/or frustrate government programs. When they did, the senatorial institutions were very poorly equipped either to recognize what they were up to or to restrain them.

To conclude, the Ruling Senate did not rule. The Senate and the colleges could decide disputes upon request, but they could neither insure nor direct action. At no time, therefore, did senatorial institutions form any more than a part of domestic administration, and this is a most important fact to keep in mind when considering the responsibilities that bureaucracy had to assume in the nineteenth century. Bureaucracy in Russia had more to do than merely respond to orders and appeals. It had also to act on its own initiative. Peter had founded the Senate with the presumption that it would impose system or at least preside over its evolution, but as it turned out, senatorial government only maintained the pretense of system. It would be the task of nineteenth-century bureaucracy to take up Peter's original presumption.

110. *Ibid.*, pp. 649–656.

CHAPTER III

The Role of Senatorial Government in the Evolution of Bureaucracy

PART ONE: DEVELOPMENT WITHIN THE ADMINISTRATION

> There is no state in which the words of politics contradict reality so much as in Russia.
>
> MIKHAIL SPERANSKII

A. INTRODUCTION

If the Ruling Senate did not rule at the close of the eighteenth century, what did it do? If the central government still had to rely on the mechanics of the old tribute-collecting hierarchy to carry out the practical tasks of government outside the cities, what did the senatorial institutions contribute to the operation and development of Russian government? The simplest answer is that they held the government-society together and made sense out of it while it underwent a profound social transformation. By the end of the eighteenth century servitors in the senatorial offices had learned not only to go through the motions of operating within a legal system but also to *aspire* to establish one. The development that Peter I had begun out of necessity Alexander I continued because he and his gentry servitors thought it was right in itself.

Before the time of Peter I, the tsar image that gave Russia its mythical identity embodied power and sanctity. The tsar's sanctity stemmed from his traditional association with the orthodox God, that is, with the Russians' belief that the tsar somehow upheld their customary way of life and their notions of justice (*pravo*). Peter seriously damaged the association of the tsar image with sanctity, and this left the tsar only his power.[1]

1. Peter did not do all this by himself. His reforms reflected ongoing changes in Russian attitudes. Serge Zenkovsky, "The Russian Church Schism," *Russian Review*, XVI (1957), 37–58, would have it that the schism of the mid-seven-

To put it another way, sanctity itself changed its nature. Before Peter's time (or before the church schism) the tsar's absolute power was holy because it purported to preserve tradition. True, notions of tradition were vague, varied, and variable in pre-Petrine Russia, but this did not prevent their sanctifying the tsar's power. Indeed, it was precisely because tradition was so inchoate and localized that only an ill-defined power could uphold it. What happened in Peter's time (or by Peter's time) was that the sanctity of the tsar's power expanded. It came to include not only the upholding of tradition but also the pursuit of purposes—such as the forming of a European-style army—that were explicitly outside and beyond the sphere of tradition. These purposes were also vague and varied, but they were clearly not traditional. We may say, therefore, that it became quite possible in the late seventeenth and eighteenth centuries to conceive of the tsar's power as opposed to tradition yet still sanctified in itself. The tsar's divinity came to transcend all concrete notions of divinity, and it became unnecessary—or at least less necessary—to seek justifications for the tsar's acts, and those of his agents, in tradition.

One result of the new attitude was that high-level statesmen could act and make policy in response to broad concepts of state necessity. Another result, however, was that it became more difficult to establish guidelines in the domestic administration for identifying and locating the tsar's power. As new arrangements and procedures were introduced, it became less clear who the agents of the tsar were and what they had the authority to do. As has been said, there had never been any consistent scheme that determined who had the authority to do what in the Russian government. Before Peter's time, however, members of the government-society had established niches for themselves in hierarchies of personal relationships, and these niches had generally embodied understandable patterns of action. Not so, when the new army began to impose its necessities. The tsar's power no longer resided solely in personal hierarchical relationships, and the servitors found it increasingly difficult to understand what their own powers and obligations were. On the lower levels of government, then, the tsar's new sanctity brought instability and arbitrariness.

The power myth alone was not enough to run an empire. The experience of the nomadic empires (see above, ch. I, sec. B) had demonstrated many times over that although personal power was a

---

teenth century was more basic to the tsar's loss of sanctity than Peter's reform. See also Michael Cherniavsky, "The Old Believers and the New Religion," *Slavic Review*, XXV (Mar. 1966), 1–39, especially pp. 27–39, concerning the relationship between Peter I and the schism in Russian mythology.

suitable myth for a war leader on a battlefield, it would not hold a tribute-collecting hierarchy together, let alone run a government. In the eighteenth century, therefore, the tsar image required a new attribute. The officers who were trying to carry their military values and behavior patterns into the countryside needed more than a belief in the tsar's power to sustain and direct them in their struggle against the archaic but practical hierarchies around which government and society organized themselves. They had to have moral convictions that would explicitly compel them to denounce bribery and to uphold system even in the face of a reality in which bribery was practical and system ridiculous. The new forms of organization—the army, the Senate, the service gentry, the budgets, the regular reports, the separation of powers—had to be moral and right, and since it was supposedly the tsar who was initiating all these new forms, he would have to stand for and embody the crusade to establish them. In the eighteenth century the tsar image *became* the aspiration to establish a legal-administrative system.

One of the clearest formulations of the new tsar myth may be found in the lessons on law and the state taught to the future Alexander II in the 1820s and 1830s when he was the heir apparent. The author was Mikhail Speranskii.[2] Speranskii maintained that the tsar's conscience was the fundamental source of Russian law. He defined conscience as "the moral feeling by means of which the intellect becomes aware of the necessities posed by social relationships."[3] Conscience originates in the individual's natural inclination to identify himself in terms of his social environment, and therefore it takes its form, or should take its form, from this environment. According to Speranskii, then, the tsar's conscience was not so much a source of law as a vehicle for the articulation of laws that already resided in society. In other words, the tsar aspired by his very nature to achieve exactly the same aim as senatorial government itself: to "find" the law that already existed in society and to impose system upon it. In Speranskii's mind the tsar *was* the aspiration to system, and it was the task of his servitors to establish (or preserve) system in Russia for his sake. This, in a nutshell, was the basic myth of senatorial government. Apart from it, neither the tsar nor his servitors could have understood themselves in the late eighteenth and nineteenth centuries. The law was there somewhere in the hearts of the people, but it was not yet clear; therefore, the only law that could guide the government resided in the consciences of the tsar and his servitors. These consciences

2. They are printed in *SIRIO*, XXX, 325–475.
3. *Ibid.*, p. 334.

were organized around a sense of duty to Russia, i.e., the belief that Russia must be organized systematically.

As with all of Speranskii's writings, it is difficult to distinguish what he said in order to please others from what he really believed. It is even more difficult to distinguish the ideas he derived from his own experience from those he simply incorporated from Western writers to suit his purposes. It may be suggested, however, that this confusion is what makes his lectures authentic expressions of a myth. Whether or not Speranskii was an original thinker, there can be little doubt that he was honestly trying to tell the heir to the throne how his government worked. Apparently Speranskii still perceived some moral significance in the Russian state after serving it for over thirty years, and he must have considered it a matter of great urgency to say something meaningful about it. The same may be said for the rather large committee of scholars and statesmen who had to approve his lectures before they could be presented to the heir.[4]

In sum, the forms of senatorial government grew up as the embodiment of the system attribute of the tsar image. From Peter's time on, Russian government servitors began to learn from experience within new administrative structures to make sense of their relationships to the tsar and to each other by believing that legal system had moral value and that it was their duty as gentry to establish (or "find") it in Russian government and society. By the 1760s this new belief began to manifest itself in their words and actions,[5] and in 1801 it was made publicly explicit in the coronation manifesto of Alexander I.[6]

It may be argued that Catherine's *Nakaz* (see above, ch. II, sec. D) was the first explicit public expression of the tsar's identity with the aspiration to establish legal system. But the *Nakaz* was not a statement of commonly accepted values, proclaimed by Catherine to reassure her servitors that she shared their values. On the contrary,

4. Another version of the senatorial myth, essentially the same as Speranskii's, may be found in the works of A. P. Kunitsyn, who taught at the Tsarskoe Lycee during the reign of Alexander I and worked with Speranskii on law codification in Nicholas I's first years. See Barry Hollingsworth, "A. P. Kunitsyn and the Social Movement in Russia under Alexander I," *Slavonic and East European Review*, XLIII (Dec. 1964), 115–129.

5. Gote, II, 194–259, especially pp. 194–201.

6. The tsars had proclaimed their identity with "law" for centuries—see, e.g., Ivan IV's pronouncement to the assembled clergy in E. Duchesne, tr., *Le stoglav* (Paris, 1920), pp. 17–25—but the law the tsar strove to preserve as an *ideal*, constituting a moral purpose in itself, did not begin to include the administrative system by which he and his servitors operated until the eighteenth century. The law "codes" of the sixteenth and seventeenth centuries were largely practical measures, not fundamental statutes. The tsar strove to enforce them, but it would hardly be accurate to say that he identified himself with them.

it was copied out of Montesquieu, Beccaria, *et al.* and delivered as a sermon of sorts to a gentry that were not yet ready to accept its propositions or even to understand them. Alexander I's manifesto, on the other hand, was drafted by Dmitri Troshchinskii, a solid "conservative," precisely for the purpose of reassuring the gentry that the tsar was with them and would henceforth embody their aspirations. This was the first clear sign that Catherine's alien ideals had become a Russian myth.[7]

It was only at the end of the eighteenth century, then, that the system attribute of the tsar image can be said to have established itself in the attitudes of politically conscious Russians. In 1801 the leading men in Russia did not yet understand how legal system worked, but they had come to believe that their country *should* be organized around one. This evolution in attitudes represents the essential contribution of senatorial government to the rise of bureaucracy. It is beyond the scope of this study to describe *how* senatorial government came to embody and to further the transformation of government and society in eighteenth-century Russia. What this chapter does is to set forth a number of indications that this was in fact what senatorial government did.

B. The Theory of Collegial Administration

Russian administrative organization had included colleges of various sorts since the fifteenth century, but no native Russian concept of development had emerged from their experience.[8] Insofar as Peter I, his servitors, and his successors were guided by ideas of national development, they followed the precepts of cameralism, a body of thought that had been taking form in central and northern Europe since the sixteenth century and had grown by 1700 into an elaborate political theory.[9]

7. *IPS,* III, 7–8.
8. See above, ch. II, n. 103; Sergeevich, pp. 270–293.
9. N. M. Druzhinin, *Gosudarstvennye krestiane i reforma P. D. Kiseleva* (2 vols., Moscow, 1946, 1958), I, 56–57. N. M. Korkunov, *Istoriia filosofii prava* (4th ed., St. Petersburg, 1908), pp. 233–294, describes the development of Russian legal thought in the eighteenth century. Russian jurisprudence, he says, pp. 251–252, depended almost entirely on Western writings during this time, in particular those of Samuel Pufendorf. Pufendorf himself was not a cameralist; none of his writings deal with practical administrative problems. But his idea that the state derived its form and power from an abstract, rational scheme of natural law, which could be discovered in existing traditions, served as a theoretical cornerstone of cameralist thought in the eighteenth century, when it rose to the level of academic discipline. See Louise Sommer, "Cameralism," in *Encyclopedia of the Social Sciences* (15 vols., New York, 1963), III, 159. Even before Pufendorf's

The cameralists generally considered collegial administration a means by which an absolute ruler who wished to increase his revenue and support a standing army could impart a measure of rational organization to a political order that rested on a variety of disparate traditional estates.[10] According to the cameralists, the ruler should not attack old institutions; rather, he should organize them in such a way as to render them more dependent on one another and, by implication, on himself. Traditional gentry assemblies and merchant guilds were not to be broken up by force but incorporated into new institutions that would represent both state and local society.[11]

On the central level the government was to be divided along functional lines, the basic divisions being foreign affairs, army (and navy), finance, judiciary, and police (internal affairs).[12] Each division was to be under a group of men—the college—appointed by the monarch in accordance with political considerations as well as professional qualifications. Theoretically, the functional offices had to have collective management because in the absence of a legal system, the king and his council would not be able to control individual ministers or keep track of what they were doing. Ideally, the colleges would serve to weaken the separate power of each branch of government in order to keep it in some kind of orderly relationship with the others.[13]

time (he died in 1694), the basic assumption underlying cameralist writings was that human welfare proceeded from the state and that therefore state interest was equivalent to it. See A. W. Small, *The Cameralists* (Chicago, 1909), pp. viii, 8–16, 26–27. On Pufendorf's idea of the state, see Krieger, pp. 39–49, 62–64, 80–81.

10. The book that served as something of an Old Testament for cameralists was Veit Ludwig von Seckendorf, *Teutscher Fürsten-Staat*, first published in 1655. A useful version of this work, incorporating some of Seckendorf's later addenda, is *Teutscher Fürsten-Staat, samt des selben Herrn Autoris Zugabe sonderbarer und wichtiger Materien* (Jena, 1737). Seckendorf's purpose was to propose a scheme for a uniform administrative system to comprise all the states of the "Roman Empire of the German Nation" (pp. 3–5), and in order to achieve this purpose he recommended the formation of collegial institutions.

R. Gneist, *Der Rechtsstaat und die Verwaltungsgerichte in Deutschland* (Berlin, 1879), pp. 120–128, traces the development of collegial institutions in Germany through the eighteenth century. See also Small, pp. 125–149, and Max Weber, *Theory of Social and Economic Organization* (New York, 1947), pp. 392–403, for discussions of the theoretical role of collegial administration in the evolution of the state.

11. Seckendorf, *Teutscher*, pp. 35–40, 61–71, 86–87.

12. B. Chapman, *The Profession of Government* (New York, 1959), pp. 12–50, describes the administrative developments in this direction that took place in Europe from the sixteenth century on.

13. Seckendorf, *Teutscher*, pp. 101–104, 160–166, 526–530. See also his *Additiones oder Zugaben und Erinnerungen zum Teutschen Fürsten-Staat*, pp. 165–170, paged separately in *Teutscher*.

In Russia, Feofan Prokopovich justified collegial organization in the following terms: "Simple people are prone to mistake an individual . . . as equal to or

On the local level collegial organs of territorial administration were to be formed partly by representatives of the privileged classes and partly by appointed officials from the central government. Representatives and agents were to cooperate in enforcing laws, carrying out orders from the central colleges, and taking care of local needs. Elected members would assure that strict functional separation between the agents of the various central colleges did not become an obstacle to their acting in response to local needs. Moreover, the elected members would impart to the government's agents a knowledge of local customs and practices, thereby furnishing a basis on which a uniform legal system could be devised and developed. The agents of the central government, on the other hand, would mediate conflicts between the estates, prevent the arbitrary exercise of authority by local privileged groups, and represent the interests of the crown.[14]

Given a country with law based only on tradition and with every position in the central government a personal privilege rather than a function, colleges offered a basis for imparting a spirit of duty and purposeful cooperation to servitors and citizens alike. Hopefully, privileged society would become involved in the work of central government and practically dependent on it. Leading men in the traditional oligarchies would come to associate their social roles with duty to the state and find honor in serving the crown in a civil capacity.[15] Experience in the colleges would teach all the members, both

above the tsar. They will not be so led astray by an impersonal, collegial body" (quoted in Hassell, "Vicissitudes," p. 11). Prokopovich may have been referring to Russian experience as well as German theory. S. B. Veselovskii, I, 14, points out that the government departments (*prikazy*) of the seventeenth century had been unable and unwilling to coordinate with one another. They had operated separately, each following its own procedures and policies. I have described this same tendency in the nineteenth and early twentieth centuries in "Some Aspects of the Imperial Russian Government on the Eve of the First World War," *Slavonic and East European Review*, XLIII (Dec. 1964), 68–90. Collegial theory may or may not have provided an effective solution to bureaucratic separatism, but we may say that the problem was real enough.

14. Seckendorf is vague on many of these points, but he does make them in one place or another, e.g., in *Teutscher*, pp. 138–139. Local courts, he says, should be partly elected, partly appointed (*ibid.*, pp. 241–242). Financial agencies, on the other hand, should be entirely made up of appointed men with their operation subject to periodic review by a body of elected men (*ibid.*, pp. 665–670).

15. Prussia is often taken to be the model for the form and development of local colleges. A brief description of the evolution that transformed the Junker nobility into state servitors is in L. W. Muncy, *The Junker in the Prussian Administration under William II: 1888–1914* (Providence, R.I., 1944), pp. 9–23. See also Gneist, pp. 120–132. A brief Russian version of the theoretical process by which aristocrats in local colleges turn into servitors, substantially the same as

elected and appointed, that they had to serve the interests of other government officials in order to accomplish their own ends. At the very least, a man sitting with a college would not be able to assert his own personal interests openly, for the simple reason that his fellow members would not share them. No matter how lacking he might be in political consciousness, he would have to learn to justify his proposals by appealing to loftier considerations, such as law, the common interest of the local area, and/or the functional purpose of the college. According to the cameralist ideal, then, colleges would foster the habits and attitudes of compromise and cooperation under law. Functional separation would not split the government apart into alien groups, as it might if a bureaucracy were introduced abruptly into a privilege-conscious society. Jurisdictional limits would constitute bases for constructive coordination rather than obstacles to it. Despite the inherent clumsiness of collegial administration, it seemed preferable to the outright imposition of alien codes and administrators on a hostile countryside. Imposed codes would have no relation to practice, and the administrators, unable to negotiate with local society or to cooperate with one another, would simultaneously disrupt society and paralyze the central government, leaving the way open to rule by arbitrary authorities, uncontrolled by either people or monarch.

So much for European theory. In essence, it was an interpretation of European experience since the sixteenth century, cooked up by German legal scholars of the seventeenth and eighteenth centuries as a basis for imperial administration and/or national identity.[16] It was by origin not a blueprint for the future but rather a number of gener-

---

the German idea, is in Mikhail Speranskii, *Proekty i zapiski* (Moscow, 1961), pp. 68–71.

16. Sommer, p. 160. As is often the case with political theories, the notion of collegial government achieved its most elaborate expression, in Germany and Russia alike, when the colleges themselves were coming under attack and losing much of their significance. D. P. Troshchinskii's essay in defense of collegial government in Russia ("Zapiska," pp. 23–162) was written in 1816, and Gneist's concepts regarding Prussian administration (pp. 272–303) date from the 1870s. The first effective collegial administrations in Europe came much earlier than the elaborate formulations of the cameralists. According to G. R. Elton, *Tudor Revolution in Government* (Cambridge, 1953), pp. 344–356, England experienced the emergence of collegial ("counciliar") administration in the central government when Thomas Cromwell "invented" it in the 1530s as a means to systematize English government. Ernest Barker, *The Development of Public Services in Western Europe, 1660–1930* (Hamden, Conn., 1966), p. 30, would have it that Cromwell got his ideas from French models. Whether French or English, however, the original colleges were practical measures, devised to cope with circumstances that differed radically from those that obtained in eighteenth-century Russia (or Germany).

alizations, not necessarily correct ones, that attempted to explain what had already happened.

In eighteenth-century Russia cameralist theory was swallowed whole.[17] By the time Peter became desperate enough to incorporate Western organization directly into his government, he was interested only in a plan (and an ideology) for reaching an ideal goal, not a basis for comprehending history.[18] His reforms and those of Catherine II embodied only one conscious departure from cameralist doctrine: instead of discouraging the meeting of traditional assemblies, he and Catherine had to form them. Peter attempted it; Catherine at last achieved it in her edict of 1775 and charters of 1785. This, however, was an adaptation of the theory, not a conscious departure. Unlike sixteenth-century Germany, eighteenth-century Russia lacked traditional estate institutions of any political significance; consequently, there were no coherent social orders or interest groups in the countryside with which the central government could communicate (see below, sec. D). For a generation or more after Peter set up the Senate, gentry corporate consciousness did not extend much beyond the guards regiments.[19] The central government, therefore, had not merely to reorganize local political institutions, as the German and Scandinavian princes were doing, but to create them. Obviously the gentry institutions that Catherine set up as a basis for her local administrative

17. The Russians had little choice. Germans did just about all the teaching of law and government in Russia until the end of the eighteenth century. See Korkunov, *Istoriia,* pp. 233–294. The first Russian professors of law were S. E. Desnitskii, who retired from the jurisprudence faculty of Moscow University in 1787, and Z. A. Goriushkin, who joined it in 1786. Only with Goriushkin, says Korkunov, did the study of Russian law as such begin. See his article "Z. A. Goriushkin, rossiiskii zakonoiskusnik," *Zhurnal ministerstva iustitsii,* I (May 1895), 97–142.

18. On Peter's frustration at trying to make a law code out of Russian practice, see V. N. Latkin, *Zakonodatelnye komissii v Rossii v XVIII v.* (St Petersburg, 1887–), I, 1–36, 525–526.

19. M. M. Bogoslovskii, *Issledovaniia po istorii mestnogo upravleniia pri Petre Velikom* (reprinted from the *Zhurnal ministerstva iustitsii,* n.d.), pp. 141–144, notes that the Russian gentry were "not ready" for collegial administration in Peter's time. A good illustration of the gentry's inability to organize itself around institutions in the early eighteenth century is D. V. Polenov's story of the government's attempts to assemble gentry delegates to draw up a new law code in 1727–1728. See his "Zakonodatelnaia komissiia pri Petre II, 1728 g.," *SIRIO,* II (1868), 394–405. The famous petitioners of 1730 gave no indication of any corporate consciousness that extended beyond factional squabbles among the residents of Moscow. When asked directly what kind of government they wanted, they were satisfied to affirm their devotion to unrestrained (and undefined) autocracy. See Slany, pp. 272–274; Marc Raeff, *Plans for Political Reform in Imperial Russia, 1730–1905* (Englewood Cliffs, N.J., 1966), pp. 41–52. The same may be said for the participants in the coups of 1740–1741 (Slany, pp. 383–385) and 1762.

colleges would form relationships with their central government very different from those that obtained in the countries of western Europe.

C. RUSSIAN SENATORIAL GOVERNMENT IN THE LIGHT OF WESTERN THEORY

The institutions of senatorial government generally failed to perform their functions systematically and often did not function at all. Slowness was their worst practical defect. The inability of the Senate and its colleges to render their decisions within a reasonable length of time caused the statesmen of the eighteenth century much more concern and produced at least as much legislation as did the relatively abstract problems of proper jurisdiction and procedure. Already in 1712, the year after the Senate's founding, one of the senators reported that the Senate was "terribly" far behind,[20] and the backlog of cases that had accumulated at Peter's death was sufficiently large to cause the leading statesmen to shuffle off much of the Senate's business onto other offices.[21] From then until Elizabeth's time the rulers tried to cope with the backlog problem by abolishing or simply ignoring the Senate and its colleges, leaving the voevodas and governors to decide matters pretty much as they pleased in their respective locales.

In Elizabeth's reign the Senate gained new prestige (see above, ch. II, sec. C). The result, however, was not orderly operation but a flood of paper: petitions and appeals from the countryside and executive decrees from the leading statesmen.[22] Slow operation did not cease to be the Senate's most urgent problem.[23] In the beginning of her reign Elizabeth concerned herself primarily with making the Senate follow proper procedures, but as backlogs mounted, her emphasis on propriety gradually gave way before the more compelling need simply to get the necessary decisions made.[24] Despite her efforts, she left a considerable backlog to Peter III when she died, to which he responded with some frenzied but seemingly ineffective commands to speed up collegial decision-making.[25] The backlog was still large when Catherine II came to the throne.[26]

20. *IPS*, I, 185–186.
21. Slany, pp. 33–37, 56–58.
22. *IPS*, II, 69–74, 245–250.
23. *Ibid.*, pp. 307–314.
24. *Ibid.*, pp. 217–223.
25. *Ibid.*, pp. 318–319.
26. Concerning the confusion in the central government at Catherine's accession to the throne, see James Duran, "The Reform of Financial Administration in Russia during the Reign of Catherine II," *Canadian Slavic Studies*, IV (Fall 1970), 485–488.

Catherine II tried to cope with the Senate's slowness by empowering the *general-prokuror* to take it over and force it to speed up (see below, ch. V, sec. D). This worked after a fashion, but the Senate did not speed up as fast as its case load expanded, and at the end of Catherine's reign the Senate's backlog was larger than it had been at the beginning.[27] As for Paul, he probably devoted more energy to speeding up the Senate than any other ruler. He expanded and reformed the Senate's chancellery and carried to an extreme the policy of disciplining the members of the central government's colleges in order to compel them to work faster. Perhaps as a result of his efforts, the Senate's backlog at the end of his reign was not larger than it had been at the beginning, though its case load had tripled.[28] Even so, the problem of collegial slowness remained a crucial one in 1801. It was one of the most pressing considerations that set Alexander I's reforms in motion.[29]

The colleges that Catherine II set up in the gubernias and uezds enjoyed an even worse reputation than those in the central government. From their very beginnings in the 1780s they were notorious not merely for slowness and arbitrary disregard of law but even for their failure to exist. Gentry participation was less than enthusiastic.[30] Their electoral assemblies were poorly attended, and the men elected often did not serve.[31] The men who actually filled the "elected" positions were often of the lowest quality.[32] Indeed, they did not even have to be gentry. A decree of 1779 empowered the governors-general to fill vacant elective positions by appointing sons of priests, merchants, graduates of Moscow University, and even state peasants.[33]

The perennial slowness of the Senate and the colleges on all levels of government produced a fundamental effect on the tsar's relationship to them. It meant that the tsar could not leave the management of the

27. *IPS*, II, 367–379, 459–462.
28. Klochkov, pp. 497–501.
29. *Ministerstvo vnutrennikh del*, pp. 10–14. In the first decade of Alexander I's reign the number of cases per year remained about at the level it had reached in Paul's time, but the backlog decreased. In 1800 the Senate decided 44,500 cases and left a backlog at the end of the year of 14,000; in 1809 the case load was 45,000 and the backlog was 6,400 (see below, nn. 115, 116).
30. See, e.g., Gradovskii, IX, 144, regarding gentry reluctance to take elected posts in the colleges.
31. Korf, pp. 120–121, 211–212, 269–270, 421–426, 575–576; Speranskii, pp. 190–191; Gradovskii, IX, 41, 127–128, 138, 146–147; "Dvorianstvo," in Brockhaus and Efron, X, 208. Lack of gentry enthusiasm for elected office was a constant feature of tsarist government from Catherine's time until 1917. Less than one-fourth of the eligible gentry voted in the elections to Catherine's Commission in 1766–1767. See Dukes, p. 68.
32. Korf, pp. 442–444, 644–647. See also below, nn. 87, 88.
33. Robert Jones, "The Russian Gentry and the Provincial Reform of 1775" (unpublished Ph.D. dissertation, Cornell University, 1968), pp. 190–193.

government to them but had always to be interfering in their operation. This is probably the main reason that the laws defining structure and procedure in the Senate and the colleges did not generally reserve powers to them but simply instructed them on how they should operate. Peter I's laws founding the Senate were lectures on how to behave, not charters of a governing institution, and the ensuing legislation regarding the other senatorial institutions followed the same pattern.[34] Catherine II began her reign by proclaiming her deep respect for the Senate as an institution, but in fact she generally regarded the senators with scorn. Her first decree-lecture to the Senate came out on 16 September 1762, to be followed by many more of the same type; that of 2 June 1794, for example, scolded the senators in Moscow because of a session at which only one of them appeared.[35]

Under the circumstances it is not surprising that the Senate and colleges never developed the habit of working independently and assuming responsibility and that they did not evolve as institutions that functioned according to their own formal procedures and purposes. Instead, they learned to depend on the direction of a higher authority who would take responsibility for what they did and what they failed to do. It would seem, then, that they did not progress toward the establishment of a legal-administrative system. Certainly they failed to live up to the expectations of the cameralist theory of collegial government.

Despite the failings of senatorial government, the Senate itself had acquired considerable prestige by the end of the eighteenth century as a high legal authority whose pronouncements had something like the force of law. In 1741, when the guards regiments set Elizabeth on the throne, she found the Senate almost defunct, and one of her first moves was to restore it (see above, ch. II, n. 58). Twenty-one years later, when Catherine II came to power, the situation had changed. Far from having to "restore" the Senate, she turned to it to entreat for its support,[36] an action that no previous ruler had ever thought necessary. From then on, the Senate was generally considered to represent the "law" in Russia. In the mythology of the government-society it became a holy repository of truth that somehow should preside over the government or at least watch over it in order to make it work properly. It came under attack in the early nineteenth century, but even then, no

---

34. See, e.g., the decree of Dec. 1718 on the duties of the Senate (*Pamiatniki*, VIII, 58–61) and the general rules regarding the colleges published on 28 Feb. 1720 (*ibid.*, pp. 72–125).
35. *IPS*, II, 333, 344.
36. *Ibid.*, pp. 331–332.

one wanted to abolish it outright. Its "opponents" generally aimed only to reform it so that it could measure up to its mythical image.[37] Mikhail Speranskii, the leading legal reformer in Alexander I's reign, based his constitutional projects on the idea that the Senate should be reorganized to form the real center of government (see below, ch. V, n. 7), and in 1825 the Decembrists thought enough of the Senate to make it the object of their plot to take over the government. There is no doubt, then, that the Senate's prestige at the turn of the nineteenth century was higher than ever before, and, as we shall see, this prestige was of no small significance to administrative development in Russia.

But prestige and the aura of legality did not bring respect for the Senate as an operating institution. The pronouncements of the Senate were laws in 1801, but they were not by any means the only laws; in any case, law in Russia was not yet a consistent guide for the behavior of government officials. In practice, official decisions on all levels— judicial, legislative, and executive alike—generally proceeded from bribes and personal influence rather than legal norms and reasoning, and no one felt any serious obligation to act consistently. No *institution* could exert authority in Russia in the early nineteenth century because the servitors of the government, including the senators, did not really know what a legal institution was. The Senate's authority, therefore, was more a matter of ceremony than of practical influence.

It is easier to illustrate the characteristic attitude of eighteenth-century governing circles toward the Senate and toward law in general than to describe it, and there is no better illustration than the story of how the Senate received its first mortal blow in 1803 at the hands of Emperor Alexander I.[38]

In June 1801, a short three months after coming to the throne, Alexander I informed the Senate that he wished to preserve its central position in the government, and he asked to be informed as to just what this position was. In August of the same year the Senate sent him a memorandum describing what it considered to be its proper role and requesting that Alexander "restore" it to supremacy over all other

37. Telberg, pp. 23–33. See also Nikolai Mikhailovich, *Le Comte Paul Stroganov* (3 vols., Paris, 1905), II, 165; Adam J. Czartoryski, *Memoirs* (2 vols., London, 1888), I, 292–293.
38. *Ministerstvo iustitsii za sto let: 1802–1902* (St. Petersburg, 1902), pp. 3–18. The narrative that follows comes largely from this source and Telberg, pp. 67–80. See also N. K. Shilder, *Imperator Aleksandr Pervyi* (4 vols., St. Petersburg, 1897–1898), II, 100–104, 109–110; *IPS*, III, 169–170; "Pototskii, Severin Osipovich," in *Russkii biograficheskii slovar* (25 vols., St. Petersburg, 1896–1913), XIV (1905), 694–704; A. V. Predtechenskii, *Ocherki obshchestvenno-politicheskoi istorii Rossii v pervoi chetverti XIX v.* (Moscow, 1957), pp. 132–135, 170–174, 203–204.

governing bodies, so that its authority would become an effective force for bringing the government into a single system.[39] Alexander considered the Senate to be a necessary safeguard against arbitrariness in his government, and he was inclined to respond favorably to the Senate's request. At the same time, however, he felt the need for effective executive organs to carry out the reforms his more progressive advisors were hatching.[40]

He resolved his conflicting needs by satisfying both at once. About a year after he received the Senate's memorandum, he issued a decree—that of 8 September 1802—affirming the Senate's prerogatives and duties substantially as the Senate had proposed. The Senate, said the decree, was the supreme governing body, generally responsible to maintain the law and to oversee the operations of all the government's agencies. No law could be enacted without first being registered by the Senate, and if a majority of the senators decided that a proposed law was "unsuitable," it was to be returned to the tsar for reconsideration. General supervision over executive and legislative processes had always been the *function* of the Senate; now Alexander was proposing to make it a matter of *prerogative*, subject, of course, to his own final authority.[41] On the same day, however, he published a manifesto that flatly contradicted his decree. It established eight ministries, the heads of which were to manage all branches of the government administration, both domestic and military. They were appointed by the tsar and were directly responsible to him, which is to say that they did not come under the Senate's control. On the same day, then, the Senate was set over the *pravitelstvo*, and the *pravitelstvo* was put under ministers who would not be subject to the Senate.

Alexander did not think his enactments of 8 September were contradictory. The ministers were to be directly and individually subordinate to the tsar, but they were also required to make their yearly reports to the tsar via the Senate. The senators had the right to examine the ministers on the basis of these reports and to demand explanations from them whenever they saw fit. Moreover, the ministers' decrees, approved by the tsar, had to be registered with the

39. Korkunov, *RGP*, II, 650–653. In fact, no one could restore authority to the Senate, because no law had ever granted any explicit authority to it. There had never been any such thing as a constitutional law in Russia prior to Alexander I's reign—with the quasi exception of Catherine II's charters of 1785 to the gentry and merchants—and although the Senate had *exercised* every kind of authority at one time or another, it had never *possessed* any.

40. For the reformers' plans of 1801–1802, see Nikolai Mikhailovich's second volume on Paul Stroganov, which contains the protocols of the "secret" committee.

41. *Ministerstvo iustitsii*, pp. 6–9; Telberg, pp. 43–47.

Senate before they could go into effect, and the Senate, be it remembered, now had the right to find them unsuitable. In 1802, then, Alexander still regarded the Senate as the center of his government. Ministerial administration was to be a necessary adjunct to senatorial government, not an alternative to it. Alexander removed any doubt concerning the value he placed on the Senate by appointing Gavril Derzhavin, an outspoken opponent of the new ministerial system, to be the first minister of justice, a position that carried with it the old title of the all-powerful *general-prokuror*. Thus the Senate did not gain all the powers it desired in September 1802, but its prestige was high and its apparent authority was greater than it had ever been before.[42]

Only three months later, in December 1802, the Senate tested its new powers by raising objections to a decree stiffening the rules regarding gentry military service. The manner of objecting was most unusual. When the Senate first acted on the decree, the members approved it without comment. Nine days later, however, one of the senators, Severin-Pototskii, made a speech against it in which he suggested that the Senate return the decree to the tsar for reconsideration.[43] Derzhavin, whose job it was to chair the Senate, informed Alexander of Pototskii's action but recommended that Alexander forbid any further discussion of the decree in the Senate on the ground that it had already been published. At the outset this was a legitimate argument. The law said that the Senate could request reconsideration of a proposed statute, but it did not prescribe how or when the Senate could make its request. Formally speaking, Derzhavin was merely proposing a constitutional amendment that would define the Senate's rights more exactly. It seems, however, that his real concern was to get this particular decree enacted, not to introduce a procedural reform. In any case, Alexander settled the constitutional issue by rejecting Derzhavin's recommendation and giving the Senate permission to discuss the decree in general session. He said to Derzhavin, "The Senate will decide and I shall not interfere."[44] The tsar's pronouncement had the force of a constitutional principle, and Derzhavin knew it. Nevertheless, he did not accept Alexander's permissive view. He continued to use every means at his disposal to block the Senate's objection.

The proposal to return the decree to the tsar came before the Senate

42. Gradovskii, I, 287–290; Troshchinskii, pp. 34–35. On the intentions of Alexander I's secret committee, see Czartoryski, I, 291–293; *Ministerstvo iustitsii,* p. 5; and Telberg, pp. 25–33.
43. *IPS,* III, 169–170.
44. *Ministerstvo iustitsii,* p. 16.

on 16 January 1803, by which time it seems to have become a popular cause both within the Senate and throughout St. Petersburg society.[45] Despite Derzhavin's vehement opposition, the overwhelming majority voted to return the decree to the tsar. But Derzhavin did not give up. Throughout January and February of 1803 he persistently refused to present the Senate's "remonstrance" to Alexander, and the issue only came to a head in March, when a deputation of senators went over his head and delivered it themselves. Alexander accepted the petition without comment, saying only that he would publish a decree on the matter. On 21 March his decree duly appeared. It denied the Senate's petition and also renounced the Senate's right to make objections to the tsar's enactments. Thus the Senate lost its new prerogative only six months after receiving it, and Alexander reversed his liberal interpretation of the Senate's rights only three months after stating it. As for Derzhavin, he got his decree through, but only at the sacrifice of the Senate's constitutional position. It seems that the foremost defender of the Senate had a rather loose conception of the prerogatives he was supposed to be defending.[46]

Another fight developed among the tsar's leading advisors during this time. It began toward the end of 1802 over Alexander's decision to allow serf owners to free their serfs, and it ended on 20 February 1803 with the publication of his famous decree making voluntary emancipation a reality. This was just a month before the Senate lost its right to raise objections to the tsar's decrees.

Alexander imposed this decree on his leading advisors against the wishes of almost all of them. Having begun thus inauspiciously, he sent it to Derzhavin in early February, ordering him to bring it before the Senate. To Derzhavin, taking care of the peasants was the sacred duty of the gentry, and he objected to their being relieved of it. He had opposed the new decree in every way he could while it was being prepared. Then, when he could no longer avoid bringing it before the Senate, he urged the senators to protest against it;[47] that is, he took a

45. *Ibid.*, p. 17. Predtechenskii, pp. 133–134, indicates that it was primarily Moscow that reacted, not St. Petersburg.

46. Derzhavin apparently had nothing to do with the decree of 21 Mar., and Telberg, pp. 72–73, would have it that he never seriously opposed the Senate's right to object to the law on gentry military obligations. This, however, is not based on evidence, only on Telberg's underlying assumption that Derzhavin had consistent views. In fact, Derzhavin, like Alexander I and just about all the statesmen of his time, was quite willing to depart openly from his constitutional beliefs in order to get a particular measure passed or rejected. See Predtechenskii, pp. 206–208.

47. According to Predtechenskii, p. 174, Derzhavin did not openly urge the Senate to protest the decree but tried to persuade one of the senators to do it.

position on the Senate's prerogatives that was exactly opposite to the one he adopted in the discussions of the decree on military service. When Alexander heard of Derzhavin's opposition, he rebuked him and sent the decree on serfdom directly to a department of the Senate for immediate and unquestioning registration and publication, leaving the general assembly of the Senate and the *general-prokuror* (Derzhavin) completely out of account. The decree was duly published on 20 February, a month *before* Alexander formally abolished the Senate's right to object to decrees.[48]

In this case Alexander did not make any constitutional declarations either for or against the Senate, and he did not tamper with the declarations he had already made. He simply ignored both the Senate and his own pronouncements in order to get his decree through. Derzhavin, on his part, urged the Senate to object to Alexander's decree at exactly the same time he was doing his best to deny the Senate the right to object to the decree on gentry military service.

To say the least, Alexander's policy toward the Senate in 1802–1803 was inconsistent, and it is arguable that the Senate's rapid rise and fall in 1802–1803 was primarily the result of his arbitrariness and indecisiveness. Alexander, however, was no more than a part of his milieu. The senators did not demonstrate any greater loyalty to a stable legal order than he did. They humbly accepted the decree of December 1802 when they first got it; yet almost all of them turned to follow an opposing leader as soon as one emerged who had the nerve to test the tsar's newly proclaimed toleration of opposition. It is doubtful that they followed Pototskii out of devotion to the Senate itself.[49] If the senators—or anyone in St. Petersburg—had felt any consistent loyalty to the Senate in early 1803, they would certainly have reacted to Alexander's blatant disregard of it when he pushed through the decree of 20 February. On this occasion, however, no senator ventured to protest or even to remark upon the tsar's contradictory behavior.

In fact, the Senate's "rebellion" did not express a demand for constitutional prerogatives or even a willingness to make use of them and rely on them. It was, rather, a crowd response by the senators to the impulsive action of one of their number.[50] They did not attempt to work out practical proposals to which Alexander could subscribe; they simply carried the matter of gentry military service before the tsar to

48. *Ministerstvo iustitsii*, p. 18.
49. The uproar over the Pototskii affair arose primarily over the substantive issue of gentry rights, not the constitutional issue. See Predtechenskii, pp. 133–134.
50. Czartoryski, I, 323, says that the Senate followed Pototskii's lead only because the members thought he had the tsar's favor.

see what he would do. The senators acted stubbornly and without policy, like schoolboys taking advantage of a carte blanche rather than statesmen exercising constitutional prerogatives. As a result of their action, Alexander found himself forced into a corner where he had to commit himself unequivocally either to Senate rule or to Senate subjugation. Under the circumstances he had no choice but to decide on subjugation. When he did, the rebellion ended abruptly. It may be concluded, then, that the senators of 1802–1803 showed very little sign of comprehending what a governing institution was supposed to do and very little practical interest in becoming one. It was not only Alexander's indecisiveness that led him to shut off the opposition he himself had declared to be legitimate. In March 1803 he had grounds for concluding that the Ruling Senate was, in fact, not fit to rule.

The attitude that Derzhavin manifested toward the Senate offers a perfect example of what Alexander had to cope with. Derzhavin was as fervent a believer in legal order as any man in Russia, but he showed little practical awareness of what systematic legality entailed. His arguments from "principle" were patently opportunistic. In early 1803 he continued to deny the Senate's right to object to Alexander's December decree on military service even after both Senate and tsar had affirmed this right, while at the very same time he was deliberately inciting the Senate to object to Alexander's February decree on serfdom. Some years later, in 1805, Derzhavin was once again to argue publicly that the Senate had the right to protest the tsar's decrees, as if Alexander had never made his declaration of March 1803. In short, Derzhavin "worshipped" both tsar and Senate as institutions possessing supreme legal authority, but in practice he did not feel obliged or even inclined to accept their pronouncements as legal norms that would guide his behavior. The law in which Derzhavin believed was essentially what Derzhavin said it was on a particular occasion, no more and no less.[51]

Perhaps the clearest indication of the general inability of Russia's statesmen in the late eighteenth and early nineteenth centuries to comprehend the nature of a legal institution is that this mortal blow to government by legal institutions was unintentional and that it went virtually unnoticed. Neither Alexander, nor Derzhavin, nor any of the senators gave any sign that they considered either of the decrees of

---

51. On Derzhavin's erratic behavior in 1802–1803, see Korkunov, *RGP*, II, 649, and *Ministerstvo iustitsii*, pp. 18–21. *IPS*, II, 512–515, gives several examples of the Russian servitors' lack of awareness of what legal institutions were in the late eighteenth century. Predtechenskii, pp. 203–208, argues that there were no statesmen in Russia in Alexander I's time, with the possible exception of Speranskii.

early 1803 to have weakened the Senate permanently.[52] Dmitri Troshchinskii, perhaps the best informed and most discerning of the defenders of senatorial government, does not seem to have been aware as late as 1816 that anything untoward happened in March 1803. According to his account, the first blow against the Senate came only in 1810, with the official establishment of the State Council.[53]

It seems, then, that the decree of March 1803 was not intentionally a constitutional act but only Alexander's response to a particular situation. Alexander just wanted the Senate to get out of the way for the time being, not to fall; otherwise he and his statesmen would not have tried so hard to resuscitate it in the ensuing decades. Indeed, such attempts did not cease to occupy the center of the stage until 1832 (see below, ch. V, sec. B), and the Russian code of laws retained provisions that proclaimed the Senate's supremacy in the government organization until 1917.[54] In short, the Senate did not lose its institutional position in 1803, because it had never had one. What happened, rather, was that it was shaken loose from the center of government by a series of conflicts that bore no relation to it, in much the same way as a farm is inadvertently destroyed when it becomes a battlefield.

Russian government in Alexander I's time was incapable of performing a constitutional act. It could neither establish a functional legal institution nor abolish one. No one in Alexander's time opposed legal system as such, and no one seriously upheld it. At best, the statesmen only used its terms when they wished to express their personal moral sentiments or to appeal to those of others.[55] The Senate had prestige, but neither it nor any other legal institution had acquired sufficient de facto authority in the central government to identify definitively what was legal and what was not. The collegial institutions had never operated as parts of a system and showed no promise of doing so.

52. Apparently, those who wrote the decree of 21 Mar. 1803—the secret committee—did not intend to destroy the Senate's control over the ministers permanently. See Telberg, pp. 79–80. Predtechenskii, p. 133, mentions that Simon Vorontsov considered the March decree to have destroyed the Senate. He seems to have been the only one.

53. Troshchinskii, "Zapiska," pp. 34–35, 60–65. Troshchinskii was one of the senators who presented the objection to Alexander in 1803.

54. *Svod zakonov Rossiiskoi Imperii* (many eds., 16 vols., St. Petersburg; all citations of this work refer to the 1892 ed. unless otherwise noted), vol. I, "Uchrezhdenie Pravitelstvuiushchego Senata," art. 1. See also *ibid.*, "Svod osnovnykh gosudarstvennykh zakonov," arts. 74–77.

55. See above, n. 51. There is no lack of testimony to this effect from contemporaries. See, e.g., Speranskii, pp. 42–43; Nikolai Mikhailovich, II, 61–63, 160–161; Czartoryski, I, 291–292. The same refrain runs through the memoirs and diaries of statesmen to the end of the tsarist period (see below, ch. VII, sec. B).

The servitors could not predict one another's behavior in any systematic way. In sum, senatorial government had made legal system holy, but after a century of operation it had not inculcated the attitudes that would make system work. By Western standards, it had failed.

D. Reasons for the "Failure" of Senatorial Government

Much of the "failure" stems from the simple fact that the authors of all our sources, official and unofficial alike, lived in the atmosphere of Moscow and St. Petersburg, and in the eighteenth and nineteenth centuries it was the custom in the capital cities to judge administrators harshly, especially those in the countryside. The vast majority of politically conscious Russians, including the government officials themselves, found deep satisfaction in condemning *chinovniki*.[56] By conjuring up and blaming all troubles on the image of a "corrupt" local administrator who was oppressing the people, cheating the state, subverting the law, blocking the execution of reform, and generally creating all the difficulties that confronted the government, a citizen of the capital cities could explain away the dilemmas of his historical situation and go on putting his faith in all manner of pipe dreams. It was easy to believe that the government had only to sweep out the wretched "ink souls" in order to find or create some sort of panacea in the countryside—holy peasants in their communes, virtuous gentry, the greatness of the Russian (Slavic) soul, communism, a constitution, freedom, industrial development, and/or some flawless reform program. Purge the clerks, and Russian virtue (or progress) would beam forth and lead the world. Given this article of faith, servitors in the central offices could live in the midst of famine, crime, injustice, mismanagement, unbalanced budgets, continual failure, and an abiding atmosphere of intrigue, and still make sense of their situation.

The image of the evil clerk was especially attractive before about 1900 (and again after 1917) because there was no reliable way of knowing what the local officials were actually doing, and one could paint one's picture of them as one chose. In the absence of an operating legal system or any meaningful standard of conduct, it was often impossible to tell whether or not an official was doing his job

---

56. Concerning this tendency in the first half of the nineteenth century, see S. F. Starr, "Decentralization and Self-Government in Russia, 1855–1865" (unpublished Ph.D. dissertation, Princeton University, 1968), pp. 14–15, 29, 31–33, 72–73.

even by watching him.[57] Everyone in the capital cities from tsar to university student was free to assume what he pleased, and it generally pleased the vast majority of them to regard those servitors of the domestic administration who were not within the circle of their own personal acquaintances as scoundrels. It is impossible to exaggerate the effect this syndrome has produced on the image of Russian government that has come down to us. It formed a basic element not only in the literature of the period but also in the laws, the administrative reports, the attitudes of the statesmen, and the policies of the government.[58] It was precisely this capital-city habit of thought, not the peculiarities of the Russian countryside, that Gogol was depicting and condemning in *Dead Souls*.[59]

57. A number of the central government's actions expressed the leading statesmen's awareness that the inspecting and overseeing of officials was an imprecise affair. See *IPS*, III, 589–597. In 1799 Paul ordered an extensive inspection of local government organs throughout Russia. Reports of its results came into the Senate in 1800, most of them denouncing the local officials for their virtually universal corruption and confusion, to which the Senate responded by denouncing the inspectors for the superficiality of their observation and the extensive harshness of their judgments. See *ibid.*, II, 764–774. Considering this inconclusive result, it is not surprising that Alexander I and Nicholas I issued a number of laws from 1817 on that curtailed the power of the Senate to censure governors for illegal actions. They were quite aware that many of a governor's actions came from his chancellery without his knowledge and that therefore he should not be condemned for them. Alexander Herzen, I, 350–352, records his meeting with a governor who could not read the papers his chancellery presented for his signature. Not that he was illiterate; he simply could not comprehend the "legal" formulas that had become customary in his gubernia by the time he took it over. Concerning the same phenomenon in the early eighteenth century before Catherine II's reforms, see below, n. 71.

58. A typical expression of this feeling, remarkable only because of the persons involved and the frankness with which they spoke, is related in the diary of Pavel A. Valuev under 23 Sept. 1866. On that day Valuev (then the minister of internal affairs) was conversing with Alexander II about the difficulties of administering western Russia. In particular, he was expressing his disgust with the russification policies of Mikhail N. Muravev, then the governor-general of Vilna. Suddenly, breaking into French, he said, "Allow me to tell you that I feel that I love my country very little . . . I scorn my compatriots." Alexander replied, also in French, "I feel it too: I don't say this to others, but I tell you that I feel as you do" (Pavel A. Valuev, *Dnevnik P. A. Valueva* [2 vols., Moscow, 1961], II, 151).

59. ". . . which of you, filled with Christian humility, will dive into the depths of his own soul, and not aloud, but in silence and solitude, in moments of isolated self-communion, will put to himself the weighty question, 'And is there not some taint of Chichikov in me also?' Why not indeed? Still you never say that of yourself; but if some acquaintance of neither very lofty nor very low rank passes by, you instantly nudge your neighbor, and say to him, almost bursting with laughter the while, 'Look, look! there is Chichikov! Chichikov has passed by!' and then, like a child, oblivious of all the respect which is due to rank and years, you will run after him, imitate him behind his back, and say, 'Chichikov! Chichikov! Chichikov!'" (Nikolai Gogol, *Dead Souls*, tr. Stephen Graham [8th ed., London, 1915], p. 194).

In reality, the "quality" of Russian officials did not constitute the main weakness of domestic administration. It only reflected a more basic difficulty—the nature of the social relationships that obtained in the countryside. As Mikhail Speranskii expressed it:

> How can a *zemskii ispravnik*, elected for a scrap of bread from among the poorest gentry, aided only by a board of similarly destitute colleagues, inspire respect for law, suppress disorders, protect property from theft and avoid ruinous lawsuits throughout an area of five or six hundred versts? In a country where landed estates are for the most part unsurveyed, where rights even to surveyed land are not clear, where the whole economy is in extreme disorder and confusion, how can there not be numerous, entangling lawsuits? How can laws have effect when they are not upheld by intelligent and enlightened officials, when these officials are still uneducated? Do you know how difficult it is for a judge to maintain his honor where there is no public opinion, no open court sessions, no responsibility, no counsel, no means for study, and finally, to sum it all up, where the very texts of the laws are known only by the notebooks of clerks, copied from one to another without any regular procedure?[60]

For one thing, Russian society in the century and a half after Peter I's reforms was a rough-and-tumble affair in which the spirit of legality and reasoned discussion did not enjoy frequent expression. Large numbers of people in all social classes were outlaws, and even those who lived within what passed for a legal framework frequently resorted to violence.[61] In the lower Volga area, says Gote, "it was not always possible to distinguish a real brigand from a man armed in his own defense."[62] In Penza in the 1760s the gentry customarily spent the winters in town because they dared not remain on their estates during "robbery season."[63]

The peasants provided an ample reservoir of manpower for criminal enterprises. According to official records, 526,000 of them ran away from their villages during the period 1719–1742, and the actual number

60. Speranskii, p. 123. Although this passage makes it clear that the government's difficulties were more than deficiencies in organizational structure, Speranskii goes on to suggest that they could all be remedied by administrative reform. Here, as in many other writings, Speranskii shifts from the role of detached observer to that of an active official who wishes to propose workable remedies and therefore to hold forth some promise that remedies are possible.

61. Herzen, I, 280–286, 300–312, relates a number of anecdotes illustrating the arbitrariness that prevailed in the 1830s.

62. Gote, I, 338.

63. This, according to their *nakaz* to the Commission of 1767. See John Sinton, "The Instructions from Kazan Gubernia at the Legislative Commission of 1767" (unpublished Ph.D. dissertation, University of Indiana, 1968), p. 108.

was probably far higher.[64] In the eyes of the government these were all hunted criminals, and the line between them and the active brigands must have been a thin one, easily crossed and recrossed.[65] The gentry were hardly less inclined to turn to crime than the peasants, and when they did, they seem to have been a good deal harder to cope with. Their serfs furnished the manpower for private armies, while relatives in high office protected them from the consequences of their escapades.[66] Such was the power of one Voronezh landholder in the late eighteenth century that a "lower land court" (the uezd *ispravnik* and his college) took an assault force and two cannon with them when they went to arrest him. Even this formidable array was repulsed with heavy losses. Nor was violence merely a matter of crime and the struggle to cope with crime. The simple conduct of government business frequently involved bloodshed. On one occasion the Vologda gubernia fiscal chamber collectively assaulted and murdered a member of another college in order to settle a jurisdictional dispute. Such cases appeared regularly in reports from all over Russia in the eighteenth and early nineteenth centuries.[67]

But violence, like the personal qualities of officials, was only a manifestation of the disorder in the eighteenth-century Russian countryside, not its essence. Crime was more a symptom of Russia's difficulties than a cause. The fundamental obstacle to the operation and development of systematic political organization was the structure—or, in Western terms, the lack of structure—of rural society itself.

At first glance, political order in the countryside appears to have been highly centralized in the eighteenth and early nineteenth centuries. Before the introduction of the local colleges, the voevodas were the uncontested centers of *formal* authority in their respective territories (see above, ch. II, n. 61), and they in turn were formally subject to the tsar's absolute authority. Catherine's reform of local government introduced some changes into this arrangement, but they did not include decentralization. Her new local colleges were not a technique for delegating authority but an apparatus to carry out the governors' commands and to enforce the central government's laws. If anything, the government's formal structure became more centralized in the nineteenth century than it had been before Catherine's time.

But centralization in rural administration was more apparent than real. If the formal administration of the *provintsii* and the gubernias

64. Kahan, p. 51; Kafengauz and Pavlenko, pp. 175–176.
65. Gote, I, 334–338.
66. *Ibid.*, pp. 334–342; Dukes, p. 19.
67. Gradovskii, I, 311–313.

had been operating in a vacuum, it might have worked like a unified hierarchy. In fact, it had to deal with the society (or societies) of rural Russia, and there were no elements in this society that lent themselves to centralized organization.

To begin with, the rural gentry in an uezd were not sufficiently conscious of common corporate rights to erect institutions around them. The gentry as a whole formed a social order of sorts, but it centered chiefly on guards regiments in the capital cities and powerful landholding families, neither of which corresponded to territorial units. Most of the wealthier gentry families held estates all over European Russia, sometimes hundreds of miles apart, and they did not identify themselves with particular areas. Even if they had, their service obligations (see above, ch. II, n. 3) and their inclination to reside in the capital cities still would have kept them away from their estates.[68] Until the nineteenth century, then, the rural population felt no traditional association with the government's units of territorial administration.[69]

The absence of any territorial social institutions in the Russian countryside should be considered in association with the attitude toward authority that prevailed there. In the eighteenth-century rural mind, both peasant and gentry, authority still resided in any man who seemed to possess "power," i.e., the capability to protect other men and to satisfy their needs (see above, ch. I, sec. A). As said before, this was primarily a personal matter. In a tribute-collecting hierarchy a man possessed authority over his subordinates by virtue of his personal relationships with them, and if he had any power other than his own, it was conceived to be that of another person (spirit) whose agent he presumably was.

Western minds and the minds of capital-city Russians have always exhibited a strong tendency to associate arbitrary personal authority of this sort with an orderly chain of command or pyramid of status, as if the one automatically gives rise to the other. But this simply was not the case in provincial Russia. The rural mind was not aware of its dependence on a structure of authority delegated in orderly fashion from echelon to echelon. Peasants, gentry, and administrative officials alike were inclined to organize themselves around separate persons, regardless of their position in any systematic order. Serfs were likely to regard the steward who managed their estate as a higher power than their owner. Likewise, they were likely to consider their owner more powerful than any government official. By the same token, the village

68. Raeff, *Origins,* pp. 46–47, 98–102.
69. See Speranskii, pp. 42–43; Troshchinskii, pp. 49–56.

elder might seem a higher power than the steward.[70] Then, too, if none of the authorities on an estate were able to impress a serf in such a way that he was confident of their power, he might seek aid (or redress) from some outside person: a local judge, a priest, the leader of a gang of thieves, the voevoda, another landholder, a magician, an inspector from the central government, or a madman pretending to be the tsar. Rural society made no distinction between these categories of authority. A person's authority stemmed entirely from his efficacy in local affairs, not from his place in a structure.

The central government's administrative agencies in the countryside suffered from the same disorder in hierarchical patterns. The clerks in the voevodas' and governors' chancelleries usually held more authority in the eyes of the populace than their chiefs. They were often able to decide a voevoda's or governor's affairs on their own and even to nullify the decisions that he did make.[71] Indeed, they dominated the offices of territorial administration to the extent that the voevodas and governors were unable even to read what they wrote. In the eighteenth century this was partly a consequence of the governors' illiteracy, but even as late as the 1830s, when most of them could read ordinary Russian, they were still unable to understand their clerks' jargon. Konstantin Pobedonostsev noted in the 1850s that the judges in the law courts were also rendered helpless by their inability to understand the complex and ritualistic machinations of their own chancelleries.[72] The clerks—like the stewards on serf estates—acquired their authority not from any system or hierarchy but from their practical relationships with those who needed their services.[73]

In short, pyramidal hierarchies of administration such as the one diagrammed in Figure 1 were visible only from the capital cities. Eighteenth-century voevodas, governors, and governors-general were

70. Confino, *Domaines*, describes the roles that stewards (pp. 39–76) and serf-elected elders (pp. 81–91) played in the management of landed estates in the eighteenth and early nineteenth centuries.
71. Gote, I, 259–260, 280, 306, 310–311; Hassell, "Implementation," p. 292.
72. Robert Byrnes, *Pobedonostsev, His Life and Thought* (Bloomington, Ind., 1968), p. 57. See Korf, pp. 442–444, regarding court chancelleries in the late eighteenth and early nineteenth centuries. On the chancelleries of the central colleges, see below, ch. V, sec. D.
73. Until 1763 a provincial servitor's formal authority and his pay were entirely determined by the rank he had acquired during his military career—that is, his personal status—rather than by the position he held in the administrative hierarchy. It is true, of course, that the position a man held usually corresponded to his former rank. Governors were ex-colonels, while voevodas were likely to be ex-captains. The fact remains, however, that even in the formal administrative structure it was personal rank, rather than position, that set one man in authority over another. See Gote, I, 327.

not *the* centers of political authority but, at best, the most powerful among a number of such centers. True, their power was virtually unlimited, but this only reflected the fact that they had no consistent and reliable way to limit anyone else's actions.[74] De facto authority in the countryside in eighteenth- and nineteenth-century Russia was "nodal," to use a geographer's term, rather than territorial. Political order, such as it was, did not form a unified whole but reposed in a number of centers—power loci—each of which exercised its influence in all directions until it ran into that of other power loci along boundaries rigidly but shakily established by a continuing experience of violence, chicanery, custom, and circumstance.[75] Occasionally there were individual voevodas and governors who acted as real centers of political authority in their territories. A man of unusual energy and ability, especially one who enjoyed the unwavering support of the tsar, could tear up and reform the political order in his territory more abruptly than would have been possible for an analogous official in any Western country. Indeed, the Russian government servitor's lore was filled with images of righteous champion-governors, men who ruthlessly destroyed "evil" and protected the "good." The champion-governor, however, was a rare exception in real life, common as it was in the mythology of the capital cities.[76] Real voevodas and governors, even the energetic ones, had to accomplish their tasks within the framework of local politics by negotiating with a hodgepodge of powerful persons and their followings. Gote's description of the central government's efforts to inspect the voevodas during the years 1725–1762 presents a capsule view of the

74. On the weakness of the "absolute" voevodas in the seventeenth and early eighteenth centuries, see Grigorev, pp. 49–51. "There was," says Grigorev, "no definite hierarchy of officials in the provinces" (p. 51). LeDonne, pp. 526–528, depicts Catherine's local institutions as essentially a disorderly pile of despots, each operating separately from the others. The same picture of the helplessness of "absolute" authority emerges from the reports of A. D. Balashev to Alexander I in the 1820s, when he was governor-general of five interior gubernias. See Predtechenskii, pp. 399–403. Balashev complained unceasingly that he was unable to organize his territory. Even with his combined military and civil powers and the sustained favor of the tsar, he could neither rule nor reform except in the old-fashioned ad hoc way.

75. T. M. Poulsen, "The Provinces of Russia" (unpublished Ph.D. dissertation, University of Wisconsin, 1963), pp. 202–205, 218–235, discusses the absence of a concept of political territory in Russia. The term "nodal" is his.

76. L. Ignatieff, "French Emigres in Russia, 1789–1825" (unpublished Ph.D. dissertation, University of Michigan, 1963), pp. 112–137, describes the service of the Duc de Richelieu as governor of Odessa and governor-general of New Russia from 1803 to 1815. Richelieu's position was not exactly the same as a governor's, and his territory was hardly typical, but he will serve as a model of a champion-governor.

"nodality" of rural administration in that time.[77] Before Catherine's reforms, it will be recalled, local government was left largely to the voevoda himself, and he had to serve as a sort of universal agent for all the functional offices and tsar's favorites in the capital cities. Without any bureaucratic system in the *provintsii*, the central government had no official information about what was going on except what it could get from the voevoda's reports and from the appeals that were sent in against him. In order to get more information, therefore, the central government resorted to dispatching special agents to the *provintsii* to make inspections.[78]

These agents were called, among other names, *komissii* (although they generally operated singly). Almost all of them were army officers, some still on active duty and some retired.[79] Usually, they went to look into specific complaints or perform specific functions, but they had wide powers to investigate, arrest, punish, and replace local officials, including voevodas and governors, if they discovered any illegal or harmful behavior.[80] They earned their pay by getting a share of the fines they levied.[81] They could remain in an area for a single season or stay for several years, though it usually happened that the longer they stayed, the more they became a part of the local oligarchy and lost their significance as a control or separate source of information.[82]

The occasions that produced calls for *komissii* were usually local squabbles between two parties at least one of which had enough influence to attract the attention of someone high up in the central government. Two stewards on neighboring estates might quarrel over a boundary; a voevoda might try to prevent a landholder from seizing a forest belonging to the crown; a local military officer might accuse a voevoda of embezzling government funds. When one of the parties in such a dispute decided to utilize his influence in the capital cities, the central government was likely to respond by sending a *komissiia*.

As soon as the local officials heard of the appointment of a *komissiia* to look into their affairs, they would begin contacting their friends and relatives in the capital cities. All the appointed officials had such con-

77. The following account comes largely from Gote, II, 46–110.
78. *Ibid.*, pp. 48–51, 84–85.
79. *Ibid.*, p. 55.
80. *Ibid.*, pp. 94–103.
81. *Ibid.*, pp. 60–63. In theory, they had to pay their expenses, including the salaries of their assistants, before they could extract any profit for themselves.
82. *Ibid.*, pp. 97–99, describes some agencies that Elizabeth established in the 1750s to combat bootlegging. Invariably, when they had worked for more than a short time in the areas they had been sent to investigate, they blended into the local hierarchies and ceased in fact to be central agents.

tacts, otherwise they could not have gotten their jobs in the first place. Likewise, the owners and stewards of large estates were not without friends in power. When the *komissiia* arrived, therefore, he faced a number of power loci—"nodes"—ready and waiting for a political struggle that might rage both in the territory and in the central offices of the government.[83]

The *komissiia* had tasks to perform, and despite the resounding phrases in his instructions, he did not ordinarily possess the power to carry them out without securing the cooperation of some of the loci in the territory.[84] In the absence of legal system, he could not be an enforcer of law, concerned only to discover violations of statutes. He was, rather, a combatant in a local faction fight. His practical aim was not to determine formal legality, which was in any case undeterminable, but to find out if possible what the real issue was and who the factions were, and then to decide matters by adding the weight of his influence to one side or the other. Of course, it often happened that there were more than two sides. His crucial problem, therefore, was to find (or organize) a side strong enough to prevail decisively with his aid. "Success" was a decision made and enforced. Right or wrong, just or unjust, it ended a local squabble, restored order, sustained the government's authority, and kept the *komissiia* himself out of jail.

Gote points out that the work of the *komissii* was very hard and their position a very difficult one. Rewards could be great, but the punishments for failure were likely to be severe, and failure was always a real possibility. Many men who were appointed to be *komissii* tried to get out of it.[85] Speaking formally, the success of a *komissiia* meant that the Senate had restored order in the countryside by telling the local "citizens" what the law was in a given case. At the same time, however, the Senate itself was acting as a tool of local politics. The officials in the central offices were using their official authority to respond to unofficial pressures from outside the administrative system.

The situation of a *komissiia* was roughly similar to that of a voevoda and/or governor when he first came into a new territory. Like the *komissiia*, the voevoda (or governor) had to contend with the entrenched authorities in his territory rather than to enforce any "law." Like the *komissiia*, the voevoda (governor) who remained too long in a territory tended to sink into local society and become a creature of local politics.[86]

83. *Ibid.*, pp. 63–74.
84. *Ibid.* See also pp. 87–92.
85. *Ibid.*, pp. 54–58, 63–72.
86. Concerning the governor's need for personal connections in the capital

The paper administrative system that Catherine's reforms established in the gubernias and uezds did not materially alter this state of affairs. If anything, the extension of senatorial organization outside the capital cities rendered its agents more vulnerable than ever to influences from rural society. As the power loci in the countryside intensified their interaction with the government, they did not change their practices to suit the formulas of the law. *Instead, they inserted their own squabbles into the central administration and compelled it to deal with them on their own terms.* Local colleges were even more likely than the voevodas had been to lose their institutional identities in a sea of local political struggles.

We have already referred to the fact that during and after Catherine's reign the bulk of the gentry were indifferent to their uezd assemblies (see above, sec. C). This allowed the few men who were politically active an inordinate amount of patronage power in their uezds. According to Jones, it was most often the marshal himself who got control of the patronage.[87] According to Romanovich-Slavatinskii, power fell into the hands of a horde of outsiders (*prishletsy*): retired officers and officials who married into the local families, or bought estates, or simply gained the favor of the governor.[88] Whoever the patrons were, they acquired all the prerogatives formally granted to the inert gentry assemblies, which meant that they not only filled the elective positions in rural administration but also played a vital role in nominating candidates for appointed positions (ordinarily, the appointment process had to begin with a recommendation by the local marshal).[89]

It may be seen that Catherine's local institutions provided a new basis on which hierarchies of personal influence could take form: hierarchies very like the ones that had always dominated the locales of Russia. Now, however, they were likely to be considerably more powerful, owing to the expansion of the government offices that they controlled. It may be said, then, that as the central government expanded its functions, it allowed local hierarchies to increase their de

---

cities, see *IPS*, III, 556. The rotation of voevodas from one area to another is described above, ch. II, sec. C.

87. Jones, "Russian Gentry," pp. 275–278.

88. A. Romanovich-Slavatinskii, *Dvorianstvo v Rossii* (St. Petersburg, 1870), pp. 490–497. Similar descriptions are in "Dvorianstvo," in Brockhaus and Efron, X, 208, and Emmons, pp. 16–18.

89. The marshal drew up a list of candidates for each position. When the assembly had approved the list, it would then be submitted to the governor and, when appropriate, to the Senate and/or ministries for final selection. This procedure was required by law after 1803 (*IPS*, III, 469–470). In practice, it usually meant that the marshal himself made the selection.

facto power in their own areas and also to intensify their de facto influence on the central offices.[90]

This is not to say that Catherine's institutions produced no significant effects on rural society and administration. If legal system did not prevail in the gubernias after 1785, at least the idea of it was inserted into formal routines and rituals; otherwise the governors would not have complained so persistently about the inconvenience they suffered from legal limits on their prerogatives throughout the period from Catherine's reign to 1905.[91] More important, Catherine's local colleges contributed to the development and expansion of communication between the government-society and the countryside. Despite their slowness, they handled far more cases and performed a greater variety of functions than the voevodas had, and the experience of working in them seems to have intensified the local gentry's awareness of their dependence on institutions, both local and central.[92] Then, too, it was the gentry marshals and assemblies who organized the reserve forces that enabled Kutuzov to drive Napoleon out of Russia.[93]

Senatorial government "failed" because society in the countryside had no institutions that were capable of interacting coherently with a systematic administration. In order to operate systematically, Catherine's administrators would have had to remain apart from rural society and to keep themselves free from any matters that did not fit their official categories and responsibilities. This they did not do, nor could they have. Catherine's colleges could not hover above the helter-skelter oligarchies of rural society as it was. They had somehow to work with rural society as it was, and in so doing they became arenas in which local "powers" contended with one another. Orders from the central government became weapons to be used by one faction against another. Reports from local officials to St. Petersburg conveyed political attacks by one faction on another rather than bona fide information. Under the circumstances a chain of command from the capital city to the countryside could easily serve as a reverse "chain" of political influence. Local factions could enlist the support of powerful friends and relatives in the central offices of the *pravitelstvo,* and as

90. Hassell, "Vicissitudes," pp. 120–124, points out that officials continued to extend their primary loyalty to the men who got them their jobs even after Catherine's reform. See also above, nn. 87, 88.

91. Concerning the governors' complaints, see Starr, pp. 38–40, 117–138.

92. Korf, p. 110. According to Klochkov, p. 435, the gentry of Catherine's time felt a quickening of social life in the rural areas following the enactment of the statute of 1775.

93. Korf, pp. 326–328.

the central government impinged upon them ever more intensively, their inclination to do this grew correspondingly more pronounced. Catherine's gentry assemblies and colleges brought greater coherence into local factional struggles only by allowing them to disrupt the entire *pravitelstvo*. Thus, as senatorial administration systematized the countryside, the countryside corrupted the administration, a two-way process that constituted the dynamic element in senatorial government and also its basic contradiction. Insofar as senatorial institutions expanded communications between tsar and people, they succeeded to some extent in accomplishing their general purpose, but this very success assured that they would "fail" to develop according to Western patterns.[94]

E. THE DEVELOPMENT OF RELATIONSHIPS BETWEEN
RURAL POLITICAL ORDER AND CENTRAL GOVERNMENT

In 1905 the general characteristics of eighteenth-century rural administration could still be found in the countryside below the uezd level. Reports of the inspections carried out by the ministry of internal affairs in 1904 and the years thereafter depicted much of the same haphazardness that had prevailed over a century before.[95] This, however, should not be taken to mean that legal-administrative system did not develop in Russia, or that it failed to make inroads on rural society. It was not the legal-administrative system that was slow to change in the eighteenth and nineteenth centuries but, rather, the social circumstances under which it developed. Generalizations about the circumstances of local government, and their broad similarity from one century to the next, serve to explain the tsarist government's "failure" to be like its Western counterparts, but they do not necessarily imply that the government itself remained unchanged. What they do suggest is that the government's evolution was complex and, in general, that the introduction of system into an essentially nonsystematic society is not a

94. A student of American urban administration has assumed that the improvement of communications between a government and its people is equivalent to the development of a unified social order and an orderly legal-administrative system. See Seymour Mandelbaum, *Boss Tweed's New York* (New York, 1965), pp. 4–16. Apparently, the study of the political processes through which immigrant populations were assimilated into American culture does not suggest that a population can tear apart a political order through the very channels of communication that the political order develops in order to rule over it. In Russia, on the other hand, this possibility has always loomed large.

95. See, e.g., a report on an inspection of the gubernia and uezd offices in Orel gubernia in 1906 in *Izvestiia zemskogo otdela* (Jan. and Feb. 1907, hereinafter cited as *IZO*), pp. 24–32, 59–62. See also below, ch. IX, sec. D.

process that necessarily conforms to plans and theories drawn up to explain what happened in another society.

Some development did occur in the relationships between rural political order and central government during the senatorial era. One way to perceive it, or at least to indicate that it occurred, is to consider some of the Russian government's attempts to survey the land in the seventeenth and eighteenth centuries.

All the surveys had the same general purpose: to provide the government with a means for communicating with society. Once the boundaries of a servitor's holdings were clearly established, the government would have a uniform basis for identifying his rights and duties, thereby regularizing and delimiting his obligations to the government and his legal relationships with other servitor-landholders. With an accurate survey, the government could estimate the tribute and the military support that it was likely to receive each year, and society could predict what the government would demand. Each would be able to predict the other's actions more reliably than was possible in the absence of land measurement, and they would be able to depend more fully on one another.

The general difficulties involved in introducing elements of system into a nonsystematic society (see above, ch. I, sec. C) all conspired to prevent the taking of a useful survey. Unsuccessful attempts to measure land boundaries succeeded one another from the sixteenth century on, causing considerable frustration to generations of Russian administrators without bringing any enduring satisfaction to the landholders. Nevertheless, the nature of the attempts to survey the land did change with time, and it is in this change that the historian can glimpse some signs of development in the rural political order and its relationships with the central government.

The survey of 1754–1762 is a good starting point. It began when someone persuaded the Empress Elizabeth that she could and should measure the land of Russia, divide it into separate lots, mark the boundaries, and draw up documents to show which person or government agency possessed each lot. Accordingly, her order of 13 May 1754 sent parties of army surveyors out to measure off the fields and, where necessary, redivide them so that each landholder, village, and government office would have his or its own separate, integral lot. Landholders who had no documents to prove their right of possession were to lose their lands.[96]

96. German, pp. 172–180. See also L. V. Milov, *Issledovanie ob "ekonomi-cheskikh primechaniiakh" k generalnomu mezhevaniiu* (Moscow, 1965), pp. 11–15. It should be kept in mind throughout the following discussion that no govern-

Elizabeth's purpose was theoretically sound. There had been no attempt at a survey since the 1680s, and no one was sure where the land boundaries were anymore. The landholders were getting into quarrels, and the disputing parties were finding it difficult to resolve their disagreements on their own. The law and customs regarding inheritance required gentry landholders to divide their estates equally among their male heirs in such a way as to split each separate field and village into shares. This made it extremely difficult for a family to maintain its holdings for more than one or two generations. Most estates consisted of a number of scattered lots, interspersed among those of other estates, none of them measured with any accuracy.[97] Under these circumstances it is not surprising that an increasing number of disputes between landholders were coming to the central government to be decided. In the absence of meaningful records, however, they were as unresolvable in the capital cities as in the provinces. A general survey, Elizabeth thought, would bring an end to the trouble.

The survey commenced in the summer of 1755, but it bogged down almost immediately. Wherever the survey parties went, they found (as one would expect) that records and land titles did not correspond to reality. Since almost no one had a clear legal claim to the land on which he resided, the original problem of confirming existing boundaries swelled up into one of parceling out the lands anew. The landholders, however, were not amenable to this sort of arbitrary reshuffling, and the attempts of the surveyors to push them about aroused strenuous opposition. Elizabeth did not press the matter. After about a year of fruitless uproar the survey was abandoned, having registered only fifty estates in Moscow uezd.[98]

At first glance, the survey of 1754 suggests nothing but another ludicrous failure on the part of the government. In the light of the previous history of land survey in Russia, however, it actually reflects considerable progress both in the effectiveness of the government organization and in the coherence of rural political order.

Consider the survey that Tsar Feodor initiated in 1680.[99] It began in

ment survey before 1905 touched on peasant land except to mark off the area inhabited and farmed by each peasant village. So far as the survey laws were concerned, peasant land was a category to be identified and marked off from other categories, not to be divided among persons.

97. Augustine, pp. 395–407.

98. N. V. Bochkov, *Istoriia zemelnykh otnoshenii i zemleustroistva* (Moscow, 1956), p. 23. Milov, p. 15, asserts that 359 areas (*dachy*) were completed. The survey did not end formally until 1762, but it was suspended in fact when war broke out with Prussia in 1756.

99. The following account comes largely from German, pp. 100–120.

response to numerous complaints from servitor-landholders that some
of the land they claimed as their own was not allotted to them in the
official registers (*pistsovye knigi*). These registers were the results of
earlier surveys of the landed estates, which usually included what
purported to be an assessment of the quantity and value of the land,
the number of people that resided on it, and an enumeration of buildings and improvements. The figures in these earlier assessments were
notoriously inaccurate. For one thing, they had all been made piecemeal, covering different locales at different times using different units
of measure. For another, the units of measure did not represent standard quantities. A variety of units of what purported to be taxable
wealth appeared in the registers—*desiatina, malenkaia sokha, bolshaia
sokha, vyta, obzha, luka, chet*. A certain number of these units were
recorded for each estate, village, or town, ostensibly indicating what it
was worth and what share of the tax it should pay. None of them,
however, were strictly measures of area or of any quantity that could
be compared on a simple arithmetic basis from one estate to another.[100]
If the tax records had one village down for two *cheti* and a neighboring
one for three, this did not necessarily mean that the former had two-
thirds as much land as the latter, or that their lands produced two-
thirds as much harvest, or that the inhabitants had two-thirds as many
dwellings. It only meant that at some time a collector had persuaded or
forced the two villages to agree that the former should pay two-thirds
as much tax as the latter. The basis for an agreement of this sort was
never clear, and it seems to have varied widely from place to place and
time to time. But the government did not care how the agreements
were made, so long as it could apportion its taxes. Whether or not the
possessions of each village or estate actually corresponded to the
portion of the tax it paid was the villagers' and estate holders' concern.
Before the 1680s, then, "surveyors" did not measure land; they only
secured the agreement of the estates and villages in a given locale on
what portion of the tax each would pay.[101]

Another reason for the inaccuracy of the registers in 1680 was their
great age. Most of them dated from the years immediately following
1626, when a fire had destroyed the central government's landholding
records and made it necessary to draw up a new set.[102] During the next
few decades the landholders had generally found it advantageous to

100. Lappo-Danilevskii, pp. 219–222, says that the *desiatina* became a uniform
measure of area by mid-seventeenth century. Such precision, however, went no
further than official documents.
101. S. B. Veselovskii, I, 17–23, 49–51, 373–377; II, 88–89, 96–102, 118–119.
102. German, pp. 73–79.

acquire land without registering it. The less of their land they registered, the less they had to pay taxes on. In the 1670s, however, the government began handing out unregistered lands to new servitors with more than usual vigor, and this changed the landholders' situation. Now it behooved them to legitimize their unofficial holdings before the government granted them to someone else[103]—thus the growing number of requests from landholders that they be allowed to register more land.

The government's problem was twofold: to satisfy the landholders and to find lands to distribute.[104] Tsar Feodor decided in 1678 that he would not simply grant the landholders' requests to legitimize their seizures. This would probably deprive the state of its lands. Instead, he ordered that a general survey be made of *all* the land, both assigned and unassigned areas. This, he hoped, would provide a basis for resolving disputes among the landholders and at the same time make more lands available for distribution.[105]

In 1680 the survey began in a few towns, and in August 1681 a general regulation came out that extended it to the countryside. Actual fieldwork began in the following month and continued through the winter of 1681–1682 until April, when Tsar Feodor died. *Streltsy* rebellions precluded any work in the following summer, and it was not until 1683 that the survey at last got going in earnest. By this time the government had scaled down its ambitions. A new order came out that required surveys only for those estate lands whose possessors requested it. This represented a rather drastic retreat from the pretensions of the regulation of 1681, which had called for the survey of all lands and even the forced redistribution of all fields held in common by more than one landholder.

Indeed, the new regulation actually proved to be too lenient. The experience of 1683 indicated that surveys by request alone would not provide the government with the records it needed. Yet another regulation came out early in 1684, calling once again for a survey of *all* lands and requiring proof of ownership from those who claimed them. This was stricter than the order of 1683; on the other hand, it did not revive the demand for forced redistribution that had been in the 1681 decree. Work on this last order went forward until August 1686, when it was interrupted, never to be resumed, by the Crimean campaign.

103. "Knigi pistsovyia i perepisnyia," in Brockhaus and Efron, XV (1895), 457–459; Bochkov, pp. 7–17.
104. German, p. 100. Chicherin, pp. 508–518, describes the lack of coherence in landholding records in the seventeenth century.
105. German, pp. 93–100.

By the time it broke off, most of the land in central Russia had been registered, a remarkable achievement considering all the difficulties involved. The new records were generally more complete and uniform than any that had been compiled before, and they would furnish the main basis for landholding until Catherine II began her survey in 1766.[106]

On the face of it, the survey of 1680–1686 appears to have been more successful than that of 1754. A closer look, however, indicates that the comparison is more complex. I. E. German has estimated the approximate time available for the fieldwork in 1684–1686, the number of men who were engaged in it, and the area they covered. According to his calculations, they could not have come close to doing all the work they claimed if they actually went out and measured the land.[107] Obviously, they did not measure the land. Their "surveys," like all that had been made before, were only products of negotiations. A completed registry of a given estate had only to be signed by the surveyors, the local officials, the owner, the neighbors, and anyone who had had anything to do with the surveying process.[108] Agreement, not accuracy, was what gave the registry its legitimacy. To read the survey regulations of 1680–1686, especially those which came out in 1681, one would think the whole of Russia was to be transformed into a well-ordered checkerboard, but in fact the new registers did not transform anything. The rectangular lots they showed should be taken as evidence not that the fields and forests of Russia were aligned in parallel columns in the 1680s, only that the tools the surveyors were ordered to use were unable to measure and register any corners except perpendicular ones.[109] The survey of 1680–1686, then, was just another reordering of the hierarchy, not a measurement. This was why it went so smoothly.

The new records did serve an important purpose. They constituted a primordial basis for orderly communication up and down the echelons of the tribute-collecting hierarchy and between the functional offices of the central government. If the registers in the central offices did not really show who held what land, at least they tallied with local records and agreed with them. Moreover, the records for different areas gave the appearance of being roughly comparable. With something resembling a uniform set of records, government and countryside could communicate with one another just a little more clearly than they had before, even though uniformity was only a pretense. A century

106. *Ibid.*, pp. 100–118.
107. *Ibid.*, pp. 112–115.
108. *Ibid.*, p. 107.
109. *Ibid.*, pp. 112–113.

later the surveyors of Catherine's reign often found the old records useful even where the land had changed hands many times and the boundary markers had disappeared.[110]

This is not to say that the old pre-Petrine hierarchy worked satisfactorily. On the contrary, the whole structure of government stood in dire need of reform when Peter came to the throne.[111] The point of this discussion of land surveys is that precisely because the old hierarchy was in some respects a going concern and an effective legal order, it could block the introduction of system all the more effectively. Elements of system such as a pretended registry of land boundaries doubtless made the hierarchy a bit more effective as an organization and as a means of communication between tsar and people, but by the same token they rendered it even more impervious to systematization than before. The better traditional society worked on the basis of bogus measures, the more capable it became of resisting the imposition of accurate measurement. Thus elements of legal-administrative system became obstacles to systematization. The pretense of system came into direct conflict with aspiration to system. It is with this dilemma in mind that Elizabeth's survey of 1754 should be considered.

The survey organization of the 1680s learned that it could not carry out an accurate survey and then resigned itself to the role of passive regulator. Its agents were under pressure to put together an orderly array of documents, and in order to do this, they allowed their survey to be formed by society. Instead of imposing system, they were content that the survey organization should represent system, i.e., that it should act systematically only when called upon to resolve a dispute. In this way, and only in this way, it was able to exert a regulating influence of sorts. By contrast, Elizabeth's survey of 1754–1762 failed to achieve anything at all. There were two reasons for this: 1) her survey was more systematically organized and technically sophisticated than any previous operation, and 2) rural political order had become more dependent on legal rules and more systematic in its application of them than it had been in the 1680s. The "law" that resided in the practical relationships in the countryside and that which guided Elizabeth's officers were both much more sophisticated than anything the 1680s had known, and this was precisely what made the gap be-

110. *Ibid.*, p. 116.
111. K. N. Serbina, *Ocherki iz sotsialno-ekonomicheskoi istorii russkogo goroda* (Moscow, 1951), presents a fascinating account of the evolution of the town of Tikhvin in northwestern Russia in the seventeenth century, showing more clearly than any statistical survey how the absence of system restricted economic development and hindered the formation of new social-economic relationships in countryside and town alike. See below, ch. IV, n. 2.

tween them all the wider. The day had passed when it would be possible to make the two "laws" correspond simply by making adjustments in the records.

The fate of the survey of 1754 indicates that there was no simple formula for the evolution of system in Russia and for the development of communications between tsarist government and rural society; yet it also indicates that development had in fact occurred. Moreover, it illustrates the kind of problem that arose with the overall evolution of senatorial government. Senatorial government embodied the same essential approach as the survey of the 1680s. It introduced some regularity into an essentially nonsystematic government, thereby strengthening its oligarchies and raising obstacles to further reform. It is not surprising, then, that although its achievements were of some positive significance for the evolution of Russian government, they appeared to many statesmen in the eighteenth and nineteenth centuries as obstacles to further progress.[112]

F. The Contribution of Senatorial Government to the Development of Legal-Administrative System

The "failure" of the senatorial institutions to act like a bureaucracy or to develop into one is not so significant as the evolution that did go forward in Russian government through the eighteenth century. By 1801, a little over a century after the survey of 1680–1686, Russian government had reached a point where bureaucratic organization could begin to take form and to act upon society—i.e., to act on its own, without sending soldiers to invade the countryside in its behalf. Before Peter's time elements of system could be found in the government, but they were being used to sustain an essentially nonsystematic hierarchy. During Peter's time the government was still unable to introduce system into society, but the new army could disrupt society in the name of system. At last, in the nineteenth century, a civil administration began to take form that could disrupt society and at the same time impart a measure of order to it.

What evolved in the eighteenth century was a symbiosis of sorts between system and the old haphazard hierarchy of nodal persons. Senatorial government did not impose system, but it did render the officials, statesmen, and courtiers so dependent upon collegial institu-

---

112. It bears repeating that this dilemma is by no means exclusively Russian. Kingsley notes that in Nigeria under the British, "modernized institutions were themselves employed to sustain archaic political structures" (p. 302). Henry Maine, *Ancient Law* (London, 1861), pp. 83–90, describes the same phenomenon in French historical development from the 1200s A.D.

tions that the process of consulting them became an accepted and vital part of government. True, the Senate and its colleges were often sidetracked, and even when they were consulted, the process was often more like a ritual than a rational decision-making process. Ultimately, however, the colleges could not be dispensed with except by replacing them with another, more effective system. Instead of dissolving into just another boiar duma presiding over a tribute-collecting hierarchy, the Senate and the local colleges continued to *represent* system over a long period of time and to lay the groundwork for new developments. The army, of course, was the goad that forced senatorial government to act and also the first training ground for its servitors, but it was in the Senate itself and its colleges that the servitors *responded* to the army's prompting, *communicated* the army's needs to society, and *organized* Russian society to the point where it could support the army without disintegrating.

Aside from the mythical prestige of the Senate, the simplest indicator of the growing influence of senatorial institutions in government and society is the number of cases it handled from year to year. Figures have not been accurately determined for all years, but those that are available give a rough indication of the increasing work load that the Senate had to handle. In the period April 1738–August 1739 it handled 391 decrees and probably a somewhat larger number of petitions: altogether not much more than 1,200 affairs in a little over a year.[113] In Catherine's time the annual case load probably averaged over 3,000,[114] increasing during the course of her reign to a high of 13,000 in 1796. Paul's brief campaign to centralize the administration sharply accelerated the rate of increase. In the year 1800 the Senate decided 44,500 cases,[115] and the volume of business continued on this level through the first years of Alexander I's reign.[116]

According to one view, the increase in the number of decrees and petitions coming to the Senate in Peter's time and throughout the eighteenth century resulted primarily from confusion.[117] Arbitrary habits of administration, together with a persistent inclination to make drastic changes in the law, rendered local authorities unable to respond to petitions or to carry out orders on their own responsibility. Consequently, undecided cases and petitions regarding the pettiest of local concerns came flooding into St. Petersburg and Moscow. Many

113. *IPS*, I, 608–609. Doubtless, the relatively informal procedures of those years allowed many cases to be dispatched without written records being made.
114. *Ibid.*, II, 497.
115. Klochkov, pp. 217–220.
116. *IPS*, III, 667.
117. See, e.g., German, pp. 146–193.

of the Senate's decisions must have been arbitrary and inapplicable. At best, they could only have resolved separate problems; at worst, they perpetrated injustices and tangled the administration. In short, senatorial government was a botch. The increasing case load was only a visible sign that a horde of parasitical clerks was gradually strangling both government and society.

From a historical perspective, this view of the Senate's development has no validity. It is true that local authorities often feared to take responsibility on themselves and were therefore inclined to shuffle a mass of petty affairs onto the central offices,[118] but the growing volume of petitions and decrees that went through the Senate reflects more than this. If the Senate's increasing work load meant no more than confusion and irresponsibility, then it should have reached its highest point in the period 1720–1740, when the central government was in chaos and the local officials had more reason than usual to be afraid. But this was precisely the time when the flow of cases to the center virtually stopped. Actually, the Russian tribute collector's traditional response to confusion and arbitrariness among his superiors has always been to put them off with false reports and bribes or simply to run away (see above, n. 101, and ch. I, sec. B), not to speed up the flow of information to them. It may be surmised, therefore, that when local officials began transferring ever more cases to the central offices, it meant that for the first time there was something resembling systematic communication between government and countryside. The Senate's confusion in the late eighteenth century proceeded primarily from the opening of new avenues of communication between government and society. As the eighteenth century wore on, systematic administration was actually beginning to impinge on the rigid chaos of Russian provincial organization, and it was becoming somewhat less practicable and even less desirable for the countryside to shrug off the central government's demands regarding procedure.

It would be foolish to suggest that the increasing volume of decrees and petitions reflected the growing satisfaction of people and government with one another. The state, after all, was still engaged in exacting tribute from its people against their will and dragging large numbers of them off to fight wars that were meaningless to them. Nevertheless, it is certainly no exaggeration to suggest that the eighteenth century witnessed an increase in the intensity of the relationship between central and local organs within the government administra-

118. See, e.g., Duran, pp. 486–488; Hassell, "Vicissitudes," pp. 88–89.

tion and in the ties between government and people. The Senate's growing case load reflected a growing awareness of mutual dependence in government and society alike that transcended the chain of personal relationships left over from the old tribute-collecting hierarchy. In short, senatorial government took some long steps toward making the Russian state recognizable to its people as a structure of concrete institutions and conscious purposes that was more than the persons who made it up.

V. I. Semevskii, whose general view of the tsarist government was one of strong disapproval, has described numerous instances that reflect a growing relationship between government and peasantry under the auspices of senatorial institutions during Catherine II's reign. We have already referred to one of these, the redistribution of peasant lands in northern Russia. Actually, Senate orders for and against land redistribution among state peasants (and peasant petitions for and against these orders) extended far beyond the northern gubernias, indicating that the state peasants, for whatever reason, were turning to governmental institutions for legal decisions (see above, ch. II, n. 108). The crown (*dvortsovye*) peasants, who numbered about 6 percent of the total peasant population in the 1760s, received even closer attention. Catherine's administration concerned itself not only with land distribution among them but also with grain reserves, migration from land-poor to land-abundant areas, famine relief, and, in a few cases, agricultural methods.[119] Other varieties of state peasant did not receive such close attention, but they all became involved with the central government to some extent. Even those who showed no interest in land redistribution indicated some sense of involvement by their apparent willingness to accept the government's census records as a basis for their rights to their lands, although the government had not intended the census for this purpose.[120] Finally, it is worth noting that Senate decisions played a significant role in the management of the factory peasants. True, these decisions were less than effective,[121] but the point here is not the effectiveness of sena-

---

119. Semevskii, *Krestiane*, II, 81–120. A recent Soviet work—E. I. Indova, *Dvortsovoe khoziaistvo v Rossii* (Moscow, 1964)—gives more emphasis than Semevskii did to the inadequacies of administration in the crown lands, probably rightly. Indova, however, does not concern herself with anything as un-Marxist as the communication between government and people that administrative activity reflects.

120. Semevskii, *Krestiane*, II, 651–676.

121. *Ibid.*, pp. 553–554. See also R. Zelnik, "The Peasant and the Factory," in Wayne Vucinich, ed., *The Peasant in Nineteenth-Century Russia* (Stanford, Calif., 1968), pp. 160–176.

torial institutions but their influence. One may imagine the peasants looking to local colleges only out of desperation, and one may find abundant evidence to show that the local colleges did not satisfy peasant needs or relieve them from arbitrary despotism. The fact remains that the senatorial institutions, and their pretense at system, exerted far more influence in peasant society than any Russian government ever had before.[122]

But the main contribution of senatorial government came from the influence it exerted on the government-society of gentry servitors. As noted earlier, a century's experience with senatorial institutions fostered the emergence in Russian gentry culture of an aspiration to impose legal-administrative system on Russia. Obviously, administrative evolution was not the only factor in this development, but by 1801 the Senate had become its institutional expression. In the words of the official history of the Senate, it came to embody "the idea of the extreme need to establish a systematic organization."[123]

The nature of the Senate's contribution to gentry culture may be seen most clearly in its relation to some developments in Russian historical consciousness in the late eighteenth century. According to Hans Rogger's excellent account, at this time a number of Russian intellectuals began seeking roots in Russian history for their vague aspirations toward progress, hoping to visualize progress in Russian terms. In the eighteenth century they had not yet found a concrete "old Russia" in whose institutions they could perceive a basis for what they were aspiring to do. Some, like Mikhail Lomonosov and Ivan Boltin, manifested a single-minded determination to find Russia's past glorious and to affirm that the glory of her eighteenth-century expansion and development was a product of native institutions, but they could offer little more than crude, unsupported assertions and vague affirmations of faith.[124] They were unable to identify anything in Russia's past that could pass for a legal system or an aspiration to it. Boltin's works of the 1790s show him to have been the most advanced of all the historians of Russia up to his time in his perception

122. Government measures to cope with famines began to purport to be systematic in the 1730s, specifically, during and after the major famine of 1734–1735. The government not only undertook to provide relief to rural areas but also, in 1736, ordered the voevodas to begin sending in annual reports of the harvests in their territories. See Gote, I, 355–356. Later on, Paul expanded the scale of the government's activity on the peasants' behalf by distributing land to state peasants and by responding more energetically to petitions from serfs who charged their owners with cruelty. See Klochkov, pp. 515–519, 525–531.

123. *IPS*, I, 51. See also *ibid.*, p. 337; Korkunov, *Ukaz*, pp. 310–315.

124. Hans Rogger, *National Consciousness in Eighteenth-Century Russia* (Cambridge, Mass., 1960), pp. 209, 214–218.

of social evolution. Yet although he claimed that "there was . . . a unity of custom, a permanence of law and belief which could be followed through all of Russian history up to the time of Peter," he was unable to identify any institution or principle that embodied or expressed this unity in terms meaningful to his own day.[125] In the 1790s, says Rogger, "the bricks for the construction of a romanticized view of the past were at hand . . . [but] the cement of a comprehensive philosophy was lacking to bind them."[126]

A decade later, in the 1800s, the picture had changed. In the debate on the Senate's role in government, virtually all the participants recognized the Senate and its colleges (and/or its departments) as native institutions. No one upheld or attacked senatorial government on the ground of its correspondence or lack of correspondence to German theory. On the contrary, all sides of the debate assumed that collegial administration *and its aspiration to legal system* were Russia's own "old order," to use Karamzin's term.[127] Depending on the point of view being expressed, the Senate was either to be safeguarded against Alexander I's seemingly reckless innovations[128] or scrapped because it was failing to develop the legal-administrative system that Russia should have had.[129] In either case senatorial institutions were taken to be equivalent to Russian tradition, and so, therefore, was their implicit aspiration to reorganize Russian government and society around a legal-administrative system. The Senate was upheld by the "conservatives" in the name of its aspiration, and those who opposed the Senate found it not only advantageous but also morally satisfying to argue on the same basis: i.e., to accept the "conservative" assumption that the senatorial aspiration to impose system on Russia was indeed Russian.[130]

125. *Ibid.*, pp. 186–252. The quotation (p. 235) is from Rogger's interpretation of Boltin.

126. *Ibid.*, p. 245.

127. Richard Pipes, ed., *Karamzin's Memoir on Ancient and Modern Russia* (Cambridge, Mass., 1959), p. 155.

128. *Ibid.*, pp. 147–156; Troshchinskii, pp. 86–101.

129. *Ministerstvo iustitsii*, p. 5.

130. Speranskii was especially apt at arguing in this fashion. In a note of 1802 (pp. 17–55) he favored the reform of Russian law around Western forms (pp. 24–28) but maintained that these forms could only be introduced on the basis of the existing Russian legal order (pp. 22–23). Actually, he did not believe that any coherent Russian legal order existed. He even acknowledged that since there was no Russian legal system in being, the would-be reformers would have to begin their work by hypothesizing one (pp. 20–22). In view of this gloomy attitude, it is difficult to say why he was so insistent that legal system should be a development out of Russian tradition. Perhaps he was simply trying to please an audience of xenophobic statesmen. Perhaps—indeed, probably—he really believed that his proposals would lead to the discovery of a latent law

Because it could pass for a tradition, senatorial government could be attacked from within the framework of Russian society rather than from without. Change could be moral and lawful as well as necessary. In 1801 "old Russia" was no longer merely a collection of quaint local customs that could only be upheld separately, each for its own sake, as it had been in Peter's time and before. Russians had learned to uphold their institutions in the name of principles; therefore, Russians could now oppose their institutions on the basis of these same principles without having to play the role of traitor or antichrist. Senatorial government had failed to serve the army's needs and it had failed to bring order to the laws, but in 1801 its failure was not greeted with relief by a hierarchy of despots as it had been in the late 1720s. Instead, it was apprehended with indignation by an elite who believed that the Senate's aspiration was both righteous and Russian.[131]

The Senate's metamorphosis into a native Russian institution is comparable to a phenomenon in the evolution of European civilization that Henry Maine has called a "legal fiction." The legal fiction, according to Maine, is a sine qua non for the introduction of "equity" into a society. By equity he means substantially the same thing I mean by legal-administrative system, except that equity refers to a quality of legal system rather than to the system itself. Equity, says Maine, exists in a legal order and characterizes it when a body of

---

(*pravo*) in the Russian consciousness. In any case, the point is that he did argue from the assumption that the aspiration to legal system in Russia was traditional and not merely necessary.

It might be suggested that Speranskii had only to read Montesquieu and other European jurists in order to come across this assumption and that he could have written his note even if there never had been any senatorial institutions. This, however, is doubtful. His appeals to Russian tradition would have made no sense if he had not been aware that "conservative" Russian statesmen were seriously pretending that "native" senatorial institutions embodied an aspiration to legal system. This, not Montesquieu, was what allowed Speranskii to proclaim openly that his proposed reforms were justified by Russian traditional values.

131. The contrast between Russian and Chinese evolution in the nineteenth and twentieth centuries offers some indication of the significance of Russia's eighteenth-century development. J. R. Levenson, "History and Value: The Tensions of Intellectual Choice in Modern China," in A. F. Wright, ed., *Studies in Chinese Thought* (Chicago, 1953), pp. 146–194, describes the impact of system on China in the nineteenth and twentieth centuries. Apparently, China experienced the same kind of external influences as Russia did in the early nineteenth century. Unlike Russia, however, she had no institution that could give system or even the aspiration to system a measure of traditional sanctity. Unlike the Russian statesmen, the Chinese were never able to discuss how they should *reform* a traditional institution in order to make it properly systematic. They could only argue and choose between a systematization that constituted an invasion of tradition and a tradition self-consciously hostile to systematization.

general principles is considered to possess higher authority than the separate rules of law.[132]

Maine noted that the evolution of equity in any society is a complex affair. In its early stages a society governs itself by rules of law in such a way that no one law can be set above another by any intrinsic quality of its own. The idea that principles of law should be the basis from which the rules are derived emerges relatively late in a society's evolution, and it comes only to a few of the more enlightened minds. These new concepts can have no basis in tradition, and even if they are enacted as rules of law, there is no obvious basis for persuading the people not only to accept them but also to subordinate all their existing traditional rules to them. Indeed, society will very likely be hostile to the imposition of equity (system). Therefore, Maine says, if the process of imposition is to be anything but one of disruption and enslavement, the people must somehow be persuaded that the new principles are more ancient and more holy than their traditional rules. Moreover, they must be convinced that their customs evolved from the principles during the course of a historical evolution. In short, the imposition of equity must begin with a historical myth, i.e., a legal fiction.[133]

Maine cites two historical developments in which a legal fiction served as the basis for introducing equity into traditional legal orders: "common" law in medieval England and "natural" law in Rome in the first century B.C.[134]

Henry Bracton, a jurist of the thirteenth century, began the process of introducing equity into English law. His major contribution, according to Maine, was to insert elements of Roman law, along with its implications of equity, into the practice of the royal courts. He did not announce that he was introducing Roman law. Instead, he wrote portions of it into the king's enactments so that they would seem to come directly from the royal authority, despite the king's express prohibition against both the use of Roman law and its teaching.[135] Bracton resorted to this gentle fraud because English society would not accept anything so alien as Roman law but would accept the king's will. As a result of his work and of similar contributions from a long series of myth-makers, the law that obtained in the royal courts of England ultimately evolved into a legal system that was assumed to have developed from native traditions.

132. Maine, p. 28.
133. *Ibid.*, pp. 24–27.
134. *Ibid.*, pp. 70–72.
135. *Ibid.*, p. 82.

Rome was Maine's other example. In the time of Cicero the *form*
of Roman government was still essentially a jumble of allied and sub-
jugated tribes that had blundered more or less by accident into the
conquest of a rather large area inhabited by alien peoples.[136] In order
to administer their new subjects and control their own armies, the
Romans needed to establish some coherence in their native political
order. Only the need was apparent, however. Formal laws and procedures suitable for imperial government were entirely lacking.
Nothing in the hierarchy of families that passed for native Roman
government suggested a basis for a centralized political organization.
In particular, there were no principles of law, nor was there any
traditional basis for deriving laws from principles, nor was there even
a coherent set of operational rules. The only element in Roman government that augured well for the introduction of a uniform administrative system was its long experience with alien tribes. From
Rome's earliest days its law had always had to include some provision
for "foreigners" who were in some way part of Rome but not full-
fledged members of Roman society.[137]

Before the first century B.C. this experience with foreigners had not
yet been embodied in native government. The closest thing to a legal
order beyond the hierarchies in each tribe and family was the law of
the praetors (*ius gentium*), a disorderly and poorly recorded assort-
ment of rules and judicial decisions that had long been used to govern
non-Roman subjects in central and southern Italy. These rules had not
all been preserved, and even those that existed in writing were not
recorded in any order that would have made them usable as a single
source of law. They were only a series of decisions that had been made
by separate authorities in separate territories to meet the needs of
separate occasions. They embodied no coherent principles. Moreover,
they were regarded as a means for governing inferior peoples and
were no more acceptable to Romans as a basis for their own law than
the regulations of a penitentiary would be to a modern American
town. The only quality the praetors' law had to recommend it was its
old age.[138]

Some Roman legal experts (jurisconsults) sensed the urgent need
for a unifying moral concept that could be associated with all Rome,
from which legal rules could be deduced that would be superior to

---

136. The oligarchic nature of Roman government in "republican" times is
described in Ronald Tyme, *The Roman Revolution* (London, 1960), pp. 10–12,
18.
137. Maine, pp. 46–48.
138. *Ibid.*, pp. 48–52, 62–63.

tribal privileges. Before and during Cicero's time a few of these experts found a means to satisfy this need by drawing upon Greek philosophy, in particular, the Stoic notion of natural law. According to the Stoics, natural law was a set of divine principles from which all rules of law in all societies should be derived. Conversely, all existing rules of law that were inconsistent with these principles should be renounced. Armed with this Greek faith, the jurisconsults undertook to transform Roman law.

Instead of wasting their time trying to persuade the tribal leaders (senators) of Rome that they should subordinate themselves and their customary notions of divinity to the principles of Greek philosophy, the jurisconsults simply asserted that the old law of the praetors was itself the natural law and that it embodied principles that were superior to all legal rules. These principles, the lawyers claimed, had already been the foundation of Roman legal order for centuries. The tribes had been a "republic" for a long time, and their customary legal rules had originated in principles of natural law. It followed, of course, that customary rules which conflicted with this alleged natural law were not authentic and would have to be changed.

By their eloquence and by virtue of the fact that most of the Roman elite were aware of the need for a new law, these legal experts were gradually able to persuade their fellow "citizens" that their traditional law was indeed systematic and that they should subordinate themselves to the principles of natural law. It was Augustus who completed this "republicization." He used the jurisconsults' ploy to its fullest by employing a bevy of intellectuals to elaborate a full-fledged republican myth not only in law but in history and poetry as well.[139]

England and Rome are by no means the only places where legal fictions were instrumental in bringing progress toward legal system. Equity (system) was slipped into European society through a long series of trumped-up traditions.[140] It may be said, therefore, that what the Senate did in Russia during the eighteenth century was quite European.

The Russian Senate was neither traditional nor systematic but only a distortion of a German theory; nevertheless, it represented the ideal of system (equity), and when politically conscious Russians agreed to call it a tradition in the early nineteenth century, it became, in effect,

139. *Ibid.*, pp. 29–68.
140. Walter Ullmann, *The Growth of Papal Government in the Middle Ages* (2nd ed., New York, 1962), pp. 54–64, describes the legal fictions from which medieval papal government and the Holy Roman Empire originated. See also Diamond, pp. 70–125, concerning the elements of legal fiction in the Lex Salica, the Pentateuch, and various old Anglo-Saxon codes.

a successful legal fiction. That the Senate was a myth was precisely what made its contribution so vital to Russia's development. If it failed to establish system, it did establish the *sanctity* of system, which meant, among other things, that society could ultimately find within itself some basis for defending, identifying, and above all making sense of itself in the face of an alien yet irresistible drive to bureaucratize its institutions.

Had Russia enjoyed several centuries of gradual development after 1801 without having constantly to compare herself with modern cultures, fight modern armies, and compete in modern markets, senatorial government might have developed further, much as the older forms of western Europe did, at a pace that would have been tolerable to its institutions. As it happened, the sanctity of system translated itself into an aspiration that would not wait for the gradual adjustment of habits. Senatorial institutions could not keep up with the expectations to which their own sanctity gave rise; thus, in the light of the aspiration around which they organized themselves, they "failed." In the light of Maine's observations, however, they succeeded. If the senatorial institutions had operated strictly according to their own myths, they would not have been corrupted and sanctified by their involvement with Russian society. They might have been flawlessly systematic, but they never would have become a part of Russia. The fact that the Senate pretended for a century to be what it was not is the key to its most basic contribution to Russia's development. As Thurman Arnold has put it, ". . . the escape of the law from reality constitutes not its weakness but its greatest strength. . . . If judicial institutions become too 'sincere,' too self-analytical, they suffer the fate of ineffectiveness which is the lot of self-analytical people. They lose themselves in words and fail in action."[141]

141. Arnold, p. 44.

CHAPTER IV

The Role of Senatorial Government in the Evolution of Bureaucracy

PART TWO: SERFDOM

> It can happen . . . that although the government may begin an action with gentle promises its last words must be grapeshot.
>
> PAVEL A. VALUEV

A. INTRODUCTION: THE NATURE OF SERFDOM

Serfdom evolved out of the same interaction between government and society that produced senatorial government. Serfdom was the social foundation of senatorial government: the major link that tied the capital cities down to the countryside and the central pillar that held the state up on its urban pinnacles, where the ruling elite could indulge themselves in higher aspirations.

What was the nature of the government-peasant relationship that serfdom embodied? It had three primary characteristics: 1) the peasants were forbidden to depart from their place of residence except by express permission from higher authority, 2) their villages were held collectively responsible for keeping order and the payment of all obligations that the government imposed upon them, and 3) legal relationships within the villages were generally neither regulated nor recognized by the central government.

The implicit assumption underlying these characteristics was that the peasantry constituted a natural resource, the proper utilization of which was vitally necessary to the state. This in itself did not distinguish them from anyone else in Russia. The primary juridical and organizational principle underlying the Russian state and all forms of Russian social order from the beginning was that a person acquired status and identity by virtue of the service he rendered.[1] The dis-

1. V. Iakushkin, *Ocherki po istorii russkoi pozemelnoi politike v XVIII i XIX v.,* vol. I (Moscow, 1890), suggests that the legal structure of landholding in Russia developed basically as a centralized organization for utilizing the land, not as a

tinguishing feature of peasant society was that its members rendered their services (or acquired status) not as individuals but as groups. It was the groups that performed services and/or rendered tribute; consequently, it was only groups that achieved social status. The state labeled the peasant groups in various ways: the names of the leaders (owners), the number of members, the land they farmed, the categories of tribute they paid, etc. At any one time the label in force could reflect actual circumstances. Usually, however, it reflected an official labeling act dating from a previous generation that no longer had any practical significance. For example, a typical peasant village of the period 1500–1800 may have been set up on lands adjoining a river bank in order to assure that a dock would be maintained there for government boats. A document may have been drawn up—probably not an accurate one even for the time it was written—to indicate how many male peasants there were, how much land they could farm, what kind of dock they were supposed to build, and what they had to do in order to maintain it. A half-century later the dock might have fallen into disuse and disrepair, the population of the village might have tripled, and the village as a whole might now be under orders from the local authorities to provide a nearby city and military garrison with fish. The records of the central government, however, would not necessarily have changed. Local agents would collect fish according to ad hoc, unwritten agreements with the villagers, while the central government would go on conceiving of the

system of rights. Even Catherine's charter to the gentry in 1785 and the liberation of the serfs in 1861, he says, were in essence schemes for organizing people to exploit natural resources. See especially pp. 79–97. Iakushkin argues that the idea of personal legal rights did not belong in Russia's legal structure, and in support of his argument he notes, p. 201, that Catherine's overemphasis on gentry rights was what rendered serfdom oppressive and rigid.

Ideological expressions of what might be called the primacy of service in Russian law date at least as far back as the early sixteenth century. See A. A. Zimin, *I. S. Peresvetov i ego sovremenniki* (Moscow, 1958), pp. 49–67, 344–424. Ivan Peresvetov, who idealized a political organization based on nothing but loyalty and service to the tsar, did not represent any official point of view (p. 426), but, says Zimin, "he mastered and reworked creatively the best expressions of Russian political thought and also took significant new steps in its development" (p. 288). In a later work—"O politicheskikh predposylkakh vozniknoveniia russkogo absoliutizma," in Druzhinin, *Absoliutizm*, pp. 18–91—Zimin goes on to demonstrate that political organization in Peresvetov's time did in fact take form around the concept of service to the central government and little else. See also the article of S. O. Shmidt, "Mestnichestvo i absoliutizm," in the same volume, pp. 168–205, and the remarks of Sergeevich, pp. 121–140, on the nature of the service hierarchy of the sixteenth and seventeenth centuries. Regarding the overall development of the gentry as servitors up through the eighteenth century, see Romanovich-Slavatinskii, pp. 401–404, and K. I. Zaitsev, *Istoricheskoe mesto ukaza o volnosti dvorianstva* (Harbin, 1938).

village as a dock with the population it had originally possessed.[2] But the inaccuracy of governmental concepts of the peasantry is not the point here. The point is that the peasants were identified by law and government, both formally and in practice, according to group functions and/or obligations. Villages had status, but their members did not. Before the nineteenth century the Russian government recognized the peasant not as a person but only as a unit of value. He might be a part of the tribute a village had to render or a basis for apportioning it. In either case he was not qualitatively different in the government's eyes from an area of land, a silver coin, or a horse.[3]

When Peter I began trying consciously to impose system on his domestic administration, his practical aim was to reorganize the government-society, not the peasantry. He wanted to make those who were supposed to be serving the state as individuals—chiefly boiars, gentry, and chancellery clerks (*kantseliarskie*)—act in cooperation with each other under a single set of laws instead of acting separately, each under his own special charter. The traditional political order that he had to work with was a simple one. The active servitors were involved primarily in the mustering and utilization of masses of peasants. As compensation for their services and also as a means to govern the countryside, many of them were granted (charged with) a number of "serfs" for their personal use. Peter's reform, therefore, had to provide for the apportioning of peasants among government offices and "private" estates, and since systematic political order demanded systematic arrangements, the peasant groups would have to be apportioned systematically. Peter I could not alter this basic necessity; he could only cope with it. This is why his idea of systematization was to give uniform definition to the social status of the higher servitors of the government and to restrict the right to use peasants to them alone.[4]

2. The above account is imaginary, but it depicts an element common to Russian experience in 1500–1800 and even later. An actual example of this type of phenomenon is the evolution of the town of Tikhvin in the 1600s. In the first years of the century warfare with the Swedes reduced it to villages. Vasili Shuiskii handed them over to a local monastery during his short and troubled reign, and his grant was later confirmed by Michael Romanov as a reward to the monks for holding out against a Swedish attack in 1613. During the ensuing century the villages grew into a center of trade and industrial crafts, but as far as the government was concerned, the inhabitants remained peasants of the monastery. It was only in 1701–1703 that Peter authorized them to call themselves a town and released them from the monastery. See Serbina, pp. 61–63, 180–181, 397, 408.

3. Zimin, *Peresvetov*, pp. 182–214, refers to the work of Feodosii Kosoi, a mid-sixteenth-century writer who recognized that the formation of the state was reducing the peasants to a completely depersonalized slavery and concluded that for them, any central authority would always have this effect.

4. It took until 1785 to establish the definition with reasonable clarity. The

By according personal legal status to state servitors in terms that fitted the existing social-political order, Peter's new system unavoidably tended to exclude the peasants more rigorously than ever. This exclusion was not in itself desirable to the tsar. It was, rather, the inadvertent by-product of his attempts to systematize government-society. In the past the state had simply failed to recognize the peasants as individuals. Now that it was trying to become a legal-administrative system, it had to define the peasants in some way, and if it could not identify them personally, the next best thing was to group them into categories. In effect, the new laws gave the peasantry the status of a mass resource.

No law ever said in so many words that the peasants were a mass resource, but just about all eighteenth-century legislation regarding the peasants had to do with ways and means for utilizing them and extracting revenue from them *as groups*.[5] Even the measures taken to protect the peasants and keep order among them were designed primarily to maintain their utility, not to grant them status or rights as individuals.[6] The more the laws said about the peasants, therefore, the closer the government came, willy-nilly, to the formal definition of peasants as a mass resource. Senatorial government not only continued the old tradition of not recognizing the serfs as persons. By the time it came to its maturity in Catherine II's time, it expressly and more or less systematically forbade them to become persons.

There was never a time when all the peasants of Russia were serfs in the strictly legal sense, "bonded" (*krepostnye*) to private owners. In the eighteenth and early nineteenth centuries a great many of them —mostly state (*gosudarstvennye*) peasants—held their lands directly

kantseliarskie (nongentry) servitors in the civil service only lost the formal right to acquire serfs in 1746. See N. F. Demidova, "Biurokratizatsiia gosudarstvennogo apparata absoliutizma v XVII–XVIII vv.," in Druzhinin, *Absoliutizm*, pp. 206–242. Even then they were not deprived of the serfs they had. Despite increasing restrictions, a few nongentry continued to hold serfs legally well into the nineteenth century. See Semevskii, *Krestiane*, I, 3–4; V. Iakushkin, p. 154.

5. From Peter's reign until Paul's, the management of the peasants who were directly under the state's purview was always entrusted to the officials who collected revenue. See *Istoricheskoe obozrenie*, I, pt. 1, 11–17. Semevskii, *Krestiane*, II, 161–193, describes some of the regulations regarding the utilization of the peasants in the eighteenth century before Catherine II's reign. See also Romanovich-Slavatinskii, p. 76; Klyuchevsky, *Peter*, pp. 91–101; Wittram, II, 159–165.

6. Wittram, II, 165–169; Ignatovich, pp. 9–25. Decrees came out from time to time prohibiting excessive cruelty toward serfs (Semevskii, *Krestiane*, I, ix–x, 2–7, 169), and although cruelty was never given precise legal definition, serf owners were punished for it in specific cases. See *ibid.*, pp. 215–221; Klochkov, pp. 524–525; Predtechenskii, p. 178; Ignatovich, pp. 64–65.

from the government without having anything to do with the formal institution of serfdom. It may be argued, therefore, that serfdom was not necessarily the most important element in the relationship between government and peasant. This, however, is to see the matter from a narrow, formalistic point of view. In practice, the relationship of unbonded peasants to government administrators was very similar to that of the serfs to their owners.[7] State peasants often found that officials, rentors, neighboring gentry, or their own village leaders ruled over them as arbitrarily (or as paternalistically) as any owner.[8] As for the serfs, most of them lived on large estates under the direct authority of stewards rather than owners.[9]

A few categories of state peasant enjoyed special legal protection throughout the period of serfdom. Military settlers (*odnodvortsy*) and non-Russian settlers from Europe such as the Mennonites were as firmly guaranteed in the possession of their land as the gentry.[10] The vast majority of the unbonded peasants, however, were de facto serfs of the crown; their persons and their lands were completely at the disposal of the government. Catherine II and Paul used large numbers of them to reward their deserving servitors, handing them out to private owners as if they were so many herds of horses. Catherine gave out a total of about 800,000 male "souls" in this fashion, most of them in western Russia. Paul, the most active peasant distributor in Russia's history, disbursed 600,000 in only five years, right at the time, be it noted, that senatorial government reached the apogee of its development. This kind of distribution practically stopped in European Russia after 1801, but in the period 1804–1836 an additional 368,000 male peasants were handed out to private owners, primarily in the

7. Zaitsev, pp. 15–20.
8. This generalization is borne out in Druzhinin's exhaustive discussion of reports from inspections carried out on the state lands in 1836–1837, in *Gos. krest.*, I, 299–475, especially pp. 346–352, 439–453. A. Leontev, *Krestianskoe pravo* (2nd ed., St. Petersburg, 1914), pp. 84–91, notes that even as late as the beginning of the twentieth century the peasants' service obligations (*naturalyne povinnosti*)—road maintenance, forest-fire fighting, auxiliary police duty—were so vaguely defined in the law that in many cases the local police, who supervised the carrying out of these tasks, could use their official authority to employ the peasants as personal servants (see below, ch. IX, n. 41).
9. In Catherine II's time and throughout the period 1785–1861, approximately 45 percent of the serfs lived on estates of more than 500 male peasants, and 80 percent lived on estates of more than 100. See Semevskii, *Krestiane*, I, 32; Emmons, p. 4; Ignatovich, p. 380.
10. Semevskii, *Krestiane*, II, vii–xxxi, gives a brief survey of the twenty-odd types of state peasants that existed in the late eighteenth century. The categories in effect in 1837 are described briefly in Leontev, *Krest. pravo* (1914), pp. 205–206.

southern and eastern parts of the empire.[11] It was only after this period that statutory law began to recognize any substantial difference between the status of unbonded peasants and that of the serfs.

It is true that state peasants and serfs were aware of differences between their respective legal statuses. Zelnik has pointed out that in some cases in the late eighteenth century involving the transfer of state peasants into private factories, the peasants who were being transferred protested explicitly against the transfer into serfdom; i.e., they consciously sought to legitimize their complaint against an undesirable transfer by claiming that since they were not serfs, they had a right not to be enserfed.[12] These protests, however, seem to have resulted primarily from the forced change of occupation, not from any change of formal category. There is no evidence to suggest that Catherine II's and Paul's massive transfers of state peasants into serfdom without change of occupation awakened any more protest from the peasants involved than did the sale of serfs by one owner to another or the transfer of an owner's serfs from one estate to another.[13]

The practice of dispensing state peasants to private owners to suit the needs of the state is only one illustration, albeit the most extreme one, of the general propensity of the government and of the Russian people in general to use peasants whenever anyone wanted them in any way he wanted to use them. In Peter I's time and after, state peasants were drafted to build cities, ships, and cathedrals and, in general, to perform any task that could be conceived for them. Semevskii tells us that the professors of Moscow University once put in a request for an allotment of peasants,[14] and as late as the 1840s, when Nicholas I was actively working to establish the legal status of the state peasants, his ministries continued to vie with each other for allotments of peasant labor without any regard for peasant rights.[15] It is also worth mentioning in this connection that it was a common—though illegal—practice up to 1861 for unbonded peasants to enserf one another.[16]

In sum, when the legal category of serfdom was finally established in the late eighteenth century, it did not distinguish one group of peasants from another but gave formal expression to a juridical re-

11. Druzhinin, *Gos. krest.*, I, 87–88.
12. Zelnik, pp. 166–173.
13. Concerning serf protests against transfers from one owner to another, see Semevskii, *Krestiane*, I, 429.
14. *Ibid.*, II, 592. An exhaustive description of the various uses of unbonded peasants in the eighteenth century is in *ibid.*, pp. 286–592.
15. Druzhinin, *Gos. krest.*, II, 276.
16. Semevskii, *Krestiane*, II, 774–775.

lationship that was to some degree common to them all.[17] Almost all the peasants were excluded from personal legal status. Almost all of them were at least potential serfs and could be made into actual ones whenever the government wanted to use them. As things stood in the early nineteenth century, the only reason that most of the state peasants had still not been officially designated as serfs was simply that the government had not yet found persons to take charge of them.

From Paul's time on, the unbonded peasants began to acquire a measure of personal legal status that distinguished them from the serfs with ever-increasing clarity. They fell into two general administrative categories: state peasants, which included the vast majority, and crown (*udelnye*) peasants, who were the property of the imperial family. Nicholas I introduced extensive reforms into the administration of both these categories, and by the end of his reign the forms of a legal-administrative system had emerged over the unbonded peasants, purporting to establish institutionalized legal relationships among them and between them and the government.[18]

But even these reforms did not signify that state and crown peasants were becoming distinct from serfs. They reflected, rather, a general development in government-peasant relationships affecting all categories of peasants in a similar way. Just as the emergence of serfdom signified a development in the relationships between the government and the peasantry as a whole, so likewise the development of a would-be bureaucratic administration over the state peasants signaled the end of serfdom for the peasantry as a whole.

B. The Historical Relationship between Peasant and Government in Russia

The exclusion of peasants from personal legal status had its deepest roots in a very old attitude that was already common among those who "governed" the area of European Russia long before Peter's time. It prevailed throughout the time of what McNeill has called "nomad empires," i.e., large-scale political orders that emerged and dis-

17. Concerning the general helplessness of the peasants before government officials, see Druzhinin, *Gos. krest.*, I, 65–69.

18. Walter M. Pintner, *Russian Economic Policy under Nicholas I* (Ithaca, N.Y., 1967), pp. 73–75, describes L. A. Perovskii's reform of the *udelyne* peasants, beginning in 1826. This was primarily a land reform, having nothing to do directly with legal status. The reform of the state peasants, carried out by Pavel D. Kiselev in 1838–1856, was more explicitly concerned with legal status. In 1850 it produced a four-volume code that gave the state peasants at least the form of civil rights. See Druzhinin, *Gos. krest.*, II, 76.

appeared in and around the east European steppe under a variety of kagans, princes, and khans from about the 700s B.C. until 1500 A.D.[19] The characteristic form of "government" in these empires was essentially a protection racket, to use a modern term, in which a gang (horde, druzhina) of warriors transcended the simple quest for booty and reorganized themselves as "protectors" to extort tribute and/or slaves from their "subjects" on a more or less regular basis. Not unreasonably, these warrior-protector gangs were inclined to regard themselves as a social order that did not include agriculturalists, shepherds, or anyone else who worked for a living. We may say, therefore, that by 1500 A.D. people who lived in and around the steppe had grown accustomed to a profound social separation between warrior-protectors on the one hand and "protected" tribute payers on the other.[20]

Originally, the separation between the gang and its subjects was not something that anyone strove to maintain. Any number of subjects might join the gang or be forced into it, and any number of warriors might drop out of the gang to take over or be enslaved by an agricultural tribe or village. The separation maintained itself as a difference between the way of life of the nomad warrior and that of the settled or semi-nomadic agriculturalist, a natural separation of attitudes that persisted no matter how many individuals switched from one society to the other.[21]

The members of each group had characteristic attitudes toward one another, stemming primarily from their functional relationship. Subject tribes and villages were likely to remain as aloof from the gang warriors as they could in order to conceal their possessions and maintain their social cohesion. Ordinarily, they did not inquire into the political and military struggles in which the gang was involved and in which their political fate was being decided. The warriors, on their part, were inclined to regard their "subjects" as an anonymous mass

19. McNeill, pp. 6–8.
20. By far the best descriptive account of this "separation" that I have seen is in Imre Boba, *Nomads, Northmen and Slavs* (The Hague, 1967), pp. 39–55, where he deals with the Avar and Khazar "empires."
21. The ease with which individuals could enter or leave a nomadic horde is demonstrated by the radical changes that occurred in the language these hordes used as they moved. See, e.g., the description of the Hun "invasion" in M. I. Artamanov, *Istoriia Khazar* (Leningrad, 1962), pp. 41–68, and that of the early Rus in Boba, pp. 107–108, 118–122. If departure from one order into the other was easy, it was also likely to be abrupt and complete. Ordinarily, a man did not live in two societies at once. S. M. Solovev, I, 223–226, says that when a member of one of the tribes in Kiev Rus joined a prince's gang (*druzhina*), he retained his position in the tribe but lost the right to pass it on to his heirs.

whose only role was to continue to live and work in their own way in order to provide the gang with material resources and, when necessary, manpower. The primary concern that the warriors felt for their human resource was to collect from it, to prevent it from running away, and to keep it from falling into any disorder or catastrophe that might diminish its contribution. They did not ordinarily inquire into *how* tribute was produced or slaves selected. An individual warrior might act now and then on his own to disrupt a village, in order to satisfy a whim or respond to a bribe, but he would not ordinarily tamper with its social structure and working methods. To the extent that he did, he became involved in the society and gave up his role of gang warrior.

When relatively stable political orders emerged in and around the steppe, the ancient, more or less spontaneous separation between warrior and agriculturalist developed from a mere expression of attitudes into forms and customs upon which people depended. The basic element in these forms, whenever and wherever they emerged, was collective responsibility, an arrangement in which each group of protected inhabitants was held jointly responsible by a tribute collector (protector) for a certain quota of tribute and/or men and for the misdeeds of its individual members. Usually, the group was forced to "elect" a leader "unanimously" from among its members. Once elected, this leader would be held personally responsible for all his electors, and the group in turn would be held collectively responsible for what he did or did not do. This arrangement became a matter of historical record in Russia as early as the 1200s A.D., when the Tatar horde introduced it into the grand princedom of Vladimir.[22] From then on, collective responsibility continued to be a basic element in Russian political organization. Most of the peasants remained under its regime until 1903.[23]

Collective responsibility served a number of practical purposes in

22. See above, ch. I, n. 24. There is almost no evidence directly relating to pre-Tatar relationships in Kiev Rus between the princes' collectors and their subjects, but it seems reasonable to conjecture that they employed similar procedures. The *Russkaia pravda* (1000s A.D.) identifies a group (the *verv*) that had to answer for its members' crimes, and Sergeevich, pp. 257–260, concludes that this was a territorial-administrative unit. Concerning local administration prior to the fifteenth century in general, see Sergeevich, pp. 249–266, 294–310, and R. E. F. Smith, *The Origins of Farming in Russia* (Paris, 1959), pp. 170–171.

23. Sergeevich, pp. 309–319, and Nosov, *Ocherki*, pp. 230–246, describe the formal establishment of collective responsibility in Russian government in the fifteenth and sixteenth centuries. On its vital role in tax collection in the sixteenth and seventeenth centuries, see S. B. Veselovskii, I, 30–35. On its general development in the seventeenth and eighteenth centuries, see Grigorev, pp. 20–26.

the tribute-collecting hierarchy that took form under the tsars of Russia in the fifteenth and sixteenth centuries. A tribute collector found it advantageous because it allowed him a crude but effective control over the tribute-paying villages and tribes while keeping his involvement in their society to a minimum. He could not keep as separate from the villages as his predecessors, the old warrior-protectors, had, because he was now answerable to his superiors on a relatively regular basis. He had to concern himself to some extent with *how* his tribute was produced. On the other hand, he continued to retain as much of the old separation from tribute-paying society as he could because, like any "superior" at any level of a tribute-collecting hierarchy, he could not operate unless he had the awe of his "subordinates" (see above, ch. I, sec. B). The tsar also was anxious to keep his collectors aloof from tribute-paying society because he, like the khans of earlier times, still had to fear that his warrior-servitors would cease to depend on his authority if they became too deeply engrossed in practical economic arrangements in their territories.[24]

Collective responsibility also became a basic element in the village (tribal) social order. The basic attitude that collective responsibility inculcated in each "peasant" was a constant fear that one or more of his fellows might leave, or fall sick, or for some other reason fail to render their share of the tribute obligation, thus increasing the burden he himself would have to bear. Unless common desperation drove all members of a village or tribe to depart (or revolt) together, they were anxious to prevent any action by any of their number that might bring punishment down on them all. Each villager, therefore, was likely to feel the need for an authority that could keep his fellows in line. When he felt this need, he found himself deeply dependent on the authority of the collector, and his sense of dependence was likely to make him genuinely anxious that his fellow villagers regard the collector with awe. Under a stable tribute-collecting hierarchy the villagers needed or wanted not kindness and "justice" for their

24. S. B. Veselovskii, I, 348–349. The concern of the tsars to keep their territorial "governors" separate from the populations over which they ruled did not cease to be an important element in Russian government until the mid-eighteenth century. G. Fletcher, *Of the Rus Commonwealth*, ed. A. Schmidt (Ithaca, N.Y., 1966), pp. 31–33, 46–47, tells us that as of the 1580s, the territorial authorities held their appointments for only one year. "They are men of themselves of no credit nor favor with the people where they govern, being neither born nor brought up among them, nor yet having inheritance of their own there or elsewhere" (p. 46). For a description of the similar policy that obtained in the seventeenth century, see Chicherin, pp. 71–74, 83–88, 298, and Grigorev, pp. 24–25; for the early eighteenth, see Gote, I, 33–35.

community but an authority strong enough to keep their neighbors from defaulting or departing.[25]

As the villagers came to depend consciously on the collector's authority, they came to depend more or less inadvertently on the separateness of the collector's society from their own. If village society needed a "chief" who possessed unchallengeable authority and would remain above the rivalries within it, then it also needed to keep its own members from becoming involved in relationships over which the chief had no control and through which his authority could be challenged. The reason for this need was that it was to an *individual* villager's advantage to seek the protection of some outside authority. For example, he might wish to depart for another estate whose "owner" or administrator had the wherewithal to give him lands and to protect him against his original chief. Or, if he got into a dispute with one of his fellows and had it decided to his disadvantage by the collector-authority, it was in his interest to find yet another man with authority who could overturn the decision of his village's collector. *Individual* peasants, then, often had reason to make contact with the government-society of tribute collectors and to find ways to manipulate its relationships. If and when they did, however, they threatened the political order within their own village and, indeed, the very existence of their society. It may be said, then, that in a regime of collective responsibility, the villagers' concern for getting everyone to pay his share produced a tendency among them to distrust those of their fellows who made contacts with men of power outside the village and to condemn any of their number who did anything to challenge the authority of their own collector.[26]

25. The authority could be either "elected" unanimously or appointed. In either case he was responsible to administrative superiors, not to the villages. See Grigorev, pp. 22–27.

26. S. B. Veselovskii, I, 261–314, 342–397. Hellie, pp. 200–259, 373–380, points out that there was a tendency in the towns and villages in the late sixteenth and early seventeenth centuries to request the central government to "bind" their members to them and outlaw their departure. Apparently the townsmen and villagers needed this in order to protect themselves from the shirking of their fellows and also from outside interference.

In Catherine's Commission some representatives from the Moslem peoples of Kazan gubernia presented complaints regarding the government's policy of granting tax relief to all Moslems who converted to Christianity. It seems that the amounts the new converts did not pay were shifted onto the shoulders of the faithful. See Sinton, pp. 176–177. Similarly, some merchants from Kazan voiced their dissatisfaction at the marriage of one of them into an aristocratic family. He became an aristocrat and thereby ceased to pay merchant taxes on his wealth, which meant that the other merchants had to increase their payments (*ibid.*, pp. 132–133). In these cases it was not absolute authority that disturbed the petitioners but the suffering imposed upon groups of taxpayers when individual

In sum, the separation of villages from rulers became a positive value in itself for villagers and rulers alike. The exclusion of tribute payers from the society of tribute collectors did not merely perpetuate itself as a social fact but gradually developed into an institution, a pillar of both territorial political order and village social order. What had once been a "natural" inclination to minimize an agricultural society's contacts with nomadic warrior bands changed under the new circumstances of regular contact into a continuing need—an institutional arrangement upon which all those involved consciously depended. Collective responsibility had the ultimate effect of allowing the village (tribe) to preserve the innocence of its isolation and to render its isolated social order dependent on this innocence. In Muscovite times and probably much earlier, both local village elders and territorial princes strove more or less consciously to maintain the separation between their respective social-political orders because they wanted to keep their respective societies intact. We have already seen (above, ch. II, sec. A) how Peter's recruiting system tended to intensify this striving.

From the fifteenth century on, the servitors of the grand prince of Moscow slowly improved their organization and expanded their political awareness. Not so, the peasants. Thanks to their reliance on the personal authority of collector-extorters, they continued to conceive of "government" as a nameless, formless conglomeration of powerful spirits (separate power loci). If, as sometimes happened, an individual villager formed relationships with one or more tribute collectors apart from the one who ruled his own village, his irate fellow villagers had to take over his share of the tribute, and he found himself separated from them. Thus individual peasants might find their way into a social order beyond the village, but when they did, they left. Peasant society as a whole retained its pristine indifference toward any social structures beyond the bounds of the separate villages. Village society continued to depend on *persons* for protection, not the government these persons ostensibly served or the laws they ostensibly obeyed.

Throughout the seventeenth, eighteenth, and nineteenth centuries the peasant villages persistently refused to tie their social orders to the state or to any larger social framework by any relationship other than the acceptance of absolute personal authority. The state peasant dele-

---

members succeeded in evading their responsibilities. It is striking in this regard that peasant complaints from Kazan against recruiting referred not to the harshness of military service but to the obligation of the villagers to go on paying the taxes for those who were recruited (*ibid.*, pp. 154–155).

gates to Catherine's Commission in 1767–1768 had nothing whatever to say about how the government should be run or what their role in it should be. All they asked in effect was to be protected from the power of local officials,[27] and the practical implication of this demand, though they may not have been aware of it, was that they wanted a patron empowered to keep government officials away—a single, all-powerful collector. It may be said, then, that as the government underwent systematization, mutual exclusion between servitor and peasant society not only did not break down but actually tended to become sharper. At the same time the peasants' dependence on the authority of an all-powerful collector did not diminish. Under these circumstances it made good practical sense to render the single all-powerful collector into an institution, i.e., the serf owner.[28] This is the primary reason that the systematization of Russia was accompanied by the institutionalization of serfdom.

As the separation between servitors and peasants became conscious, individual peasants did not necessarily become less free to move out of their villages into the status of servitor. On the contrary, as the government service rapidly expanded from the sixteenth century on, it probably became all the easier for individuals to rise to higher social position. The social orders themselves, however, became less comprehensible to each other than ever. As the society of the servitors developed, the mass of the peasants only kept on following their old ways.

The historical development of territorial political order in and around the steppe was, of course, much more complex than the preceding paragraphs have indicated. Doubtless, the religious conversion of the major political leaders in the area to Islam and Christianity played a fundamental role. There were also the evolution of technology, the rise and fall of trade routes, the long-continuing sparsity of population, and, more important than any of these factors by themselves, the way they related to one another at particular times and places. But the purpose of this discussion is not to show how political order evolved in Russia. The point is that the old pre-Christian and pre-Islam attitudes of steppe and near-steppe society,

27. Gote, II, 204; Grigorev, pp. 121–123.
28. See Chicherin, pp. 515–526, and above, ch. III, sec. D, for a description of peasant attitudes toward external authority in the seventeenth century. Zaitsev, pp. 15–18, gives an account of eighteenth-century legislation that reflects the government's intention to make the serf owners into all-powerful, all-responsible collectors. He notes, for example, that serf owners had to feed their serfs in times of famine, to answer for civil damages caused by their serfs, and to make good their serfs' tax arrears. A more detailed account of the serf owners' responsibilities is in Ignatovich, pp. 9–29.

especially the natural separation between nomadic warriors and sedentary agriculturalists, persisted into the political and social orders that emerged later and continued to exert their influence long after the nomads themselves disappeared.

Following the collapse of the western Roman Empire, western Europe lived through several centuries under a political order that in some respects resembled the one described above. In Europe, however, the separation between peasants and other classes achieved formal legal definition at a much earlier date. When the Tatars were sweeping through Russia, dragging thousands of men out of their tribes and pressing them into their fighting bands, it had long since become virtually impossible for a peasant of western Europe to become a member of the warrior class, even if he knew how to fight. The warrior class had already progressed so far toward transferring its identity from practical function to legally defined status that the "warriors" were beginning to develop interests, occupations, and even values that were quite unconnected with war.

The institutionalization of status barriers in the West made them more rigid in the eyes of particular individuals at particular times, but it allowed the barriers themselves to develop into increasingly abstract forms, subject to debate, negotiation, analysis, measurement, and justification. They became, therefore, measurable, changeable in form, and above all purchasable. In the West an individual peasant was not likely to sneak into the aristocracy or be dragooned into it, but he could recognize aristocratic status as an entity in itself. He could define his relationship to aristocracy as a whole rather than to this or that aristocrat.

Eventually, by the end of the eighteenth century, the "people" of Europe could be taught to claim aristocratic "liberties" en masse. Why? Because these liberties had been defined within the framework of a legal-administrative system. Men had learned to organize themselves around definitions; that is, they had come to attribute more importance to myths of abstract legal categories than to practical functions. In Russia, on the other hand, abstract legal forms did not begin to insert themselves into society until the eighteenth century, and although peasant exclusion did not prevent individual peasants from going their own way, the practical gap between warrior and peasant social orders remained much wider for a much longer time than it did in the West.

Why did peasant exclusion last longer in Russia? The question is much too involved to be answered here, but it is worth mentioning that scholars have generally distorted the matter by asking why

Russia followed a different and peculiar path instead of "normal" European patterns. Actually, Russian development before the eighteenth century was relatively straightforward and simple. Warriors served the tsar; peasants cultivated the soil. When a warrior required the services of peasants, he dragged them off and set them to work; when a peasant needed the services of a warrior, he bribed one. However undesirable this crude and unprogressive way of life may have been, it was not peculiar or outlandish. It is Europe's development that is difficult to account for. It is not especially useful to ask why peasant exclusion should have lasted longer in Russia. A better question is: why should a more or less natural tendency like peasant exclusion have broken down in western Europe? How was it that Europeans acquired the highly unnatural aspiration to twist their social relationships into rational patterns that could be manipulated in the name of abstract purposes?[29]

C. The Contribution of Serfdom

Serfdom not only furnished the social underpinning of senatorial government but also played a role of its own in the systematization of Russia. Two contributions are especially important: 1) it constituted an arrangement by which senatorial government could extend elements of legal system into the countryside, and 2) in some areas it provided a reasonably effective basis for establishing order in newly settled lands.

Since legal system demands that personal status be defined and protected according to general principles of law, Catherine's charter to the gentry (1785), which formally recognized the serfs as their private property, was essentially progressive. The intention behind it was to create a citizenry who would serve the state voluntarily, motivated by the conviction that by so doing they were upholding their own rights.[30] Peter III had freed the gentry from compulsory service

29. Much of the answer lies in the differences between Roman Catholicism and Eastern Orthodoxy. These are portrayed from a blatantly but revealingly Orthodox point of view in E. Benz, *The Eastern Orthodox Church* (New York, 1963), pp. 43–53, 94–98, 208. E. Kantorowicz, *The King's Two Bodies* (Princeton, N.J., 1957), pp. 42–97, 189–235, 273–286, describes the Roman church's long struggle to conceptualize itself and its relation to society in abstract terms, while V. V. Zenkovsky, *A History of Russian Philosophy* (2 vols., London, 1953), I, 1–50, points out the Russian church's lack of interest in conceptual form and its emphasis on mystic experience and undefined power as opposed to rational abstract purposes.

30. See Leontovitsch, pp. 24–29, and Zaitsev, pp. 3–4, concerning the "liberalism" of the charter.

in 1762, and the law of 1775 had made them the leading element in local government. By 1785, therefore, it seemed vitally important to complete the process of making them into citizens by establishing their rights in law.

These rights were basically devices for administrative reform, not personal attributes. They expressed the conviction of Catherine and her leading statesmen that Russian government would work better if its servitors were property-holding citizens rather than helpless and inflexible puppets who had no status except that which their personal association with their superiors gave them.[31] The presumption was that the new citizen gentry would identify themselves not by Western notions of individual self-interest but by their inclination to regard state service as equivalent to both moral duty and social status.

> We hope [said Peter III's manifesto of 1762] that the whole noble Russian dvorianstvo [gentry], appreciative of our generosity to them and their descendants, will be inspired by their most dutiful loyalty to Us . . . not to absent or hide themselves from service, but to enter it with pride and enthusiasm, and continue it in an honourable and decent manner to the extent of their ability. . . . Those who have not been in service anywhere, but spend all their time in sloth and idleness, and do not subject their children to any useful education for the benefit of the fatherland, these We, as they are negligent of the common good, command all Our obedient and true sons to despise and scorn, and they will not be allowed to appear at Our Court, or at public meetings and celebrations.[32]

> . . . at every time [said Catherine's charter of 1785] . . . when the service of the dvorianstvo is necessary . . . to the general good, then each noble dvorianin is bound at the first summons from the autocratic authority to spare neither labor nor life itself for the service of the state.[33]

But if Catherine wanted to extend legal system into the country-side, what kept her from guaranteeing personal rights to all the people? Why did she explicitly deny them to the serfs? After all, she disapproved of the serf owners' arbitrary authority. In a memorandum on the subject to A. A. Viazemskii, she once went so far as to say, "If we do not agree to some moderation in a situation that is intolerable to human beings, then sooner or later they [the serfs] will take their own measures against our will."[34] In the course of her reign she made

31. See Korf, pp. 114–135; Zaitsev, pp. 15–27.
32. Quoted in Dukes, p. 43.
33. Quoted in *ibid.*, p. 227.
34. Quoted in N. M. Druzhinin, "Prosveshchennyi absoliutizm," in *Absoliutizm*, p. 436.

several attempts to formulate practical proposals to regulate serfdom. In 1765, for example, she encouraged a few enlightened gentry to establish the Free Economic Society, and in the same year she prompted the new society to solicit essays concerning the desirability of giving the serfs hereditary tenure on the lands they farmed (see above, ch. II, n. 94).

But introducing legal regulation to serf estates proved in practice to be a difficult affair. The central government lacked the machinery to impose laws on serf estates. This Catherine herself tacitly acknowledged in 1767, when she forbade serfs to appeal to the government against their owners. Worse, the response to her efforts to stimulate discussion of reform indicated that neither the gentry nor any other element of the population would have cooperated in the legal regulation of serfdom even if they could have been made to understand what it meant. The 500-odd delegates to Catherine's Commission (1767–1768) were asked at one point to consider introducing legal regulations of serf status into the new law code they were supposed to be drawing up. It was suggested that the serfs be guaranteed civil rights, hereditary land tenure, and fixed obligations to their landlords. The Commission's general reaction was to reject the proposal and also the whole idea of imposing laws on the serf estates. The primary reason the speakers (chiefly M. Shcherbatov) gave was that formal regulations would give government officials the right to interfere on the serf estates. Since government officials were generally corrupt, they would not in fact introduce formal regulations but only constitute additional arbitrary authorities who would disrupt village society and demand bribes.[35] Actually, most of the discussion on serfdom that went on in the Commission was not concerned with legal regulation. The delegates were much more interested in the question of who would enjoy the privilege of owning serfs. The gentry delegates defended the view that only they should have the privilege, while the delegates from the other classes—including cossacks, military settlers (*odnodvortsy*), and other types of state peasant—demanded it for themselves as well.

When the Commission failed to recommend any legal regulation of serf estates, Catherine formed a smaller committee to consider the matter. To this eleven-man body she assigned the task of drawing an a system of regulations that would define the legal status of all the peasants of the empire, serfs and unbonded peasants alike. Knowing that most Russian gentry were unable to digest such an idea, Catherine

35. Semevskii, *Krestianskii vopros*, I, 95–120; Dukes, pp. 112–125.

picked Baltic German noblemen and the most enlightened Russians she could find to do the job. The little group worked for over a year. They discussed peasant status in great detail, bringing up most of the arguments that would preoccupy the government for the next eighty years. In the end, the members submitted a project, but it contained no adequate provision for regulating the relations between serfs and owners. Serfdom was arbitrary, the committee admitted, but as some of the delegates in the general Commission had already suggested, Russia was a country full of petty despots, and it was a great advantage to the peasant to be at the mercy of only one.[36]

Under the circumstances that confronted Catherine in the 1760s, an edict granting civil rights to the serfs would have sounded strange indeed, and it certainly would not have been enforced. Instead of protecting the serfs, it would very likely have undermined the personal status of her gentry servitors, rendering them indifferent to state service and economic enterprise alike. Understandably, Catherine decided that the best thing she could do in order to extend legal rights (system) into the countryside was to continue to limit serf owning to the gentry, organize these new citizens into local colleges, and do what she could to foster in them the aspiration to legal system. Senatorial government could not work and system could not develop except on the basis of serfdom.

The idea that serfdom might be a viable basis for introducing legal system into peasant society continued to attract supporters throughout the era of serfdom. In 1810 Alexander I considered publishing a draft manifesto calling for the general conversion of the state peasants to serfs in the hope that serf owners could take care of them and develop them better than the government could.[37] Later, in the 1820s and 1830s, Nicholas Mordvinov, one of the leading "progressives" of the time, felt compelled to advocate serfdom because he observed that without it the peasantry would be rendered helpless before the bureaucracy.[38] Alexander II, the tsar-liberator himself, still cherished the hope in 1856 that the serf owners would lead their serfs into legal system (see below, n. 85).

Serfdom played yet another role in the development of Russia. In Catherine's time it was still a part of the process by which the government imposed a measure of organization on newly settled territory.

36. Semevskii, *Krestianskii vopros*, I, 126–147. See above, ch. III, sec. D, for a discussion of "despotism" in the eighteenth-century countryside.
37. Druzhinin, *Gos. krest.*, I, 147–151.
38. See H. Repczuk, "Nicholas Mordvinov (1754–1845): Russia's Would-Be Reformer" (unpublished Ph.D. dissertation, Columbia University, 1962), pp. 205–218; Druzhinin, *Gos. krest.*, I, 127–130, 149.

Take, for example, Catherine's land policy in Malorossiia, or, as it is commonly called, the left-bank Ukraine. Russia acquired the area only after Peter's death; consequently, serfdom had never been formally established there, and when Catherine came to the throne, the peasants could still move to new lands without government interference. In 1763 Catherine appointed P. A. Rumiantsev to be her governor-general in Malorossiia (*glavnyi malorossiiskii komandir*) and instructed him to take a census in order to introduce the soul tax. Malorossiia, she said, was not bringing the state "the slightest income." Rumiantsev was to determine whether peasant migration constituted an obstacle to revenue collection, and if he found that it did, he was to stop it "by any suitable means." It would be up to Rumiantsev to determine what these means would be.[39]

Not surprisingly, Rumiantsev did find that peasant movement stood in the way of revenue collection, and for twenty years off and on he worked to stop it. The method he used most often was to distinguish "landholders" from "peasants" in each area and then to empower the former to force the latter to farm land and pay taxes. Distinguishing "gentry" from "peasants" took a long time, but at last, in 1783, Rumiantsev was able to issue a decree forbidding peasant movement in Malorossiia, the effect of which was to bind the "peasants" to the estates of the "landholders."[40] It required only the charter of 1785 to complete the process of enserfment.

In short, Catherine's attitude toward serfdom was quite different in Malorossiia from what it was in Great Russia. In the relatively disorderly and disorganized borderland, she considered it expedient to set up that same arbitrary serfdom which she wished to reform and limit in the central gubernias.[41]

In New Russia (i.e., the steppe along the northern shore of the Black Sea) and the Don Cossack oblast, yet another policy was in force during Catherine's reign. Her law of 22 March 1764 ordered, in effect, that peasants in these areas be allowed to move about as they wished and to settle without interference.[42] The clear implication was that runaway serfs from other areas would be free if they could get

---

39. Semevskii, *Krestianskii vopros*, I, 152.
40. *Ibid.*, pp. 153–159, 226–227.
41. The enserfment of Malorossiia was less than successful. The estates were so scattered that not only villages but individual serfs were shared by owners. It was not uncommon in the 1850s for a left-bank serf to have three owners, to do one day's fieldwork per week for each of them. Serf owners in Malorossiia, says Ignatovich, pp. 223–224, were generally more inclined to overwork their serfs than elsewhere. See also below, n. 122.
42. *PPSZ*, 12099.

to New Russia or the Don oblast. Here again the government suited its policy to its need. In New Russia and the land of the Don Cossacks the main problem was not to establish legal rights or even to provide for orderly tax collection and land use but first of all to settle and occupy the land. Accordingly, Catherine opened the territory to settlement in patent disregard for the laws that obtained in the rest of the country, and she kept it open throughout her reign.

Catherine's peasant policies, then, originated not in any social ideal but primarily in the conditions and practical problems she met with in different areas. If her legislation reflected any concept of constitutional development, it was that arbitrary serfdom constituted a valid political order at a certain stage of settlement or social-economic development, but that it had somehow to be replaced at a later stage by another, yet more advanced form of rural management that would fit peasant society into a centralized, Russia-wide legal-administrative system.

This "constitutional" idea corresponded to a policy of settlement that the Russian government had been using since the time of Ivan IV. There were many variations, but the essential process began with the opening of new lands to settlers and ended with the confirmation of the leading settlers (or military officers) as serf owners (or patriarchal "hetmen").[43]

This policy involved the government in a contradiction. On the one hand, the tsar had to prevent peasants in relatively long-established areas from abandoning their lands. If he did not, collective responsibility for taxes would create disproportionate burdens on the peasants who continued to live in their villages, ultimately forcing all peasants to move and making taxation impossible. On the other hand, new lands had to be settled, and in order to encourage this, the government frequently made it legal for peasants to abandon their lands and tax obligations if only they could reach the new territory without being caught on the way. Thus laws that encouraged the settlement of new lands flatly contradicted the legal orders prevailing in the

43. *Istoricheskoe obozrenie*, IV, 5–11. See also V. I. Koretskii, "Krestianskaia kolonizatsiia i osobennosti protsessa zakreposhcheniia na iuge Rossii v kontse XVI v.," *Ezhegodnik po agrarnoi istorii vostochnoi Evropy 1964 god* (Kishinev, 1966), pp. 96–103.
Enserfment was only one method of organizing newly settled areas. In no area of settlement in the eighteenth and nineteenth centuries was it the only one, and in some places it was used very little. Astrakhan, Tavrid, Orenburg, and Samara gubernias, for example, had very small serf populations, about 15 percent of the total or less in 1858. In Saratov, Kherson, and Ekaterinoslav gubernias the percentage was higher, but in none of them did it go much above 40 percent. See Ignatovich, pp. 69–71.

settled areas. Contradictions notwithstanding, the policy of allowing free settlement and then enserfing the settlers seems to have served the needs of the state, and this seemed more important than consistency. In the period 1500–1800 the state had simultaneously to bind peasants to the land and also to settle new lands, and this was what the state did.[44]

Paul's law of 12 December 1796 forbade unauthorized land settlement in all areas of the empire, thereby "binding" a number of peasants in the Black Sea area to "owners." This marked the last frontier enserfment.[45] After Paul's time the government gave up its old policy of utilizing the more or less natural evolution of frontier society from free settlers into serf owners and serfs and instead undertook to oppose the further spread of serfdom. In the early nineteenth century virtually all settlement of Russia's open country was carried out under administrative direction, and serfdom was outlawed in all the territories where it had not yet been introduced.[46]

To sum up: serfdom was still, in Catherine's time, a vital element in the Russian state. Serfs and owners needed each other, and the government could neither exist nor develop without arrangements for utilizing the peasants en masse as laborers and settlers. Moreover, serfdom played an important and progressive role in the senatorial quest to bring legal system to Russia, even though the granting of civil rights to the gentry in 1785 was predicated on the denial of them to the serfs. For all its inadequacies, then, serfdom was a going concern in the period 1785–1861, not merely an evil and an obstacle to progress.

Had serfdom been nothing more than an evil, its abolition would have been a relatively simple matter. As it was, however, Russia still

44. Concerning the contradiction in the Muscovite government's legislation on peasant movement in the period 1450–1650, see J. M. Culpepper, "The Legislative Origins of Peasant Bondage in Muscovy" (unpublished Ph.D. dissertation, Columbia University, 1965), and his article of the same title in *Forschungen zur osteuropäischen Geschichte*, XIV (Berlin, 1969), 162–237.

45. Semevskii, *Krestianskii vopros*, I, 227–228; J. Blum, *Lord and Peasant in Russia* (Princeton, N.J., 1861), pp. 418–419. Paul's measures brought an end to free peasant movement in the empire except for occasional arbitrary administrative acts such as the temporary opening of the Kuban steppe in 1832 to all settlers who could make their way to it. See *Materialy dlia istorii krepostnogo prava v Rossii* (Berlin, 1872), pp. 18–19; Ignatovich, p. 306. According to *Istoricheskoe obozrenie*, II, 22–28, all peasants, serf and nonserf alike, were free to settle in Stravropol (the Kuban) and Orenburg gubernias from then until 1843.

46. From 1827 to 1844 laws came out expressly forbidding the transportation of serfs into the various border areas—Finland, Bessarabia, Congress Poland, Siberia, Transcaucasia, and, at last, Transcaspia. See Semevskii, *Krestianskii vopros*, II, 543–546; Blum, pp. 419–420.

needed serfdom in the early nineteenth century. Neither the gentry servitors nor the government could act except by using peasants. How, then, could they grant the peasants the right not to be used? If the evolution of the Russian state had rendered the peasantry unable to conceive of government except as an alien power that used them for incomprehensible purposes, then how could the government renounce this power and still continue to command the peasants' support? The rise of senatorial government forced these questions upon the attention of politically conscious Russians, and, as we shall see, senatorial institutions proved unable to furnish satisfactory answers within the framework of their own pretensions and aspirations.

D. Retreat from Serfdom: 1785–1855

THE DILEMMA

The basic reason that serfdom had to be done away with was that the assumptions underlying it conflicted with the myths of senatorial government. The institution that made possible the social-political development of 1711–1855 turned out to be intolerable to the social-political order that the development produced. As we have seen, serfdom took form on the implicit premise that the peasantry constituted a mass resource. In the end, however, serfdom made possible the emergence of government institutions and social aspirations that made no sense if the Russian state depended for its existence on the use of the peasantry as a mass resource. In Catherine's reign this dilemma was not yet a practical problem, only a matter for academic heart-bleeding. In the following decades, however, social-economic developments in the countryside transformed moral agonies into social tensions, and by the 1850s these tensions had become sharp enough that the humiliating defeat in the Crimea brought on a crisis, rendering the demand for reform irresistible.

The most obvious and familiar manifestation of the dilemma of serfdom in the period 1785–1855 was the widespread use of "barshchina" agriculture on the serf estates. In barshchina agriculture the serfs farmed a portion of the plowland on the estate for their own sustenance and paid for it by working part of the time—usually half—on the plowland reserved for the owner.

The use of barshchina labor was widespread mainly because the serf owners of that time found it profitable to produce grain and other agricultural products for the market, and they believed that barshchina labor was the most productive method for exploiting their lands.[47] Not surprisingly, a substantial proportion of the steadily increasing quantity of marketed grain came from barshchina fields, and the percentage of serfs who rendered their dues to their owners in the form of labor rose from a little over 50 in the 1790s to around 70 in the 1850s.[48]

The trouble with barshchina agriculture was that it did not favor the introduction of new techniques. Worse, it actually militated against progress. Consider the serfs' situation. In general, they had no obvious motive to adopt new methods. They worked only because their ancient tradition of collective responsibility demanded it of them; consequently, most of them did only what they had to do within the limits of their traditional conceptions of agriculture.[49] For the typical nineteenth-century peasant, changing his farming methods to achieve greater productivity was something like trading in his parents for a more suitable pair. Moreover, the unprogressive majority inadvertently prevented occasional forward-looking individuals from introducing new methods, because all the peasants in a village had to work their strips in each field according to a common schedule. If one peasant let his animals graze a few days longer, none of his colleagues could plow and plant. Indeed, the main problem, as

47. Kahan, p. 50; Confino, *Domaines*, pp. 21–22, 75–76; V. A. Markina, *Magnatskoe pomeste pravoberezhnoi ukrainy vtoroi poloviny XVIII v.* (Kiev, 1961), pp. 47–51. A. I. Koshelev, writing in the 1850s, offered an alternative explanation for the expansion of barshchina. He noted that the increase in population and improvement of agriculture had rendered the land more valuable and caused the landowners to raise the dues (obrok) the peasants paid. This had caused the peasants to fall into arrears, and in order to collect from them, the owners had resorted to exacting payment in labor—thus the expansion of barshchina. See his "Zapiska," in *Otmena krepostnogo prava na Ukraine, Sbornik dokumentov i materialov* (Kiev, 1961), pp. 61–66.

48. The development of serf agriculture before 1861 is an enormously complex and much disputed subject. Milov's careful study of survey documents (*Issledovanie*) suggests, pp. 176–271, especially p. 265, that barshchina evolved in very different ways in different areas and that generalizations about it as an all-Russian phenomenon are virtually useless. Emmons, pp. 21–25, offers a good concise summary of scholarly opinion on the problem, but it is already out of date. So far as I know, the best discussion in English on the newest trends in Soviet scholarship is Daniel Field's review of I. D. Kovalchenko, *Russkoe krepostnoe krestianstvo v pervoi polovine XIX veka* (Moscow, 1967), in *Kritika*, V (Winter 1969), 31–45. Suffice it to say here that if barshchina did not expand relative to obrok in all parts of Russia, there were certainly not many places where it diminished.

49. M. Confino, *Systèmes agraires et progrès agricole* (Paris, 1969), pp. 225–236, 327–333. Feodot Udolov, a servitor of Catherine's time, expressed the basic "incentive" in barshchina labor in the following succinct terms: "Above all it is necessary to assure that the cultivators of the soil . . . understand that they do not engage in agriculture . . . for their own profit but because they are obliged to serve the sovereign first and after him the estate owner and all society. They are unconditional tributaries and they should not dream of impossible goals incompatible with their condition" (quoted in Confino, *Domaines*, p. 95).

Confino has said, was not primitive methods in themselves but the social relationships that had grown up around them. Three-field agriculture could not be changed without breaking up the repartitional commune,[50] the commune could not be broken up without consolidating the land into integral farms,[51] and no consolidation could be effective without changing the customs and laws regarding inheritance.[52] A peasant who wanted to adopt a more modern system of crop rotation on his lands had not only to quibble about techniques but also to challenge the foundations of his society.

As for the serf owners, they were virtually as helpless before tradition as their serfs. Above all, they lacked capital.[53] The return on an investment in new methods of cultivation is always relatively small and slow in coming; consequently, even those few who had capital often preferred to invest it in commerce or industry.

What the serf owners did have was an abundance of cheap, ignorant, and virtually uneducable labor and, in many cases, more land than they could farm. Given these circumstances, it was more or less natural for the owners to get the most out of their land by forcing their serfs to work as much of it as they could in any way they could.[54] Unfortunately, this tended to strengthen even more the already formidable bulwarks against agricultural development in the Russian countryside. Forced labor had to be regulated, and the most workable basis for regulation was the peasants' own primitive farming methods. Once a serf owner got his regulations established, therefore, he found himself not only allowing his serfs to farm the land in their customary way but forcing them to do so. For the sake of good order and the productivity of the whole village, the serf owner was likely to prevent an individual peasant from violating the customary ways of his associates, even if the violation promised a rise in productivity. Despite its immediate expediency, then, barshchina agriculture put even a would-

50. Confino, Systèmes, pp. 276–282.
51. Ibid., pp. 282–294.
52. Ibid., pp. 294–300.
53. Ibid., pp. 282–283, 312, 349. Confino, Systèmes, pp. 236–239, also points out that a number of serf owners who tried new techniques not only failed to get any favorable results but lost a good deal of money. This made a bad impression on the gentry as a whole.
54. Ignatovich, pp. 160–165. A recent study—B. G. Litvak, "Ob izmeneniiakh zemelnogo nadelia pomeshchichikh krestian v pervoi polovine XIX v.," in Ezhegodnik po agrarnoi istorii vostochnoi Evropy, 1963 god (Vilna, 1964), pp. 523–524—points out that serf owners generally tried to provide all available lands to their serfs for cultivation in the period 1800–1855. In the areas Litvak studied, cultivated land per capita did not decrease during this period, and he believes this to have been generally the case in all of Russia except for the western gubernias.

be progressive owner in the uncomfortable position of having to uphold outmoded agricultural techniques and freeze his serfs into
customary ways that he himself knew were uneconomical.[55]

It will be recalled that in the old relationship between government
servitors (collectors) and peasants, the peasants had worked according to their own custom, while the "servitors" or "owners" had tapped
their villages—much as a beekeeper taps his hives—without forming
binding legal relationships with them. In 1785–1855, with the spread
of barshchina, this relationship was not changing to one in which
each peasant learned to work for himself in hopes of maintaining or
improving his standard of living. Here and there peasants and serfs
learned to work as free laborers and respond to material incentives,[56]
and the number of industrial enterprises that employed wage labor
increased steadily.[57] Nevertheless, the predominant tendency on the
serf estates was not to adopt new methods but only to farm as much
land as possible in the old way.

It seemed very doubtful in the first half of the nineteenth century
that anyone would have benefited economically from the elimination
of barshchina by government fiat. Interference on the serf estates
represented a grave risk not only to the national economy but to the
welfare of the serfs themselves. One indication of the seriousness of
this risk came in 1841, when the government forcibly terminated the
long-term leases by which the Polish gentry of western Russia had
been farming almost all the state lands there, utilizing state peasants
for barshchina labor (see below, sec. E). According to the government's information, the results of this termination were catastrophic.
Production for the market ceased on land where the leased estates
had been, revenue fell off sharply, and the value of the land decreased. Much of the arable land was left to weeds, while estate
improvements, such as mills and gardens, were abandoned. Government, former rentors, and peasants all suffered alike.[58] However in-

55. Confino, *Domaines*, pp. 104–105, notes that any increase in the barshchina
obligation generally caused the peasants to impose a rigid conservatism on their
farming methods.

56. For examples of this, see H. Rossovsky, "The Serf Entrepreneur in Russia,"
in H. G. J. Aitken, ed., *Explorations in Enterprise* (Cambridge, Mass., 1965),
pp. 341–370.

57. See *Istoriia SSSR* (2 vols., Moscow, 1954), II, 8–19.

58. *Istoricheskoe obozrenie*, III, pt. 1, 29–31. The same expulsion of gentry
rentors from the state lands occurred in the Baltic gubernias. Here results seem
to have been different. The peasants took over the pre-existing estates and ran
them effectively on their own. The reason, according to the historian of the
ministry of state domains, was that the Baltic peasants, unlike the White Russians
and Ukrainians, had learned from their German masters to work their lands on
separate plots and, in general, to organize their labor systematically.

effective barshchina agriculture may have been, then, there was
reason to believe that it was not something that could easily be swept
out of the way.[59]

Thus it seems that "modernization" was not broadening the social
horizons of the peasants in 1785–1855. Serf villages did not generally
learn to cope with the market, or to face necessities, or to make choices
on their own. The only impact they felt, if any, was the command to
work longer hours in the same old way. As for the state peasants, they
did not even feel this. Their revenue burden was relatively light and
their land relatively abundant; consequently, they generally felt little
inclination to produce, let alone change their methods of cultivation.[60]
In general, the peasant communities just continued in their old ways,
used and protected as they always had been by an external authority
in the name of purposes that were meaningless to them.

The peasants were not necessarily growing poorer in a material
sense in the early nineteenth century, not even the serfs.[61] Their basic
troubles stemmed not from poverty but from a social situation that
prevented them from facing their own problems. As the government-
society was moving ever more rapidly into modern relationships,

59. It is of interest that a number of gentry in the early nineteenth century
were hostile to innovation on moral grounds. They opposed new techniques, and
also the tendency of some peasants to abandon agriculture for manufacturing,
simply because they believed traditional agriculture to be godly. See Confino,
Systèmes, pp. 142–148, 239–262. Regarding similar gentry beliefs in the morality
of traditional agriculture in Catherine's time, see Augustine, pp. 412–425.

These sentiments were essentially similar to those that moved many of the
peasants, and it is worth emphasizing that they were not merely reactionary.
Many Americans of the time, among them Thomas Jefferson, felt the same way.
So did Lev Tolstoi and Mahatma Gandhi.

60. I. D. Kovalchenko, "O tovarnosti zemledeliia v Rossii v pervoi polovine
XIX v.," in *Ezhegodnik . . . 1963*, pp. 469–486, thinks that state peasants increased their share of marketed grain during the period 1800–1855. Whether or
not he is right, it may still be said that they *generally* did not increase their
productivity or improve their methods. Confino, *Systèmes*, pp. 215–218, 347–348,
says that significant agricultural progress occurred only in the Baltic area.

61. A. A. Skerpan, "The Russian National Economy and the Emancipation,"
in A. D. Ferguson, ed., *Essays in Russian History* (Hamden, Conn., 1964), pp.
200–201, maintains that the lot of the serfs actually improved up to 1861. Emmons, pp. 25–29; Daniel Field, "The End of Serfdom" (unpublished Ph.D. dissertation, Harvard University, 1968), pp. 52–76; and Confino, *Systèmes*, pp. 91–
142, 313–314, 350–359, indicate that serfdom may well have been the most
practical arrangement for using the resources at hand to maximize production
but that the serf estates may nevertheless have been operating at a loss. Ignatovich, on the other hand, pp. 94–165, insists that the serfs were getting much
poorer in 1800–1855. For a general discussion of early nineteenth-century views
on the possibilities of serfdom as a progressive socio-economic system, see
Semevskii, *Krestianskii vopros*, II, 140–145, 163–179, and Skerpan, pp. 169–177.
See also above, nn. 37, 38.

necessities, and political ideals, peasant society was sinking into a helpless and anachronistic futility. On the serf estates barshchina was rendering the owners as helpless as the serfs, because when it did work reasonably well, it made them dependent on the helplessness of their own serfs. In effect, then, the expanding market was driving both government and peasants into a cul de sac. It was progress, not backwardness, that was rendering Russian society helpless. Progress under the aegis of serfdom was not developing rural society but actually freezing it into an immovable and uninfluenceable block, seemingly helpless in itself and incapable of being helped, able only to grip itself with its own internal tensions until some outside force intervened.[62]

The politically conscious gentry knew by the 1850s that serfdom needed reform. Well as they knew it, they could not organize themselves to rectify the potential social disintegration that was building up in the countryside. Even those gentry who resisted the inclination to victimize their serfs could do no more than leave them to their old subsistence agriculture and to keep parceling out more land to them as their numbers increased.[63] In the 1850s, then, serfdom stood revealed as a solid obstacle to the growth of anything like a state and/or a modern economy. It was not, however, an evil that men of good will could join together and destroy. It was, rather, a working arrangement on which men of good will depended whether they liked it or not.

It has been noted that in the period up to 1785 the dilemma that serfdom posed to senatorial government manifested itself in the explicit exclusion of the peasantry from personal legal status. After 1785 this exclusion did not grow milder, as Catherine and her successors hoped. Instead, the serf owners' attempts to increase production on their estates tended to stiffen the formal exclusion that Catherine had established into a helpless hostility between peasantry and gentry. All this was not yet the whole of the dilemma of serfdom. There was one more aspect of the peasants' alienation from the "enlightened" elements in Russian society, more elusive and intangible and yet more enduring than either of the above manifestations, lasting on long after the forms of serfdom had been done away with.

During the first half of the nineteenth century a few gentry servitors

62. Leontev, "Volostnoi sud," pp. 21–29, describes how this phenomenon evolved (and persisted) from Catherine's time to the early 1900s.
63. Later in the century A. N. Engelgardt believed that the gentry could help the peasants develop new working organizations, but his own attempts in the 1870s indicate how much this demanded from anyone who tried it. See his *Iz derevni* (Moscow, 1937), pp. 104–126, 163–177.

began to react against what they regarded as the evils of serfdom and to devise schemes for breaking down the legal exclusion of the peasantry. They felt, as A. I. Koshelev expressed it in his famous appeal, that:

> Abolishing our right to dispose of people as if they were things— or cattle—is as much our own emancipation as it is theirs. We are under the yoke of a right that destroys the humanity in us, more so than it does in the peasants. Look closely at the village life of the land-owners; attend their idle and trivial congresses; converse with them; take part in the gentry assemblies or go among the gentry in the towns and in the capital; observe their occupations and listen to their talk. See how devoted they are to sloth, inactivity, luxury, and corruption, and then you will not wonder that in law courts and administrative offices they act senselessly and heedlessly. Rather, you will wonder that with such men, affairs do not go worse then they do. If the blindness that comes with owning men has not possessed you wholly, you will say: "Yes, the rapid emancipation of the serfs is yet more necessary for the gentry than for the serfs themselves." [64]

Seemingly, this kind of attitude and the activities it inspired should have helped to bridge the gap between the gentry and the peasantry. In fact, however, the very men who concerned themselves with the problem of peasant exclusion were inclined to formulate their ideas and programs solely around their own crusades to "help," "save," or "develop" the peasants without regard for the values and hopes of the peasants themselves. We have noted that when the "enlightened" gentry of the late eighteenth century spoke of government, they were not thinking of what really went on in the offices of the administration. In the nineteenth century, when they began to regard the peasantry more closely, they had to resort to yet another flight from reality. Instead of discussing the people who actually inhabited the countryside, the capital-city gentry adopted the habit of referring to the peasants as if they were abstract concepts derived from current schemes of social and economic development.[65] Generally speaking, it was these structures to which the enlightened gentry drew close and on which they came to depend, not the peasants in the countryside. What their theorizing and organizing did, therefore, was to set

64. Printed in *Otmena . . . na Ukraine*, p. 66.
65. See above, ch. I, sec. C. Good examples of this theorizing may be found in the second and third volumes of N. Tourgueneff, *La russie et les russes* (3 vols., Paris, 1847). Druzhinin, *Gos. krest.*, I, 130–164, gives a good survey of the discussion of the peasantry that went on among the government's ministers during Alexander I's reign. Concerning Western theories about economic and legal arrangements that various Russians hoped would unleash progress among the peasants, see Skerpan, pp. 161–229.

them apart from the peasants as decisively as formal laws and economic practice had ever done. This was why the gentry's moral commitment to "save" or "guide" the peasantry did not bring them closer
to rural realities but only resolved their own socio-psychological
dilemmas. In effect, the nineteenth-century peasant had to provide
not only labor for the gentry servitors but psychotherapy as well.[66]
    It is true that the attempts of politically conscious Russians to con-
ceptualize peasant society improved their understanding of it. Toward
the end of the nineteenth century the capital cities began to discover
concepts regarding the peasant way of life that were tolerably accurate
reflections of reality. Knowledge, however, did not narrow the gap
between peasantry and government-society. A servitor (politician,
agitator) who understood peasant society could manipulate it more
effectively than one who did not, but it was precisely this manipula-
tion of the peasants—to achieve purposes they themselves did not
comprehend—that had always set government-society apart from the
peasantry. The knowledgeable servitor (or capital-city idealist) was
only a serf owner in academic robes.[67] All capital-city concepts of
the peasantry—informed or uninformed, liberal, radical, humane, or
reactionary—were alien to the peasants, and so were the capital-city
Russians who cherished them. They all derived from the fact of life
that the peasants were objects of legal-administrative system rather
than parts of it and that they had somehow to be changed or handled
so as to make them serve its purposes.
    To conclude, neither legal-administrative system nor the capital-
city aspiration to extend system to peasant society narrowed the gap

66. The best contemporary description I have seen of the gentry servitors'
moral commitment to the peasantry and of the peasant exclusion that was
historically inherent in it is in Kavelin, *Krestianskii vopros*, pp. 3–36. An excellent
scholarly treatment of the intellectuals' need to construct images of the peasantry
is Alan Pollard, "Consciousness and Crisis: The Self-Image of the Russian Intelligentsia, 1855–1882" (unpublished Ph.D. dissertation, University of California,
1968), especially pp. 46–119.
67. The alienation between gentry servitors and peasants came into the open in
the course of the populist movement of the late nineteenth century. Any attempt
the populists made to guide the peasants and to advance them had to begin
with the peasants' own helplessness and their willingness to be used. If the attempt
worked at all, then the peasants ceased to be willing to be used, thus undermining
the whole scheme of development. See R. Wortman, *The Crisis of Russian
Populism* (Cambridge, 1967), pp. 44–46, 59–60, 62–94. Engelgardt's experiments at "improving" the peasants in the 1870s led him at last to imply that up-
lifting them required something like total supervision. See pp. 119–123, 176–181,
271–299, 388–403. Engelgardt shrank from this extreme conclusion, but his description reflects an all too common evolution in Russian capital-city attitudes
toward the peasantry. He began with a desire to save them and progressed almost to the point where he felt compelled to dominate them.

between capital-city society and the peasants. On the contrary, the legal structure, economic needs, and psychology of government-society all militated to throw up a complex variety of obstacles to the formation of relationships of mutual dependence between government and peasants. Senatorial government brought the forms of law and citizenship to a small number of Russians, but in so doing it rendered them dependent on the exclusion of the vast majority from personal legal status. As a result, the capital cities—i.e., the government-society— became increasingly inclined to conceive of the peasantry not only as a mass to be utilized but also as a mass that had to be changed in order to close the gap between it and the state.

The evolution of senatorial government in the eighteenth century institutionalized the use of the peasants as a mass resource. Bureaucracy—i.e., ministerial government—was the institutional expression of the impulse to reform and manipulate the peasants. After 1801 senatorial government attempted to reform its institutions in order to enable them to carry on a crusade for active reform, but since this implied the reform of peasant society, it also implied an attack on senatorial government itself. This was the underlying reason that the ultimate effect of the introduction of the ministries in 1802 was to subvert senatorial government and to replace it with a new kind of administration (see below, ch. V, sec. B).

ATTEMPTS AT REFORM

Despite the manifest difficulties involved, the tsars of the late eighteenth and early nineteenth centuries were invincibly determined to reform serfdom. Catherine's search for ways to grant legal status to the peasants suggests that by 1785 the central government had already come to feel some responsibility to organize the peasants themselves rather than merely to organize the gentry so that they could use the peasants. In the years thereafter the rulers never tired of expressing their desire—verbally, legislatively, and administratively—to extend system to peasant society and to eliminate the arbitrariness that prevailed in rural Russia. The question was: how?

The obvious answer was that the serf owners had to do the job. Throughout the period 1785–1861 they constituted all there was of political order in the countryside and the only conceivable means for carrying out reforms there. Of necessity, the government's attitude toward them was ambivalent. The central government's agents often quarreled with individual serf owners and they were fond of criticizing the landholding gentry in general,[68] but the administration and

68. Romanovich-Slavatinskii's book, published by the ministry of internal af-

the gentry were too dependent on one another to allow a clear, two-sided political struggle to develop between them. At no time did the central administration permit its reforming aspirations to bring it into outright opposition to the serf-owning gentry. In 1855–1861, when the debate on serfdom became more or less public, something like a sustained, two-sided struggle did take place, but even then the two sides were not the government administration and the serf owners. On the contrary, administrators, capital-city society, and rural gentry all divided themselves into factions vaguely for and against the autonomy of the serf estate.[69]

It would be somewhat inaccurate, then, to label the evolution of the government-society's relationship to the peasantry in the period 1785–1861 as a withering away of serfdom or a gradual usurpation of local gentry institutions by an ever-growing bureaucracy. What was going on was an evolution in serf estates, gentry institutions, and central administration all at the same time. Serfdom was basic to all three, and it would demand their mutual development and cooperation to bring serfdom to an end. The abolition of serfdom was not some force descending upon Russia from the outside. It was, rather, a step forward in the evolution of serfdom itself, taken by those very institutions that had come to depend on serfdom. Like senatorial government, serfdom had to grow in order to destroy itself. There could be no retreat from serfdom until and unless the serf owners themselves were sufficiently well organized to conduct it.

Any Russian who consciously favored some sort of progress or reform in the countryside during the period 1785–1861 had a choice of three basic means to achieve it: 1) he could affirm that the serf owners would bring progress if the government would only leave them free to act as patriarchal, moral leaders over the serfs; 2) he could believe that the local gentry would do more good if the government imposed regulations on them and made them manage their estates within a framework of laws to which they themselves would be subject; 3) finally, if our Russian did not believe that the gentry would have a good effect in any capacity, he had perforce to believe that a reform could somehow be carried out by some sort of central administration

---

fairs, contains most of the standard criticisms that the ministry officials directed at the gentry in the early nineteenth century. For an indication of gentry hostility to the central government, see Druzhinin's description of their opposition to Kiselev's reform in *Gos. krest.*, II, 525–527, 534–535.

69. Emmons, pp. 51–68, 87–89, 224–318, and Field, pp. 131–263, describe the conflict that arose between gentry and ministry of internal affairs in 1859–1861, making it quite clear that in this context the term "gentry" actually refers to factions in both central government and gentry assemblies.

—elected, autocratic, dictatorial, or sublime—without any help from the serf owners at all.

These basic approaches were essentially contradictory to each other. The practical effects that stemmed from pursuing any one of them tended to negate those of the others. It did not make much sense simultaneously to impose laws upon the serf owners, send administrators to shoulder aside both them and their laws, and still go on hoping that they would feel some incentive to carry out the government's wishes on their own initiative. Nevertheless, it proved practically impossible in the period 1785–1861 to pursue any one of the approaches to the exclusion of the others.

The story of the government's active efforts to introduce legal system to the peasantry begins with Catherine II. At one point or another she tried all three of the approaches mentioned above. In her Commission she at least suggested limiting the serf owners' arbitrary power by imposing regulations on their estates. By confirming gentry civil rights in 1785, she was trying in effect to encourage the serf owners to use their arbitrary power to develop peasant society on their own initiative (see above, sec. C). Finally, she worked on a small scale to find ways in which the central administration could influence the peasants by its own action.

Catherine's experiments with government-administered reform deserve brief description. She offered a few crown (*dvortsovye*) villages a variety of incentive schemes to adopt more rational agricultural methods and to make independent, self-reliant farmers of themselves. The specific nature of each scheme is not known, but most of them involved some sort of land consolidation and agronomic improvement. Seed, tools, and animals were lent or provided, and rewards were promised to those families who increased production. Some successes and/or lessons may have come from these experiments, but all work on them seems to have stopped after 1773, perhaps because at least one of the experimental villages engaged in rioting at the time of Pugachev's rebellion. These experiments were not merely agricultural but social as well. Catherine was seeking a formula by which the government could reorder peasant society to make it amenable to systematic administration. By implication (or at least hindsight) this was an incipient attack on serfdom by the central government's own agents.[70]

70. Semevskii, *Krestiane*, II, 144–156. The government's experiments followed upon some similar attempts by a few enlightened serf owners and were to some extent an imitation of them. These attempts date from the 1740s. See Druzhinin, *Gos. krest.*, I, 57. According to Confino, *Systèmes*, p. 189, the notions of crop

Paul continued all three approaches. He handed out state peasants to private owners on a grand scale, thereby indicating that he put his trust in serf owners to do something intelligent with the peasantry on their own. At the same time he disciplined the serf owners more rigorously than any autocrat before or since his time, often confiscating the estates of owners who were convicted of cruelty to their serfs.[71] According to his son, Nicholas I, Paul said that he was giving out land and peasants to the gentry in order to establish them as "*politseimeistery*," who would be responsible to the government for "everything that occurred" on their estates. "Russian government," said Paul, "will be unable to do without such methods for a long time to come."[72] In Paul's view the gentry were to be all-powerful on their own estates, but the tsar in turn would hold them absolutely responsible and would exercise despotic power over them. The owners would be free from statutory constraint, but their actions would be subject to the tsar's judgment. The tsar (and Senate) would protect the serfs against their owners not by legislation but by hearing their appeals and deciding each case according to its merits.[73]

Discipline, however, was only one of Paul's approaches. He enacted a few scattered statutes to regulate serf estates, the most famous being his law limiting barshchina labor to three days a week. In addition, he attempted to establish the legal status of the unbonded peasants. He organized self-governing volosts (counties) among the state peasants and established a separate ministry with its own local agents to look after the *udelnye* peasants of the imperial family.[74]

---

rotation that informed both the earlier gentry experiments and Catherine's were not agronomically sound. This, however, does not diminish their significance as administrative developments.

In addition to her experiments, Catherine also made some feeble beginnings at establishing elective institutions in the villages. She provided for the election of police officers (*sotskie, piatidesiatskie,* and *desiatskie*) from among the peasants (instruction of 19 Dec. 1774, in *PPSZ*, 14231), and she allowed the court (*dvortsovye*) peasants a considerable degree of autonomy (Semevskii, *Krestiane*, II, 117). In 1787 she (or, rather, Potemkin) made provision for elected village courts on the state lands in New Russia, and in 1790 she ordered that these institutions be extended to Perm, Tobolsk, Iaroslavl, and Vologda gubernias. See *Istoricheskoe obozrenie,* I, pt. 1, 20–21; Leontev, "Volostnoi sud," pp. 21–22.

71. Klochkov, pp. 524–525. On Paul's harsh disciplinary methods in the central administration, see above, ch. III, n. 28.

72. "Materialy i cherti k biografii Imperatora Nikolaia I i k istorii ego tsarstvovaniia," *SIRIO,* XCVIII, 246. See also Druzhinin, *Gos. krest.,* I, 147.

73. Klochkov, p. 531. Both Alexander I and Nicholas I shared Paul's faith in direct government intervention in specific cases. See Korf, pp. 622–633; above, n. 6.

74. For a brief description of Paul's volost reform, see Leontev, "Volostnoi sud," pp. 23–24.

Contradictory attempts to limit the power of the serf owners by law, encourage them to act on their own, and expand the central administration so that it could impose "order" on its own, all went forward on a much larger scale during the reigns of Alexander I and Nicholas I. The least effective approach was the first one, as the statesmen of Catherine II had foreseen when they opposed her efforts to regulate the serf estates in 1768. Serfdom did not lend itself to partial regulation by one rule at a time. Several of the tsars tried to forbid the sale of serfs without land, but with all their power they never put a stop to it. Alexander I could not even prevent their sale at public auction within sight of the Winter Palace.[75] A serf owner's power was either arbitrary or it was not. Limiting it in one aspect and leaving it unlimited in another did not change the nature of the relationship but simply made a farce out of the would-be limits.[76]

Both Alexander and Nicholas recognized the pointlessness of separate regulations, but they did not cease to enact them.[77] Nicholas I began his reign with threats that he was going to see to it that the serf owners did their "Christian duty" or suffer punishment,[78] and he ultimately went so far as to enact the law of 12 February 1853, which held absentee serf owners criminally responsible for the actions of their overseers.[79] All this came to very little. The government's efforts to impose specific limits on the serf owners' powers while leaving the framework of serfdom intact were for the most part ineffective throughout the era of serfdom.

The second approach, expanding or at least guaranteeing the serf owners' power in hopes of persuading them to establish institutions on their own initiative, seemed more promising (see above, sec. C). The most important policy stemming from it was the consistent but more or less passive one of upholding gentry property rights. Both Alexander and Nicholas persistently rejected any legislative proposals and ad-

---

75. Tourgueneff, II, 100–110.

76. The frustrations involved in trying to regulate the serf estates by law are clearly reflected in the discussion that developed in the government around Nicholas I's project of 1844 to guarantee some sort of rights to household serfs. See "Materialy . . . k biografii Nikolaia I," pp. 208–248.

77. Semevskii, *Krestianskii vopros*, I, 239–256, describes Alexander I's laws and projects to regulate serf conditions, and his second volume takes up those of Nicholas I. See also Ignatovich, pp. 51–68.

78. Semevskii, *Krestianskii vopros*, II, 2–17. The frequency of official prosecutions against serf owners actually did increase during Nicholas's reign, especially after the 1830s. See *Materialy . . . krepostnogo prava*, pp. 18, 31, 83–84, 153–154, 166–169. In 1854, 193 serf owners were on trial for negligence or cruelty to their serfs. See *ibid.*, pp. 262–263.

79. *Ibid.*, p. 262.

ministrative acts that threatened the property guarantees set forth in
the charter of 1785. Also of significance were Nicholas's efforts, especially the law of 6 December 1831, to enhance the authority of the
gentry assemblies and marshals—though at the same time compelling
them to work more closely with the central administration.[80]

Alexander and Nicholas each passed one major law designed to
encourage serf owners to introduce legal relationships to their estates
on their own initiative. Alexander's law of 20 February 1803 allowed
owners to petition the tsar for permission to free whole serf villages
along with the land they cultivated.[81] Nicholas's law of 4 April 1842
allowed an owner to enter into contractual relations with his serfs
rather than freeing them outright. If an owner and his serfs wished,
Nicholas's law allowed them to draw up a contract (*inventar*) that
1) marked off the land to be used by the serfs from that which the
owner kept for his own purposes, and 2) specified what payments and
obligations the serfs would render to the owner for the land allotted to
them. Once signed by owner and serfs and approved by the government, the contract became law, and the serfs possessed legal rights
in accordance with its provisions.[82]

Neither Alexander's nor Nicholas's attempts to evoke the gentry's
cooperation produced significant practical results,[83] but both tsars
placed high hopes in them. We have seen how Alexander disregarded
his newly rejuvenated Senate and brushed aside his *general-prokuror*
in order to push through the 1803 law. Nicholas I kept his closest
advisors busy on the 1842 law for several years, and he thought it so
important that when it came at last to the State Council for final
approval, he himself attended the meeting and presided. He did this
only five times during all of his thirty years on the throne (see above,
n. 82). In his speech to the State Council he called his proposed law a
step toward the development of a new order in the countryside. The
government, he said, did not yet know how to reform serfdom, but
under the terms of the new law individual serf owners would be able
to gain experience, and this would show the government the way.
"When the serf owners who desire to make use of this decree submit
projects suited to local pecularities and various types of agriculture,

80. See Korf, pp. 584–633, for a full description of Nicholas I's policies along
these lines.
81. An English translation of the law is in B. Dmytryshyn, ed., *Imperial
Russia* (New York, 1967), pp. 133–135.
82. The enactment of the law of 1842 is described in "Materialy . . . k biografii Nikolaia I," pp. 105–121, 268–271. See also Druzhinin, *Gos. krest.*, I,
612–623.
83. Semevskii, *Krestianskii vopros*, II, 210–211.

then our consideration of them . . . will tell us . . . the details of what can and must be done."[84] Despite the negligible results of the laws encouraging serf owners to act on their own, the approach they represented was of vital importance throughout the first half of the nineteenth century. Indeed, when Alexander II came to the throne in 1855, he still believed that it was the best one for the government to take.[85] In his first speech to the gentry after the Crimean War, in March 1856, he adhered to his father's old custom of reassuring them of their rights and requesting their cooperation (see below, sec. E). At that point he still hoped he might get it.

The third approach, experimenting with direct administrative action on the peasants, developed into massive operations under Alexander I and Nicholas I. Beginning in 1810, Alexander ordered his most trusted servitor, Alexei Arakcheev, to set up military colonies. Their ostensible purpose was to reduce the cost of the army and to lighten the burden of recruiting on the peasants, but Alexander's fondest hope was that the army's experiments in management would uncover an administrative path to a general peasant reform.[86] Certainly the experiment was large in scale. By the end of Alexander's reign there were about 370,000 male peasants enrolled in the colonies.[87] Nevertheless, as the colonies multiplied, the hope that they might become a basis for a general peasant reform seems to have disappeared. In 1824 Arakcheev himself recommended that they not be expanded further.[88] His reforms, it seems, were too abrupt. Moreover, the idea of involving the army directly in rural administration appealed neither to the gentry nor to the domestic administration nor to the army.[89]

In 1835 Nicholas I embarked on a new peasant reform, this time on a much broader scale. He ordered Mikhail Speranskii and Pavel D. Kiselev to work out plans for an administrative system that would encompass all the state peasants, of whom there were 7.8 million

84. Quoted in *Gosudarstvennyi Sovet, 1801–1901* (St. Petersburg, 1901), pp. 64–65.
85. Druzhinin, *Gos. krest.*, II, 536–537.
86. Ferguson, dissertation, p. 57.
87. "Istoricheskoe obozrenie voenno-sukhoputnogo upravleniia, pp. 418–424; Ferguson, dissertation, pp. 85–171. About one-third of the Russian army came from the colonies.
88. Ferguson, dissertation, pp. 198–199. Actually, Nicholas I did enlarge the colonies further, but after 1831 they no longer embodied any fundamental changes in the peasants' way of life. See A. D. Ferguson, "Russian Military Settlements, 1825–1866," in Ferguson, *Essays*, pp. 107–128, and also his dissertation, pp. 216–229.
89. On the army's opposition, see P. P. Evstafev, *Vosstanie novgorodskikh voennykh poselian* (Moscow, 1934), pp. 45–51.

(males) at the time, comprising about 40 percent of the total peasant population.[90] Speranskii and Kiselev spent about two years getting a project together. In 1838, with the establishment of the ministry of state domains and the appointment of Kiselev as its first head, the government began to carry out reform programs in the villages. In the following two decades a series of legislative enactments and executive programs actually granted formal civil status to the state peasants and attempted a good deal more in the way of land reform, improvement in agricultural techniques, and various types of village reorganization.[91]

Kiselev's reforms were by far the most extensive action the government had ever undertaken in the peasant villages. In the end, however, his administration discovered more obstacles in the way of government-sponsored social change than paths toward it. Kiselev believed that "in Russia nothing is begun and nothing is done without the involvement and leadership of the government,"[92] but he had also to admit that "improvements introduced by force can neither succeed nor endure."[93] By 1856, the year of Kiselev's dismissal, his new ministry had performed a number of valuable experiments and accumulated an unprecedented amount of information about the peasantry. But twenty years of effort had not produced a sound procedure for modernizing the state peasants; nor had it suggested an administrative approach to the introduction of legal system to all peasant society, though this had been Kiselev's and Nicholas I's ultimate purpose.[94] At the end of Nicholas's reign the central administration was still very far from being able to replace the serf owners and their local institutions.

Ultimately, all three approaches to the introduction of legal system in the countryside bore some fruit. Attempts to regulate the serf owners and to secure their voluntary cooperation had achieved few concrete results, but they had kept the problem before the eyes of the capital cities and the rural gentry.[95] By the 1850s the gentry were much better prepared at least to discuss reform than they had been in Catherine's time, and in view of the central administration's continuing inability to act in the countryside and its undiminished need to rely on

90. The 40 percent figure comes from the *reviziia* of 1835. See Druzhinin, *Gos. krest.*, I, 45. Kiselev's own inspections of 1836–1841 produced an estimate of over 44 percent. See *ibid.*, II, 4. Concerning the work of Speranskii and Kiselev, see *ibid.*, I, 490–493; II, 4–8.

91. Druzhinin's second volume gives an exhaustive description of Kiselev's reform.

92. Quoted in "Materialy . . . k biografii Nikolaia I," p. 212.

93. Quoted in Druzhinin, *Gos. krest.*, II, 236.

94. *Ibid.*, I, 612–621.

95. Blum, p. 551; Semevskii, *Krestianskii vopros*, I, 112–113; II, 76–77.

the gentry, this educational achievement was of no small importance. The impact of the third approach, culminating in Kiselev's large-scale measures, was probably greater than the other two, but it was two-edged. On the one edge, Kiselev's reform produced much of the experience and information that was necessary to conceive of and enact the statute of 19 February 1861. Many of his former aides played vital roles in the enactment process. A. I. Levshin and E. Lode, for example, probably drafted the rescript of 20 November 1857, the first public proclamation to commit the government to freeing the serfs with land within a relatively short period of time.[96] Yet another long-time Kiselev henchman, Ia. A. Solovev, and Kiselev's nephew Nicholas Miliutin played leading roles in drafting the Liberation Statute itself.

On the other edge, Kiselev's reform (to say nothing of Arakcheev's) gave rise to widespread disillusionment in the capital cities regarding the possibilities of direct government action to bring legal system to the peasantry.[97] Alexander II and the majority of his leading statesmen deplored the effects of Kiselev's long rule over the state peasants, and to some extent their inclination to oppose any direct government action in the countryside arose directly from what Kiselev had done.[98] A. F. Orlov, the man who secured Kiselev's dismissal in 1856, was chairman of the "secret committee" that Alexander formed in January 1857 to commence the reform of serfdom. Among its members were Vasilii A. Dolgorukov, V. F. Adlerberg, P. P. Gagarin, and Mikhail N. Muravev (Kiselev's replacement as minister of state domains and his arch-foe).[99] All these men were outspoken opponents of Kiselev's system and of any measures that smacked of direct administrative interference in serf estates.

96. Druzhinin, *Gos. krest.*, II, 553–555, describes the roles played by Kiselev's former aides in drafting the rescript. Levshin worked for eleven years under Kiselev, and Lode, one of his most radical idea men, served even longer. See *ibid.*, I, 479–483; II, 195–199. On Levshin's role in drafting the rescript, see Emmons, p. 56; A. A. Kornilov, *Ocherki po istorii obshchestvennogo dvizheniia i krestianskogo dela v Rossii* (St. Petersburg, 1905), pp. 164–169, 205–206, 215–230; A. Rieber, *Politics of Autocracy* (Paris, 1966), pp. 42–43; and Levshin's own memoir, "Dostopamiatnyia minuty v moei zhizni," *Russkii Arkhiv* (1885), kn. 8, pp. 475–557.

97. Druzhinin, *Gos. krest.*, II, 455, 522–539, describes the opposition to Kiselev in detail.

98. *Ibid.*, p. 534, describes Valuev's reaction to Kiselev's reform. Alexander II expressed his low opinion of government bureaucracy rather often. In a typical note—to Lanskoi in 1858—he said flatly that the government administration was incapable of guaranteeing legal rights to anyone. See G. A. Dzhanshev, *Epokha velikikh reform* (St. Petersburg, 1907), p. 40.

99. P. A. Zaionchkovskii, *Otmena krepostnogo prava v Rossii* (3rd ed., Moscow, 1968), p. 68. Not only these "conservatives" disparaged Kiselev's reform. Many "liberals" also thought ill of it, e.g., Tourgueneff, II, 72–76.

In 1856 Alexander II dismissed Kiselev from his ministry and, at Orlov's suggestion, sent him off to Paris as ambassador. In April 1857 he appointed Mikhail N. Muravev, then minister of the crown (*udelnye*) lands, to take over the ministry of state domains with the explicit purpose of destroying Kiselev's organization and reducing the state peasants to the patrimonial, semi-serf status under which the crown peasants lived.[100] Muravev was so hostile to the extension of central government agencies into the countryside that he actually proposed turning the state peasants over to private owners. It was in the government's best interests, he said, to give out the state lands to private persons on long-term leases and perhaps even under permanent tenure. In short, Muravev wished not only to preserve serfdom but to extend it.[101]

Muravev's attempt, launched with the tsar's determined support, lasted about a year. He made elaborate inspection tours, found the usual widespread corruption and ineptitude, and formulated projects, all designed to wipe out the effects of Kiselev's bureaucratizing reforms.[102] All for naught. On 20 June 1858 Alexander abruptly reversed himself. He ordered that Kiselev's system be maintained on the state lands and also extended to the crown (*udelnye*) lands.[103]

No one knows exactly what was going on in Alexander II's mind in 1856–1858. Druzhinin speaks of his "vacillations" but makes no attempt to account for them.[104] It is clear, however, that Alexander and many of his leading statesmen were reacting negatively to Kiselev's reform during the first two years of reign. It may be said, then, that the experience of Kiselev's reform produced an ambiguous effect on the government-society's attitude toward serfdom. It laid the administrative groundwork for the Liberation, yet it seems to have bred a general lack of confidence in the central government's capacity to act in the countryside and a corresponding inclination to trust in the serf-owning gentry to reform serfdom on their own. It is of interest that Kiselev himself was opposed to the full emancipation of the serfs in the 1850s (as he had been all along), and so, it seems, were some of his former

---

100. Druzhinin, *Gos. krest.*, II, 536–538.
101. *Ibid.*, p. 547.
102. *Ibid.*, pp. 542–549. Muravev's "invasion" is described colorfully if imprecisely in N. V. Shelgunov, *Vospominaniia* (Moscow, 1923), pp. 74–80. Shelgunov was on Muravev's staff at the time.
103. Druzhinin, *Gos. krest.*, II, 550–551. The law of 20 June 1858 is in (*Vtoroe*) *polnoe sobranie zakonov Rossiiskoi Imperii* (55 vols., St. Petersburg, 1830–1884, hereinafter cited as VPSZ), 33326. Concerning the changes Muravev did make, see *Istoricheskoe obozrenie*, II, 63–72; IV, 47–54.
104. Druzhinin, *Gos. krest.*, II, 549.

subordinates, especially Levshin, the man who drafted the rescript of November 1857.[105]

In sum, all three approaches to the reform of serfdom failed to provide any means to liberate the serfs or any practical plan of reform. Serf owners and government had become somewhat better organized and increasingly aware of their mutual dependence, but they had also grown more hostile and distrustful of one another. Mutual reliance and tension arose between them during the same period of time and from the same historical process, intensifying their interaction yet also raising serious obstacles to their cooperation. Consequently, the government's policy toward serfdom did not cease to be ambivalent and contradictory in the last years before the Liberation.

E. ENACTMENT OF THE LIBERATION: 1856–1861

In its final form the Liberation turned out to be a combination of the three approaches and also of their contradictions, which made it a very risky affair. Contradictions that had formerly been implicit in separate, scattered actions were now thrust together in a single program and thereby rendered explicit and inescapable. At one time and in one single act the government violated the gentry's rights, deprived them of a portion of their wealth, and abruptly imposed a mass of regulations upon them, knowing full well that it had to rely on the gentry themselves to do all this.

The dangers of gentry noncompliance with the Liberation seemed very real during the years when it was being prepared.[106] In 1857–1859 the gentry were commanded to express their views on serf reform, and most of them took advantage of this command to declare their opposition to the programs that were ultimately adopted in the Statute of 1861.[107] The tsar's response was to dismiss them abruptly from the enactment procedure and to forbid them to discuss the matter further. The gentry were not merely ignored; they were assembled, asked to organize themselves sufficiently to formulate their views, and *then* abruptly thrust aside—all in all, a peculiar way to treat the only men

105. In July 1857 Kiselev cautioned Alexander II against freeing the serfs. See Zaionchkovskii, *Otmena*, pp. 76–77. On Levshin's views, see Druzhinin, *Gos. krest.*, II, 553–556, and Roger Portal, ed., *Le statut des paysans libérés du servage: 1861–1961* (Paris, 1963), p. 100. According to Levshin's own note, pp. 509–512, his idea of serf liberation did not include providing them with land until some later date. Moreover, he did not want to begin any kind of liberation in Russia proper until it had first been tried out in the Lithuanian gubernias.

106. Emmons, pp. 224–242, 271–281, 344–347, describes various measures taken by the government to cope with gentry discontent in 1857–1861.

107. Field, pp. 214–216.

who could put the government's peasant policies into effect. Alexander II's maneuvers united the gentry in opposition to the government as they had never been before, at the very time when he most needed their services.[108] On the face of it, then, the process by which the Liberation was enacted was essentially self-defeating and absurd. The Statute of 1861 was an act of desperation that never would have occurred had it not been for the crisis in which the government found itself in 1856–1861.

Before dealing with the decision-making of 1856–1861, it will be instructive to study an administrative action that was in many ways a precedent for the Liberation, though no one seems to have thought of it as such in 1856. This was the campaign that went forward in the period 1844–1852 under the direction of D. G. Bibikov, governor-general of Kiev, to draw up *inventari* (cadastres, inventories—in effect, legal guarantees of serf rights to the land—see above, sec. D) on the serf estates in southwest Russia. Southwest Russia, or right-bank Ukraine, was Bibikov's territory. It consisted of the three gubernias of Kiev, Podoliia, and Volyniia, which formed the southernmost part of the area acquired by Russia in the Polish partitions. Rural society there was made up almost wholly of Polish, Roman Catholic gentry on the one hand and predominantly Orthodox Ukrainian peasants on the other.

As governor-general of Kiev (from 1838 to 1852), Bibikov was virtually a military dictator, and he seems to have been in an exceptionally good position to carry through an active reform. The formal powers of his office were practically unlimited (see above, ch. II, sec. E); moreover, he enjoyed the personal confidence of Nicholas I. Because of these advantages and also his unusual energy, Bibikov was able to carry through a program that was, according to Semevskii, the most effective that the government ever undertook "to benefit the serfs" before the Liberation itself.[109]

The campaign to introduce estate inventories began with the decree of 15 April 1844, which was directed to all of western Russia (i.e., all the area acquired in the Polish partitions), including Bibikov's Southwest and the gubernias of "Lithuania" (the Northwest) and White Russia: Vilna, Grodno, Kovno, Vitebsk, Mogilev, and Minsk. This decree required serf owners—almost all of whom were Poles—to sub-

---

108. Emmons, pp. 260–265. The gentry projects of 1858–1859 are discussed in *ibid.*, pp. 266–298; Portal, pp. 55–92, 109–113; and Kornilov, *Ocherki*, pp. 119–312.

109. Semevskii, *Krestianskii vopros,* II, 504.

mit lists of their "immovable properties" to the gubernia administrations, identifying the lands their serfs cultivated and the duties they had to perform in payment. Such lists already existed on the Polish serf estates and had been in use long before the Polish partitions, but they were only tax-collecting devices. They had never had anything to do with legal guarantees for the serfs. According to the decree of 1844, the formal filing of these lists would render the serf-cultivated fields inviolable by the landowners, and the obligations the serfs owed their owners would be fixed according to what the lists described. In short, the owners' power over their serfs was to be limited by law.

These limits seemed very sharp in Nicholas's day. Kiselev had recommended that they be imposed on gentry estates throughout Russia in 1841, but Nicholas and his advisors had changed this recommendation into what became the decree of 4 April 1842, which only *allowed* Russian serf owners to draw up inventories in agreement with their serfs if both serfs and owners so desired (see above, sec. D). Even this rather mild request for cooperation was generally thought to be extreme in the 1840s. Bibikov's forced inventories, then, represented a flat violation of gentry rights. Enforced as they were by a resolute and hostile administrator, they constituted a harsh imposition, threatening gentry political influence and social status almost as much as the Liberation Statute itself.[110] Nicholas never would have enacted such a drastic measure had not the Polish gentry constituted at that time the strongest and most dedicated antigovernment element in the empire. Nicholas and Bibikov intended not to destroy serfdom as such or to bring social reform to the countryside but simply to weaken the political power of the government's foes.

Bibikov made his hostility to the Poles quite clear from the very beginning of his term of office. He deplored the government's failure to reward the peasants for not having joined their Polish owners in the rebellion of 1831. As he said in 1839, "During the last rebellion the orthodox peasants displayed an irreproachable loyalty to the government, but . . . afterward, they were given back to their former owners and had to endure cruel persecution. From the government they received nothing whatever for their services, and now they feel very cool toward it."[111]

Bibikov introduced several measures calculated to "free" the

110. The initial "agreements" between the serfs and their owners (*ustavnye gramoty*) that were made in 1861–1863 as the first step in the process of liberation were essentially *inventari*. See P. A. Zaionchkovskii, *Provedenie v zhizn krestianskoi reformy 1861 g.* (Moscow, 1958), pp. 99–101.

111. Quoted in Semevskii, *Krestianskii vopros*, II, 484.

peasants in his area from the domination of institutions still surviving from the days of Polish overlordship. He secularized the Roman Catholic church's lands and introduced the Russian civil code.[112] If Kiselev had not prevented him, he would have handed out the state lands (and peasants) in southwest Russia to deserving Russian gentry (former government servitors) in order to establish a force of loyal landholders.[113] As it was, he abruptly terminated the leases under which the Polish gentry had been farming most of the state lands in his area and set the state peasants directly under Kiselev's administration, doing this much faster than even Kiselev himself desired.[114] By 1844, Bibikov's position was quite clear: he was no friend of the Polish gentry. He did not wish to reform anyone, nor did he concern himself with "progressive" or humanitarian purposes. His campaign to introduce inventories was essentially a tactical measure carried out under the aegis of an army of occupation.

In accordance with the decree of April 1844, Bibikov set up a committee of elected gentry delegates and government agents in each of his gubernias to make up the inventories. The committees labored for two years, and in 1846 they had their inventories. But Bibikov was not satisfied. He complained that the inventories did not follow any standard form and that in any case they were largely trumped up. It would be necessary to check every one. But, he continued, "there are no means for this; we have no competent officials."[115] Bibikov suggested that the government issue a standard form on the basis of "general regulations" and that the inventories be redone.

In response to Bibikov's suggestion, Nicholas issued a new decree on 26 May 1847, this one to apply only to the Southwest. It stated explicitly and in some detail that the serfs' plots were to be inviolable, and it set forth a number of rules limiting the serfs' obligations to their owners. The gentry marshal in each uezd was to read these rules aloud to the serfs on each estate in the presence of the uezd police commandant and the local priest, and each priest was to keep a copy of the decree so that he might explain it to the peasants whenever they inquired about it. Another decree—that of 10 September 1847—ordered trial by military court-martial for any serf owner in the Southwest accused of violating the new rules.[116]

112. German, pp. 277–278.
113. Druzhinin, *Gos. krest.*, II, 33–35; Semevskii, *Krestianskii vopros*, II, 493–494.
114. *Istoricheskoe obozrenie*, III, 29–31. The law of 25 Dec. 1841 terminated the leases.
115. Quoted in Semevskii, *Krestianskii vopros*, II, 494–495.
116. *Ibid.*, p. 497.

By 1847 a battle between gentry and central administration was clearly in progress. The sides, however, were not clear. Bibikov's key agents were not officials in his own organization but the gentry marshals and gentry-elected police commandants, i.e., Polish serf owners. As in the rest of European Russia, gubernia gentry marshals were selected by the minister of internal affairs (in theory, the tsar) from a slate of two candidates nominated by the gubernia gentry assembly. Uezd marshals and police commandants were elected to their posts by the propertied gentry, subject to the approval of the governors— ultimately the minister of internal affairs.[117] Marshals and commandants alike were members of the Polish gentry, selected, or at least nominated, by their peers. It would seem that they constituted a doubtful means for carrying out an attack on their own constituents. Be this as it may, Semevskii's account of the reform in the Southwest shows quite clearly that the commandants and marshals were Bibikov's most reliable agents in his attack on their associates.

The decree of 10 September 1847 urged serfs to appeal to the gentry marshals if their owners violated the rules regarding inventories. Some serfs did so, but it often happened that when they sent delegates to the marshal in the uezd town, their owner quickly called out the local police captain (*stanovoi pristav*—see below, ch. V, n. 89) to punish them for their "revolt." The delegates would return from their visit with the marshal to find that the police had beaten and intimidated a substantial number of their constituents. This happened often enough to call forth an order from Bibikov directing the police captains (that is, his own subordinates) not to interfere in quarrels between serfs and owners but always to call in the police commandants. The commandants, it seems, were men of higher quality and more reliable.[118]

The rules of May 1847 proved too rigid to be workable. Grain does not ripen in accordance with schedules or labor contracts. A strict limit on the number of days the serf had to work for his owner each week was inapplicable during harvest time. In 1848, therefore, the government issued yet another decree introducing new rules that allowed for local and seasonal variations, and the composition of inventories began all over again. Only in 1852 were they at last com-

117. This was essentially the arrangement that Catherine had established (see above, ch. II, sec. D), except that the Senate's power of final approval for gentry-elected offices had been taken over by the minister of internal affairs. The Polish gentry elected the same officials under the same laws as did their counterparts in the interior gubernias, with one exception: in most western gubernias only those gentry could be elected who had done at least ten years of government service. See Korf, pp. 548–550, 566–567.
118. Semevskii, *Krestianskii vopros,* II, 497–498.

pleted to the government's satisfaction.[119] In that year Bibikov went off to St. Petersburg to become minister of internal affairs, and the battle between administration and gentry in the Southwest came to an end. It was a victory over traditional gentry privilege, but the gentry themselves seem to have won it.

Admittedly, the reform in the Southwest was the product of a unique situation and a unique administrative action. When Bibikov became minister of internal affairs in 1852, one of his first acts was to issue a decree—that of 22 December 1852—ordering that his rules regarding inventories in the Southwest be put in force in the remaining gubernias of western Russia. As minister, however, Bibikov was unable to enforce his decree, and on 15 April 1854, with the Crimean War already in progress, Nicholas I set it aside, replacing it with an order that the gentry of western Russia form committees to set up their own rules for drawing up inventories. There the issue rested until 1857.[120] Perhaps if the Crimean War had not intervened, Bibikov could have accomplished something in western Russia from his ministerial post, but the prospects were not promising in 1854. As a minister of the central government, he could not pursue and push the landowners of all western Russia with the same concentrated vigor that had served him so well when he had enjoyed the powers of a governor-general and had had a smaller area to contend with.

The fact remains that Bibikov could not have carried out his reform in the Southwest without the cooperation of the gentry. He had units of the Russian army available, but they only gave him the power to make threats. If the gentry had failed to organize themselves to carry out his commands, Bibikov could have used his regiments to punish

119. *Ibid.*, pp. 499–503. Zaionchkovskii, *Otmena*, pp. 59–60, would have it that the inventories were not in fact satisfactory. What he means, however, is simply that they did not change the peasants' situation fundamentally within a short time after they were completed. It is doubtful, however, that Bibikov himself expected this much. The inventories were only an administrative change, not a social reform; the best that could have been expected from them was a gradual withering away of the landowners' power. A report from the governor of Kiev on 17 Dec. 1863 says that up until 1861 the peasants of Kiev "had been almost completely dependent" on the landowners: "*Within the limits established by the inventories*, the peasant economy depended completely on the landowners. . . . Even the domestic affairs of the peasants were structured and their quarrels, such as they were, decided, according to the advantage of the landowners or their agents" (quoted in *Otmena . . . na Ukraine*, p. 288; italics mine). After one decade, then, Bibikov's rules remained in effect but had not yet given rise to social reform. This was unsatisfactory only in the light of utopian expectations. Ignatovich, pp. 204–208, 218–220, acknowledges that the inventories introduced more effective regulations into the serf estates, and this, after all, was what they were intended to do.

120. Semevskii, *Krestianskii vopros*, II, 511–513.

them, but with all his authority and all his regiments, Bibikov could not have compelled the gentry to organize *if they had not been capable of it.* He could make it "necessary" for the Polish gentry to obey his commands, but he could not compel them to recognize the necessity and respond to it collectively in the way he desired. With all due recognition for the administration's unique and vital contribution to Bibikov's reform, then, we are forced to conclude that an equally vital sine qua non for its success lay in the ability of the Polish gentry in the Southwest to organize themselves.

Why was Bibikov able to rely on the very gentry whose privileges he was attacking? One of his subordinates, Iu. F. Samarin, suggested at least the beginnings of an answer when he compared the serf estates in the Southwest with those in Malorossiia across the Dnepr.[121]

In the 1850s Malorossiia was profoundly disorganized. It was the only area in European Russia in which the government had not yet been able to carry out a survey of the land. As we have seen, peasant migration there had been effectively halted only in the 1780s, when a crude gentry society had been identified officially (and somewhat artificially) for the first time. Most of the gentry estates in the area were still interstripped with each other. Indeed, they would remain in this condition until after 1906, a clear sign that much of gentry society was not far removed from that of the peasants.[122]

It was Samarin's opinion that it would actually be a harder task to establish estate inventories in Malorossiia than it had been in the Southwest, despite the fact that the gentry of Malorossiia were loyal, Orthodox Russians while those of the Southwest were disloyal, Roman Catholic Poles. As Samarin saw it, the reliability of the gentry did not depend so much on their political attitudes or even their national identity as it did on the degree to which they were capable of organizing themselves. "However little sympathy the Poles have for the peasantry, they have been governing themselves in orderly fashion for a long time. In Malorossiia, however, [the Russian gentry] have not."[123] Let the gentry of the Southwest speak Polish, adhere to the pope, and hate the tsar. No matter; they were capable of sustained cooperation among themselves. One could conduct negotiations with them and make lasting arrangements. Were the gentry of Malorossiia

121. *Ibid.,* pp. 509–510.
122. Bochkov, pp. 76–82, 102. In 1906 the *average* surveyed plot (*dacha*) in Chernigov and Poltava gubernias contained strips of land belonging to three villages, four large landholders, and twenty-seven small landholders, all of them scattered about among each other. This sort of thing existed here and there in other areas, but in Malorossiia it was typical. See also above, n. 41.
123. Quoted in Semevskii, *Krestianskii vopros,* II, 509.

relatively loyal? No matter; their loyalty was no use to the government or to the cause of peasant reform unless they could articulate their common interests and act within a recognizable institutional framework. To put Samarin's views in modern terms, the Malorossiian gentry could not organize themselves around a common awareness of their dependence on legal-administrative system, whereas the Polish gentry could. Consequently, the Malorossiian gentry could be neither used nor governed in orderly fashion, whereas the Poles could.

Samarin's observations point to an important and continuing feature in the domestic administration of the Imperial Russian government: namely, that no matter how "absolute" the "power" of the central government was, it could not force society to reform until the members became capable of formulating their own interests and policies. If the tsarist statesmen wished to reform rural society without shattering it, they had somehow to find and strengthen those very institutions that would be likely to oppose the government. The whole history of the tsarist government's struggle to impose system on the countryside unfolded within the framework of this seemingly paradoxical "axiom." The abolition of serfdom, for example, had to be delayed until the serf owners themselves were ready to carry it out *and also to oppose it.*

It is very doubtful that anyone consciously followed Bibikov's example during the enactment of the Liberation. In 1852–1854, when Alexander II was still the heir apparent, he was one of the most active opponents of Bibikov's attempts to impose inventories on western Russia.[124] Nevertheless, Bibikov's experience does make a certain amount of sense of the way the Liberation developed. Both Bibikov and the "liberators" had to formulate their programs in the absence of usable bureaucratic agencies, and they both had to rely on elements in the countryside that were hostile to the programs and to the central administration. There was only one major difference between Bibikov's reform and the Liberation from an administrative point of view. Bibikov intended from the beginning to force change on a recalcitrant gentry and only later discovered that he had to rely on them; Alexander II believed at the outset that it would be not only undesirable but physically impossible to force the gentry to revamp their institutions. Both reforms evolved inadvertently, and their similarity was also inadvertent. Both evolved from experience, not preconceived ideology or purpose, and this is what makes their evolution instructive concerning the practical problems that faced would-be reformers in tsarist Russia.

124. A. A. Kornilov, *Obshchestvennoe dvizhenie pri Aleksandre II* (Moscow, 1909), p. 13.

It remains to discuss the decision to "liberate" the serfs in 1856–1861. As has been said, the government did not originally intend to assault the gentry. In 1855–1856 politically conscious Russians were generally agreed that the military setback in the Crimea had given rise to a crisis and that some sort of reform had to be introduced.[125] It seemed, therefore, that the formulation of specific measures would not present any serious difficulties. K. D. Kavelin wrote up an optimistic program of reform in 1855 in which he assumed that gentry and bureaucracy would work hand in hand.[126] At about the same time Dmitri Miliutin, war minister from 1861 to 1881, was arguing that universal conscription was necessary to the development of a modern army and pointing out that conscription would be impossible under serfdom.[127] Surely, then, the time was ripe to rally serf owners and government together to work out sweeping reforms.

But the reformers' optimism was shortlived. Until Alexander II signed the Liberation Statute on 19 February 1861, neither government nor rural gentry ever reached a consensus on how serfdom was to be reformed, nor was anyone able to find a suitable basis for cooperation between them. The process of enactment was not to be one in which some knowing and far-sighted person or persons devised a statute and struggled for years against the opposition of stupid reactionaries to get it through at last. The Statute took form in the course of a frenzied and disorderly debate that often involved more than two sides, and by the time it was enacted, it had far outstripped the assumptions and intentions of those who had commenced its enactment.

Historians have long proceeded on the utterly unwarranted assumption that since the Liberation Statute was an idea, it must have begun with the man or men who first articulated it. They have dug up several "real authors." We have Kavelin, whose paper of 1855 attracted much attention in government and court circles (see above, n. 126); Baron Haxthausen, whose note of June 1857 Alexander II read and agreed with;[128] A. M. Unkovskii and A. A. Golovachev, gentry marshals from

125. Rieber, pp. 11, 23–30.
126. Printed in his *Sobranie sochinenii* (4 vols., St. Petersburg, 1897–1900), II, 5–88. According to D. J. MacIntyre, "Constantine Dmitrievich Kavelin" (unpublished Ph.D. dissertation, State University of Iowa, 1966), pp. 106–121, 130, the note was well received in St. Petersburg society.
127. A serf who went in the army was automatically freed. Universal conscription, therefore, would have liberated all male serfs fit for military duty within a generation or so after its introduction. See Miliutin's note of 29 Mar. 1856 in *Otmena . . . na Ukraine*, pp. 95–96, and Zaionchkovskii's introduction to Dmitri A. Miliutin, *Dnevnik D. A. Miliutina* (4 vols., Moscow, 1947–1950), I, 17.
128. Zaionchkovskii, *Otmena*, pp. 74–75, discusses Haxthausen's note. Druzhinin, *Gos. krest.*, II, 558, testifies to its influence on Alexander II.

Tver gubernia, who composed a memoir and presented it to the tsar in December 1857;[129] and at last Nicholas Miliutin, Ia. A. Solovev, E. Lode, Iu. F. Samarin, and Vladimir A. Cherkasskii, all of whom played leading roles in drafting the Statute.[130] With all due regard for the genius and contributions of these men, the fact that their notions bore some resemblance to the Liberation Statute does not necessarily testify either to their foresight or to the stupidity of the men who opposed them. Above all, their early advocacy of radical reform does not demonstrate that the process of enactment was a matter of other men coming to recognize what good ideas these innovators had.

As said before, Kavelin predicated his proposals of 1855 on a co-operative gentry. In August 1857, when he observed that the gentry were not cooperating, he abandoned his own project and concluded that the abolition of serfdom would be decades in coming.[131] His proposals, therefore, can hardly be called guides for the subsequent steps taken to enact the law of 1861. Haxthausen's notions (see above, n. 128) were too general to be called practical proposals. Unkovskii and Golovachev set forth a specific program, but they, like Kavelin, failed to take into account that their views were acceptable to only a small minority of the gentry and that the enactment of their proposals would demand some kind of imposition from above. In 1859, as soon as they saw that the government was pushing the gentry into reform by decree, both of them turned vehemently against the enactors of the Statute and the Statute itself. Unkovskii maintained his opposition to the point of refusing to participate in its execution.[132] However useful his and Golovachev's earlier notions may have been, then, they were no guiding light for a tsar who was engaged in stuffing a reform down the gentry's throats while trusting in them to carry it out.

Turning to the enactors themselves, it must be acknowledged that

129. Kornilov, *Ocherki,* pp. 180–185; Portal, pp. 86–87. The memoir is translated in part in Emmons, pp. 427–443.
130. On Miliutin, Solovev, and Lode, see Portal, pp. 100–101, and Druzhinin, *Gos. krest.,* II, 555. On Samarin and Cherkasskii, see Boris E. Nolde, *Iurii Samarin i ego vremia* (Paris, 1926), pp. 112–135.
131. MacIntyre, pp. 137–144.
132. Emmons, pp. 248–255, 263, 334. Emmons would doubtless disagree with the above interpretation of Unkovskii's views. Nevertheless, it is drawn largely from his discussion. Unkovskii's candidacy for the role of "real author" suffers even greater damage from his unseemly willingness to mix his constitutional demands for local autonomy and modern justice with less altruistic notions: that the serfs were getting too much land (Zaionchkovskii, *Otmena,* pp. 114–115) and that the gentry should retain their dominant position in the countryside (Emmons, p. 255). Such proposals may demonstrate Unkovskii's ability to make political compromises, but they were not the sort of thing to inspire the government's confidence in him as a guide to action.

they were brilliant and able men, but they were also typical capital-city minds, capable of talking at length and in detail about laws and reform programs without saying anything meaningful about who would enforce and carry them out against what opposition. The implication that lay hidden in all their ideas was that if worse came to worst, regiments could be sent. Take Nicholas Miliutin, for example. Leroy-Beaulieu calls him "the purest representative of Russian official-dom."[133] His contribution to the development of a coherent program of action cannot be doubted. As deputy minister of internal affairs in 1858–1861, he played a leading role in selecting the editing commission (see below, pp. 185–186) and also in managing it.[134] Nevertheless, his notions concerning *who* was to carry out his programs were less than well developed. He was fond of saying that he believed the "liberal" gentry would carry through the Liberation despite "intrigues" in the bureaucracy and the court,[135] but he himself became the main force behind his ministry's activities to prevent the gentry from playing any role in the enactment process. In the event, it was Miliutin's activities that drove many "liberals" into opposition.[136]

The real implication of Miliutin's faith in the cooperation of "liberal" gentry came into somewhat clearer focus in 1863, two years after the Liberation, when Alexander called upon him to impose a peasant reform in Poland. Here he could no longer pretend that he would have "liberal" gentry to work with, and in their absence he turned without hesitation to regiments.[137] "It is necessary," he wrote from Poland in late 1863, "to act in a dictatorial manner. We cannot think of proceeding in any other way."[138] In Poland in 1863–1866, as in Russia in 1858–1861, Miliutin the reformer was essentially Alexander II's hatchet man:[139] a proper successor to Bibikov, though he seems to have lacked Bibikov's ability to use people without resorting to outright force.[140]

133. Anatole Leroy-Beaulieu, *Un homme d'état russe* (Paris, 1884), p. 4.
134. *Ibid.*, pp. 41–45. Field, however, pp. 288–303, 415–475, suggests that Rostovtsev's role in the editing commission was far more important than Miliutin's.
135. Leroy-Beaulieu, pp. 76–79.
136. Emmons, pp. 219–222, 228–234, 329.
137. Leroy-Beaulieu, pp. 153–154, 217–218. See also S. J. Zyzniewski, "Miljutin and the Polish Question," in H. McLean *et al.*, eds., *Harvard Slavic Studies*, IV (The Hague, 1957), 243–246.
138. Quoted in Leroy-Beaulieu, p. 221.
139. *Ibid.*, pp. 171–174.
140. See *ibid.*, pp. 250–257; R. F. Leslie, *Reform and Insurrection in Russian Poland, 1856–1865* (London, 1963), pp. 236–240.
A detailed and valuable study of Miliutin's activities and attitudes before 1858 may be found in W. B. Lincoln, "Nikolai Alekseevich Milyutin and Problems of State Reform in Nicholaevan Russia" (unpublished Ph.D. dissertation, University of Chicago, 1966). As Lincoln shows, pp. 120–121, 146–152, Miliutin believed throughout his active life that reform in Russia could only come from a

The other "bureaucratizers" all shared Miliutin's general attitude to some degree. Samarin, Cherkasskii, and Solovev were also called to Poland in 1863 to apply their experience at attacking gentry to the rebellious Polish aristocracy, and they all seem to have performed well.[141] Solovev and Lode had worked for Kiselev before the Liberation and had demonstrated their cheerful readiness to assume that the government could administer any law or reform they enacted so long as it looked orderly on paper.[142] As for Samarin, the henchman and admirer of Bibikov, it is worth noting that he spent twelve days in the Petropavlovsk fortress in 1849 for writing a denunciation of the Baltic German noblemen together with a demand that the government deprive them of their political rights and set a purely Russian administration over the Baltic gubernias, this despite the obvious fact that these territories were the best administered in the empire.[143] In the late 1850s Samarin seems to have been somewhat more frank about what the Liberation would represent than his bureaucratizing colleagues. He justified his advocacy of radical reform by maintaining openly that even ill-advised and harsh government action was better than no action at all,[144] a much more satisfactory statement of the bureaucratizers' policy than the rhetoric about "liberal" gentry, "effective" organization, and "dedicated" agents that Miliutin and Solovev were fond of using to avoid considering the means they might have to employ.

It would seem, then, that the Liberation Statute was not an especially good idea except from hindsight. It was not obvious in the late 1850s that serfdom had to be done away with immediately in order to avoid some impending catastrophe. Most of the spokesmen who believed this believed it for the wrong reasons, and in any case they generally ignored the practical problems involved.[145] Given the central

central government administration backed by an autocrat and that any prior consultation with the social groups to be affected by the reform would only hold things up and distort the government's purposes. Lincoln also shows, however, pp. 28–30, 37, that Miliutin had little use for the bureaucracy as it was and that he scorned the majority of his colleagues in it. He regarded routine bureaucratic work as a degrading and stultifying waste of time suitable only for lesser beings. Miliutin's projects, then, were not without contradictions, and they were not very reassuring to a tsar who had to consider the *means* to action.

141. Leroy-Beaulieu, pp. 192–196.

142. Druzhinin, *Gos. krest.*, II, 195–206, describes Lode's experiments with radical land reform in Samara and Saratov and gives Solovev's evaluation of them.

143. Nolde, pp. 35–49.

144. *Ibid.*, pp. 68, 73.

145. Concerning the irrelevance of most of the ideas advanced by would-be emancipators in the decades preceding 1861, see Skerpan, pp. 184–193, and

administration's weakness at the time, it could be and often was argued soundly and reasonably that the safest thing for the government to do was to let the matter ride for a time and try to use more subtle means to push the gentry into doing something on their own.[146] Of the highest-level statesmen who completed the enactment of the Liberation in 1861, many of them started out in 1856 as either indifferent (Ia. I. Rostovtsev) or opposed (Grand Duke Konstantin and Alexander II) to the idea of the central government's imposing radical reform on the gentry.[147] Only under the pressure of events did these men reluctantly come to accept a reform that ultimately resembled Bibikov's attack on the Poles more than it did any of the high-sounding projects of the late 1850s.

In sum, the enactment of the Liberation was not a matter of a few far-sighted intellectuals persuading the statesmen to accept a preconceived plan or policy; nor was it a deliberate finding of facts and gathering of opinions in order to arrive at the best of all possible decrees; nor was it a judicious balancing of interests to achieve the compromise that came closest to satisfying everyone. It could not be any of these things, because no one at any stage of the enactment had any notion of what to do that was both coherent and practicable. What produced the Liberation Statute was a disorderly series of blundering gambles taken by men who hardly knew they were gambling. The end result in 1861 was not a culmination of reasoned judgment but a desperate attempt to escape the trap into which the statesmen's own experimentation had driven them. Had Alexander not been trapped, it is doubtful that he ever would have issued the Statute of 1861, which was itself the most desperate gamble of all.

It must be emphasized that the bureaucratizing liberals were not

---

Alexander Gerschenkron, "The Problem of Economic Development in Russian Intellectual History of the Nineteenth Century," in Edward Simmons, ed., *Continuity and Change in Russian and Soviet Thought* (Cambridge, Mass., 1955), pp. 15–33.

146. See Zaionchkovskii, *Otmena*, pp. 68–74.

147. Rostovtsev only began to favor the complete separation of the serfs from their owners in June 1858. See Druzhinin, *Gos. krest.*, II, 557–558. As for the Grand Duke Konstantin, he wrote to Kavelin in Oct. 1857 that he thought there should be a long postponement before the serfs were separated from their owners. See MacIntyre, p. 144.

Lanskoi, minister of internal affairs in 1855–1861, also played a leading role in the enactment, and most authorities—Rieber, pp. 31–32, is an exception—claim that he, too, was initially either opposed or indifferent to any immediate reform of serfdom. This is what Levshin, p. 548, his direct subordinate, said about him. Druzhinin, *Gos. krest.*, II, 537, says that Lanskoi was "lacking in initiative." Field, pp. 246–247, says that Lanskoi was not an abolitionist by conviction but acted like an advocate because of his belief in organizational discipline, i.e., obedience to the tsar.

less intelligent or less balanced than the relatively conservative servitors and gentry. Quite to the contrary, they saw further and more
clearly than most of their contemporaries. They were, however, a part
of capital-city society, and they were to some extent prisoners of its
illusions. In 1861 Alexander had more to do than simply realize the
correctness of their proposals; he had to accept the necessity of taking
a chance on them.

The question of serfdom began to evolve into a crisis when Alexander II made a speech to the Moscow gentry on 30 March 1856,
expressing his wish that the serf owners do something about it. There
was nothing in the speech itself that Nicholas I (and even Catherine
II) had not already said many times,[148] but Alexander was speaking
virtually in public to an audience that had at last begun to give some
serious consideration to the reform of serfdom. Words that had been
little more than moral sermons before the 1850s were now germane to
a growing debate. In 1856 the salons were already in the habit of
going into a frenzy of interpretation at every word Alexander uttered,
trying to find some sign of the great things he was going to do. Thus
his remark to the Moscow gentry that he wanted them to do something
about serfdom was taken by many of the winterpalaceologists of the
day as a statement of his intention to act.

It seems, however, that most serf owners did not draw this conclusion. The vast majority of them felt neither compulsion nor inclination to move toward reform on their own.[149] After all, Alexander was
also dismissing Kiselev and Bibikov from their ministerial posts, and
this suggested anything but an intensification of government pressure.
For a year and a half after Alexander's speech the gentry assemblies
remained unanimously silent on the subject of reform, and by the
summer of 1857 the government had concluded that the serf owners
were not going to respond. Alexander's secret committee—which he
had appointed in early 1857 to consider the problem of serfdom—
recommended in effect that since the gentry were not yet ready for
reform, it should be postponed indefinitely. Alexander approved this
recommendation.[150]

Then came the break. In the early fall of 1857 a note came in from

148. In 1842 Nicholas said to his State Council, "There is no doubt that serfdom as it is presently constituted is an evil . . . but to abolish it now would
make matters worse." Nevertheless, he continued, change must come eventually
if peasant uprisings like Pugachev's were to be avoided. See "Materialy . . . k
biografii Nikolaia I," pp. 114–115. For Catherine II's statement, see above, sec.
C.

149. See Field, pp. 159–244, 652–668.

150. Zaionchkovskii, *Otmena*, pp. 79–82.

the governor-general of the Northwest—the "Lithuanian" gubernias of Vilna, Grodno, and Kovno—informing the minister of internal affairs that the gentry in his territory wanted permission to draw up a program for liberating their serfs.

The request of the Lithuanian gentry was hardly encouraging in itself. For one thing, it was less than spontaneous. The ministry of internal affairs had exerted considerable unofficial pressure to get the gentry to make it.[151] For another, the gentry were obviously not striving for reform. Their request indicated that they intended to free their serfs *without land,* an idea that had been denounced repeatedly by Nicholas I and his statesmen on the ground that it would lead to a worse victimization of the peasants than they had suffered under serfdom.[152]

In fact, the request was only a move to forestall any renewal of Bibikov's old campaign to force inventories on the serf estates. The gentry of the Northwest, over 90 percent of whom relied on barshchina labor to farm their lands, calculated that if they "freed" the peasants without land, they would frustrate any attempts by the government to turn over parts of their estates to the serfs in permanent tenure.[153] The Baltic gentry had played this trick about a half-century before. Alexander I had tried to force them to accept inventories on their estates in 1804,[154] but they had escaped this annoying limitation on their political power by securing his permission in 1816–1819 to free their serfs without land. In 1857 the Lithuanian gentry were attempting to do exactly the same thing.[155] Indeed, they had already tried to play the Baltic trick twice before, in 1848 and again in 1854.[156]

Nevertheless, for all its limitations, the note from the northwestern governor-general provided the government with the spark it needed. The ministry of internal affairs submitted it to Alexander with the recommendation that he allow the Lithuanian gentry to draft a program of emancipation. The ministry also set forth a few principles on which the program should be based, mainly that it offer not only personal freedom to the serfs but also ownership of their house lots and hereditary tenure on sufficient cultivated land to support them-

151. Levshin, pp. 484–486. See also Emmons, pp. 60–62; Zaionchkovskii, *Otmena,* pp. 82–83.
152. See, e.g., "Materialy . . . k biografii Nikolaia I," p. 116; Field, pp. 36–38. The gentry's request suggested that they would follow the example of the Baltic gubernias, where the serfs had been freed without land in 1816–1819. See Levshin, pp. 524–525.
153. Bochkov, p. 86.
154. See Predtechenskii, p. 176.
155. Bochkov, pp. 40–41.
156. Leslie, p. 72.

selves. Alexander approved the ministry's recommendations and turned them over to his secret committee, ordering that august assemblage of anti-reformists to embody them in a reply to the serf owners of the Northwest. The resulting document was the rescript of 20 November 1857.[157]

Not satisfied with addressing himself only to the gentry of the Northwest, Alexander published his rescript to all the gubernias of European Russia, proclaiming to the people at large that all serfs were to be freed, that their house lots were to be sold to them as their personal property, and that they were to have hereditary tenure on enough plowland to support themselves. The gentry in each gubernia were "invited" to elect committees to compose detailed recommendations for how this was to be carried out in their respective gubernias.[158]

In retrospect, it is clear that the rescript of November 1857 marked the point of no return.[159] The tsar had promised publicly that the serfs would be freed, and there could be no turning back from his fundamental commitment. There had been no real threat of peasant violence before. Now, however, the peasants had concrete expectations, and the government-society's old fear that a reform of any kind would arouse the peasants' hopes and plunge them into revolt grew more intense.[160] But fear of peasant violence was no longer a reason for

157. Field, pp. 119–131.

158. P. I. Iakushkin, "Velik bog zemli russkoi," in *Russkie ocherki* (3 vols., Moscow, 1956), II, 118–119, describes the reaction to the November rescript among the peasants. Henry Troyat, *Tolstoy* (New York, 1967), p. 191, describes the rejoicing among the liberal intellectuals. A letter from Ivan Turgenev to Lev Tolstoi said of the rescript: "The event so long awaited is now at hand, and I am happy to have lived to see it." Prince Vladimir A. Cherkasskii, *Kniaz Vladimir Aleksandrovich Cherkasskii* (Moscow, 1879), p. 276, also refers to the general jubilation in Russia when the rescript was published.

159. As Dzhanshev says, "All the lots were cast" (pp. 21–22).

160. Emmons, p. 223, and Field, pp. 170–171, both maintain that peasant violence was not actually serious in 1857–1861. Soviet scholars, on the other hand, lay great stress on it as a sign of rising peasant rebelliousness. Violence did reach higher levels in 1857–1861 than it had in the early 1850s. According to S. B. Okun's introduction to *Krestianskoe dvizhenie v Rossii v 1857-mae 1861 gg.* (Moscow, 1963), pp. 11–14, the average annual number of peasant disturbances in the period 1850–1856 was 59. In 1857 there were 100; in 1858, 378; in 1859, 161 (excluding the widespread riots in favor of the prohibition of alcoholic beverages); and in 1860, 108. The most violent years prior to the 1850s had been 1826 (104 outbreaks) and 1848 (161 outbreaks). A more recent study—B. G. Litvak, "Dvizhenie pomeshchichikh krestian v velikorusskikh guberniiakh v 1855–1863 gg.," in *Ezhegodnik . . . 1964*, p. 563—asserts that there was a far stronger wave of peasant disruption in 1858 than in any other year in the nineteenth century before 1861.

But if peasant violence was somewhat more widespread in 1858 than in the years preceding, it was still far from overwhelming. Somewhat less than 10 percent of the serf owners experienced some form of resistance. See *ibid.*, p. 564. On the

inaction. On the contrary, according to a police report for 1858, it was now hesitation that posed the greatest danger. Having promised the reform, the tsar had to get it enacted as rapidly as possible.[161]

The enactment of the November rescript was in some respects a theatrical display. Alexander and the reforming officials of the ministry of internal affairs seem to have come to the end of their rope by the fall of 1857 and to have given up the possibility of serious reform within the near future. The petition from the Northwest was a final blow of sorts, a new and yet more vivid display of the serf owners' indifference and hostility. Instead of becoming even more discouraged, however, Alexander (and his ministry of internal affairs) reacted, intentionally or unintentionally, by transforming the serf owners' opposition into an affirmation of reform. Alexander did not denounce the serf owners of the Northwest for trying to sidestep the government's demands. On the contrary, he thanked them profusely for their loyal support and affected to welcome their proposals.[162] His rescript began with the expression "Fully approving the intentions of the representatives of the gentry of Kovno, Grodno, and Vilna gubernias as agreeing with my views and desires. . . ."[163] Alexander even carried the comedy into his personal correspondence. On 22 November he wrote a note to his friend Bariatinskii, then viceroy of the Caucasus, saying, "The great question of the emancipation of the peasants has just taken its first step forward. The gentry of three Lithuanian gubernias have just asked me to free their peasants. Naturally, I have consented by sending a rescript to Governor-General Nazimov, setting forth the general bases on which they can proceed. . . . God grant that the gentry of the rest of the Empire will soon follow their example."[164]

It is difficult to account for this sort of talk in an intimate letter to a

---

other hand, it is probably quite true that the *threat* of peasant violence was growing. Certainly many statesmen believed this. In mid-1858 Rostovtsev proposed that governors-general be established throughout Russia to act against possible rebellions, and for a while Alexander was inclined to approve the idea. See Dzhanshev, pp. 40–43.

161. Zaionchkovskii, *Otmena*, pp. 98–100, 108.

162. Kornilov, *Ocherki*, pp. 161–163. Levshin, pp. 524–528, claims that as deputy minister of internal affairs, he was instrumental in making and carrying out the ministry's policies during this time. He also claims that he favored the Baltic method of emancipation, which means on the face of it that his words and actions make no more sense than Alexander's. Field's account of the enactment of the rescript (see above, n. 149), on which I have relied, disregards much of what Levshin says, probably rightly.

163. Quoted in Kornilov, *Ocherki*, p. 170.

164. Quoted in Rieber, p. 111. In one sense Alexander's "hope" was fulfilled. The Lithuanian gentry did what they could to evade the provisions in the rescript (Leslie, pp. 73–75), and the Russian serf owners followed their example.

close friend except by calling it a sort of party line, or "ideology," or myth that Alexander had to believe and wanted desperately for everyone else to believe.[165] The tsar proclaimed that he and the serf owners were in agreement; ergo, it became the fact that they were in agreement. This was absurd from an objective point of view, but as a myth it suited the government's situation perfectly. With the help of rhetoric, Alexander could begin his attack on the serf owners while trying to secure their support, yet he could still sound as though he was making sense.

During the following year Alexander came to the realization that abolishing serfdom was not going to be easy. Responses to his rescript from serf owners throughout European Russia indicated that the majority wanted no drastic change in the existing relationships on their estates. The owners were not entirely cynical or backward, as some of the Statute's advocates claimed,[166] but the practical suggestions their local committees put forward convinced the government that they were resisting any serious reform. What most of them wanted in effect was that Alexander should leave the serfs to their owners and keep the central administration out of the countryside.[167] Even as they were voicing this desire, however, a number of them seem to have been taking away some of the lands formerly reserved for their serfs' use, in preparation for the time when the government would require that the serfs be granted their allotments in perpetuity.[168]

Sometime in the summer of 1858 Alexander began to disregard the gentry. Instead of leaving it up to their gubernia committees to draft the reform, as the November rescript had proposed, he transferred the whole business of enactment to the central government.[169] In March 1859 he appointed an editing commission from among the known advocates of radical reform and ordered it to draft a detailed program of

165. Field, p. 153, opines that Alexander's letters to Bariatinskii were generally stilted and formal, not intimate. Certainly the tsar-liberator's remarks on the November rescript and the Liberation bear this out.

166. Kornilov, *Ocherki*, pp. 177–181.

167. *Ibid.*, pp. 87–100, 113–119; Dzhanshev, pp. 127–146; Portal, pp. 55–92; Field, pp. 159–244.

168. Zaionchkovskii, *Otmena*, pp. 95–98; Druzhinin, *Gos. krest.*, II, 557.

169. Every student of the Liberation has his own preference for *the* date when Alexander II made his final decision not to rely on the gentry. If there must be such a point, I think Druzhinin's choice is the most convincing. According to him, Alexander's order of 20 July 1858 to his new minister of state domains (see above, sec. D) was the first unambiguous sign that he had given up all hope of voluntary gentry support. It will be recalled that this was the order that abruptly reversed Alexander's intention to do away with Kiselev's organization by commanding the new minister of state domains, Muravev, to extend it to the crown lands.

serf reform in St. Petersburg.[170] No longer would Alexander seek cooperation in the composition of the reform. The tsar and his hatchet men would issue a command, and the gentry would have to obey.

Between early 1859 and late 1860 Alexander's select minority of radical bureaucrats got his statute drafted. In its final form it went much further than the rescript of November 1857 by demanding that the peasants *own* their allotments of plowland outright rather than holding them in hereditary tenure.

Opposition to the projected statute was widespread in the government by the time it got out of the editing commission. Half of the commission's own members refused to sign it,[171] and although the secret committee—now renamed the "chief" committee—obediently gave their formal approval, most of them were still as opposed to government action as ever. Reluctantly they brought it to Alexander in January 1861, whereupon he took it to the State Council in person.[172] Despite his presence at the first session and his flat command that the Council approve the project, a substantial majority of the members rejected a number of key clauses. Undaunted, Alexander approved the minority opinions, and at last, on the evening of 18 February 1861, the Statute came to him for his final signature.[173] He dated it the 19th in honor of his coronation day, although it was not actually published until 5 March.[174]

170. On the establishment of the editing commission, see Emmons, pp. 216–218.

171. Field, p. 475.

172. On the continuing hostility to the Liberation among the members of the chief committee, see Emmons, p. 321. Alexander took the project directly from the chief committee to the general session of the State Council, bypassing its departments, where the Council usually made its decisions. See V. G. Shcheglov, *Gosudarstvennyi Sovet v Rossii* (Iaroslavl, 1903), p. 111. These tactics were precisely the same ones Nicholas I had used in 1842, when he, too, had felt a strong desire for the government to act (see above, n. 82).

173. Dzhanshev, pp. 70–71; Zaionchkovskii, *Otmena*, pp. 122–123; *Gosudarstvennyi Sovet*, pp. 94–99.

174. Zaionchkovskii, *Provedenie*, pp. 23–24, 40–61, makes much of the delay in publication. To him it is conclusive evidence of the government's overwhelming fear of peasant revolt, stemming from what he believes to have been a capitulation by the government to the gentry's demands during the deliberations of 1858–1861. Fear there was, but Zaionchkovskii cites evidence indiscriminately from 1858 and 1861 without noticing that the more extreme plans for military government in 1858 had been consciously abandoned long before 1861 and never again revived. Valuev's diary entry for 21 Jan. 1861 contains the most probable explanation for the delay. See *Dnevnik*, I, 61. Lent began on 8 Mar., and the peasants would be drunk for a week or more before then. In all likelihood, Alexander originally intended to wait until the first Sunday in Lent (12 Mar.) but for some reason changed his mind. Actually, the public reading of 5 Mar. took place only in the capital cities. The greater part of Russia did not hear of the Liberation until Lent—per Alexander's original intention.

It is also arguable that the delay in publication was simply a result of the

It was a dangerous matter to rely on the gentry to carry out a decree while disregarding their express wishes, but Alexander had little choice. In 1858–1861 he was already out on a limb. His rescript of 20 November had changed the abolition of serfdom from a vital but vague necessity into a concrete guarantee of government action that could not be withdrawn. In 1858, when the serf owners' largely useless petitions and projects came flooding in, together with urgent requests from the government's agents to produce the promised reform as soon as possible, the trap shut tight on Alexander II. Everyone in Russia looked to him, but the majority of his people—serf owners, statesmen, and peasants alike—would be opposed to anything he did.

It is worth pointing out that Alexander's position in 1858–1861 bore some resemblance to that of Peter I in 1719–1723 (see above, ch. II, sec. A) and that of Stalin in 1925–1929. In 1719 Peter ordered his gentry to take a census and to collect a new tax in their locales based on the male population. In 1722–1723 it became apparent that the gentry would not get him either census or revenue, whereupon he quartered his army on the countryside to get its revenue for itself. Stalin's forced collectivization of 1930 amounted to the same operation, though he used "workers" instead of soldiers. In 1858–1861 Alexander II contemplated the unpleasant but very real possibility that further pressure on the gentry would either provoke their resistance or disorganize them, resulting in either case in widespread disorder and peasant violence. In this event he would have had to dispatch the army into the countryside, à la Peter I and Stalin. Indeed, Alexander seriously considered making just such a move in 1858 (see above, n. 160). In the end, massive military action proved unnecessary, but the possibility of it deserves emphasis in order to indicate more clearly the risks Alexander was facing and to set the "Liberation" into its proper historical perspective.[175]

F. Significance of the Liberation

It is history that in spite of the dubious origins of the Liberation Statute, the serf owners carried it out. The method used to organize

---

Senate's slowness in preparing it. See Dzhanshev, pp. 72–97. The confusion and general ineptness that accompanied the publication argue for this latter interpretation. For descriptions of the government's blundering, see P. I. Iakushkin, pp. 125–127, and E. P. Pertsov, "Zapiski sovremennika o 1861 g.," *Krasnyi Arkhiv*, XVI (1926), 126–151.

175. Zaionchkovskii, *Otmena*, pp. 152–157, and *Provedenie*, pp. 40–55, describe the military precautions taken in Jan.-Feb. 1861 against possible violence. As said above (n. 174), he grossly exaggerates the matter, but the government was in fact apprehensive.

them was somewhat more dictatorial than the technique Bibikov had used in the Southwest. The ministry of internal affairs selected "arbitrators" (*mirovye posredniki*) from among the serf owners in each locale to supervise the negotiation of contracts between owners and serfs. There was one arbitrator in each *uchastok,* or four to six in each uezd—about 1,700 in all.[176] Ideally, these new officials were to exercise something close to absolute authority over the negotiations between owners and serfs in their *uchastki.* They were authorized to settle most of the disputes that arose during the course of the Liberation, and their approval was required on all the official agreements that the owners made with their former serfs regarding the division of the land. They were appointed officials, but once they were appointed, no higher authority could call them to account unless they violated the law. Even then, only the Senate was empowered to act against them and/or discharge them.[177] Nicholas Miliutin, who was still deputy minister of internal affairs in early 1861, selected the first arbitrators from among those serf owners who were known to be in agreement with the reform.[178] In this way he established a crusading elite of sorts who were relatively free from potentially hostile administrators and influential enough in their locales to direct the activities of their neighbors, if their neighbors cooperated.

On the whole, they did cooperate. Within three years the basic contracts (*ustavnye gramoty*) were signed, specifying the amount of land the serfs were to keep and the amount of "rent" (obrok) they would pay the owners until they purchased their allotments for good. By 1870 most of the serfs, together with the *udelnye* peasants, had completed the purchase of their allotments and commenced paying for them.[179] There was, it is true, far more peasant violence in April, May, and June of 1861 than there had been in any comparable period of time since Pugachev, but it never reached threatening proportions.[180] Thereafter, the frequency of collective protests decreased rapidly in

176. V. G. Chernukha, "Pravitelstvennaia politika i institut mirovykh posrednikov," in N. E. Nosov *et al.,* eds., *Vnutrenniaia politika tsarizma* (Leningrad, 1967), pp. 197–238.

177. Zaionchkovskii, *Otmena,* pp. 148–150, describes the administrative structure within which the arbitrators worked. See also below, ch. VI, n. 9.

178. Emmons, pp. 330–331; Chernukha, pp. 202–203.

179. Zaionchkovskii, *Provedenie,* pp. 112–113, 142.

180. Emmons, pp. 324–326. By Soviet estimates there were well over a thousand outbreaks following publication of the Statute in 1861 and over 800 in 1862. See Okun, p. 16; L. M. Ivanov, ed., *Krestianskoe dvizhenie v Rossii v 1861–1869 gg., Sbornik dokumentov* (Moscow, 1964), pp. 18–20. Zaionchkovskii, *Provedenie,* p. 65, indicates that the highest incidence of violence came in Apr.–May 1861. The number of peasants directly involved, however, never amounted to more than 2–4 percent of the population. See L. M. Ivanov, pp. 7–8.

rural Russia, and from 1865 to 1900 massive peasant disruption ceased almost entirely.[181] Thus, despite all the very sound reasons for Alexander II to be fearful in 1861, his reform worked.[182] Despite all the very sound reasons the serf owners could find for not cooperating, it was they who made it work.

There were many cases in which the owners interpreted the Liberation Statute to serve their own interests and to keep their former serfs dependent on them.[183] Doubtless, some of the concessions they made to their serfs proceeded only from fear of violent opposition. The fact that about half the serfs did not sign the initial contracts regarding how much land they were to get indicates that tension between serfs and gentry became stronger and more overt after the Liberation than it had been before.[184] In short, the rural gentry of the 1860s did not always act like humanitarian idealists. On the contrary, they seem to have been trying to serve their own interests as best they could.

Much has been made of this. Volumes of statistics and case studies have been compiled to demonstrate that the gentry acted only to serve themselves when they carried out the Liberation.[185] The result of all this work, however, is noteworthy more for its exhaustiveness than its relevance. Doubtless, a diligent historian could compile equally accurate and equally meaningless volumes of documents to demonstrate that a considerable proportion of the gentry suffered from colds while they were carrying out the Liberation. This, however, would not demonstrate that it was only their illness that drove them to implement the law of 19 February. Likewise, the fact that the gentry acted in their own interests bears no necessary relation to the historical significance of what they did, except in an argument with someone who insists that the gentry were all motivated solely by idealism.

What is of historical interest is not the degree to which the Russian gentry were pure in heart but, rather, the fact that they acted in

181. See A. Nifontov *et al.*, eds., *Krestianskoe dvizhenie v Rossii v 1881–1889, Sbornik dokumentov* (Moscow, 1960), pp. 17–23; P. A. Zaionchkovskii, *Krizis samoderzhaviia na rubezhe 1870–1880-kh godov* (Moscow, 1964), pp. 480–481.

182. In *Provedenie*, pp. 88–99, Zaionchkovskii describes the work of the arbitrators with all the hostility he can squeeze out of the evidence, but he is forced to acknowledge that they did the job. Even P. I. Iakushkin, pp. 142–149, who was far from favorable to the government as a whole, praises the achievement of the arbitrators.

183. The most graphic evidence of owners' transgressions against their former serfs that I have seen is in the layouts of some of the villages that emerged from the reform, in P. N. Pershin, *Zemelnoe ustroistvo dorevoliutsionnoi derevni* (Moscow, 1928), e.g., pp. 191–229.

184. Zaionchkovskii, *Provedenie*, pp. 99–113.

185. E.g., *ibid.*, pp. 144–361; L. M. Ivanov.

cooperation with one another to carry out a program they did not approve of in spite of a great many excellent reasons for not doing so. To speak within the framework of gentry mythology, they were obeying their tsar even while he broke their law, seized a portion of their wealth, usurped their status, and sharply curtailed their role in local government. To speak in terms more meaningful to the present day, they were holding their country (society, world) together at a time when neither traditional forms nor practical considerations made it clear what their country was or why anyone should hold it together. Despite all difficulties, the gentry could perceive that a rather vague but very real entity—we are justified in calling it a corporate society— was posing necessities to which they felt compelled to respond, and they organized themselves around this common feeling. They not only "obeyed" the tsar à la Derzhavin, according to their own free interpretation of what he wanted. They also accepted the supreme authority of the tsar's law and attempted more or less consistently to abide by it. Nothing like this had ever happened before in Russia.

Compare the gentry of 1861 with their grandfathers of 1801. It will be recalled that at the beginning of the 1800s the politically conscious gentry depended on each other to *aspire* to bring legal system to Russia. Derzhavin, the *general-prokuror* in 1802–1803, was a highly moral man, and there have been few rulers in history more prone to idealism than Alexander I. Both were intensely loyal to Russia and highly intelligent men. Yet in 1801–1803 neither Derzhavin, nor Alexander I, nor any of the gentry of St. Petersburg felt themselves restrained or "trapped" into sustained collective action by their moral sentiments regarding the institutions of Russian government. Did they affirm that the Senate was a symbol of Russian law and justice? Nevertheless, their affirmation of the Senate, however fervent, did not "trap" them into behaving in any consistent fashion toward it. Alexander I could issue a decree one day and disregard it the next, and no one objected or even thought his behavior unusual—except, of course, for those who happened to disagree with the substance of his action. The Russian statesmen of that time were conscious of their dependence on the Senate as a symbol and a glorified chancellery, but not as a part of a working legal-administrative system.

The gentry of 1861, on the other hand, had become conscious of their dependence on one another to behave in certain ways within a Russia-wide legal framework; otherwise they would not have felt themselves to be trapped by a mere law. Alexander II and his gentry servitors were neither more nor less idealistic than their forebears of 1801, but their sense of being trapped in common by laws and contracts meant that legal-administrative system had acquired institutional force in the government-society.

The gentry's new awareness of dependence was perceptible in both their resistance to the enactment of the Liberation and their acceptance of the Liberation Statute. In 1856–1860 they struggled against the government to preserve the legal structure of serfdom. This we may call a movement in the name of principles of *law*.[186] On the other hand, the tsar's command of February 1861 reorganized the gentry around a common recognition of a principle of *purpose*, i.e., the carrying out of the Liberation. Thus at about the same time the gentry were achieving a measure of cooperation in opposition to the central administration, they were also cooperating to carry out its commands. In both these movements they were demonstrating a common awareness of their mutual dependence and an ability to comprehend, articulate, and organize themselves around an operational system.

What the Liberation signifies is that after a century or more of conscious effort to cultivate the "spirit of law" in Russia, the tsars and their henchmen had at last found an authentic social response to the forms of legal-administrative system. System, in other words, had become to some extent an operational myth in the government-society. To be sure, bureaucracy was not yet ready to act in the countryside in the 1860s, but when and if it did act, there was a society in most of European Russia that would know how to aid and/or oppose it within the framework of a legal system. The hierarchy of bribery and personal influence had not disappeared, but a small part of the population—unfortunately only a very small part—had learned to organize themselves and to function in new ways. The gentry would never learn to love the central government's agencies, but their performance in the 1860s showed that the government could communicate something besides naked authority to them and that they in turn could communicate something besides bribes and faction fights to the central government. For the first time in Russian history a chain of command became conceivable in domestic administration.

Senatorial government and serfdom left behind them the social order that bureaucracy needed, but in their own peculiar way. The more or less orderly interaction between government and society that took place during the enactment and execution of the Liberation involved only about 2 percent of Russia's population,[187] and these 2

---

186. See Field, pp. 159–244, 316–344; Emmons, pp. 249–259, 416–418, indicates that the gentry "movement" of 1859–1862 provided a basis for the subsequent growth of the zemstvo "movement."

187. Ignatovich, p. 380, points out that in 1858 the number of serf owners

percent organized themselves primarily around relationships within their own social order. They did not form ties with the mass of the people. Thus the Liberation did not by any means put an end to the peasants' social isolation. The absence of legal relations with the peasantry came to bureaucracy as a problem not yet resolved. Senatorial government had proven itself unable to cope with it, and bureaucracy itself was in no way prepared to tackle it—not in 1802, when the ministries were established, nor yet in the 1860s, when the government finally abandoned the institutions of senatorial government. After 1861, then, the chief problem and the most characteristic feature of Russian bureaucracy would be the absence of orderly communication between it and the peasant society for whose welfare and good order it had, willy-nilly, assumed full responsibility.

---

who were eligible to participate in the gentry assemblies came to about 24,000—not a very large citizenry, to be sure.

CHAPTER V

The Emergence
of Bureaucracy: 1802-1862

> If the Emperor gives the Senate any real power, he will tie his
> hands so tightly that he will no longer be able to carry out all those
> measures that seem necessary for the welfare of his people.
>
> NIKOLAI NOVOSILTSEV (1802)

> The tsar, lulled by brilliant reports, does not have a true under-
> standing of the present situation of Russia. Standing on an inac-
> cessible height, he does not have the means to hear. No truth dares
> to come to him, nor can it, for all ways to express ideas are closed—
> there are no representatives, no public opinion, no appeals, no pro-
> tests, no controls. . . . In his own office, each minister imagines
> himself to be an autocratic tsar and he too has no opportunity to
> find out the truth about his own organization.
>
> MIKHAIL POGODIN (1854)

A. The Founding of Ministerial Government

Ministerial government came into being on 8 September 1802, when
Alexander I issued a manifesto establishing eight ministries: war, navy,
foreign affairs, justice, internal affairs (minister or ministry hereinafter
referred to as the MVD), finance (hereinafter referred to as the MF),
commerce, and education.[1] In themselves these ministries did not constitute a new form of organization, nor did Alexander intend them to
be new. His aim was essentially the same as his predecessors': to improve the machinery of senatorial government by setting up auxiliary
functional offices to streamline its operation.[2]

1. The ministries of war, navy, and foreign affairs did not change their functional responsibilities to any great extent in the ensuing century, but the number
and composition of the domestic ministries varied considerably. Responsibility
for the state lands, for example, was at first divided between the MVD and the
MF; then, in 1810, it was shifted entirely to the MF; and at last, in 1837, it was
assigned to the newly created ministry of state domains. Thus the above list of
ministries is only an illustration of the general nature of executive organization
after 1802, not a description.

2. *IPS*, III, 5–7. Compare Alexander's intentions with Catherine's in the early
part of her reign (*ibid.*, II, 350–353). Marc Raeff, *Michael Speransky, Statesman
of Imperial Russia* (The Hague, 1957), pp. 43–45, would have it that Alexander

But the creation of the ministries produced an unforeseen result. The manifesto of 8 September ordered each minister to consult with his fellows before making his reports to the tsar, and since the ministers reported regularly in the first years of Alexander's reign, they met frequently and made many of the government's most important decisions. In practice, their meetings became an institution.[3]

The new "Committee of Ministers" (*Komitet Ministrov*) instantly became very powerful. Its members were favorites of the tsar; moreover, the manifesto of 8 September assigned the new ministry of justice to the *general-prokuror*, thereby making this erstwhile powerful official a member and compelling him to submit his decisions to his fellow ministers for their consideration. It will be recalled that the *general-prokuror* was the director of the Senate. He represented the Senate before the tsar and, in turn, conveyed the tsar's commands to it. Thus, when the manifesto of 1802 required him to consult with his fellow ministers before making his reports, it meant that the Senate's communications with the tsar had ordinarily to travel via the Committee of Ministers and undergo its scrutiny.[4] Despite its unofficial nature, then, the Committee was in a position to dominate the Senate.

The intensity of the Committee's activity indicates that the ministers took their power seriously. They met forty-three times during 1803,[5] and during the next few years, when Alexander was absent from St. Petersburg for long periods of time, they acted on and off as a center of administration. The first formal statement of the Committee's functions and procedures came in the decree of 5 September 1805, enacted by Alexander as he departed for the battlefront. Two subsequent laws—those of 31 August 1808 and 20 March 1812—gave it substantially the form it was to have until 1905.[6]

The statute of 1 January 1810 established a new supreme body, the State Council (*Gosudarstvennyi Sovet*), to preside over the govern-

I and his more progressive advisors were consciously attempting to "bureaucratize" Russian government in the early years of the reign. Raeff, however, uses the term "bureaucracy" in an eighteenth-century cameralist sense, e.g., pp. 74–75. In this book, as I have said, bureaucratization refers specifically to the transformation from a collegial administration, which thinks it is finding law in society, to a system of government departments identified by function, which strives to impose reforms on society in order to allow its offices to function properly (see above, ch. I, sec. B). In this context it may be said that neither Alexander I nor his progressive advisors were *consciously* striving to bureaucratize the government.

3. On the accidental origin of the Committee of Ministers, see *IPS*, III, 209–213, and Nikolai Mikhailovich, I, xxviii. See also below, sec. B.

4. Muravev, pp. 320–321.

5. Nikolai Mikhailovich, I, xxxii.

6. Lazarevskii, I, 454–457; *Istoricheskii obzor deiatelnosti Komiteta Ministrov* (5 vols., St. Petersburg, 1902), I, 4–21.

ment as a sort of legislative body and sometime supreme court. Originally, this was intended to be only a temporary measure, designed to prepare the way for a sweeping constitutional reform. The ultimate purpose of its author, Mikhail Speranskii, was to revitalize the Senate as the highest organ of government and to do away with the Committee of Ministers. But Speranskii fell from favor in early 1812, before his last project could be enacted, and Napoleon's invasion put a long halt to further reforms.[7]

In 1818 Alexander made another attempt to establish order among his new supreme organs and to set the Senate at the head of government, but it was no more successful than Speranskii's had been.[8] Nicholas I tried again in 1826. He formed a committee of his most trusted servitors, including Speranskii, and instructed them to devise an orderly scheme of government that would subordinate the ministries to the Senate and do away with the Committee of Ministers as an institution. The committee labored until 1832 and submitted projects for revitalizing the Senate, but Nicholas did nothing with them.[9] Thus the manifesto of 1802 and the laws of 1805–1812 had the ultimate effect of reducing the Senate to a subordinate position and formally establishing ministerial government (bureaucracy) in the general form it would take until 1906.

In the first decades of their existence the new "supreme organs," the State Council and the Committee of Ministers, operated in most disorderly fashion.[10] Their functions and their authority were so poorly defined that despite the power that some of their members could wield, the organs themselves hardly functioned as institutions at all. The State Council occupied a high position during 1810 and 1811 because the tsar regularly attended its weekly general sessions. In early 1812, however, with Speranskii's fall from favor, it ceased to be a center of administrative coordination. Its powers relative to other supreme organs remained considerable, though vague, but it lost any effective control it may have had over the individual ministers.[11] As for the Committee, its rise toward formal status did not increase its control over its members. On the contrary, the ministers seem to have found formalized association an annoying constraint rather than a

7. *Ministerstvo iustitsii*, pp. 32–33; Korkunov, *RGP*, II, 669. The statute is in *PPSZ*, 24064. Speranskii's project for a revitalized Senate had been approved by the State Council and confirmed by Alexander by the time Napoleon came. It needed only printing to become law. Nevertheless, it was abandoned after the war. See Shilder, *Imperator Aleksandr*, III, 6–7.
8. *IPS*, III, 127.
9. *Ibid.*, pp. 142–145, 165–166.
10. See Korkunov, *RGP*, II, 236–241.
11. Shilder, *Imperator Aleksandr*, III, 1–10, 35–48.

means to coordinate their efforts.[12] From about 1810 on, attendance at their meetings fell off sharply.[13]

It seemed to many statesmen in the latter years of Alexander I's reign that the Committee of Ministers was growing more powerful. In fact, it was the individual ministers, if anyone, who were taking over.[14] Supposedly, they were responsible to both Council and Committee, but since they took their orders directly from the tsar (or from the tsar's personal secretary, Alexei Arakcheev), neither of the supreme organs had any solid basis for holding a minister accountable for his actions. In the years following, Nicholas I increased the arbitrary power of the individual ministers further by having them submit reports that he could sign and make into laws without the Committee or Council ever seeing them.[15]

For all its arbitrariness, however, ministerial government continued to be a recognizable organizational structure from 1810 on. The State Council, the Committee of Ministers, and the separate ministries remained the leading institutional elements in tsarist administration until October 1905.

B. General Considerations Regarding the Impact of the Ministries

What was new about the ministries? Stated simply, it was the formal identification of each minister by the functions he was responsible for performing *in coordination with the other ministers*. A minister did not operate entirely on the basis of orders from the tsar to carry out this or that particular mission all by himself. The rules that guided his actions did not merely isolate him from other servitors and keep him from interfering with them. Each minister's authority and his role in government depended to some extent on his relationships with his colleagues within a common scheme of organization.[16]

Before the nineteenth century the tsar's executive agents had been virtually omnipotent individuals sent out to accomplish specific mis-

12. Lazarevskii, II, 170, 177–178. See also *IPS*, III, 433–434.
13. *Istoricheskii obzor . . . Komiteta*, I, 12–13.
14. Shilder, *Imperator Aleksandr*, IV, 4–6. According to Schcheglov, p. 47, one high official noted that each minister had become "a tsar in his own area."
15. Eroshkin, pp. 185, 251. Sometimes Nicholas submitted the ministers' decisions to the State Council *after* he had approved them. In other words, he commanded the Council to accept them. In these cases he was using the Council as a rubber stamp instead of ignoring it outright—insulting it rather than disregarding it. See A. E. Presniakov, *Apogei samoderzhavii* (Leningrad, 1925), p. 45.
16. Troshchinskii, pp. 62–71, 89–92; Pipes, *Karamzin's Memoir*, pp. 227–228; Korkunov, *RGP*, II, 233–241.

sions or to rule over territories. Some of them, to be sure, had been formally designated as heads of seemingly functional offices—*prikazy, ekspeditsii*, etc.—but they had never been brought together on a systematic basis to coordinate their work. Despite their formal designations, therefore, even the *prikazchiki* were identified not by functions—i.e., by parts of a task—but by whole tasks. The purpose of "organization" was not to provide a framework, within which servitors could operate, but to separate them, so that each could be held absolutely responsible for his actions.[17] In practice, this was still the case with Catherine's and Paul's pseudo-ministerial offices, though, as we shall see, the outlines of systematic functional division did begin to emerge in the late eighteenth century.

Pre-ministerial executive agents had not been omnipotent in an absolute sense. They had had specific tasks to carry out, and their authority had been limited to some extent by the nature of these tasks. An agent assigned to build ships would not ordinarily have been called to account for his methods of selecting and supervising his labor gangs, but he might have been imprisoned for exceeding his authority if he had used his laborers to build a mansion for himself.

Nevertheless, the old-style agent was omnipotent in the sense that his purposes and authority were substantially his own. His powers proceeded almost exclusively from the orders the tsar gave him personally, not from a general framework of regulations that set forth the manner in which agents were to relate to each other. The orders that an old-time omnipotent agent received did not tell him to get a certain amount of money from the MF and to secure the cooperation of the MVD's police in a certain area in order to set up some sort of functional organization, such as, for example, a network of schools. Instead, the tsar would simply tell one of his trusted servitors to go out and build a school, taking whatever measures might prove necessary, including the collection of revenue and the negotiation of some sort of agreement with the local population. It will be recalled that when Catherine II sent Rumiantsev to set up a revenue system in Malorossiia, she told him not how to do it but only to use "any suitable

17. See, e.g., Troshchinskii's note of 1816, pp. 89–93, defending senatorial (collegial) administration. In Alexander I's time only a very few tsarist statesmen were capable even of recognizing the need for systematic cooperation among administrators identified by function. Speranskii (pp. 21, 70–74), Simon Vorontsov, and the members of Alexander's secret committee referred to it in a general way from time to time (Predtechenskii, pp. 137–138), but none of these "progressives" realized that there were problems involved in making men cooperate in an organization. The secret committee, for example, had nothing more to offer on the subject than their recommendation that the ministers should be men who agreed with each other politically. See *ibid.*, pp. 136, 207.

means" (see above, ch. IV, n. 39). In sum, the old-time omnipotent agent's orders did not limit his power precisely but instead rendered him absolutely responsible, at least in theory, for the success or failure of his mission, leaving the exact nature of his power to be determined by what he took to be the needs of the situation in which he found himself.

The voevoda had been this sort of official (see above, ch. III, sec. D). Throughout the seventeenth and eighteenth centuries he had operated according to his own separate instructions, designed for him alone. When he took over a territory, he was not bound by the actions of his predecessors, nor did his actions bind his successor. It was only in 1649 that the government began even to try to compel the "office" of each voevoda to maintain a permanent record of the orders that the tsar sent to it, so that orders sent to a given territory would be binding on all the men who came to govern it.[18] It was only in Peter's time that the government made its first serious attempt to impose a common administrative framework on the voevodas in the different territories. Needless to say, the practical effect of these measures was less than instantaneous. The voevoda's de facto authority never ceased to depend largely on his own instructions, his own abilities, and his personal relationships at the court of the tsar. His formal relationships with other agents consisted of little more than a few rules designed to keep him and them out of each other's way.

Ministers could not operate effectively in this kind of isolation. A minister was ultimately answerable to the tsar alone, but his actions could not proceed simply from his reactions to his own day-by-day experience. Before a minister acted, he was supposed to tell his colleagues what he and his ministry were going to do, how much it would cost, and how it would affect their operations; this meant that he had to know these things himself, or at least he had to act as if he knew. He had to predict the results of what he was going to do, so that his colleagues could instruct their subordinates accordingly.

The ministries did not actually function systematically in 1802–1862. An individual minister who enjoyed the confidence of the tsar could often override the wishes and interests of his colleagues and interfere in matters that were quite beyond his official concern. Moreover, there was a general lack of systematic communication between the central offices and the agencies in the countryside. The MF, for example, was supposedly responsible for managing something called the financial system of the empire, but in the early nineteenth century no such system existed except in the capital cities. The simple notion

18. Chicherin, pp. 88–92.

of auditing the financial accounts in the gubernia administrations did not begin to enter into administrative practice in the tsarist government until 1837, and the first set of accounting regulations appeared only in 1846.[19] Before this time a central office had no basis for checking on its local agencies except the appeals and disputes that were brought before it and the occasional inspections it carried out.[20] The same situation prevailed in the army, where the first personnel accounting system was set up only in 1833.[21] Given the absence of an operational system outside the capital cities, then, a minister's orders were likely to produce unforeseen and unintended results when they were carried out.[22]

Nevertheless, the ministers did bring something new to the tsarist government. Their collective responsibility to act like a system, though often ignored in practice, was a serious matter. As we shall see, the ministers were engaged until the very end of the tsarist regime in frenzied efforts to systematize their relationships, indicating that frequent transgressions of system did not reduce their common dependence on it. Unfortunately, this dependence also rendered their organizations massively arbitrary in relation to society as a whole.

Pre-ministerial agents had been powerful as individuals, but their very arbitrariness had enabled them to work directly with existing social-political relationships. Their freedom from systematic coordination had allowed them to act as they saw fit in response to any situation or problem. They could respond to any appeals, settle any disputes, and tap any resources without regard for formal constraints, serving both people and tsar as the situation demanded. In a sense, the omnipotent agent had *communicated* between tsar and people, making the purposes and needs of each at least crudely intelligible to the other. Tsar and people could not see or comprehend each other directly, but an old-time agent could translate the tsar's vague intentions into practically effective actions and decisions, whereas his freedom of action allowed at least some elements in the population to use him to their own advantage through personal negotiation and bribery.

Senatorial government had been able to get along with omnipotent agents throughout its development. Indeed, it could not have existed

19. "Materialy . . . k biografii Nikolaia I," pp. 503–522. The law that first introduced gubernia audits was that of 30 Dec. 1836. See *VPSZ*, 9812.

20. Concerning the absence of effective supervision (*nadzor*) in the government before the 1860s, see Starr, pp. 37–56.

21. *Ibid.*, p. 327. Concerning the introduction of systematic information into the governors' annual reports from 1837 on, see below, ch. VIII, sec. B.

22. Troshchinskii, pp. 46–49.

without them. Despotic agents might ride roughshod over this or that college in specific instances, but in no case did they threaten the very existence of senatorial government. On the contrary, senatorial institutions depended on omnipotent agents to assume responsibility for accomplishing those tasks and resolving those issues that the colleges could not cope with on their own.

The ministries were an entirely different affair. They were opposed to the freewheeling operations of omnipotent agents and, indeed, to the senatorial colleges as well. Neither of these essentially haphazard devices for communicating between tsar and people conformed to the would-be systematic framework within which the ministers were trying to work. Not only did the ministers and their agents find it difficult to make ad hoc arrangements with rural society on its own terms; they could not but oppose the ad hoc arrangements that already existed between government and society, and they tended to oppose any college or personal agent of the tsar that presumed to form any more such arrangements.

As said before, ministerial government was geared not to find the law but to make it. Unlike the Senate, which had tried to work within a systematic framework but had not been responsible for imposing it on the government as a whole, the ministers' responsibility to the tsar was absolute. They were absolutely responsible to the old aspiration to system, which meant that they were collectively responsible to the tsar for the imposition of system on the whole of Russian society. Unlike the old-time omnipotent agents, the ministers were not content merely to violate the existing legal relationships of the countryside from time to time in order to accomplish this or that specific aim. When a minister found officials following procedures that did not conform to his own prescriptions, he wanted to root them out entirely.

It was the combination of the ministers' senatorial pretension to system and their absolute responsibility to the tsar that rendered them more arbitrary from the point of view of Russian society than the old-time omnipotent agents had ever been. The ministers often seemed to be destroying society by their seemingly arrogant insistence on the necessities of their own organizational framework. Although the ideal aim of ministerial government was the same as that of senatorial government—to extend legal-administrative system to Russia—the two orders clashed head on from the beginning.

Alexander I and his statesmen did not intend that the ministers should pursue purposes and nourish attitudes that conflicted with those of senatorial government. Nikolai N. Novosiltsev, the member

of Alexander I's secret committee who originally proposed the requirement that the ministers discuss each other's reports to the tsar, intended only to regularize the operations of the *pravitelstvo*, not to
establish new governing bodies over it.[23] Likewise, we have seen that
when Speranskii gave the State Council a measure of formal status
in 1810, he was striving to subordinate the ministries to the Senate and,
ultimately, to get rid of the Committee (see above, n. 7). It may be
said, then, that the basic institutions of ministerial government took
form and developed on their own momentum, quite apart from the
intentions of the men who did the most to bring about their formal
establishment.[24]

The rise of ministerial government had to be inadvertent. In effect,
it was attacking the senatorial institutions in both form and principle,
but those statesmen who wanted reforms could not say, even to themselves, that effective ministerial action implied the destruction of
senatorial government. No advocate of political, administrative, or
social reform in nineteenth-century Russia professed to believe that
bureaucracy should expand or that society should change in order to
accommodate itself to bureaucratic operation.

Take Count Stroganov, for example. As a member of the secret committee of 1801–1802, he was one of the leading founders of bureaucratic government, yet he considered himself to be an enemy of
bureaucracy. In order to escape the contradiction between his desire
for the government to act as an organization and his belief that it
should not be bureaucratic, he resorted to fantasy. According to his
vision, the emperor would reform the administration in secret in order
to get all the bad men out of it and then set up an orderly judicial
system and inaugurate a reform program. The new program would
provide for the distribution of land to the peasants, including the
serfs. Each family would receive its own integral plot of land. When
the land had been distributed (he did not say how this was to be
done), the peasants would be granted the rights of citizens, and at this
point the secretly reformed central administration would gracefully

23. Korkunov, *RGP*, II, 235–236; Nikolai Mikhailovich, II, 104–109.
24. Predtechenskii, pp. 136–140, indicates that the secret committee agreed to
the need for a formally unified committee of ministers in the spring of 1802
but then shrank back from the idea when they began to perceive its radical
implications. Predtechenskii, however, labors under the unwarranted assumption
that Alexander I and his secret committee had realistic conceptions of administration. Actually, the evidence he cites suggests the contrary; see especially excerpts
from Stroganov's writings on pp. 90–109. Predtechenskii, p. 142, concludes that
the reforms of 1802 produced no essential change in the government but only
gave impetus to *biurokratizatsiia*. My account differs from his only in its insistence
that the impulse to *biurokratizatsiia* did mark an essential change.

disappear. In subsequent years negotiations among the new citizens under the new courts would give rise to law.[25]

Stroganov was not some half-demented revolutionary. On the contrary, he was an educated, intelligent, highly respected Russian statesman of the early nineteenth century. His thinking was typical, not outlandish. Speranskii had a similar fantasy in 1802: a "program" for the gradual elimination of serfdom, in which a select group of young gentry would be educated in western Europe and then sent out into the countryside, incognito, to find the law. While they were poking around, Speranskii said, they could take the opportunity to persuade their less enlightened brethren to give up their serfs.[26] Like Stroganov, the youthful Speranskii avoided open advocacy of a bureaucratic attack on senatorial government by relying on what might be called the mythical power of enlightenment.

Another fantasy that appealed to many tsarist statesmen both before and after the Liberation was the mythical power of paper. This vision included no image of *who* was to carry out reforms but only lists of instructions that would somehow put themselves into effect simply by being printed on paper. Of course, if printed instructions had the power to unite and direct government-society, then there need be no talk of a bureaucratic attack on senatorial government. Instead, senatorial opposition could be denounced as "bureaucratic" formalism —a "bad" adherence to the letter of the law rather than a "good" enthusiasm for its spirit. Armed with the myth of paper power, a reforming bureaucrat could hatch the most preposterous scheme of reform and still see himself as a defender of senatorial government against *biurokratizm*.[27]

Consider D. A. Gurev. He was MF from 1810 to 1823 and should have known better, but he wrote up a project in 1823–1824 at Alexander's behest calling for the granting of allotments to the state peasants in hereditary tenure, each household to receive no less than fifty-four acres. Village lands were to be redivided so that each household had its own integral plot, and three-field agriculture was to be abandoned. In order to carry all this out, an administrator was to be

25. Nikolai Mikhailovich, II, 1–5, 19–25. See also above, n. 24.
26. Speranskii, pp. 50–55.
27. Splendid examples of this attitude may be found in "Zapiska Grafa Dmitriia Nikolaevicha Tolstogo," *Russkii Arkhiv*, no. 5 (1885), pp. 38–40, and in some proposals Mikhail N. Muravev made for reform when he became governor of Mogilev in 1828. See D. A. Kropotov, *Zhizn Grafa M. N. Muraveva* (St. Petersburg, 1874), pp. 254–257. Tolstoi (uncle of Dmitri A. Tolstoi, MVD in 1882–1889) was director of the department of police in the MVD in 1861–1863. He wrote his note shortly after he resigned. Muravev was the man who led the attack on Kiselev in the 1850s (see above, ch. IV, sec. D).

set up in each volost, because, said Gurev, the peasants were too backward to act on their own. This pipe dream, which was quite beyond the government's capability even in 1914, was actually submitted to the State Council in 1824 and given serious consideration. Several of the members thought it a sound idea, and there is no telling where it might have gone had Alexander's death not put an end to the matter.[28]

Kiselev, the most notorious bureaucratizer in the government before the 1850s, never indulged himself in the dreams of Alexander's day, but he held as firmly and sincerely as any of his predecessors to the senatorial belief that government-imposed reform was essentially a method of finding and articulating the law under which the people lived.[29] Unlike Stroganov and his associates, Kiselev did not hide from the implications of his bureaucratizing by burying himself in fantasy. He recognized the negative effects of government-imposed reform when he saw them, and his way to avoid seeing the basic contradiction between bureaucracy and senatorial government was simply to call off his reform programs on the state lands whenever they aroused determined opposition. In practice, he generally introduced and carried out only those reforms that had the peasants' consent,[30] which is why his reform of the state lands was at best moderate and at worst stultifying and self-defeating. Kiselev probably was doing the best that could be done under the circumstances, but the point here is that even he failed to recognize the basic dilemmas involved in a social reform carried out through direct administrative action. When one of his programs failed to go forward, he did not speak of contradictions between bureaucracy and senatorial institutions but resorted to the usual capital-city images of peasant backwardness and corruption in provincial administration.[31]

Even after the forms of senatorial government passed away in the 1860s, its law-finding ideal remained stuck in the government-society and in the personalities of politically conscious Russians. Very few men ever stopped trusting in some variation of the old collegial notion that a legal code (or perfect justice) lay hidden in the customs and practices of the inhabitants of the empire: waiting for some combination of enlightened men, printed instructions, economic development,

28. Druzhinin, *Gos. krest.*, I, 154–164; *Istoricheskoe obozrenie*, I, pt. 1, 23–25.
29. *Ibid.*, pt. 2, pp. 8–10.
30. For example, he accepted the peasant commune as it was, because he knew that the government lacked the means to change it. See Druzhinin, *Gos. krest.*, I, 632. On the face of it, this does not appear to have been a major intellectual achievement, but in the St. Petersburg milieu of would-be reform, such restraint betokened wisdom far beyond the ordinary.
31. *Ibid.*, II, 128–130.

sound plans and policies, revolutionary ideology, and/or local autonomous institutions to find it and set it down in proper form. Instead of trying to see the contradiction between senatorial aims and bureaucratic action, politically conscious Russians generally strove not to see it, mainly because seeing it would have prevented them from making sense of what they were doing and would have precluded any systematic action to cope with the problems they faced. Those who did stop trusting in senatorial aims did not find any alternative ones. Usually, they fell into indifference and despair or took up some active form of nihilism. Social reform carried out by a bureaucracy whose agents realized, albeit dimly, that what they were doing was revolutionary would not come in Russia until after 1905.

Pavel Valuev (the MVD in 1861–1868) is an extreme example of a statesman who despaired.[32] Valuev, be it noted, was an exceptionally perceptive, sensitive, and competent man, seemingly no more or less paranoiac than his colleagues. During his term of office he presided over the processes of liberating the serfs and installing the zemstvoes; that is, he lived and worked for years at the heart of a momentous social revolution. He was one of the most important of the leaders whose activities put an end to senatorial government and set the stage for the relatively unhindered expansion of bureaucracy.[33] He above all others should have had some inkling of the significance of what he was doing. In fact, however, he did not. In everything he did as a statesman his conscious aim was to further the development of senatorial government. He could see with appalling clarity that nothing he or the government was doing was really leading to the establishment of an effective legal system, but he did not conclude from this that his government might be serving some other purpose or approaching some other end. All he could see was that his work was in vain and that the government hovered on the brink of collapse. The actual effect of his work, therefore, was not something he could intend, or foresee, or believe in. Unlike most of his colleagues, he could look at what he was doing without taking refuge in fantasies, but he was never able to accept bureaucracy as a conscious purpose. Paragon of bureaucratizers that he was, he nevertheless loathed bureaucracy.

Since the statesmen of the nineteenth century could not conceive of the growth of ministerial government as a purpose, they could not comprehend, explain, or proclaim the achievements of ministerial

---

32. Valuev's diary for the 1860s is full of doom crying. See, e.g., *Dnevnik*, II, 100, 140–141, 202.

33. Valuev's activities and ideas in the early 1860s are described in Starr, pp. 202–208, 297–368.

government as such. The only defense bureaucracy had was its claim that each of its reforms and institutions promised to fulfill this or that aspiration of senatorial government or to keep this or that senatorial institution from collapsing. Since the ministers' practical programs of reform actually served to undermine senatorial government and, indeed, many of their own basic values, these programs were invariably difficult to defend against informed opposition. This was why a statesman who opposed reform was often able to advance sound arguments in support of his position, whereas those who favored reform usually found nothing to support their plans but specious arguments and banal slogans. Given this general situation, wherein the basic processes of development could not be discussed intelligently except by those who opposed the development, the issues raised in the statesmen's debates and the aims the government pretended to be pursuing tended to be somewhat irrelevant to real needs and problems. It is not surprising, therefore, that nineteenth-century statesmen had difficulty foreseeing the consequences of their actions and that the evolution of ministerial government should have been largely inadvertent.

C. The Breakup of Senatorial Government

It was senatorial government that broke up, not the Senate itself. In 1802 the Senate possessed no *formal* authority; consequently, it cannot be said to have lost any formal prerogatives in the following decades. Nor did it lose its sanctity as a symbol of legality. As for the Senate's activity, it actually expanded in volume during Alexander's reign. In 1824, 86,000 cases came to the Senate—over twice the work load of 1805[34]—and in 1819 its chancellery employed about 1,300 ranking servitors,[35] as opposed to somewhat less than 800 in 1801.[36] Its work seems to have fallen off in Nicholas I's latter years, but until 1842 at least, it remained well above its 1802 level of operation.[37] The Senate continued throughout the nineteenth century to arbitrate disputes between government agencies whenever the ministries thought that a question of law was involved, and it played a major role, though not always effectively, in upholding the rights of local institutions.[38]

34. *IPS*, III, 440.
35. *Ibid.*, p. 264.
36. Klochkov, pp. 184–185.
37. In 1842 the Senate's administrative staff was cut back and its salaries reduced. See *IPS*, III, 264–265.
38. *Ibid.*, pp. 598–603. By the 1860s it had become the practice to submit interministerial disputes over legality to the Senate and those that had to do with expediency to the Committee of Ministers. See Lazarevskii, II, 182.

Its position as supreme court in criminal and civil cases actually became more secure and more clearly defined after the 1860s.[39]

What took place in 1802–1862 was a gradual change in the Senate's role in government and, consequently, a change in its position relative to the other supreme organs. In 1802 the Senate was the de facto center for the management of government, but its influence derived primarily from the simple fact that it did the bulk of the work. In the ensuing decades the ministries gradually took over the Senate's work, and the government's local agencies gradually cut down on the reports they made to the Senate. At the same time the ministries began to utilize the Senate as a regulative body to help keep order among themselves while they ran the government. In effect, the Senate became much less a mediator between government and society and much more a referee among the ministries, and its decisions had increasingly to be made in terms dictated by the imperatives of ministerial pseudo-system rather than by its relationships with rural society.[40] Instead of protecting law from government agencies and participating actively in the communication between tsar and people, the Senate became an element in an executive organization whose implied aim was to impose system on both tsar and people.[41]

The Senate lost its managerial functions relatively slowly. The reforms of 1810–1811 subordinated the central colleges to the ministries and ordered the government's agents in the local colleges to carry out directives from the ministers *as well as from the Senate.* From 1811 on, the *sovetniki* in the gubernia *pravlenie* (see above, ch. II, sec. D) took orders from both MVD and Senate. Likewise, the assessors of the gubernia fiscal chamber came under the jurisdiction of the MF.[42]

In the following two decades the all-important power of appointment passed into the hands of the ministers. The tsar and/or Senate continued to make formal appointments to the administrative offices of government, but acceptance of the appropriate ministries' recommendations grew to be more or less automatic. The tsar began to accept the recommendations of the MVD for the appointment of civil governors,[43] and in 1831 Nicholas I granted the ministries the authority to appoint many local officials directly. To the MF he assigned the

39. Concerning the Senate's later development, see below, ch. VII, sec. A.

40. Korkunov, *RGP*, II, 648–669, describes the Senate's transformation. See also *IPS*, III, 447–451; Lazarevskii, I, 452–457.

41. See Korkunov, *RGP*, II, 351–364, for a general discussion of the changes from collegial to ministerial (*edinolichnoe*) administration in Russia.

42. Gradovskii, IX, 137; Troshchinskii, pp. 42–44; *Ministerstvo iustitsii*, pp. 32–33.

43. *IPS*, III, 556.

assessors of the gubernia fiscal chamber and the uezd treasurers; to the MVD, the *sovetniki* in the gubernia *pravlenie;* and to the minister of justice, the appointed judges on the gubernia and uezd courts.[44]

The Senate continued to exert considerable influence on the local colleges until about 1830. There were cases into the 1820s when the MF had to go through the Senate in order to get the fiscal chambers to carry out orders, and it often happened that collisions between the Senate's orders and those from the ministries were resolved in the Senate's favor.[45] In the 1830s, however, Nicholas speeded up the process of whittling away at the Senate's influence in the countryside. A series of measures gradually reduced its prerogative to demand reports and restricted the types of appeal that it heard against local administrators.[46] Most of these appeals came to be handled by the ministries, ultimately by the Committee of Ministers or the State Council.[47] In addition, Nicholas gradually eliminated most of the elected officials in the gubernia and uezd colleges and concentrated authority in the hands of appointed agents. In 1837 the gubernia *pravlenie* ceased to operate as a college and became in effect the governor's executive office (see below, ch. IX, sec. C). In the same year the number of elected men in the "lower land court"—the police organ on the uezd level—was reduced (see below, n. 87). Alexander II finished what Nicholas had begun. In 1862 he replaced the lower land court and its elected police commandant with an appointed servitor of the MVD.[48] Similarly, in 1866 the gubernia fiscal chamber and the gubernia chamber for the management of the state lands both came under single agents (*upravliaiushchie*) from their respective ministries.[49] In short, the absolute volume of business that the Senate handled does not seem to have decreased markedly during the first half of the nineteenth century, but its de facto managerial role in the government organization gradually faded away.

D. THE RISE OF MINISTERIAL GOVERNMENT

ORIGINS: THE PROCURACY

It bears repeating that in 1802 senatorial government was still no more than a pretense at legal-administrative system. The Senate and its

44. *Ibid.*, pp. 474–476.
45. *Ibid.*, pp. 438–441, 458–461.
46. *Ibid.*, pp. 461–464, 589–595.
47. *Ibid.*, pp. 504–505; *Ministerstvo vnutrennikh del*, p. 51.
48. Lazarevskii, II, 220–221; Korkunov, *RGP*, II, 439–440; *Ministerstvo vnutrennikh del*, p. 132.
49. Korkunov, *RGP*, II, 454; *Ministerstvo finansov*, I, 429–430; *Istoricheskoe obozrenie*, III, pt. 2, 26.

colleges did not generally make their decisions through collective deliberation; they only maintained a facade while essentially arbitrary authorities made their decisions for them.

The practice of violating collegial procedures in order to make the colleges operate began at the very birth of senatorial government. In March 1711, less than two weeks after the Senate was first established, a number of officials (*fiskaly*) were appointed to maintain surveillance over the government offices to see that they obeyed the decrees of the Senate.[50] In 1722, when the *fiskaly* had proven themselves inadequate, the procuracy was set up. The procuracy went a step further than the *fiskaly*. The decree of 27 April 1722 specifically authorized the *general-prokuror* (the head of the procuracy) to supervise the Senate itself, while his subordinate *prokurory* were to keep watch on its colleges and agencies.[51] From then on, it was the responsibility of the *general-prokuror* and his organization to make the Senate and the colleges decide their affairs at a speed that would allow the government to discharge what it regarded as its responsibilities.

German cameralist theory did not say much about how colleges could be made to work if they did not work properly on their own; thus the evolution of the tsarist procuracy bore little relation to Western theory. The procuracy originated from European models, but these Western agencies only maintained surveillance over administrators and, when necessary, brought them before the high councils of government to be judged and punished. No Western office of surveillance had ventured actually to manage the administration directly and preside over the entire government. Only the Russian procuracy presumed to take over all the functions and prerogatives of domestic administration and, as it were, to manage the law itself.[52]

In sum, the procuracy was a key element in eighteenth-century

50. The decree of 5 Mar. 1711 is in *Pamiatniki*, VIII, 46–47.
51. Printed in *ibid.*, pp. 211–215. The relevant clause is no. 9. Among other things, it required the *general-prokuror* to keep an hourglass before him at the meetings of the Senate. Every time there was a division in the Senate, he was to turn the glass over. When the sands ran out, debate had to stop and a decision had to be rendered. According to Chernov, p. 18, this law also made the Senate answerable to the *general-prokuror* for faulty decisions.
52. Muravev, pp. 245–271. Heinrich Fik, the expert from Holstein who did most of the preparatory work that led to the establishment of the procuracy, did not make any recommendation for setting the *general-prokuror* over the Senate. See *ibid.*, pp. 268–271. Veretennikov, pp. 1–26, has concluded that the actual construction of the procuracy was the work of Peter himself, with Aleksis Makarov, the head of his chancellery, performing the mechanical task of drawing up the decree. Foreign influence, French as well as Swedish, cannot be denied, but Veretennikov asserts that Peter's law of 1722 owed more to Russian experience than to foreign models (see above, ch. II, n. 55).

collegial government. It provided the colleges with authorities who were responsible for getting tasks accomplished, while the colleges, on their part, provided the procuracy with a measure of legality and regularity. It is in this unique symbiosis that the roots of ministerial government are to be found.

The most important element in the power of the procuracy was its control over chancelleries. The *general-prokuror* directed the Senate's chancellery, and his subordinate *prokurory* directed the chancelleries of the major colleges and offices in the central government. The chancelleries, in their turn, dominated the colleges. Their clerks were generally better trained and more experienced than the college members. Some of them were able to read more than official formulas, whereas the ranking officials who sat in the colleges were often illiterate former army officers who knew little or nothing of the procedures of civil administration.[53] In practice, the clerks arranged the materials to be brought before the colleges, set up agendas, and drafted decisions, leaving the colleges themselves little to do but give their approval.[54] By taking over the chancelleries, then, and adding their formal authority to the clerks' de facto influence, the *prokurory* reduced the colleges they were supposed to be supervising to little more than rubber stamps. With the massed clerical skill and routines of his chancellery and with the power to use his "surveillance" to manipulate his college, a *prokuror* could generally get the members to do as he and the clerks wished.[55]

According to the letter of the law, a *prokuror* was supposed not to influence his college's decisions substantively but only to speed up the process of making them. Since the colleges did not generally work fast enough on their own, however (see above, ch. III, sec. C), his function was not so much to keep his college on its toes and enforce rules upon it as to keep the members from getting in the chancellery's way. Whenever for some reason the spirit of harmonious indifference among the college members failed and they attempted to discuss their cases

53. Lazarevskii, II, 74. On the low educational level of both elected and appointed servitors in Catherine's gubernia colleges, see above, ch. III, sec. C. Gote, I, 260–270, traces the emergence of a separate "caste" of chancellery clerks (*kantseliarskie*) in the eighteenth century as a social status below that of the gentry and an administrative level below the Table of Ranks. I. Andreevskii, *O namestnikakh, voevodakh, i gubernatorakh* (St. Petersburg, 1864), p. 137, tells us that the first law requiring the governors to have any knowledge of civil administration came out only in 1841. The career of P. Kh. Obolianinov is suggestive. He remained practically illiterate all his life; yet from 1783 on, he followed a successful career in the civil service, rising to the post of *general-prokuror* in 1800–1801. See P. I. Ivanov, pp. 77–79.
54. Lazarevskii, II, 15–16.
55. *IPS*, II, 152–153, 312–313, 366–374.

and challenge their chancelleries—that is, when a college actually functioned as cameralist theory prescribed—the backlog of unmade decisions quickly built up, and the machinery of government jammed.[56] This is the basic reason that the procuracy did not serve the Senate but instead developed into a machinery for forcing the senatorial institutions to serve the *general-prokuror*.

In the late eighteenth century the *general-prokuror* became a de facto dictator over the senatorial institutions and something like an executive manager of domestic administration. Prince A. A. Viazemskii, *general-prokuror* during most of Catherine II's reign, frequently sent orders directly to colleges via the *prokurory* in their chancelleries without troubling to consult the Senate and without allowing the colleges any freedom to decide the matter on their own terms.[57] At its highest point of development, then, "collegial" government in Russia operated under the de facto rule of a military-like chain of command. The better senatorial government worked, the less collegial it became.

Outside the capital cities the power of the *general-prokuror* was relatively weak. He had subordinate *prokurory* in some gubernias in Elizabeth's time,[58] and Catherine set up regular agencies of the procuracy in all gubernias and uezds, but their practical role seems to have remained insignificant.[59] Until Catherine's death in 1796 the governors-general exercised greater influence in the countryside than any central administrative office, and they were responsible to the ruler alone, not to the Senate or the procuracy. With these territorial lords in control of the countryside, the *general-prokuror's* dictatorial power was confined largely to the capital cities.

As has been said, the procuracy followed a checkered career in its first decades. It was active until Peter died, mainly because the *general-prokuror*, P. I. Iaguzhinskii, was one of Peter's favorites. Indeed, such was Iaguzhinskii's personal power that Peter presented

56. All the tsars and higher statesmen of the eighteenth and nineteenth centuries were inclined to regard collegial discussions as a waste of time. As Nikita Panin said in his memorandum of 28 Dec. 1762, if the Senate worked as the law required, "the flow of business in the administration of the state would often come to a halt; instead of quick decisions there would be endless arguments . . . " (printed in English in Raeff, *Plans*, p. 55). In general, the idea that discussion should produce decisions by itself has not thrived in Russian government in any period of its history (see below, ch. VII, sec. B).

57. Lazarevskii, I, 451–452. The *general-prokuror* hired and fired all the procuracy's agents in the gubernias and uezds without any interference from either the Senate or the governors. See *IPS*, II, 368.

58. *IPS*, II, 251–253.

59. Muravev, pp. 304–305, 313–315.

him to the Senate in 1722 with the words "This is my eye, through which I shall see everything. . . . Do what he tells you."[60] But Iaguzhinskii lost his position not long after Peter's death,[61] and from the time of his fall until 1740, when Prince Trubetskoi was appointed to the office, the procuracy and the Senate ceased to play a significant role in government (ch. II, n. 26).

Trubetskoi remained in office and kept Elizabeth's favor for over twenty years until 1760. During his long service he brought considerable prestige to Senate and procuracy alike. He expanded the network of *prokurory* in central and local government offices and laid the foundation for Catherine II's and Paul's efforts to transform the procuracy into a full-fledged executive administration.

Catherine appointed A. A. Viazemskii to be *general-prokuror* in 1764, and he held office until his death in 1793, during which time he (and Catherine) brought the authority of the procuracy to its highest point. On the one hand, he expanded the official responsibilities of the *office* of *general-prokuror*, while on the other he *personally* acquired a number of functions that he performed through other agencies.[62] Catherine assigned these extra-procuracy functions to Viazemskii as a person, not as *general-prokuror*, but the reason she assigned them to him was that his position as *general-prokuror* made him the most promising agency for mobilizing the government's resources to perform them. Thus the new organizations that Viazemskii formed were initially dependent not only on his personal standing but also, to some extent, on the authority attached to the position of *general-prokuror*. By the end of Viazemskii's term of service, a structure of formally separate functional agencies had come into being, each connected to the other by the power of a single government office, the *general-prokuror*. This development paved the way for the introduction of the ministries.

Of particular importance was the part Viazemskii played in reorganizing the finances of the central government. During the 1770s he used his sweeping authority as *general-prokuror* to set up an embryonic state treasury, though he kept this new executive apparatus quite apart from the organization of the procuracy. In 1780 he took over the treasury officially, but he continued to keep it separate from the procuracy throughout his term of office.[63] After he died (in 1793),

60. Quoted in P. I. Ivanov, pp. 2–3.
61. Veretennikov, pp. 104–107.
62. Viazemskii's formal positions are described in *IPS*, II, 377–379, and Klochkov, pp. 227–228.
63. P. I. Ivanov, pp. 47–50; *IPS*, II, 371, 423–426; Klochkov, pp. 384–385.

the two organizations were assigned to two different men,[64] and in 1796 Paul confirmed the separation between them by law.[65]

As *general-prokuror*, Viazemskii was already a combination of what was later to become the MVD and the ministry of justice. The hierarchy of *prokurory* and college chancelleries was in effect an incipient MVD, whereas a sort of ministry of justice resided in the Senate and the lower courts. With the formation of the separate state treasury as an embryonic MF, Viazemskii had three separate, quasi-ministerial organizations under him, representing a framework of relationships that would guide the evolution of domestic administration on all levels from Catherine's time on.

EARLY EVOLUTION OF THE MINISTRIES

The driving force behind the emergence of proto-ministries during Catherine's and Paul's reigns came chiefly from the countryside, from the enormously expanded responsibilities (and case loads) acquired by the senatorial institutions as a result of their sudden and presumptuous extension into an unreceptive rural society. By 1802 the impact of these responsibilities had been massive, but as yet it had only disrupted the government, not transformed it. Catherine's and Paul's reforms in the central offices were only hasty expedients, and their new departments had few ties with the gubernia and uezd colleges. In 1802, therefore, the new ministers found no agencies outside the capital cities that they could employ for their own ends. They knew nothing of conditions in the gubernias, and they had no systematic way to inform themselves. Yet it was their official responsibility to reorganize the government into a uniform, all-inclusive system.

It would be many decades before the ministers began to work themselves out of this predicament. In the 1830s they had not yet established anything like systematic communication with the gubernias and uezds. Kiselev's inspections of the state lands in that decade revealed that there was still a general ignorance of the laws and an absence of supervision in the provincial offices. It often happened that the positions called for in the regulations were not even occupied, let alone supervised or managed.[66] In subsequent years Kiselev's new agencies "discovered" 9.7 million acres of state lands whose existence the government and its local agents had never suspected.[67]

64. Klochkov, pp. 231–239.
65. *Ibid.*, pp. 159, 385–389. See also Duran.
66. Druzhinin, *Gos. krest.*, I, 354–364, 439–453; Gradovskii, IX, 41, 137–138; "Materialy . . . k biografii Nikolaia I," pp. 472–474.
67. *Istoricheskoe obozrenie*, III, pt. 1, 16–17.

Given the absence of coherent administrative organization outside the capital cities, it is hardly surprising that the ministries could not begin immediately to act as parts of a single machine. In practice, the conduct of their separate functions often required each one to act independently, knocking the others out of the way or avoiding them entirely, much as the old-time omnipotent agents had done.

The MF, for example, assumed general responsibility for collecting revenue in 1821, when the state treasury came under his jurisdiction. Yet he had no agencies of his own to collect it.[68] Revenue was coming in from the countryside through the workings of a social order that was neither systematic, nor amenable to systematic organization, nor even definable in general terms.[69] Gubernia and uezd administrations generally kept aside what they needed from their revenue before passing on what was left to the central treasury. Attempts to audit their accounts to determine how much they were keeping aside only began in the 1830s. In short, the MF of the early nineteenth century did not know how his revenue was collected in each area, nor did he have any consistently reliable way of finding out. All he heard from the countryside were reports of this or that obstacle to effective collection, to which he would respond in the old eighteenth-century fashion by ordering the local officials, whoever they were, to eliminate the obstacle, whatever it may have been, in any way they thought best. If a road needed repair, get it fixed; it did not matter how or by whom. If a peasant village failed to pay its allotted taxes, the order would go out to take whatever measures were necessary, though the minister could not know what these would be. All he knew was that his status vis-à-vis the other ministers, his standing with the tsar, and his capability to achieve any purpose whatever—ideal, humane, necessary, or corrupt—depended primarily on his ability to get revenue.

The MVD, on the other hand, was responsible for "good order" in the countryside,[70] but he could not define the bases for "order" any more than the MF could comprehend the methods by which revenue was collected. Occasional reports of violations of "order" came to him from the local colleges, but he had little basis for understanding what the colleges meant. He would generally respond by ordering the sup-

68. There were, of course, gubernia fiscal chambers and uezd treasurers (see *Ministerstvo finansov,* I, 36), but as we have noted, these local agencies were still closely tied to the Senate.

69. See *Istoricheskii obzor . . . Komiteta,* I, 98–113.

70. This became clear only in 1819 at the earliest, when the ministry of police was eliminated and its organization absorbed into the MVD. See *Ministerstvo vnutrennikh del,* pp. 23–24, 33; Eroshkin, pp. 200, 204; *Ministerstvo finansov,* I, 42.

pression of the violation, whatever it was, by any suitable means. If a horse were stolen, find the thief; but how this was to be done or by whom was not clear. If a peasant village refused to obey its owner, persuade or force it to obey; but the minister had no idea what obedience entailed. All he knew was that his status vis-à-vis the other ministers, his standing with the tsar, and his capability to achieve any purpose whatever depended to a considerable degree on his ability to keep violence, "crime," famines, and epidemics at a minimum.

In theory, and to some extent in practice, there was a solid basis for coordination between the MF and the MVD. The MF knew that he could not get revenue from a disorderly countryside, and the MVD recognized the need for revenue. But the nature of their operation rendered coordination extremely burdensome in practice. We may imagine a typical incident in which a governor calls up the peasants from a number of villages to repair a road that he expects the tsar to use on one of his trips. Imagine further that this sudden labor draft comes at harvest time and prevents many of the peasants from bringing in their grain, thus rendering them unable to pay their taxes for that year. If news of the resulting revenue deficit filters up to the MF, he might protest to the MVD, demanding that the MVD reprimand or restrain the governor. The MVD might take the matter up with the governor, but it would be difficult to verify the reports the MF had received. The local official who dragged the peasants out on the road might claim that his victims had received compensation for their losses, or that care had been taken to leave enough peasants in the villages to complete the harvest, or that the peasants had been released in time for the harvest but had gotten drunk and arrived home too late. The governor would have no reliable way to determine whether the official was telling the truth or not, let alone prove his conclusions to the satisfaction of the MVD or the MF. Lacking agents of their own, neither MVD nor MF could obtain verified, reliable reports; therefore, their attempts to check on the incident would be far more likely to produce friction between them than cooperation.

Generally speaking, any ministerial intervention in local administration brought disruption. Orders from ministers were very often not enforced or even published in the gubernias. Whenever one of them was, the volume of disputes and appeals rose sharply, flooding the central offices with obscure squabbles to be resolved. The central offices could not understand local issues, yet they had to make decisions. Unlike the colleges, the ministers were responsible to act, not merely to observe formulas. In practice, therefore, they were obliged to act blindly. They could, of course, see reports, appeals, orders, and sometimes even the persons involved in the matters they decided, but they could not see any coherent relationship among all these elements. Insofar as they affected to act as a system, therefore, they acted blindly.

It was in the nature of things that conscientious officials who had often to issue orders blindly should feel compelled to extend their subordinate organizations further into the countryside. It was natural for a minister to hope that a more elaborate system would allow him to see what he was doing and thereby to cooperate more effectively with his colleagues. Driven by their functional responsibilities and their pretense to system, the ministries had no way to fend off the wave of appeals and disputes or to keep local issues from setting them at odds with one another, except to send out more agents and issue more rules. Their only way to deal with the disorder they created was to intensify their impact on society and, ultimately, to change it into more systematic form.[71]

In the early part of the nineteenth century the ministers could often minimize the clashes between their "organizations" by letting disputes go undecided or by allowing them to be resolved informally on the local level according to the needs of the situation. Ministerial organizations were only beginning to take form, and the conflicts among them were not yet coherent enough to be massive and sustained. The confusion introduced into all levels of government by the ministers' attempts to exercise their vague powers could be explained away by referring to "outdated" colleges, the "moribund" Senate, the "reactionary" Arakcheev, the "mystical" Alexander I, the "interfering" and "tyrannical" Nicholas I, and, of course, the "corruption" of local officials. As the century wore on, however, the ministries became better organized, and their efforts to perform their duties brought their conflicts into sharper focus. Consequently, their clashes became more frequent, more sustained, and more clearly associated with the ministries themselves.[72]

As we have seen, the domestic ministries spent the first thirty-odd years of their existence acquiring the more or less exclusive prerogative to issue orders to and receive reports from the gubernias. Aside from the relatively small-scale activity of the ministry of the crown (*udelnye*) lands in the late 1820s (see above, ch. IV, sec. D),

71. Starr, pp. 17–19, has shown that the number of personnel in gubernia and uezd agencies increased from two to four times in the 1830s and 1840s.
72. The interministerial clashes of the late nineteenth and early twentieth centuries are discussed in chs. VIII and IX.

there was no attempt to build new agencies in the countryside along-side Catherine's colleges or to impose new programs on the existing agencies.[73] Only in the mid-1830s, when the ministries had established their predominance in the organs of local administration, could they begin to consider initiating reforms on their own. It was also in the mid-1830s that at least a few statesmen began to give up the con-viction that the government had to contrive a perfect legal system and work out all-encompassing plans before any active reform could begin.

The passionate need to find a more or less universal system of ab-stract plans and principles has never ceased to be a characteristic element in Russian political thought, but it has never been taken more seriously than in the reign of Alexander I and the early years of Nicholas I. The last grand effort to set up a legal-administrative sys-tem out of formulas came in 1826–1832. Nicholas appointed Speranskii to head the second section of his chancellery—the codification sec-tion—and at the same time included him on a committee of top-level statesmen to draft a new plan of administrative organization. One of the committee's reports in 1827 expressed Nicholas's intention in a nutshell: "Orderliness in the gubernias will be established only when the administration and the courts in all areas have been brought under precise and uniform rules; when all areas are set under a single, supreme, central administration, each to be administered on the same common basis."[74]

Speranskii's second section worked up a law code of sorts and Nicholas published it in 1832,[75] but the top-level committee's pro-posals regarding a general administrative system went nowhere (see above, n. 9). In 1832 the committee ceased to meet, and from then on both Nicholas I and Speranskii gave up waiting for the perfect framework. Instead, they began to take up specific reforms in the legal order of the countryside and to work out limited programs of practical administrative action.[76] They had reached the point where they accepted the need for reform even if it had to be carried out

73. *Istoricheskoe obozrenie*, IV, 18–27.

74. Quoted in Gradovskii, I, 321. For a brief description of the work of legal reform in 1826–1832, see Shcheglov, pp. 45–50. According to Presniakov, *Apogei*, p. 31, it was clear in 1826 that it would take administrative action rather than constitutional reform to straighten out the countryside. This, however, is his hindsight. The impossibility of constitutional reform did not become clear to Nicholas I before 1831–1832.

75. This was the first edition of the *Svod zakonov*, numbering fifteen volumes. Concerning its significance and its general nature, see N. M. Korkunov, "Znache-nie svoda zakonov," in his *Sbornik statei*, pp. 77–96.

76. *IPS*, III, 142–166; Korkunov, *RGP*, II, 669. Pintner has noted that the period 1836–1843 was a time when Russian government moved into an "era of state-sponsored economic change" (pp. 121–122).

without a coherent plan or all-encompassing general purpose. In 1835 Nicholas began to meet more or less regularly with a variety of secret ministerial committees to discuss practical reforms, not the least of which was Kiselev's.[77]

The reforms of the 1830s and 1840s suffered severely from a lack of funds. Their basic purpose was to increase revenue,[78] but it was the army, not the domestic administration, that was to receive the additional funds. From the mid-thirties on, the budgeted expenditures of the domestic ministries actually decreased.[79] The desire for reform was there in the 1830s, but the resources, to say nothing of the constitutional framework, were lacking.[80] The reforms that were enacted, therefore, were necessarily modest ones.

The first basic step in reorganizing the ministerial agencies in the gubernias and uezds was a law issued in 1837, making official the de facto elimination of the post of governor-general in the interior gubernias (except for Moscow and St. Petersburg).[81] This was a significant decision. The possibility of governing Russia through separate territorial organizations, each of them under their own "viceroy," had been a part of Russian political thought since Peter the Great, and the desire for such an arrangement still flourished in the early nineteenth century. In his last years Alexander I made an attempt to set them up as permanent institutions.[82] His purpose, it seems, was to use them as a check on the power of the ministers.[83]

An organization in which governors-general played a vital role could not have been ministerial. Governors-general held rank and status equivalent to the ministers' and sat with them as equals in the Committee of Ministers. Neither they nor the ministers had any clear

77. "Materialy . . . k biografii Nikolaia I," pp. 101–283, describes the meetings of the secret committees in the 1830s and 1840s. Baron Korf, the author of this account, became the head of the chancellery of the Committee of Ministers in 1831, and this involved him in most of the meetings. The ones he describes were all devoted to the consideration of practical reforms.

78. See A. D. Bilimovich, *Ministerstvo finansov, 1802–1902* (Kiev, 1903), pp. 12–44.

79. *Ministerstvo finansov,* I, 628–629. Even Kiselev's ministry of state domains received very little to work with in proportion to the total revenues that came in from the state lands. See Pintner, pp. 170–173; *Istoricheskoe obozrenie,* I, pt. 1, 96–101.

80. Starr, pp. 20–22, 28, has found evidence that expenditure on domestic administration increased slightly in the period 1830–1855. Whether expenditures increased or decreased, the fact remains, as Starr points out, that the government did not spend enough to carry out effective reforms.

81. Gradovskii, I, 321–323; *Ministerstvo vnutrennikh del,* pp. 60–62.

82. G. Rauch, *Russland* (Munich, 1953), pp. 56–58.

83. Predtechenskii, p. 398.

authority over one another, and in the border areas, where governors-general continued to operate until 1917, conflicts between them and the ministers were continuous.[84] A good expression of the basic attitude that kept them in tension appears in a note of 1839 from the governor-general of Siberia to the MVD: "You are neither my predecessor, my chief, nor my judge. . . . My rank is higher than yours, and therefore whenever you have occasion to pass judgment on my work, I request that you communicate it directly to His Imperial Highness."[85]

It may be said, then, that Nicholas's act in 1837 marked a decisive turning point in favor of ministerial bureaucracy. The official removal of the governors-general from the interior gubernias left the way open to the domestic ministries to establish agencies of their own in the gubernias and uezds. These agencies would take their orders directly from their ministerial superiors in St. Petersburg and, hopefully, would not lose themselves in the factional struggles that had formerly merged central officials and gentry landowners into a purely local political arena.[86]

A series of centralizing measures followed closely upon the elimination of the governors-general. An order calling for regular financial audits of gubernias offices came out in 1837, and Nicholas issued a number of new organizational rules designed to create something like an executive organization under ministerial direction in each gubernia. The governor was already an agent of the MVD (see above, sec. C), and these new rules served to strengthen his authority as such. In essence, they reduced the number of elected men in the uezd police administration and set up a new police network in the uezds that was directly subordinate to the governor (and the MVD).[87] A few years later, in 1845, the gubernia *pravlenie* was stripped of its few remaining prerogatives and converted wholly into an executive organ of the governor.[88]

The new police network is of special interest. It was set up in subsections, called *stany*, of each uezd. In each *stan* a police unit was established under a new official, the police captain (*stanovoi pristav*).[89] The police captain was supposed to be appointed from among the

84. Concerning interaction between ministers and governors-general in the early nineteenth century, see *Istoricheskii obzor . . . Komiteta*, I, 94–113; II, pt. 1, 107–118.

85. Quoted in *IPS*, III, 552–553.

86. *Ministerstvo vnutrennikh del*, pp. 60–64.

87. See Gradovskii, IX, 142. The most important of these reforms were embodied in the laws of 3 June 1837, printed in *VPSZ*, 10303–6.

88. *Ministerstvo vnutrennikh del*, pp. 40–41, 59–65; Gradovskii, IX, 140–141.

89. *VPSZ*, 10305, p. 465. Meshcherskii, I, 243, says that there were on the average two or three *stany* in each uezd as of the 1850s.

landowning gentry of the gubernia in which he held land, according
to nominations made by the gentry assemblies. But the law did not
say this had to be, only that it would be "preferable." Moreover, the
law gave the governor concrete grounds for rejecting gentry nominations. It required, for example, that retired military officers be given
preference over other candidates.[90] In short, the police captains were
essentially hirelings of the central administration. As we have seen,
Bibikov found that in practice the police captains in the Southwest
usually did what the local gentry told them to do despite their oaths of
service. Nevertheless, their establishment did indicate that the central
government aspired to impose ministerial authority on the countryside.

With the reform of the *pravlenie* and the introduction of the *stan*
police, the governor was in a much better position to play the role of
executive director. His orders were still legally subject to the approval
of his *pravlenie,* and he continued to depend on the gentry-elected
uezd police commandant to carry them out, but the *pravlenie* now
consisted of his own subordinates, and the working police organizations in the *stany* were at least formally separated from gentry control.[91]

Along with the increase in the governor's authority came the beginnings of functional specialization in the gubernias, corresponding
to organizational divisions in the capital cities. An agent of the MF
replaced the vice-governor as chairman of the gubernia fiscal chamber,
thus introducing a measure of separation between the governor's authority and the financial system.[92] This marked a new stage in the
tendency to isolate revenue collection under a separate agency, subject only to the MF in St. Petersburg. In previous years a series of
moves had separated specific revenues from the jurisdiction of the
fiscal chamber itself. Customs collection had come under a separate
organ, then mining, then salt, and at last, in 1832, the forests.[93] To the
extent that these agencies had gotten away from the pre-1837 fiscal
chamber, they had escaped from gubernia-level control of any kind
and become tools of the MF. With the reform of 1837, the fiscal
chamber itself followed the same path.

In the same year that the fiscal chamber gained quasi-independence
from the gubernia administration and came under the MF, Kiselev
was completing preparations for his reform of the state peasants. On

90. *VPSZ*, 10305, p. 466.
91. Starr, pp. 38–45, points out that the governors were still severely handi-
capped after 1837 by complex procedural rules.
92. *Ministerstvo finansov*, I, 222–224. Eroshkin, p. 235, says that the vice-
governor retained his chairmanship until 1845.
93. Bilimovich, p. 12.

1 January 1838 he formed the ministry of state domains from what had been a department in the MF and set up gubernia agencies directly subordinate to himself to replace what had been sections in the gubernia fiscal chambers. We have already noted that Kiselev's new ministry was significant as an instrument for carrying out a peasant reform of unprecedented scope. It is also noteworthy as an organizational innovation that expressed a new faith in the efficacy of a ministerial organization. Kiselev's agencies undertook to bring almost half the population of Russia under a single ministry. In theory, at least, the new agencies were answerable only to their ministerial superior, not to any local colleges or agencies of other ministries and not even to the governors.

Functionally specialized offices whose agents operated apart from all the others were no novelty in Russian government. The agencies of the postal system, for example, had long enjoyed almost complete autonomy from all other local authorities, including the governors. The ministry of the crown (*udelnye*) lands had been autonomous ever since its establishment in 1797. But Kiselev's ministry operated on a far larger scale than any of its predecessors. Moreover, it began its operations only a few years after the Senate had lost the greater part of its executive powers in local government. Thus the autonomy the new ministry enjoyed was somewhat greater than had ever obtained in the tsarist government before. It is true that Kiselev's reform had only moderate goals, and it did not come anywhere near achieving even these. Nevertheless, the founding of the ministry of state domains did express an emphatic and, indeed, unprecedented commitment to nonmilitary bureaucratic administration as an agency of social reform.[94]

In sum, the innovations of 1835–1837 not only introduced significant changes in the central government's agencies in rural Russia but also initiated the first serious move by a ministry to act upon rural society through its own organs. This is not to say that in 1837 Nicholas suddenly transformed the old senatorial government into an active bureaucracy. On the contrary, the government continued to operate pretty much as it always had in the countryside. At best, the innovations of 1837 began to shift the government organization in the gubernias from one kind of political arena, in which local squabbles were the bones of contention, to another, more generalized arena, in which factions sometimes identified themselves with all-Russian issues.

94. For further discussion of Nicholas's tendency to put his faith in ministerial government, see below, ch. VIII, sec. B.

E. GOVERNMENT BY PERSONAL AGENTS OF THE TSAR: 1802–1860s

Before taking up the period 1861–1905, we must discuss one more aspect of the burdens the ministers inherited in the 1860s: the degree to which domestic administration continued to depend on the operation of personal, omnipotent agents during the first half of the nineteenth century.

If the history of the rise of legal-administrative system in Russia had been a steady progression, it would be possible to speak of a series of steps by which colleges and/or bureaucratic systems gradually replaced omnipotent agents as the instruments of government. This progression did take place, but it was not steady. The employment of despotic agents, answerable to the tsar for the consequences rather than the legality of their actions, did not decline at an even pace by easily recognizable stages. Arbitrariness did not slowly give way before system; rather, it assumed different forms as the growth of system produced new dilemmas. We have seen that the erection of serfdom into a legal institution actually secured the arbitrary authority of the serf owners over their serfs. Similarly, the introduction of gubernia and uezd colleges was accompanied by the establishment of all-powerful governors-general, responsible only to the ruler. Finally, the growing effectiveness of administrative procedures in the eighteenth-century Senate depended on the assumption of dictatorial authority by the *general-prokuror*. In short, the rise of system in the eighteenth century was everywhere accompanied by the parallel development of arbitrary authority.

There was a fairly continuous trend in the history of the tsar's personal agents from Peter's time on, even if it was not a steady one. Throughout the eighteenth century there were roughly two types: those, like the *prokurory*, who were set over the portion of the government that pretended to be sytematic, and those, like the governors-general and the serf owners, who were set entirely outside the Senate's area of operation to manage areas and affairs that the tsar could not even pretend to cope with by systematic means. The first type was responsible for making institutions function; the second was responsible either to accomplish specific tasks or to govern territories. As might be expected, the development and expansion of system brought with it a general trend for the former type of agent to extend its area of operation at the expense of the latter. From 1762 to the 1860s the *general-prokuror* and his successors, the ministers, expanded their operations and pretensions. The governors-general, on the other hand, were eliminated in the interior gubernias (1837), and the serf owners were stripped of their formal authority over the peasants (1861). As of the 1860s, then, omnipotent agents who operated outside the "systematic" part of the government were virtually eliminated from domestic administration in European Russia.[95]

During the latter part of Alexander I's reign and the first part of Nicholas I's, while personal despotic agents *outside* the systematic sector of government were being swept away, such agents were being employed more intensively than ever *within* the central administration, chiefly under the auspices of His Majesty's Own Imperial Chancellery. The tsar's chancellery acquired its official title only in 1826, but it had been managing the central administration since about 1818, when Alexei Arakcheev, the tsar's secretary, became virtual dictator of Russia.[96]

The helplessness of the administration in Alexander I's last years— no longer senatorial and not yet ministerial—has been described above. Arakcheev had before him a chaos of supreme organs, ministries, and colleges in which legal cases and administrative disputes could be appealed from one office to another without any effective restraint. Whenever an office decided a matter, its chief or chiefs had to fear that the case would be reopened once more and its decision challenged. Under the circumstances there was considerable temptation not to make decisions, and those that were made often took a long time. All offices had great difficulty keeping up with their work loads. The ministers were the ultimate decision-makers; consequently, there was a tendency to refer all decisions to them. When Arakcheev came to power, they were buried in cases.

Arakcheev's solution to the problem was to take severe disciplinary measures to force the offices of government to decide their affairs as fast as they came in, much as his old master, the Emperor Paul, had

95. It will be recalled (see above, ch. IV, sec. E) that in 1858 Alexander II briefly considered the temporary establishment of governors-general in order to maintain public tranquillity during the enactment of the Liberation. Aside from crisis situations of this sort, however, extra-system omnipotent agents did not again come into use in the interior gubernias during the tsarist regime. On their employment during the revolutionary upheavals of 1905–1907, see Santoni, and N. N. Polianskii, *Tsarskie voennye sudy v borbe s revoliutsiei 1905–1907 gg.* (Moscow, 1958).

96. V. N. Stroev, *Stoletie Sobstvennoi Ego Imperatorskogo Velichestva Kantseliarii* (St. Petersburg, 1912), pp. 5–124. Arakcheev seems to have managed Alexander I's correspondence from 1812 on, but he did not undertake to involve himself in the management of the government as a whole until after the Napoleonic Wars (*ibid.*, pp. 5–18).

tried to do.[97] His method was understandable and even traditional under the circumstances he faced. It is arguable that he had no alternative, given the general reluctance in his time to enact any organizational reforms without first finding a "foundation." Nevertheless, Paul's experience had already demonstrated the limitations of overly harsh discipline. Although Arakcheev was probably able to bring some immediate relief to this or that administrative tangle, his very achievements nourished a fatalistic irresponsibility among the officials, thus defeating the general purpose of his interference. Whether or not Arakcheev himself was at fault, the events in St. Petersburg on 14 December 1825 revealed that the government's paralysis had reached alarming proportions. Russian administrators had generally ceased to identify the domestic administration with any meaningful purpose, and both civil and military branches found themselves without clear direction.[98] When Nicholas came to the throne, he dismissed Arakcheev and established His Majesty's Own Imperial Chancellery to replace him.

Nicholas set up his new chancellery in sections. The first undertook to supervise personnel assignments throughout the government and to keep watch on what the personnel were doing;[99] the second worked on the codification of the law; and the third assumed responsibility for overseeing society as a whole, including the government administration.[100] There were other sections, but these three were the most important.[101] The first section continued to exist until 1917, although its power to operate came under systematic control after 1858, when

97. *Gosudarstvennaia kantseliariia: 1810–1910* (St. Petersburg, 1910, hereinafter cited as *Gos. kants.*), pp. 72–75.

98. The absence of leadership in the government in Dec. 1825 is amply documented. See, e.g., T. Schiemann, *Geschichte Russlands unter Kaiser Nikolaus I* (4 vols., Berlin, 1908), II, 1–33.

99. Concerning the extensive supervisory activities of the first section, see Stroev, pp. 143–159, 183–185.

100. See S. Monas, *The Third Section* (Cambridge, Mass., 1961), pp. 62–64, 93–107.

101. The fourth section was set up in 1828 after the death of Alexander I's mother, the Empress Marie, to manage the charitable and educational institutions she had founded. See N. K. Shilder, *Imperator Nikolai Pervyi* (2 vols., St. Petersburg, 1903), II, 188–190. The fifth was established under Kiselev in 1836 to initiate his reform of the state peasants. The sixth existed for only a few years, from 1842 to 1845, for the purpose of establishing the new office of viceroy of the Caucasus. See Eroshkin, p. 196. The administration of the institutions of the Empress Marie was taken out of His Majesty's Own Imperial Chancellery in 1880 and remained a separate institution thereafter. See *ibid.*, p. 261. Kiselev's fifth section continued to exist on paper until 1856, but it had no importance after 1 Jan. 1838, when Kiselev became minister of state domains. After 1846 it received no funds. See *Istoricheskoe obozrenie*, I, pt. 1, 100.

224   *The Systematization of Russian Government*

the ministers managed to get its inspection office eliminated. From then on, it ceased to play any vital role in government.[102] The second section was primarily a study group. It produced a quasi law code in 1832 and worked until 1882 to keep it up to date. In the latter year the section was incorporated into the chancellery of the State Council.[103] The third section held the most sweeping powers. It consisted of two parts. One was the corps of gendarmes, a military elite picked for their high personal morality and their intense desire to serve the state.[104] The other was the third section proper, which constituted the central authority over the gendarmes and also over a network of secret police who supposedly worked together with the gendarmes.

The gendarmes were the most unique feature of the third section and the most significant. Gendarme officers were personal agents of the tsar, *explicitly charged to act according to conscience rather than formal law*. A typical instruction from the corps commander, A. Benkendorf, to one of his gubernia-level officers reads as follows:

> Your own characteristic sentiments of nobility and righteousness will undoubtedly arouse the respect of all classes; and then your title, fortified by the people's confidence, will achieve its purpose and bring great benefit to the state. All will see in you an official who can carry the voice of suffering humanity through me up to the throne of the tsar and quickly bring the defenseless and voiceless citizen under the supreme protection of the tsar emperor. So many . . . illegal and unending disputes that you can bring to an end; so many men with evil intentions, striving to seize their neighbor's property, will become afraid to carry out their ruinous intentions when they come to believe that the innocent victims of their greed have a short, direct path to the protection of imperial majesty. On this basis, you will acquire many collaborators and helpers very quickly—citizens who love their fatherland and truth and who desire peace and order will guard your every step and help you by their useful counsel, thus serving as co-workers in behalf of the good intention of their tsar.[105]

102. Stroev, pp. 207–234, 285–289. P. A. Zaionchkovskii, *Rossiiskoe samoder-zhavie v kontse XIX stoletiia* (Moscow, 1970), pp. 109–111, points out that in 1894 the first section acquired greater power than before over the hiring, firing, and promotion of government servitors. There is no indication, however, that this expansion gave it any significant role in the government's operation.

103. Stroev, pp. 264–265.

104. P. S. Squire, *The Third Department* (Cambridge, 1968), pp. 85–86, 91–95. Squire estimates that the corps numbered well over 4,000 officers and men by 1855. By the late 1870s the total number of all types of gendarmes had reached about 13,000 (Zaionchkovskii, *Rossiiskoe samoderzhavie*, p. 174), and their numbers continued to rise in subsequent decades.

105. Quoted in Shilder, *Imperator Nikolai*, I, 468–470.

Gendarme officers were assigned to every gubernia and large city, charged not only with hearing appeals against wrongdoing but also with exercising surveillance over government and society and furnishing the tsar with information on what was happening.[106] Each gendarme officer had the power to inspect government offices and, if necessary, to remove, replace, and bring accusations against the incumbent officials.[107] But the gendarmes had more to do than make reports and see that things ran properly. They were to inspire confidence in the people and infuse a sense of purpose into the domestic administration by setting an example of dedicated, loyal, and honorable service. Given the dilemmas involved in the government's pretensions and aspirations, Nicholas seems to have decided that its purposes could be conveyed not by way of rational explanation but only by the living example of impeccably virtuous and conscientious servitors.

The third section kept up its political surveillance until its elimination in 1880, and the corps of gendarmes continued to operate as an elite police force under the MVD until 1917. But the original role of the gendarmes does not seem to have survived the reign of Nicholas I. By the 1850s, if not before, personal virtue coupled with arbitrary authority had done as much as it could toward the introduction of a facade of coherent organization and purpose in the government. Thereafter, the gendarmes generally confined themselves to their police functions and left bureaucracy to the bureaucrats.[108]

It is arguable that His Majesty's Own Imperial Chancellery had already ceased to play a predominant role in domestic administration by 1840. Korf's reports on Nicholas's secret committees of the late 1830s and 1840s clearly indicate that from 1835 on, it was primarily the ministers who were making the vital decisions (see n. 77). Monas notes that by 1840 the administrative work of the third section had already "petered out into a more or less normalized routine."[109] The new police organization of 1837 came under the MVD, not any part of the chancellery, and it is significant that Kiselev decided in 1837 to take his reform program out of the chancellery and put it under a ministry. Kiselev prepared his reform in 1835–1837 as head of the fifth section, but when he began to carry it out, he requested and got

106. See Squire, pp. 57–77.

107. These powers were not explicitly set forth in any law, but they could be exercised in practice because the agents of the third section were responsible only to their chief and he was answerable only to the tsar. See *ibid.*, pp. 177–181, 184–185.

108. A list of the third section's official functions during the period 1855–1880 indicates that it no longer concerned itself with the management of government organization. See Eroshkin, pp. 256–257.

109. Monas, p. 231.

the MF's department of state domains—i.e., a functioning organ of the bureaucracy—and assumed the title of minister (see n. 101). Apparently he conceived this to be the most effective position from which to direct his reform.[110] As for the third section's role in Kiselev's reform, Druzhinin's exhaustive study never brings up the subject. Kiselev had ultimately to set up his own surveillance to keep track of his organization.[111]

Squire would have it that the power of the third section increased steadily until the end of Nicholas's reign and especially after its reorganization in the late 1830s under L. V. Dubelt. As evidence, he notes that the number of cases it handled each year continued to increase[112] and that the size of its organization may have increased substantially after the 1830s.[113] Unfortunately, Squire does not make a clear distinction between administrative supervision and police work, and the available evidence does not allow him to discuss the evolution of the gendarmes' administrative supervision at all. It is impossible, therefore, to arrive at a definite conclusion regarding the degree to which omnipotent agents from the tsar's chancellery continued to be the "pivot" of the domestic administration after the 1830s.

It is my impression, however, that despotic personal power gradually became a less essential feature of administration as the ministries gradually built up their organizations. It is hard to imagine the gendarmes retaining their aura of virtuous detachment over a long period of time. As Mikhail Speranskii once pointed out, "trusted" omnipotent agents cannot stay apart from the regular offices of government for very long.[114] In order to keep themselves informed and to exercise their authority intelligently, they have to become directly involved in administration. But as soon as this happens to an agent, he ceases to exercise surveillance and becomes instead a part of the administrative order with which he is associated, fully as dependent on it as it is on him. This was what happened to the procuracy in the eighteenth century (see above, sec. D), and it was very likely what happened to the first and third sections of the chancellery by 1840.[115] The *police* work of the third section continued to swell in volume after the

110. *Istoricheskoe obozrenie*, I, pt. 1, 25–27, describes the changeover from section to ministry.
111. Druzhinin, *Gos. krest.*, II, 100–101.
112. Squire, p. 232.
113. *Ibid.*, p. 105.
114. Speranskii, pp. 105–106.
115. Concerning this general tendency in Russian government, see George L. Yaney, "Law, Society, and the Domestic Regime in Russia in Historical Perspective," *American Political Science Review*, LIX (June 1965), 379–390.

1830s, and this was probably the reason that its impact on capital-city society became more noticeable and onerous to politically conscious Russians. There is no convincing evidence, however, that gendarmes continued to act as all-powerful agents in *administration* after the 1830s.

Some memoir accounts from gendarme officers who served in the gubernias during Nicholas's reign describe occasions when they used their authority to force high officials to cooperate with one another.[116] This did not make them exceptional. Any official could play a leading role in gubernia administration if he had the requisite energy and personal influence, and just about all officials who wrote memoirs claimed that they had indeed played such roles at one time or another. In short, agents of the corps of gendarmes were in much the same position as were the agents of the major ministries, and they exercised the same kind of authority; that is, they were bureaucrats serving a bureaucracy within the limits of their particular functions. If the corps was ever really an assemblage of administratively untrammeled knights, it did not remain so for long. The principles and purposes Nicholas I set for it in 1826 did not become a characteristic feature of its administrative activities, nor were they basic to Nicholas's own administrative policies.

Generally speaking, 1840 marks the end of the period when men of "virtue," with no functional responsibilities of their own, would play any essential role in the management of domestic administration in European Russia. From then on, the ministries would run the domestic administration. If arbitrary power was to be exercised, they and their subordinates would exercise it.[117] The profound instability of tsarist administration in the two or three decades after the Napoleonic War does not in any way refute the general assertion that legal-administrative system was making constant progress during the period—resolving its problems and creating new dilemmas as it went along, slowly increasing its revenues and widening its contacts with society. The third section did not represent a regression to eighteenth-century disorder; nor was its use of despotic agents a characteristic feature of nineteenth-century administration. In essence, it was a temporary emergency measure.

It was the last of its kind. After the 1830s there would be yet more occasions when omnipotent agents would be officially appointed to

116. See Squire, pp. 186–191.

117. In his later years Nicholas I tended to ignore the supreme organs—State Council, Committee of Ministers, and Senate—even more than he had before and to govern directly through the ministers themselves. See "Materialy . . . k biografii Nikolaia I," pp. 219–220, 256–257.

respond to this or that crisis, but they were all of the extra-system type (see above, sec. B). None of them took over and ran any part of the government bureaucracy in order to improve its operation. Occasionally, a "dictator" like Mikhail Loris-Melikov (1879–1880) or Dmitri Trepov (1905–1906) would attempt to use the bureaucracy, but they would either do it on the bureaucracy's own terms, as Loris-Melikov did, or fail to act effectively, as Trepov did (see below, ch. VIII, sec. C). After the reign of Nicholas I no agent would ever again be *explicitly* empowered to break into the administration and twist it around to suit his conscience or the tsar's tastes. The tsars were still able to act arbitrarily, but when they wished to act through their government, they had to do so through a minister or group of ministers.

F. Conclusion: The Nature of Ministerial Government in the 1860s

To sum up this lengthy description of the heritage that came down to the government of the 1860s, the ministers were the legitimate descendants of the old-time omnipotent agents, yet they were obviously not omnipotent agents themselves. On the other hand, they were not the heads of a functioning administrative system that operated within a formal, systematic legal framework. Indeed, it is impossible to describe them in other than historical terms. They were the products of a long process, in the course of which aspiration and pretension to system became the main basis for legitimate political authority, including the tsar's. On the other hand, they were rulers over a government organization that was manifestly incapable of operating on a systematic basis. Arbitrary authority, therefore, had not been eliminated. It remained a vital element in government operation at all levels. What had been achieved was a measure of assurance that arbitrary authority would only be exercised by ministers; that is, *it would only be exercised on behalf of functional responsibilities that derived from a system.* To put it another way, arbitrary authority would be exercised primarily in order to impose system on society rather than to cope with society as it was. This was, in a nutshell, what the ministers could do that senatorial government had been unable to do.

The historical background of tsarist bureaucracy points to its most vital characteristic in the period 1861–1905. By the late 1850s the domestic administration was becoming conscious of the need to act arbitrarily in the name of system, and it was beginning to establish an organization that could act this way. The need for such action had not disappeared in the course of Nicholas I's reign. On the contrary, it had become more urgent, and when Nicholas's heir decided to "free" the serfs, it suddenly became massive and unavoidable.

The continuing need for arbitrary authority was not a result of backwardness, or of the tsar's stupidity, or of the gentry's corruption and selfishness. We are accustomed to assuming that the elimination of arbitrariness in government is invariably a desirable achievement. In the late nineteenth century, however, the Russian government had to be, above all, an organization that was able to operate arbitrarily in order to uphold and extend system. Bureaucracy in Russia from 1861 to 1905 did not know and could not know what it was doing or even what it was trying to do. It had to experiment, and an experimenter cannot be confined by laws. If the ministers could not act arbitrarily in the name of system, system could not exist. Arbitrariness —the power to act without guide in violation of any prescribed limits—was not a handicap or a misfortune. It was an absolutely necessary capability of whoever or whatever was to govern Russia.

CHAPTER VI

General Introduction to the Study of Tsarist Bureaucracy in 1861-1905

In the understanding of the Russian people the sincere conviction prevails that it is within the power of government authority to be concerned with everything touching the welfare and the needs of the people. In all cases of public misery, whenever it assumes considerable proportions, the people turn to the authority of the Tsar with their hopes and their trust. Considering the weak development of the habits of self-help among the population, the whole burden of coping with public misfortune falls inevitably upon the government.

SERGEI WITTE (1893)[1]

A. THE REFORMS OF THE 1860s

It will be recalled that the reforms of the 1860s virtually eliminated elective collegial posts within the agencies of the central administration. The intention was to replace the colleges with bureaucratic agencies on the one hand and separate elective institutions on the other. The new elective institutions were to operate apart from the central administration to perform those governmental functions that the central administration felt itself unable to handle on its own.[2] Accordingly, two locally elected, more or less autonomous government institutions were introduced to the countryside. The Liberation Statute established peasant villages (*selskie obshchestva*) and volosts, and the zemstvo statute of 1 January 1864 set up the zemstvoes (*zemskie uchrezhdeniia*). The village and volost administrations were elected

1. Quoted in Von Laue, p. 35.
2. Korkunov, *RGP*, II, 533–534; N. K. Brzheskii, *Naturalnye provinnosti krestian i mirskie sbory* (St. Petersburg, 1906), pp. 133–134.
Starr's recent study of the intentions behind the establishment of the zemstvoes suggests that they were highly complex. Valuev viewed the new institutions as integral parts of the *pravitelstvo*, whereas M. A. Korf, Reitern, and others viewed them as local organizations primarily concerned with local affairs. See Starr, pp. 366–367. Here, however, I use the word "separate" in a different sense. I am speaking of the structural difference between the old colleges, made up of both elected and appointed officials, and the new zemstvoes, which were entirely elective. Concerning this distinction, Valuev, Korf, and other reformers were in substantial agreement.

and staffed exclusively by peasants, whereas the zemstvoes represented all classes. The volosts were territorial units, averaging sixty to an uezd. Their jurisdiction, however, extended not to all areas and inhabitants within their boundaries but only to peasants and to the lands allotted to them in accordance with the Liberation Statute.[3] The zemstvo, on the other hand, exercised jurisdiction over the whole territory of its uezd (or gubernia), including all its inhabitants.

The basic element in the zemstvo organization was the uezd assembly (*sobranie*), a body of thirty to fifty delegates who were elected every three years by all classes of the population. Each uezd assembly elected delegates from among its members to the gubernia assembly, and these also served three-year terms. The main functions of the uezd and gubernia assemblies were to levy taxes, assign funds to finance the operations of their administrative organs, and elect executive officers—chiefly the chairman of the directorate (*predsedatel zemskogo uprava*), who managed the zemstvo's administrative organs.

In theory the zemstvoes represented all classes, but in fact they consistently adopted policies and programs that suited gentry interests and aspirations throughout the period 1861–1905. Until about 1890 they generally had little contact with the peasants, exerted little influence on them, and took little interest in them. The peasants, for their part, remained largely indifferent to the zemstvoes until the end of the tsarist regime. The peasants had the formal right to elect delegates indirectly to the uezd assembly—about a third of the total number—but the law and their own indifference assured overwhelming predominance in the assembly to the owners of large estates, most of whom were gentry.[4] The peasants did pay taxes to the zemstvo— far more than their share—and they were supposedly subject to any laws that their uezd assemblies passed, but the taxes were collected and the laws enforced by the central government's police, not by the zemstvo itself. Finally, the peasants had the right to appeal their legal

3. Leontev, *Krest. pravo* (1908), pp. 14–15, points out that despite laws limiting the jurisdiction of the volost authorities to peasant society, the subordination of elected peasant officials to the police gave the former de facto functions as authorities over the whole territory and everyone in it. On the other hand, the experience of Engelgardt, pp. 226–229, in 1878 suggests that the landed gentry could easily resist the volost elders' pretensions to territorial authority. Most volosts contained six to twelve villages.

4. B. Veselovskii, *Istoriia zemstva za sorok let* (4 vols., St. Petersburg, 1909–1911), I, 46–47; II, 55–130. The zemstvoes were only set up in thirty-four gubernias—those, generally speaking, in which there were a considerable number of Great Russian gentry. Only three of the thirty-four—Viatka, Olonets, and Perm— lacked gentry institutions. See M. M. Kataev, *Mestnyia krestianskiia uchrezhdeniia, 1861, 1874, i 1889 gg.* (3 pts., St. Petersburg, 1911), III, 5–6.

disputes to the zemstvo courts—the justices of the peace (*mirovye sudy*) that the uezd assemblies elected to handle certain categories of criminal and civil cases—but in practice they rarely availed themselves of the opportunity.[5] Even when they did, the courts had to base their verdicts on village custom rather than the relatively modern legal order that governed nonpeasant society. In short, the contacts between zemstvoes and peasant villages provided very little basis for mutual influence or the development of relationships of mutual dependence. The zemstvoes were at least as alien to peasant society as was the central government, and their overall effect was to reinforce the social separation between gentry and peasants. It was only in the 1890s that a significant number of assemblies began to interest themselves actively in the development of peasant society, chiefly through the establishment of primary schools, hospitals, and agricultural stations. Even this tendency reflected primarily the changing inclinations of the gentry rather than growing peasant participation.[6]

PEASANT INSTITUTIONS

It must be acknowledged that Alexander II's reforms embodied a tendency, or at least an intention, to assure the elected volost officials some degree of administrative autonomy. A number of legal provisions enacted in the 1860s set specific limits to the authority of the central government's servitors over the volost officials. Moreover, some nonpeasant authorities were physically removed from all participation in peasant affairs: in 1861 the serf owners and their stewards, in 1863 and 1866 the officials of the crown and state lands respectively,[7] and in 1874 the arbitrators (see above, ch. IV, sec. F). From then until 1889 the only nonpeasant officials who could exercise authority in the volosts were the police. It is arguable, therefore, that intervention by central government officials in the volosts decreased

5. Peter Czap, "The Influence of Slavophile Ideology on the Formation of the Volost Court of 1861 and the Practice of Peasant Self-Justice between 1861 and 1889" (unpublished Ph.D. dissertation, Cornell University, 1959), p. 156, notes that peasants generally avoided the justices.

6. B. Veselovskii, I, 25–26, 46–89; II, 152–232. See also below, ch. IX, sec. D. Of course, there were some exceptions to the zemstvoes' general unconcern for peasant society in the 1860s–1870s. The work of Ivan Petrunkevich is perhaps the most outstanding one. Concerning his career, see Charles Timberlake, "The Birth of Zemstvo Liberalism in Russia" (unpublished Ph.D. dissertation, University of Washington, 1968). The difficulties he experienced in getting his zemstvo interested in the peasants prove the rule.

7. See Druzhinin, *Gos. krest.*, II, 566–570. The administrators of the state and crown lands departed not immediately but only as the terms of the Liberation Statute were put into effect in their territories.

somewhat during Alexander II's reign. Only in 1878, when the rural police were expanded, did the number of officials empowered to deal with peasants increase (see below, ch. VII, n. 3).

Whatever the actual burden on the peasants at any particular time, however, there was no time in the period 1861–1905 when their institutions enjoyed real administrative autonomy. This was owing in part to the nature of the government's laws regarding the peasants and in part to the nature of the peasants' customary law.

The Liberation Statute actually increased both the central administration's power and its inclination to intervene in village affairs, mainly by introducing a massive code of government regulations regarding the villages, most of them drawn from the rules that Kiselev had tried to put into effect on the state lands. They concerned such diverse subjects as land division, sanitation, epidemic diseases, village and family relationships, religious practice, and "general morality" (see below, ch. IX, n. 40). Such rules were rarely enforced, and therefore they were of small import in themselves, but their existence, together with their nonobservance, allowed police officials to *threaten* to enforce them, thereby providing a lever by which they could interfere in the volosts arbitrarily. What effective limit could there be to the authority of an official who was legally responsible for the moral condition of the peasants under his jurisdiction, especially if the peasant way of life, including its customary legal order, was largely immoral in the light of the government's regulations?[8]

The final seal on the peasants' administrative subordination was provided by the regime of collective responsibility and customary law. According to the Liberation Statute, the members of each village were collectively responsible to the central government for the payment of direct taxes, including the performance of state labor duties (*naturalnye povinnosti*) and the payments on the debt that the peasants owed the government for their allotment lands. As in the past,

8. Korkunov, *RGP*, I, 479. The defenders of serfdom had always protested against the regulation of serf estates because they feared that a multitude of laws would oppress the serfs rather than protect them.

The phenomenon of local despots rendered powerful by an abundance of laws rather than by their absence may be said to have begun to enter into peasant life when Catherine II published the law of 19 Dec. 1774 establishing peasant-elected police and an unprecedented number of unenforceable regulations. See Grigorev, pp. 116–119. In the 1840s–1850s Kiselev's well-meant laws seem only to have added to the burden. According to one contemporary, they only served "to constrict the village population with empty formalities and to weaken the community" (Druzhinin, *Gos. krest.*, II, 535). Druzhinin observes that state peasants were helpless against the power of officials before Kiselev's reform (*ibid.*, pp. 65–69) and that they were still helpless thereafter, despite all the formal limits on police power (*ibid.*, p. 570).

collective responsibility rendered the de facto authority of the village over its members virtually absolute. The inhabitants of a village had to answer for each other; consequently, their general inclination was to value strict and decisive authority more highly than the preservation of individual rights. Collective responsibility might not by itself have fostered arbitrary rule in the villages if the peasants had possessed a sense of legal system or a framework of systematic administration. In fact, however, the vagueness and formlessness of peasant customary law allowed elected peasant authorities to exercise broad powers, and they could do this to suit their own purposes, or those of the police, or those of any person of influence in the area, peasant or nonpeasant.[9]

In sum, the combination of peasant custom and collective responsibility rendered volost and village administration into a hierarchy of arbitrary authority and set it under a government police force that derived de facto arbitrary power from the supposedly enlightened rules it was ordered to enforce. This is not to say that all peasants suffered oppression, only that peasant society enjoyed no systematic protection against oppression.

The authors of the Liberation Statute did not intend to isolate the peasant legal order permanently but only to protect the villages from the interference of their former owners.[10] Nevertheless, the effect of the Statute was to perpetuate the separation of formal legal system and peasant custom.[11] By explicitly setting the peasant villages and volosts outside legal system under their own customary law, the Statute not only *allowed* them to define and punish crimes and to

9. N. K. Brzheskii, *Ocherki iuridicheskogo byta krestian* (St. Petersburg, 1902), pp. 65–67; Czap, "Influence," pp. 68–69.
   From 1861 to 1874 the arbitrator had considerable authority over the peasants. So long as he existed, the police did not enjoy uncontested authority in the villages. Czap, "Influence," pp. 149–150, has suggested that the arbitrators actually kept the police from entering into the direct administration of the villages until 1874; Starr, pp. 197–198, points out that the police had fewer official responsibilities in the villages after 1862, and he concludes from this that their influence became weaker. Both authors give too much weight to formal jurisdictional limits. Legal rules never meant much in rural administration, and they meant virtually nothing in the peasant institutions of 1861–1905. The police had as many practical grounds for interfering in the villages before 1874 as after, though it is doubtless true that after 1874 they had a somewhat clearer field in which to operate. In 1889 a land captain (*zemskii nachalnik*) was appointed in each *uchastok* to govern the peasants. He constituted a check on the local police, but since he himself was a subordinate of the governor and ultimately of the MVD, he cannot be called a check on the police organization as a whole.
   10. Leontev, *Krest. pravo* (1914), pp. 67–68.
   11. Leontev, "Volostnoi sud," pp. 23–26, 34–35; Czap, "Influence," pp. 122–143.

resolve civil disputes according to their own custom but *forced* them to do so. Peasant inheritance, for example, was defined in each volost chiefly by what the inhabitants collectively believed it to be, and no individual peasant could escape this collective belief even if he wanted to.[12] Before 1889 individual peasants enjoyed a theoretical right to take at least some of their disputes and accusations to the courts and agencies of the central legal system, and their elected authorities could appeal against any illegal orders they received from the police, *but no one could appeal against custom.* Decisions in the peasant courts were substantively final. The regular courts in the government's legal system could only hear appeals against faulty procedures, not against the decisions themselves.[13] After 1889 the land captains (see below, ch. IX, sec. D) heard substantive appeals against volost courts, but they were charged to follow custom in their decisions whenever possible.

In short, custom provided no clear and consistent basis for judging cases; yet both peasants and higher authorities were generally forbidden to decide peasant legal affairs on any basis other than custom. In its efforts to guarantee peasant autonomy, the post-Liberation government actually held up the evolution of system in the villages and, in effect, preserved that arbitrary police authority against which it hoped to protect the peasantry. Law did not protect the individual peasant against his community; therefore, it could not effectively protect the peasant community against authorities external to it.

THE ZEMSTVOES

By contrast, the zemstvoes operated entirely within the government legal system, and this made it possible to separate their administrative organizations to some extent from the central bureaucracy. Indeed, it was the purpose of the enactors of the zemstvo statute to divorce the functions of the zemstvoes as much as possible from those of the central government (see above, n. 2). The zemstvoes had to perform various duties that the central government assigned to them—chiefly

12. Brzheskii, *Ocherki*, pp. 71–101.
13. Leontev, "Volostnoi sud," pp. 34–35. It is true that throughout the period 1861–1905 only small-scale crimes and disputes were adjudged by peasant courts. Cases involving relatively large sums or serious crimes had to be handled in government courts. Even the government, however, decided peasant cases according to custom, at least in civil disputes, except where it actually conflicted with statutory law. It may be said, then, that no institution of government offered the peasant an escape from village custom. The government might interfere now and then in peasant life, but it had no way to release peasants from their own society.

the operation of the lower courts and the maintenance of roads—and
they had to suffer some restraint in the amount of revenue they collected, but within these limits the statute of 1864 allowed them to
preside over the development of the local economy as they saw fit.
The formal administrative autonomy of the zemstvoes might have
had no more practical significance than that of the peasant volosts
had it not been for the introduction of a new system of law courts
into nonpeasant society in 1864.[14] The new courts were partly under
the central government and partly under the zemstvoes. Below the
uezd level a zemstvo-elected justice of the peace took care of minor
crimes and civil disputes.[15] On the uezd level there was a judge
(uezdnyi chlen okruzhnoi sudy) appointed for life by the central
government, and in each okrug (approximately equivalent to a gubernia), a court of appeal, likewise appointed for life. Above these
were thirteen judicial chambers, each of them having jurisdiction
over about a half dozen gubernias, and at the top of the court system
were the fourth and fifth departments of the Senate, which served in
effect as a supreme court.

The creation of a modern legal system reflected and furthered the
tendency of the 10–20 percent of the population who were not peasants to become conscious of their dependence on a systematic legal
order. The "citizens" of Russia were beginning to rely on one another
and on the officials of the government administration to operate
according to formal rules instead of putting their faith in personal
bribes and pressures. They both could and would bring a zemstvo
official before a judge or administrator for violating their legal rights.
This was a practical thing to do because the zemstvo official operated
in the same legal framework as the central government, and a judge
knew approximately what a zemstvo executive should and should not
do. Unlike the peasant elder, therefore, a zemstvo executive was not
free from judicial interference. Because he was not free to act arbi-

14. The publication of the first Svod zakonov in 1833 was followed in the 1840s
by the enactment of civil and criminal codes. The procedural code of 20 Nov.
1864 constituted the last step in the construction of a more or less modern legal
system in Russia. The new courts began operating in most of European Russia
in 1866, and, unlike the zemstvoes, they were extended to most of the rest of the
empire within a few years. In the nine gubernias of western Russia they were
not set up until 1879. See Ministerstvo iustitsii, pp. 103–112, 146–147.

15. In those gubernias where there were no zemstvoes, the justices were appointed by the minister of justice. They were eliminated in most of European
Russia in 1889 by the same law of 12 July that established the land captains. See
arts. 1–30 in the law of 12 July 1889, in Sbornik uzakonenii o krestianskikh i
sudebnykh uchrezhdeniiakh preobrazovannykh po zakonu 12-go iiuliia 1889
goda (St. Petersburg, 1895), pp. 149–165.

trarily, he could not obey arbitrary commands from the central government's officials even if he wished. Thus there were both formal and de facto assurances that zemstvo executives would not become the mere tools of the central government or buttress their own power by bribing the central government's officials. Uniform judicial system, with its effective guarantee of individual civil rights, was an important institutional basis for zemstvo administrative autonomy. Conversely, its absence in the peasant institutions was the most serious flaw in their supposed administrative autonomy.

Taken in toto, the reforms of the 1860s set the central bureaucracy and a small minority of the population of the thirty-four zemstvo gubernias under a single, self-consistent legal system that excluded the peasants. The new laws separated the central administration from the zemstvoes by putting them under a common judicial system, but they failed to separate the central administration from the volosts because they did not and could not put them under a common judicial system.

The separation between zemstvo and central bureaucracy produced, or at least implied, a number of changes in rural political organization. In their new zemstvoes the gentry gained a measure of protection from the central government's interference. The agencies of the central government, on the other hand, were somewhat more free than they had been from the informal influence of the gentry. Instead of relying on gentry-elected servitors within its ranks, the government could use the new zemstvoes as institutions.

Ideally, the zemstvoes could take care of local governmental problems, such as education and medical care, that the central government was not equipped to handle. At the same time they could serve as an amalgamating force in society that would give recognizable form to local needs and aspirations and communicate them to the central administration. Before the 1860s gentry institutions had been little more than hierarchies for distributing patronage. They had dominated both local society and central government agencies without really giving corporate identity to the one or serving the other. The zemstvoes, on the other hand, constituted something like self-governing bodies of citizens, capable of formulating common interests and pursuing common purposes.

The improvement of political organization in the locales had another side to it. With the partial separation of local gentry society from government service, the new "citizen-gentry" had no further call to trouble themselves about the peasants. While the peasants were being set directly under the police and made collectively responsible to them, the citizenry of the zemstvoes were excluded from peasant society and absolved of any responsibility for peasant welfare. The onset of system, then, did not unite peasant laws and institutions with those of the gentry. What it did do was to cut the citizenry off from the peasantry and leave the peasantry bonded to the bureaucracy. The inescapable implication of this state of affairs was that the ministries were assuming full responsibility for peasant welfare. Here and there a zemstvo might help out with the peasants, but the ministers were responsible for them.

B. New Responsibilities of the Ministries after 1861

It has been noted that one characteristic difficulty of Russian administration from Peter's time until the Liberation was the sharp disparity between the ideals of system and the practical requirements of operation. The officials could not adhere to system and still get their work done even if they wanted to. Usually, therefore, they did what seemed necessary and expedient from day to day while pretending and aspiring to operate according to system. Chains of command and office routines were established, forgotten, and re-established unendingly, but outside the capital city no standard system emerged. When an official in a gubernia or uezd actually functioned with a purpose in mind larger than the satisfaction of his own whims or the demands of his superior, he generally found that he had to work according to custom and social structure in his locale, utilizing his formal prerogatives to influence and manipulate local factions in whatever ways he could. Very little that he did resembled coordination with other members of a systematic organization; consequently, if the rules of system came to him at all, they came as a burden—more faked reports, more facades, more formalistic constraints—not as a mechanism to be used or relied on.

   The "triumph" of the ministries in the 1860s did not change this situation. Ministerial government did not overcome its rivals by its own powers and capabilities but only assumed their responsibilities by default as they broke down in the face of their own dilemmas. The fall of senatorial government did not resolve the problems of domestic administration but only dumped them into the ministers' laps. Indeed, the problems were now harsher than ever. The authors of the Liberation Statute had hoped that legal system would evolve by itself in the new peasant villages and volosts,[16] but as this hope

16. Leontev, *Krest. pravo* (1914), pp. 101–108, and Skerpan, pp. 172–180,

quickly proved illusory, the ministers faced the terrible necessity of acting directly in the name of system upon a society that was unable to comprehend system or respond to it. This was no liberation. It was, rather, a naked bureaucracy confronting a helpless society head on.

When it became apparent that legal system was not extending itself by spontaneous social and economic evolution to include the peasantry, the bureaucracy of 1861–1905 had to face a number of conflicting responsibilities. First, like all earlier forms of Russian government, it had to collect revenue, muster recruits, and do whatever else was necessary to maintain the state's military power. Second, since its servitors organized themselves around their common commitment to system, they had to make some attempt to operate systematically. Third, since the ministries (chiefly the MVD) dealt directly with the peasants and allowed no other institution to become involved with them—no serf owners, no governors-general, no all-powerful gendarmes—they were committed to act in order to introduce system *whether their programs could be carried out by properly systematic operation or not.* If and when the government acted upon peasant society, it would have no system to guide it, only its compulsion to act. Unconsciously but inescapably, the government bureaucracy after 1861 was forming itself for an onslaught on peasant society, and this was the key element in its development throughout the period 1861–1905.

C. The Compulsion to Attack the Peasantry

As stated above, the enactors of the Liberation did not intend that there be an onslaught on the peasantry. On the contrary, they consistently rejected any measures that would encourage government interference in the villages. In the ensuing decades, however, legal system did not develop in the villages. Worse, a substantial minority of the peasants suffered increasing impoverishment and social disorganization (see above, ch. I, sec. C), and as their condition grew worse, the pressure on the ministries to act increased sharply.

This pressure was not explicitly directed toward ministerial action. Almost all concrete recommendations for action were combined with demands for the elimination of one or more elements in the existing legal-administrative system in order to "allow" the peasants to develop on their own. These demands, however, came ultimately to the tsar,

---

describe the intentions of the members of the editing commissions when they drafted the Liberation Statute.

and their implication was much clearer than their explicit proposals. In one way or another they all said "You are responsible," and to this naked fact of life the tsar had only three ways to respond: 1) a manifesto proclaiming his hope that the peasants would learn to take care of themselves;[17] 2) a manifesto proclaiming his hope that the zemstvoes would take care of social and economic problems, each in its own area;[18] and 3) a decision to act.[19] In the decades after 1861 the "tsar's will" tried all three of these at one time or another. Whenever it was the third, the tsar turned to his ministers, and he turned to them because he had no other agencies at his disposal.

It is conceivable, of course, that the government could have relied on the gentry zemstvoes and gentry institutions. After all, the gentry had carried out the Liberation, thereby demonstrating their loyalty and their ability to organize themselves to do the tsar's bidding. But the Liberation had also shown that the gentry would not organize themselves to act except when the tsar ordered. They might perform specific tasks that the tsar assigned to them, but he could not rely on them to assume general responsibility for rural welfare. They had demonstrated their inability to take the initiative in reform programs before the 1860s, and they continued to demonstrate it in their zemstvo assemblies for several decades thereafter.[20] As said before, zemstvo participation in the social and economic development of rural society as a whole became a significant phenomenon only in the 1890s, and even then it grew only slowly and sporadically in this or that uezd or gubernia. What the tsar needed in the late nineteenth century was a means to systematic action in the countryside, and although his bureaucracy suffered from many shortcomings, it seemed a more promising agency than the gentry zemstvoes.

Dmitri Miliutin, war minister from 1862 until 1881, was one of the leading upholders of zemstvo autonomy among the statesmen of his time, but his notion of it did not include zemstvo leadership or responsibility. "In Russia," he wrote in 1864–1865,

> reform can be carried out only by authority. We have too much disturbance and too much divergence of interests to expect anything good from the representation of these interests. . . . Besides, our reforms must cover the whole empire; any exceptional usages in this or that locale will harm the unity of the state, giving rise to separatism

17. E.g., that of 19 Feb. 1861.
18. E.g., the recommendation of the Kakhanov commission's subcommittee (1881–1883) in Tsentralnyi gosudarstvennyi istoricheskii Arkhiv Leningrada (hereinafter cited as TsGIAL), f. 1317, op. 1, d. 71, vol. II.
19. E.g., the statute of 12 July 1889 establishing the land captains.
20. V. Trutovskii, *Sovremennoe zemstvo* (Petrograd, 1914), pp. 146–148.

and rivalry. . . . Strong authority does not preclude the personal liberty of the citizen or self-governing institutions. . . . But he who desires the true welfare of Russia . . . should firmly renounce anything that can weaken the unity of authority.[21]

Another sometime believer in zemstvo autonomy, Pavel Valuev, put it this way in a note in the early 1860s:

His majesty has made it clear that the basic principles underlying zemstvo administration are to be the unity and independence of the local interests of each gubernia and uezd. Matters touching local interests are to be entrusted to local institutions. . . . [But] the unity of the central administration, the force and integrity of state authority, cannot yield to the demands of local interest, however important and legal they may be. The zemstvo administration is only a special organ of the state. Its rights and powers come to it from the state. The zemstvoes have their place in the organism of the state and they cannot exist outside it. Like the other parts of the organism, they are subordinated to those general conditions and regulations that are established by the central government.[22]

The implication of Miliutin's and Valuev's views is clear, though neither of them saw it: centralized bureaucracy was the government's most likely means for introducing social reform. Indeed, it was more than a means. It had emerged since 1802 in response to the compulsive need of politically conscious Russians for governmental action to bring legal system (perfect justice) to their country. From the 1860s on, the sense of functional responsibility became the main generator of the impulse to change the countryside in accordance with capital-city ideals and needs. The zemstvoes offered no viable alternative to action by the central bureaucracy. The only serious question they posed was how the ministers were to use them.[23]

21. Quoted in Zaionchkovskii's introduction to Miliutin's *Dnevnik*, I, 31–32.
22. Pavel A. Valuev, *Obiasnitelnaia zapiska k proektam polozheniia o zemskikh uchrezhdeniiakh i vremennykh pravil dlia ikh uchrezhdenii* (St. Petersburg, 186–), p. 26.
23. Starr, pp. 110–376, presents a detailed description of the government's projects for local autonomous governing bodies in the 1850s and 1860s. He points out that a number of them, especially the ones produced in the MVD, were designed explicitly to allow the central government to act more effectively. These plans, however, had little in common with visions of ardent zemstvoists, inspired by their new political rights, springing forward to turn their uezds into blooming gardens. Such visions proceeded from a conviction that the central government should refrain from acting, not that it should be enabled to act effectively. Obviously, when I speak of the irrelevance of local autonomous institutions to the problem of government action, I am referring only to zemstvoist visions, not to the MVD's projects. As for these projects, some of them were relevant to the problems of a centralized bureaucracy trying to invade a society. So far as I can see, however, they did not offer any alternative to this bureaucracy.

D. The Dilemmas of Ministerial Action

As said before, the impetus to bureaucratic onslaught on the country-side found expression, from the 1830s on, in a tendency to expand and multiply the local agencies of the separate ministries. Each agency was a separate body, subject to its own ministerial superior in St. Petersburg, and since the governors themselves were only agents of the MVD, the new agencies constituted separate centers of authority in the gubernias and uezds. Each was responsible to its own home office in St. Petersburg; none was responsible to any recognizable social or administrative institution in the territory in which it operated. As these agencies expanded, therefore, they tended to undermine the coherence and unity of territorial administration.

The multiplication of autonomous ministerial agencies began to cause problems even before the Liberation. From the 1830s on, there was a continual struggle between the gubernia-level ministerial organs on the one hand and the governors and their police on the other, and these local conflicts created interministerial tensions at the highest level of government. The governors almost invariably held ranks lower than those of the ministers, and the law prevented them from interfering on their own with the ministerial agents in their territories. In order to discharge their responsibilities, therefore, they often had to appeal to the MVD for support, and these appeals were likely to develop into jurisdictional disputes between the MVD and the other ministers. In this way the old conflicts between governors-general and central administrators, which had been left to the tsar to resolve, were now transformed into a disruptive force within the ministerial bureaucracy itself. Like senatorial government, ministerial bureaucracy could introduce elements of system into its organization only at the price of communicating ever more of the countryside's disorder to the capital cities. The ministries' onslaught on the peasants tended to be self-defeating in the villages, while in St. Petersburg it plunged the ministries into paralyzing conflicts with one another.[24]

These organizational dilemmas help to make intelligible the seemingly erratic evolution of the tsarist government's domestic programs during the period 1861–1917. The ministers of that time had a propensity for forming committees, gathering materials, drafting projects, and then enacting nothing; the laws they did pass seemed to mark sharp, unintelligent reversals in policy. Many scholars—and many of the officials themselves—have taken this seeming aimlessness and paralysis to reflect the sloth, corruption, and political backwardness

24. See my article "Some Aspects," pp. 68–90; below, ch. VIII, sec. A.

of certain statesmen and/or classes. Others have attributed all vacillations in policy to the statesmen's fears of "revolutionary" violence[25] or the insidious personal influence of "reactionary" charlatans and fools who managed to get close to the tsar.[26] But the effects of violent crowds and reactionary courtiers on government action have been consistently exaggerated. Contemporaries and historians alike have generally ignored the simple fact that governing Russia in the period 1861–1917 was a colossally difficult task involving a number of utterly unprecedented problems, the solution of which demanded contradictory policies.

E. Evolution of the Government's Attitude
toward Peasant Reform: 1861–1905

We are attempting to study the tsarist government as a social structure that evolved out of its interaction with the people, chiefly the peas-

25. See e.g., Zaionchkovskii, *Krizis,* pp. 7–18.

26. A typical example of the personal-influence approach to the study of tsarist policy is L. G. Mamulova, "Zemskaia kontrreforma 1890 g.," *Nauchnye doklady vysshei shkoly: Istoricheskie nauki,* no. 4 (1960), pp. 60–85.

The readiness of tsarist servitors to believe in the insidious personal influence of those whose views were opposed to their own is illustrated by a story taken from the diary of Alexander A. Polovtsov, the imperial secretary from 1883 to 1892. In early May 1885 Petr A. Shuvalov informed the Grand Duke Mikhail Nikolaevich (president of the State Council) that Mikhail N. Katkov had told him (Shuvalov) that he (Katkov) had been to see the tsar (Alexander III) to express his disapproval of a project then in the process of passing through the State Council. According to Shuvalov, Katkov claimed that the tsar had agreed with him and told him to go to Konstantin Pobedonostsev and Mikhail Ostrovskii (members of the State Council holding ministerial posts) and encourage them to oppose the project in the Council meeting. The grand duke hastened to pass Shuvalov's story on to Polovtsov (that is, the manager of his, the grand duke's, chancellery). When Polovtsov heard the story, he grew angry at this back-door politicking. He recommended that the grand duke ask the tsar to name Katkov to the State Council, where he would have to make his attacks openly and answer for them. If the tsar refused this request, the grand duke was to ask permission to resign his post. The next day the grand duke went to the tsar (his nephew) and did as Polovtsov had suggested. The tsar replied that he had not seen Katkov for several months and had never discussed the project at hand with him. See Alexander A. Polovtsov, *Dnevnik A. A. Polovtsova* (2 vols., Moscow, 1966), I, 322–324.

The story shows that Katkov could indeed make his influence felt in the government without occupying any official post. On the other hand, it illustrates the strong tendency among the high statesmen to exaggerate such unofficial influence and to believe that intrigues were being hatched against them by their opponents. Polovtsov and Shuvalov were both capable statesmen with long experience in a variety of high posts. Polovtsov was one of the most level-headed and perceptive of all the nineteenth-century statesmen and one of the least inclined to dream up intrigues that were not there. Examples of such intrigue-imagining appear far more frequently in the memoirs and diaries of more excitable servitors such as Valuev, Sergei Witte, and Dmitri Miliutin, to say nothing of Pobedonostsev.

ants. After 1861 the nature of this interaction underwent some changes, and the attitudes of the government's servitors changed accordingly. Speaking broadly, the period 1861–1905 was essentially a time when the tsarist government awoke to the responsibilities it had unwittingly assumed toward the peasants in 1861. The awakening was gradual, mainly because it took a long time for the enduring trends that the Liberation had set in motion to make themselves felt. The physical completion of the Liberation—the actual allotting of lands to the liberated peasantry—required more than two decades, and it was not until the 1870s that leading statesmen were forced to the conclusion that the peasantry as a whole were in serious difficulty. It took until the late 1880s to decide that the central administration would have to take action, and yet another fifteen years passed before it decided what the action would be. Only in 1906 did a coherent program of peasant reform actually commence.

There were a few statesmen as far back as the 1860s who believed for various reasons that the central government should play an active role in the development of the peasantry. A. E. Timashev, MVD from 1868 to 1877, tried in 1869 to convert the arbitrators into permanent agents of his ministry in order to provide the central government with an organization that could devote itself to peasant reform. But this attempt and others of a similar nature were opposed for many years by the majority of Alexander II's ministers, most decisively by his brother, the Grand Duke Konstantin Nikolaevich.[27] In Alexander II's time, says A. A. Polovtsov, both "rightist" and "liberal" statesmen labored under the very real dread of any return to what they considered to have been the over-bureaucratization of Nicholas I's reign, and they generally opposed any measure that openly extended ministerial power into society.[28]

In the Great Liberator's last years fear of bureaucracy began to give way to a fast-growing compulsion to do something to cope with the crisis in the countryside. The reforms proposed under the "dictatorship" of Mikhail Loris-Melikov in 1879–1881 reflect both new compulsion and old fear. On the one hand, the would-be dictator wanted to subject the peasants to a drastic land reform. On the other, he assumed that such a reform would somehow be accepted by the peasants voluntarily and that the central administration would have

27. Kataev, II, 56–58. For a full discussion of the attempts from 1864 on to convert the arbitrators into *pravitelstvo* agents, see Chernukha, pp. 225–234.
28. See Polovtsov, *Dnevnik* (1966), I, 448–449; above, ch. IV, sec. D. On Polovtsov, see below, ch. VII, sec. B.

little more to do than issue regulations.[29] He used the same sort of jargon-play with regard to the zemstvoes. He affected to recommend greater autonomy for them but tied their freedom to expectations that they would cooperate with the central government's policies.[30] It may be said, then, that Loris-Melikov had come to recognize the need for bureaucratic action but was not yet ready to call for it openly.

In the period 1861–1881 the government's policies and actions in the countryside reflected two basic beliefs regarding peasant reform: 1) that the government's purpose was to allow society to develop on its own, and 2) that the government's actions should be completely planned in advance so that they might be carried out within the framework of a uniform legal-administrative system. These beliefs were essentially senatorial. The only thing that distinguished them from the convictions of the early nineteenth century (see above, ch. III, sec. C) was their implied assumption that society was not merely going to express its innate legal order but to undergo some sort of change in the natural course of events.

The first belief found expression in the major reforms that were actually introduced during Alexander II's reign. The zemstvoes and law courts of 1864, the town dumas of 1870, and the practice of encouraging private enterprise to develop Russia's industry were all calculated to *allow* society to develop. The military reform of 1874 was exceptional in that it had some aspects of a government-directed social reform, but it was not designed primarily to achieve domestic purposes.

The second belief found its expression in some reforms that the statesmen tried to introduce. During the late 1860s and 1870s a number of commissions made investigations of local government and the revenue system. They submitted lengthy reports, but the gist of most of their recommendations was that although reforms were needed, they would have to come as part of a general scheme. In the early 1870s, for example, everyone agreed that revenue collection was in drastic need of reform. A new system was drafted in 1870–1873 and sent out to the gubernia administrations and zemstvoes for comment. All the responses agreed on the need for change, but most of them said that the change had to be much more sweeping than a mere alteration in tax-collecting methods. Peasant institutions would have to undergo a thorough overhaul. Unfortunately, the responses made no concrete suggestions as to *how* such fundamental social changes

29. Zaionchkovskii, *Krizis*, pp. 347–348.
30. See *ibid.*, pp. 216–219.

could be introduced. The only specific remarks in them had to do with reasons why this or that reform would be impracticable.[31] Recommendations of this sort were typical of the material the central government got whenever it asked its agencies for suggestions.[32] It is not entirely reprehensible, therefore, that the central administration refrained from any massive executive action throughout Alexander II's reign. All it did was to go on searching for master plans while waiting hopefully for society to transform itself and to resolve the dilemmas of its transformation on its own. There was, of course, no end of government interference in the countryside, but this was largely of the old, uncontrolled variety. Bureaucracy per se was not interfering, only demonstrating its continuing inability to control and direct its own agencies.

The decision to act in the countryside without waiting for a comprehensive plan began to gain force in 1885 with the dismissal of Mikhail S. Kakhanov as deputy MVD and the shelving of his commission's report (see below, ch. IX, sec. D). In 1885–1890 Alexander III and Dmitri Tolstoi (his MVD) mustered sufficient determination to enact a two-part program into law against the resistance of almost all the other ministers and members of the State Council. The first part took the form of a statute that was enacted in July 1889, setting up the land captains; the second was the statute of June 1890, which introduced a number of reforms in the zemstvoes.

The land captains were agents of the MVD set up on the *uchastok* level, six to ten in each uezd, to preside over the peasant volosts. The statute of 1889 gave the new officials virtually absolute authority over the volosts and allowed them to work directly under the governors, free from the confusion of the regular multi-ministerial administration. The main idea was that they should have freedom of action *under the direction of the MVD,* much like that which the old omnipotent agents of the eighteenth century had enjoyed *directly under the tsar.*

31. See *Svod otzyvov gubernskikh prisutstvii po krestianskim delam i zakliuchenii gubernatorov po proektu preobrazovaniia podushnoi sistemy sborov sostavlennomu v ministerstve finansov* (2 vols., St. Petersburg, 1873).

32. Similar piles of vague recommendations without any useful suggestions about their implementation may be found in the report of the Valuev commission —*Doklad vysochaishe utverzhdennoi* (26 *maia 1872*)—and that of the ministry of justice's commission on volost courts—*Trudy komissii po preobrazovaniiu volostnykh sudov* (7 vols., St. Petersburg, 1873). But the production of these relatively short-lived bodies is dwarfed by the shelf-fuls turned out by the *Komissiia o gubernskikh i uezdnykh uchrezhdeniiakh*, which went on grinding out studies and projects long after the reforms of the 1860s had come into being. See the MVD's report on the *Komissiia* in 1881, in TsGIAL, f. 1317, op. 1, d. 102.

The main reason they were to have freedom of action was that they would have to operate without any clear plan or concrete purpose. They did not know what peasant society was like or what to do with it; consequently, they would have to work for a while and gain experience before they could formulate the laws they should follow. Tolstoi, the leading enactor of the 1889 statute, frequently implied that his land captains represented a peculiar kind of reform, one that had to go into effect before precise guidelines and aims could be formulated.

Tolstoi died in the spring of 1889, and his successor, I. N. Durnovo, seems to have been a less capable man. The second part of the program, therefore, was enacted with somewhat less determination than the first, though it was imbued with the same spirit. The statute of June 1890 gave the zemstvo administrations substantially greater freedom of action than they had previously enjoyed but made the administrators responsible to the central administration, chiefly the MVD, as well as to the assemblies of elected delegates. This brought the zemstvo administrations much closer to being agencies for carrying out central government politices in the countryside.[33]

The extension of government agencies into the countryside did not immediately produce dramatic results. Primary schools and hospitals were established at a much faster rate than ever before, but measures of actual social change in the 1890s consisted of little more than tinkering with the peasants' tax and debt obligations in order to allow hardship cases to postpone their payments. After 1900, however, the tempo of reform quickened measurably. Collective responsibility was abolished in 1903. In 1904 virtually all the peasants' arrears in their debt payments to the government were abruptly written off—ostensibly to celebrate the birth of an heir to the throne. In November 1905 the debt the peasants had owed the government for their allotment land since the 1860s was canceled. By then the so-called Stolypin reform had already been drawn up in the offices of the MVD, and in the following year the government at last began its long-awaited program of bureaucratically organized peasant reform.

During the same period in which rural administration was feeling its way through experience toward comprehensive action, the government gradually intensified its intervention into private industry.[34]

33. "Novoe zemskoe polozhenie," *Iuridicheskaia letopis*, I (Oct. 1890), 299–300 (probably by N. M. Korkunov). The law of 13 June 1890 required, among other things, that the MVD approve the election of the chairman of the zemstvo directorate. See *ibid.*, p. 341. See also ch. IX, sec. D.

34. Regarding the evolution of government industrial policies, see Gindin, pp. 3–94.

Government-sponsored industrialization and government-imposed agrarian reform came together in the period 1881–1905, both arising out of piecemeal actions and evolving into increasingly comprehensive programs. Both, therefore, reflected a radical departure from the assumptions underlying the Liberation and the regime of Alexander II. As actions, however, they constituted a more or less natural outgrowth of the Liberation.

F. Conclusion

The development of the tsarist government's attitude toward peasant reform in 1861–1905 was not merely a continuous vacillation in the capital cities from one political conviction or prejudice to another. It proceeded basically from relationships between the government-society and the peasantry. New elements emerged in these relationships after the Liberation and gradually imposed themselves on the awareness of the local administrators. Awareness, however, did not mean enlightenment. The administrators did not recognize new developments and then unite themselves around measures to deal with them. In most cases they recognized only the practical difficulties they encountered in their everyday work. They found themselves unable to perform their functions or achieve their purposes, and they fell to blaming one another and pressing for new laws that would free them from interference. Conflicts on the lower levels of the administration communicated themselves to the statesmen in the capital city; as the statesmen reacted, they, too, came into conflict. Ultimately, the nature of the government began to change, reflecting and furthering the developing interaction between its lower echelons and the peasantry. The following three chapters will undertake to describe this process in somewhat greater detail.

CHAPTER VII

The Constitutional Framework
of Ministerial Government

I do have convictions, strong ones. Those who think I do not are wrong. But I consider myself obliged to learn the views of the sovereign emperor first of all, as is my duty according to my oath of fidelity and submission. If I establish by some means, direct or indirect, that the sovereign's attitude toward something is different from mine, I consider it my duty to abandon my convictions and even work against them, with . . . even more energy than if I were guided by my own private opinion.

VICTOR PANIN[1]

Any government must be based on some kind of principle. At present, our principle is the delimitation of authority. Authority is not viewed as a means but as a purpose, or a right, or a possession. We demand obedience, but in whose name do we demand it? Only in the name of the duty to obey and the right to give orders. But it remains to be proven that either of these is really useful—that commands from one side and submissiveness from the other are enough to secure the well-being of the fatherland. Without new forms, well-being cannot be secured. We are turning into a vicious circle and we don't want to find a way out of it.

PAVEL VALUEV (1866)

As used here, the term "constitutional framework" carries no necessary implication of representative government. The constitutional ideal that the tsarist government was trying to establish in the nineteenth century—insofar as it was trying to establish one—envisioned an administration in which no servitor would be above the law. The tsar would retain his absolute authority, but he would use it to prevent all other persons in the empire from transgressing the law. Ideally, every element in ministerial government but one aspired to operate under a single consistent code of regulations, the one exception being the tsar's personal responsibility to sustain this code.

1. Quoted in Field, pp. 594–595. Panin was minister of justice in the early years of Alexander II's reign.

A. The Supreme Organs

The formal structure of ministerial government divided itself roughly into two parts: the supreme organs (*verkhovnye organy*) and the subordinate organs (*podchinennye organy*). The most important of the subordinate organs were the ministries, and since the main task of the supreme organs was to hold the ministries together, the most important of them were the three that had to do with interministerial coordination: the State Council, the Committee of Ministers, and the Senate.[2] The "supremacy" of the State Council stemmed primarily from its duty to consider legislative projects and annual budgets and to make recommendations to the tsar regarding them. The Committee of Ministers also considered legislative projects now and then, but its primary function in the second half of the nineteenth century was to decide specific matters that arose in the course of the administration's activity. Usually these decisions were executive in nature, affecting only particular cases. Sometimes, however, they contained general legal rules, and these had the same force as the recommendations of the State Council.[3] The Committee, in other words, was as "powerful" as the State Council. The Senate was in part a judicial body, but its first department was a high administrative court whose primary function was to decide disputes concerning the legality of the actions and policies of the subordinate organs.[4]

The supremacy of the supreme organs, like that of the eighteenth-century Senate, resided in functions rather than prerogatives. The State Council formulated recommendations concerning proposed legislation, but it did not possess the exclusive prerogative to legislate. Likewise, the Committee of Ministers made recommendations to the tsar with regard to executive matters, but it was by no means the sole source of such recommendations. As for the Senate, it generally decided only those cases that the ministers submitted to it. If the tsar chose, he or his ministers could legislate, issue executive orders, and render judicial decisions through any of the supreme organs or with-

2. See Lazarevskii, I, 449, and Korkunov, *RGP*, II, 2–6, on the distinction between supreme and subordinate organs.
3. The law of 9 June 1878, which established the semi-military *uriadniki* in the rural police organizations of the European Russian gubernias, was enacted through the Committee of Ministers. See Zaionchkovskii, *Krizis*, pp. 67–68.
4. Korkunov, *RGP*, II, 6. Some legal scholars do not list the Senate as a supreme organ (e.g., Lazarevskii, I, 458), partly because its subordination to the minister of justice rendered its formal position ambiguous. Be this as it may, the Senate played a major role in the business of coordinating the ministers and compelling their agencies to adhere to the law, whether it was "really" supreme or not. See Lazarevskii, II, 138, 164–166, 182.

out consulting supreme organs at all. In 1861–1905 the possibility that the tsar would do these things was very real.

A number of permanent supreme organs functioned alongside the three main ones. Each one taken by itself played only a peripheral role in domestic administration, but their presence in the government is of some significance to our discussion.

The Council of Ministers (*Sovet Ministrov*) was probably the most important of them, or would have been had it been utilized. Alexander II set it up in 1857 (officially in 1861) for the purpose of considering legislative proposals from individual ministers before their submission to the State Council. In order to unite the ministers firmly behind their collective decisions and to impart authority to them, he ordered that the meetings of the Council of Ministers should always be presided over by the tsar himself. In theory, with the tsar's signature on all its decisions, this was the most supreme organ of them all. In fact, however, it virtually ceased to exist shortly after founding. Its archives indicate that in all its history, this would-be ministerial legislature handled only ninety-six matters, almost all of them before 1865. It continued to exist on paper until October 1905, when it was drastically transformed into something resembling a Western-style cabinet, but after about 1870 it only met on exceptional occasions.[5]

Polovtsov offers two explanations for the atrophy of the Council of Ministers. On the one hand, it proved inadequate for handling high-level executive problems because it had too many members who were prone to leak secrets.[6] On the other, it was unsuitable as a legislative body because the tsar's participation rendered it too powerful vis-à-vis the State Council. According to Polovtsov's paraphrasing, Alexander III expressed this idea in February 1887: "Pobedonostsev often urged me

5. Zaionchkovskii, *Krizis*, pp. 21–22; *Istoricheskii obzor . . . Komiteta*, III, pt. 1, 5–16; IV, 76. According to Zaionchkovskii, the Council of Ministers never met between 1881 and 1905. This is substantially true, but Polovtsov's diary describes a meeting of 16 Mar. 1899, called at the request of Witte to decide whether or not the government should encourage the investment of foreign capital in Russia. See Alexander A. Polovtsov, "Dnevnik A. A. Polovtseva [*sic*]," *Krasnyi Arkhiv* (106 vols., 1922–1941), XLVI (1931), 120–121. Since this was not a legislative decision, it may be said that the Council of Ministers had no *legislative* meeting in the period 1882–1904 and that it did not play any significant role in coordinating the ministers during this period.

The decree of 18 Feb. 1905 (*TPSZ*, 25853) revived the Council briefly by ordering it to draft legislation to carry out constitutional reforms. For several months it worked on a number of projects until a decree of 6 Aug. 1905 (*ibid.*, 26657) relieved it of this, its last responsibility. From then until its transformation in October, it remained inactive.

6. Polovtsov, *Dnevnik* (1966), I, 315.

to consider projects in the Council of Ministers before bringing them before the State Council; but in the first place this would be an expression of my opinion, which would hamper the State Council's consideration, and in the second place the Council of Ministers has so many members that further consideration in the State Council would be a waste of time. . . ."[7]

There were yet other permanent supreme organs. His Majesty's Own Imperial Chancellery, which had enjoyed so much power in the first decade of Nicholas I's reign, continued to be a supreme organ throughout the tsarist period. After 1894 it was supposed to be the final arbiter in all personnel matters—promotions, awards, dismissals, etc.[8] Two other formally supreme organs, the "ministry" of the imperial household and the imperial chief apartment (*imperatorskaia glavnaia kvartira*), concerned themselves primarily with the imperial family.[9] The military council, admiralty council, finance committee, and guardianship council were all supreme organs.[10] The military and admiralty councils were lawmaking bodies for the army and naval organizations, empowered in many cases to enact orders and regulations without going through the State Council or the Committee of Ministers.[11] The finance committee was in practice little more than a discussion group that made recommendations regarding the financial policies of the government. On paper, it sounded like a pre-revolutionary Gosplan, but it did not often play a role in the coordination of the ministries.[12]

7. *Ibid.*, II, 19.
8. See above, ch. V, n. 102. Zaionchkovskii, *Rossiiskoe samoderzhavie*, pp. 109–111, considers the imperial chancellery's new personnel functions to have been nothing more than crude measures to insure the political reliability of government servitors. Whether or not they also embodied a serious attempt to standardize personnel policies and reduce petty despotism in government offices is a question that awaits further study.
9. Korkunov, *RGP*, II, 6. The "ministry" of the imperial household was a ministry in name only. Baron Fredericks, who held the post from 1897 until 1917, testified before the examining commission of the Provisional Government that he had never attended a meeting of the Council of Ministers (the chief coordinating body for the ministers after Oct. 1905) and did not even know where it met. See *Padenie tsarskogo rezhima* (7 vols., Leningrad, 1924), V, 33–34.
10. On the guardianship council, see Lazarevskii, I, 464, and Korkunov, *RGP*, II, 265–269. The list of supreme organs varies somewhat from one author to the next. The government's own publication, *Statesman's Handbook for Russia*, I, 50, lists the military and admiralty councils and the finance committee. Korkunov, *RGP*, II, 6, on the other hand, does not list these but does include the ministry of the imperial household and the imperial chief apartment. W. Gribowski, *Das Staatsrecht des russischen Reiches* (Tübingen, 1912), p. 83, lists the holy synod as a supreme organ.
11. Lazarevskii, I, 407.
12. *Ibid.*, pp. 462–463. The finance committee's action on 2 Jan. 1897, putting Russia on the gold standard, was exceptional (see below, pp. 271–272).

Finally, there was the imperial office for receiving petitions, an essentially judicial body empowered to hear appeals in judicial cases against the decisions of the Senate. From 1884 to 1895 it was attached to the State Council, but in the latter year it was renamed his majesty's chancellery for receiving petitions and was separated from the Council to become a supreme organ in its own right.[13]

In addition to the permanent supreme organs, there were always a number of more or less temporary bodies in existence that exercised "supreme" prerogatives within limited functional jurisdictions. The tsars often appointed temporary committees or commissions to draw up decrees, supervise the execution of a policy, or oversee the government of a territory. Some, like the secret committee that drafted the new regulations regarding the tsar's family in 1885, were called together only to draft one law and then dismissed.[14] Others, like the committee for the Siberian railroad, remained active for several years or even decades and acquired a measure of institutional status.[15] One of the most important of this type was the chief committee for the management of rural society, which operated from 1861 until 1882 to supervise the implementation of the Liberation Statute. Its work carried it into such a profusion of legislative, judicial, and executive functions that they had to be parceled out at the time of its dissolution to a number of organs—legislative matters to the State Council and judicial cases to the newly created second department of the Senate. Other "temporary"

13. *IPS*, III, 202–203.

14. When, in 1885, Alexander III felt the need to set new limits to the number of the tsar's relatives that should be officially designated as members of the imperial family, he called together Alexander Polovtsov (the imperial secretary), I. I. Vorontsov-Dashkov (minister of the imperial household), and the Grand Duke Vladimir Aleksandrovich (his brother) to determine how to go about it. Polovtsov had already drafted a proposal that set forth Alexander's general intentions, and the group approved it. It was then shown to A. V. Adlerberg (former minister of the imperial household), who made a few changes, after which it was discussed and approved once more by all the above. All this took place in Jan. 1885. Sometime later, another, more formal ad hoc commission was appointed to draft the final legislation, and it presented its draft to the tsar in June 1886. He approved the draft, and it was enacted into law in the decree of 2 July 1886 (*TPSZ*, 3851) without ever coming before any of the permanent supreme organs. It subsequently appeared in the next edition of the *Svod zakonov* as the major part of the "Uchrezhdenie imperatorskoi familii," vol. I, pt. 1, bk. 2. In effect, these two ad hoc commissions were supreme organs during the short time of their existence, despite their extreme informality. See Polovtsov, *Dnevnik* (1966), I, 274–282, 393–398, 401, 434–435, 544.

15. *Svod zakonov*, vol. I, pt. 2, bk. 3, "Uchrezhdenie komiteta sibirskoi zheleznoi dorogi." According to Sergei Iu. Witte, *Vospominaniia* (3 vols., Moscow, 1960), I, 434–437, this committee, established in 1891, was essentially a gimmick to get legislation passed without having to go through the State Council or the Committee of Ministers, where it was likely to meet with opposition.

committees managed various border areas from time to time, usually during periods when the regular administration was undergoing reform. At one time or another there were committees for western Russia, Poland, Finland, the Baltic gubernias, the Caucasus, and Siberia.

Ordinarily, the "supreme" temporary committees were smaller replicas of the Committee of Ministers, exercising the same kind of influence in a particular matter or a special field of action that the Committee was supposed to exercise over the whole government.[16] They generally included a few ministers, members of the State Council, senators, and/or relatives of the tsar. When one of them engaged in legislative work, it generally confined itself to submitting draft projects to the State Council for approval. It sometimes happened, however, that the tsar would approve a special committee's decision before it went to the Council, and this was tantamount to forcing its acceptance. In short, the special committees, like the Council of Ministers, could be used by the tsar and his ministers to bypass the regular supreme organs entirely[17] or to overcome resistance in the State Council by presenting projects already approved by the tsar.

It may be said that the large number and variety of supreme organs, both temporary and permanent, reflected the weakness of system in the tsarist government and also helped to perpetuate it. So long as a minister who had the tsar's support could choose or create the supreme organ that was to put through his legislation, he obviously did not have to recognize the authority of any one supreme organ. So long as the three supreme organs responsible for coordinating the ministries did not control the legislative, executive, and judicial processes, they could not impose system on the ministers. Thus individual ministers enjoyed considerable freedom of action.

THE STATE COUNCIL AND THE COMMITTEE
OF MINISTERS

The membership of the State Council increased from about thirty in 1810, to sixty in mid-century, to over eighty by 1905. All the ministers were ex officio members, and the regular members, all appointed by the tsar, were men who had served many years in the bureaucracy or

16. Lazarevskii, II, 178–184.
17. Zaionchkovskii, *Provedenie*, pp. 370–372, 405–406, describes two occasions in 1863 when tsar-confirmed decisions of the chief committee for the management of rural society became laws without the participation of the regular supreme organs.

the army and risen to high rank. The term of office was generally life-long, although in theory the tsar could dismiss the members at will.[18]

General sessions of the Council began each year in early October and usually ended in May or early June. When he chose, the tsar could preside, but in practice he rarely did. Alexander I met regularly with the Council in 1810–1811, but after Speranskii's fall in April 1812 he never attended another meeting. Nicholas I attended only five meetings of the Council during his thirty-year reign,[19] and the last time a tsar presided over the State Council for any but ceremonial purposes was when Alexander II forced the Liberation Statute through in 1861.

The major part of the Council's work went on in its standing committees, which were called departments (*departamenty*). Originally there were four of these, but one of them, the military department, existed only on paper after Nicholas I's reign. An additional active department was established in 1899, bringing the number of functioning departments to four. The members of the departments—four to eight in each—were appointed by the tsar from the body of the Council. They met once a week while the Council was in session, and their meetings generally lasted about four hours. By contrast, the general meeting of the Council, which was also a weekly event, usually lasted only about one hour. The departments formulated the Council's decisions. In most cases they agreed unanimously, and all the general meeting had to do was accept their proposals. When a department's vote was split, however, the general session had to debate and decide between two or more points of view.

The general meetings were not mere formalities. Opposition and debate were relatively rare in them only because the Council customarily handled its disagreements elsewhere. Whenever a member wished to oppose a departmental project, he stated his desire prior to the general meeting in which the project was to be voted on, and in most cases the project was then returned to the department for reconsideration with the participation of the objecting member. In a

---

18. On the structure and membership of the Council in the nineteenth century, see Korkunov, *RGP*, II, 89–96. The tsars almost never dismissed members except at their own request. See *ibid.*, II, 91. In one case Alexander III ordered a member (Prince Liven) to request his own dismissal because of his involvement in land fraud—see Egor A. Peretts, *Dnevnik E. A. Perettsa* (Moscow, 1927), p. 117 —but this sort of thing seems to have been exceptional. If a tsar wanted to get an undesirable out of the Council, his most likely method seems to have been to allow him not to attend the meetings and to let it be known informally that he should not. Even this relatively mild form of dismissal seems to have been a very rare phenomenon.

19. Korkunov, *RGP*, II, 61–85; *Gosudarstvennyi Sovet*, pp. 42–59, 62–68.

sense, then, the general meetings did play an important role in making the Council's decisions, but the process of arriving at the decisions was relegated almost entirely to the departments.[20]

The Committee of Ministers consisted of the ministers, the heads of the departments of the State Council, the head of the codification section of the State Council (after 1882), and the imperial secretary (after 1893).[21] In addition to these basic members, required by law, the tsar could appoint anyone he chose to the Committee, permanently or temporarily, and he did this often enough to render its membership somewhat less stable than that of the Council. Moreover, the governors-general met with it as voting members when they were in the capital city.[22]

Like the Council, the Committee met once a week except in the summer months.[23] Attendance varied from about ten to twenty. The tsar could attend and preside, but this happened only rarely in Alexander II's reign and never thereafter. A permanent chairman ran the meetings, though this was largely a ceremonial function somewhat analogous to that of the Council chairman. Before the 1860s the same man chaired both Council and Committee at once; thereafter, the posts were separate. There is little point in identifying the formal functions of the Committee. The law's prescriptions do not fall into neat categories, and in practice the Committee made all kinds of decisions on demand: executive, legislative, and judicial.

The chancelleries of the Council and the Committee played a vital role in interministerial coordination, especially the chancellery of the Council, called officially the imperial chancellery (*gosudarstvennaia kantseliariia*). The imperial chancellery was not so much an auxiliary body as an organ in its own right, possessing de facto powers that were not inferior to those of the Council itself.[24] The imperial secretary (*gosudarstvennyi sekretar*), who managed the imperial chancellery, was appointed directly by the tsar, and neither the Council nor its chairman had any formal authority over him. The sense of the law was

20. V. I. Gurko, *Features and Figures of the Past* (Stanford, Calif., 1939), pp. 22–34; Korkunov, *RGP*, II, 89–157.
21. The minimum membership of the Committee was prescribed in *Svod zakonov*, vol. I, pt. 2, bk. 2, "Uchrezhdeniia soveta ministrov i komiteta ministrov," arts. 14–17. See also Shcheglov, pp. 136–137.
22. See Korkunov, *RGP*, II, 241–242.
23. *Ibid.*, p. 253.
24. See *ibid.*, pp. 100–101, 253. Korkunov suggests that the crucial role played by the chancelleries of the State Council and the Committee of Ministers was one of the features of Russian government that distinguished it from western European states.

that the secretary was to cooperate with the chairman of the Council, not necessarily to obey him.[25] Indeed, two statutes enacted in 1893 and 1901 gave the secretary formal prerogatives of his own far more significant than those of the chairman. He acquired the right to initiate legislation, became a member of the Committee of Ministers, and, most significant of all, took over the codification section of the Council, which gave him the right to instruct the Council on the legality of its decisions.[26] In effect, then, the chancellery enjoyed virtual autonomy from the Council, though the two bodies were inseparable parts of a single institution.[27]

The imperial chancellery's prerogatives and its influence in governmental decision-making stemmed from its ability to serve the government's practical needs. By the 1890s the imperial secretary's organization contained over half as many high-ranking servitors as the Council itself (forty-eight), and all of them were appointed by the secretary. The primary practical function that this massive machinery performed was to research the projects and cases that came before the Council, to prepare its decisions, and to keep records of the deliberations behind each decision.[28] It did much more than serve the Council, however. It performed the same functions on behalf of the more or less temporary interministerial committees and commissions that acted now and then as supreme organs,[29] which meant that the chancellery sometimes worked on projects that the Council never saw at all. In the course of time the chancellery's archive grew into a practical foundation for governmental unity, and its officials acquired a fund of technical and legal knowledge that made them indispensable whenever problems

25. *Svod zakonov,* vol. I, pt. 2, bk. 1, "Uchrezhdenie gosudarstvennogo soveta," arts. 155–160.

26. Shcheglov, pp. 136–137, 177–181.

27. Polovtsov's accounts of his everyday work as imperial secretary in 1883–1892 suggest that the degree to which the chancellery was subordinate to the Council depended to a considerable extent on the personalities of the Council chairman and the secretary. Polovtsov himself was able to play a leading role in the government, owing to the weakness of the then chairman of the State Council, Grand Duke Mikhail Nikolaevich. See Polovtsov's *Dnevnik* (1966) (Zaionchkovskii's introduction), I, 7. It is true that Polovtsov once described Mikhail as his *nachalnik* (chief), and he often found it necessary to consult with Mikhail before taking any decisive steps. He refrained from having regular audiences with the tsar largely at Mikhail's insistence. Nevertheless, Polovtsov's diary entries make it clear that as long as he was imperial secretary, he actually exercised much more influence in the administration than did Mikhail. See, e.g., *ibid.,* pp. 358–359.

28. *Gos. kants.,* p. 4.

29. *Ibid.,* pp. 188–193, describes the work the imperial chancellery did for the chief committee for peasant affairs in 1858–1861, when this committee was enacting the Liberation Statute.

arose that called for interministerial coordination. Gurko would have it that the experience of the chancellery's officials at interministerial decision-making made them the best administrative talents in the government.[30] Since the *functional* role of the chancellery in the practical processes of interministerial coordination was much more sweeping and inclusive than the *formal* role of the Council, and since the chancellery's work furthered and supported interministerial coordination, it may be said that the State Council and its chancellery, taken together, were much more effective in coordinating the ministries than the formal powers of the Council suggest. To a lesser degree, the same generalization applies to the Committee of Ministers and its chancellery.[31]

The imperial chancellery's rise to importance actually preceded that of the State Council. In Nicholas I's time, when the Council itself was hardly more than a rubber stamp, the chancellery was handling the affairs of the secret committees that drafted his key legislation. Baron Korf, who was imperial secretary in the 1830s and 1840s, was a member of most of the committees.[32] In the 1850s, therefore, when Nicholas and his successor began to use the State Council more actively, the imperial chancellery was in a position to furnish the kind of information that would help to make the Council's deliberations more meaningful.[33]

All in all, the chancelleries of the State Council and the Committee of Ministers were important elements in the evolution of formal bureaucracy out of the disorganization of the early nineteenth century. Their development accompanied the gradual elimination of His Majesty's Own Imperial Chancellery and its powerful third section from any active role within the administration, which suggests that the "triumph" of bureaucracy in the 1860s marked the ascendancy of the archivist and legal researcher over the gendarme.[34]

30. Gurko, pp. 35–51. Gurko worked in the imperial chancellery in the 1890s until 1902, when he followed Pleve into the MVD.
31. P. P. Mendeleev, who worked in the chancellery of the Committee of Ministers in 1904–1909, indicates that his office developed along the same lines as the imperial chancellery. See bk. 2 of his untitled notebooks in the Russian Archive at Columbia University. One of the auxiliary functions of the chancellery of the Committee of Ministers was to take care of the administrative work for the committee of the Siberian railroad. See *Svod zakonov*, vol. I, pt. 2, bk. 3, art. 5. Concerning the general importance of the chancellery of the Committee of Ministers, see Korkunov, *RGP*, II, 253.
32. *Gos. kants.*, pp. 72–73, 178–182.
33. *Ibid.*, pp. 174–175.
34. *Ibid.*, pp. 24–73, describes the evolution of the imperial chancellery under Nicholas I. On the gradual decline of His Majesty's Own Imperial Chancellery, see above, ch. V, sec. E.

In the late nineteenth century the Senate consisted of about forty members, appointed by the tsar from among his high-ranking servitors. It never met in general session during the period 1861–1905 except on rare ceremonial occasions. The work was all done in the separate departments, and each of them functioned practically independently in its own sphere. The so-called general meetings of the Senate were actually meetings of two or three departments, held to decide certain types of cases.[35]

During the period 1861–1905 only two of the departments, the first and the second, played important roles in administration. The first was essentially an administrative court that handled cases in which the legal powers of the government's administrative organs were called into question. Zemstvoes or gentry marshals could complain to the first department against a governor who issued illegal commands to them,[36] and if two organs of the central government got into a jurisdictional dispute, this also was likely to go to the first department. The second department was established in 1884 to take over the judicial functions of the chief committee for the management of rural society. It decided cases involving elected administrators in peasant volosts and villages, including jurisdictional clashes between the volosts and the agencies of government and also certain types of appeals from individual peasants against their own elected officials.

No special provisions in the law gave any general description of the Senate's role in administrative disputes. The clauses in the *Svod zakonov* purporting to describe the Senate stated that it was the highest executive organ of the government, but these anachronisms from the eighteenth century had no practical significance whatever.[37] The actual administrative jurisdiction of the first and second departments resided in a mass of separate provisions, each one stipulating a particular type of dispute that should be subject to the Senate's decision. By 1905 the number of these provisions was considerable: thus, although the jurisdiction of the two departments was not defined in general terms, it had become very broad. It had grown up, as it were, with ministerial government itself.[38]

35. *IPS*, III, 378–380.
36. Korkunov, *RGP*, II, 586–591. See also above, n. 4.
37. Lazarevskii, I, 457–458. The clauses giving the Senate sweeping executive powers are in *Svod zakonov*, vol. I, pt. 2, bk. 4, "Uchrezhdenie Pravitelstvuiushchego Senata," especially art. 1. See above, ch. III, sec. C, concerning the Senate's "loss" of its supreme position in 1802–1803.
38. *IPS*, IV, 104–107. At no time were the Senate's decisions absolutely guaranteed to be final, though in practice the vast majority of them were. Zaionchkovskii,

The independence of the first and second departments of the Senate was considerably weakened by their close contact with the ministries. A Senate department could not act on a case that involved a ministry until it had sent all relevant materials to the minister's own chancellery for consideration and received the minister's recommendations.[39] When the department did at last begin its deliberations, the minister, or one of his deputies, had to participate. According to the law, the participating ministerial officials had no vote in the final decisions in the sessions they attended,[40] but Polovtsov tells us that this formal limitation had no significance after 1861 because the tsar customarily made all the deputy ministers senators,[41] thereby giving each ministry at least one vote in all senatorial deliberations. Considering the large variety of affairs that the Senate departments had to decide unanimously,[42] one vote was enough to make it extremely difficult for the Senate to challenge any minister, except in cases where the ministers wanted to use the Senate either to challenge one another or to escape responsibility for this or that decision.

B. "Weaknesses" in the Supreme Organs

I have put quotation marks on the word "weaknesses" because the features of tsarist legal structure that I am about to describe were not necessarily weaknesses in fact. They were, rather, discrepancies between what most Russian statesmen and legal scholars regarded in 1861–1905 as "efficient" administration and the arrangements that actually obtained in the government organization. Tsarist statesmen and legal scholars generally agreed in 1861–1905 that if the supreme organs were to impose systematic coordination upon the ministries, they had first of all to make and enforce legal rules that would be superior to the orders that the ministries themselves issued.[43] As we shall see, however, the formal structure of the tsarist government did not embody any clear distinction between law and administrative decree, and this was the fundamental "weakness" in the supreme organs during the period 1861–1905, or so most Russian statesmen believed.

Rossiiskoe samoderzhavie, pp. 175, 178, cites a number of instances in Alexander III's reign when the Committee of Ministers and even the State Council persuaded the tsar to reverse the Senate's decisions.

39. The regulations requiring this are in *Svod zakonov*, vol. I, pt. 2, bk. 4, arts. 56–57.

40. *Ibid.*, arts. 8, 35, 98, 120–133.

41. Polovtsov, *Dnevnik* (1966), I, 477. The law allowed a senator to hold other positions in the government. See *Svod zakonov*, vol. I, pt. 2, bk. 4, art. 7.

42. *Svod zakonov*, vol. I, pt. 2, bk. 4, arts. 103–119.

43. Korkunov, *Ukaz*, pp. 310–313. See also above, Introduction, n. 1.

According to Korkunov, the tsarist government took its first conscious step toward introducing a distinction between law and command on New Year's Day of 1810, when Alexander I established the State Council.[44] Reading from a script written by Speranskii, Alexander publicly acknowledged that he could not keep order among the branches of his administration (ministries) unless he set permanent collegial institutions over them with prerogatives defined by law. There were to be several such bodies, but the State Council was to be the uppermost one, "the focal point of all the affairs of the supreme administration."[45]

Later on, in the period 1861–1905, many leading statesmen, including the tsars themselves, continued to speak and act as if they intended the State Council to be the supreme legislative organ of the government. They did not believe it should dictate to the tsar, but they generally agreed in principle that the tsar's authority could be more effectively exercised if he acted only through regular channels. Statutes should have been enacted according to a special procedure, and they should not have been changed or abrogated except by this same procedure. The decisions of the State Council, confirmed by the tsar, should have taken precedence over the enactments of all other government organs. A minister's orders should not have had the force of law *in themselves* unless they had first been submitted to the State Council for consideration.

It depended entirely on the tsar himself whether or not the ministers actually made laws without consulting the State Council. His approval gave any order the force of law no matter what its source, even if it contradicted earlier legislation. Thus the Council's enactments could only be consistently superior to those of the separate ministers if the tsar refrained from confirming the orders of separate ministers. The first principle of tsarist constitutional theory, therefore, was that the tsar should generally refrain from approving ministerial orders, or at least that someday he should stop doing it. The second principle was that the tsar should not interfere with the Council's deliberations.

Some indication of these ideals can be found in the constitutional laws that were in force in 1861–1905. Article 47 of the fundamental laws declared that "the Russian Empire is administered on the firm foundations of positive laws, institutions, and regulations enacted by the Autocratic Authority."[46] There were laws, in other words, and they

44. Korkunov, *RGP*, II, 32.
45. Shilder, *Imperator Aleksandr*, III, 2–4. The quotation is from Alexander's manifesto of 1 Jan. 1810, in *PPSZ*, 24064.
46. *Svod zakonov*, vol. I, pt. 1, bk. 1, "Svod osnovnykh gosudarstvennykh zakonov,"

were "firm." The tsar had the absolute power to change them, but he would only exercise it in accordance with definite procedures. Some other provisions give the impression that such procedures actually existed. Article 50 of the fundamental laws provided that "all drafts of laws (except those that apply exclusively to the armed forces) are to be considered in the State Council." Taken by itself, this suggests that if the State Council did not control the making of laws, it was at least guaranteed a role in the legislative process. The Council's participation in the enactment of a measure was what made it a law as opposed to an administrative order.[47] Two other articles, 72 and 73, gave the Council's would-be legislative prerogative some additional protection. In effect, they said that only a law considered by the State Council could amend or abolish an extant rule that the Council had previously enacted.[48] In other words, the ministers could not issue any orders, not even with the tsar's approval, that contradicted previous enactments of the Council.

It is true that articles 72 and 73 did not by themselves eliminate the possibility that the ministers would enact tsar-approved laws on their own. They did not prevent a minister from issuing orders with the force of law that did *not* contradict the Council's previous enactments. Presumably, however, the Council would pass more and more laws in the course of time, and the area covered by these laws would gradually expand, thus limiting ever more closely the subjects concerning which any governing body outside the Council could enact legislation. If articles 72 and 73 were enforced, therefore, the Council would gradually build up a monopoly on the legislative process. Even if there was no clear distinction between the Council's laws and the ministers' decrees in the late nineteenth century, the implicit intent of the constitutional laws was that time would ultimately give rise to one. As Korkunov said, "It is impossible not to see a clearly expressed striving [in the laws] to create in our government a division in the exercise of supreme authority into legislative and administrative systems."[49]

Despite the above articles, the State Council did not enjoy the sole prerogative to legislate during the period 1861–1905. Under a strict interpretation of article 50, enactments that did not go through the State Council lacked the force of law, but other fundamental laws explicitly provided for such "legislation." Article 80, for example, allowed

47. There was yet another article in the *Svod zakonov* (vol. I, pt. 2, bk. 1, "Uchrezhdenie gosudarstvennogo soveta," art. 95) affirming that "all" laws had to be considered in the State Council before enactment.

48. Korkunov, *RGP*, II, 40–41.

49. *Ibid.*, pp. 12–13. See also Korkunov, *Ukaz*, p. v.

the tsar to entrust "a definite degree of authority . . . to positions and persons acting in His name and by His order," which meant that the tsar could authorize any agency, supreme or subordinate, to legislate. In the light of article 80, article 50 established not a single legislative process but at best only the pretense of one.

The decree of 5 November 1885 rendered the formal significance of the Council even more doubtful by proclaiming explicitly that all acts of the tsar were of equal force no matter how they were enacted.[50] A law (*zakon*), said the statute of 5 November, was any "Royal order signed by His Imperial Majesty or State Council opinion confirmed by Him."[51] The Russian code (*Svod zakonov*) was to include all such *zakony* that had the character of general legal rules, and it was also to include orders from the tsar "formulated by the supreme organs" if these orders contained rules not yet expressed in any *zakon*. Presumably, these latter referred to "temporary" laws enacted outside the State Council. Indeed, the law of 5 November was itself enacted outside the normal procedures. It was an opinion not of the Council but only of the Council's department of laws. The tsar signed it, making it a law, without the Council as a whole ever considering it. Moreover, it established a procedure for editing the new *Svod zakonov* that excluded the Council's general session.

In effect, then, any minister acting on the tsar's instructions possessed the *formal* power to issue decrees with the full force of law. It is true that such orders almost invariably applied only to specific cases; they were, in other words, executive rather than legislative in nature. Some of them, however, found their way into the *Svod zakonov* as full-fledged legal rules. In any case, all tsar-approved ministerial orders—legislative, executive, and judicial—represented an anomaly in the constitutional framework because the authority behind them was not the law but only the tsar's command. They were "laws" in themselves, even if they violated statutes properly enacted through the State Council.

A number of statutory provisions assured that tsar-approved orders, enacted without the participation of the State Council, would have force on all levels of the administration. The practical distinction between a law and an administrative order, said Korkunov, lay fundamentally in the right of the courts to pass on their relative "juridical strength."[52] In tsarist administration, however, both officials and judges were expressly forbidden to evaluate the validity of the tsar-approved laws and orders that came down to them. Despite the articles of law

50. Korkunov, *RGP*, II, 29–31.
51. *TPSZ*, 3261.
52. Korkunov, *Ukaz*, pp. 302–303, 356–359.

that suggested a distinction between *zakony* and administrative orders, no one in the government was able to draw it.

The Senate, it will be recalled, was forbidden to prevent the passage of any tsar-approved enactment, whether it contradicted an existing law or not.[53] The judicial code of 20 November 1864 forbade all law courts to "decide cases on the basis of contradictions between laws,"[54] and article 65 of the fundamental laws prohibited executive offices from weighing the relative authority of the orders they received from their superiors.[55] When a judge or official found that two tsar-approved enactments of any kind contradicted one another, he was not to compare their validity or weigh the authority of their respective enactors but to decide the case at hand according to the "spirit" (*dukh*) or "general sense" (*obshchii smysl*) of the law as a whole. The case at hand was to determine the decision, not the law itself. Judges and administrators might decide cases that the laws did not cover, but such decisions were to apply only to one case and not to any other.

The implication of these rules was that low-level servitors had broad powers vis-à-vis the population but no power at all to influence or interpret the formal structure under which they worked. Judges and officials had considerable latitude to get their affairs decided, but they were compelled to phrase their decisions so as to appear to be adhering to the letter of their laws and orders. Thus the law remained until 1906. Throughout the period 1861–1905 a tsar-instigated order from an individual minister had exactly the same weight as a tsar-approved decision of the State Council.

To conclude the discussion on the weaknesses of formal structure, the constitutional framework of tsarist Russia in 1861–1905 set forth a number of formal distinctions between laws and decrees but also allowed the ministers to break them down. The compilers of the *Svod zakonov* offered no discussion of this anomaly or any formal indication that they were even aware of it. Worse, the anomaly was not an old, out-of-date tradition that would gradually disappear with the spread of enlightenment. On the contrary, it was a new development, growing into an ever greater disparity as bureaucracy expanded.

In theory, it would have been far more desirable to allow the provincial officials to interpret the constitutional framework under

53. This rule was preserved in the *Svod zakonov*, vol. I, pt. 2, bk. 4, art. 202, until 6 June 1905 (see below, pp. 272–273). The Senate could evaluate the relative strength of laws *subsequent* to their enactment in response to appeals from low-level courts and administrators, but its deliberations, as we have noted, went on under the watchful eyes of the ministers.

54. Quoted in Korkunov, *RGP*, II, 40.

55. *Svod zakonov*, vol. I, pt. 1, bk. 1.

which they supposedly were operating. It is true, moreover, that a mere stroke of the tsar's pen would have made it possible for his officials and judges to weigh the validity of one legal rule against another on the basis of clearly established principles. In fact, however, none of the tsars made the stroke. On the contrary, they repeatedly reaffirmed their prohibition against interpretation and even strengthened it during the course of the nineteenth century.

One may conclude from this that the tsars were stupid, but it may also be suggested—this is the main point to be made in the following two chapters—that they had some reason for taking the stand they did: namely, that the government administration continued to operate in a disorderly fashion outside the capital cities throughout the period 1861–1905. Existing laws did not conform to principles of any kind, they could not immediately be made to conform to principles, and, in any case, the servitors in the countryside could not be relied on to interpret the law according to principles. Under these circumstances it is understandable that the high-level statesmen should have entertained a profound distrust for the officials in the countryside. It is equally comprehensible that tsarist lawmakers should have been reluctant to expose their contrived legal code to all the interpretations that might be derived from its application to the far corners of the empire. Provincial officials had to be allowed to decide matters, but there had to be some way to prevent these scattered decisions from becoming a part of the central organization. The ministries had not only to give the appearance of being systematic, be it remembered, but also to act; if every decision with legal force had somehow to be fitted into the central system, the central system would lose the ability to act.

In sum, the anomaly in the tsarist legal-administrative system suited the system's needs. It resided in the process of imposing system, not in the tsar's personal prejudices or those of his advisors. The "weakness" of the legislative process was a mark not of the government's backwardness but of its aspiration to be systematic while imposing system on rural society by administrative action.

EVOLUTION OF THE STATE COUNCIL: 1861–1905

To many statesmen, the cause of systematic legality seemed to be losing ground in 1861–1905, especially after 1880, and they believed that the main indication of this decline was the diminishing legislative role of the State Council.[56] Why did they believe the Council was losing

56. In his latest work Zaionchkovskii points to numerous other indications of growing arbitrariness in the highest levels of government. See *Rossiiskoe samoderzhavie,* pp. 98–111.

its legislative role? Because the ministers could sometimes get legislation approved by the tsar without submitting it to the Council, and, this failing, they could sometimes persuade the tsar to interfere in the Council's deliberations.[57]

That the Council actually declined, however, is open to doubt. To my knowledge, no one has proven or even attempted to prove that ministerial violations of the Council's prerogatives actually became more frequent or more extreme as time went by. Indeed, if anyone ever does try to count the number of violations and measure the degree of their illegality, I think he will fail, because he will be unable to determine exactly what a violation consisted of and because he will have no reliable way to distinguish actual violations from rumored ones. The number of times the tsar bypassed the Council cannot be determined because the rules about when the Council should have been consulted were not clear even to the statesmen themselves. Likewise, interference in the Council's deliberations was so often perpetrated informally and in such a variety of ways that the instances of it cannot possibly be listed and numbered with any accuracy. In short, no thorough study of the State Council's evolution in 1861–1905 exists; even if it did, I doubt that it would justify any definitive generalization regarding the rise or fall of constitutional legality in the tsarist government. What can be said is that the evolution of the Council and the "spirit of legality" during the tsarist government's last decades is an extremely complex question and that scholars have not generally recognized how complex it is.

The description that follows does not prove or disprove anything. What it does, hopefully, is to suggest that "decline" is not an adequate term to describe the evolution of the State Council (or the spirit of legality) during the period 1861–1905.

It is certainly true that many of the matters the Council handled had very little to do with legislation. From 1810 on, the Council was saddled with a mass of essentially judicial decisions, many of which it still had to contend with to the end of the nineteenth century. Moreover, the number of essentially managerial decisions brought before the Council seems to have increased sharply in the last decades of the nineteenth century, partly because lower-level administrators were not allowed to interpret their instructions for themselves and partly be-

57. Even the official history of the State Council reports somewhat wistfully that the Council reached its highest prestige in the period 1856–1874. See *Gosudarstvennyi Sovet,* pp. 121–124. Polovtsov testifies repeatedly to its decline in the 1880s (e.g., *Dnevnik* [1966], II, 199–200, 363), and Gurko, p. 23, believed that it had even less influence in 1894–1905 than in the 1880s. See also Lazarevskii, I, 406–407; Zaionchkovskii, *Krizis,* pp. 19–22; Eroshkin, p. 251.

cause the ministers often found it useful to resolve disputes between their organizations by letting the Council—or one of the other "supreme" organs—decide them.[58] To take one example of a "managerial" decision: in the session of 1905–1906, in the midst of revolutionary turmoil and dramatic constitutional reform, the Council found time to discuss at some length the question of whether a certain doctor working at the girls' school in St. Petersburg should receive civil service status.[59]

But not all the Council's managerial decisions were petty. In early 1906 Petr N. Durnovo, then the MVD, submitted drastic programs of police-military action to the Council. After some debate and amending —reflecting Durnovo's disagreements with other ministers—the Council gave its approval.[60] This was hardly an unimportant decision, nor was the act of rendering it a mere formality. True, the ministers were using the Council as a tool to resolve their own differences and unite the government, but the discussions in the general meetings were not merely ritualistic ceremonies. The Council was actually telling the ministers something they could not determine on their own, and this was the case with most of the Council's managerial decisions, petty and important ones alike. The Council's managerial responsibilities— like those of the Committee of Ministers—were not so much a sign of disorder as a characteristic feature of a legal system in which lower administrative and judicial levels found it difficult to interpret the law.

We turn now to the evolution of the Council's legislative "prerogative." On the one hand, it must be acknowledged that there were many occasions when the tsar and his ministers connived to bypass the Council. In 1866 Alexander II allowed Pavel Valuev (his MVD) and Petr Shuvalov (head of the third section) to enact a law through the Committee of Ministers without even publishing it or including it in the "Full Collection of Russian Laws," to say nothing of submitting it to the Council.[61] In 1878 he acted through the Committee of Ministers

58. Gurko, pp. 29–30. See also *Istoricheskii obzor . . . Komiteta*, IV, 1–16, 26–27.

59. *Otchet po deloproizvodstvu Gosudarstvennogo Soveta za sessiu 1905–1906* (St. Petersburg, 1906), pp. 79–84. The majority decided forty-nine to twenty-eight for the doctor, and the tsar solemnly confirmed their opinion.

60. Santoni, pp. 376–423, describes the discussions of Durnovo's measures in the State Council.

61. Valuev, erstwhile champion of systematic administration, thought it proper (*udobno*) to enact the law of 25 Nov. 1866 through the Committee of Ministers, thus bypassing both the Council and the Grand Duke Konstantin's chief committee for the management of rural society. This law gave the governors-general and, where there were none, the MVD the right to remove arbitrators (see above, ch. IV, sec. F) from their positions temporarily if they had undesirable political views. See Chernukha, pp. 231–232.

to establish the *uriadniki* (see above, n. 3), and in 1880 he abolished the salt tax by approving a recommendation from the MF without consulting any supreme organ at all (see below, n. 66). Alexander III, in his turn, sometimes enacted laws through the Committee of Ministers in order to avoid debate, and Sergei Witte was occasionally able to persuade Nicholas II to legislate without the Council.[62]

On the other hand, the ministers occasionally interfered in the Council's deliberations. Before discussing the development of this interference, it will be necessary to say a word about the mechanisms by which it was perpetrated.

The main constitutional basis for ministerial interference in the Council's deliberations was the tsar's legal right to approve minority opinions. Until 1906 the Council's majority votes (like those of all the other supreme organs) did not constitute official decisions that the tsar had to accept or reject as such. Whenever the Council's vote was not unanimous, the law required that both majority and minority opinions be sent to the tsar, and he could choose either one. If he chose the minority variant, he had to publish it as his own decree, not as the opinion of the State Council, but since an enactment had only to be considered by the Council in order to be a "higher" law, such a decree was fully as "high" legally as a tsar-confirmed majority.[63]

The tsar's right to approve minority votes constituted a lever by which a minister could exert pressure on the Council to accept his projects if and when the tsar supported them. Each minister was a member of the Council, and if the tsar mentioned to one of them that he supported one of the minister's projects, the favored one could then proceed to uphold it—or threaten to uphold it—against all opposition, safe in the assurance that he needed only a minority to bring it before the tsar and get it enacted into law. He had only to let it be known that he had the tsar's support for a project, and the members of the Council were faced with what often amounted to an ultimatum. It sometimes happened that a member absented himself from a session rather than oppose what he thought to be the tsar's opinion, and some members, especially the ministers, actually supported measures they did not approve of in order to avoid an open clash with the tsar.[64]

In the minds of the tsarist statesmen of the late nineteenth century, legality and the Council's integrity seem to have suffered more from

62. Regarding Alexander III, see Polovtsov, *Dnevnik* (1966), II, 128–129. On Witte, see his *Vospominaniia*, II, 259–261, and also above, n. 15.

63. *Svod zakonov*, vol. I, pt. 2, bk. 1, arts. 80, 116–117. The Council began submitting both majority and minority opinions to the tsar in 1812, though the law did not formally require it until much later. See Korkunov, *RGP*, II, 81.

64. Gurko, pp. 29–30.

the tsar's approval of a minority vote than from his bypassing the Council entirely—despite the fact that the former was technically legal while the latter was technically a violation of article 50 of the fundamental laws.[65] Even statesmen who were concerned with legality were not averse to persuading the tsar to put out a legal rule in the form of a personal decree (*imennoi ukaz*) in his own name, or a tsar-confirmed (*vysochaishe utverzhdennoe*) opinion of a supreme organ other than the State Council, or a tsar-approved order (*vysochaische povelenie obiavlennoe*) from a minister. This sort of thing could be tolerated so long as matters that were clearly the concern of the State Council were not too blatantly or too often kept from it. Polovtsov, an ardent upholder of the Council, often participated approvingly in ad hoc conferences formed to enact legislation without consulting the Council (see, e.g., above, n. 14). Apparently he did not take such bypassing, technically illegal as it was, to be a serious violation of what he considered to be the Council's prerogatives.[66]

To take up now the Council's "evolution" in 1861–1905, the period is generally supposed to have begun with a sort of golden age in which the Council enjoyed a degree of respect and freedom from outside interference that it had never known before (see above, n. 57). The tsar-liberator's predecessors had interfered in the Council whenever it pleased them, and on a few occasions they had done it openly. In 1821, for example, Alexander I had scolded the united departments of the Council for voting against some tax proposals that his MF had submitted, and the Council had humbly withdrawn its objections.[67] Nicholas I did much the same thing in 1839, when the general session of the Council voted seventeen to seven against some recommendations

65. Polovtsov felt that the tsar's acceptance of minority opinions belittled the Council and all it stood for. See, e.g., *Dnevnik* (1966), I, 134, 228–230.

66. I know of only one tsarist statesman in the entire period who disapproved of bypassing the State Council *even when he favored the legislation involved*. This was Egor A. Peretts, imperial secretary from 1878 to 1883. In Nov. 1880, when the MF got the tsar to abolish the salt tax without consulting the State Council, Peretts was pleased that the measure was passed but sincerely horrified at the way it had been done. When he ventured to protest, however, he found himself alone. Not Alexander Abaza, the "liberal" MF; nor Mikhail Loris-Melikov, the "reforming" MVD; nor Konstantin Nikolaevich, the "constitutionalist" chairman of the State Council, whose business it was to uphold the Council's prerogatives; nor the tsar-liberator himself saw anything seriously wrong in bypassing the Council and, indeed, all the supreme organs. See Peretts, *Dnevnik*, pp. 11–14. Peretts, of course, was hardly a typical Russian statesman. His uniquely Western attitude probably derived at least in part from his origin. He was a Jew who had been converted to Lutheranism at an early age.

67. *Gosudarstvennyi Sovet*, pp. 34–37. Alexander I accepted the Council's minority votes in one-third of the decisions on which the Council split. Four of them were a minority of one. See *ibid.*, pp. 23–25.

regarding currency reform submitted by Egor Kankrin, then the MF. At Kankrin's urging, Nicholas order the Council to reconsider. When some of the members balked, Nicholas sent a note to the chairman, ordering, in effect, that Kankrin's views be accepted. The chairman read Nicholas's note to the general meeting, whereupon the members decided to adopt Kankrin's views without further discussion.[68] So far as I know, this sort of direct, public pushing around did not take place in Alexander II's reign or at any time thereafter. Even in January 1861, when Alexander came before the Council to order it to accept the Liberation Statute, he did not interfere in its debates, as Nicholas I had done in 1842, nor did he make any public move to silence the opposition (see above, ch. IV, sec E). In any case, the enactment of the Liberation Statute saw Alexander II at his most arbitrary. He never came before the Council again except for ceremonial purposes, and although he approved minority votes on a number of occasions, he generally left the Council to itself, especially during the period 1865–1881, when his brother, the Grand Duke Konstantin, was presiding over it.[69]

The tsar-liberator had no special respect for institutional prerogatives, judging from his readiness to accept minority opinions from the Committee of Ministers and other deliberative bodies.[70] The honor he showed to the Council seems to have come primarily from his regard for his brother Konstantin and, perhaps, from Konstantin's ability to bully the Council into doing what Alexander wanted.[71] In any event, it seems that in Alexander II's reign the Council enjoyed about fifteen years of relative freedom from outside interference. By 1881 a consensus of sorts had emerged among the high-level statesmen to the effect that ministerial interference in the State Council's deliberations was improper and that a minister should not prevail upon the tsar to go against a majority.[72]

68. *Ibid.*, pp. 83–84. *Ibid.*, pp. 78–83, and Shcheglov, pp. 96–99, describe other occasions on which Nicholas I interfered openly in the Council's proceedings. On Nicholas I's inclination to ignore and/or bypass the Council in his later years, see above, ch. V, n. 15.

69. Concerning the minority votes that Alexander II approved, see *Gosudarstvennyi Sovet*, pp. 110, 118–119.

70. See, e.g., Valuev, *Dnevnik*, II, 57, 101, 160–161, 460–462. It will be recalled that Alexander II's respect for the Council did not preclude his bypassing it (see above, n. 66).

71. Regarding Konstantin's despotic habits as chairman of the State Council, see Polovtsov, *Dnevnik* (1966), I, 387–388; II, 363. During the period 1865–1881, when the Grand Duke Konstantin was president, I know of only two occasions when Alexander II accepted a minority vote, both of them involving Dmitri Tolstoi's educational reforms. In both cases Konstantin voted with the minority. See *Gosudarstvennyi Sovet*, pp. 118–119.

72. Polovtsov, *Dnevnik* (1966), II, 281–282, 446–447.

When Alexander III came to the throne, he dismissed his Uncle Konstantin to replace him with yet another uncle, the Grand Duke Mikhail Nikolaevich, and this change brought an end to the Council's royal protection. Mikhail, who held his new post until 1903, had no stature in the government or in the royal family. Apparently he was a man without any opinion of his own who allowed the tsars under whom he served to make an "ornament" of him.[73] He consistently refused to oppose either Alexander III or Nicholas II no matter what they did to the Council; consequently, the Council was left with no defense except the consensus regarding its prerogatives that had built up among the statesmen in the 1860s and 1870s.

Alexander III was especially prone to approving the Council's minorities. According to the Council's official history, there were fifty-seven split votes during his reign, and in nineteen of them he sided with the minority.[74] Moreover, he did not shrink from amending the Council's decisions, both majority and minority. On one occasion, in 1886, he actually went so far as to accept a project that had been voted down in the departments of the Council eighteen to one. The one was the war minister, who had himself introduced the project. Alexander III rejected the eighteen—including most of his own ministers— and the general meeting of the Council had no choice but to approve the measure.[75] This case was exceptional,[76] but on the whole it seemed to many statesmen that Alexander III's relatively frequent approvals of minority opinions reflected his ministers' inclination to disregard the Council's deliberations. The ministers preferred to rely on the tsar's support or to curry favor with anyone who stood close to the tsar, rather than strive to form majorities in the Council or among their fellow ministers. Such behavior did not favor the development of legal-administrative system even by tsarist standards.[77]

A number of incidents in Nicholas II's reign indicate that the Council's legislative activities were still subject to violation. The most

73. See above, n. 27. Polovtsov often asserts this: see, e.g., *ibid.*, I, 388; II, 132.

74. *Gosudarstvennyi Sovet*, p. 185. This compares closely with Alexander I's record (see above, n. 67).

75. Korkunov, *RGP*, II, 88–89.

76. There was one other similar incident. In 1892 Pobedonostsev ventured to stand alone in the general meeting of the Council in opposition to a proposal of the minister of education (Ivan D. Delianov). The vote was thirty-eight to one against him, and Alexander III backed the one. See Polovtsov, *Dnevnik* (1966), II, 411, 418, 510. In this case Alexander was stopping a project, not pushing it through, thus insulting both the Council and his own minister simultaneously.

77. It may be said, however, that Alexander III showed less inclination to by-pass the Council in the last decade of his reign. See Zaionchkovskii, *Rossiiskoe samoderzhavie*, p. 98.

notorious one before 1905 occurred in January 1897. During the preceding year the Council had been putting up a fight against a proposal from Witte, then the MF, to put Russian currency on the gold standard. In the face of this determined opposition, Witte persuaded Nicholas to adopt a procedure that seems to have been unprecedented. The currency reform was already before the Council, but Witte presented it to another "supreme organ," the finance committee, on 2 January 1897, and prevailed upon Nicholas to chair the meeting. The finance committee approved Witte's proposal, and Nicholas signed its decision, thus making it a law. Its publication on the following day brought the Council's deliberations to an abrupt end.[78] In this case Nicholas II not only utilized the Council's weak legal position to undermine it, as Alexander III had often done. He openly violated both formal law and informal consensus regarding proper legislative procedure.[79]

In 1905–1906 the legislative "prerogatives" of the Council were violated even more patently in a series of decisions strongly reminiscent of the mortal blow the Senate had suffered a century earlier (see above, ch. III, sec. C). On 6 June 1905 Nicholas II enacted a law stating more precisely than ever before that all legislation had to go through the State Council, and he even went to the length of empowering the Senate to refuse to publish any laws that the Council had not considered.[80] In effect, he was dragging up Alexander I's old prescription of September 1802 that the Senate was to have the right to refuse to publish laws that were not properly enacted. Like Alexander I's

---

78. Witte, *Vospominaniia*, II, 95–97.

79. Polovtsov, "Dnevnik," *Krasnyi Arkhiv*, XLVI (1931), 111–118. I know of only one case that even remotely resembles Nicholas's interference. In 1873, during Alexander II's reign, a project was submitted to the Council by the minister of education. After the project had already been taken under consideration by the Council, the leading statesman of that time, Petr Shuvalov, whose official position was head of the third section, conceived the desire to amend it. In December he and a few others persuaded Alexander II to issue a rescript directing the Council to introduce the new amendments into the project. The Council did as it was told, and it enacted the law in toto in May 1874. This was enough of a violation of the Council's prerogatives to infuriate its president, Grand Duke Konstantin. He and Shuvalov almost got into a serious conflict. See Valuev, *Dnevnik*, II, 285–287, 506.

But Nicholas II's interference in 1897 was far more extreme than Alexander II's rescript of 1873. The rescript did not constitute a law in itself but only inserted some provisions into a project that was before the Council. The Council did get to pass on the law in the end, and the only interference it suffered was the compulsion to adopt Shuvalov's amendments.

80. M. Szeftel, "The Legislative Reform of August 6, 1905," in A. Marongiu, ed., *Mélanges: Études présentées à la Commission Internationale pour l'Histoire des Assemblées d'États* (Palermo, 1967), p. 141. The law of 6 June 1905 is in *TPSZ*, 26345.

measure, the law of June 1905 ostensibly brought the supreme organs —especially the Council—to the pinnacle of their influence.

As it turned out, however, their new power was no less illusory than the Senate's had been in 1802–1803. It was only two months later, on 6 August 1905, that Nicholas approved the law that established the "Bulygin Duma" without consulting the State Council at all and without referring to the law of 6 June (see above, n. 5). From then on, major reforms flowed thick and fast—constitutional, administrative, and social. Just about all of them, including a new edition of the fundamental laws and a drastic reorganization of the Council itself, were enacted entirely without the Council's participation by a disorderly pile of ad hoc committees and informal conversations between the tsar and his henchmen.[81]

If the tsarist government's spirit of systematic legality resided solely in the State Council's legislative role, and if the tsar's continuing readiness to interfere in the Council's proceedings and/or bypass it implied that the Council's legislative role was declining, then it must be admitted that in 1905 legal system was still far from being a predominant feature of tsarist government organization.

But it remains doubtful that the Council's legislative prerogative actually declined during the period 1861–1905. A few incidents do not demonstrate a trend, and even if they do—even if someone were to prove that the government violated the Council's prerogatives more freely as time went by—there are any number of circumstantial explanations for this. Polovtsov, for example, seems to have thought that the main reason for what he considered to be the decline of the Council was the simple fact that in 1861 Mikhail replaced Konstantin as chairman. Similarly, it is often assumed that Alexander III and Nicholas II were personally more inclined to be arbitrary than the tsar-liberator.

And even if someone were to prove that the tendency to violate the Council's legislative prerogatives was a fundamental one, there is still no reason to believe that the diminution of this prerogative was

81. Some of the enactment procedures are described in detail in M. Szeftel, "Nicholas II's Constitutional Decisions of October 17–19, 1905 and Sergius Witte's Role," in *Album J. Balon* (Namur, Belgium, 1968), pp. 463–472, 483–488, and also Szeftel, "Legislative Reform," pp. 137–142. Apparently there still remained a shadow of legality in the minds of the statesmen. On 22 Nov. 1905, Polovtsov says, the tsar ordered that the laws passed by the Council of Ministers should go through the State Council in order "to give them a firm, legal basis" ("Dnevnik," *Krasnyi Arkhiv*, IV [1923], 88). But this concern for legality is less than impressive in view of the fact that a great many of the laws had already been enacted and put into effect. In any case, the tsar's wish was disregarded. None of the constitutional legislation of 1905–1906 ever got to the State Council.

equivalent to the decline of the Council itself, let alone the spirit of legality. As we have seen, the Council's legislative function was by no means its only significant feature. It was also evolving into a managerial device for coordinating the ministries.

We have seen that the imperial secretary acquired more power to direct the Council in 1893 and 1901. The statute (*uchrezhdenie*) of 7 May 1901 stripped the Council of just about all its judicial responsibilities and streamlined its decision-making processes, with the obvious intent of making it more serviceable to the ministers. The Council's departments were empowered to form commissions within the Council to take over some of the burden of preliminary consideration, a practice that had already become common without benefit of formal sanction during Alexander III's reign. Moreover, the statute broadened the powers of the ministers, recognizing their right to report individually to the tsar on matters that were before the Council and allowing them somewhat greater freedom to make decisions on their own without submitting them to the Council.[82]

Whether or not these changes actually made the Council into a more effective managing directorate, they do suggest the government's aspiration to do so. In fact, there are some indications that the Council became more effective. It enacted the police reforms of 1905–1906 (see above, n. 60), though neither Alexander II nor Alexander III had entrusted such matters to it in the crisis of 1878–1882. Moreover, in 1896 and 1899 it handled some rather delicate laws for easing the peasants' redemption debt,[83] measures of social experimentation of the sort that previous tsars had usually enacted in secret committees.

To sum up the discussion of the State Council's evolution in 1861–1905, it was a complex affair in which consistent trends are difficult to perceive. I have pointed out that there is no convincing reason for believing that the Council's legislative prerogative gradually lost its force during the period 1861–1905. In any case, the development of legal-administrative system and legislative prerogative had no necessary connection in the short run.

What was developing—or failing to develop—was not necessarily a constitutional order along Western lines, as many enlightened Russians thought, but machinery for social action. So long as the aspiration to system made sense to only a tiny part of the population, the growth of an operational system produced anomalies rather than a coherent order. So long as systematization produced anomalies, its furtherance required disciplined organization, not the supremacy of law. As said

82. Shcheglov, pp. 136–137, 163, 173–187.
83. *Ibid.*, pp. 164–165.

before, ministerial government was essentially a crusade, not a legal order, and in 1861–1905 it was preparing more or less unconsciously for an invasion, not a constitution. In the absence of an operational legal system, it should not surprise us if the tsars used the State Council primarily to manage an organization rather than to preserve a nonexistent legality.

The hope that the Committee of Ministers would evolve into an executive center of government was even less promising in 1861–1905 than the State Council's aspiration to be a legislature. Article 61 of the statute on the Committee specified that "the Committee itself has no executive power,"[84] and in fact it was not very active in any capacity in the late nineteenth century. The number of affairs it handled fell off in the 1880s and 1890s, at the very time when the government was growing more complex and requiring more active coordination at the center. In 1882 it handled 1,831 affairs; by 1893 the number had fallen to 1,416. Less than half of these had anything to do with the domestic ministries, and the Committee did not do very much even with those ministerial projects that did go through it. In 1893, a typical year, the Committee acted upon 703 proposals from the ministers (many of them from the war and naval ministries). Of these, it confirmed 618 without any change and 79 with minor changes and additions. Only 6 suffered substantial changes.[85] This may say something for inter-ministerial cooperation, but not for the institutional significance of the Committee.[86] As an institution for the general management of government, the Committee had become quite insignificant by 1905. In August 1903, when Sergei Witte surrendered his position as MF and became chairman of the Committee, he felt that he had fallen from power.[87]

84. *Svod zakonov*, vol. I, pt. 2, bk. 2.

85. *Istoricheskii obzor . . . Komiteta*, IV, 470–472, shows the declining annual case load of the Committee in the 1880s and early 1890s. On at least one occasion the Committee undertook to coordinate the ministries actively—in the matter of famine relief in 1891–1892. See *ibid.*, IV, 37–38, 134–150. This, however, seems to have been an exception. Aside from its consideration of the ministers' projects, the Committee performed a number of special tasks, for example, the issuing of charters to joint stock companies. See *ibid.*, V, 119–124; Korkunov, *RGP*, II, 247–252. The categories of affairs officially charged to the Committee are listed in *Svod zakonov*, vol. I, pt. 2, bk. 2, art. 26.

86. Zaionchkovskii, *Rossiiskoe samoderzhavie*, pp. 98–99, maintains that the Committee of Ministers played a more important role in government than did the State Council during Alexander III's reign. The grounds for his assertion: the Committee frequently made decisions, especially in 1885–1894, that flatly violated the law. Zaionchkovskii's implicit assumption is that the significance of an organization in the tsarist government was in direct proportion to the number of times it violated the law—a very Russian way of understanding institutions but not an entirely accurate one.

87. Witte, *Vospominaniia*, II, 245–247, 259–261.

CONCEPTS OF LEGALITY IN THE TSARIST BUREAUCRACY

If the evolution of the supreme organs did not hold forth much promise that the aspiration toward systematic legality was actually bringing
system to the tsarist government, the attitudes of the leading statesmen of the period present an even less encouraging picture. True,
many of them believed that the prerogatives of the supreme organs
should be upheld at least in theory, and they all seem to have looked
forward to some future time when a law really would be clearly
distinguishable from an administrative decree. Most of them, however,
did not believe that Russian government was ready for the rule of law
in their own time.

Pobedonostsev, to take the most notorious example, remained convinced throughout his long career in government that no formally
constituted body could govern Russia. This is not to say that he favored
arbitrary rule. On the contrary, he believed fervently that men who
held power should show respect for law and do what they could to
strengthen the constitutional framework of the government. But he
held to the conviction that the tsar should rely on the personal virtues
of his servitors to maintain and develop legality rather than trusting in
institutions to govern his servitors. "Institutions are of no importance,"
he said to Polovtsov in 1884. "Everything depends on individuals."[88]
Apparently this was a sentiment he was very fond of repeating.[89]

Pavel Valuev was somewhat more inclined than Pobedonostsev to
believe in the authority of institutions. He favored the inclusion of
elected gentry representatives in the State Council and often expressed
his dissatisfaction with personal authority as a principle of government.
Nevertheless, he entered the following characteristic remark in his
diary under 6 January 1876:

> The extreme friability of our [governmental] structure makes it neces-
> sary that we have an element of authority. [In Russia] the fascination,
> the spectre, of authority is all the power that the state has. Our new
> people view authority from the fashionable vantage point of so-called
> progress, and most of them see only arbitrariness in it. . . . They
> portray authority by their denunciations, as if it were a personal,
> special attribute of one or another person rather than a social force,
> entrusted for the attainment of social and state purposes.[90]

88. Polovtsov, *Dnevnik* (1966), I, 215. On Pobedonostsev's views concerning
state organization in general, see his *Reflections of a Russian Statesman* (London, 1898), pp. 252–271, and *Pisma i zapiski* (2 vols., Moscow, 1923), I, 68–69.
89. See, e.g., Polovtsov, *Dnevnik* (1966), I, 60.
90. Valuev, *Dnevnik*, II, 324. When Valuev spoke of the desirability of constitutional government, he was usually referring to his disapproval of the way his
fellow ministers behaved and his fervent wish that they show greater respect for

Apparently Valuev also recognized personal authority as a social force, despite his desire to replace it or at least limit it with institutions.

Sergei Witte, who was responsible for the "liberal" manifesto of October 1905, did not at any time believe Russia to be ready for a government whose servitors would be subordinated to legal system. His manifesto was a tactic devised to cope with revolutionary violence, not an expression of his convictions. More indicative of his views on government organization are his accounts of his own administrative methods. Writing in the years just before World War I, he noted gratefully that only the "confidence of the Emperor" had made it possible for him to introduce the gold standard in 1897 (see above, n. 78), and this was the case with all his programs to industrialize Russia.[91]

If any man in the government stood for legality, it was Alexander Polovtsov. From 1851 to 1883 he served in the Senate and devoted himself to upholding what there was of a judicial branch in the tsarist administration.[92] When, in 1883, he became imperial secretary—i.e., the business manager of the State Council—his position became identified with the Council's procedures, and he acquired the strong conviction that they should be respected. Throughout his term of office, until 1892, he acted as the chief guardian of the Council's prestige, sometimes venturing to oppose Alexander III himself when that most decisive of tsars violated what Polovtsov considered to be the Council's prerogatives.[93] His activity brought him into a treacherous arena of political conflict with the ministers, especially those favored ones who were wont to use the tsar's support to pressure the Council. Moving from the Senate to the Council, he said, was like going from the practice of civil law into the conduct of international relations.[94] He had to keep in constant touch with the more powerful ministers, now trying to restrain them, now helping them maneuver their legislative proposals through the Council, living in the constant (and frequently justified) apprehension that if they became impatient with the Council, they would either bypass it or usurp it. In short, if any man in the tsarist

---

law. See, e.g., *ibid.*, pp. 92–93, 140–141. It seems to me that what he really wanted was not so much the introduction of new institutions as an improvement in the quality of the servitors. As far as political theory is concerned, then, he was in Pobedonostsev's camp. Regarding his respect for legal system in action, see above, n. 61.

91. Von Laue, pp. 67–68, 142–144. Witte included several stories in his memoirs about how he used the tsar's favor to avoid the State Council and the Committee of Ministers. See, e.g., *Vospominaniia*, I, 434–437.

92. Polovtsov, *Dnevnik* (1966), I, 19.

93. See, e.g., *ibid.*, pp. 192–197, 226–228.

94. *Ibid.*, p. 19.

government could be called an upholder of law *in practice*, Polovtsov was that man.

How did this shining knight of legality conceive of the law he was upholding? Clearly, even he did not see it as a legal system. Law for him was no self-consistent body of legislation that all subsequent government enactments had to take into account. It was, rather, the prerogatives of the State Council and, more particularly, those attached to his own office and that of the Grand Duke Mikhail.[95] As said before, his diary gives no indication that he was disturbed when the tsar approved projects *before* they came to the State Council, and he himself often participated in drafting them. For him, the Council was not an institutional embodiment of systematic legality but only an office that carried out certain specific functions and possessed certain prerogatives. It did not govern; it only deserved the respect of those who did. Who did govern? According to more than one entry in his diary, he thought that the government would be best run by a small circle of stalwart, virtuous statesmen who would carry out the tsar's orders, give him good advice (preferably in secret), and maintain a regime of law through the staunchness of their characters and the purity of their intentions. In his opinion Russia had enjoyed its most effective political order in the time of Catherine II, when, he said, "the mechanism of our government was more satisfactory."[96] In sum, his concept of good government was basically similar to the old senatorial arrangement, in which trusted agents of the tsar did what was necessary for state and people while taking care not to violate each other's prerogatives.[97]

Polovtsov, be it remembered, was not some sort of eccentric left over from the past. He was an enlightened and shrewdly practical statesman who knew the government's workings as well as any man in

95. On one occasion Alexander III proposed calling a special conference to discuss an affair under consideration in the Council. Polovtsov thought this to be a direct affront to the Council and to the Grand Duke Mikhail. Mikhail, Polovtsov thought, should resign, unless the tsar appointed him to head the special conference. See *ibid.*, p. 382. The implication is that Mikhail's prestige was of greater importance than the Council's or, alternatively, that Mikhail's personal prestige was the vital element in the Council's influence. In either case Polovtsov was more concerned with personal prerogatives than proper procedure.

96. *Ibid.*, p. 300.

97. But Polovtsov's ideas regarding the *function* of his elite were quite bureaucratic. "I am not a believer in making law according to theory," he once told Alexander III. "I believe it is much better to raise legislative questions only as life calls them forth and to resolve them by specific measures—in a carefully planned direction, of course" (*ibid.*, II, 18). In other words, Polovtsov did not expect to find the law in society and then codify it; he hoped, rather, to develop it out of administrative action.

Russia and whose concern for legality was far more consistent than that of the vast majority of his colleagues.[98] His concept of legality cannot be dismissed as quaint conservatism. It expressed, rather, the only workable concept that the Russian government knew.

Anyone who wishes to dismiss Polovtsov's idea of good government as irrelevant will have a hard time finding a more serviceable one among the men who had some experience with the practical problems of government in 1861–1905. Generally speaking, the political philosophies that prevailed among the statesmen in the period 1861–1905 simply did not give any serious consideration to legality. As noted above, Pobedonostsev's tsar-and-his-trusted-henchmen concept of government had many adherents. This was a sort of personality cult championed by such statesmen as Dmitri A. Tolstoi, minister of education from 1866 to 1879 and MVD from 1882 until his death in 1889; V. K. Pleve, MVD in 1902–1904; and Petr N. Durnovo, MVD in 1905–1906. Insofar as these statesmen considered the problem of legality, they believed that it should be upheld by the conscientious exercise of absolute power by virtuous servitors.

A variant of this idea was the notion that virtuous servitors should not uphold the legal order as it was but instead sweep it aside in the name of a progress that was holier than law. This view did not come fully into its own until after 1917, but it had its share of adherents in pre-revolutionary Russia: Nicholas Miliutin the liberator,[99] Dmitri Miliutin the liberalizer of the army,[100] Sergei Witte the constitution

98. See Zaionchkovskii's introduction to Polovtsov's diary, *ibid.*, I, 5–6, 14–15. Polovtsov makes it abundantly clear that he does not approve of unsystematic governing practices. See, e.g., *ibid.*, II, 417. His imaginary elite (like Pobedonostsev's) were men devoted to legality.

99. See above, ch. IV, sec. E, for a discussion of Nicholas Miliutin's idea of good government.

100. Dmitri Miliutin's implicit authoritarianism has been referred to above (ch. VI, sec. C). It is worth adding that he thought highly of the dictatorial regime of Paul I (Klochkov, p. 90) and enthusiastically associated himself with the dictatorial reforms of Mikhail Loris-Melikov in 1879–1881. He had little use for men who opposed ideals and theories of law to the practical problems of government (see, e.g., his *Dnevnik*, II, 83; III, 82), such as his friend Kavelin (*ibid.*, III, 278). As a practicing statesman, he was as prone as any of his colleagues to see points of view that disagreed with his own as products of the machinations and intrigues of his personal enemies (e.g., *ibid.*, I, 77–80, 107–109). His idea of good government recognized only one principle: national unity. In its name he wanted to abolish class distinctions (*ibid.*, p. 32) and the separate legal categories under which the various nationalities in the empire lived. See F. Miller, "Dmitri Miliutin and the Reform Era in Russia, 1861–1881" (unpublished Ph.D. dissertation, University of California, 1963), pp. 32–33, 136. He also wanted to unite the zemstvoes and central bureaucracy into one vast apparatus. See *Dnevnik*, I, 57–58.

Alexander III "dismissed" Miliutin from the government in 1881 not because

writer,[101] and Petr Stolypin the peasant reformer.[102]

All of these men—upholders of old legality and coordinators of administrative activity alike—were fond of repeating phrases that had to do with legal system, but none of them put forward any practical conception of it, mainly because there was none that would fit what they were doing, i.e., running the government in violation of what there was of a constitutional framework on the basis of the tsar's personal favor. For all its defects, then, Polovtsov's concept of law was the only practical one that ministerial government had available to it, and it can be taken as a fair approximation of what the tsarist servitors strove to maintain (or create) on those occasions when they were moved to maintain (or develop) legality. Bureaucracy had overwhelmed senatorial government, but in 1905 it still had not brought forward any better notion of an operational legal system than had been available when it first appeared. From the beginning to the end of its evolution, the only coherent claim that ministerial government could make with regard to legality was that, in practice, it upheld the senatorial variety at least as well as the senatorial institutions had.

C. Preliminary Inquiry into the "Weaknesses" of the Supreme Organs

This section is called a preliminary inquiry because the study of the lower levels of the government in chapters VIII and IX constitutes a more complete explanation. The purpose here is only to offer some interpretive remarks on the supreme organs in the light of the situation they confronted.

We have seen that the three main supreme organs did not have

Miliutin wanted to free anyone from the power of the autocrat (see *ibid.*, IV, 96–97) but because the tsar's ministers were divided into two paranoiacally irreconcilable factions. Alexander had to choose one or the other if there was to be a united ministry. In Apr. 1881, when Alexander III had been in office only a month, the leaders of Miliutin's faction—himself, Loris-Melikov, and Abaza—flatly refused to remain in the government if the tsar would not follow their recommendations. As it happened, the tsar's choice went against Miliutin's side, but the actual making of the choice was itself quite in line with Miliutin's own ideal of good government. He also believed that the tsar's ministers should be all of one mind (*ibid.*, pp. 57–58). In short, the views, talents, and psychological peculiarities of Dmitri Miliutin were much like those of his brother. What they both wanted above all was a bureaucratic organization capable of changing Russian society. If law could not be supreme in such an organization, so be it.

101. See above, n. 91.

102. Stolypin had little understanding of or respect for the niceties of formal legality. See A. Meyendorf, "A Brief Appreciation of P. Stolypin's Tenure of Office" (unpublished manuscript in the Russian Archive at Columbia University), booklet 1, p. 28; booklet 3 ("Agrarian Question"), p. 5.

sufficient power to render the ministers dependent on them for collective decision-making. Ministers who wished to act decisively were apt to seek the tsar's support rather than the cooperation of their colleagues or of the members of the State Council. Indeed, in some cases an individual minister was able to overturn or disregard decisions already made in one of the supreme organs; that is, he could persuade the tsar to authorize the violation of his, the tsar's, own laws. In general, then, the supreme organs constituted a less than perfect basis for insuring systematic interministerial coordination. The constitutional framework exercised a certain degree of restraint on the ministers, and in practice it resolved most of the disputes that arose among them, but no one could be sure in any particular case if its restraints would actually govern the ministers' behavior.

The tsar had the formal authority to coordinate the ministries and enforce regulations upon them, but after the 1860s the growing size and complexity of the administration limited his ability to keep control of it in his own hands or to act upon it in accordance with his own judgment. The organizational power that each ministry could generate expanded rapidly, and as a result the ministers came to be ever more limited and driven by their disparate functional responsibilities.[103] Instead of being a coordinating force that imposed common purposes on the ministers, therefore, the tsar was gradually becoming a tool for this or that minister to use. Given the tsar's inability to direct this massive machinery, and given the absence of an operational system of interministerial coordination, the central government as a whole became ever more dependent on the personal authority of the separate ministers for whatever coordination there was. Each minister had to make his own arrangements as well as he could from day to day, now cooperating with his colleagues, now seeking to use the tsar's authority to force them to do his will. The ministers' ability to function along these lines became the main practical basis—the framework—for the government organization.[104] It was this situation that

103. Lazarevskii, I, 147–152.

104. See Korkunov, *Ukaz*, pp. 220–245; Lazarevskii, I, 37–47, 147. Otto Hintze, *Staat und Verfassung* (Leipzig, 1941), pp. 303–306, 383–386, has suggested that these generalizations regarding the power of separate ministers apply to any government in which the ministers are responsible to the monarch. The first legal scholar to recognize the trend toward administrative discretion in modern government was Lorenz von Stein, who spent most of his life in the service of the Austrian government. See Korkunov, *Ukaz*, pp. 1–7; W. Schmidt, *Lorenz von Stein* (Eckernförde, 1956). Korkunov asserted that although European legal theory "started out by completely denying to the executive authority any right to enact general rules, it is now [in the 1870s–1890s] allowing it an ever wider prerogative. This change in the concept of the executive decree came with the growth of a new attitude toward the functions of the executive power" (*Ukaz*,

forced the latter-day tsars to become the servants, as it were, of their ministers.

It would seem that the ministers of 1861–1905 should have found it in their interest to create and preserve a constitutional framework within which they could coordinate effectively, and that therefore the period should have seen a steady development in the influence and effectiveness of the supreme organs. Such a tendency did manifest itself, but it was not the only one operating. As we shall see (below, ch. VIII), the ministers often had to operate separately on an ad hoc basis in order to discharge their respective functions, and constitutional limitations threatened to render them immobile. Thus, despite their need for a stable and reliable framework within which they could coordinate, they do not seem to have been able to commit themselves to one. This was the main practical reason for the "weakness" of the supreme organs.[105]

Two points must be emphasized regarding the State Council's role in government. First, it did continue to act as a legislative organ throughout the period 1861–1905 on no more solid basis than the consensus among the government servitors regarding its prerogatives (doubtless owing in part to the real dependence of the ministries on the Council's chancellery). There was an excess of petty affairs and useless oratory in the general meetings (as in all legislatures in all times), but the debates often contained much more than mere rhetoric, and the voting did not always reflect indifference on the part of the members. The ministers frequently had to defend their projects against intelligent opposition, and they often had to suffer rejection or amendment even after they had gotten the tsar's preliminary approval.[106]

Second, it will not do to assume that the State Council's prerogatives

---

p. 29). P. Woll, *Administrative Law* (Berkeley, Calif., 1963), describes much the same development of informal executive procedures in modern American government as Stein and Korkunov pointed to in the imperial governments of the late nineteenth century. In the United States in the present day the independent regulatory commissions of the federal government combine executive, legislative, and judicial functions (Woll, pp. 1–3), but, as Korkunov would point out, this does not necessarily mean they are reducing the "law" that resides in the statutes to meaninglessness. It only means that executive function is expanding faster than legal regulation.

105. Lazarevskii, II, 158–167; Korkunov, *RGP*, II, 38–41.

106. In practice, the State Council could and often did amend proposals that the tsar had already approved. See Korkunov, *RGP*, II, 85. Polovtsov, *Dnevnik* (1966), II, 18, suggests that the best men in the Council were likely to oppose a minister even more vigorously if he brought forward proposals already approved by the tsar.

should have been enforced more firmly than they were, or that it would necessarily have been a good thing to impose Western standards and forms on the tsarist administration more rapidly. Obviously, the power of persons to usurp laws was not an ideal element in an organization pretending and striving to be a modern bureaucracy. Even under the best of tsars the continuing existence of formally established personal power reinforced the tendency to depend on persons rather than to rely on the general conformity of one's fellow servitors to behavior patterns that fit some sort of institutional framework.[107] Under a weak or incompetent tsar the government could easily fall into a confusion of factional disputes and intrigues and lose all power to influence the course of events. When the tsar did act decisively, on the other hand, his commands often subverted what there was of law and gave one or two of his agents sufficient de facto personal power to act arbitrarily in their own interests, sometimes to the injury of both government and people. All this notwithstanding, there is no basis for assuming that the proper solution to the problems of government-imposed systematization was more rapid and uncompromising systematization at the highest levels of government. Such an assumption is no more or less reasonable than the notion that the tsarist government might have coped more successfully with its problems had it compelled all its subjects to speak Russian. In fact, the government's efforts to "russify" its subjects almost invariably did more harm than good to state and people alike, and forced conformity to Western modes of organization would have been (and perhaps actually was) equally disastrous. The assumptions underlying the movements for forced russification and paper systematization came (and still come) from the same fallacy: that the tsar's power, being absolute, could effectively prevent people from living and relating to one another according to their custom and at the same time compel them to adopt new ways according to the government's prescriptions.

In short, there is no reason to assume—as almost all historians of Russia do—that the "weaknesses" of the supreme organs were actual weaknesses.[108] When and if scholars learn more about the process of

107. Korkunov, writing in the early 1890s, indicated "that under the present administrative system there is no body established for the general consideration of state problems in all their legislative aspects; that this lack is the main cause for the disorderliness and confusion that exists in all parts of the organization; that the strength and permanence of the law require that such a body be established . . ." (*RGP*, II, 72). See also Weber, *Theory*, p. 402.

108. A recent work that repeats the pious assumption that a constitution should have been stuck onto the government long before 1906 is G. Kennan, "The

systematization in general and the workings of the Imperial Russian State Council in particular, these "weaknesses" may well turn out to have been bases for effective operation. It deserves emphasizing in this regard that the period 1861–1905 began with a reform enacted in autocratic fashion against the wishes and immediate interests of rural society and government-society alike, whereas it ended with the establishment of a pseudo-constitutional order by the extensive use of obviously illegal procedures. In both cases the existence of a supreme organ with well-established prerogatives would have made effective government action impossible. No amount of logic can lead from this kind of experience to the conclusion that the creation of a supreme organ with a monopoly on the legislative process constituted the *only* proper aspiration of tsarist bureaucracy. Indeed, one could argue that the overly rapid introduction of legal restraints on authority may actually have weakened the state and contributed to its downfall.

The purpose here, however, is not to decide whether autocracy was effective per se, only to render the Russian variety of it intelligible. The following chapters will indicate that the institutional "weakness" of the supreme organs in the Russian government of 1861–1905 originated in large part in the practical problems and dilemmas that the subordinate organs and territorial administrations had to face, not in the congenital stupidity, brutality, rapacity, sloth, or "backwardness" of the tsar and his statesmen or in any "defect" in the supreme organs themselves.

The tsar's absolute authority has been regarded for so long only according to the categories of holy and evil that its real nature has been almost totally buried in irrelevant sermons. Actually, it did not at any time in history enable the tsar to govern as he wished. There have never been any words in any language by which a ruler could convey an enforceable command to his subordinates that they co-operate with one another in any way except that which they already knew. When the tsar wanted his subjects to act collectively, he had to work through existing forces and groups. Whatever the tsar may have wanted his supreme organs and his ministries to be, when he worked through them, he had to take them as they were. Alexander I and Speranskii learned this when they tried to introduce constitutional reforms in 1801–1812, and Alexander II learned it all over again when he set out to reform serfdom. At no time has autocracy ever been a simple matter of dallying with puppets.[109]

Breakdown of Tsarist Autocracy," in Richard Pipes, ed., *Revolutionary Russia* (Cambridge, Mass., 1968), pp. 6–7.
    109. Korkunov, *Ukaz*, pp. 130–191.

"Authority," says Korkunov, "is only a conventional expression to designate the causes that produce the influence of the state."[110] It is a legal relationship, and like all legal relationships, it derives from men's awareness of their dependence on one another. If a ruler enjoys absolute authority, it is only because his subjects depend on one another to act as if they believe in it. Its supposed absoluteness is not the ruler's own; it resides in the attitudes of those who recognize it. It follows that the ruler is not free to trifle with these attitudes or the institutions and behavior patterns that express them. Supposing that a forward-looking ruler successfully forces his followers to adopt a new law, it is still their concept of his power that they are obeying, not the new law itself. Supposing that he succeeds in imposing a reform that modifies his own power, his very success perpetuates in some degree his subjects' inability to find a better way to organize themselves. In the end, then, they are likely to go on depending on him even though he does not want them to.

I do not mean to say that an absolute autocrat cannot possibly introduce legal system into the relationships among his followers. Were this true, there would be no need to write this book. The point is that the establishment of system requires much more than an autocrat's act of will. It requires nothing more or less than changes in the social relationships among those who have been depending on the autocrat's authority.

None of the nineteenth-century tsars had any illusions regarding the "power" to which they have been so much accused of "clinging." They and their statesmen believed, with excellent reason, that as yet Russia had no other way to organize herself than to believe in the myth of an all-powerful tsar. The tsar held the power of final decision not because he knew what to do or because he was necessarily able to do anything even if he did know, but because his servitors—not to mention the population—were unable to find any other commonly acceptable basis on which they could decide practical questions for themselves.[111] As Polovtsov once said, "The autocracy they talk so much about is only an external form; an exaggerated expression of an absence of internal content."[112] As Alexander II said in June 1857, "There is no one to help me."[113]

110. *Ibid.,* pp. 177–178.
111. Valuev reports that Alexander II "opposed the establishment of a constitution not because he was jealous of his authority, but because he was convinced that it would harm Russia and would bring to her dissolution" (*Dnevnik,* I, 181).
112. Polovtsov, *Dnevnik* (1966), I, 99.
113. In conversation with Kiselev. Kiselev's report of Alexander's words is quoted in Zaionchkovskii, *Otmena,* p. 76.

CHAPTER VIII

The Ministries

Even now Russians do not like strict definition in laws and are
very little inclined to identify their activities with precise legal
forms.

v. i. sergeevich (1883)

A. Introduction

In this study the term "ministry" is used to refer to any administrative
agency in the central government the head of which was not formally
subordinate to any other such organ. Not all such agencies were
formally designated as *ministerstva*. The holy synod, the state auditing office (*gosudarstvennyi kontrol*), and the chief administration of
agriculture and land settlement fit the above definition, though they
lacked the official title. For our purposes, and for all practical purposes
in the tsarist government, they were ministries. Their heads enjoyed
the same kind of relationship with the tsar and, in general, behaved in
the same fashion as did the ministers.

The number of ministries did not change appreciably during the
nineteenth and early twentieth centuries. Initially, the law of 8
September 1802 set up eight of them (see above, ch. V, sec. A), and
in 1811 the number increased to twelve. In 1905, when the membership of the Council of Ministers became a matter of strict constitutional definition, there were fourteen organizations whose chiefs were
members. Nine of these played significant roles in domestic executive
organization: education, finance, internal affairs, justice, ways of
communication, commerce and industry, the chief administration of
agriculture and land settlement, the holy synod, and the state auditing
office.

In Alexander I's time the titles of the ministries and their subdivisions (variously called departments, chief administrations, sections, *et al.*) changed around with bewildering rapidity, and there
were additional switches from time to time throughout the century.
Certain features, however, did not change. There was always an MVD,
and the governors were always more or less subordinate to it (see
above, ch. V, sec. D). There was always an MF, a ministry of justice,
and one of education. Organs for the management and development

of communications, commerce, and agriculture existed throughout the century, but at times they were only departments in the MF or MVD rather than independent ministries.

The three major ministries not involved directly in domestic administrative organization—foreign affairs, war, and the admiralty—always possessed separate status and enjoyed special prerogatives. Questions of foreign policy and military organization almost never came under the purview of any interministerial committee or any of the main supreme organs except when the budget was under discussion or when some project of military reform came up—such as Miliutin's reorganization of the recruiting system—that had ramifications outside the army and navy proper. Domestic ministers (and governors-general) occasionally became involved in foreign policy matters by the nature of their activities or because the tsar saw fit to consult them personally, but they almost never took part in formal commissions officially empowered to make recommendations.[1]

Domestic ministries were roughly of two types. The ministries of finance, internal affairs, and justice, and the state auditing office, were organs of general management, or general ministries, meaning that they were involved in the overall functioning of the government and its interaction with society. Those of commerce, agriculture, education, and communication, and the holy synod, on the other hand, performed specific functions. They were not involved in managing the government organization as a whole, and therefore the other government agencies did not require their continual cooperation in order to carry on their work. Of the general ministries, justice and the state auditing office did not carry out programs or assume responsibility for social conditions but only played regulatory roles. They were involved in the general management of the government, but they were not responsible to do anything but follow and enforce rules. The MF and the MVD, on the other hand, were universally involved in government and society and also universally responsible for conditions and events throughout the empire. All branches of government were

1. During most of the period 1722–1882 the minister of foreign affairs (and before him the chairman of the college of foreign affairs) was the only government servitor to hold the rank of *kantsler,* the highest of the fourteen ranks in Peter I's Table of Ranks. This had no practical significance in either the eighteenth or the nineteenth centuries, but it symbolized the separateness and prestige associated with the business of foreign affairs. See "Obozrenie prezhnego i nyneshnego sostoianiia ministerstva inostrannykh del," *SIRIO,* XXXI, 165–178. Speaking practically, the administrative autonomy of the ministry of foreign affairs rested on the separateness of its problems, the tsar's close interest in foreign affairs, and the small size of its budget. The latter feature freed it from dependence on the MF.

vitally dependent upon the MF and the MVD not only to enforce rules but to act. These two ministries, therefore, exercised enormous power, and they were subject to enormous pressures. They were the kingpins, so to speak, of domestic administration in 1861–1905, much more a vital center of operation than the supreme organs. This chapter focuses its attention largely on them.

We have noted that from the beginning of the nineteenth century the MF had basically to supply the government with revenue, and the MVD had to keep order. They kept these general functions throughout the century, but the nature of the functions themselves changed markedly. As they did, the two ministries came into a conflict of aims and interests that grew steadily sharper throughout the period 1861–1905.

For the MF, the change came with the government's growing dependence on commercial and industrial development. In 1725 almost 60 percent of the state revenue had come from tribute exaction in the form of the soul tax. In the 1760s this proportion had already fallen to about 40 percent, and it continued to decrease as trade and industry developed.[2] By the 1880s revenue from the salt tax and the soul tax, which were both direct taxes for all practical purposes, had fallen to such a small proportion of the total state revenue that they could be abolished without serious loss to the treasury.[3] In the same decade the peasants' redemption debt, which was a de facto direct tax, was reduced by about one-fourth.[4] In 1903 collective responsibility, the foundation of Russian tribute collection ever since the 1200s A.D., was abolished. The manifesto of 11 August 1904 wrote off all arrears on the redemption debt, and the decree of 3 November 1905 canceled the debt itself as of 1 January 1907.[5]

2. Troitskii, p. 214. In 1864 the soul tax still produced slightly more than 20 percent of the state's ordinary revenues (Gindin, p. 28), but this figure fell much lower after 1866, when industrial development began to accelerate (*ibid.*, p. 30), despite sharp increases in amount in the direct taxes up to 1881 (*ibid.*, pp. 34–35).

3. Landless peasants were allowed to stop paying the soul tax in 1881–1883, and it was virtually eliminated for all classes in 1885–1887. See Leontev, *Krest. pravo* (1914), p. 46. The salt tax rested on a more or less standard necessity of life; thus, in practice, it produced the same kind of burden on the peasants as the soul tax. The revenue loss occasioned by abandoning these taxes was made up by increases in indirect revenues.

4. Poliakoff, pp. 38–40.

5. *Ibid.*, p. 64. The peasants generally understood the redemption payments to be a tax, and the government established the amounts of the payments in relation to the dues the peasants had paid earlier. See *ibid.*, pp. 14–15, 35–36, 45–47.

It should be noted that the old tribute collecting never entirely disappeared.

We may say, then, that by the end of 1906 the central government's revenue (but not that of the zemstvoes and peasant institutions) was coming almost entirely from commerce and industry—indirectly from the economic distribution system rather than directly from the peasants and their lands (see above, ch. I, sec. C). The MF was becoming more and more concerned to bring the population into the market as interdependent producers and consumers, to tax their purchases and sales rather than their persons. No longer could the government simply leave the peasantry in their isolated villages and take whatever "tribute" their primitive practices might provide.

The new direction in peasant taxation did not reflect any desire on the part of the MF to relieve the peasants of their tax burden.[6] Quite to the contrary, he meant to intensify it by changing the manner of paying. Economists refer to the process that the MF was furthering by the euphemism "raising the level of demand," and the MFs of the late nineteenth century were fond of articulating their goals in jargon of this sort in order to make them sound like some sort of emancipation. When the MFs expressed their wish to allow the peasants to sell, mortgage, and rent their lands, they generally spoke of "freeing" them from the chains of tradition. What they wanted, however, and what they had to want, was to extend and strengthen the market.

The change in the MVD's responsibility for order came at first from the liberation of the serfs and then from the growing impact of commercial and industrial development. The Liberation, which took till 1887 to complete, made the peasantry "free," which meant that the MVD became directly responsible for their general well-being and would have to devise some administrative means for discharging this responsibility. Rural "society" after 1861 was no longer a number of estate owners and managers to be harassed into taking care of the inhabitants of their lands. Now, in the eyes of the government-society, it had suddenly become an amorphous and disorganized mass of people, utterly without leadership, whose actions and behavior patterns were not immediately predictable nor even perceivable but upon whose productivity and good order the state depended. By the 1870s the MVD had already noticed that the rapid tumble into the marketplace was destroying all the society the peasants knew and reducing

---

Peasants continued to render "natural" obligations such as road labor and police work until the end of the tsarist regime. See Brzheskii, *Naturalnye povinnosti*, pp. 1–91.

6. On MF attitudes regarding the peasants' taxes during the 1860s–1880s, see Gindin, pp. 31–35.

large numbers of them to a profound helplessness, the chief manifestations of which were massive starvation and anarchy (see above,
ch. I, sec. C).

When the MVD tried to do something about the peasants' difficulties, its efforts brought it into conflict with the MF. While the MF
was engaged in "raising the level of demand" and "freeing" the
peasants from tradition, the MVD was deploring the destruction of
peasant society and calling for leadership in the villages.[7] The resulting tension between the two ministries forms the main thread in the
story of domestic administration in the tsarist government in the
period 1861–1905. The clash between market and peasant society
produced effects all through the government, but its most consistent
and dramatic manifestations appeared in the relations between the
MF and the MVD, the organizations least able to escape from the
dilemmas of Russian government as a whole.[8] It is not far-fetched,
therefore, to regard the MVD-MF conflict as the result of the *impact*
of Russian society on the bureaucracy that was attempting to govern
it or, alternatively, as the Russian government's *response* (albeit not
a conscious one) to the needs of Russian society.

Organizational conflict between MF and MVD did not always
plunge the ministers into personal opposition; nor did all the personal squabbles between the two ministers during the period 1861–
1905 proceed from the basic tension between their organizations.
Indeed, none of the ministers seem to have been more than dimly
aware at best that there was a basic contradiction between the purposes of the two ministries. The contradiction was clearly a very important element in the social environment of the tsarist government,
but its importance, like that of other conceptualized elements in

7. When the interministerial conflict reached its culmination in the first years
of the twentieth century, Max Weber observed that the MVD was leading the
peasantry against the capital cities while the MF was organizing the capital cities
for an assault on the villages. See his "Zur Lage de bürgerlichen Demokratie in
Russland," *Archiv für Sozialwissenschaft und Sozialpolitik*, XXII (1906), 338.
This is a fair approximation. Polovtsov thought that the main cause of the feud
between Witte and Ivan L. Goremykin (the MVD) in the late 1890s was that
Witte wanted a peasant "reform" and Goremykin was preventing its enactment.
See Polovtsov, "Dnevnik," *Krasnyi Arkhiv*, XLVI (1931), 122.

The conflict manifested itself within the new industrial society, not only between it and the countryside. A. F. Vovchik's recent study of government policy
with regard to worker organization from the 1880s to 1905—probably the best
documented one in existence—describes in detail the development of tension
between the two ministries in this area. See *Politika tsarizma po rabochemu
voprosu v predrevoliutsionnyi period* (Lvov, 1964), e.g., pp. 134–148. Vovchik
labels the MVD side "police bonapartists" and that of the MF "enlightened protectors of capitalism" (p. 146).

8. See Yaney, "Some Aspects," pp. 68–90.

society—free competition, class struggle, etc.—was general and pervasive, not necessarily immediate and specific in any given situation or event.

As said in the previous chapter, we are studying the ministries primarily in order to find causes for the anomalies in tsarist legal-administrative system. Nevertheless, the point must be made and emphasized at the outset that the degree of practical cooperation attained by the ministries increased markedly during the course of the nineteenth century. Despite the "failure" of the supreme organs to instill formal unity among the ministries after 1861 in the form of a constitutional framework, the ministerial organizations grew more effective and became increasingly inclined to cooperate with each other even as the tensions between them grew sharper. The contradiction between growing tension and growing cooperation is only apparent. The government servitors were becoming more interdependent, and it was more or less natural that this should have forced them to coordinate and at the same time provoked them into fights. As Ihering and Korkunov have suggested, conflict and law have a common origin.[9]

There are several indications that the ministers felt a growing need for systematic cooperation among themselves in 1861–1905. The most apparent were the procedures they developed to facilitate it. In 1872, for example, they began to print their legislative projects and distribute them to each other for comments before submitting them to the State Council or other supreme organ.[10] More basically, their operations furthered the steady expansion of the imperial chancellery's role in government (see above, ch. VII, sec. A). But the most telling indication of growing interministerial cooperation may be seen in the informal understandings that emerged among the ministers regarding their behavior toward each other. Throughout the period they maintained a sort of professional courtesy toward one another, setting effective though unofficial limits to the actions that any one of them could take unilaterally.

The substance of these understandings cannot be outlined exactly, largely because there is little concrete evidence relating to them. I have already alluded to the consensus among the statesmen regarding the prerogatives of the State Council, especially their inclination to regard the tsar's acceptance of a minority opinion from the Council as a violation of "legality." Another unwritten rule of interministerial

9. The classical expression of the idea that conflict over the law's meaning is the primary source of its strength is Rudolf von Ihering, *The Struggle for Law* (Chicago, 1879). See also Korkunov, *Ukaz,* pp. 189–190.

10. *Gos. kants.,* pp. 298–300. Concerning other measures of this nature, see below, sec. B.

cooperation was that no minister should call independently for a senatorial inspection. The dispatch of senator-inspectors to the ends of the empire with almost unlimited powers was one of the Senate's oldest functions, dating back to Peter's time.[11] In the nineteenth century the Senate could not initiate these inspections on its own but had first to receive an order from the tsar, and after 1837 the tsar issued orders for inspections only upon a request from one or more ministers. In 1801–1855 about eighty were carried out,[12] but between 1861 and 1905, when the ministers were in full command, there were only eight, the last of which came in 1882. Three of these were made in the period 1862–1875, four during the "crisis" of 1880–1881 at the request of Mikhail Loris-Melikov, and one more in 1882.[13] As the official history of the Senate says, there were very few inspections after 1861, and almost all of them were for exceptional occasions.[14] Apparently the ministers were reluctant to use them, mainly because a call for a senatorial inspection by any one minister usually brought down upon him the same kind of disapproval that arose if he tried to approach the tsar unilaterally regarding a measure that had already been placed before the State Council.[15]

In general, informal understandings among the ministers constituted a powerful restraint on unilateral action even in the absence of formal sanctions. As Lazarevskii has pointed out, whenever a minister went over the heads of his colleagues to get the tsar's support, he incurred their displeasure, and this was no small risk. Only ministers

11. See E. S. Paina, "Senatorskie revizii i ikh arkhivnye materialy (XIX-nachalo XX vv.)," in *Nekotorye izucheniia istoricheskikh dokumentov XIX-nachala XX veka* (Leningrad, 1967), pp. 147–155.

12. About fifty in Alexander I's reign and thirty in Nicholas I's. See *IPS*, III, 616–632; Paina, pp. 156–164.

13. Paina, pp. 165–168. The official history of the Senate says there were eighteen senatorial inspections in 1861–1905, the last one coming in 1892, but that only ten of these were of any significance. See *IPS*, IV, 185–186, 507–508. A few senatorial inspections were made in 1905–1912 in connection with the revolutionary movement of that time. See Paina, pp. 168–170.

14. *IPS*, IV, 185–187.

15. It is certain that the ministers' disinclination to call for senatorial inspections was not due to any failing in the inspections themselves or any lack of need for them. N. M. Druzhinin has described two major inspections made in connection with the Liberation, one in 1862–1863 and the other in 1870. His account shows that the inspectors collected much valuable information and that the discrepancies they uncovered clearly demonstrated the need for many such visitations. True to form, however, the ministers agreed not to act on their reports and recommendations. See N. M. Druzhinin, "Senatorskie revizii 1860–1870-kh godov," *Istoricheskie zapiski*, LXXIX (1967), 139–175. See also *IPS*, IV, 187–189.

who were very sure of the tsar's continuing support could undertake it.[16]

Ministers did try now and then to act unilaterally to get the tsar's support (see above, ch. VII, sec. B). Indeed, Valuev maintained that during his term of office as MVD in 1861–1868, most of the ministers readily sought the support of the tsar against their colleagues if they had any hope of getting it. "Among us," he says, "there is no kind of behavior toward one's colleagues that is accounted frivolous, careless, or even treacherous. The sense of personal dignity and the respect for a few basic principles regarding public activity are so little developed and so unsophisticated that one expects no very delicate treatment from one's colleagues. What weighs most heavily with us is immediate expediency and facile hopes for advantage."[17]

This is not an objective description of the tsarist government's high-level servitors in the 1860s,[18] but even if it were accurate, the fact that Valuev felt so strongly is one more indication that respect for proper procedure was already making itself felt in his time. Valuev's bitter words express his awareness of a rather well-developed and sophisticated code of ethics for government servitors, the correctness and practicality of which he took so much for granted that he never bothered to defend it. His own anger makes it clear, despite his protestations, that by the 1860s high-level servitors were coming to a consensus concerning the ways in which ministers should and should not use the tsar's authority.

Personal reminiscences of other nineteenth-century Russian statesmen give abundant indication that they not only disapproved of but actually scorned their peers who either tried to gain the tsar's support against their colleagues or sacrificed professional considerations in order to please the tsar. I have never found a diary or memoir of any nineteenth-century tsarist statesman that failed to express this scorn. Polovtsov, for example, was fond of denouncing Mikhail Ostrovskii, minister of state domains in the 1880s, for "caring only that he please those in power."[19] Those who made accusations of this sort were often guilty of the practices they affected to scorn, but if the ministers were sinners, it is still significant that they *and the tsars* regarded unilateral action by any one of them as a sin.

16. Lazarevskii, II, 182.
17. Valuev, *Dnevnik*, II, 410.
18. Had Valuev been consistent in his analysis of the behavior of his fellow statesmen, he would not have been so fond of blaming their difficulties on the pusillanimity of Alexander II. See, e.g., *ibid.*, pp. 438–440.
19. Polovtsov, *Dnevnik* (1966), I, 220–221.

Even statesmen who more or less regularly sought the tsar's support at least professed to disapprove of the practice. Pobedonostsev enjoyed an especially black reputation for using his personal influence with the tsar to get this or that project past the objections of the other ministers. In 1883, for example, he got excited about starting a "volunteer fleet" and tried to get Alexander III's support for it over the head of the minister of the navy.[20] But even Pobedonostsev took pains to deny allegations that he was using his influence with the tsar to get by other ministers.[21] Polovtsov records numerous instances in his diary when he confronted Pobedonostsev and others with accusations of this kind of behavior, and although their answers were not always satisfactory to him, they were always anxious to deny the accusations or to justify themselves by pleading urgent necessity.[22]

It is true that the ministers never reached the point where they openly advocated any formal limitation on the tsar's authority to interfere in the government as he saw fit. Moreover, it must be acknowledged that their informal consensus did not produce uniformly desirable results: it could obstruct action as well as render it possible. The fact remains, however, that the ministries did show signs of depending on one another ever more closely in 1861–1905, and although our discussion emphasizes the difficulties that stood in the way of system and the "flaws" that emerged within it, this should not obscure the substantial development that actually occurred in interministerial coordination even in the absence of a constitutional framework for it. In practice, the ministers were coming to expect their colleagues to be at least as loyal to interministerial organization as to the tsar.

B. The Rise of Rational Order in the Ministries

The basic difficulty that the ministries faced was not any defect in their formal systems but, rather, the dilemmas into which the rise of

20. In this case Alexander III backed the minister, despite Pobedonostsev's pressure and despite Alexander's own favorable attitude toward the fleet. "Actually it is a shame," he said, "to abandon this useful project . . . ," but in the face of "the convictions of the naval minister," it should not be continued. See Alexander III's letters to Pobedonostsev of 17 and 21 Mar. 1883, in Pobedonostsev, *Pisma i zapiski*, I, 302–304.

21. Polovtsov, *Dnevnik* (1966), I, 411–412.

22. See, e.g., *ibid.*, p. 413. The appointment of I. A. Vyshnegradskii to the State Council in Apr. 1886 seems to have caught the statesmen by surprise. Polovtsov accused a number of them of exercising influence on Vyshnegradskii's behalf, and although this would not have been illegal, all seemed anxious to deny that they had had anything to do with the matter and to blame someone else. They all acted as if they were acknowledging that a wrong had been done.

rational order in the government was leading. Before discussing the ministries' difficulties, therefore, it is necessary to describe the evolution of system in their organizations.

The clearest indication I have seen of this evolution comes from two articles published in 1964 by N. P. Diatlova and R. Iu. Matskina, two archivists who work in the Central State Historical Archive in Leningrad.[23] Diatlova offers a general description of the annual reports made by the governors to the tsar during the period 1801–1917, and Matskina describes the annual reports of the ministers. The original purpose of both articles was only to discuss the value of these reports as historical sources. So far as I could determine in conversation with Matskina (in early 1966), she was utterly unaware that she had written anything more than an aid to scholarly research. She insisted that her purpose in writing the article was only to describe the kinds of information that could be found in the ministerial reports and to estimate its value to historians. In writing their archival guides, however, both Matskina and Diatlova found it relevant to trace the more or less steady development of the reports from the relatively crude form they took in the early nineteenth century to a much higher level of sophistication by 1905. In so doing, they have inadvertently illuminated the evolution of rational organization in the tsarist bureaucracy in the nineteenth and early twentieth centuries far better than any historical work I know of. A discussion of the articles follows.

THE GOVERNORS' ANNUAL REPORTS

Diatlova's article sets out to describe changes in the form, content, and distribution of the governors' annual reports. These changes, she says, reflect the entire course of the domestic administration's development throughout the nineteenth and early twentieth centuries: "Evolution in . . . the governors' reports was called forth by life itself—by the steady development in the economy, in the social-political life of Russia, and in all branches of the government administration."[24] To be sure, Diatlova adds, the governors remained agents of despotism to the

---

23. R. Iu. Matskina, "Ministerskie otchety i ikh osobennosti kak istoricheskogo istochnika [*sic*]," pp. 209–226, and N. P. Diatlova, "Otchety gubernatorov kak istoricheskii istochnik," pp. 227–246, in *Problemy arkhivovedeniia i istochnikovedeniia* (Leningrad, 1964). Diatlova's article will be cited hereinafter as Diatlova, article, to distinguish it from the longer and more detailed report on which the article was based. The report, which bears the same title, is unpublished and undated, but a typed copy is kept in the TsGIAL. It will be cited hereinafter as Diatlova, report.

24. Diatlova, article, p. 235.

end. They "took no great interest in learning the true situation in their gubernias," and their reports never did rise to a level that made them wholly satisfactory to the central offices.[25] Even as late as 1912 V. Kokovtsev, MF from 1906 to 1914, complained that the governors' reports were too disorganized to be used effectively.[26] Nevertheless, the governors improved their work as time went by, and their reports came to play, in Diatlova's words, "a key role in the central government's policy making." A. S. Ermolov, minister of agriculture from 1894 to 1905, said in 1897 that the statistics in the governors' annual reports constituted for the central government "the only source of information on the area of land being cultivated, the nature of the crops being raised, and the number of cattle."[27]

The governors' annual reports to the tsar began when the September 1802 manifesto ordered the civil (and military) governors to make annual reports to the MVD. The first ones were submitted in 1804, and they continued to come in each year from then on. Until 1837 they came to the MVD. All that the tsar and the other ministers saw was the information the MVD took from them to make up his own annual report.

The years 1835–1837 marked the real beginning of the evolution of the governors' reports. As has been noted, this was a time of significant reforms in gubernia administration. The governors expanded their police forces and brought them more directly under central control, the governors-general were formally abolished in most of European Russia, the MF tightened its control over gubernia and uezd financial institutions, and the ministry of state domains commenced its reform of the state peasants. It was also in 1835–1837 that the governors' reports began to go directly to the tsar.[28] From then on, Nicholas I used them as one of his most important means for directing and controlling the ministries.

His method was as follows. Upon receiving the reports, he read them, wrote comments in the margins, and then sent them to the Committee of Ministers. Theoretically, these marginal notes had the force of law, but they were not published as such. Some were merely questions or specific orders regarding a particular matter, while others constituted a legal basis on which the ministers, individually or collectively, could issue directives having the force of law.[29] When the

25. *Ibid.*, p. 240.
26. Diatlova, report, p. 25.
27. *Ibid.*, p. 64.
28. *Ibid.*, p. 28.
29. The tsar's marginalia continued to be an important basis for government action, both executive and legislative, until 1905. Some notes were mere expres-

tsar-annotated governors' reports came to the Committee of Ministers, the royal marginalia

> were reported in the Committee . . . and a short record was kept of the matters of interest in the report and of the Committee's deliberations. After this, printed excerpts from the reports together with the tsar's remarks, accompanied by the [Committee's] journal or special letters of instruction, were sent to the ministries concerned— to each according to its jurisdiction. . . . In the Ministries, this material was distributed among the appropriate departments, which in their turn carried on correspondence with other offices and with local organs concerning matters of interest in the reports.[30]

In Nicholas I's time the governors' annual reports were of greater significance to the central offices than they were in later decades, when other sources of information began to become available both inside and outside the government organization. The ministries were only beginning to acquire local organs of their own, and for a long time they had to get what information they could from the governors and the local colleges. Under these circumstances the tsar's monopoly on the governors' annual reports gave him a considerable measure of initiative. Until 1881 only three copies of each report were made, and the tsar was the only central "institution" that could use them systematically as a basis for making decisions and issuing orders. Under these circumstances the ministers were much more dependent on the tsar and to some extent on the Committee than they would be later in the century. Doubtless, Nicholas felt a need for such a system. In 1837 he was extending the ministers' organizations a long way into the countryside, and he wanted to keep an eye on them.

Nicholas soon found the governors' annual reports unsatisfactory. They contained more vague expressions of opinion than solid information, and each one was organized in a different way. Lacking any standard form, the reports could not be compared with each other systematically, and general information could not be compiled. In short, they were hardly adequate as instruments for directing an organization pretending to be a state.

---

sions of sentiment. He might scribble "Delighted" or "Glory to God" after a report of a success. The only action that would result, if any, would be the granting of a medal to some official. On the other hand, if he approved a concrete suggestion—sometimes merely by underlining it—this generally produced instructions to one or more ministers. A collection of these marginalia for the years 1895–1901, together with reports of actions taken in response to them, is in *Svod vysochaishikh otmetok po vsepoddanneishim otchetam za 1895–1901* (7 vols., St. Petersburg, 1897–1904).

30. Diatlova, report, p. 29.

In 1842 Nicholas published a law setting up a standard form for the reports to follow and requiring the gubernia offices to maintain their records according to standard procedures. From then on, the annual reports became gradually more standardized and more useful to the central government.[31] Despite these improvements, the governors' annual reports continued to leave much to be desired. Apparently their expansion to include ever more categories of information proceeded more rapidly than the development of standard formulas to comprehend the categories. Even so, the reports grew immensely more valuable in the following decades ("incomparably better"), especially following the enactment of sweeping changes in the report forms by the laws of 13 April 1869 and 19 June 1870.[32]

The content of the reports also began to improve in some respects in the 1840s,[33] but the gathering of gubernia statistics that could be compiled in the capital city began to develop into something serious only with the law of 26 December 1860.[34] To take one example of the quality of information available to the governors, the police presumably *improved* the accuracy of their population count in the 1860s by utilizing parish registers (*metricheskie knigi*) of marriages, births, and deaths.[35] These registers were not especially reliable, but in the 1860s they still seem to have constituted a more accurate basis for counting the population than all the records and reports the young bureaucracy could muster. How valid, then, were the figures in the governors' reports of the 1860s regarding more complex matters such as acreage under cultivation, annual harvest yields, and the like?[36]

In the next few decades the picture changed considerably. The statistical sections of the reports expanded and improved in quality throughout the latter half of the nineteenth century. By 1898, Diatlova says, they had become the most valuable part of the reports.[37]

31. Diatlova, article, p. 230.
32. *Ibid.*, p. 231.
33. The flow of information from countryside to capital city seems to have undergone a general improvement in the 1840s and 1850s. A collection of secret police reports to the MVD for the period 1836–1856 (*Materialy . . . krepostnogo prava*) reflects a year-by-year increase in the number of details furnished and a gradual improvement in the organization of information.
34. Diatlova, article, p. 241.
35. Diatlova, report, pp. 59–60.
36. One indication of the inability of the gubernia offices to gather or to compile statistics is in Herzen's description, I, 288, of how it was done in Viatka when he worked there in the early 1840s. He once saw a clerk adding up the deaths for the year according to the causes of death. After adding together all types of violent deaths and getting a total, he then added both this total and the different kinds that made it up into the figure for deaths of all kinds.
37. Diatlova, report, pp. 56–57.

The distribution of the governors' annual reports remained severely restricted until well after the Liberation. A separate statistical section was printed and circulated directly to the ministries from 1870 on,[38] and in 1879 the governors were granted the right to send printed copies to each other.[39] Until Alexander III's reign, however, the descriptive part of the reports—that which the tsar received directly from the governors and annotated—continued to be essentially a document by which the tsar controlled the ministers.

It was Alexander III, not his father the tsar-liberator, who at last broke down the old system of Nicholas I and converted the governors' reports into vehicles for interministerial coordination. In 1881, the first year of his reign, he ordered that the reports, together with his marginal notes, should be printed and that each minister should receive a copy of his own prior to the meetings of the Committee of Ministers in which they were to be discussed.[40] Before 1881 each minister had received only those parts of the reports that the Committee directed to him personally. After 1881 each ministry maintained a full collection of the governors' reports.

Alexander III's order to print the governors' annual reports and to distribute them to the ministers in advance indicates that government organization had undergone considerable development during the previous forty years. According to Nicholas I's old arrangement, the information from the governors—i.e., the "people"—came to the Committee of Ministers only via the oracular tsar, a procedure devised for the purpose of keeping a tight rein on the newly powerful ministers. Alexander II seems to have shared his father's desire to restrict the power of individual ministers. He not only retained his oracular role but also seems to have deliberately appointed ministers who were not in agreement so that they would constrain one another.[41] The impatient Alexander III, on the other hand, wanted above all that his ministers act. Unlike his father, he did what he could to improve communications among them and between them and their gubernia agencies, even at the risk of weakening his own and the Committee's control over them.

Not that Alexander III was surrendering his power to the bureaucracy; he was simply using it in a way that was more suitable to his aims and to the nature of the organization he was manipulating.

38. Diatlova, article, p. 231.
39. *Ibid.*, p. 237.
40. Diatlova, report, p. 29.
41. Concerning Alexander II's inclination to keep his ministers divided, see Rieber, pp. 55–56. See also Dmitri Miliutin's statement in *ibid.*, p. 40, and Valuev's in *Dnevnik*, II, 438–440.

Judging from the way he handled his ministers, he was the first tsar to conceive of the government administration as essentially a reforming agency, and his manner of ruling may be taken as a reflection not merely of his own personality but primarily of the development that the administration had undergone since the 1830s. If there was a demand for the distribution of the governors' annual reports in 1881, it is reasonable to suppose that the servitors found them an aid to communication among themselves. Moreover, they had reason to regard such communication as desirable and necessary.

The development in the use of the governors' annual reports from 1837 to 1881 is one of the clearest indications that the servitors of the tsarist government were learning from their experience to depend on one another to work systematically. Whatever Nicholas I may have consciously intended to do in 1835–1837, his reforms in those years embodied a general decision to govern through ministries rather than gendarmes, all-powerful inspectors, and secret agents. From then on, he exercised his authority primarily through centralized system rather than the personal virtues of special, all-powerful agents. As noted before, the third section lived on after the 1830s, but after 1837 it developed no further as a means for the tsar to run his government.

What did develop after 1837 was a degree of system in ministerial organization and a steady improvement in the quality of information that came to it from the "people." In 1881 the tsar could no longer play the oracle. No longer could he keep each minister dependent on him by issuing separate orders and making it difficult for him to know what his colleagues were doing. Alexander III *had* to allow his ministers to utilize and interpret his orders to suit their collective purposes. He *had* to transfer a large measure of initiative to his ministers because he recognized, at least implicitly, that the government's ability to act depended on the ministers' collective ability to cooperate with one another on their own. The tsar could still pick his ministers after 1881, but he could no longer manage his government by manipulating them individually, ordering each one of them to do this or that task or make this or that change. As Nicholas II's activities demonstrated, the tsar could sometimes disrupt his government by trying to run it on his own, but he could not manage it. Only the ministers could manage it, and they could only manage it if they could make their organizations coordinate.[42]

42. In Nicholas II's time it was not uncommon for a minister to challenge the tsar on technical grounds. Take, for example, a governor's report from Baku gubernia in 1895, requesting a change in judicial procedures. Next to the governor's request the tsar wrote, "Give this serious attention." Two ministers responded to the tsar's suggestion by arguing that the proposed change was not

Except for the wider distribution of the governors' annual reports after 1881, Nicholas I's basic arrangement for their use remained in force until 1917. The tsars never surrendered their prerogative of seeing the reports and commenting upon them before any of the ministers did. In 1856 and again in 1897 the MVD proposed that the reports should come first to its central offices and only then be sent on via the Committee of Ministers to the tsar. On both occasions the tsar and most of his ministers rejected this idea on the ground that if the governors lost their direct access to the tsar, the tsar would lose one of his ties with the "people."[43] To put it in more prosaic terms, if the governors had had to report through the MVD, the MVD's power over them would have become so great that even the tsar would have been unable to restrain him. If the tsar could not allow a constitutional framework to hamstring his ministers and prevent them from acting, neither could he give any single minister a legal basis for dominating his colleagues.

THE MINISTERS' ANNUAL REPORTS

The development of the governors' annual reports from 1801 to 1917 presents a reasonably simple picture of growing regularity and procedural uniformity in the central government organization and its local agencies. The annual reports of the ministers, however, reflect a more complex evolution. To be sure, the ministers' reports, like those of the governors, conveyed more and better information as the century progressed, indicating the same growing regularity and procedural standardization. On the other hand, the ministers—chiefly the MF and the MVD—were often able to avoid making reports, and their tendency to do so grew more marked as time went by.

The ministers' annual reports were intended to be devices for systematic coordination, but in Alexander I's reign they never came close. Until 1810 they were supposed to go from the individual ministers to the Senate and thence to the tsar. The law of September 1802 called upon the Senate to form special committees to look over the reports and, when it seemed necessary, require additional information from the ministers before sending the reports on to the tsar. This was to have given the Senate a means to supervise the ministries and in some measure to coordinate them. In fact, the whole matter degenerated into a mere formality from the beginning. The Senate was pushed aside,

---

necessary, and with that the matter seems to have been dropped. See *Svod . . . otmetok* (1895), pp. 8–9.

43. Diatlova, report, p. 30.

and the ministers' reports went directly to the tsar.[44] Apparently, separate, uncorrelated reports were not satisfactory to Alexander I. In 1810 he ordered that they be submitted via the State Council, and until the end of his reign this was the way it was done. The State Council, however, represented no real improvement. After 1812 it never made any attempt to correct the reports or standardize their form but only filed copies of them in the archive of the imperial chancellery.

Nicholas I tried to use the ministers' annual reports more effectively. In the rescript of 30 September 1826 he ordered that the reports for 1826 be presented in the Committee of Ministers on 1 January 1827, so that the Committee could look them over before sending them on to the tsar. The tsar would then read them, make comments in the margins, and send them back to the Committee for distribution and action, in much the same way as he would distribute the governors' reports after 1837. This procedure remained in force from 1827 to 1858.[45]

Superficially considered, Nicholas's reign was the time when the handling of the ministers' reports was at its most orderly stage. Indeed, the formal machinery looked so impressive on paper that on one occasion Nicholas tried to extend it one step further. In 1827 he ordered the Committee to compile all the ministers' reports into one big general survey, to be put into printed form, presumably as a basis for a common administrative policy. The attempt failed. The reports came in at different times and covered different periods, and it proved virtually impossible to produce a meaningful compilation of the information in them. Only one general survey was ever put together, that of 1831, but it was never printed and no more were compiled. The Committee's inability to compile its members' reports reflects their low quality. Though regularly submitted, they contained little information of the type from which policies and orders could be derived, and therefore they were of little value as instruments of coordination. Apparently Nicholas could get reports whenever he wanted them, but there was virtually nothing to report.[46]

Alexander II attempted to improve the quality of the ministers' annual reports and to use them more rigorously as instruments of coordination. His decree of 11 April 1858 ordered that the ministers submit their reports to special commissions, to be made up of members

44. Matskina, pp. 210–211. See also *IPS*, III, 416–431, for a more detailed account.

45. Matskina, pp. 211–212. The procurator of the holy synod and the ministers of finance, communications, and the imperial household were allowed to go on submitting their annual reports directly to the tsar.

46. *Ibid.*

of the State Council and other high dignitaries appointed by himself. The commissions were to study the reports and to submit them to the Committee of Ministers with their comments, whereupon the Committee was also to consider and comment upon them. Only then were they to come to the tsar.

The practical result of Alexander II's efforts was the virtual elimination of annual ministerial reports. Some special commissions were actually set up, but after only a few years they stopped meeting, and the ministers began either to delay their reports for periods of several years or to stop making them altogether. The MVD made his last annual report in 1863, the MF in 1864; from then on, the other ministries took up the practice of making only one report for each five or six years. After 1881, Matskina says, the ministers made annual reports only when it pleased them. In 1899 Nicholas II expressed a desire to receive reports from all ministries, but even then not all responded. This is not to say that annual reports stopped coming in entirely. At the end of the century the holy synod and the ministries of agriculture, education, and justice were in fact submitting them with some regularity, and communications handed one in now and then. There were only two domestic ministries that submitted none at all: the MF and the MVD.[47]

The ministers did not cease reporting to the tsar altogether. On the contrary, they continued to make regular reports in person[48] and often submitted special memoranda either on their own initiative or on the tsar's. In addition, they published a mass of books and periodicals full of statistical information and discussions of their activities and policies. Matskina's investigation indicates that neither the MF nor the MVD nor any of the ministries lacked the necessary information to make annual reports. They received information regularly from the gubernia administrations and from their own subordinate organs, and both of

47. *Ibid.*, pp. 212–213. The MVD did make one report after 1863; it covered the years 1895–1898.

Zaionchkovskii, *Krizis*, pp. 24–25, expresses the belief that the MF and the MVD actually made annual reports but that they have since been lost. He suggests that they may have gone down with a boat that capsized while hauling archives from Petrograd to Moscow in the hectic days of early 1918. Matskina, however, has found no record of the reports in the journals of the Committee of Ministers, and this appears to be conclusive evidence that the reports were in fact never submitted. To be more precise, if they were submitted to the tsar himself and disposed of by him, they never went to the Committee of Ministers either before or after he got them. This, says Matskina, p. 214, is highly unlikely. In his latest work Zaionchkovskii seems to accept Matskina's conclusion. See *Rossiiskoe samoderzhavie*, p. 13.

48. According to Witte, *Vospominaniia*, I, 285, it was Alexander III's custom to hear a report from each minister once a week.

these sources improved and expanded after the 1860s.[49] Moreover, both MF and MVD received annual reports from their own departments. In the MF, for example,

> the Department of Manufacturing and Internal Trade . . . asked the governors and the *gradonachalniki* [prefects] of the port cities to get information about trade, shipbuilding, ship traffic, and sailors' guilds. As a rule, the governors and *gradonachalniki* got the information requested of them. The Department also received reports from offices at the wharves and from the larger private companies. In general, reports from the departments, kept in the ministerial chancelleries, obviously came in with impressive regularity.[50]

What, then, was the reason for the ministries' failure to make regular annual reports after the early 1860s? "It appears," Matskina says, "to have been their desire not to submit their activities to anyone for discussion or control."[51] But Matskina's answer does not go far enough. She does not explain how it was that the MF and the MVD were able to evade the law that required them to submit annual reports. It was the tsar who wanted the reports, not the supreme organs, and there was nothing to prevent him from demanding them. Nicholas I had gotten reports regularly throughout his reign,[52] and it seems reasonable to surmise that the MF and the MVD could not have opposed his successors on any ground other than very basic practical difficulties. The tsar himself must have seen good reason to allow the MVD and the MF not to make annual reports after 1864, even though this represented a violation of his own law.

What was his reason? Apparently the ministers' annual reports were not only sources of information but also—like the governors' annual reports—instruments for subordinating the ministries to a framework of systematic coordination. When a minister submitted an annual report, he could expect it to produce orders that would require his regular cooperation with other ministers. Conversely, if a minister wished to avoid submitting his organization to collective supervision, he had somehow to escape the requirement of making annual reports. Although the MF and the MVD had no objection to de facto cooperation with the other ministries, the evidence suggests that they

49. Matskina, p. 216.
50. *Ibid.*, pp. 216–217.
51. *Ibid.*, p. 214. IPS, III, 417–426, notes that in the first decade of the nineteenth century the breakdown of the ministerial reports to the Senate came from the same cause. The Senate's perusal of the reports of 1802–1803 was satisfactory, but the ministers did not wish to submit to the control of the Senate, and they were influential enough to refuse to do so.
52. Matskina, pp. 214–215.

consistently avoided any arrangement that would commit them to definite and formal relationships with their colleagues. Systematic frameworks developed *within* the ministries in 1861–1905, but relationships *among* them continued to be essentially ad hoc.

The continuing failure of the MF and the MVD to make annual reports in such a way as to subordinate themselves formally to a common system is one of the clearest indications we have that tension between the ministries was not merely a matter of the personal characters of the ministers, or the inherent weakness of the supreme organs, or the tsar's personal compulsion to retain his arbitrary authority, or the absence of a constitution. In essence, it was a manifestation within the bureaucracy of the government's interaction with Russian society.

C. The Split between the MVD and the MF

THE IMPACT OF RATIONAL ORDER ON MINISTERIAL GOVERNMENT

If the nationwide organizations of the MF and the MVD had been merely hierarchies of chiefs and henchmen, like those that had formed under the old-style omnipotent agents, they probably could have gotten along well enough by dividing off their respective areas of operation and leaving one another alone. Quarrels would have arisen, but they would have been personal and limited in scope, not clashes between operating principles that could shake the whole government. The ministries not only were powerful, however, but also pretended to be parts of a single system. Not only that, but their functional responsibilities rendered them unavoidably interdependent in practice, to the point where they could not escape interacting with one another on all levels in order to do their jobs. The MVD needed the MF's funds, and the MF relied on the MVD's executive organization in the countryside. The gubernia fiscal chamber relied on the police to collect taxes, and the governor relied on the fiscal chamber to approve his expenditures.

In the early nineteenth century the main problem in the relationship between the two ministries had been their inability to impose an orderly definition of their respective functions on the local organs of government (see above, ch. V, sec. B). In that time neither ministry had developed the directions and policies that characterized it at the end of the century, and the tension between them was more or less amorphous and incidental, taking the form of specific disputes rather than consistent divergences in attitudes.[53] Indeed, if any consistent views can be perceived in the policies of the two organizations, they seem to have been the opposite of the ministries' later positions. The MF in Nicholas I's time, still heavily dependent on its "tribute" from the countryside, seemed anxious to preserve the social status quo there and was suspicious of bureaucratic innovations.[54] By contrast, the MVD manifested an inclination to sweep rural institutions aside and to extend the agencies of the central bureaucracy as far into the countryside as it could, an impulse that reached its ultimate expression in the enactment of the Liberation.[55]

In the 1860s the local organs of the ministries were as yet far from perfect orderliness, but they had made some progress. During Nicholas I's reign, specifically from the mid-1830s on, the first serious steps had been taken to impose financial accountability on the gubernias (see above, ch. V, sec. B). This development reached its culmination in the decree of 22 May 1862, which set up a formal procedure—including the participation of the State Council—for compiling and publishing an annual budget on the basis of estimated revenue and expenditure.[56] With the introduction of a formal, published budget, the MF became more closely associated with central bureaucratic organization, while at the same time the elimination of serfdom gave the MVD such an overwhelming preponderance in local government relative to the other ministries that it lost some of its impetus to attack the countryside and became more closely identified with territorial administration as it was. In the 1860s, then, the ministries began to diverge into a new kind of conflict.[57]

It was also in the 1860s that the split between the MF and the MVD achieved institutional form on the gubernia level. As has been said, the gubernia fiscal chamber came unequivocally under the MF's command in 1866, thereby achieving virtual autonomy within the territorial administration. In the years thereafter the MF's organs expanded and multiplied in the gubernias and uezds, bringing it a considerable measure of real power, enough by the 1890s to allow it to contend on approximately equal terms with the MVD, though

53. See Starr, pp. 28–56, for an excellent description of administrative amorphousness in local government during Nicholas I's reign.
54. See Pintner, pp. 63, 72–73, 76–81.
55. Nicholas Miliutin's "radical" attitudes have been referred to in ch. IV, sec. E. It will be recalled that the MVD was intimately involved in the enactment of the Liberation and that its officials were among the most "radical" of the enactors.
56. *Ministerstvo finansov*, I, 404–407.
57. Starr, pp. 350–354, describes some of the first signs of this divergence in a dispute over zemstvo reform between Valuev, the MVD, and Reitern, the MF, in the early 1860s.

the MVD's police continued to collect direct taxes in the countryside until 1899.[58]

The growing power of the MF made interdependence between it and the MVD final and inescapable. Neither organization could ignore the other or push it aside, and this meant that the need for cooperation between them became crucial during the same span of years in which they were developing toward a basic conflict of interest and purpose. Organizational progress simultaneously multiplied both the sources of conflict between the ministries and the opportunities available to them for blocking each other. System in interministerial relations not only expressed the dependence between the ministries but heightened it, simultaneously allowing them to act together, creating antagonism between them, and providing each of them with the means to render the other impotent.

If the ministries did not operate accordng to a common set of rules and procedures, they still had to operate together in some fashion. The tsar could not manage his government except through them. When combined action did become necessary, therefore, the tsar adopted the practice of working through a single ministry, either the MVD or the MF. By giving a minister his personal support, the tsar could impart to him at least temporary freedom of action, i.e., enough predominance over his equally powerful colleague to enable the favored organization at least to bypass the agents of its rival. In practice, the tsarist government of the late nineteenth and early twentieth centuries worked best when either the MF or the MVD was able to manipulate his own organization and those of the lesser ministries without having to suffer interference from the other. If the tsar's power could not coordinate the ministries, it was still strong enough to keep one of them out of the other's way.

It was chiefly because of this fact—because of the needs called forth by the development of system—that the tsar's personal favor continued to play such a vital role in government during the period 1880–1905. With the two most powerful ministries in domestic administration locked in mutual dependence and drastic contradiction, only an essentially arbitrary authority could compel the one to allow the other to act. This was why the statesmen had to safeguard the tsar's authority and not let it be shackled by a constitutional framework or even a framework of systematic coordination. This was why they could not demand that *all* orders be issued via supreme organs or that *all* information be channeled through them. Even the tsar's favor would have

58. *Ministerstvo finansov*, I, 408, 418–483; Bilimovich, pp. 42–44, 49–50. See also below, ch. IX, sec. D.

been unable to stir the ministries to action if there had been a formal system that purported to unite the MF and the MVD, because any such system would have allowed the agents of one to block those of the other on all levels. This is the basic reason a constitutional framework did not take form despite the general desire of tsar and statesmen to form it.

All the tsars and statesmen knew that the granting of favor and arbitrary power to one minister threatened the integrity of every governing institution from the supreme organs to the peasant villages—an integrity that they themselves devoutly wished to maintain and inculcate. It is hard to imagine them repeatedly resorting to the means of a favored minister out of some sort of mania for power, or religious mysticism, or personal whim, or stupidity. This or that tsar may have been inclined to mysticism, or a prey to whims, or stupid, but the tsar's personality was hardly a basic factor in government organization. What was more significant was the compelling necessity that forced the last two tsars, regardless of their own inclinations or limitations or those of their statesmen, to resort to the rule of a favored minister—either the MF or the MVD—whenever they wanted the government to do something other than write laws or maintain oligarchies.

THE USE OF FAVORED MINISTERS

The tsarist government never made it a conscious, long-term goal to organize itself around the tsar's personal support of the MF or the MVD. It did not begin to adopt the device until 1880, and even then Alexander II only blundered into it while he was reacting to a crisis.

In the first half of the century, dictators' favorites—most notably Arakcheev, Kiselev, and Bibikov—were neither MVD nor MF. Arakcheev, who played the role from 1816 to 1825, was the tsar's personal secretary, and he ran the military colonies through an organization that was entirely separate from both domestic and military ministries (see above, ch. IV, sec. D). Kiselev, who governed 40 percent of Russia's population from 1838 to 1856, was minister of state domains. As such, he had control of an organization that was at least theoretically separate from the rest of the government on all levels, operating without either interference or cooperation from other ministries.

Arakcheev's and Kiselev's ability to operate without having to rely on the MF or the MVD indicates how weak the organizations of these ministries were and, in general, how decentralized in practice the domestic administration was during the first half of the century. This was the time when Governor-General Bibikov could introduce inventories on the estates of the Southwest by working with the gentry and ignoring the central ministries, especially the MVD's police (see above, ch. IV, sec. E). It was also the time, be it recalled, that Nicholas was able to force the MVD and the MF to make reports to him through the Committee of Ministers.

The reign of Alexander II (1855–1881) was something of an interlude in the evolution of ministerial government. It saw the enactment of major *legislative* reforms, a steady but slow improvement in the bureaucracy's routine operation, and general socio-economic progress throughout the country. In comparison with the reigns that preceded and followed, however, Alexander II's was a time of *administrative* inaction (see above, ch. VI, sec. E). The domestic organization developed and expanded, but only its parts operated. Alexander II's statesmen consistently stopped short of any attempt to bring all of them together in a single program. Consequently, the dilemmas of ministerial government did not become crucial until a crisis arose at the end of the reign. It was only in 1880 that Alexander II found himself governing by backing a single minister consistently.[59]

The main reason for the government's executive inaction in 1860–1880 was simply that the statesmen of the time did not perceive any workable means for setting the bureaucracy into coordinated motion. Unable to form any practically acceptable concept of themselves or their situation, they could not very well initiate collective action on the basis of some common program on which they all agreed. All they could do was react to problems individually from day to day by devising temporary expedients.[60] The following statement by Dmitri Miliutin is typical of not only his own state of mind throughout the reign but also that of his colleagues:

. . . all our governmental structure demands basic reforms from top to bottom. Autonomous village administrations, zemstvoes, uezd and

59. In the early 1870s Petr A. Shuvalov, then the head of the third section, used the tsar's favor for a short time to establish a measure of informal cooperation among at least a few of the ministers (see above, ch. VII, sec. B). This, however, was no more than a personal arrangement. See Valuev, *Dnevnik*, II, 284–285, 311. As head of the third section, Shuvalov had no functioning organization upon which the other ministries depended, and he was unable to initiate reforms. His inefficacy only serves to demonstrate that personal influence at the top levels of government was no longer enough, by itself, to move the domestic administration or even to get free of it. Zaionchkovskii discusses a number of reforms enacted under Alexander III that had already been drawn up or at least proposed in Alexander II's time. See, e.g., *Rossiiskoe samoderzhavie*, pp. 200–201. Before 1880, it seems, the administration could envision reform programs but could not enact them.

60. Valuev, who was as close to understanding the situation in Alexander II's government as anyone, repeatedly referred in his diary to the government's lack of direction and his own sense of aimlessness. See, e.g., *Dnevnik*, II, 136–137, 140–143, 187, 303, 382.

gubernia offices, and central and supreme institutions as well—all have outlived their time; all must be given new forms. . . . Such a colossal task is beyond the capacity of our present-day statesmen, who are completely unable to rise above the point of view of a police chief or even a sergeant. In recent years, the leading administrators have been intimidated by the insolent assertions of socialist propaganda, and they think only of protective police measures instead of acting against the most basic evils. . . . I am convinced that present-day people are unable to accomplish the task that confronts them or even to understand it.[61]

Alexander II seems to have feared the prospect of collective ministerial action; his ministers all thought so, at any rate. They were fond of denouncing him for indecisiveness and for playing them against one another (see above, n. 41). But Alexander II's personal weaknesses were not so paralyzing as his inability to conceive of his government in other than senatorial terms. As said before, he still clung to the same notion that had informed Alexander I's servitors: namely, that the purpose of a legal-administrative system was to keep each minister in his own separate compartment rather than to unite them in a single program of action.[62]

In this regard the ministers of the 1860s were no more enlightened than their ruler (see above, ch. VII, sec. B). None of them proposed or even tried to propose a coherent basis for government action other than the tsar's exercise of autocratic power.[63] True, a number of them

61. Miliutin, *Dnevnik*, III, 139–140. He wrote this in 1879, when he was at the height of his power.

62. See Alexander's letter to Prince Bariatinskii of 20 May 1857. The letter was concerned with a quarrel between Bariatinskii and the war minister, but in the course of his remarks on this specific matter Alexander expressed a general view on the proper relationship between subordinate organs: "The War Minister is as responsible before me for his job as you are for yours, and it is my duty to see to it that neither the one nor the other of you exceeds the limits assigned to him" (quoted in Rieber, p. 105). This was not the view of a bureaucratic manager. So far as I know, Alexander II never expressed an awareness that he had to form a single machinery out of his ministries in order to achieve general purposes.

63. Some illustrative proposals for action by autocratic power were those submitted in 1868 by B. Obukhov, then governor of Pskov. Obukhov believed that it was the government's proper aim to march the Russian peasantry into legal system as rapidly as possible. One of his proposals, which expressed his general concept of reform very well, was to forbid marriage to all peasants who could not pass a literacy test. See B. Obukhov, *Russkii administrator noveishei shkoly* (Berlin, 1868), p. 52.

The MVD looked upon Obukhov's proposals with favor. He was promoted to deputy minister shortly after submitting them. In the rest of the government, however, he made no impression. In fact, his proposals were extreme and unworkable. That they should have come from a man who had had long experience

favored vague schemes for introducing elected representatives into the central government or setting up local autonomous institutions that might act on their own. But none of this imaginative reasoning bore any relevance to the problem of how the government was to act (see above, ch. VI, n. 23). The closest Alexander II's statesmen could come to conceiving of administrative action was to think up new ways to legislate, as if the bureaucracy could cope with its problems by concocting "sound," "properly enacted" laws.[64]

In short, the general condition of Russian statesmen after 1700—their inability to perceive any meaningful purpose in what they were doing, combined with the necessity for acting and thinking as if they did—was especially acute in the 1860s–1870s. It was a time of disillusionment, frustrating inactivity, and lack of direction. This is what produced the statesmen's overpowering inclination to denounce one another. Mutual denunciation was perhaps the only device that allowed them to keep their sanity.

It was only in the "crisis" situation of 1878–1882 that Alexander II began to act decisively to remedy the ills of rural society. In February 1880 he resorted to the extraordinary measure of granting one of his generals, Mikhail Loris-Melikov, such sweeping authority as to make him virtually dictator of Russia.

Loris-Melikov's dictatorial powers first came to him along with the official title of "chief of the supreme administrative commission." He quickly learned, however, that virtual dictatorship and the tsar's full support did not convey the means to act. In less than a month he asked for and got the third section, and in the summer of 1880, when the third section also proved inadequate, he eliminated both the supreme commission and his dictatorship in order to assume the post of MVD, bringing the third section with him into the ministry.[65] At the same time he used the tsar's favor to fill the other ministerial posts with men who were in general agreement with his plans and could be counted on to support him.[66]

Loris-Melikov's move into the MVD was clearly a tactical venture, not a conscious institutional reform. He and his tsar blundered into it

in local administration and had been an ardent emancipator in the late 1850s (*ibid.*, pp. v–viii) only emphasizes the difficulty of formulating programs of action in the countryside.

64. Rieber, p. 55, refers to Valuev's belief in adding zemstvo-elected representatives to the State Council. For Dmitri Miliutin's similar notion, see Zaionchkovskii's introduction to Miliutin's *Dnevnik*, I, 72.

65. Zaionchkovskii, *Krizis*, pp. 155–157, 164–165, 224–230.

66. See Peretts, *Dnevnik*, especially p. 7, and A. E. Presniakov's introduction to it, pp. vii–viii.

in desperation at what they considered to be a moment of national emergency. But Loris-Melikov's maneuvering had more than tactical significance. He was actually the first man to set ministerial government in motion on its own terms. As it happened, he lost his leading position shortly after the death of Alexander II and thus did not carry out any of his reform projects.[67] He did observe, however, that if he had the tsar's support, together with direct control over a single ministry, he would be in an optimal position for conducting reform programs, and he at least began to act on this basis.

In the mid-1880s, after several years of attempting to *legislate* peasant reform from the center and to strengthen local institutions so they could carry it out, Alexander III's statesmen decided to initiate and to *administer* it from the center. Alexander dismissed the Kakhanov commission (see below, ch. IX, sec. D) in 1885, renouncing with unmistakable finality its idea of entrusting reform to local autonomous institutions.[68] In 1886 he gave preliminary approval to a project from his MVD, Dmitri Tolstoi, concerning a law that would entrust peasant society to local "land captains," agents of the MVD whose primary purpose would be to introduce unified authority into the countryside. Tolstoi's project was based on his belief that authority (*vlast'*) had to be established by government action before there could be any talk of law or local institutions; therefore, the new agents were to combine in themselves both judicial and executive powers. They would be neither restricted nor guided by law in their activities and judgments. More important, they would be able to operate without having to suffer any of the formal constraints of bureaucratic coordination. In theory, they represented a return to the old eighteenth-century device of omnipotent agent; the important difference was that they were not the tsar's agents but the MVD's.[69]

The merits of Tolstoi's project are of no concern to us at this point. What is significant is his position in the government and the way he used it to build an organization in the countryside. He was able to get his project through the other ministers and the State Council only because the tsar backed him consistently against their opposition throughout the three years it took to complete the process of enactment. Tolstoi's relationship with Alexander III in 1886–1889 resembled the working agreements that had developed between Alexander II and Loris-Melikov in 1880–1881. Like Loris-Melikov, Tolstoi found him-

---

67. Zaionchkovskii, *Krizis,* pp. 207–212, 216–220, 239–258, 283–292, describes Loris-Melikov's projects.

68. Kataev, II, 115–116.

69. The land captains are discussed in greater detail in ch. IX, sec. D.

self in the position of favored minister and used it to push for reforms. Going beyond Loris-Melikov, Tolstoi actually got some of his projects enacted, though he died a few months before the process was completed.

Death interrupted both Loris-Melikov and Tolstoi before they could get their programs underway—Alexander II's in 1881 and Tolstoi's in 1889—but in 1889 at least a beginning had been made. The MVD's land captains actually came into existence, and their operation during the following fifteen years brought the government a long step closer to the villages. The alliance of tsar and favored minister (MF or MVD) had gained the status of precedent. Experience suggested that it was the only organizational arrangement that would allow the *pravitelstvo* to act in the countryside.

Following Tolstoi's death in 1889, Alexander III grew increasingly absorbed in the industrial development of Russia, in particular the construction of the trans-Siberian railroad, and he found himself relying on Sergei Witte, who seemed to be the government's best railroad manager. Witte began his government career in 1891 by taking over the newly founded department of railroad affairs in the MF. In this capacity he set up a government-managed system of railroad rates and fares. Early in 1892 he moved up to the post of minister of ways of communications, and in August of the same year Alexander appointed him MF.[70] As MF, Witte said, he was in a better position to develop Russia's railroad network than if he had remained minister of communications. Many high-level statesmen were not favorably disposed toward his ambitious schemes for railroad building and industrial development. If he had not had the funds and the power of the MF organization in addition to the tsar's support, he could not have carried them through.[71]

Witte retained the MF and the support of the tsar for about ten years,[72] and under this relatively long alliance Russia "enjoyed" an unprecedented spurt in urban and industrial development, fostered and led by the government under the direction of the MF. Sheltered and bolstered by the favor of the tsar, Witte was able to overcome his opposition in the supreme organs and at least to sidestep that of the

70. Witte, *Vospominaniia*, I, xii, 256.

71. See *ibid.*, p. 433; above, ch. VII, n. 15.

72. The tsar accepted Witte's nominations for those ministerial posts that were vital to the furthering of his projects for economic development. M. I. Khilkov, minister of communications from 1894 to 1905, was Witte's man (Witte, *Vospominaniia*, II, 24–25), as was A. S. Ermolov, minister of agriculture during the same period (*ibid.*, I, 348–349). Until 1905 the department of commerce and industry was directly under the MF.

MVD in the lower levels of the administration. In rural Russia, how-ever, his power to bypass the MVD's territorial administration was severely limited, and here the tsar's power was of no avail to him. In the end he was unable to introduce any serious reforms in peasant society.[73]

Witte lost the tsar's active support in 1902, when Nicholas II ap-pointed his mortal enemy, V. K. Pleve, to be MVD. In 1903 he was dismissed from his ministry, and for a short time the government op-erated on the basis of an alliance between tsar and MVD, devised to restore order and to produce a much-needed peasant reform.[74] But Pleve was assassinated in July 1904, and this left the government in the middle of war and domestic crisis without a favored minister. It was to be more than a year before Nicholas II found a competent replacement.

The year 1905 saw the central government at its nadir of weakness and paralysis. Practical administrators did not stop trying to rally be-hind a dictator in order to set the government in motion once again, but none of them seem to have realized that the dictator would have to be either the MF or the MVD. Since 1880 the tsars had been unable to govern from a framework set over both MF and MVD, and in 1905 the opposition between the two ministries had reached an unprece-dented degree of bitterness. This was the least likely time for any out-side leader, no matter how capable, to try to force them to work together.[75]

73. The MF did manage to make a few gains in the countryside. See below, ch. IX, sec. D.

74. Some considerations and projects coming from the MVD's work on peasant reform in 1902–1903 were published in 1903. See *Trudy redaktsionnoi komissii po peresmotru zakonopolozhenii o krestianakh* (2 vols., St. Petersburg, 1903). This work, carried out under Gurko's direction, was the primary source from which the so-called Stolypin land reform came. Gurko, pp. 135–168, gives an account of it. Pleve was not himself a leader in peasant reform (*ibid.*, p. 135), but his subordinates made a major contribution to it.

75. The conflict between the two ministries over labor organization had reached the point by 1903 that they were both creating rival worker groups in order to oppose each other's influence (see above, n. 7). The conflict between them over the peasant question was such that in 1902–1906 they operated two entirely separate investigations of rural society. Witte's investigation, begun a few months before his dismissal, was carried out against Pleve's heavy-handed opposition. Two governors were fired for cooperating with it too enthusiastically. See D. N. Liubimov, "Russkaia smuta, nachala deviatisotykh godov, 1902–1906" (unpub-lished manuscript in the Russian Archive at Columbia University), pp. 44–48. Despite Pleve's displeasure, Witte's committees produced fifty-eight volumes of reports, one from each gubernia, and twenty-three volumes of topical summaries. The results were officially compiled in S. I. Shidlovskii, *Obshchii obzor trudov mestnykh komitetov* (St. Petersburg, 1905). Concerning the MVD's conclusions, see above, n. 74. Actually, the two investigations came to much the same con-

As it was, Nicholas II had a run of bad luck in 1904–1905 in the men he picked for the leading posts in his government. His reaction to the incomprehensible blundering that produced Bloody Sunday (9 January 1905)[76] was to name one Dmitri Trepov to approximately the same kind of overall dictatorship that Loris-Melikov had taken up, and rejected, in 1880.[77] Trepov lacked the abilities of Loris-Melikov. He never had the wit to use his power to take over a ministry. Instead, he satisfied himself with the formal prerogative to issue orders to the police forces.[78] As 1905 wore on, his helplessness became increasingly apparent. By the end of the year he seems to have fallen into semi-hysterical inactivity. He issued enough futile orders to the MVD's police to deprive the proper MVD (Bulygin) of responsibility for his own organization, yet he himself never assumed it. By the fall of 1905 he had virtually ceased to issue orders, thus leaving the MVD and the police without direction of any kind.[79]

Driven to desperation by a general strike in October 1905, Nicholas II published a manifesto promising a constitution—meaning that the supreme organs were not only to secure their control over the ministries but also to deprive the tsar formally of his right to enact laws on his own authority.[80] Judging from the immediate result, this was probably a tactical blunder. It was done under the threat of rebellion rather than willingly, thus conveying to all rioters, actual and potential, the intoxicating realization that the government was helpless before them. All forms of opposition instantly intensified and expanded in scope.[81] On the other hand, the October manifesto may have done more good than harm in the long run. It gave the government the appearance of greater legality than before without really preventing the tsar from ruling directly through his ministers in practice. What better

clusions. By 1903 interministerial conflict over rural reform was almost entirely concerned with organizational questions, not issues.

Finally, a recent investigation refers to conflicts in these years between the MVD's police agents and the MF's money dealers in western Europe. See James Long, "The Economics of the Franco-Russian Alliance, 1904–1906" (unpublished Ph.D. dissertation, University of Wisconsin, 1968), pp. 13–15, 51–54.

76. See Sidney Harcave, *First Blood* (New York, 1964), pp. 76–79, 82–97. Even Liubimov, pp. 173–184, who was then chief of the MVD's chancellery, could not say exactly how the slip-up occurred.

77. Liubimov, pp. 202–204.

78. *Ibid.*, pp. 266–267.

79. *Ibid.*, pp. 268–272, 297–308.

80. Szeftel, "Nicholas II's Constitutional Decisions," and Witte, *Vospominaniia*, III, 3–56, describe the enactment of the manifesto. Such was the emergency at the time it was signed that there was talk of the royal family's having to abandon Peterhof. See Witte, *Vospominaniia*, III, 37–38.

81. Harcave, pp. 199–212.

government could Russia have had? The fact remains that October 1905 was a bad time to look weak, and in the ensuing months the tsarist government came very close to blundering into some sort of collapse.

As it turned out, the principle of government by one minister reasserted itself. On 18 October, the day after the manifesto was published, Petr N. Durnovo, head of the department of post and telegraph in the MVD, seized control of the ministry on his own initiative and began to issue commands of a most arbitrary nature, in order first to break the strike among his own telegraph workers and then to stop the riots and strikes throughout Russia. Confronted with a fait accompli, Nicholas reluctantly appointed Durnovo as MVD on 23 October.[82] At this point the government was beginning to reassert that control over the course of events which principles could not give it. On 19 October Witte was formally appointed chairman of the newly constituted Council of Ministers, and he proceeded to use his position to put all the resources of the government behind Durnovo. By the end of 1905 Durnovo had put down the worst strikes and mutinies and restored the administration to a measure of confidence in itself, firing fifteen governors and countless other officials in the process.[83]

The history of the device of the favored minister did not end with Durnovo's ascendancy in the last months of 1905, but in the following years this singular method of government was blended with more complex techniques, giving rise to developments that fall outside the scope of this work. It was only in the period 1880–1905 that the favored minister was the primary means to resolve the dilemmas of ministerial government.

It is arguable that the favored minister was an arbitrary, oppressive, and self-defeating method of administration that should have been abandoned long before 1905. Lazarevskii implied this in the early 1900s when he said that a good legislature could correct defects in a bad administration, whereas a good administration could not remedy the errors of a bad legislature.[84] Proper lawmaking, in other words, could repair administrative defects, and therefore there was no need to give this or that minister arbitrary power. The historical validity of this generalization is doubtful. Korkunov's observation that a state can

---

82. The most detailed account of Durnovo's "takeover" that I have seen is in Liubimov, pp. 344–361. See also Gurko, pp. 413–448.

83. Liubimov, pp. 354–355. Witte, *Vospominaniia*, III, 57–330, would have it that he was responsible for all the successes in 1905–1906 and Durnovo was to blame for all the mistakes, but his account is grossly inaccurate. Santoni offers a detailed account of Durnovo's activities and policies in late 1905 and early 1906.

84. Lazarevskii, I, 51.

exist without law but never without an administration seems more useful for the purpose of understanding Russian experience.[85] In any case, the argument I am advancing here is that the use of the favored minister was not an organizational defect that could have been eliminated by men of good will but a viable administrative technique devised to cope with real problems. It did not cause interministerial tension but was caused by it, and interministerial tension was a manifestation of the Russian government's response to Russian society: a result of the growing involvement of government servitors and of all capital-city society in the destruction and regeneration of peasant society.

D. Conclusion

This chapter has indicated that elements of an operational legal-administrative system did emerge in the tsarist government in 1861–1905, that these elements gave rise to the conflict between the MF and the MVD, and that this conflict made the formation of a systematic constitutional framework impossible.

There is little use in offering value judgments between one form of government and another, but the Russian experience does point to one standard for such a judgment that has received little attention from historians: the principle that a state should respond to its people. This does not mean that all major questions of state should be decided by mass elections or that statesmen should formulate their policies in order to please mobs. The tsarist government's primary concern was not with anyone's "will," not the majority's and not the tsar's. Will, like the state, is an expression of social relationships, not their essence. When a government responds to its people, therefore, it does not necessarily conform to anyone's desires or expectations. What it does, rather, is to recognize, give expression to, and organize itself around the social relationships of mutual dependence in which it is rooted and from which it derives its characteristic features. Communication with society is its first commandment, and all abstract notions—tsar, majority, law, constitutional principles, ideological aims, national identity, and public opinion—are only devices for carrying it out. The tsarist government's first concern was to respond and to go on responding to society, not to measure itself against theoretical patterns of political behavior, or the express desires of its subjects, or even the convictions of the members of government-society. If the strain of the response ultimately proved too much for it, this was still infinitely

85. Korkunov, *RGP*, II, 221–222.

better for all concerned, including posterity, than if the government-society had found a way to isolate itself from the "people" by imposing upon itself a sterile conformity to what its members thought it should do.

None of the above discussion is intended to demonstrate beyond any doubt that the tsar's peculiar relationship with the MF and the MVD was superior to any other arrangement. Nothing I have said proves that the constitutional reforms of 1905 were harmful or irrelevant or that they could not perhaps have come earlier. It is not my purpose to show that such institutions as the Duma, the Provisional Government, the Petrograd Soviet, or even the one-day Constituent Assembly of 1918 were farces. Actually, these bodies were quite as serious and successful as ministerial government. The only point I want to make is that the use of the favored minister was an intelligible arrangement. It proceeded basically from the attempts of practical men to cope with real problems.

It cannot be assumed that the main problem of government in Russia at any time before or after 1905 was simply to eliminate arbitrariness and to protect the formal law by setting up "Western" supreme organs of one sort or another. Many of the statesmen thought this was the problem, but this only illustrates a characteristic that all varieties of political order in Russia have shared: their slogans and ideological aims have been almost completely irrelevant to the real problems of society and even to their own actions. No regime in Russia should be measured against the liturgical formulas that its servitors and supporters repeated. Russian government in all eras should be comprehended against the background of the problems with which it had, consciously or unconsciously, to cope. The fundamental problem it faced in 1861–1905 was not how to subordinate itself to system but how to act in order to impose system on itself and society as a whole.

CHAPTER IX

The Local Organs

> [The Liberation Statute] established communal organization among
> the peasantry in principle, but when it defined the commune's rela-
> tionships with the state, it resorted to legal formulas (indeed, it
> would have been difficult to avoid this). These formulas froze
> the living spirit of the people's custom, which does not fit easily
> into superficial precision, especially when this precision comes from
> completely alien legal principles. It was the necessity of making the
> Statute of 19 February correspond to an administrative framework
> fundamentally contradictory to the essential quality of the people's
> way of life that gave rise to the internal contradictions that have re-
> sulted from its enactment.
>
> Article in a Russian journal of 1883[1]

The conflict between the organizations of the MVD and the MF had
its deepest roots in the evolution of gubernia and uezd administration
from the passive senatorial order of Catherine II's time toward a centralized bureaucratic executive organization capable of carrying out
active programs of reform in the countryside. The evolution was slow
and uneven. In 1905 bureaucracy was only beginning to impose its
discipline on practical relationships at the uezd level. On the gubernia
level, however, the influence of local peculiarities on the administration did grow steadily weaker, and it was here that the central government's struggle to set up bureaucracy produced its most noticeable
effects. It was primarily in the gubernia offices that the ministries of
the late nineteenth century found themselves at cross-purposes.

This chapter begins with a study of the relatively clear organizational development that went forward on the gubernia level in 1861–
1905 and proceeds from there into a discussion of uezd administration,
including both the regular offices of the central administration and the
local autonomous institutions. The overall purpose is to describe what
happened on the gubernia level and to account for it by pointing to
persistent incoherence in uezd administration. The chapter concludes
with a brief survey of the relatively rapid extension of MF and MVD
agencies below the uezd level during the last two decades of the period, the purpose being to show how bureaucratic development just

---

1. *Rus*, no. 3 (1883), p. 33, quoted in Prugavin, p. 35.

before 1905 heightened tensions in the gubernia and central offices but also increased their effectiveness.

A. THE ELEMENTS OF GUBERNIA ADMINISTRATION

PERSONAL AUTHORITY OF THE GOVERNOR

"Personal authority," as the term is used here, refers to those prerogatives of the governor that resided in his general responsibilities for managing his territory as personal agent of the tsar. It is useful to distinguish these prerogatives from those that proceeded from the governor's formal relationships with other agencies, because, as will be seen, this distinction provides a rough measure of the evolution of the governor's position during the course of the nineteenth century. In 1800 the governor was essentially a viceroy of the tsar. By 1905 his effective authority proceeded chiefly from his official relationships with the MVD, the gubernia *pravlenie* (see below, sec. C), the various gubernia-level standing committees, and the zemstvoes. Personal authority gave way to bureaucratic. The despot gave way to the manager.

The old laws giving the governor his personal authority were never removed from the *Svod zakonov.* No administrative reformer decided consciously to abolish personal authority and substitute bureaucratic organization for it. What happened in the second half of the nineteenth century was that personal authority became less and less useful as a means for coping with the problems the governors had to face. New laws had to be introduced to give the governor more specific prerogatives, expressed in terms of his relations with other officials.

It will be recalled that Catherine II made the civil governor the highest power in the gubernia (in the absence of a governor-general) but also entrusted a measure of formal authority to the gubernia colleges and the autonomous institutions of the gentry. In the decades before the Liberation the colleges were either done away with or relegated to passive, routine functions, while the gentry institutions gradually lost most of their administrative functions and political authority (see above, ch. V, sec. C). The governor's personal authority remained, and its importance as a basis for territorial organization became greater as competing institutions gradually disappeared. Of the old senatorial institutions, then, the governor was the most important survivor in the 1860s. In the ensuing decades his authority would be one of two key elements in gubernia administration, the other being ministerial agencies, a relatively new phenomenon that began cropping up in the gubernias in the 1830s.

In the first half of the nineteenth century the governor played a dual role. On the one hand, he was the *nachalnik* (chief) of the gubernia, a position originally reserved by Catherine II for the governor-general (see above, ch. II, sec. D). In this capacity he was the personal agent of the tsar, responsible directly to the crown for everything that occurred or failed to occur in his territory. In other words, the governor-*nachalnik* could act as omnipotent agent, disregarding the prerogatives of the colleges and flouting regulations whenever it pleased him.[2]

When a governor acted as *nachalnik*, however, he was only ordering a particular person or office to do one particular thing, not establishing policies or operating through commonly accepted routines. Legal, organizational operation in the gubernias had at least to pretend to proceed according to some set of rules, and the rules that applied were the Senate's, not the governor's. As we have seen, an omnipotent agent could often ignore the Senate's jurisdictional regulations in this or that case, but one thing he could not do was to eliminate the Senate's rules and replace them with his own. Thus, although these rules did not necessarily guide the actual operation of the gubernia and uezd offices, their existence did enable the gubernia colleges to resist any attempt to alter the formal basis of their operation.

In order to use the gubernia offices as an organization, the governor had to adopt his second role, that of civil governor per se. In this more circumscribed role he shed the broad personal responsibilities of the *nachalnik* and became in effect an agent of the Senate, responsible to the central departments of the Senate for the proper operation of the gubernia colleges. He exercised this authority primarily by presiding over the colleges in accordance with relatively well-defined procedures, not by handing out direct orders to whomever he pleased.[3] It may be said, then, that the governor-*nachalnik* could exercise considerable authority over separate individuals but that only the civil governor could hope to impose consistent policies on the gubernia offices.

As we have seen, however, colleges were hardly appropriate tools for executive action. Their purpose, like that of the governor-*nachalnik* himself, was simply to preside over society as it was, and this in fact was all they could do. For all his vast powers, then, the pre-Liberation governor was not an executive director. The offices under him were designed not to be used consistently to accomplish long-range purposes

2. See Herzen's description of a "despotic" governor of the 1830s, I, 274–349.
3. Korkunov, *RGP*, II, 437.

but only to decide disputes, hear appeals, suppress disturbances, and, in general, to cope in ad hoc fashion with specific problems as they arose. The governor could supervise the colleges, or interfere with them, or ignore them, but he could not use them systematically as an executive organization. In short, he was in no position to reform or reorganize either society or government, not even if he and/or his superiors wanted to.[4]

In 1837–1862 the governor acquired a police organization entirely subordinate to himself (see above, ch. V, sec. D), and from then on, his administrative position began to change. As civil governor he began to act more like the director of an organization, while his *nachalnik* role slowly disappeared. Gubernia administration gradually acquired the implicit responsibility not only to keep the countryside in order but to do something with it so that the peasants might become what the capital city wanted them to be.

The governor's constitutional position did not change. The old contradiction between broad, vague responsibilities and precisely defined means of action remained enshrined in the law throughout the period 1861–1905. Article 275 of the laws regarding gubernia administration required that the governor act only through legally established offices and procedures, whereas many other articles (e.g., 294–300, 314, 322–324) still held him to the *nachalnik*'s general responsibilities for the morality, sobriety, and welfare of the people.[5] What did change was the governor's relationships with the other organs of government. The new agent-director had more authority over the police organization than the old presiding chairman had been able to exercise over the gubernia colleges. On the other hand, he was much more dependent on the offices of the central government than the old *nachalnik* had been.

MINISTERIAL AGENCIES IN THE GUBERNIAS

As we have seen, the general idea behind the reforms of the 1860s was to clear the gentry out of peasant administration, not to put a bureaucracy into it. In effect, the reformers had assumed that the peasants would be able to look after themselves. No permanent machinery was set up in the 1860s to extend the governor's executive power into the vacuum left by the elimination of serfdom, mainly because most of

4. See Mikhail Muravev's description of the organization he had to work with when he was governor of Mogilev in his annual report of 1830, quoted in Kropotov, pp. 251–253. Muravev expressed sublime confidence in his ability to remedy administrative disorder in his gubernia if the tsar would give him full support (ch. V, n. 27), but this was only part of the "champion governor" fantasy.

5. *Svod zakonov,* vol. II, pt. 1.

Alexander II's administrators did not want any such machinery (see above, ch. VI, sec. E). In the following decades, however, it turned out that the peasants were not able to look after themselves, and the need for a means to administer programs of social reform grew more pressing.

The central government's response to the new needs of the late nineteenth century was to expand the organizations of the various ministries outward from the capital cities. New agencies began to appear in the gubernias, each of them subject to its own ministry, and the governor found himself at the head of a disorderly mass of offices that neither he nor anyone else could control. Already, in the 1860s, the governor's authority no longer comprehended the whole of the administrative organization that was operating in his territory, and in the ensuing decades the proportion of the total administrative activity in his gubernia that was subject to his authority grew steadily smaller. The governor's authority did not cease to be the most important institutional basis for maintaining the coherence of territorial administration,[6] but the bureaucratization of the administration neither provided him with the tools he needed to govern nor immediately gave rise to any alternative institution. On the contrary, the most obvious effect of bureaucratization in the late nineteenth century was the disintegration of territorial political order. The more effectively the central government functioned, the more difficult it became for the local organs to govern their respective territories.[7] These contradictory tendencies ultimately gave the tsarist government of 1861–1905 its peculiar character.[8]

Obviously, not all the ministries were involved in gubernia administration. Foreign affairs and navy had nothing to do with the governors, and although the war ministry had army units in all areas, they played no regular role in domestic administration except in the war ministry's own territories (e.g., the Don Cossack oblast). In the interior gubernias the governors had to do with the army only in wartime and on those occasions of civil disturbance when the police required the assistance of troops.[9]

6. It will be recalled that the governors' annual reports to the tsar continued to play a significant role in the central government's operation throughout the tsarist period.

7. The general problem of the replacement (or usurpation) of territorial government by ministerial is discussed in Korkunov, *RGP*, II, 341–342, and described in *Istoricheskii obzor . . . Komiteta*, IV, 309–312.

8. See Starr, pp. 38–45, for a description of gubernia administration during the period 1837–1862.

9. In case of emergency the governor decided when troops should be used and where. Only tactical control was left in the hands of the army. See S. D. Urussov, *Memoirs of a Russian Governor* (London, 1908), pp. 31–33.

Of the ministries and departments whose local organs were engaged in domestic administration, the majority communicated directly with their subordinates in the gubernias and uezds without having to co-ordinate with the governors. Some of them—e.g., the organs of the ministry of commerce and industry (until 1905 a department in the MF), those of the ministry of communication, and those of the mining department in the ministry of state domains[10]—operated in territorial divisions that did not even coincide with the gubernias and uezds. Of those that organized their agencies along gubernia boundaries, many had no formal connection with gubernia administration or the governors—e.g., the holy synod, the organs of the state auditing office, and the branches of the state bank. The gubernia and uezd organs of the ministry of education were closely tied in with the gubernia administration, but they, too, were free of the governors' direct authority.[11]

The governor had the right to inspect all the above offices and to report any infractions of the law to their respective ministerial superiors, but in practice even this small shred of authority became a dead letter in the late nineteenth century. The governor lacked the staff to undertake the supervision of specialized functional offices. Even if he had had more inspectors, the law they would have had to enforce would have consisted primarily of ministerial regulations that often contradicted each other.

A number of ministerial agencies were required by law to collaborate with the governors in a limited fashion, and these formed what there was of a territorial government. Taken together, they included almost all the agencies that had to do with peasant society. The most important institution for unifying them was, of course, the governor's authority. In addition, however, a variety of laws called upon these ministerial agents to participate in a number of standing committees,

10. The mining department was in the MF before 1874 and in the ministry of state domains from 1874 to 1905. In 1905 it was switched once again to the MF, and its local organs were set under the gubernia administrations.

11. Korkunov, *RGP*, II, 418–422, 422–444; Lazarevskii, II, 228–230. The governor's relationships with these separate agencies were covered in arts. 407–409 of the *Svod zakonov*, vol. II, pt. 1. From the 1860s on, the gubernia and uezd organs of the ministry of education were subject to supervision by councils consisting of officials from other ministries and elected members from the zemstvoes. In 1874 the ministry strengthened its control over the local schools, but its agents on the gubernia and uezd levels had to go on working with councils throughout the tsarist period (uezd councils were chaired by the gentry marshals). To some extent this integrated them with the regular administration, but it did not subject them to the governor himself. See Korkunov, *RGP*, II, 421–422; *Svod zakonov*, vol. II, pt. 1, arts. 272–273. On the administrative changes in the ministry of education of the 1860s–1870s, see A. Sinel, "Educating the Russian Peasantry," *Slavic Review*, XXVII (Mar. 1968), 53–59.

most of which were under the chairmanship of the governor or vice-governor.[12] There were committees with specific functions, such as the one that managed the recruiting of soldiers (*gubernskoe po voinskoi povinnosti prisutstvie*), and committees that resembled, at least on paper, institutions for general administration of the territory, such as the general gubernia board (*obshchee gubernskoe prisutstvie*)[13] and the gubernia statistical committee.[14] Figure 2 shows how one of these committees, the gubernia board (*gubernskoe prisutstvie*), which was set up in 1889 to take care of peasant affairs, tied some of the ministerial agents together in a collective decision-making process.

The ministries whose agencies were involved in the gubernia and uezd committees were those of internal affairs, finance, state domains (from 1894 to 1905 this was called the ministry of agriculture and the state domains), and justice. Aside from the MVD, the most important of these was the MF. Those of its local organs that operated as part of the gubernia administration or in connection with it were the fiscal administrator, the administrator of excises, and, after 1883, the local section of the peasant land bank.[15] Under the fiscal administrator's jurisdiction were the tax inspectors, established in the uezds in 1885 and in the *uchastki* in 1903.[16]

The ministry of state domains had an agency on the gubernia level from 1837 on. It was initially collegial, but in 1866 its director, an agent of the ministry, became sole head. For several decades thereafter this

12. Korkunov, *RGP*, II, 440–441, gives a partial list of the gubernia-level standing committees that were established after 1860. See also *Svod zakonov*, vol. II, pt. 1, art. 14.

13. The general gubernia board brought together the *pravlenie* (see below, sec. C), the fiscal administrator, the administrator of the state domains, and the gubernia *prokuror*. See *Svod zakonov*, vol. II, pt. 1, arts. 441, 474.

14. The membership of the statistical committee was very flexible. It could include just about anyone the governor wanted. It was not a governing body in the sense that it maintained any existing machinery, but the provisions that set it up made it a potential instrument for reform and development of just about any kind. See *ibid.*, arts. 605–627.

15. The peasant land bank was headed by a council on which the ministry of agriculture (state domains) and the state auditing office were also represented. Appointees of the MF, however, constituted a clear majority, thus assuring that the bank would adhere to the ministry's policies. The council had local organs, called sections (*otdely*), one for each two gubernias. See "Bank," in Brockhaus and Efron, I (1891), 927–929.

16. Lazarevskii, II, 240–253. The main function of the fiscal administrator and his organization was to oversee all aspects of financial management in gubernia administration. The decree of 12 Mar. 1903, printed in *IZO* (Jan. 1904), p. 9, set up tax inspectors on the *uchastok* level. The *uchastki*, it will be recalled, were subdivisions of the uezd, equivalent to but somewhat smaller than the *stany* and averaging about eight to an uezd. Concerning the significance of the tax inspectors, see below, sec. D.

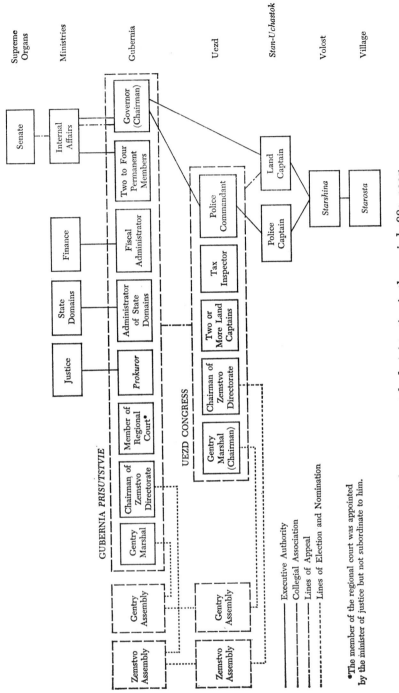

Figure 2. The gubernia board and its place in territorial administration in the period 1889–1905.

Source: *TPSZ*, 6196, arts. 104–112.

agency had little to do but preside over the exploitation and conservation of the state lands, but in 1894, when the central ministry took on general responsibility for agriculture in Russia, its gubernia directors began to expand their functions accordingly. In 1902 the gubernia agricultural administration split off from that of the state domains to take charge of the broader problems of agricultural development, leaving the gubernia-level administrators of the state domains to manage the state lands as before.[17]

The law courts came under the administrative direction of the ministry of justice, but from 1864 on, they constituted something like a separate area of government. The *prokurory*, who were now little more than prosecuting attorneys, were subordinate to the ministry. The judges, however, were appointed for life, and no administrative body, either minister or governor, could interfere with or participate in their judicial decisions.[18] On the other hand, both judges and *prokurory* were in a position to influence executive action by participating in many of the gubernia and uezd boards and committees as voting members.[19]

B. The Conflict between Governors and Ministers

From the governors' point of view, autonomous courts of law guaranteed not the supremacy of law but its powerlessness. They constituted one of the many organs that a governor could not control but for whose activities he was ultimately responsible. Judges and *prokurory* could impede his operations by their action on the gubernia and uezd com-

17. Each of the "gubernia" agencies that managed the state domains had to cover two or three gubernias. This was a result of the personnel cutbacks that followed the Liberation. See Korkunov, *RGP*, II, 458–459.

18. By Western standards Russia did not have an absolutely independent judiciary. Certain kinds of judicial decisions, especially those involving political crimes, were referred to administrative bodies instead of the courts. See Zaionchkovskii, *Rossiiskoe samoderzhavie*, pp. 153–162, 167–168. Now and then a judicial decision made in the Senate was revoked by the tsar at the request of the Committee of Ministers. See *ibid.*, pp. 174–178. Finally, there were cases in which the tsar's pardon overturned criminal convictions. Apparently these were very frequent in 1905 and after, when Nicholas II pardoned a considerable number of pogromists. See John Bohon, "Reactionary Politics in Russia: 1905–1909" (unpublished Ph.D. dissertation, University of North Carolina, 1967), pp. 12–13. Despite these violations of judicial autonomy, however, it is clear that the courts were not administratively subordinate to either the central ministries or the governors.

19. The executive role of the *prokurory* in the gubernias during the period 1861–1905 is described in Muravev, pp. 434–448. It bears mentioning that the gubernia surveying offices also came under the jurisdiction of the ministry of justice, and these were indeed administrative agencies, subject, like the others, to a minister's authority rather than the governor's.

mittees, and their courts exercised authority over the population
without being formally subject to his influence. Worst of all, they
enforced many of the rules and regulations that shielded other ministerial organs from his authority. In a uniform legal-administrative
system a separate judiciary is a means of preserving order. In the
territorial administration of tsarist Russia, however, the order it strove
to preserve was not in itself orderly. While bringing a measure of legal
rights to the population, the courts were also playing an important
part in inflicting a facade of bureaucratization on local government,
thereby *insuring* that it would be disorderly.[20]

As has been suggested, the governor's legal position vis-à-vis the
ministerial agencies was a very weak one. He could neither appoint
nor discharge them on his own. He had the power to block appointments that the ministers made, but once an agent took office, the
governor lost all direct personal power over him.[21] When a governor
did not like what an agent was doing, he could not simply order him
to stop. He had, perforce, to appeal to the agent's ministerial superior,
and in this relationship the governor was at a distinct disadvantage.
The ministers usually outranked him, and they were much closer to
the tsar. More important, the law explicitly required a governor to
allow all ministerial orders to go into effect without any complaint or
even consultation unless he could show them to be illegal.

It is true that the governor could issue regulations of his own on the
basis of the law's general commands that he do whatever he thought
necessary to keep order and preserve morality and welfare. But his
enactments had no more force than his own authority as *nachalnik*
and no basis except his personal conviction that they were necessary

20. This, at least, was how many of the governors and their subordinates felt.
The memoirs of the conservative poet Afanasii Fet (Shenshin) record a conversation between himself and a governor that took place sometime in the 1870s–
1880s. See his *Moi vospominaniia* (2 vols., Moscow, 1890), II, 149–151. Fet was
working as a justice of the peace (see above, ch. VI, sec. A) in Orel gubernia
and found himself involved in settling a strike. He ended it by persuading the
workers to sign an agreement to return to work under certain conditions. Most
of them returned to work, but some did not. Fet understood this to be a violation
of the agreement, and he arrested as many of the offenders as he could find. When
the *prokuror* of the regional court heard about this, he said to Fet, "You acted
splendidly, with energy and intelligence, but illegally." Fet then went to the
governor, an old friend of his, who said that he would like to support Fet but
that the law would not allow it. Fet would have to let the arrested men go. If he
did not, the governor said, "the uezd committee of justices can inflict disciplinary
action on you, and the arrested men can sue you for damages." Writing in 1890,
when he was on the point of taking a job as land captain, Fet opined, "I concluded long ago from bitter experience that the local legal institutions were power-
less and entirely unsuitable to rural life."

21. *Svod zakonov*, vol. II, pt. 1, art. 286; Korkunov, *RGP*, II, 443.

for the general welfare of the gubernia.[22] Did his general responsibilities give him the authority to order the fiscal administrator to set up a poor-relief program? Some parts of the law implied that they did, but not explicitly. The fiscal administrator's instructions from the MF, on the other hand, were clear enough, and they gave him ample basis for rejecting any such order.[23] If the governor really wanted his program, he would have to get the approval of the MF himself, and whether or not the MF could be persuaded depended not so much on conditions in the gubernia as on those that prevailed in St. Petersburg.

After the 1860s, then, the governor's convictions no longer sufficed to override the specific limits that the law imposed on his actions. His new agencies came armed with specific goals and specific rules of their own. Moreover, their purposes and programs were relatively measurable. When they met with interference from the governor or his police, they could often brush these less precise authorities aside with statistics and systems of regulations that would not tolerate the random inconsistencies to which the governors were accustomed. In short, a *nachalnik* could not manage the new bureaucracy. When it came to a confrontation between the all-powerful governor, acting in the name of a vague notion like "good order," and the lowliest clerk, acting according to the relatively specific rules of his ministerial organization, the clerk had the advantage, because in the late nineteenth century system connected him ever more effectively to the head of his ministry. The more of these agencies there were and the more systematically united they were to their respective ministries, the weaker the governor's personal authority became.

As for the ministerial organs, they could defy the governors, but they themselves were not able to establish effective territorial organizations. The gubernia standing committees did not control and direct their disparate members any better than the governor did. On the whole, therefore, gubernia administration seemed to work poorly.[24]

The picture was not uniformly dark. Lack of systematic coordination on the gubernia level did not preclude efficient operation but only

22. *Svod zakonov,* vol. II, pt. 1, art. 421. See also Korkunov, *RGP,* II, 443–445; Lazarevskii, II, 37–38.

23. *Svod zakonov,* vol. II, pt. 1, arts. 1043, 1050, stated that the governor could not give the fiscal administrator orders or interfere with his activities except in cases where the law specifically required it. Art. 564 said that the gubernia *pravlenie*—i.e., the governor's executive office—and the fiscal administrator were on the same administrative level and that neither could give the other orders.

24. For a general description of the weakness of formal order in gubernia and uezd administration in the late nineteenth and early twentieth centuries, see D. Pestrzhetskii, *O prepodavanii uzakonenii o krestianakh* (St. Petersburg, 1905), pp. 4–7. Pestrzhetskii worked in the land section of the MVD in the early 1900s.

failed to guarantee it by any systematic means. The possibility always existed that an unusually energetic and capable governor could command the confidence of the officials and political leaders in his territory and drive them into effective action by the force of his personality (see above, ch. III, sec. D). In fact, administrative efficacy varied enormously from gubernia to gubernia, depending largely on who was in office.

In 1906–1907, for example, the MVD carried out inspections in Orel and Kaluga gubernias. According to the reports, the government offices in Orel worked poorly, while those in Kaluga ran relatively smoothly. In Orel in January 1906 the inspector found approximately 27,000 uncompleted affairs in the files of the gubernia offices, many of which had been resting there without action for well over a year. During 1905, a year of famine and unprecedented peasant violence, the gubernia board (*gubernskoe prisutstvie*) had met only twenty times.[25] In Kaluga the situation was radically different. The total number of cases awaiting action in January 1905 was only 134, and most of these had been initiated within the previous two months. The gubernia board met regularly every week and sometimes more often. During the famine emergencies of 1905–1906 it had met up to four times per week.[26]

The difference between Orel and Kaluga illustrates the possibilities of variation in all echelons of local government. Inefficiency and corruption were no more guaranteed than their absence.[27] The point, then, is not that all gubernias and uezds necessarily failed to organize themselves during the period 1861–1905 but that the advent of ministerial systems broke up traditional order in territorial government before a *systematic* territorial administration could take form. The resulting disorder tended to give rise, more or less in the course of things, to continual conflicts between governors and gubernia-level ministerial organs. This in turn created tension between governors and ministers.

C. Subordination of the Governors to the MVD

If the growing power of the ministries undercut the personal authority of the governors and yet failed to pull the territorial organization together, the fact remains that gubernia administration did hold together during the period 1861–1905. It did not solve the problems of

---

25. *IZO* (Jan. 1907), pp. 24–32.
26. *Ibid.* (Oct. 1907), pp. 425–451.
27. This applies to all echelons. In Orel gubernia there were individual officials who were doing their jobs conscientiously. See e.g., *ibid.* (Feb. 1907), p. 62.

rural social development to the satisfaction of most contemporaries, but it did muster sufficient strength and coherence to preserve order among the peasants during a social transformation of unprecedented harshness. Moreover, an active agrarian reform did at last begin to go forward after 1905 within its organizational framework. The question is: if neither central system nor the personal authority of the tsar's governors was able to manage the gubernias, what did manage them? The answer, in brief, is that the governor maintained a semblance of authority over the ministerial systems by keeping his role as agent of the tsar and at the same time subordinating himself to one of the ministers—the MVD—thereby bolstering his personal power with the more modern and effective authority that a ministerial organization could afford to its agents.

The governors' subordination to the MVD began to develop as far back as 1802 (see above, ch. V, sec. C). Like many developments in the tsarist government, it did not come as a conscious reform but evolved from a more or less random accumulation of decrees over a period of decades.

After the 1820s, it will be recalled, the MVD's recommendations to the Senate became the normal basis for hiring, firing, and transferring governors. From the 1830s on, the MVD gradually extended its control over the internal order of business in gubernia administration.[28] In 1831 it acquired the power to appoint the councilors (*sovetniki*) to the gubernia *pravlenie*. In 1845, when the *pravlenie* ceased to operate as a college and became in effect the gubernia chancellery, these *sovetniki* became in effect directors of functional departments.[29] But this change in form did not diminish the prerogatives of the *pravlenie*. Orders from the ministries to their gubernia organs still had to go via it, and it could still object to them if they were illegal.[30] Thus, when the individual *sovetniki* took over virtually all the functions that had been assigned to the *pravlenie*, it meant that the MVD gained at least formal control over the exercise of the *pravlenie*'s old prerogatives, and the MVD in turn made it a policy to delegate its authority over the *sovetniki* to the governors. Nicholas I's laws did not spell it out, but their effect was

28. By 1905 this control had expanded considerably. *Svod zakonov* (1912 ed.), vol. II, art. 528, gave the MVD explicit power to regulate the internal order of business in the gubernias. Arts. 372–376 in vol. I (1912 ed.), which specified the responsibilities of the MVD's department of general affairs with regard to the supervision of the governor, included a provision requiring that the very furnishings of the governor's home be ordered through the department.

29. *Ministerstvo vnutrennikh del*, pp. 63–64.

30. Its method of opposition was to appeal to the Senate (first department), whose decision regarding the legality of the order was binding. See Korkunov, *RGP*, II, 446–447.

to recognize formally the subordination of the *sovetniki* to the governor and thereby to give him the prerogatives of the *pravlenie*. This was one of the basic steps in the evolution of the governor from his old dual role, as tsar's personal agent and presiding chairman over colleges, to a single functional role, as executive agent of the MVD.[31]

The governor's growing dependence on the MVD did not put an end to his conflicts with ministerial agencies in his gubernia but only transferred them to the capital city into the lap of the MVD himself, transforming them into a problem in interministerial relations. At base, the new problem was only another manifestation of the old conflict between territorial despots, like the eighteenth-century governors-general, and functional offices in the central government, like the Senate and the colleges. In the eighteenth century, however, tension had developed in a random, day-by-day fashion between a would-be administrative organization and arbitrary agents that operated outside the organization—i.e., between the administrative hierarchy of senatorial government and the omnipotent agents of the tsar. In 1861–1905, with the effective subordination of all gubernia agencies to their respective ministries, the same tension manifested itself entirely within the would-be legal-administrative system of ministerial government. What had been a series of random personal conflicts, settled arbitrarily by a variety of informal arrangements between the persons and agencies involved, now became a matter of formal record, systematically compiled, giving rise in time to an impulse in the contending parties—i.e., the ministries—to express their differences in general, ideological terms and to identify themselves with consistent policies and aims.

The evolution of system, then, did not unify the government. Instead, it polarized the *pravitelstvo* into sustained conflicts. Systematic communication was putting Russia together and tearing her apart at the same time.

In the preceding chapters we have suggested that the inability of the tsarist statesmen to organize themselves around a unified system of supreme organs stemmed from a basic conflict between the MF and the MVD. In the last few pages we have indicated that this conflict, in its turn, originated in tensions between territorial governors and the agencies of functional ministries. The question remains: what precisely was transpiring in the gubernias and uezds in 1861–1905 that was

---

31. See Gribowski, pp. 98–101; "Gubernskoe pravlenie," in Brockhaus and Efron, IX (1893), 844; Lazarevskii, II, 233–253.

blowing up into interministerial conflicts in St. Petersburg? The answer is that the MVD-police hierarchy was taking form.

As has been said, the central government's police organization in the countryside came into being between the 1830s and the 1860s. From the beginning it was under the governor's command, but he did not hold this command on his own as the tsar's personal agent. The center of police organization was in St. Petersburg in the MVD, and the governor's authority over the police in his area came to him only by virtue of his subordination to the ministry.[32] In theory, at least, the police organization extended directly from St. Petersburg to the peasant through a line of command running from MVD to governor, to uezd police commandant, and at last to the police captain on the *stan* level (see Figure 2).

Until 1889 the police were the only government officials that could work with the peasants in an executive capacity.[33] Neither ministries nor zemstvoes could carry out their own orders or enforce their own rules that applied to the peasants; they could only issue their orders and rules to the police and then leave it to the police to carry them out. This meant, among other things, that although the governor could not control the ministerial agencies in his gubernia directly, he could at least curtail their power to operate in the countryside and exert an influence on what they did. The police were not likely to be enthusiastic in carrying out an order the governor did not support, and in practice, therefore, it behooved the gubernia ministerial agents to secure the governor's cooperation when dealing with the peasants.[34]

There was nothing essentially wrong with the formal structure of the police hierarchy. The governor was entrusted with the execution of orders intended for the local police organization, and he also actually ran the local police organization. His authority within the police organization was commensurate with his responsibility, and his re-

32. *Svod zakonov,* vol. II, pt. 1, art. 642, gave the MVD's department of police formal control over all the local police throughout European Russia; arts. 656–669 and 694 gave the governor and his *pravlenie* control over the police in his gubernia.

33. "Politsiia," in Brockhaus and Efron, XXIV, 329–330. The clauses establishing police authority over villages and volost administrations are in *Svod zakonov,* vol. II, pt. 1, arts. 717–718. See also above, ch. VI, sec. A.

34. If the police failed to carry out a legal order from any of the gubernia-level offices, the law allowed the office to appeal to the *pravlenie.* See Lazarevskii, II, 233–238. What a legal order was, however, varied from office to office. The fiscal administrator could issue orders directly to the police in cases where the law specified his right to do so. See *Svod zakonov,* vol. II, pt. 1, arts. 680, 708. The gubernia administrator of state domains, on the other hand, could only issue orders to the police "when necessary" and then only via the governors. See *ibid.,* arts. 756, 1132.

sponsibility as head of the police was expressed in sufficiently clear and systematic form to insure, at least on paper, that the central ministry could support him effectively and exercise a measure of supervision over his operations. This was a consistent arrangement if nothing more.[35] The inadequacies of the MVD's police organization proceeded not from its own administrative order but from two basic weaknesses: 1) the police were ill-trained and undermanned, and 2) they were required to act as a catch-all executive organization.

It is doubtful that the operating police organizations in the *stany* measured up to the requirements set forth in the law in 1861–1905, but even if they did, they were still appallingly inadequate. The police reform of 1903 called for an increase in the *stan* police to an average of about forty appointed, salaried officers, and this small force was supposed to manage a rural population of about 70,000.[36] As to their qualifications, the law of 1903 required only that they be literate, "able to compose protocols, and generally familiar with the police service and with the duties of the police in apprehending criminals."[37] These were not high standards, yet they were more exacting than the ones in

35. "Politsiia," in Brockhaus and Efron, XXIV, 328–330. There were perennial difficulties in the central offices. Dmitrii N. Tolstoi, director of the department of police in 1861–1863, complained that the MVD of his day had no effective machinery for supervising the police in the gubernias. The department of general affairs received all police reports and kept files but did nothing with them except to publish a journal "that no one read." The land section compiled legislation, the minister's chancellery handled questions of "internal policy," and the department of police did nothing but keep up meaningless routines. None of these offices had regular access to the information that came to the department of general affairs (see above, ch. V, n. 27). Tolstoi was more prone to exaggeration than most memoir-writing Russian statesmen, but there is probably something to what he says. Nevertheless, disorder at the center does not belie the emergence of a formal chain of command extending down from the center, nor does it lessen the significance of this emergence.

36. There were also the *desiatskie* and *sotskie*, peasants who were elected by their fellows against their will and usually without pay to aid the government police. These, however, were less than reliable as executive agents. See Brzheskii, *Naturalnye povinnosti*, pp. 68–85.

Part of the less than forty appointed police in each *stan* consisted of the *uriadniki*, who were introduced in 1878. Before 1903 there was an average of eleven of these in each uezd, which made less than two for each *stan*—even less in the interior gubernias, since most of the *uriadniki* were concentrated in western Russia. In any case, the *uriadniki* did not work in the *stany* on a regular basis. They were attached to the uezd and gubernia offices so that they could be concentrated in those areas where they would be most needed. See Zaionchkovskii, *Krizis*, pp. 67–68. According to the law of 1903, the regular *stan* police (*strazhniki*) were supposed to be *reinforced* so that there would be one for every 2,500 people (decree of 5 May 1903 in IZO [Jan. 1904], p. 31). Presumably, there were fewer of them before 1903.

37. This was the requirement for the *uriadnik*. The *strazhnik* had only to be able to read and write. See the decree of 5 May 1903 in IZO (Jan. 1904), p. 31.

force before 1903. If it is assumed that the salaries of the police bore some relationship to their competence, then it is safe to surmise that the actual abilities of the *stan* police did not transcend the legal minimum. The salary established in 1862 did not change until 1903, when it was raised to 200–400 rubles annually.[38]

However glaring the inadequacies of the servitors in the police system, they probably did not constitute so serious a flaw as the multifunctional use of the police. A small force can still be efficient, and an ill-trained one can at least be systematically supervised, but no administration in the world can operate smoothly if it has to take its orders from a half-dozen different authorities, each of whose aims and regulations contradict those of the others. The police had to collect taxes (only arrears after 1899), gather a variety of statistical information, see to it that the laws regarding military service were carried out, and generally enforce all regulations and carry out all orders that the central ministries chose to issue. Beyond these relatively specific responsibilities, they were answerable for the morality, sobriety, loyalty, and religious feeling of the peasants under their jurisdiction.[39] Obviously, this was too much for the, at best, barely literate *stan* police, and the burdens imposed on them increased enormously as the number and functions of the ministerial organs in the gubernias increased.

As bureaucratic system expanded outward from St. Petersburg, the governor and his police intensified their struggle to keep bureaucratic chaos out of the villages, but it was a losing fight. Harassed with orders they could not carry out and laws they could not enforce, the police in the *stany* generally ignored the central administration as best they could and carried on according to the despotic methods that had obtained in the countryside for centuries.[40] An investigation of 1902– 1903 brought forth the following statement from one of the peasant-

---

38. According to the decree of 5 May 1903, the *uriadniki* were to receive 310– 400 rubles and the regular *stan* police 200–240 rubles (per year). It is relevant to compare these figures with other salaries of the time. In 1894 the average annual wage of a volost clerk (*pisar*), an official hired and paid by the peasants themselves, was 326 rubles. In the same year the average pay of a volost elder was 204 rubles. See Brzheskii, *Naturalnye povinnosti*, p. 174. The average annual pay for zemstvo employees in Voronezh gubernia, which was typical of European Russia in general, was 400 rubles in 1910. See Trutovskii, p. 49.

39. Some of the duties of the police on the uezd level and below are described in *Svod zakonov*, vol. II, pt. 1, arts. 681–684, 711, 726–747, 783–828.

40. The Kakhanov commission (1882–1885) described the overburdening of the police by the ministerial agencies in the reports it submitted in 1885. See TsGIAL, f. 1317, op. 1, d. 71, vol. II, 101–104. See also Leontev, *Krest. pravo* (1914), pp. 84–90; Brzheskii, *Naturalyne povinnosti*, pp. 49–65.

elected policemen regarding the despotic habits of the *stan* police. His duties, said the peasant, amounted

> to being a slave of the police captain and his men, especially his clerks. . . . One peasant-policemen had to stand duty for two weeks; six days as his normal tour and six days extra because he couldn't get a kitten out from under a barn. . . . When the *uriadnik* [police officer] comes, we have to meet him and escort him around like a governor. Two peasant-policemen go before him and two behind, as he goes from village to village shouting reprimands. . . . The *uriadnik* visits a friend and stays the whole day and night, and the peasant-policemen stand out in the bitter cold watching his horse. That's what we are policemen for![41]

All defects notwithstanding, the MVD-police hierarchy continued to the end of the regime to represent an important unifying element in gubernia administration. The police monopoly on executive operation in the countryside constituted the basic means by which the governor could impose some degree of coherence on the government's relationships with the peasantry. For a time, it kept the confusion and conflict among the ministerial agencies at least one level away from rural society. If the "reactionary" MVD could not stop the assault of the city and the market on peasant society, at least its police could cushion the blows by preventing a direct confrontation between the villages and the growing horde of uncoordinated functionaries who were striving to bring the blessings of legal-administrative system and economic development to them. Indeed, if one considers the government of rural Russia from the point of view of the social conditions that obtained there rather than Western standards, the rural police might even be passed off as an effective organization. Since the time of Peter I the basic task of Russian government, conscious or unconscious, had been not only to extend legal system into the countryside but also to provide a buffer against system for the sake of those to whom it came as an attack rather than a result of their own rational choice.[42] In 1861–1905 the police, the governors, and the MVD were the buffer, consciously so, and considering the problems they faced, they seem on the whole to have done rather well at it.[43] They constituted an interim device,

41. Quoted in Leontev, *Krest. pravo* (1914), p. 85.

42. Concerning the general need for such a buffer in countries undergoing rapid economic development, see Karl Polanyi, *The Great Transformation* (Boston, 1957), pp. 156–166.

43. It bears mentioning that in 1888–1891 the cost per inhabitant of the Russian police organization was somewhat less than one-sixth that of the British and less than one-half that of the Austrian. See "Politsiia," in Brockhaus and Efron, XXIV, 337. In Russia, be it remembered, the police did much more than police work.

maintaining a measure of unity in territorial administration in a time when there was little other basis for it.

Despite its achievements in the countryside, the MVD-police hierarchy produced a number of adverse effects on the government organization as a whole. By strengthening the authority of the governor, the police organization deepened the conflict between the MVD and the MF. Moreover, it obstructed the growth of systematic coordination on the gubernia level and of constitutional framework in the capital city. It is not surprising that "progressive" elements in capital-city society should have considered the MVD to be backward and heretical, an evil obstacle to progress, prosperity, and the government's aspiration to bring system to Russia.[44] By the same token, it was no less to be expected that bureaucratic system should have been regarded as an illness by the MVD and by all those who wanted to cope with and stave off the processes that were destroying the peasant way of life.[45]

D. ORGANIZATION BELOW THE GUBERNIA LEVEL

The preceding sections have outlined the intrinsic problems that faced the tsarist administration in 1861–1905 and suggested an explanation for them. The main point has been that the most basic problems and the most significant developments in the administration arose from the interaction of the administration with society, chiefly the peasants. As yet, however, we have kept to the higher levels of government and left out of account the interaction itself. We have, in other words, discussed the manifestations of the government's difficulties rather than their roots.

The reason for this omission is simply that the roots are not nearly as visible and identifiable to the historian as the manifestations. Given the general practices among the local organs of faking reports, bribing inspectors, and making unwarranted accusations, one finds little reliable evidence regarding what went on below the gubernia level in rural Russia in 1861–1905. What evidence there is does not convey an impression of sustained political struggles that involved broad issues or

44. When the Provisional Government put the tsarist ministers on trial, the MVD-police organization was specifically singled out as one that "could not operate without committing crimes" (*Padenie tsarskogo rezhima*, I, xi).

45. The similarity between the MVD's attitudes and those of the populists is striking. See, e.g., F. Venturi's discussion of N. G. Chernyshevskii's views in his *Roots of Revolution* (New York, 1966), pp. 143–168. The only real difference between "reactionaries" and agrarian radicals was that the reactionaries based their ideas on the practical requirements of administration, whereas the radicals generally based theirs on their fantastic expectations of how the peasants would behave when they were "free" from government domination.

coherent organizational forms. From the administrator's point of view, the uezds and below were a chaos, and this is what is to be portrayed in the following pages, together with some signs of evolution toward systematic order.

No generalization can be made about uezd-level government in the period 1861–1905 that is both clear and accurate. The laws regarding the uezd expressed no unifying principles, and in any case the administrators did not adhere to them with any precision either in their actions or in the structure of their organization. Procedures varied widely from place to place, and the roles the uezd officials actually played seem to have borne little relation to their formal assignments. Uezd administration operated more as a family than a system. Its unity and its ability to act were almost entirely dependent on personal, informal arrangements.[46]

The old colleges of partly elected and partly appointed servitors were by and large done away with in the 1860s, and it seemed that in the post-reform era the central government's officials would be able to work separately from the local autonomous institutions of the gentry.[47] In fact, however, the majority of the uezd agencies continued after the 1860s to take the form of standing committees—colleges, in effect—that included elected members as well as appointed officials. Until 1889 the "general board of uezd police administration" included elected men,[48] and in the period 1874–1889 the permanent member of the "uezd board for peasant affairs" was elected by the uezd zemstvo assembly.[49] In short, the separation between central administration and local autonomous institutions did not take effect on the uezd level either in law or in practice.[50]

46. Concerning the lack of unity in uezd organization in 1861–1905, see Lazarevskii, II, 255–257. A number of inspection reports testify to disorderliness in uezd administration throughout the period. See, e.g., Druzhinin, "Senatorskie revizii," pp. 169–170, which describes the situation in Perm gubernia in 1870, and the senatorial reports of 1880–1881, in TsGIAL, f. 1317, op. 1, d. 71, vol. II, 105–116, 224; f. 1317, op. 1, d. 11, ll. 3–5. One of the senator-inspectors, S. A. Mordvinov, *ibid.*, l. 361, said that the explanation for the discrepancies in uezd administration lay in the officials' habit of disregarding laws and duties alike. Reports of inspections carried out by the MVD in 1903–1914 show much the same state of affairs. See, e.g., *IZO* (Jan. 1907), pp. 24–28.

47. Lazarevskii, II, 74–76, 220–221.

48. "Politsiia," in Brockhaus and Efron, XXIV, 328–329.

49. "Elected" is not quite the right term. The uezd zemstvo assembly nominated two candidates, and the governor forwarded them to the MVD along with his comments. The MVD made the final selection. See Kataev, II, 92–93.

50. "Uezd," in Brockhaus and Efron, XXXV (1902), 134–136, gives a descrip-

If collegial administration outlasted the 1860s, so did its defects. The new colleges rarely met except as a formality. The members usually evaded the burdens and embarrassments of collective decision-making, either by making one of the members the head of the chancellery and letting him make all the decisions or by dividing the case load among themselves and accepting each other's recommendations.[51] The uezd board for peasant affairs offers an illustration. During the short span of its existence—1874 to 1889—it consisted of three members: the permanent member (selected by the gubernia zemstvo assembly), the police commandant, and the gentry marshal. The law assigned definite functions to each of these and also required them to make certain decisions as a college. According to Leontev, however, what most of them actually did was simply to divide the territory of the uezd into three parts and leave all the functions and decisions in each area to one of them acting by himself.[52]

In the late nineteenth century, then, the time had not yet come when the offices in St. Petersburg could draw their jurisdictional lines down to the uezd level or even separate their uezd agents from local society. This is not merely to repeat old saws about the arbitrary despotism of the local police and their interference with the "progressive forces" in society. The point here is that since there were no clear lines in practice between local autonomous institution and uezd administration or between the parts of the uezd administration, the relationships between government and society were *mutually* arbitrary, much as they had been in the eighteenth century.

Unlike the gubernia, with its governor, the uezd had no single authority who could exert consistent pressure upon the administrative organs to conform to a unified regime. There were two chief personages: the gentry marshal, elected every three years by the local landholding gentry, and the police commandant, appointed by the governor with MVD approval. A third official, the chairman of the uezd zemstvo directorate (see above, ch. VI, sec. A), began to play an increasingly important role from about the 1880s on.[53]

To take up the gentry marshal first, it may be said in general of both

---

tion of the uezd-level collegial bodies that were operating in the late nineteenth century. See also *Svod zakonov*, vol. II, pt. 1, art. 15.

51. *Svod zakonov*, vol. II, pt. 1, art. 70, authorized gubernia and uezd committees to split up the work unless they were specifically prohibited from doing so. For other provisions regarding the colleges of 1861–1905, see arts. 26–169.

52. Leontev, *Krest. pravo* (1914), pp. 131–133.

53. Lazarevskii, II, 255–258. Uezd marshals were often elected to be chairmen of zemstvo directorates and held both their offices simultaneously. See B. Veselovskii, III, 212, 217–224.

uezd and gubernia marshals that they possessed great political power in their territories and that their administrative responsibilities, like those of the eighteenth-century governors, were all-encompassing and vague rather than functional and specific. Indeed, since the marshal was not directly subordinate to any organ in the central government, his responsibilities were even less well-defined than those of the old governor-*nachalnik*, and his involvement in local politics was much deeper. His authority, therefore, was personal rather than managerial, which suggests that his power to manipulate administration tended to decrease as the officials began to function as agents of a bureaucracy. In fact, there are indications that the marshals' administrative role was no longer significant in the 1900s, and in the absence of any evidence that his activity actually diminished after the 1860s, it seems reasonable to suppose that it was not he who ceased to function but, rather, the uezd administration that grew up around him and passed him by.

The marshal's decline certainly did not come from the central government's policies or intentions. On the contrary, the government's enactments continued throughout the period 1861–1905 to expand the marshal's formal role in administration and to strengthen his political influence. He was included on all the standing committees—in the uezds he was usually the chairman—and his approval continued to be necessary to secure appointments to many government posts until the end of the tsarist regime.[54] In 1906 he was made chairman of the uezd-level board that carried out the agrarian reforms of 1906–1917.

Nevertheless, despite the extensive participation in administration that the formal law allowed to the marshals, it is doubtful that they actually participated. Take, for example, the board that carried out the agrarian reforms of 1906–1917, the uezd land settlement commission. The gentry marshal chaired it, but this did not necessarily make him an active administrator. The first major instruction concerning the execution of the reforms, that of 19 September 1906, set up a quorum for the commission, making it possible for it to do business without the marshal there.[55] Similar arrangements existed for the other boards in which the marshals were involved—necessarily so, because many of the marshals seem to have spent the better part of their time outside their territories.

---

54. In 1887 Dmitri A. Tolstoi, then the MVD, referred to the marshal as "the closest supporter of the government's authority in the management of local affairs" (TsGIAL, f. 1149, t. 4, d. 44, ll. 17–18). From the 1870s on, the central government often appointed former marshals to high positions in its offices. See B. Veselovskii, III, 584–589.

55. The instruction is printed in *Pravitelstvennyi vestnik* (20 Sept. 1906), p. 2.

Two memoirs, written by men who held the office of gentry marshal in the late nineteenth and early twentieth centuries, suggest the marshal's waning role in local administration.

The memoirs of A. N. Naumov,[56] who became the gubernia gentry marshal in Samara in 1905, show him to have been very conscientious in the performance of his duties, and his eventual promotion to high office in the central government (he became minister of agriculture in 1915) gives a measure of objective support to his own portrayal of his work. Naumov repeatedly refers to himself as an idealistic servitor who worked for the government as a matter of conscience. Deeply moved by the famine of 1891, which occurred when he was attending St. Petersburg University, he decided to give up the joys of the city and a promising singing career to dedicate himself to the provinces, where he could "devote himself wholly to the service of the people."[57] His memoirs reiterate constantly his belief in the gentry as the real strength of Russia, and the picture that emerges from the story of his provincial career as land captain, zemstvo administrator, and gentry marshal depicts the gentry as the main support of local government.[58] Naumov's notions bear no necessary relation to reality, but they do indicate that he himself was an energetic upholder of the gentry marshals as important figures in local government in the early 1900s. It is significant, therefore, that even his account should imply that the marshal did not play a vital *administrative* role.

Naumov tells us that he served three consecutive terms as gubernia marshal, extending from 1905 to 1914. In 1909, during his second term, the Samara zemstvo elected him as their representative to the State Council, where he served until 1915.[59] From 1909 to 1914, then, he was able to do an adequate job as gubernia gentry marshal in Samara while spending seven months of each year in St. Petersburg, over 800 miles away. Naumov does not venture any explanation for this—how such a central figure as he claimed the marshal to have been could have regularly absented himself from his place of duty for more than half the year over a period of five years without seriously disturbing local administration—but the explanation seems apparent: the gubernia gentry marshal did not play an active administrative role on a regular basis.

Another memoir of the same type—that of Prince A. D. Golitsyn—

56. A. N. Naumov, *Iz utselevshikh vospominanii, 1868–1917* (2 vols., New York, 1954).
57. *Ibid.*, I, 119.
58. E.g., *ibid.*, II, 129–130.
59. *Ibid.*, I, 234.

suggests that the same generalization applies to the uezd marshal.[60] Golitsyn was also a strong believer in the gentry as the basic element in Russian local government. He was elected chairman of an uezd zemstvo directorate in Kharkov gubernia in 1900, uezd marshal in 1901 and again in 1904, and chairman of the gubernia zemstvo directorate in late 1905. Thus in the years 1901–1907, when he occupied the position of uezd marshal, Golitsyn was almost continually preoccupied with other duties. Moreover, he was absent from the uezd for long periods of time. He spent most of 1904 in the Far East with the Red Cross, and in 1906–1907 he held a full-time administrative post in the gubernia capital. At the same time he was giving a great deal of time and energy to developing his private estates, building and operating a distillery there, and founding and editing a newspaper. The latter task kept him in St. Petersburg throughout most of 1907.[61]

According to their own accounts, then, both Naumov and Golitsyn were admirable men, competent officials, and energetic benefactors of their country. They make it clear, however, that they did not give a great deal of time to the job of gentry marshal.

The only explanation for the inactivity of the gentry marshal that I can perceive is that the marshal's authority, somewhat like that of the governor-*nachalnik* before the 1830s, was personal, unsupported by any ministry and unidentified by any specific responsibility. As organs of functional administration gradually became identifiable on the uezd level, the marshal's administrative role was bound to decline, just as the governor-*nachalnik*'s had. In 1905 uezd administration remained far less sophisticated than gubernia organization, but it was at least beginning to reach the stage where functional officials were rendering personal authority irrelevant to administrative activity.

It should be kept in mind that if the inactivity of the gentry marshal as a functioning administrator was a common phenomenon, it was not necessarily universal.[62] Throughout the period 1861–1905 individual marshals could work as administrators if they chose to do so, and apparently some did. In no part of Russian government did the possibility not exist that a strong personality could exercise great influence on his colleagues far beyond what his official position allowed.[63] The

60. A. D. Golitsyn, "Vospominaniia" (unpublished manuscript in the Russian Archive at Columbia University), p. 10.

61. *Ibid.*, p. 223.

62. A. D. Samarin, Moscow gubernia marshal in the early 1900s, forbade the uezd marshals in his gubernia to leave their uezds. See Kissel-Zagorianskii, "Les mémoires du General Kissel-Zagorianskii" (unpublished manuscript, in Russian, in the Russian Archive at Columbia University), p. 119.

63. In 1913, when the first awards for land settlement work in the agrarian

point here, however, is that whatever an individual marshal might do, his formal authority was no longer in itself a promising means to administrative action in 1905. If it had been, Naumov and Golitsyn would have utilized it, or at least they would not have thought of the peremptory attention they gave to their duties as devoted service.

The passivity of the uezd gentry marshal, where he was in fact passive, left the police commandant to form what there was of a center for the uezd level of rural administration. The commandant occupied a position superficially analogous to that of the governor on the gubernia level.[64] Like the governor, he was a vital link in the MVD-police chain of command, and until 1889 all executive activities in his territory that pertained to the peasants were carried on under his direction. Neither the uezd agencies nor the zemstvoes could act in the villages except through his subordinates. For all his formal prerogatives, however, he lacked the authority to compel uezd agencies to act as he wished. Like the governor, he could often block his fellow servitors and make life unpleasant for them, but he could not act in an administrative capacity except by negotiating with them and securing their support.

The uezd, however, was very different from the gubernia. Jurisdictional battles loomed large on the gubernia level because the agencies involved were directly in touch with their own ministerial superiors, and the degree to which each of them could depart from his own instructions was relatively small. The uezd servitors, on the other hand, received almost all their orders from the governor himself.[65] True, the governors had very little control over the motley collection of instructions they passed on to the uezd level. Even so, the uezd did get most of its orders all in one lump from one source, and this allowed the servitors a great deal more de facto leeway for interpretation and negotiation than the ministries would tolerate in the gubernia capitals.

---

reform were handed out, 153 marshals received them, including both gubernia and uezd marshals. See *Izvestiia kantseliarii komiteta po zemleustroitelnym delam* (May 1913), p. 107; (Dec. 1913), p. 274. Of these, at least a few must have merited their awards by their active work, though it is doubtful that they actually managed the land reform in their territories. Finally, it must be recorded that a delegate in the Council of the United Gentry claimed in 1908 that three-fourths of the uezd marshals resided permanently in their uezds. See G. Simmonds, "The Congress of Representatives of the Nobles' Association, 1906–1916" (unpublished Ph.D. dissertation, Columbia University, 1964), pp. 199–200.

64. Engelgardt, p. 314, notes that the police commandant's importance in uezd administration increased after the 1860s.

65. Lazarevskii, II, 232–233. Art. 58 of the fundamental laws (*Svod zakonov*, vol. I, pt. 1, p. 15) required that only the gubernia *pravlenie* should publish laws in the gubernia, which meant in effect that the governor himself did it (see above, sec. C).

Uezd administrators were closely involved with local society. In part, this was a matter of tradition. Until 1837 the uezd police had been entirely under the management of elected gentry servitors, and although elected servitors in pre-Liberation Russia were hardly representatives of their constituents, they were not agents of a bureaucracy either. It was only in 1862, almost a century after the establishment of the governors, that the police commandant became an appointed servitor. The uezd was only beginning to feel the presence of bureaucratic organization in the 1860s, and in the following decades it continued to bear the mark of its heritage. At the end of the nineteenth century most of the ranking servitors in the uezds—the *stan* police captains, the police commandants, the land captains—were still gentry who resided in the same gubernia, if not the same uezd, in which they worked.[66]

It was not only tradition that tended to keep the uezd servitors closely involved in local politics. An even more significant factor was the proximity of the uezd organization to local society and its continuing remoteness from the central ministries. Uezd servitors and their agents actually had to carry out the central government's orders. They had to confront the population directly, not merely to hand papers down to subordinates. Unenforceable orders from the capital city may have dismayed a gubernia servitor, but he did not often have to translate them into actions, and he did not have to contemplate the results his actions produced. In most cases he had only to relay orders to the governor for dissemination to the uezds and let the lower echelons worry about their relevance.[67] Uezd servitors, on the other hand, had to deal with the population directly, and when orders came down that were inapplicable, they were more likely to drive a servitor into cooperation (and/or collusion) with influential persons in local society than to stimulate any real effort at obedience.

In short, uezd administration had no solidly established central institution that corresponded to the governor in the gubernia. The chief concern of administrative agents, autonomous institutions, and collegial bodies alike seems to have been to arrive at ad hoc jurisdictional agreements that would allow each of them to operate on his own. Each man sought the protection of a local patron or faction and held jealously to whatever prerogatives and routines he could establish for himself,

66. The law suggested that the police captains be selected from among the local gentry (see above, ch. V, n. 90).

67. Art. 58 of the fundamental laws (see above, n. 65) required that the *pravlenie* publish laws absolutely without change, and art. 65 made this rigidly explicit. Neither the letter nor the spirit of any law was to be touched by its executors.

exercising his official influence to suit his purposes. The most an official had to do for the central government was to keep his records neat and his formal reports to the gubernia officially correct.

The police commandant was in much the same situation as his colleagues, but he was also generally responsible for his uezd, and there were times when he had to find the means to act in order to cope with real problems and disputes. In such cases he usually had to depend more on the local support he could command than on the backing of his distant superior in the gubernia capital. The governor was in no position to exert any consistent influence in the uezd. Such practical unity as could be achieved, therefore, had to take form primarily among local elements.[68]

To sum up, it may be said that during the period 1861–1905 uezd administration continued to reflect the incoherence of local society. Protected to some extent by the MVD-police hierarchy, it remained essentially collegial and resisted the growing pressure toward bureaucratization that emanated from the capital cities. On the other hand, it also played a part in social development. In 1905 there were indications that system was developing in the quasi-collegial uezd regime. Perhaps the most convincing was the agrarian reform of 1906–1917. Its effects are disputed, but its organization was indisputably a controlled executive bureaucracy that extended from capital-city ministers down to uezd operators, effectively uniting zemstvo and government agents on the uezd level in a single enterprise.[69]

LOCAL AUTONOMOUS INSTITUTIONS

On its lowest level the tsarist government administration worked with a variety of local autonomous institutions in 1861–1905. Three of them operated in the rural areas of European Russia: 1) uezd assemblies of landholding gentry (see above, ch. II, sec. D), 2) uezd zemstvo assemblies, and 3) peasant villages and volosts (see above, ch. VI, sec. A).

The gentry assemblies, dating from Catherine II's time, were the oldest. Considered as elements in administrative evolution, however,

68. Regarding the governor's weakness as a manager, see above, sec. A. One typical illustration of the nature of administrative discipline in the countryside comes from an article by an observer of peasant society. See G. I. Kulikovskii, "Arteli obonezhia," *Etnograficheskoe obozrenie*, XIII (1892), 207. Kulikovskii notes that an order from the forest department, published on 19 Sept. 1868, was read to the peasants to whom it applied only in 1873.

69. See my "Imperial Russian Government," pp. 177–268; "Concept," pp. 282–293; and "Agricultural Administration in Russia from the Stolypin Land Reform to Forced Collectivization," in James Millar, ed., *The Soviet Rural Community* (Urbana, Ill., 1971), pp. 3–35.

they were not the most significant of the local institutions in 1861–
1905. Their political influence, like that of the gentry marshals, continued to be considerable throughout the period. In 1905 they were
still electing the gentry marshals, and they still had the right to
nominate candidates for many appointed positions in the central government's local organs. After 1905 the assemblies even achieved national identity in the form of the Council of the United Gentry, the
leaders of which are supposed to have exerted considerable influence
on Nicholas II in 1906–1917.[70] Be this as it may, the importance of
gentry assemblies as agencies of government gradually diminished as
the central government and the zemstvoes expanded their administrations into the countryside. It was in the zemstvo assemblies that the
landholding gentry of the late nineteenth and early twentieth centuries
played their most vital managerial role.[71]

The Zemstvoes

The relationships that the reforms of the 1860s established between the
central government on the one hand and the zemstvoes and peasant
institutions on the other have been described in chapter VI. It will be
recalled that the original purpose of the zemstvoes was to take care of
those problems of local government in which the central administration did not wish to involve itself. On this premise the statute of 1
January 1864 allowed the separate zemstvoes considerable latitude to
develop, each according to its own lights and resources and the needs
of its own locale.

What did the zemstvoes do with their latitude? One estimate of
their performance in the 1860s–1870s may be found in the reports of
the senatorial inspections in 1880–1881 and in the reports of a subcommittee (*soveshchanie*) of the Kakhanov commission, which met in
the MVD in 1882–1883 to discuss the inspection reports and make

70. It is a dogma of Soviet scholarship that the Council of the United Gentry
dictated the agrarian reforms of 1905–1906. See, e.g., S. M. Dubrovskii, *Stolypinskaia zemelnaia reforma* (Moscow, 1963), pp. 105–113. The evidence for this,
however, is not convincing, even to Dubrovskii. The first meeting of the council
took place in May 1906, after the reform was already drafted and the greater
part of it enacted. As Dubrovskii himself had to acknowledge, "The gentry actually
repeated what the administration had formulated" (p. 113). On the influence of
the council in later years, see Simmonds, pp. 191–200.
71. B. Veselovskii, II, 55–105. A little over half of the delegates to the uezd
zemstvo assemblies were gentry, but the gubernia assemblies were over 80 percent gentry before 1890 and about 90 percent thereafter. See Trutovskii, pp.
19–21. Similarly, the uezd zemstvo directorates were about 72 percent gentry
and officials (in 1903) and the gubernia directorates over 94 percent. See B.
Veselovskii, III, 432–434.

recommendations for reform (Mikhail S. Kakhanov was deputy MVD and chairman of the commission).

The inspectors generally agreed that one of the basic defects in local government lay in the zemstvoes' lack of means to exercise the powers granted to them by the statute of 1 January 1864.[72] The subcommittee —of which the inspectors were members—repeated this general assertion in its report[73] and concluded that the police monopoly on executive power in the peasant villages posed the most serious obstacle to zemstvo activity. Throughout the inspectors' reports and the subcommittee's discussions, the view was often repeated that the zemstvoes, despite their handicaps, had accomplished a great deal by 1880. The majority of the subcommittee concluded that if the zemstvoes had not been active enough, it was due primarily to government interference, chiefly that of the police, not to the zemstvoes' lack of initiative.[74]

This optimistic view of the early zemstvoes did not proceed unequivocally from the evidence the senators gathered, much of which actually showed the zemstvoes in a bad light. In fact, the subcommittee's conclusions were highly interpretive, and there is some doubt about the disinterestedness of those who arrived at them. One of the inspector-senators was Alexander Polovtsov, whose views on government have been discussed above (ch. VII, sec. B). He believed in gentry rule in the countryside and the employment of independently wealthy gentry to fill the highest posts in the government. Wealthy gentry made the best servitors, he once said to Alexander III, because they were loyal yet not subservient.[75] In the 1860s he had opposed the abrupt abolition of serfdom,[76] and, as will be seen, his desire for a more independent zemstvo in 1880 reflected nothing more than an intention to restore some of the authority that the gentry had lost twenty years before.

Polovtsov's belief in gentry dominance reflected that of the zemstvo assemblies themselves during their first thirty years. According to Veselovskii, whose general view of the zemstvoes is by no means unfavorable, most of them used their autonomy not to develop the countryside but primarily to further the material interests of the gentry and to minimize the effects of the Liberation. Only a very few of the

---

72. TsGIAL, f. 1317, op. 1, d. 109, l. 10.

73. *Ibid.*, d. 71, vol. II, 221. Zaionchkovskii lists the members of the subcommittee in *Rossiiskoe samoderzhavie*, p. 219.

74. E.g., TsGIAL, f. 1317, op. 1, d. 71, vol. II, 223; d. 109, ll. 74–75.

75. Polovtsov, *Dnevnik* (1966), I, 236–237.

76. *Ibid.*, p. 155.

assemblies showed any interest in bringing reform to their territories or even in governing them.[77]

In part, this was because of the obstacles put in their path by the central government and its agents. The law of 21 November 1866, for example, set limits to the zemstvo's right to tax. It is wrong, however, to assume that all the constraints that the central government placed on the zemstvoes were no more than manifestations of the bureaucracy's distrust of local autonomous institutions. The law of 1866, like many other measures, was intended not to curtail the zemstvoes' activities but to prevent the landholding gentry from using their dominant position in the uezd assemblies to force an unduly large proportion of the tax burden on other classes of the population. Reitern, who was MF in 1866, noted that the gentry-dominated assemblies were trying to shift the zemstvo tax burden onto trade and industry; in order to prevent this, he got the November law enacted. He was protecting the towns, he said, not preventing the zemstvoes from raising taxes per se.[78] The long-range effect of his law was to favor the towns and to impose a disproportionate share of the tax burden on agriculture,[79] but it hardly constituted a significant limitation on zemstvo activity.

Before the 1890s no law prevented the zemstvoes from raising their land taxes—i.e., the taxes the gentry paid—but in fact, says Veselovskii, the zemstvoes generally showed no inclination to do so. Nor did they make any attempt before the 1890s to reform their utterly arbitrary methods of assessing the land, methods by which they consistently forced a grossly disproportionate share of the tax burden onto the peasants.[80] During the 1890s and 1900s many of the gubernia zemstvoes had their statisticians draw up land registers to serve as a basis for a fair assessment, but as of 1906 the uezd assemblies had still not adopted them.[81] Indeed, there was a considerable amount of land that the zemstvoes did not tax at all—almost all of it belonging to the gentry.[82] The only reform in zemstvo taxation that the early zemstvoes favored with any consistency was an income tax, but this was only another gimmick to get the towns to pay a greater share of the taxes.[83] The idea of extending credit to peasant villages to enable them to buy

77. B. Veselovskii, II, 15–105, especially pp. 55–59. See also III, 202–203.
78. *Ibid.*, I, 105–107. Finance ministers continued to be suspicious of zemstvoes until after 1900. See, e.g., *ibid.*, pp. 74–75, 127.
79. *Ibid.*, pp. 107–108.
80. *Ibid.*, pp. 44–87. See also M. A. Sirinov, *Zemskie nalogi* (Iurev, 1915), pp. 12–117, 167.
81. B. Veselovskii, I, 81, 86.
82. *Ibid.*, pp. 78–86. In the period 1871–1901 the gubernia zemstvoes' statisticians found a total of 84 million acres that were not being taxed.
83. *Ibid.*, pp. 155–161.

land found significant support in the early zemstvoes, but even this seeming display of social consciousness, says Veselovskii, was calculated to keep the price of land high, not to help the peasants.[84]

Admittedly, at all times a few zemstvoes expressed some aspiration to do something useful for their territories, and government officials did set obstacles in their way.[85] On the whole, however, the zemstvoes showed little inclination to act on their own before the 1890s except on behalf of their gentry members.

In the light of Veselovskii's study, the recommendations of the Kakhanov commission's subcommittee and those of the inspecting senators suggest, more than anything else, a return to the unrestricted gentry dominance over the countryside that had characterized local government before 1837.[86] The subcommittee proposed that the uezd zemstvo assembly take over the administration of rural areas, including the police agencies.[87] Exclusively peasant volosts and villages were to be done away with, and a new volost administration was to be established to govern not only peasants but the whole population.[88] It would be financed entirely by the uezd assembly, and run by a new chief, the *volostel*, elected by the assembly for a six-year term.[89] The *volostel* had to be a local inhabitant[90] with at least a high school education.[91]

84. *Ibid.*, II, 61–77.

85. The zemstvoes' activities during the first decades of their existence have been described in a number of works. See especially G. B. Sazonov, *Obzor deiatelnosti zemstv po selskomu khoziastvu, 1865–1895 g.* (4 vols., St. Petersburg, 1896), a publication of the ministry of agriculture. Sazonov was anxious to show how active the zemstvoes had been, and his account lists all their projects on agricultural improvement down to the pettiest. In spite of his positive approach, however, he was unable to find much evidence of activity in the zemstvoes before 1890.

Concerning government interference with the zemstvoes, see B. Veselovskii, III, 357–358, 471, and Zaionchkovskii, *Rossiiskoe samoderzhavie*, pp. 209–215.

86. This was not Veselovskii's own view. Quite to the contrary, he believed that the central government held the zemstvoes down and kept them from developing in a properly liberal direction. With all due regard for Veselovskii's scholarship, however, his own evidence plainly contradicts his belief. One cannot demonstrate that the vast majority of zemstvo delegates were profoundly antiprogressive throughout the period 1864–1905 and then conclude that the zemstvoes would have been progressive if the central government had only left them alone. What Veselovskii suggests (see especially III, 413–419), though he and other crypto-bureaucratizers in the zemstvo movement of 1905–1917 did not wish to recognize it, was that from 1858 to 1905 a progressive minority in the rural gentry was ultimately able to prevail over a hostile majority *because* it had support from some elements in the central government.

87. The project is printed in TsGIAL, f. 1317, op. 1, d. 71, vol. II, 7–100.

88. *Ibid.*, ll. 7, 22.

89. *Ibid.*, l. 62.

90. *Ibid.*

91. *Ibid.*, l. 8.

Election by the zemstvo, said the subcommittee, would insure that the *volostel* would have the confidence of the local population.[92] And what was this zemstvo? Ideally, it would be a congress of all "property owners" in the uezd,[93] but in the 1880s this meant it was essentially a gentry organ, as the subcommittee freely acknowledged.[94] So was the new volost administration.[95] If the *volostel*, with his high school education, was to be a local inhabitant, he would almost invariably have to be from the gentry. Kakhanov's subcommittee was really saying, then, that the gentry should control the countryside. If the central government had orders to communicate to the countryside, these orders should be delivered to and carried out by elected gentry, just as they had been before 1837. The new volosts were to be free from the governor's interference except in cases where laws and orders from the central government specifically allowed him to act.[96] The *volosteli* were to be answerable only to the uezd zemstvo directorate.[97] In short, the conclusions of the senatorial inspectors and their subcommittee came from much the same kind of reasoning as that of the serf owners of the 1850s, and their frequent use of the slogan "all-class" to refer to the zemstvo does not alter this fundamental similarity.[98]

Granted that the gentry of 1880 were a world apart from those of the 1830s, granted also that they were to grow rapidly more broad and national in their outlook in the following generation, they were still, in 1880, not all that far from their elder brothers of the 1850s–1860s who had had to be shoved into the Liberation of the serfs and whom the government had specifically banned from peasant administration for fear that they would use any power granted to them to perpetuate serfdom. This was especially true of the gentry in the uezd zemstvo assembly, and these were precisely the ones to whom Kakhanov's subcommittee wished to entrust the future development of rural Russia. Strangely, this subcommittee (i.e., the majority of its members that approved its project) has been passed down in the history books as "liberal," whereas the land captains, who worked as

92. *Ibid.*, l. 62.
93. *Ibid.*, ll. 27–30.
94. *Ibid.*, l. 22.
95. *Ibid.*, ll. 56–60.
96. *Ibid.*, l. 22.
97. *Ibid.*, l. 30.
98. The subcommittee specified that its project embodied not a real all-class government but only a suitable mechanism for developing one. See *ibid.*, l. 58. Translated from ideological into descriptive language, this meant that former serf owners should reassume their old responsibility (and power) to lead the peasants forward.

servitors of the government rather than delegates of local privilege, have been labeled "reactionary."[99]

Given the real nature of the Kakhanov subcommittee's proposals, its opinion that the government bureaucracy had been responsible for the zemstvoes' inaction before 1880 appears to have been a product more of the members' ideology than of their observations. Veselovskii's description, on the other hand, is the more convincing in that it comes from a man who believed in the autonomy of the zemstvoes and generally opposed government interference in their development. In the 1880s the tsarist government had reason to doubt that the zemstvoes were capable of carrying out reform programs in rural Russia. This is not to say that the zemstvoes "failed" during the 1860s–1880s or that their contribution and development were not significant. The only point being made here is that in the 1880s there were legitimate reasons for government decision-makers to consider them unpromising as vehicles for rural reform.

To return to the evolution of the zemstvoes, Veselovskii tells us that they began to expand their operations with much greater speed after the famine of 1891. The famine was by no means the only cause of the "awakening," but it accelerated a trend that had been going forward rather slowly. If the gentry zemstvoes' major concern before the 1890s had been only to minimize the revenue the gentry had to pay and to keep the price of their land high, they did begin to act thereafter as if they were aware that their own welfare depended ultimately on that of the peasantry.[100] They began building and running schools and hospitals and gathering statistics on a much larger scale than before. Aided by subsidies from the newly formed ministry of agriculture, a few of them even inaugurated some modest programs to improve peasant agriculture.[101]

As the zemstvoes expanded the scope of their activities, their administrative apparatuses likewise expanded, and their officials came into ever closer contact with the organs of the central government. Not surprisingly, a good deal of friction developed. Of course, the zemstvoes had been grappling with the MVD-police hierarchy since their

99. Zaionchkovskii, for example, refers to the subcommittee's project as "a significant step forward . . . on the way toward . . . bourgeois monarchy" (*Rossiiskoe samoderzhavie*, p. 225), and he terms the statute on the land captains a "counterreform" (*ibid.*, p. 366). See also his *Krizis*, pp. 478–479.

100. B. Veselovskii, II, 78–79.

101. *Ibid.*, I, 252–268, describes the programs in general. Concerning the zemstvo schools, see especially *ibid.*, pp. 586–587. On the programs of agronomic aid, see *ibid.*, II, 16–20, 137, and above, n. 85.

founding in 1864, and the landholding gentry had been in conflict with any and all government agencies long before then (see above, ch. III, sec. E). Before the 1890s, however, the fight had generally been of a different sort. The traditional concern of the gentry and the zemstvoes had been not primarily to organize themselves and to act but primarily to keep their taxes at a minimum and maintain their local social-political order against outside interference.[102] The method for doing this had been to appeal to the first department of the Senate whenever an official violated the legal "rights" that the zemstvoes (or gentry assemblies) enjoyed. To put it more realistically, whenever a faction in a zemstvo assembly had tried to invoke the official authority of its colleagues who were serving as police, the opposition could invoke the statutes that limited the police by appealing to the Senate in the name of the assembly as a whole. This kind of conflict did not cease in the late nineteenth century, but as the zemstvoes began to expand their administrative organizations and to act like functioning agencies, a new kind of conflict with the central government developed, the kind that develops between functional agencies which depend on one another in order to operate.

The new conflict emerged primarily on the gubernia level, where most of the zemstvoes' new activity was going forward.[103] While most of the uezd zemstvoes continued to oppose all forms of government interference and to contend with the central government in much the same way they always had, the gubernia zemstvoes began to interfere in local society, i.e., to play the role of modernizing, bureaucratizing invaders. As they did, they found themselves in conflict with the MVD-police hierarchy, which by the 1890s had come to see itself as an upholder of local society against the corrosive effects of bureaucracy.

This new kind of gentry-police conflict was exactly the reverse of the one in the 1850s–1860s. Now the gubernia zemstvoes were sending bureaucrats into the countryside, and the police were trying to hold rural society together. After 1890, therefore, the gubernia zemstvoes found themselves increasingly dependent on the invasion from the capital cities rather than opposed to it, and they began to take the same attitude toward the MVD-police hierarchy as did the agencies of the MF and the functional ministries.

It will not do to push the similarity between the newly active gubernia zemstvoes and the MF's agencies too far. Zemstvo administrators encountered a variety of opposing forces in the central govern-

102. See B. Veselovskii, III, 289–312.
103. A few uezd zemstvoes became more active (*ibid.*, p. 389), but the main stimulus to action came on the gubernia level (*ibid.*, pp. 412–413).

ment, and they were not consistently on either side in the conflict between MVD and MF. Their relationship to the MVD could not help but be ambivalent. If the MVD's police often put obstacles in the way of the zemstvo administrators (see above, n. 85), the general concern of the ministry for local order and prosperity often led it to encourage the zemstvoes' demands for government aid. In the 1890s the MVD appeared for a time to be the champion of the zemstvoes, while the MF seemed to be leading the opposition. Ivan L. Goremykin, MVD in the late 1890s, supported a proposition to extend zemstvo institutions to western Russia, while Witte, the MF, not only opposed him but also strove to impose new limits on the zemstvoes' right to tax.[104]

But Witte was not opposing the zemstvoes' activities as such. Actually, his attacks expressed roughly the same attitude as that of the gubernia zemstvo activists. In the main, he objected to persistent irregularities and injustices in the uezd zemstvoes' land taxes, and he opposed the MVD's attempts to bring the zemstvoes under the control of the police hierarchy.[105] If successful, these attempts would have empowered the MVD to keep the MF (and the gubernia zemstvo activists) entirely out of the countryside. In 1898, when Witte was still ostensibly opposing the zemstvoes, he got a law through (that of 29 October) that purported to impose a standard system of land assessment on them. His law of 12 June 1900 required that the MF and the MVD approve annual increases of more than 2.5 percent in zemstvo property taxes.[106] With these measures enacted, Witte abruptly changed his policy and began to use his new power of approval to permit zemstvo tax increases far in excess of any that had been allowed before. At the same time he encouraged the functional ministries, chiefly agriculture, to expand their subsidies to the zemstvoes.[107] As far as the gubernia zemstvoes were concerned, then, the MF was more or less consistent in its support of their aspirations to reform, despite the seeming fluctuations in its policy toward the zemstvoes as a whole.

The statute of 12 June 1890 concentrated most of the zemstvoes'

104. Sergei Iu. Witte, *Samoderzhavie i zemstvo* (Stuttgart, 1903), describes the dispute. See especially pp. 3–4, 54–55, for his expressions of opposition to the zemstvoes.

105. *Ibid.*, pp. 176–177. In 1900–1902 the MVD's plan to extend zemstvoes into western Russia included a proposal to make the assemblies there nonelective, i.e., to put them entirely under the MVD's control. See B. Veselovskii, III, 514–515.

106. B. Veselovskii, III, 533–534. Witte's initial project of the law of 1900 required that *all* such increases be approved by the central government. It was amended in the State Council to produce the milder version.

107. Sirinov, pp. 173–174; B. Veselovskii, I, 15; T. I. Polner, *Zhiznennyi put Kniazia Georgiia Evgenievicha Lvova* (Paris, 1932), pp. 58–59.

dealings with the *pravitelstvo* at the gubernia level. It set up a new gubernia-level standing committee, the gubernia board for zemstvo and municipal affairs, chaired by the governor and including both government administrators and delegates from the gubernia zemstvo.[108] The new committee was empowered to decide almost all varieties of dispute between zemstvoes and central administrators, and unless the governor objected, its majority opinions were final. This meant that the uezd zemstvoes had to let the gubernia organization handle their disputes with the *pravitelstvo*. The statute also required that all petitions from the uezd zemstvoes to the central government be submitted via the gubernia zemstvo assemblies, which were empowered to decide whether or not to submit each petition and to do the actual submitting.[109] From 1890 on, then, the gubernia zemstvo assembly and the new gubernia-level committee provided relatively easy channels for communicating uezd-level affairs to the gubernia level and translating them into a relatively consistent and recognizable conflict between the governor, representing the MVD-police hierarchy, and the gubernia zemstvo.[110]

As the gubernia zemstvoes began to learn to conceive of themselves as functional organizations in relation to the agencies of the central government, the uezd assemblies by and large continued to concern themselves primarily with local squabbles. Those landholders who did come to believe in some kind of reform were likely to despair of accomplishing anything in the uezd, and their natural inclination was to try to get out: either to get themselves elected as delegates to the gubernia assembly or to take up a post in gubernia administration, zemstvo or *pravitelstvo*, where the atmosphere was more congenial to ideas of change. A more or less natural split seems to have developed between zemstvo men who stayed in the uezd assemblies and their delegates in the gubernias, and as the gubernia zemstvoes intensified their activities and expanded their executive organizations, the split

108. Aside from the governor, the members were the gubernia gentry marshal, the vice-governor, the fiscal administrator, the *prokuror* of the regional (gubernia) court, the chairman of the gubernia zemstvo directorate (elected by the gubernia zemstvo), the elected "head" (*golova*) of the gubernia capital city, and one elected delegate from the gubernia zemstvo assembly. See *Svod zakonov*, vol. II, "Polozhenie gubernskikh i uezdnykh zemskikh uchrezhdeniiakh," art 8. A permanent member, appointed by the central government, was added in 1900. See B. Veselovskii, III, 362.

109. B. Veselovskii, III, 400–401.

110. See the discussion of the statute in "Novoe zemskoe polozhenie," pp. 306–310, 334–335, and B. Veselovskii, III, 418–420. Veselovskii opines that the statute was the main basis for the growing power of gubernia zemstvoes over the uezds in the 1890s and 1900s.

widened.[111] A sign of the time was Dmitri N. Shipov's resignation as head of the Moscow gubernia zemstvo directorate in 1899. According to his own account, he was the leading advocate for centralization in the zemstvo organization, and it was primarily protests from the uezd assemblies that drove him to resign.[112]

The gubernia zemstvo activists began to develop an ideology of sorts in the 1900s. Despite the growing gap between themselves and their constituencies, they began to make much of their close association with the "people" and to believe that their status as elected men gave them a position in gubernia administration that was unique and exalted.[113] According to this new ideology, the agents of the central government were invaders of the land, not builders. Far from representing the real interests of the inhabitants, their work was harmful. The zemstvoes, on the other hand, "represented" Russia, both rural and urban.[114] From an objective point of view, this was poppycock, no more or less far-fetched than the tsar myth from which the ministers derived their legitimacy. The gubernia zemstvoes did not represent their constituencies in the countryside. What they were trying to do, after their reorganization at the hands of the central government in 1890, was to impose their essentially capital-city notions on their backward constituents, just as the "progressive" ministries were trying to impose systematic limitations on the MVD-police hierarchy.

One indication of the zemstvo movement's operational concept of representative government may be found in the views of two of its most important leaders: Dmitri Shipov, chairman of the Moscow gubernia zemstvo directorate from 1893 to 1899 and first president of the all-Russian zemstvo congress, and Georgii E. Lvov, chairman of the gubernia zemstvo directorate in Tula from 1903 to 1905 and president of the congress after Shipov resigned in 1906.

Shipov's notion of representation had very little in common with the Western idea of it. He did not believe that representative institutions should limit the authority of the tsar. Legally, he said in his memoirs,

111. B. Veselovskii, I, 135–136; III, 413–429. The gubernia zemstvoes adopted the practice of granting matching subsidies to uezd zemstvoes in order to push them into reform. This, it seems, was the only way they could exert any positive influence in the uezds. See *ibid.*, I, 131–132.

112. Dmitri N. Shipov, *Vospominaniia i dumy o perezhitom* (Moscow, 1918), pp. 32–51. The gubernia assembly did not accept Shipov's resignation, and he remained in office until 1903. See B. Veselovskii, III, 422–423.

It is worth adding that the agrarian reform of 1906–1914, which was initiated in a time of MVD ascendancy, was carried out through the uezd zemstvoes, much to the chagrin of the gubernia-level activists (see below, n. 128).

113. See, e.g., Trutovskii, pp. 221–222; Shipov, pp. 27–30.

114. Trutovskii, pp. 132–144.

the tsar's power was absolute and unlimited. Autocracy was limited only by morality, not by law. The institution of the autocrat constituted not "a limitation on power in the name of a juridical concept but a self-limitation in the name of the autocrat's consciousness of his moral duty to express the voice of the collective conscience of the people."[115] In other words, the government was organized basically around the moral feelings of its servitors and people, and since the tsar had the highest sense of duty, he had the highest authority. Legal reform, then, had to be introduced by developing the people's consciousness of their duties rather than their rights.[116] This concept of government was hardly appropriate for a leader whose authority rested on election by his constituents. Shipov did not really believe that his being elected made him responsible to an electorate. To him, the essential significance of his "popular" support was the guarantee it should have given him to have regular access to the all-powerful tsar. What he wanted was equal status with the ministers.[117]

Lvov's views carried a similar implication.[118] He did not concern himself as much as Shipov with theories about autocracy but addressed himself to what he considered to be the practical problems of administrative organization. In 1905 he did not join in the debate over political theory but instead bent all his efforts to getting an executive organization into operation in the countryside.[119] Lvov "considered himself a representative of the problems at hand, not of his electors," said one of his associates. "In his eyes, the zemstvo directorate was more important than the assembly."[120]

It may be said, then, that the leaders of the zemstvo movement had more on their minds than representing their constituents back in the uezd. Indeed, their efforts brought them willy-nilly into the forefront of the attack on their constituents. By implication, at least, the zemstvo "movement" was not much less authoritarian, bureaucratic, and centralist at heart than the tsarist government itself.

It is worth adding that the degree to which even the uezd zemstvo represented the "people" or commanded their confidence is disputable. Notes from the report of the senatorial inspection in Samara gubernia in 1880–1881 indicate that less than 25 percent of the eligible

115. Shipov, p. 271.
116. *Ibid.*, pp. 267–269.
117. *Ibid.*, pp. 261–265.
118. Polner, pp. 93–96, 99–102.
119. *Ibid.*, pp. 109–113.
120. *Ibid.*, p. 109.

voters participated in zemstvo elections there,[121] and even a zemstvo activist like Trutovskii had to acknowledge in 1913 that indifference to zemstvo elections was still general throughout European Russia.[122] Apparently the "awakening" of the masses to their need for zemstvoes was at best only beginning when World War I broke out. The electorate seems to have been almost as indifferent to the zemstvo leaders as the leaders were to the wishes of the electorate.

From 1890 to 1905 legislation regarding the zemstvoes tended generally to strengthen relationships of mutual dependence between gubernia zemstvo directorates and ministerial agencies. The statute of 12 June 1890 streamlined zemstvo administration and granted government ranks to zemstvo servitors.[123] From 1894 on, the ministry of agriculture helped to sponsor numerous congresses in which zemstvo agronomists could meet and exchange views, and in the early 1900s other ministries began to do the same for other professions.[124] More important, the government began to expand its financial support to the zemstvoes. In the late 1890s the central government took over most of the zemstvoes' obligatory expenditures,[125] and in 1904 it undertook to pay off all arrears in zemstvo revenue.[126] As said before, despite the limitations imposed by the law of 12 June 1900 on the amount of taxes that the zemstvoes could collect, the government actually allowed zemstvo revenues to increase more rapidly in the early 1900s than ever before (see above, n. 107). Not satisfied with relieving pressure on zemstvo budgets, the government subsidized zemstvoes directly, or, to put it another way, the ministries carried out a growing number of their reform and relief programs through zemstvo organizations. In 1905–1906 the central government contributed 3.6 million rubles to a famine-relief campaign that the all-Russian zemstvo congress conducted, about half the total cost.[127] After 1906 government subsidies

---

121. TsGIAL, f. 1317, op. 1, d. 109, ll. 71–72. B. Veselovskii, III, 141–147, notes that zemstvo assemblies suffered a great deal from absenteeism in the 1860s and 1870s.

122. Trutovskii, pp. 181–185. His view is supported in considerable detail in the sections on separate gubernias in the fourth volume of B. Veselovskii's *Istoriia*.

123. B. Veselovskii, III, 441–443.

124. See *ibid.*, pp. 377–384, regarding the ministry of agriculture. On the other ministries, see Polner, p. 96.

125. B. Veselovskii, I, 241–243; II, 332–333.

126. *Ibid.*, I, 189–202, especially pp. 191–192. From 1904 on, the government continued to collect its own and the zemstvoes' taxes together, but all arrears were charged to the government's share.

127. Polner, pp. 134–136. The zemstvo campaign absorbed only a fraction of

to zemstvoes grew to massive proportions, as did government-zemstvo collaboration in general.[128]

Two elements in the increasing collaboration between zemstvoes and central administration are worth noting. On the one hand, the zemstvoes came to represent a potential basis for opposition to the government; on the other, they played a vital role in the government's campaign to bring system to the countryside.

After 1900 a demand became audible among the zemstvo activists for an all-Russian zemstvo organization, and in 1904 this "movement" actually produced a "congress" that continued to meet until 1917, despite sporadic government efforts after 1906 to discourage it.[129] As has been said, neither Shipov nor Lvov, the principal leaders of the movement, were opponents of autocracy—not, at any rate, in 1905–1906. They were practical executives who did most of their work in collaboration with government agencies and whose policies implied nothing more than an aspiration to acquire the same prerogatives for their zemstvo organizations as the ministers had. What they wanted, in essence, was a formal, all-Russian organizational center whose head would have regular access to the tsar. Nevertheless, Shipov and Lvov and their zemstvo associates clashed with the high-level statesmen of the central government from the early 1890s on, and in the heady days of 1905 they acquired the public image of an opposition to autocracy and bureaucracy.[130]

But there were also indications that practical collaboration was bringing the zemstvoes into productive relationships with the *pravitelstvo*. One of these was the growing inclination of the servitors to transfer back and forth between government and zemstvo organizations and to use the zemstvo as a place to begin a career in the government. Take F. V. Shlippe, for example. He began his career as a gentry marshal in early 1905, was elected to the Moscow gubernia

---

the 173 million rubles that the central government spent on famine relief in 1906–1907.

128. See above, n. 69. Trutovskii, pp. 151–154, reports with considerable exaggeration that the zemstvoes became solidly pro-government after 1905. B. Veselovskii is referring to much the same phenomenon when he says that the zemstvoes became "tools of reaction" (IV, 85). Veselovskii strongly disapproved of the central government's policies after 1906, especially its decision to work through uezd zemstvoes instead of the gubernias. See *ibid.*, pp. 49–85. Nevertheless, he was forced to admit that zemstvo work expanded in scope under the new regime. See *ibid.*, pp. 99–152.

129. Polner, pp. 130–165, and Trutovskii, pp. 132–143, describe the birth of the all-Russian zemstvo congress out of an administrative base in the Moscow gubernia zemstvo directorate during the course of the Russo-Japanese War.

130. Polner, pp. 55–56, 66–90, 112–121. On the conflicts of the 1890s, see Shipov, pp. 100–130.

zemstvo assembly in 1906, and in 1907 was appointed to a government post—permanent member of the Moscow gubernia land settlement commission. In 1911 he was promoted to vice-director of the department of agriculture in the ministry of the same name, but he gave this up in 1912, when he heard of his election as chairman of the Moscow gubernia zemstvo directorate. Apparently the switch to government service in 1907 did not hurt his standing in the zemstvo. Nor did his switch back to the zemstvoes in 1912 hurt his career in government. In 1914 he was offered the post of assistant director of the land section in the MVD.[131] Shlippe's career was by no means exceptional in the 1890s–1900s.[132] It epitomizes the merging of zemstvo and government into an increasingly coherent legal-administrative system in which each party had its own functional roles to play.

The simultaneous development of political conflict and effective administrative coordination between zemstvoes and *pravitelstvo* was not exceptional or even paradoxical in the context of ministerial government. Organizational unity and polarization into hostile camps were manifestations of the same basic phenomenon: an increasing awareness of mutual interdependence between gubernia zemstvoes and central government.

If the roles and aims of the gubernia zemstvoes had come to resemble those of the ministerial agencies by 1905, it is not surprising that their attitudes should also have been similar. Zemstvo activists, like ministerial agents, were demanding greater freedom of action and more financial support from the central government. In lieu of a ministry to back them, the zemstvo administrators demanded an all-Russian organization that would coordinate and supervise them and give them direct access to the tsar. All these demands required implicitly that the central government evolve into an effective bureaucracy that could support and work with the zemstvoes while controlling its own agents sufficiently well to give de facto protection to zemstvo

131. See F. V. Shlippe, "Memoirs" (unpublished manuscript, in Russian, in the Russian Archive at Columbia University), pp. 87–92, 113–115, 123–130, 152.

132. B. Veselovskii, III, 584–589, gives a list of zemstvo men appointed to high government posts from the 1870s on. It is of interest that in Viatka gubernia the ties between central administration and zemstvoes were especially close. See *ibid.*, IV, 667–669. Viatka had a very small gentry population, and many of its zemstvoes were predominantly peasant. See *ibid.*, pp. 197–201. It seems that zemstvo-government collaboration was not entirely a development within the gentry class.

In a story written in 1896 Chekhov has a rural landholder advise his brother to enter government service via elected office. "You will be noticed in Petersburg and asked to go there," he says. "Active men on the provincial assemblies and town councils are all the fashion there now" (A. Chekhov, "Three Years," in *Peasants and Other Stories,* ed. Edmund Wilson [New York, 1956], p. 91).

autonomy.[133] It was to be expected, therefore, that zemstvo activists would be hostile toward the MVD-police organization. As said before, however, this was no longer the hostility of local society toward its invaders. The gubernia zemstvoes had joined the invasion.

Peasant Volosts and Villages

Before we discuss the invasion of peasant society, it is relevant to introduce a brief description of the legal-administrative order that was to be invaded. To begin with, all officials were elected, regardless of their own wishes, from among the resident heads of households. Elections were conducted in the village assembly (*skhod*), which was made up of all the heads of households in the village.[134] The majority of Russian peasants lived in small villages—under fifty households— and therefore the village assembly usually managed the village's affairs directly. There was, however, an executive head of the village, the village elder (*starosta*), who was elected by the assembly for a three-year term to do the everyday work of governing. In addition, the law required that each assembly elect a tax collector (*sborshchik podatei*) and a number of police (*desiatskie* and *sotskie*) to perform their functions independently of the *starosta* under the direct command of the *stan* police and/or the land captain.[135]

The village assembly also selected a number of delegates to the volost assembly, where they served three-year terms. The volost assembly normally performed no function except to meet once a year to elect the volost government. This consisted of a volost elder (*starshina*) and a court (*sud*) of four members, all of whom served three-year terms.[136] The volost elder, unlike the village *starosta*, had a regular administrative board (*pravlenie*), which he was supposed to

133. As Shipov wrote to Witte in Nov. 1905, "The most frightening and pernicious thing about this threatening time in which Russia is living is the absence in the government organization of any definite program, based on definite political convictions, which could guide government policy by its imperatives. Only under such a program is it possible to command the belief and support of the nation" (Shipov, p. 374).

134. Leontev, *Krest. pravo* (1914), p. 74.

135. Brzheskii, *Naturalnye povinnosti*, pp. 69, 85–86, 155–156. The inspections of 1880–1881 found that there was about one *desiatskii* for every 100–200 peasants and one *sotskii* for every 4–10 *desiatskie*. See TsGIAL, f. 1317, op. 1, d. 71, vol. II, 161–188. The law of 5 May 1903 eliminated the *sotskie* and required that there be one *desiatskii* for every 25–30 households. See Brzheskii, *Naturalnye povinnosti*, p. 85.

136. V. A. Beer, *Kommentarii novykh provintsialnykh uchrezhdenii 12 iiuliia 1889 goda* (Moscow, 1894), p. 248. According to the Liberation Statute, members of the volost court served one-year terms, but the law of 28 Apr. 1887 changed this to three. See Zaionchkovskii, *Rossiiskoe samoderzhavie*, p. 255.

consult in the course of his work. The membership included all the village elders and tax collectors of the volost.[137] Volost administration was sufficiently complex to warrant the hiring of a clerk (*pisar*).[138]

The absence of real autonomy in the peasant institutions has already been discussed. It deserves repeating that if the volosts did not enjoy de facto institutional status, neither were they under the central government's effective control. The government agents who exercised supervision over peasant society were the land captains (after 1889) and the police. But all these officials had was power, not control. They could interfere in peasant administration at their pleasure, but they could not govern the volosts directly any more than the voevodas of the seventeenth and eighteenth centuries could manage their territories (see above, ch. III, sec. D). The tiny staff of land captains and police in each uezd could not have handled the legal affairs of 200,000 peasants even if they had been familiar with the extremely varied customs in the multitude of villages that came under their purview.[139] What they actually did, therefore, was to rely on volost and village administrators to do whatever governing was done.[140]

As said before, the authority of peasant officials and, likewise, the restraints on their authority still resided in nothing more firm than a number of habitual practices that could vary according to the impulses of the moment. Neither central government nor electorate could understand what the elected peasant officials had to do; thus the ever-increasing presence of the central government in peasant society generated a great deal of power without imposing corresponding controls. A volost *starshina* could be a tyrant over the weak, yet helpless before influential families, tavern keepers, money lenders, or horse thieves.[141]

The elements of the situation are illustrated in the following story

137. Leontev, *Krest. pravo* (1914), pp. 78–80, says that the introduction of the land captains reduced the *pravlenie* to an empty formality.

138. In the 1890s most clerks received higher salaries than the volost elders (see above, n. 38). On peasant administration in general, see Leontev, *Krest. pravo* (1914), pp. 71–112.

139. Kissel-Zagorianskii, pp. 43–44, notes that the land captains had no knowledge of or training in peasant custom. V. V. Tenishev, *Administrativnoe polozhenie russkogo krestianina* (St. Petersburg, 1908), pp. 63–70, records a number of cases illustrating the land captain's inability to control the volosts or to protect peasants against one another.

140. Leontev, *Krest. pravo* (1908), pp. 14–15.

141. Tenishev, *Administrativnoe polozhenie*, pp. 47–48. Tenishev thought that the frequency with which the volost elder misused his power decreased significantly in the years after the introduction of the land captain. Land captains, however, were not a solution to the problem. At best, says Tenishev, they were a stopgap measure.

of peasant law enforcement, taken from the studies of an amateur anthropologist at the turn of the century.

When the villagers became convinced that Anna had really stolen the linen, they decided to march her around the village carrying the stolen linen and to take all her own linen to sell for drink as a lesson to others. When the holiday came, Anna dressed up in her good blouse. They smeared her blouse with tar and tore off her kerchief. Then they unrolled one of her linen pieces and tied it to her hands so that her arms were bound behind her, and in this way they led her about the village. Two peasants went ahead, beating on oven doors with sticks, and behind them came two more, leading Anna with the linen. The whole village came out to watch. All of them laughed at Anna and some of the children threw dirt clods at her.

Anna walked proudly, with her head high, paying no attention to the mockery. The peasants were surprised to see her still smiling instead of lamenting as women usually did when led about in this way. They led her through the whole village and then to the creek, where they got her all wet, saying that they had to wash the tar off her blouse. When she was soaked through, the peasants took her home and untied her hands. For drink, they took only the piece of linen they had tied her with.

When she was free, Anna ran into the doorway and grabbed a chain hanging on a hook. She came running out with it and began to strike out with it at any peasants she could see, male or female. Seeing this, the *starosta* ordered her to stop and to go into the barn that the village used for a public hall and to stay there under arrest for twenty-four hours. Three peasants ran after Anna to put her into the barn. Seeing this, Anna threw the chain away and ran into the hemp field and hid.

Some peasants from another village advised Anna to go to the land captain and complain to him that the peasants had robbed her. This is what Anna did. The land captain called in the *starosta* and asked him if the story was true. The *starosta* told him everything in detail, adding that this was the way the village had been handling its offenders since time immemorial. The land captain forbade him to do it again, and as a punishment he ordered the *starosta* to stay in the volost for two days under arrest.

The *starosta* went home, called a meeting, and announced that Anna had complained against the village to the land captain for her illegal punishment and that the land captain had forbidden them to do any such thing again and had put him, the *starosta*, under arrest for two days. The peasants at the meeting summoned Anna's husband Sergei and his brother Simeon, and they decided to punish her in the following manner. First of all, the husband should beat her with a knout before all the peasants; then the village would take some of her property for drink and she would be subjected to every kind of mockery and abuse.

Coming to the house, the peasants ordered Sergei to bring out his wife. Anna came out. They asked her why she had complained against them to the land captain as if she had been innocent. Anna began to ask forgiveness. Then the *starosta* ordered Sergei to teach his wife to be obedient to the village court. They gave Sergei a knout—a good strap—and ordered him to give his wife thirty lashes without mercy. If the village saw that he was going easy on his wife, then they would do the job for him.

Sergei ordered his wife to lie down on the ground. Anna stood silently, without answering or even hearing him. Then Sergei went up to his wife and tried to force her down. Anna grabbed him by the hair and began to pull at him. The peasants dragged Sergei away and knocked Anna down. One held her by the legs and another by her head and hands. Sergei began to beat his wife with the knout with all his strength. After thirty blows, the *starosta* stopped Sergei and took away the knout. When the husband went to get his wife's clothes to give them to the village to sell for drink, he found that they were not in her trunk. Anna had taken them to her relatives in Balashev.

From then on, Anna's family cursed her for her behavior, and she began to lead a dissolute life, openly and wholeheartedly. She quarrelled with her husband every day. All the villagers scorned and mocked her, and the children often threw clods of dirt at her, shouting "hurrah." At last, she decided to go away. She got her passport from her husband and went to the town of Orel, and then to Odessa, where she still lives.[142]

This was the "incoherence" that rural administrators faced during the period 1861–1905—the unadministrable and unteachable village. By 1905 land captains, police officers, zemstvo statisticians, and *narodniki* had all broken their teeth on it, and there it still was, still shielded from the world around it by its old autonomy of bribery and passivity, as if nothing had changed since the days of Ivan the Terrible. This was the "mass" that the central government contemplated in the 1880s, when Alexander III decided to act upon the countryside through his own administration.[143]

142. Quoted in V. V. Tenishev, *Pravosudie v russkom krestianskom byte* (Briansk, 1907), pp. 41–43.

143. Changes did occur in the volost legal-administrative order in 1861–1905, but they did not seem to be making the villages any more coherent. One indication of what was going on may be seen in the following comment from a gubernia committee (Samara) formed in 1899 to consider a project for a new set of instructions to the land captains: "When the institution of the peaceful arbitrator was in operation [i.e., in 1861–1874], the life of the Russian village, only recently freed from serfdom, was not so complex as it is now. It took the

But how was he to act? The gubernia administration was divided by the conflicting interests of its sections; the uezd offices were not effectively subordinated to their confused superiors, let alone usable as agencies for any active reform; the zemstvoes seemed uninterested as yet in reform of any kind; and the MVD-police hierarchy not only was unable to carry out reforms but was rapidly losing its ability to keep bureaucratic agencies out of the villages. In short, the need for rural reform and reorganization was clear by 1880, but neither the means to reform nor the direction it was to take was immediately perceivable. If the government was to act, therefore, it could not lose time searching for perfect and permanent plans and laws. It would have to settle for ad hoc courses of action that might at least begin to cope with the worst problems for at least a short time. This, in essence, was what Alexander III believed.

EXTENSION OF THE MF AND THE MVD INTO THE
COUNTRYSIDE, 1885–1905

The extension of the MF from the gubernia level downward into the countryside began in 1885. In that year it acquired the authority to set up a tax inspector (*podatnyi inspektor*) in each uezd to check on financial operations. In 1899 these inspectors took over from the police the task of collecting the regular yearly revenue, including redemption payments, from the peasants.[144] In 1903, with their extension down to the *uchastok* level, they assumed the additional responsibility of collecting arrears (see above, n. 16). By 1905, then, the elected village tax collectors had come under the effective jurisdiction of the MF, and bureaucratic specialization had at last penetrated to peasant society. Peasant-elected officials had come under three separate authorities. The *starosty* and *starshiny* were taking orders from the land captains (MVD), the village tax collectors were responsible to the tax inspectors (MF), and the village police were still directly subordinate to the *stan* police captains (MVD).

The almost simultaneous extension of the MF's tax inspectors and

---

arbitrator only a very short time to collect all the information he needed to decide affairs assigned to him. Now, a rather large part of the population in a majority of Russian villages is constantly absent and thus forced to defend their interests in their home villages from a distance. Peasants are changing residence in unprecedented numbers, and this demands the resolution of many affairs in their places of origin. In the contemporary village, so many aspects of life have come under administrative regulation . . . that the land captains can hardly handle the affairs assigned to them" (quoted in *Sbornik zakliuchenii gubernskikh soveshchanii po proektu nakaza zemskim nachalnikam* [2 pts., St. Petersburg, 1899], I, 8–9).

144. Eroshkin, p. 312; *Ministerstvo finansov*, II, 359.

the MVD's land captains down to the *uchastok* during the period 1885–1905 commenced the replacement of the MVD-police hierarchy in peasant government by a vastly more systematic and more closely supervised regime.[145] By 1905 the old aspiration to extend system into the countryside (see above, ch. V, sec. B) was bringing interaction between government and peasant into a new stage that would reach its culmination in the agrarian reforms of 1906–1930. Government bureaucracy was racing to embrace Russian society in a single order; at the same time industrialization and urbanization were sharpening tensions between city and country. One result was the improvement and extension of legal-administrative system. Another was that this very system compelled the government to expose the contradictions in itself and in society and to assume responsibility for resolving them. The very success of ministerial government intensified its dilemmas (see above, ch. VI, sec. D). One expression of this intensification can be seen in the growing conflicts within the zemstvoes and between them and the central government. Another was the growing conflict between MF and MVD in the countryside.

We have considered the inability of rural society to cope with such large-scale systematic orders as the all-Russian market and ministerial government. We have observed how this inability gave rise in 1837–1862 to the MVD-police hierarchy, thereby setting the stage for a sustained conflict between MF and MVD. Finally, we have described some manifestations of the MF-MVD conflict in the gubernia administrations, the ministries, and the supreme organs.

At this point it will be useful to describe briefly the role, or roles, that the land captains played in the process of extending bureaucracy into the countryside. In a sense, these peculiar agents epitomized the whole development of legal-administrative system in Russia. They constituted a means to extend system into peasant society and also a bulwark against the extension of system. Like Catherine II's governors-general (see above, ch. V, sec. E), they were absolute authorities above the law; yet their purpose was to establish law. They extended and improved the operation of one part of the government—the MVD-police hierarchy—but in so doing they exacerbated the conflict between MVD and MF. As will be seen, they seem to have made a substantial contribution to the introduction of legal-administrative system to the countryside in the period 1889–1905, but their very success quickly rendered them obsolete and called forth radical changes in

145. Brzheskii, *Naturalnye povinnosti,* pp. 13–15.

their administrative roles. It is hoped that this very brief description of their evolution will suggest some explanation of why the MF and the MVD made great strides toward bringing the countryside under their control, thereby removing to some extent the original basis for the conflict between them, while at the same time their progress rendered the conflict ever more violent and irreconcilable.

In the 1880s Dmitri Tolstoi, MVD and enactor of the statute on land captains, was one of those who were warning against the harmful effects of bureaucratization on peasant society. The division of local government into functional branches, he said, was rendering both it and the peasant villages helpless to organize themselves. In 1887 he described uezd administration as follows:

> The attitudes of the majority of local institutions and officials toward their duties are extremely formalistic. They fear more than anything else that they will go beyond the limits of the functions assigned to them and almost always prefer to avoid taking part in any matter that could possibly be construed to fall within the province of another agency and in the execution of which they might be subject to accusations, however preposterous, of exceeding their authority. Under the circumstances it often happens that a peasant or even a landowner, acting to protect his rights, is shuttled from one official to another and receives no satisfaction. Obviously, such occurrences cannot go unnoticed among the people and cannot fail to disrupt in them their respect for authority and their sense of legality.[146]

And further: ". . . experience has made clear . . . the unsuitability in our fatherland of a system of local administration based on strict functional divisions and of a separate judicial power in the lower instances. It was inevitable that these conditions should have produced an absence of strong government authority in the uezd."[147] Under these circumstances strictly functional agents like the tax inspectors would only make the situation worse. Tolstoi concluded that a new kind of agent was needed.

The land captain was not an entirely new institution. He represented an adaptation of the "peaceful arbitrators" (*mirovye posredniki*) who had carried out the Liberation in the 1860s. Tolstoi wrote in 1887 that his aim was "to re-establish the arbitrators in a modified form corresponding to contemporary needs and recent experience."[148]

146. Note from the MVD to the imperial secretary of 25 Feb. 1887, in TsGIAL, f. 1149, t. 4, d. 44, ll. 10–11.
147. Tolstoi's note of 5 Feb. 1887, in Kataev, III, 1.
148. Note of 25 Feb. 1887, in TsGIAL, f. 1149, t. 4, d. 44, l. 15. For an interesting discussion of the MVD's views on peasant administration during the period 1861–1889, see Peter Czap, "P. A. Valuev's Proposal for a Vyt Adminis-

To some extent, then, the land captain was a product of historical evolution.

The evolution began in 1861, when the government lacked the means to operate as an administration in the countryside and therefore resorted to the arbitrators to carry out the Liberation. The arbitrators, it will be recalled, were given broad powers to act apart from the regular legal-administrative order in the gubernias. Within the general limits of the law they could issue and enforce commands of their own according to what they thought were the needs of the situation, and their decisions had the force of law in the peasant villages. Appeal coud be made against them to the uezd congress (*sezd*), a meeting of all the arbitrators in an uezd under the chairmanship of the uezd gentry marshal. Beyond the uezd there was the gubernia board for peasant affairs, a college made up of gubernia-level officials and elected gentry. In sum, the arbitrators enjoyed a de facto power over the peasants that bordered on the despotic, and there was almost no possibility of appeal against them except to the government's administrative agencies.[149]

The arbitrators held their powers because the task they had to perform could not be prescribed or planned in advance. Detailed laws could not be written; therefore, the government elected to trust in the personal virtue and practical competence of the arbitrator as the only available guarantee that he would act for the good of the state. His personal virtues were supposedly assured by requiring that he be of the landholding gentry and that he be selected by the MVD (see above, ch. IV, sec. E). Thus the arbitrator was an omnipotent agent of sorts, operating on the basis of his personal qualities rather than legal rules. His job, however, was specific and temporary. The enactors of the Liberation intended that he confine his activities to carrying out the Liberation and that when he completed his task he should cease to exist. He was not by origin an institution for the government of the peasants.[150]

Despite the intentions of the enactors of the Liberation Statute, the

tration, 1864," *Slavonic and East European Review,* XLV (July 1967), 391–410. Czap indicates that the legal provisions governing the land captains did not resemble those governing the arbitrators. There can be little doubt, however, that Tolstoi was indeed much influenced by the experience of the arbitrators. See Chernukha's more detailed study of MVD policy in 1864–1870, pp. 225–235.

149. See Leontev, *Krest. pravo* (1914), pp. 126–129; "Mirovoi posrednik," in Brockhaus and Efron, XIX (1896), 423–425. Unlike the land captains, however, the arbitrators had very little formal authority over the volost administration. See Kataev, II, 51–56.

150. Kataev, I, 15–119, describes the discussion that accompanied the enactment of the provisions regarding the arbitrators in the Liberation Statute.

arbitrators lasted on after the bulk of the work had been carried out. The judicial reform of 1864 transferred most of their judicial powers to the newly established justices of the peace (*mirovye sudy;* see above, ch. VI, sec. A). At the same time, however, their administrative jurisdiction was somewhat broadened.[151] In 1869 the MVD proposed replacing the arbitrators with permanent officials who would work directly under the MVD to manage the villages and volosts.[152] This notion remained alive in the MVD from then on, but it found very little favor in the rest of the government. In the end the law of 27 July 1874 did away with the arbitrators in most gubernias, and the peasants were left more or less to themselves.[153] Actually, the law of 1874 only gave formal recognition to what had already happened. The arbitrators had ceased to do anything but routine work from about 1863 on.[154]

The law of 1874 established a new uezd-level standing committee to govern the peasants and to assume responsibility for bringing the peasant legal-administrative order into correspondence with that under which the rest of the population lived. This was the uezd board for peasant affairs (*uezdnoe po krestianskim delam prisutstvie*), made up of the police commandant, the gentry marshal, and a permanent member "elected" by the gubernia zemstvo assembly. The gubernia board for peasant affairs, which had existed since 1861, was retained, and it continued to operate in a general supervisory capacity over the new uezd board. From 1874 to 1889 these two boards, together with the police, constituted all the agencies of peasant government that the central government possessed.

The enactors of the law of 1874 wanted primarily to preserve the autonomy of the peasant institutions and to avoid a return to the "guardianship" that Kiselev's ministry had exercised over the state peasants before the Liberation. With this purpose in mind, they set

151. *Ibid.,* II, 42.
152. *Ibid.,* pp. 56–58. See also above, ch. VI, sec. E.
153. Leontev, *Krest. pravo* (1914), pp. 129–131. Arbitrators continued to function in areas where there were no *mirovye sudy* (i.e., some uezds of Perm and Bessarabia gubernias and all of the nine western gubernias). See Chernukha, p. 237.
154. A large number of inspection reports and statements of local officials testified to the general inactivity of the arbitrators after 1863. See *Zapiska ot MVD k chlenam glavnogo komiteta ob ustroistve selskogo sostoianiia* (27 Mar. 1873), pp. 13–19; the report of Senator S. A. Mordvinov's inspection of Voronezh gubernia in 1880–1881, in TsGIAL, f. 1317, op. 1, d. 11, l. 361; Kataev, II, 83–84; Leontev, *Krest. pravo* (1914), pp. 126–128. Chernukha, pp. 221–225, suggests that criticisms against the arbitrators for inactivity after 1863 came primarily from former serf owners, who wanted them to be more energetic in the collection of peasant taxes and obrok payments.

strict limits to the jurisdiction of the uezd board. It could consider appeals from the peasants not against the substantive decisions of the volost courts but only against the procedures the court had followed in this or that case.[155] But even if the board had possessed greater power, the members had neither the knowledge of local custom nor the time to supervise all the peasant villages in their uezd.

Not surprisingly, neither peasantry nor government found the new uezd board satisfactory. In 1873, even before the board was set up, an extensive investigation of volost and village institutions had found that the peasants were dissatisfied with any institution that made subtle distinctions between procedure and substance. What they wanted was a power above the volost, easily available to them and also strong enough to overrule the decisions of their own officials.[156] The government was equally dissatisfied, mainly because it found itself even less able to enforce its laws in rural Russia than it had been before 1874. In 1878, for example, it was embarrassed to learn that its agents—the uezd boards—could not enforce limits on the taxes the volost administrations collected.[157] In short, the "autonomy" that prevailed in the period 1874–1889 pleased no one.

The land captains were set up initially in thirty-six gubernias. Like the arbitrators, they were nominated by the gentry assemblies from among the local landholding gentry and selected finally by the MVD. Unlike the arbitrators, they took orders from the MVD and could be dismissed by him if they did not perform satisfactorily. They operated by themselves, one in each *uchastok,* under the immediate supervision of an uezd congress made up of themselves, the head of the uezd zemstvo directorate, and the police commandant, all under the chairmanship of the uezd gentry marshal. For judicial affairs the uezd judge attended; for financial matters, the tax inspector. On the gubernia level a new board was established as a higher instance of appeal, called simply the gubernia board. It included the governor (as chairman) and a number of gubernia-level administrators (see Figure 2).

The relationships of the land captains to the peasants embodied much the same kind of despotic authority that the police had enjoyed. Unlike the police's authority, however, their power proceeded directly from explicit statutory provisions. The law specifically allowed the land captain 1) to make rules for the peasants in his *uchastok,* 2) to arrest and try any peasant who violated the rules, and 3) to

155. Kataev, II, 95–96.
156. Czap, "Influence," pp. 142–143; Kataev, II, 55–56.
157. Kataev, II, 106–112.

pronounce sentence upon the unfortunates he himself had accused and convicted for violating his rules. Moreover, he could discharge the peasants' "elected" officials practically at will.[158] Not only was his authority absolute; it was virtually exclusive. Other government officials, including the police, could do very little in the villages without his approval. In many respects, then, the land captain was a miniature governor-general, a personal agent of the central government responsible for all that went on among the peasants in his territory and possessing absolute personal authority over them.

This, at least, was the theory. In fact, bureaucracy was fast becoming too strong in the countryside to be coped with by an omnipotent agent, even one who had a ministry and a law behind him. The land captains doubtless did better than the police at maintaining some coherence in the volosts, but in the not very long run their personal authority proved inadequate to cope with the deluge of orders from the ministries. By 1905 it had become clear that the land captains could not continue to operate as the statute of 1889 prescribed. True, the land captains were extended to Vilna, Grodno, and Kovno gubernias in 1901, indicating that at least some ministers thought they were making a contribution, but this had to be done against a contrary vote in the State Council of thirty-four to nineteen.[159]

In any case, this was about the time that even the MVD ceased to believe in the use of arbitrary agents in the countryside. Already in 1897 the land section (in the MVD) had sent some draft regulations to the gubernia administrations, asking for their suggestions regarding possible methods for imposing limits on the land captains. Responses varied widely, but the majority recommended that the land captain's powers be subject to more systematic control. Even those who sought to preserve his absolute authority generally spoke of it as an administrative device to be employed only so long as the peasants remained incapable of governing and protecting themselves.[160]

---

158. See the "Polozhenie" (statute) of 12 July 1889, in *TPSZ*, 6196, arts. 22–31.

159. Kataev, III, 108–119.

160. The gubernias' responses are in *Sbornik zakliuchenii*. Art. 2 of the draft, for example, suggested that the land captain's power to influence the village assemblies should be carefully delimited by law (I, 13), and just about all the gubernias agreed that some form of legal limitation was needed (I, 13–79). It must be acknowledged that Nicholas II remained a fierce supporter of the land captains' absolute authority at least until the early 1900s. Any favorable remark about them, no matter how banal, was sure to arouse the warmest sentiments of gratitude and friendship in him. See his marginal comments on governors' annual reports in the late 1890s in *Svod . . . otmetok*, e.g., the report from Viatka for 1901 in the volume for that year, published in 1904, on p. 8.

In 1902 the land section of the MVD began to work consistently to limit the land captain's arbitrary power. V. I. Gurko, who took over the section in that year, inspected fifty land captains in three gubernias during the spring of 1905. His general verdict was that although they had made an important contribution to the bringing of order to the villages, they were no longer able to do the job they had set out to do.[161] In August of the same year the MVD issued a long-awaited *nakaz* (instruction) to the land captains. Its effect is impossible to determine because the new laws and constitutional reforms of the following year rendered it obsolete, but its obvious intent was to limit the land captain's power and to bridge the gap that separated him from the rest of the administration.[162] Articles 129–131, for example, restricted the land captain's power to tamper with the volost court, and article 141 limited the ways in which he could influence the volost administration. Not content with imposing formal restrictions on the land captains, the land section began publishing reports of its inspections of them in its monthly journal (the *IZO*); that is, they began to issue detailed public denunciations against those land captains who were not discharging their responsibilities properly. By 1905, then, the land captains' role was already undergoing rapid change, primarily at the hands of their own ministry.

If the land captain's absolute authority was a transitory phenomenon, it was still important in its time. In the period 1889–1905 he served as a stopgap measure to maintain some sort of order in the villages, and, more important, he took a few steps toward organizing the peasants themselves.[163] His long-range contribution toward the dual process of introducing system into the countryside is not subject to measurement or even verification. Obviously, it must have been at best a very limited one in such a short period of time. It is at least arguable, however, that his experience created a framework of sorts, a communication between administration and peasant that was clearer and more meaningful than what had existed before. Some of the leading men in the agrarian reform of 1906–1917 believed that its programs could not have begun without the foundation he had established.[164] In a sense, the land captain set the same process in motion in

161. *IZO* (May 1905), p. 202.

162. See *Nakaz zemskim nachalnikam* (St. Petersburg, 1905).

163. Leontev, "Volostnoi sud," pp. 36–39; Tenishev, *Administrativnoe polozhenie*, pp. 47–48; and Brzheskii, *Naturalnye povinnosti*, pp. 155–156, all disapprove of the land captain, but all acknowledge that he improved volost administration and made it more orderly.

164. This was the late Vladimir Gsovsky's opinion. See also A. A. Kofod, *Russkoe zemleustroistvo* (2nd ed., St. Petersburg, 1914), p. 52.

the *uchastok* that Catherine II's governors-general had initiated in the gubernias over a century before.

The land captains were much criticized throughout the period 1889–1905 as a step backward from Alexander II's reforms.[165] In the last decade P. A. Zaionchkovskii has erected this negative view into a historical interpretation in his exhaustive studies of the motives of those who had to do with the enactment of the statute of 12 July 1889.[166] Zaionchkovskii refers to a number of journalists, courtiers, and high-level statesmen of the 1880s who subscribed to the belief that the privileges of the hereditary gentry should be not only maintained but expanded. From this he concludes that the government's desire to protect gentry interests constituted the principal motivation from which the institution of the land captain derived.[167] The land captains, so Zaionchkovskii says, were established not to serve the state but to please the gentry.

In fact, concern for gentry privilege proceeded basically from faith in gentry usefulness to the government or, to put it in ideological terms, from faith in gentry virtue. But gentry virtue was not a sober conviction of the sort that leads to the formulation of policies. The tsarist government built railroads because its statesmen believed they would carry goods and passengers more effectively than horse carts, but this was not the kind of faith the government placed in the gentry. The statesmen could see a railroad, and they could grant lands to it with the assurance that certain results would be forthcoming. Gentry privilege was not like this. The government tried to rely on the gentry only because there seemed to be nothing else. No one thought gentry virtue was a fact. It was at best a desperate hope, a myth of the same type as slavophile commune worship and liberal faith in the magic of elections; it was one of the ideological straws that capital-city men grabbed at in order to render their actions and proposals intelligible to themselves. Gentry morality (usefulness, privilege) was

165. Leontev, *Krest. pravo* (1914), p. 134, notes that their introduction was one of the most universally condemned government actions in the second half of the nineteenth century.

Capital-city opinion notwithstanding, it is of interest that the populist writer P. I. Iakushkin had praised the arbitrators of the 1860s for being able to do precisely what the land captains were set up to do, i.e., render immediate decisions as the situation called for them—executive, judicial, or legislative. This, said Iakushkin in the 1860s, pp. 142–149, was what the peasants needed and wanted.

166. See his "Zakon o zemskikh nachalnikakh 12 iiuliia 1889 goda," *Nauchnye doklady vysshei shkoly*, no. 2 (1961), and, more recently, *Rossiiskoe samoderzhavie*, pp. 366–396.

167. Zaionchkovskii, "Zakon o zemskikh nachalnikakh," pp. 45–50.

never a policy in itself but rather an exalted way of talking about policies, a way to express the government's practical needs in terms that would allow the servitors to conceive of the government as meaningful to themselves. It did not produce the concept of the land captain or any particular idea of reform. It neither justified the absolute power of the land captains nor required it by force of logic. Depending on how it was used, the myth of gentry virtue could have provided a rationale for any kind of reform—administrative, constitutional, democratic, or even revolutionary. It was at least as basic to Kakhanov's proposal to make the uezd zemstvo the supreme arbiter in the countryside as it was to Tolstoi's land captains.

The practical reasoning behind the land captains stemmed from the realization that legal system would neither work nor develop by itself in the countryside and from the belief that only one-man rule held forth any hope of exerting a direct and immediate influence on peasant institutions. Every Russian administrator knew that omnipotent agents were a dangerous expedient and that over a period of time they were unworkable and self-defeating. Throughout the period 1861–1905, however, virtually all Russian statesmen agreed that the situation in the countryside was desperate, and a number of them, especially Dmitri Tolstoi and Alexander III, were willing to resort to desperate measures to cope with it.[168] The decree announcing the publication of the statute of July 1889 said specifically that its purpose was to do something about the "absence of authority" in the villages.[169]

The statute of 1889 did require the land captains to be of the gentry, and statesmen who supported it did believe the gentry to be more virtuous than other men, but this was primarily a matter of rhetoric. Once Tolstoi and his henchmen decided that one-man absolute rule in the countryside was an administrative necessity, they had to explain it away to a government dedicated to the development of legal system. Of course, they could point to the need for drastic action, but another necessary justification was that the person who was to be entrusted with absolute authority possessed a higher morality and reliability than the common run of men. Gentry virtue was this justification. It was a myth twisted to suit the government's practical purposes, not a purpose in itself. It appealed to Tolstoi primarily because it made sense out of something he thought he had to do.

The myth of gentry virtue had a broader foundation than the simple

168. The senatorial *revizii* of 1880–1881 had made it clear to all segments of opinion in the government that administrative disorder in rural society was a serious and growing problem (see above, nn. 40, 46).
169. *TPSZ*, 6195.

need to justify a new administrative procedure. The enactors of the statute of 1889 sincerely believed that the hereditary gentry were the foundation of the state and that they had to be drawn into and kept in its high offices. Quite apart from traditions of service that went back to Peter I's time, the landholding gentry had in fact carried out the Liberation, and in the 1880s they were still virtually the only enlightened people in Russia who not only talked about the countryside but also lived and worked in it. Moreover, there was a strong tendency among some elements in capital-city society of the nineteenth century to admire England and to believe that Russia would do well to follow the English pattern of land ownership—i.e., large estates farmed by tenants according to the dictates of noble landowners who were all educated in a few elitist schools to believe they were Roman Stoics after the images of Cicero and Marcus Aurelius.[170]

But none of these mythical foundations had much to do with reality. The Russian gentry of the late nineteenth century had given no indication that they could carry out a reform. Indeed, the shortage of qualified gentry—to say nothing of virtuous gentry—was one of the most

170. As minister of education in 1866–1880, Dmitri Tolstoi had set up the classical gymnasia on the assumption that the primary need of Russia's educated classes was to receive a standard education in Latin language and Roman Stoic virtue. One of the prime movers behind this scheme was the journalist Mikhail N. Katkov. On his notions regarding the gentry and England, see Katz, pp. 86–98, 148–155. Katkov shared these general views on the gentry and the English model with a number of statesmen. See Edward Thaden, *Conservative Nationalism in Nineteenth-Century Russia* (Seattle, 1964), pp. 157–178. For a brief description of the English model, see W. Schiff, "Die Agrargesetzgebung der europäischen Staaten vor und nach dem Kriege," *Archiv für Sozialwissenschaft und Sozialpolitik,* LIV (1925), 91–93.

There was a movement among some of the gentry in the 1880s–1900s to preserve (or create) a landholding aristocracy in Russia. Its followers advocated the establishment of inheritance by primogeniture and tried to block admission to gentry status by promotion in government service. Nongentry should be admitted, they said, only by acquiring enough land to meet minimum requirements (see below, n. 176). Their most practical and insistent demand was for the extension of government credit to landholders. Concerning this movement, see Iu. B. Solovev, "Pravitelstvo i politika ukrepleniia klassovykh positsii dvorianstva v kontse XIX veka," in Nosov, *Vnutrenniaia,* pp. 239–280; L. P. Minarik, "Kharakteristika krupneishikh zemlevladeltsev Rossii kontsa XIX i nachala XX v.," in *Ezhegodnik . . . 1963,* pp. 639–708; and A. M. Anfimov, *Krupnoe pomeshchiche khoziaistvo evropeiskoi Rossii* (Moscow, 1969), pp. 43–47. The government's response to the demand for credit on gentry estates was quite generous (Gindin, pp. 66–105), and a number of laws were enacted in the 1890s to help the gentry maintain their estates and make them productive (Iu. B. Solovev, pp. 240–250). Even in these matters, however, the government was not supporting the gentry as a value in itself, nor was it catering to their interests out of weakness. Basically, the statesmen were seeking an instrument to carry out reforms in rural Russia.

telling arguments advanced against the statute of 1889.[171] Alexander
III himself acknowledged the shortage in a marginal note of 30
January 1889 in which he stated that the zemstvoes' justices of the
peace would have to be eliminated in rural areas "in order to assure
that the necessary number of reliable land captains will be available."[172] But even the "reliable" gentry in no way resembled Cicero's
fantasies, and the Russian policy-makers knew it. Mikhail N. Katkov,
one of the most ardent believers in an English-Ciceronian landed
gentry, was highly critical of the Russian variety as they were in the
flesh. Their virtue was not something he actually saw, only a hope he
clung to because he could see no other basis for government action in
the countryside.[173]

In any case, the ideal servitor that the land captain was supposed to
embody bore no resemblance to any existing aristocracy, English or
otherwise. According to Tolstoi's notion of the ideal Russian gentry,
they were "established by the state, in the name of and for the satisfaction of the needs of the state, as servitors . . . upholders of the
old tradition of unflinching loyalty to the Throne and conscientious
service to the people."[174] Tolstoi's gentry were not primarily inheritors
of a tradition but crusaders serving a cause. For Tolstoi, "loyalty to
the Throne" meant primarily the abandonment of privilege and the
destruction of traditional social relationships in the name of unquestioning service to the state.[175] When he referred to virtuous gentry, he
was talking not about good landholders but about government servitors
to whom he had to allow a measure of independent authority. By contrast, most of the gentry-virtue crowd—those who looked to the

171. See, e.g., Boris Mansurov's note of 15 Dec. 1888, in TsGIAL, f. 1149,
t. 4, d. 44, ll. 765–768.
172. *Ibid.*, l. 853.
173. Katz, pp. 87–88, 150.
174. Quoted in Kataev, III, 17–18.
175. K. Golovin, a believer in gentry virtue who bitterly opposed the statute
of 1889, accused Tolstoi of putting all his faith in government officials rather
than landowning gentry, "as if a uniform would guarantee the suitability and good
intentions of a *chinovnik*" (Golovin, II, 53).
Vladimir P. Meshcherskii once expressed an idea of gentry virtue that corresponded closely to Tolstoi's in an anecdote about Prince Vasilii A. Dolgorukov,
head of the third section from 1856 to 1866. When a deranged student tried
to shoot Alexander II in 1866, Dolgorukov went to Alexander and offered his
resignation. Alexander refused, saying that the shooting was no fault of Dolgorukov or his organization. But Dolgorukov insisted on resigning; even if it
wasn't his fault, he said, he should take the blame in order to reassure public
opinion that measures were being taken and wrongs being righted. This, said
Meshcherskii, was a "real Russian nobleman" (II, 17–18).

English model—believed that landholding, not service, was the prime source of virtue.[176]

Zaionchkovskii is correct in asserting that Tolstoi *said* he was re-establishing the influence of the hereditary gentry in the countryside. Perhaps this is what he actually thought he was doing. The fact is, however, that he repeatedly stated his belief in the land captains as a "first step" toward reform, which suggests that he saw them basically as a means to act, not as an institution to be preserved.[177] The statute of 1889 did actually furnish a means to act, and in the end it did not maintain the influence of the landholding gentry. Its practical effect was to extend bureaucracy into the countryside and to weaken traditional privilege. It will be recalled that in 1897, less than a decade after the establishment of the land captains, the MVD was already seeking ways to impose administrative controls on them in order to make them over into full-fledged bureaucrats. The establishment of the land captains constituted not a retreat from the Liberation but a continuation and development of the practical measures by which the Liberation had been carried out.

E. Development of Gubernia-Level Coordination

The main purpose of this chapter has been to trace the conflict between the MVD and the MF to roots in the interaction between government and rural society. It has been suggested that these roots lay in the evolution of the MVD-governor-police hierarchy from the 1830s on, which proceeded in turn from the helplessness of rural society and from the basic need to maintain some sort of unity in territorial government while the central government was extending its ministerial agencies into the countryside. Conflicts broke out on the gubernia level between the governor-police organization and the ministerial agencies—the former concerned to keep each territory in order and the latter to render the empire as a whole into a coherent system and develop its economy. Coherence in the separate ministries allowed these conflicts to be transferred to St. Petersburg, where they

176. In early 1896 an all-Russian conference of gubernia gentry marshals approved by a substantial majority proposals to make it harder to attain gentry status by government service and easier to do it by acquiring land. See Iu. B. Solovev, pp. 257–258.

177. TsGIAL, f. 1149, t. 4, d. 44, l. 4. See also A. Pazukhin, *Sovremennoe sostoianie Rossii i soslovnyi vopros* (Moscow, 1886), pp. 7–12, 37–38, 44–60; Gurko, pp. 146–147. Pazukhin, says Zaionchkovskii, *Rossiiskoe samoderzhavie*, p. 366, was the man who first thought up the idea of the land captains and wrote the initial draft of the statute of 1889.

created, among other things, a gap between the MF and the MVD. This gap, in turn, rendered the central ministries unable to function within a single system and served to exacerbate the conflicts between their gubernia agencies. Under these circumstances the tsarist government was unable to establish a unified system of regulation through which it could control local organs. Thus it was inherently incapable of carrying out any large-scale program of executive reform during the period 1861–1905.

In order to make these points, I have perforce slurred over some significant developments in operational system and executive coordination that went forward in the gubernia organizations despite the difficulties involved, and it is time to say a word about them.

Above all, gubernia administration needed a device for securing systematic cooperation among ministerial organs. The only institutions that held forth any promise of developing in this direction were the gubernia-level standing committees. Here ministerial agents could make collective decisions that might hopefully be binding upon them all and give a measure of institutional form to gubernia administration as a whole. As has been noted, there were a number of these boards, some permanent and some temporary, usually comprised of the heads of ministerial organs and presided over by the governor or vice-governor. Their membership was always flexible, in order to allow any administrative official or local figure to participate in decisions that fell under his jurisdiction.

By 1905 the most significant of the standing committees as far as rural government was concerned was the gubernia board (*prisutstvie*), the inter-agency regulatory body for peasant affairs that was set up along with the land captains in 1889 and remained the chief gubernia-level governing body for the peasants until 1917. The membership of the board is shown in Figure 2.

The gubernia board had little formal authority to do anything but supervise routine operations, hear appeals, and decide disputes in such a way as not to set any formal precedents or establish any general rules. No agreement among the members could have any force beyond the particular case at hand because they each took their orders from a separate superior. A single order from any ministry, with or without the tsar's imprimatur, could prevent that ministry's agent from honoring any precedent or abiding by any rule established in the gubernia board.

On the face of it there seems to have been no reason for the members of the board to want to work through it and to use it as a means to coordinate with their colleagues. To use the board meant to rely on it and to accept its rulings as binding. But why do that if the other members could not in fact be depended on to observe the rules and if one's own superior in St. Petersburg might issue orders that contradicted the local rulings? If such a board possessed any real legislative power, it threatened a ministerial agent's freedom of action without offering any of the reciprocal advantages of formal cooperation. Was it not simpler to deal directly with the governor on those occasions when some degree of coordination was necessary? Was it not also more convenient for the governor to work directly with the separate administrators than to go through the formal procedures of the board? In 1904–1906, when the zemstvoes formed an all-Russian congress to organize medical support for the army in Manchuria, no one suggested that they work through the gubernia board or any other gubernia standing committee in order to get the administration organized behind them. Instead, the government fell back on the more familiar method of using the governor's police power to clear the regular administration out of the zemstvoes' way. Circulars went out (6 October 1904 and 6 December 1905) directing the governors to "remove any obstacles" to the zemstvoes' work, but there were no orders to rally an administrative organization to their support.[178] Obviously, the gubernia level did not yet possess an administration that could organize itself around a program.

These considerations make it all the more significant that some of the gubernia-level standing committees, chiefly the gubernia board itself, not only continued to exist in the late nineteenth century but actually expanded their organizations. The most important formal improvement was the introduction of permanent members.[179] The statute of July 1889 appointed two of these to the gubernia board, and by 1905 the number had grown to four in most gubernias. Supposedly, they took care of administration, peasant appeals, famine relief, and peasant emigration to Siberia respectively, although in practice they seem to have distributed the work as it suited them.[180] The permanent members were appointed by the governor (with MVD approval) from among the gentry, normally on the basis of previous administrative experience. Unlike their colleagues, they belonged to no other standing committees and had no duties apart from the affairs of the gubernia board itself. They personally supervised the chancellery and

178. Polner, pp. 131–135.
179. On the general use of permanent members in gubernia-level committees after 1900, see Lazarevskii, II, 253. Korkunov, writing in the 1890s, foresaw their usefulness—see *RGP*, II, 684–690, especially p. 689.
180. See the report of an inspection of five gubernia administrations in 1907, in *IZO* (Apr. 1908), p. 240.

saw to the scheduling and arrangement of the board's business. The permanent members generally seem to have dominated the gubernia boards. Other members had little to do but approve their decisions.[181]

The significance of the permanent members lies not so much in what they had accomplished by 1905 but, rather, in the trend they reflected. The growing use of them suggests that tsarist administrators were coming to see some value in institutions of coordination on the gubernia level in spite of all the perfectly sound reasons for trying to evade them and to keep their power at a minimum. The introduction of permanent administrative staffs with voting privileges and executive powers had the obvious purpose of giving real force to the inter-agency decisions of the standing committees, even though this constituted a constraint on the ministries themselves.

It has been noted that government organs on the uezd level cooperated effectively to carry out the agrarian reforms of 1906–1914, and it has been suggested that their performance reflects their development toward a systematic order during the preceding decades. The same may be said for the standing committees on the gubernia level. Initially, in 1906–1907, the organizational framework within which the agrarian reforms were carried out consisted only of a permanent interministerial committee in St. Petersburg and the uezd-level commissions that actually operated in the field. By 1909, however, an executive bureaucracy had emerged under the ministry of agriculture, and its center of operation and coordination turned out to be a committee on the gubernia level, comprised of ministerial agents and elected representatives and dominated in practice by a permanent member who was himself an agent of the ministry of agriculture. In at least one case, then, a gubernia-level standing committee was able to coordinate the ministerial agencies in an effective executive program (see above, n. 69). The gubernia-level committees of 1905 were at least potentially viable as institutions of territorial government in European Russia, and it may be surmised that in the preceding decades the growing interdependence of the ministerial agencies was gradually producing systematic working relationships as well as conflicts in the gubernias.

In conclusion, disorder was not the most basic feature of the tsarist government in 1861–1905. On the contrary, the emergence of recognizable polarized conflicts was only a part of the essential development in Russian government during the nineteenth century, from a

181. Lazarevskii, II, 253–255. It will be recalled that a permanent member was also introduced to the gubernia board for zemstvo and municipal affairs in 1900.

long-standing and deep-seated social amorphousness toward a Russia-wide structure of more or less systematic relationships. The year 1905 saw not only a climax of social upheaval but also the beginning of an unprecedented consolidation of administrative system, seemingly diverse tendencies that were in reality parts of the same phenomenon: the imposition of system on the Russian countryside. Violent conflicts between bureaucratic system and personal authority, and between central and local institutions, were not consequences of some defect in the constitutional structure of the government, nor did they proceed from any inherent disorderliness in Russian society or Slavic personality. They arose from the aspirations of administrators on all levels to govern Russia effectively. Indeed, they could not conceivably have arisen if the servitors had not aspired to govern effectively, each according to his own concept of duty.

CHAPTER X

Conclusion

All histories which narrate the death and not the life of peoples, of states, of institutions, of customs, of literary and artistic ideals, of religious conceptions are to be considered false.

BENEDETTO CROCE

The purpose of this book has been to describe the organization that in 1905 was about to go creaking and blundering into a comprehensive program of action to impose social change on the Russian peasantry—the first such program actually to be carried out in Russian history. The impulse to impose social change for its own sake may be said to have come to life in the time of Peter the Great, though in his time and for more than a century thereafter it was no more than an implication in the government's policies and actions. Senatorial government arose not from any conscious desire to force change on Russian society but simply from the need to make it support a military organization. Insofar as senatorial institutions embodied a social ideal, it consisted of the implicit assumption that legal-administrative system would emerge in Russia by itself if the government only kept its records properly and prevented disorders, famines, and epidemics from getting out of hand. It was only after 1861, when the apparatus of serfdom and senatorial institutions was finally cleared out of the way, that the necessity for government-imposed social change began to grow into an unavoidable demand for immediate action. True, there had been conscious attempts before 1861 to impose social change: chiefly Arakcheev's and Kiselev's. These, however, had not proceeded from necessity. The military colonies could fail and Kiselev could soften his programs, but the government waddled on. Only in the 1900s did Russian statesmen come to feel that Russia's fate rested on the success or failure of their efforts to change the villages.

Enlightened Russians never abandoned the old senatorial assumption. They never ceased to believe that social change would somehow take place by itself, without any unpleasant interference from on high, if only the capital cities could settle on a proper law, or policy, or ideology. Catherine II's procuracy, Alexander I's ministers, Kiselev's reforms of the state domains, Alexander II's Liberation, and Alexander

III's land captains were all presumed by their creators to be nothing more than government reorganizations that would *allow* society to develop. None of them were expressly designed to impose social change, because if anyone had acknowledged that he intended to change the people, he would have had to admit to himself and his colleagues that he was advocating an invasion against them.

The agrarian reform of 1906–1914 was also conceived by men who had no intention of imposing social change. The enactors all insisted that they wanted only to *allow* individual peasants to change their way of life, and they took pains to show how their proposed measures would make it possible for the peasants to do what they "really" (naturally) wanted to do. Unlike all previous programs, however, the agrarian reforms of 1906–1914 did accompany a sweeping social change that was in large part government-imposed.[1]

What changes had occurred in 1711–1905 that allowed the government-society and the peasantry to react to each other in relatively systematic fashion from 1906 on? I have not answered this question fully, but I have tried to describe some changes that occurred in government-society during the eighteenth and nineteenth centuries in order to give an indication of the problems it faced in 1905 and the means available to it for coping with these problems.

In the eighteenth century senatorial institutions were founded to establish uniform standards of legality, but they did not do this. Instead, they devoted themselves to cranking out ad hoc decisions to suit the immediate circumstances of each case entrusted to them. Their work neither produced nor maintained permanent, consistent legal norms. On the other hand, their experience gave rise to an aspiration to bring systematic order to the government-society and, ultimately, to the peasantry.

In the nineteenth century, ministries were established for the purpose of reorganizing senatorial government into a single administrative system. Instead of doing this, however, they developed into separate organizations, each with its own purpose. Far from strengthening senatorial government, they were driven by their functional responsibilities into an attack on its "corrupt" ad hoc procedures, and when they completed their attack, they found themselves involved, willy-nilly, in a full-scale invasion of rural society itself. At the same time their diverse functional responsibilities prevented them from establishing any uniform institutional basis for their own mutual coordination.

1. See Yaney, "Concept," and "Agricultural Administration."

Ministerial government, then, embodied a complex historical development that included seemingly contradictory tendencies. Bureaucracy arose from the government-society's absurd aspiration to cut itself off from its old hierarchical ties with rural society and at the same time to force rural society to follow its lead. "Flaws" in the bureaucracy, chiefly its "failure" to establish some institutional basis for interministerial coordination, reflected the government-society's continuing need and aspiration to communicate with peasant society and seek roots in it.

We have seen that in 1905 absolute personal authority was still a major element in the tsarist government at all levels of its organization. "Supreme" organs, which were supposed to guarantee systematic legality and interministerial coordination, remained susceptible to subversion or violation. Under the circumstances one might well ask whether any systematization really took place in the tsarist government in 1711–1905. Was there any essential difference, for example, between the actions and attitudes of Gavril Derzhavin in 1801–1803 and those of Sergei Witte in the 1890s?

The answer is yes. It is true that neither Derzhavin nor Witte was willing to accept the constraints of systematic legality, but their reasons were very different. For Derzhavin, political action consisted of currying and using the tsar's favor primarily in order to impose his personal views on the government's legislation and to maintain his personal status against attacks by personal rivals. Witte also curried and used the tsar's favor against personal rivals, but he had much more to do than this. Unlike Derzhavin, Witte derived his personal power and his purposes almost entirely from the organization for whose functioning he was responsible, i.e., his ministry. He had not only to please the tsar but also to make his ministry work, and in his day there were reliable ways to *measure* and *identify* the success or failure of its work. In 1905 ministerial organizations were recognizable entities. They had relatively clear responsibilities that were either met or not met, and it was relatively difficult to manufacture successes or conceal failures by resorting to oratory or friends in power. In 1905 a statesman had to serve his own organization in order to win his fights. This was what distinguished Witte from Derzhavin, and this distinction represents the essential achievement of ministerial government in the nineteenth century.

A. The Impact of Systematization

ON PEASANT SOCIETY

By 1905 a worldwide economic order and a Russia-wide legal-administrative system had impinged upon the villages of Russia, giving rise to a new network of social relationships. The chief characteristic that distinguished this new order from traditional society was the tremendous power accruing to an individual who was able to take part in it. In the old order a man could only manipulate his fellow villagers to serve the very limited purposes that custom embodied. In the new order he could initiate actions, such as borrowing money or bringing a legal suit, that could evoke predictable reactions on a truly massive scale. True, the individual in the new order was vulnerable to influences beyond his control. A depression in Germany, an international crisis in Africa, or a new law from St. Petersburg— each could "ruin" him. Even so, the new order could outlast the ruin of any number of its members, and the power it afforded to its successful members was infinitely greater than that which the traditional hierarchies of the Russian countryside could generate.

In each area a few individuals suddenly acquired power of a high order. By utilizing their "freedom" to act according to laws that were far beyond what local notions of right and wrong could comprehend, they availed themselves of capital while their neighbors fell into debt. They learned to depend on the very legal-administrative system that was rendering their neighbors helpless. At the same time, as they became aware of the new order and learned to depend on it, their old village society became irrelevant to them, and they were likely to abandon it, together with its values and constraints.

The impact of market and bureaucracy on peasant society, then, was doubly disastrous. On the one hand, it left the peasants at the mercy of forces their customary relationships of mutual dependence could not comprehend. On the other, it assured that whenever an individual peasant learned to manipulate the new forces, he would separate himself from his fellows and leave them as helpless as ever. Indeed, he might even victimize them himself. Thus the effect of market and bureaucracy was to assure that peasant society would remain helpless. Modernization not only brought calamities; it assured that the peasants would not be able to respond collectively to them.

Russian peasants were not the only people in the world to experience the glories and degradations of systematization, but in Russia the experience came relatively suddenly and drastically to a great mass of people who were far less prepared to cope with it than their brethren in Europe. The massive famines of the 1890s and 1900s in the grain-producing areas suggest a more profound cultural shock than anything that occurred in the West.

A. I. Shingarev's investigation of a village in Voronezh gubernia in 1902–1903 brought to light a story that epitomizes the peasants' condition.[2] The local zemstvo had established an orphanage about a decade before Shingarev came. In a very short time the building filled to capacity, and the authorities were forced to take care of the overflow by placing orphans with peasant families, each of which received an allowance from the zemstvo to cover the cost of maintenance. After a few years the zemstvo observed that the orphans placed with families suffered a rather high mortality rate. Fifty-two out of sixty died in the period 1891–1900. Some families lost an orphan as often as every two years, and they no sooner buried one than they returned for another. What the families were doing, it seems, was starving the orphans while using the zemstvo allowance to keep themselves alive.[3]

It will not do to explain away this kind of behavior by referring to oppressive government (as Shingarev did), nor will it suffice to say that the peasants were backward. The peasants who took in orphans in order to starve them were not backward at all; they were quite advanced. They were responding individually to the zemstvo's reform, improving their situation while learning to take care of themselves. No advocate of "progress" could ask for better results. On the other hand, the willingness of the more advanced peasants to starve children before the indifferent eyes of their fellow villagers indicates that the zemstvo's efforts at reform were rendering peasant society helpless.

This is not to say that the zemstvo caused children to die who otherwise would have lived. On the contrary, the net effect of the orphanage was probably to save lives. What the zemstvo did was to impose an alien standard on the village regarding the proper care of orphans, thereby dramatizing the village's inability to measure up to it. The orphanage did not cause the peasants to lose the ability to act collectively. They had never possessed this ability. It taught them, rather, to *believe* they were losing their unity and that therefore they were becoming helpless. Given this belief, they actually did become unable to act collectively even in customary ways.

ON GOVERNMENT

Throughout the period under study Russian statesmen continued to hold the personal authority of the tsar and his agents above the law

2. A. I. Shingarev, *Vymiraiuschchaia derevnia* (2nd ed., St. Petersburg, 1907), reprinted as a part of K. M. Shuvaev, *Staraia i novaia derevnia* (Moscow, 1937). Voronezh is in the heart of the grain-producing region.

3. *Ibid.*, p. 14.

even as they labored to establish legal institutions that would limit personal authority. One of my main purposes has been to seek out the historical roots of this seeming paradox, and it is appropriate to include some remarks on it here.

One word of caution. We are concerned here not with all elements in the tsar's personal authority, only with those which made it meaningful and practically necessary to administrators. Obviously, the tsar image was traditional and Orthodox, and on this basis it still appealed to the imaginations of backward peasants and ignorant priests. But traditional elements only explain why the tsar image had symbolic and ceremonial importance. They do not explain why many enlightened Russians continued to rely on it and organize themselves around it in 1905. The following discussion takes up only those attributes of the tsar image that made it a vital part of the government-society's development toward legal-administrative system.

From the perspective of 1905, the most significant development that systematization had brought to Russia during the preceding two centuries was the transformation of the "pile of islands" that had made up the old tribute-collecting hierarchy into two profoundly contradictory elements: an urban society resting on a system of distribution, and a hierarchical rural society resting on the social isolation of the villages. In 1905 these elements had been identified, but they were not organized around a conscious political struggle. Fortunately so, because if such a fight had come into the open, it would have been a destructive zero-sum affair in which one side's victory would have meant the other's annihilation. This was no labor-management dispute, or class struggle, or interministerial conflict, or gap between intelligentsia and government. In these latter conflicts both sides have to depend on one another as they struggle, and their warfare can be a means of communication, leading to a continuing accommodation. Not so in a conflict between urban distribution and traditional hierarchy. Each can only exist by destroying the other; thus an open fight between them produces nothing but destruction. In the 1900s industrialization and enlightenment were threatening to deepen the conflict and thereby to plunge Russia into an aimless, massive bloodbath. One aspect of the tsar's personal authority, then, was the inability of any institution to bridge these two irreconcilable elements in any consistent way. Personal authority was quite possibly the only conceivable basis (device) for holding them together within a single political order, precisely because its purposes and decisions did not have to be consistent or even explicit.

Not only did the government-society require the tsar image in order to symbolize the unity of Russian society as a whole; it also needed personal authority as a practical means to organize itself. Interaction between government and rural society had begun in Peter's time as an attack on traditional hierarchies, and the government-society had subsequently evolved both as the attack and as the structure being attacked. This combination produced an arrangement in which servitors went on working in the traditional manner while pretending to be parts of a system. In order to work together and depend on one another, they formed tight little groups—hierarchies of pretenders— each one organized in fact around customs, rituals, and liturgical slogans of its own but pretending to be part of a functioning organization. By transforming laws and orders into rituals, each subordinate was able to use legal system to evade his superior's control and to escape responsibility for accomplishing his tasks. Despite all laws and commands to the contrary, therefore, the government's officials were not susceptible to systematic control. It often happened that they could be moved to action only by the threat of arbitrary force. Thus system slowly inserted itself into the government through a series of violent conflicts between those who felt a moral impulse to impose the reality of system on government and those for whom the introduction of an operational system meant the shattering of all the government they knew, i.e., their rituals and pretenses. Reform from on high set in motion a self-perpetuating cycle, continually establishing hierarchies that pretended to be systems and then disrupting them in the name of system. There was no way to break the cycle. The government could only cope with its contradictions from day to day on an ad hoc basis.

Under the circumstances government-society learned from experience to conceive of legal-administrative system not only as a moral obligation but also as a hated imposition. As Russians slowly learned to organize themselves systematically, the basis for their organizations was always at least partly their common opposition to administrative direction. If a servitor attacked the pretense of legality in the name of authentic system, he conceived himself to be attacking "formalistic bureaucrats." If, on the other hand, he was involved in an organization that was working reasonably well on the basis of established pretenses, then he was inclined to join with his fellows in opposing the interference of "arbitrary bureaucrats." In either case the servitor and his colleagues felt themselves to be in league against legal-administrative system, the hated *biurokratiia*. Whatever a servitor was opposing, the formal law that hid corruption or an arbitrary crusader who was breaking the formal law, he called his enemy *biurokratiia* and saw himself as a defender of "freedom" against system. All members of the government-society could agree to at least one thing: they hated the system they were creating. Systematization strengthened hostility to government authority in all its aspects at the same time that it brought order to its organization. When this hostility evolved from the old struggle between subordinate and superior into the new bureaucratic struggle between ministerial apparatuses, it meant that society was "progressing," but hostility and tension did not disappear from the government organization.

Given the opposition to system inherent in the process of systematization, the image of the absolute tsar made a certain amount of sense to those who served the Russian state. The tsar embodied both pretense and aspiration to system, both the authority of system-in-being and the hope of progress toward "real" system. His personal authority stood behind the whole edifice of government administration but also remained apart from it, holding forth a vague promise of salvation from its disastrous effects but also the hope that someday it would really work. As long as a man could believe that the tsar's power was absolute, the madness of legal-administrative system was sane. The moral, patriotic Russian could not give his loyalty to legal-administrative system per se, but he could obey a tsar who ordered him to accept or impose its demands and restraints. Thus the autocratic tsar was not only a symbol but also a practical basis for making and enforcing vital governmental decisions. This was why the progress of system in Russia did not displace the myth of personal authority. System grew up under the aegis of the tsar image and remained dependent on it. System made sense to most members of the government-society only if they could believe that it was the expression of the tsar's will.

It is necessary at this point to remind the reader of the approach from which the above remarks have been made. I am not evaluating the tsarist government, only relating the attitudes and actions of its servitors to its historical experience in order to render their behavior intelligible. If I deny that tsarist absolutism was essentially peculiar, or backward, or evil, this does not mean that it was normal, or modern, or good. Above all, it does not mean that the forms of tsarist autocracy were inevitable, any more than the continued existence of the Russian state from 1711 to 1905 was inevitable.

At every stage of the tsarist government's evolution, men *chose* to follow this or that path and *decided* that they would have to act in certain ways to follow it. Their actions produced responses in other men, with results generally unforeseen, and then they had once again to choose and decide. They could at any time have chosen differently or simply refused to choose, and as a result the Russian state might have evolved in a very different way or not at all. The tsar, his servitors, and all politically conscious Russians sensed that vague "forces" were compelling them to do unpleasant things, but these "forces" arose from their own moral urgings and beliefs, not from any abstract necessity hovering eternally above them. If a scholar of today can perceive more clearly than the Russians of tsarist times the nature of the necessities they faced and the implications of what they said and did, it does not follow that these necessities were above and beyond the Russians of that time—inevitabilities into which they were driven like helpless sheep. The scholar's hindsight only renders necessities intelligible to himself; it does not impose them on the past.

Nothing, nothing whatever, forced the Russians of 1711–1905 to depend on the tsar's authority except they themselves through their own choices and actions, their willingness to accept the consequences of their choices and actions, and, fundamentally, their awareness of their mutual dependence. All the circumstances, dilemmas, and historical "laws" that can be perceived in Russia's development played their roles only because the actions and beliefs of the Russians brought them into play. The perpetuation of the institutionally absolute tsar, then, was not unavoidable. It was what Russians chose for a long time to do in order to express their awareness of their mutual dependence.

A legal system did develop in Russia in the two centuries before 1905. By the end of the nineteenth century law courts with judges appointed for life were conducting public jury trials under a judicial code that provided higher instances of appeal and procedural rights for defendants. Judges frequently abrogated orders and actions of the executive administration on the grounds of their illegality, and administrators generally had to comply with the judges' decisions. For those who lived within the law, legal rules formed a basis of sorts on which a citizen could predict the behavior of his fellows and depend on his predictions.

Most contemporary observers rated the Russian judiciary on a par with its European counterparts. The most celebrated defects in Russian justice stemmed from the power of the police to arrest and convict men of "political" crimes without recourse to the courts and from the unrestrained use of postal clerks to read people's mail. But these practices, however unfortunate, affected only a tiny minority of suspected revolutionaries and high-level statesmen. The fundamental defect of Russian legal system was that only about 10–15 percent of the population lived within its framework. The peasant villages still organized themselves around local custom, which meant that although a peasant could be arrested and tried for violating a law, he was not often in a position to seek the protection of the courts on his own behalf. Russian legal system worked well enough in 1905, but it did not cover much of the Russian population.

There was also an administrative system in 1905, certain parts of which worked very well. Railroads, the postal system, institutions of higher learning, and financial administration all possessed reasonably effective organizations. Since the 1880s institutions of local government had been establishing networks of hospitals, elementary schools, and agricultural aid stations. Russian government organization as a whole was good enough in 1905 to enjoy excellent credit in the international money market and to make it desirable, if not always easy, for foreign firms to build and operate industrial plants almost anywhere in Russia. As with the judiciary, however, administrative system did not extend into the countryside. Below the gubernia level there was little more than a confused mixture of influential landholders, arbitrary tribute collectors, and semi-literate police, all of whom were more harassed by system than organized by it.

According to just about everyone who had occasion to record his opinions in that time, including the government officials themselves, Russian government was not operating as it should. The events of 1905 seemed to confirm this opinion. Russia lost a war, suffered major revolutionary outbreaks and famines, and almost went bankrupt. The administration lost confidence in itself to such a degree in the fall of 1905 that it almost perished in its own indecision.

As it turned out, however, Russia's legal-administrative system had not only its structure but also remarkable vitality. In 1905–1906 the government launched a number of constitutional reforms that strengthened the power of legal system over administration by establishing a formal legislative process. At the same time it initiated a sweeping executive program to reduce the countryside to order and develop peasant society into an operational legal system. On the whole, these measures were successful up to the outbreak of World War I, at least in terms of capital-city aspirations. For the first time in history the administration in the countryside began to act somewhat like a system, and peasant society began to reorganize itself around systematic legal relationships. All this suggests that the evolution of Russian government from 1711 to 1905 had produced not only the forms of a legal-administrative system but also a considerable potential for its further development.

Unfortunately, vitality was not all that systematization had produced. By 1905 the government had studied the peasants with some care and learned a great deal about them, but all it had learned was problems, not solutions. Traditional behavior patterns now stood revealed as abuses, and everyone could see that the old organization through which the government had been coping with the peasants was shot through with corruption, brutality, and bigotry. The facts were there in 1905, and there was no escaping them. The tsar had wanted to know how his society was run; now he knew. Now that he did know, his responsibility suddenly extended itself far beyond what any statesmen had ever contemplated. What had been social structure now became a number of evils that required instant correction, and the government had to do the correcting. Any suggestion that rural society should be allowed to work out its own difficulties was no longer admissible. The government in 1905 not only possessed a system with some vitality; it was committed irrevocably to system. Its organization, therefore, was committed irrevocably to massive and rapid social reform.

The government's situation in 1905 was analogous to that of our zemstvo in Voronezh gubernia. It will be recalled that the zemstvo introduced a measure to serve the public welfare; i.e., it built an orphanage. In effect, however, the zemstvo was doing much more. It was attacking a practice—the abandonment of orphans—that had always played an important role in the village economy, and it was denouncing this practice as evil. Suddenly the orphans were not something to be ignored; they were a problem. Suddenly the zemstvo found itself responsible for achieving the general aim that its limited action had only implied, even if it lacked the resources to do so. It brought an orphanage to the peasantry; ergo, it must now take care of all orphans. It had taken one step toward eliminating the evil it was denouncing; as a result, it had to assume full responsibility for the evil. In the absence of sufficient resources—human and material—for the immediate construction of new orphanages, what could the zemstvo do in the face of the public wrath its own efforts had awakened? The answer we have already seen, and we have also seen that the practical results of its laudable efforts were not altogether positive. In precisely the same way the effects of the tsarist government's reforms were not altogether positive even when they were effectively carried out. When the government uncovered evils, it did not simultaneously find the means to cope with them. When it did act to correct the evils that it found, its efforts did not teach the peasants to organize themselves and to depend on one another. On the contrary, progress taught everyone in Russia to blame the government for the existence of the "evil" it was striving to correct.

It may be said, then, that there were three elements in the tsarist government of 1905: the forms of system, the potential for organizational development and constructive social change, and the dilemmas that development was producing. These were the fruits of a remorseless progress that had thrust 160 million people into close interaction before they had developed a full awareness of their mutual dependence. Russia was being enlightend and organized, but the very success of her leaders' efforts was rendering both government and society helpless.

B. The Myths of Ministerial Government

As we have noted, Henry Maine considered that the introduction of equity (system) into a society with no traditional basis for it could destroy the society. He also believed, in mid-nineteenth century, that this was a real danger in "non-progressive"—i.e., non-European—societies. These societies, he said, were threatened by an alien equity that would come upon them with such force as to deny them the luxury of a legal fiction. Lacking a false past, the members of a non-European society would probably find equity acceptable only if it promised future development toward some desirable goal.[4] They would only accept the bonds of system in the name of a fantasy about the future.

Maine's insight has been fully borne out by Russian history ever since the early nineteenth century. Russian government-society's mythology has never been without an element of legal fiction, in particular the "tradition" of the Senate (see above, ch. III, sec. F). Even so, the gradual but seemingly irresistible ascendancy of bureaucracy over senatorial government has reflected a persistent tendency among politically conscious Russians to derive their moral identity from future expectations rather than contrived legends.

The basic future-myth of Russian capital-city society in 1861–1905 was that the peasantry would somehow undergo social change in accordance with this or that ideological fantasy. Aspiration to bring social change to the countryside, reflecting as it did an expanding social consciousness in the capital city, was certainly a desirable phenomenon from any point of view, but it created an atmosphere of utopian expectation at the very time that Russia's rapid economic development was destroying peasant society. The combination of utopian social vision with a calamitous reality gave rise to an abiding sense of failure and frustration among all political groups, including

4. Maine, pp. 75–78.

the government servitors and the tsars themselves. Frustration, in turn, lent a frenzied quality to the aspiration to social change, plunging politically conscious Russians into a vicious cycle of mania and despairing indifference, translating good intentions and elaborate plans into desperate and sporadic actions.

Under these psycho-social circumstances the central government became the natural object of all expectations, including even the hopes of those groups who worked to destroy it. The net effect of rising social consciousness in late nineteenth-century Russia was a powerful and continuing impetus to develop an effective, centralized administration and at the same time to blame whatever central administration there was for all the disappointments and frustrations that systematization produced. All capital-city ideologies, whatever their specific content, served to strengthen the impetus to bureaucratic expansion and also to intensify and organize opposition to bureaucracy.

As has been said, capital-city illusions regarding the efficacy of this or that ideology of social change cannot be dismissed as products of some sort of mental illness, or childishness, or escapism, or backwardness. They constituted myths that made sense of a real need for action. Unfortunately, however, there was sharp disagreement among these future-myths, and the upholders of each one exhibited a strong tendency to attack all the others. Given the practical absurdity of all the government-society's myths, the best defense for any one of them was an elaborate demonstration of how foolish the others were. As a result, we have at hand a great quantity of evidence to the effect that all action in 1861–1905 was futile. Generally speaking, however, attempts to prove the absurdity of this or that program were and are beside the point. Capital-city myths—like all myths—did and could derive their validity not from practical feasibility but primarily from the degree to which they were capable of mobilizing the government-society for action.

It may be argued that a myth which roused the government to action by creating false hopes would bring disaster. This, however, is not necessarily true. Both the Liberation and the agrarian reforms of 1906–1914 were enacted on the basis of false hopes and could not have been enacted without them. Yet they were not disasters.

It could be argued further that a program of action that led into dilemmas held no promise of success.[5] This too is untrue, and it is

5. This argument has always been a favorite among Western students of Russia, especially in the last twenty years. American and European scholars never tire of pointing to gaps between ideology and reality in the Soviet Union and then

the purpose of the following section to point out in a general way why it is untrue. Paradoxical as it may seem, practical dilemmas not only made government action difficult and absurd but also drove capital-city Russians into action. Dilemmas could paralyze politically conscious Russians and at the same time transform their sterile theories, idle dreams, and vague hopes into stern moral commands that had somehow to be obeyed.

It is instructive to compare the moral impetus behind government action and bureaucratization in Russia in 1861–1905 to the phenomenon Max Weber perceived in the self-doubting Calvinist of the sixteenth and seventeenth centuries. According to Weber, the Calvinist's belief in predestination left him helpless before the inescapable conclusion that all action on his part was futile. God had already decided whether he was to be saved or damned, and nothing he could do would change this. Yet the Calvinist did not fall into indifference. Quite to the contrary, the very hopelessness of action lent a moral quality to it, spurring him on to labor consistently rather than sporadically to acquire the visible tokens of salvation. Similarly, the politically conscious Russian of the eighteenth and nineteenth centuries could perceive both the iron necessity for reform in the countryside and the futility of all concrete attempts to achieve it, and his very despair drove him into action. The more appalling the dilemma, the more consistent and/or ruthless he became.

The difference between Weber's Calvinist and a morally sensitive capital-city Russian of 1861–1905 lies in the content of their respective myths. The Calvinist's dilemma involved only himself and God. He had no way to tell whether he had been marked for eternal blessedness or eternal damnation, but he could look into himself to seek signs of good or evil tendencies that would indicate what God had willed for him. Naturally, he was inclined to emphasize the good he found and to suppress or repress whatever he regarded as evil. If he could organize himself so that he saw nothing but holiness in his thoughts and feelings, he could hope for salvation. Despite the harsh dictum that conscious, purposeful striving for blessedness was futile, he could still strive to assure himself that he had already been blessed by mobilizing all his feelings and urgings into a convincing semblance of blessedness. Indeed, it was precisely his acceptance of the utterly hopeless doctrine of predestination at the hands of a rigorously rational God that forced him to seek such assurance.

concluding from their observations that ideology must somehow change if the state is not to collapse. Generally speaking, American students of government do not know what a myth is; consequently they have no idea what a government is.

This continual reorganizing and disciplining of all the senses often produced a very well-organized and resolute man, however "neurotic" he may appear by modern standards. Above all, self-mobilization produced a relatively consistent man. The Calvinist's struggle to associate himself with rationalized blessedness had to be a day-by-day affair. Experience was always threatening to lay bare some basic flaw and throw the poor man's entire identity into a cocked hat. Thus a Calvinist's efforts to cope with the contradiction between his ideal self and the reality within him taught him self-discipline and rendered him exceptionally capable of engaging in long-term projects that required sustained effort. The "virtues" produced by Calvinism corresponded closely to the qualities that enable a man to accumulate capital, and many Calvinists did indeed accumulate capital. Some of them came to believe that the accumulation of capital was a visible sign of blessedness, and they pursued their trades with moral fervor, not merely for the sake of gain.[6]

The dilemma of the politically conscious Russian proceeded from a different world view. Unlike the Calvinist, he did not identify himself with a rationalized personal God and a universe governed by unforgiving laws. For him, God was something of a given. Orthodox Russians have feared God and sought his love as intensely as anyone, but they have not been so inclined as Westerners to define and codify what God demanded of the individual. Generally speaking, Orthodoxy has assumed morality to be a relatively simple matter, not a rational structure that must somehow fit into an unequivocally logical universe. Orthodox believers, therefore, have not characteristically found their own individual sensations and urgings hopelessly at odds with the unwavering expectations of a logical God. The capital-city Russian's individual relationship with God did not pose an unresolvable dilemma; hence it did not generate a force such as that which early Calvinists felt. The enlightened Russian did not learn to repress his own feelings and make himself systematic in order to secure his own personal salvation. He did see himself as part of a rationalized universe and he did confront its dilemmas, but his experience taught him that his people were hopelesly at odds with his universe, not he

---

6. Weber's ideas with regard to the significance of Calvinism in the rise of capitalism have been much discussed and partly refuted. He was probably wrong to insist that Calvinism was a prerequisite for the rise of capitalism, but it is valid to say that Calvinism was an extreme expression of that rationalizing quality that has been inherent in all forms of Western Christianity. The psycho-social dilemma that Weber saw confronting the Calvinists confronted all Western Christians to some degree, and it is probably true that the resulting passion for consistency had much to do with the rise of modern economic organization.

as an individual. The laws of the enlightened Russian's universe were as unforgiving as those laid down by the Calvinist's rationalized God, but it was Russian society that they did not forgive. It was Russian society, therefore, whose "salvation" was at stake. The dilemma that aroused the capital-city Russian's moral fervor and caused him to repress the evidence of his senses was his society's dilemma, not his own; consequently, his moral identity resided primarily in his concept of society and his relation to it, not in his concept of himself. Insofar as he felt himself to be morally responsible, he felt obliged to answer for his "people" and to assure himself relentlessly of their "blessedness," not to answer for his personal urgings or to assure himself of his own individual oneness with the universe. Instead of escaping his own personal doom by organizing himself into a semblance of blessedness, he escaped from the obvious absence of system in Russian society by assuring himself that Russian society was fundamentally "just" and by striving to impose a facade of (or crusade toward) system on all his relationships with it.

For an enlightened Russian, the demands of system were fully as much a part of personal identity as the Calvinist's rational God was for him. The Calvinist crusaded, as it were, against himself, and this inner, psychological crusade made him value proper *behavior* for its own sake. A member of government-society in Imperial Russia crusaded against his people rather than himself, and this social crusade organized him around consistent social attitudes, to the point where he came to value proper *attitudes* for their own sake. Psychologically, however, the enlightened Russian was very close to Weber's Calvinist. Both inadvertently made a fetish of system. Both sensed dilemmas in their respective identities, and their respective dilemmas implanted a moral impetus to act and to organize themselves consistently: the one as a separate individual, the other as part of a social movement.

Calvinist and Russian social attitudes were radically different. In practice, a Calvinist's economic action was intensely social, and his aim to accumulate capital rendered him heavily dependent on his community, yet both action and aims proceeded from his individual relationship with God. For a Calvinist, God was the demanding standard. The community was a given, a presupposition to which it was not necessary to give much thought. Men who fitted Calvinist asumptions were in the community, those who did not were out, and that was that. The Calvinist community was not itself an object of moral fervor.

Like the Calvinist, the capital-city Russian found psychological release from his dilemma in action, but since he conceived of himself as part of a social movement rather than as a separate individual, he was not so likely to find his release in individual enterprise and the accumulation of money as in the operation of an army, or reform program, or organization. The Russian's satisfaction at forming, running, or joining an organization was fully as egotistical, personal, and religious as any Calvinist's, but he was likely to understand his actions and aims as contributions to the "rise" of Russian, or Slavic, or human civilization. The Calvinist's actions and aims contributed as much to community, nation, and civilization as the Russian's, but he understood them primarily as steps he was taking for his own personal salvation.

It may be suggested that Weber's Calvinist got his social attitudes, in particular the inclination to take his society for granted, from living in a social order in which the myth of system had developed out of legal fictions. Legal-administrative system was part of his birthright, not a means to his salvation. Our ministerial Russian, on the other hand, made society the object of his moral fervor and the locus of his identity because system had come to his social order primarily as a promise of future achievement.

Given the vastly different social attitudes that Western and Russian modernizing myths have embodied, it is not surprising that government-society in Russia should have arrived at an ideal of legal-administrative system somewhat different from the Western model. In the West law grew into modern form as a definition of individual rights. Ideally, it walled off each man in his own cell and assured him that he could wrestle with God in his own way without fear of interference. Modern Western man has seen individual rights as the basic element in legal relationships, and he has been inclined to believe that his duties to the state spring only from them. His ideal of legal system carries the implication that an individual owes nothing to his fellow men except whatever practical effort is necessary to keep the walls around each individual in good repair. This is not to say that modern Western man has no feeling for his fellow men, only that he has not traditionally derived his moral aims from his concept of society.

If legal relationships in the Russian government-society derived from the common attitudes of its members toward society, then it is clear that uniformity of attitude was the most likely basis for coordination. As we have seen, however, the servitors of different ministries and departments held very different attitudes toward society, derived primarily from their very different functions and purposes. As each ministry organized itself effectively, its servitors tended to identify its practices and purposes with those of the whole state. In effect, however, this meant that they conceived of the state as an agency of their ministry rather than the reverse. In 1905 government officials believed in the legal-administrative system as a whole and adhered to it not from their consciousness of their dependence on one another to behave systematically but from the individual compulsion each of them felt to affirm that the functions he himself was performing and the purposes he was serving were vitally necessary to the state.[7]

Moral fervor was all very well; without it, ministerial government never would have evolved. Nevertheless, the ideologies of plan, program, and function that spurred ministerial servitors (and all politically conscious Russians) into their invasion of the countryside did not nurture the habits of coordination and compromise that have imbued legal-administrative system in the European world. Europeans have not characteristically depended wholly on collective action for their salvation (identity); consequently, they have found it relatively easy to make compromises concerning state policies and purposes. For Russian servitors, on the other hand, the government organization was itself their salvation. This is why the different ministries in the tsarist government resembled different religions. This is also why the ideological spirit that united the tsarist government also created such profound disharmony in it.

C. The Significance of Tsarist Experience

The Imperial Russian government was the first in history to attempt—albeit inadvertently—to introduce radical social change into a backward society. Its servitors were the first men to sense the necessity of forcibly uprooting social order in order to preserve political order. The Prussian state was imposed on society from above, but not in the absence of traditional institutions that could mobilize and organize themselves to participate in the process. Prussian monarchy did not destroy or create society but only reformed and reorganized it. The Austrian empire attempted for some centuries to impose a single state on a scattering of traditional societies, each one very different from the others. In Austria, however, "society" was not an amorphous cloud of scattered villages. Each society was coherent and institutionalized in itself, possessing a historical identity (legal fiction) of its own.

7. For further discussion of this point, see my "Some Aspects."

Austrian history, therefore, was not basically one of government-imposed social change but of a long negotiation between central government and a number of local institutions, most of which were as "modern" as the government. As for the Ottoman empire, the idea of imposing social change on its subjects never entered its statesmen's minds except as a matter for idle conversation. In the French, British, and Dutch colonial empires this or that official or magnate dabbled in social reform but only as a small-scale experiment, never as a desperate measure undertaken to save the empire from collapse. Russia, in short, was the very first state to stake its existence—consciously or unconsciously—on its attempts to impose social change on its subjects by administrative means.

In the 1970s government-imposed social change is no longer unique, but the tsarist experience is still relevant. It would be foolish to say that the policies and programs of the tsarist government should be taken as models for any present or future state that engages in government-imposed social change. The history and conditions of the Eurasian steppe were unique, and in any case what the tsarist government did was largely haphazard and unconscious, as is typical of operations that have no historical precedent. In the late twentieth century, however, there is still much to be learned from the story of how Russian administrators gradually became aware of the difficulties and dilemmas involved in contrived social change, and how they kept themselves united in the face of what they took to be their continual failures.

Selected Bibliography

The evolution of the Russian state between 1711 and 1905 is too broad a topic to allow any pretense at including all relevant sources. The following list mentions only materials actually cited in the book plus a very few additional works important enough to demand mentioning. Most of the published materials listed here are available in the United States. For a good list of basic published works on the Imperial Russian government, see M. Szeftel, "Russia before 1917," in John Gilissen, ed., *Bibliographical Introduction to Legal History and Ethnography* (Brussels, 1966).

Aitken, H. G. J., ed. *Explorations in Enterprise.* Cambridge, Mass., 1965.
———, ed. *The State and Economic Growth.* New York, 1959.
Amburger, E. *Geschichte der Behördenorganisation Russlands von Peter dem Grossen bis 1917.* Leiden, 1966.
Amos, M. S. "Roscoe Pound." In *Modern Theories of Law.* London, 1933.
Andreevskii, I. *O namestnikakh, voevodakh, i gubernatorakh.* St. Petersburg, 1864.
Anfimov, A. M. *Krupnoe pomeshchiche khoziaistvo evropeiskoi Rossii.* Moscow, 1969.
———. "Zernovoe khoziaistvo Rossii v gody pervoi mirovoi voiny." In *Materialy po istorii.*
Arnold, Thurman. *The Symbols of Government.* New Haven, Conn., 1935.
Artamanov, M. I. *Istoriia Khazar.* Leningrad, 1962.
Augustine, W. R. "Notes toward a Portrait of the Eighteenth-Century Russian Nobility." *Canadian Slavic Studies,* IV (Fall 1970), 374–425.
Avrekh, A. Ia. *Stolypin i tretia duma.* Moscow, 1968.
"Bank." In Brockhaus and Efron, I (1891), 927–929.
Barker, Ernest. *The Development of Public Services in Western Europe, 1660–1930.* Hamden, Conn., 1966.
Barnard, Chester I. *Functions of the Executive.* Cambridge, Mass., 1938.
Barnett, H. G. *Anthropology in Administration.* Evanston, Ill., 1956.
Baykov, A. "The Economic Development of Russia." *Economic History Review,* VII (Dec. 1954), 137–149.
Beer, V. A. *Kommentarii novykh provintsialnykh uchrezhdenii 12 iuliia 1889 goda.* Moscow, 1894.
Benedict, Ruth. "Myth." In *Encyclopedia of the Social Sciences.* 15 vols. New York, 1937. XI, 178–181.
Benz, E. *The Eastern Orthodox Church.* New York, 1963.

Berliner, Joseph. *Factory and Manager in the USSR*. Cambridge, Mass., 1957.

Bilimovich, A. D. *Ministerstvo finansov, 1802–1902*. Kiev, 1903.

Blau, P. M. *Dynamics of Bureaucracy*. Chicago, 1955.

Blum, J. *Lord and Peasant in Russia*. Princeton, N.J., 1961.

Boba, Imre. *Nomads, Northmen and Slavs*. The Hague, 1967.

Bochkov, N. V. *Istoriia zemelnykh otnoshenii i zemleustroistva*. Moscow, 1956.

Bogoslovskii, M. M. *Issledovaniia po istorii mestnogo upravleniia pri Petre Velikom*. Reprinted from the *Zhurnal ministerstva iustitsii*. St. Petersburg, n.d.

———. *Petr I: Materialy dlia biografii: Tom pervyi, Detstvo-iunost, Azovskie pokhody*. Moscow, 1940.

Bohon, John. "Reactionary Politics in Russia: 1905–1909." Unpublished Ph.D. dissertation, University of North Carolina, 1967.

Braibanti, Ralph. "Public Bureaucracy and Judiciary in Pakistan." In LaPalombara.

———, ed. *Asian Bureaucratic Systems Emergent from the British Imperial Tradition*. Durham, N.C., 1966.

Brandt, Karl. *Management of Agriculture and Food in the German-Occupied and Other Areas of Fortress Europe*. Stanford, Calif., 1953.

Brockhaus, F. A., and I. A. Efron. *Entsiklopedicheskii slovar*. 41 vols. plus 2 supplementary vols. St. Petersburg, 1891–1907.

Brown, Norman. *Life against Death*. London, 1959.

Bruun, Geoffrey. *Europe and the French Imperium*. New York, 1963.

Brzheskii, N. K. *Naturalnye povinnosti krestian i mirskie sbory*. St. Petersburg, 1906.

———. *Ocherki iuridicheskogo byta krestian*. St. Petersburg, 1902.

Burns, C. D. *Government and Industry*. London, 1921.

Byrnes, Robert. *Pobedonostsev, His Life and Thought*. Bloomington, Ind., 1968.

Cambridge Economic History of Europe, vol. VI. Cambridge, 1965.

Carson, George. "The State and Economic Development; Russia, 1890–1939." In Aitken, *The State and Economic Growth*.

Chapman, B. *The Profession of Government*. New York, 1959.

Chayanov, A. V. *The Theory of Peasant Economy*. Homewood, Ill., 1966.

Chechulin, N. D. *Ocherki po istorii russkikh finansov v tsarstvovanie Ekateriny II*. St. Petersburg, 1906.

Cherepnin, L. V. *Obrazovanie russkogo tsentralizovannogo gosudarstva v XIV–XV vekakh*. Moscow, 1960.

Cherkasskii, Vladimir A. *Kniaz Vladimir Aleksandrovich Cherkasskii*. Moscow, 1879.

Cherniavsky, Michael. "Khan or Basileus: An Aspect of Russian Medieval Theory." *Journal of the History of Ideas*, XX (Oct.–Dec. 1959), 459–476.

————. "The Old Believers and the New Religion." *Slavic Review*, XXV (Mar. 1966), 1–39.

————. *Tsar and People*. New Haven, Conn., 1961.

Chernov, A. V. *Gosudarstvennye uchrezhdeniia Rossii v XVIII veke*. Moscow, 1960.

Chernukha, V. G. "Pravitelstvennaia politika i institut mirovykh posrednikov." In Nosov, *Vnutrenniaia*.

Chicherin, B. *Oblastnyia uchrezhdeniia Rossii v XVII-m veke*. Moscow, 1856.

Commons, J. R. *Legal Foundations of Capitalism*. Madison, Wis., 1959.

Confino, M. *Domaines et seigneurs en Russie vers la fin du XVIII siècle*. Paris, 1963.

————. *Systèmes agraires et progrès agricole*. Paris, 1969.

Culpepper, J. M. "The Legislative Origins of Peasant Bondage in Muscovy." Unpublished Ph.D. dissertation, Columbia University, 1965.

————. "The Legislative Origins of Peasant Bondage in Muscovy." *Forschungen zur osteuropäischen Geschichte*, vol. XIV. Berlin, 1969.

Czap, Peter. "The Influence of Slavophile Ideology on the Formation of the Volost Court of 1861 and the Practice of Peasant Self-Justice between 1861 and 1889." Unpublished Ph.D. dissertation, Cornell University, 1959.

————. "P. A. Valuev's Proposal for a Vyt Administration, 1864." *Slavonic and East European Review*, XLV (July 1967), 391–410.

Czartoryski, Adam J. *Memoirs*. 2 vols. London, 1888.

Demidova, N. F. "Biurokratizatsiia gosudarstvennogo apparata absoliutizma v XVII–XVIII vv." In Druzhinin, *Absoliutizm*.

Diamond, A. S. *Primitive Law*. London, 1935.

Diatlova, N. P. "Otchety gubernatorov kak istoricheskii istochnik." In *Problemy arkhivovedeniia*.

————. "Otchety gubernatorov kak istoricheskii istochnik." Unpublished report kept in TsGIAL.

Doklad vysochaishe utverzhdennoi (26 maia 1872) komissii dlia issledovaniia nyneshnego polozheniia selskogo khoziaistva i proizvoditelnosti v Rossii: Prilozheniia. 7 vols. St. Petersburg, 1873.

Donnelly, A. *The Russian Conquest of Bashkiria: 1552–1740*. New Haven, Conn., 1968.

Druzhinin, N. M. *Gosudarstvennye krestiane i reforma P. D. Kiseleva*. 2 vols. Moscow, 1946, 1958.

————. "Prosveshchennyi absoliutizm." In Druzhinin, *Absoliutizm*.

————. "Senatorskie revizii 1860–1870-kh godov." *Istoricheskie zapiski*, LXXIX (1967), 139–175.

————, ed. *Absoliutizm v Rossii (XVII–XVIII vv.)*. Moscow, 1964.

Dubrovskii, S. M. *Stolypinskaia zemelnaia reforma*. Moscow, 1963.

Duchesne, E., tr. *Le stoglav*. Paris, 1920.

Dukes, Paul. *Catherine the Great and the Russian Nobility*. Cambridge, 1967.

Dunn, Ethel. "Educating the Small Peoples of the Soviet North: The Limits of Cultural Change." *Arctic Anthropology,* V, no. 1 (1968), 1–31.

Duran, James. "The Reform of Financial Administration in Russia during the Reign of Catherine II." *Canadian Slavic Studies,* IV (Fall 1970), 485–596.

"Dvorianstvo." In Brockhaus and Efron, X (1893), 203–218.

Dzhanshev, G. A. *Epokha velikikh reform.* St. Petersburg, 1907.

Eck, A. *Le moyen age russe.* Paris, 1933.

Eisenstadt, S. N. *The Political Systems of Empires.* Glencoe, Ill., 1963.

Elton, G. R. *Tudor Revolution in Government.* Cambridge, 1953.

Emmons, Terence. *The Russian Landed Gentry and the Peasant Emancipation of 1861.* Cambridge, 1968.

Engelgardt, A. N. *Iz derevni.* Moscow, 1937.

Erikson, Erik. *Young Man Luther.* New York, 1958.

Eroshkin, N. P. *Ocherki istorii gosudarstvennykh uchrezhdenii dorevoliutsionnoi Rossii.* Moscow, 1960.

Etnograficheskoe obozrenie. 55 vols. Moscow, 1889–1902.

Evstafev, P. P. *Vosstanie novgorodskikh voennykh poselian.* Moscow, 1934.

Ezhegodnik po agrarnoi istorii vostochnoi Evropy 1963 god. Vilna, 1964.

Ezhegodnik po agrarnoi istorii vostochnoi Evropy 1964 god. Kishinev, 1966.

Ferguson, A. D., ed. *Essays in Russian History.* Hamden, Conn., 1964.

———. "The Russian Military Settlements, 1810–1866." Unpublished Ph.D. dissertation, Yale University, 1954.

———. "Russian Military Settlements, 1825–1866." In Ferguson, *Essays.*

Fet, Afanasii. *Moi vospominaniia.* 2 vols. Moscow, 1890.

Field, Daniel. "The End of Serfdom." Unpublished Ph.D. dissertation, Harvard University, 1968.

Firsov, N. N. *Petr III i Ekaterina II.* Petrograd, 1915.

Fletcher, G. *Of the Rus Commonwealth.* Ed. A. Schmidt. Ithaca, N.Y., 1966.

Foster, George M. *Traditional Cultures and the Impact of Technological Change.* New York, 1962.

Gentile, Giovanni. *Theory of Mind as Pure Act.* London, 1922.

German, I. E. *Istoriia russkogo mezhevaniia.* 2nd ed. Moscow, 1910.

Gerschenkron, Alexander. "Agrarian Policies and Industrialization: Russia 1861–1917." In *Cambridge Economic History of Europe.*

———. "The Problem of Economic Development in Russian Intellectual History of the Nineteenth Century." In Simmons.

Gierke, Otto. *Natural Law and the Theory of Society, 1500 to 1800.* 2 vols. Cambridge, 1950.

———. *Political Theories of the Middle Ages.* 2nd ed. Cambridge, 1951.

Gindin, I. F. *Gosudarstvennyi bank i ekonomicheskaia politika tsarskogo pravitelstva (1861–1892 gody).* Moscow, 1960.

Gneist, R. *Der Rechtsstaat und die Verwaltungsgerichte in Deutschland.* Berlin, 1879.

Golitsyn, A. D. "Vospominaniia." Unpublished manuscript in the Russian Archive at Columbia University.

Golovin, K. *Moi vospominaniia.* 2 vols. St. Petersburg, 1908, 1910.

Golubinskii, E. *Istoriia russkoi tserkvi.* 2 vols. Moscow, 1880, 1900.

Goodnow, F. J. *Comparative Administrative Law.* 2 vols. New York, 1893.

Gosudarstvennaia kantseliariia: 1810–1910. St. Petersburg, 1910.

Gosudarstvennyi Sovet. *Stenograficheskii otchet.* 13 vols. St. Petersburg, 1906–1917.

Gosudarstvennyi Sovet, 1801–1901. St. Petersburg, 1901.

Gote, Iu. V. *Istoriia oblastnogo upravleniia v Rossii ot Petra I do Ekateriny II.* 2 vols. Moscow, 1913, 1941.

Gradovskii, A. D. *Sobranie sochineniia.* 9 vols. St. Petersburg, 1899–1904.

Gribowski, W. *Das Staatsrecht des russichen Reiches.* Tübingen, 1912.

Grigorev, Vladimir A. *Reforma mestnogo upravleniia pri Ekaterine II: Uchrezhdenie o guberniiakh 7 noiabria 1775.* St. Petersburg, 1910.

Gruzinskii, A. "Iz etnograficheskikh nabliudenii v Rechitskom uezde Minskoi g." *Etnograficheskoe obozrenie,* vol. XI (1891).

"Gubernskoe pravlenie." In Brockhaus and Efron, IX (1893), 844.

Guins, G. K. "Sovetskoe pravovedenie i psikhologicheskaia teoria prava L. I. Petrazhitskogo." *Vestnik Instituta po Izucheniia SSSR,* XXVII (May–Aug. 1958), 64–79.

Gurko, V. I. *Features and Figures of the Past.* Stanford, Calif., 1939.

Hägerstrom, Axel. *Inquiries into the Nature of Law and Morals.* Stockholm, 1953.

Harcave, Sidney. *First Blood.* New York, 1964.

Hassell, James. "Implementation of the Russian Table of Ranks during the Eighteenth Century." *Slavic Review,* XXIX (June 1970), 283–295.

———. "The Vicissitudes of Russian Administrative Reform, 1762–1801." Unpublished Ph.D. dissertation, Cornell University, 1967.

Hellie, Richard. "Muscovite Law and Society: The Ulozhenie of 1649 as a Reflection of the Political and Social Development of Russia since the Sudebnik of 1589." Unpublished Ph.D. dissertation, University of Chicago, 1965.

Herzen, Alexander. *My Past and Thoughts.* 6 vols. New York, 1926.

Hintze, Otto. *Staat und Verfassung.* Leipzig, 1941.

Hoebel, E. A. *The Law of Primitive Man.* Cambridge, Mass., 1954.

Hollingsworth, Barry. "A. P. Kunitsyn and the Social Movement in Russia under Alexander I." *Slavonic and East European Review,* XLIII (Dec. 1964), 115–129.

Huizinga, J. *Homo Ludens.* New York, 1950.

Huntington, Samuel. *Political Order in Changing Societies.* New Haven, Conn., 1968.

Iakushkin, E. I. *Obychnoe pravo.* 4 vols. Iaroslavl, 1875, 1896; Moscow, 1908, 1909.

———. "Zametki o vliianii religioznykh verovanii i predrassudkov na narodnye iuridicheskie obychai i poniatiia." *Etnograficheskoe obozrenie,* IX (1891), 1–19.

Iakushkin, P. I. "Velik bog zemli russkoi." In *Russkie ocherki.* 3 vols. Moscow, 1956. II, 118–195.

Iakushkin, V. *Ocherki po istorii russkoi pozemelnoi politike v XVIII i XIX v.,* vol. I. Moscow, 1890.

Ignatieff, L. "French Emigres in Russia, 1789–1825." Unpublished Ph.D. dissertation, University of Michigan, 1963.

Ignatovich, I. I. *Pomeshchich i krestiane nakanune osvobozhdeniia.* Leningrad, 1925.

Ihering, Rudolf von. *The Struggle for Law.* Chicago, 1879.

Indova, E. I. *Dvortsovoe khoziaistvo v Rossii.* Moscow, 1964.

Istoricheskii obzor deiatelnosti Komiteta Ministrov. 5 vols. St. Petersburg, 1902.

Istoricheskoe obozrenie piatidesiatiletnei deiatelnosti ministerstva gosudarstvennykh imushchestv 1837–1887. 5 vols. St. Petersburg, 1888.

"Istoricheskoe obozrenie voenno-sukhoputnogo upravleniia s 1825 po 1850 goda." *SIRIO,* vol. XCVIII (1896).

Istoriia Pravitelstvuiushchego Senata. 5 vols. St. Petersburg, 1911.

Istoriia SSSR. 2 vols. Moscow, 1954.

Ivanov, L. M., ed. *Krestianskoe dvizhenie v Rossii v 1861–1869 gg., Sbornik dokumentov.* Moscow, 1964.

Ivanov, P. I. *Opyt biografii general-prokurorov i ministrov iustitsii.* St. Petersburg, 1863.

Izvestiia kantseliarii komiteta po zemleustroitelnym delam.

Izvestiia zemskogo otdela.

Jones, Robert. "Catherine II and the Provincial Reform of 1775." *Canadian Slavic Studies,* IV (Fall 1970), 497–512.

———. "The Russian Gentry and the Provincial Reform of 1775." Unpublished Ph.D. dissertation, Cornell University, 1968.

Kafengauz, V. V., and N. I. Pavlenko, eds. *Ocherki istorii SSSR: Period feodalizma: Rossiia v pervoi chetverti XVIII v.* Moscow, 1954.

Kahan, Arcadius. "The Costs of Westernization in Russia." *Slavic Review,* XXV (Mar. 1966), 40–66.

Kankrin, E. E. "Kratkoe obozrenie rossiiskikh finansov." *SIRIO,* vol. XXXI (1880).

Kantorowicz, E. *The King's Two Bodies.* Princeton, N.J., 1957.

Kaplan, Herbert. *Russia and the Outbreak of the Seven-Years War.* Berkeley, Calif., 1968.

Kataev, M. M. *Mestnyia krestianskiia uchrezhdeniia, 1861, 1874, i 1889 gg.* 3 pts. St. Petersburg, 1911.

Katz, M. *Mikhail N. Katkov.* The Hague, 1970.

Kaufman, A. A. *Pereselenie i kolonizatsiia.* St. Petersburg, 1905.

Kavelin, K. D. *Krestianskii vopros.* St. Petersburg, 1882.

———. *Sobranie sochinenii.* 4 vols. St. Petersburg, 1897–1900.

Kazimirov, N. *Krestianskie platezhi i zemskaia deiatelnost v moskovskoi gubernii.* Moscow, 1906.

Keenan, Edward L. "Muscovy and Kazan, 1445–1552: A Study in Steppe Politics." Unpublished Ph.D. dissertation, Harvard University, 1965.

Kennan, G. "The Breakdown of Tsarist Autocracy." In Pipes, *Revolutionary Russia.*

Kingsley, J. D. "Bureaucracy and Political Development with Particular Reference to Nigeria." In LaPalombara.

Kissel-Zagorianskii. "Les mémoires du General Kissel-Zagorianskii." Unpublished manuscript, in Russian, in the Russian Archive at Columbia University.

Kistiakovskii, B. A. *Sotsialnyia nauki i pravo.* Moscow, 1916.

Kliuchevsky, V. O. *History of Russia.* 5 vols. New York, 1960.

———. *Peter the First.* New York, 1961.

Klochkov, M. V. *Ocherki pravitelstvennoi deiatelnosti vremeni Pavla I.* Petrograd, 1916.

"Knigi pistsovyia i perepisnyia." In Brockhaus and Efron, XV (1895), 457–459.

Kofod, A. A. *Russkoe zemleustroistvo.* 2nd ed. St. Petersburg, 1914.

Koretskii, V. I. "Krestianskaia kolonizatsiia i osobennosti protsessa zakreposhcheniia na iuge Rossii v kontse XVI v." In *Ezhegodnik . . . 1964.*

Korf, Sergei A. *Dvorianstvo i ego soslovnoe upravlenie za stoletie 1762–1855 godov.* St. Petersburg, 1906.

Korkunov, N. M. *General Theory of Law.* Boston, 1909.

———. *Istoriia filosofii prava.* 4th ed. St. Petersburg, 1908.

———. "O nauchnom izuchenii prava." In Korkunov, *Sbornik statei.*

———. *Russkoe gosudarstvennoe pravo.* 6th ed. 2 vols. St. Petersburg, 1908, 1909.

———. *Sbornik statei N. M. Korkunova.* St. Petersburg, 1898.

———. *Ukaz i zakon.* St. Petersburg, 1894.

———. "Z. A. Goriushkin, rossiiskii zakonoiskusnik." *Zhurnal ministerstva iustitsii,* I (May 1895), 97–142.

———. "Znachenie svoda zakonov." In Korkunov, *Sbornik statei.*

Kornilov, A. A. *Obshchestvennoe dvizhenie pri Aleksandre II.* Moscow, 1909.

———. *Ocherki po istorii obshchestvennogo dvizheniia i krestianskogo dela v Rossii.* St. Petersburg, 1905.

Koshelev, A. I. "Zapiska." In *Otmena . . . na Ukraine.*

Kovalchenko, I. D. "O tovarnosti zemledeliia v Rossii v pervoi polovine XIX v." In *Ezhegodnik . . . 1963.*

Krasnyi Arkhiv. 106 vols. 1922–1941.

Krieger, L. *The Politics of Discretion.* Chicago, 1965.

Kropotov, D. A. *Zhizn Grafa M. N. Muraveva.* St. Petersburg, 1874.

Kulikovskii, G. I. "Arteli obonezhia." *Etnograficheskoe obozrenie,* XIII (1892), 203–209.

Kushner, P. I., ed. *The Village of Viriatino.* Tr. Sula Benet. New York, 1970.

LaPalombara, J. G., ed. *Bureaucracy and Political Development*. Princeton, N.J., 1963.

Lappo-Danilevskii, A. *Organizatsiia priamogo oblozheniia v moskovskom gosudarstve so vremen smuty do epokhi preobrazovanii*. St. Petersburg, 1890.

Latkin, V. N. *Zakonodatelnye komissii v Rossii v XVIII v*. St. Petersburg, 1887–.

Lazarevskii, N. I. *Lektsii po russkomu gosudarstvennomu pravu*. 2nd ed. 2 vols. St. Petersburg, 1910.

LeDonne, J. "The Provincial and Local Police under Catherine the Great, 1775–1796." *Canadian Slavic Studies*, IV (Fall 1970), 513–528.

Leontev, A. *Krestianskoe pravo*. St. Petersburg, 1908.

———. *Krestianskoe pravo*. 2nd ed. St. Petersburg, 1914.

———. "Volostnoi sud i obychnoe pravo." *Zhurnal iuridicheskogo obshchestva pri S-Peterburgskogo Universiteta*, XXIV (Nov. 1894), 26–55.

Leontovitsch, V. *Geschichte des Liberalismus in Russland*. Frankfurt am Main, 1957.

Leroy-Beaulieu, Anatole. *Un homme d'état russe*. Paris, 1884.

Leslie, R. F. *Reform and Insurrection in Russian Poland, 1856–1865*. London, 1963.

Levenson, J. R. "History and Value: The Tensions of Intellectual Choice in Modern China." In A. F. Wright, ed., *Studies in Chinese Thought*. Chicago, 1953.

Levshin, A. I. "Dostopamiatnyia minuty v moei zhizni." *Russkii Arkhiv* (1885), kn. 8, pp. 475–557.

Lincoln, W. B. "Nikolai Alekseevich Milyutin and Problems of State Reform in Nicholaevan Russia." Unpublished Ph.D. dissertation, University of Chicago, 1966.

Litvak, B. G. "Dvizhenie pomeshchichikh krestian v velikorusskikh guberniiakh v 1855–1863 gg." In *Ezhegodnik . . . 1964*.

———. "Ob izmeneniiakh zemelnogo nadelia pomeshchichikh krestian v pervoi polovine XIX v." In *Ezhegodnik . . . 1963*.

Liubavskii, M. K. *Lektsii po drevnei russkoi istorii do kontsa XVI veka*. Moscow, 1918.

Liubimov, D. N. "Russkaia smuta, nachala deviatisotykh godov, 1902–1906." Unpublished manuscript in the Russian Archive at Columbia University.

Long, James. "The Economics of the Franco-Russian Alliance, 1904–1906." Unpublished Ph.D. dissertation, University of Wisconsin, 1968.

MacIntyre, D. J. "Constantine Dmitrievich Kavelin." Unpublished Ph.D. dissertation, State University of Iowa, 1966.

McNeill, W. H. *Europe's Steppe Frontier: 1500–1800*. Chicago, 1964.

Maine, Henry. *Ancient Law*. London, 1861.

Maitland, Frederick W. *The Constitutional History of England*. Cambridge, 1963.

———. *Township and Borough*. Cambridge, 1898.

Mamulova, L. G. "Zemskaia kontrreforma 1890 g." *Nauchnye doklady vysshei shkoly: Istoricheskie nauki*, no. 4 (1960), pp. 60–85.

Mandelbaum, Seymour. *Boss Tweed's New York.* New York, 1965.

Mannoni, O. *Prospero and Caliban.* New York, 1964.

Markina, V. A. *Magnatskoe pomeste pravoberezhnoi ukrainy vtoroi poloviny XVIII v.* Kiev, 1961.

Materialy dlia istorii krepostnogo prava v Rossii. Berlin, 1872.

"Materialy i cherti k biografii Imperatora Nikolaia I i k istorii ego tsarstvovaniia." *SIRIO*, vol. XCVIII (1896).

Materialy po istorii selskogo khoziaistva i krestianstva SSSR, vol. III. Moscow, 1959.

Matskina, R. Iu. "Ministerskie otchety i ikh osobennosti kak istoricheskogo istochnika [*sic*]." In *Problemy arkhivovedeniia.*

Matthews, G. T. *The Royal General Farms in Eighteenth-Century France.* New York, 1958.

Meinecke, Friedrich. *Cosmopolitanism and the National State.* Princeton, N.J., 1970.

———. *Die Idee der Staatsräson.* Munich, 1957.

Mendeleev, P. P. Untitled notebooks in the Russian Archive at Columbia University.

Meshcherskii, Vladimir P. *Moi vospominaniia.* 3 vols. St. Petersburg, 1897–1912.

Meyendorf, A. "A Brief Appreciation of P. Stolypin's Tenure of Office." Unpublished manuscript in the Russian Archive at Columbia University.

Miliutin, Dmitri A. *Dnevnik D. A. Miliutina.* 4 vols. Moscow, 1947–1950.

Miller, F. "Dmitri Miliutin and the Reform Era in Russia, 1861–1881." Unpublished Ph.D. dissertation, University of California, 1963.

Milov, L. V. *Issledovanie ob "ekonomicheskikh primechaniiakh" k generalnomu mezhevaniiu.* Moscow, 1965.

Minarik, L. P. "Kharakteristika krupneishikh zemlevladeltsev Rossii kontsa XIX i nachala XX v." In *Ezhegodnik . . . 1963.*

Ministerstvo finansov, 1802–1902. 2 vols. St. Petersburg, 1902.

Ministerstvo iustitsii za sto let: 1802–1902. St. Petersburg, 1902.

Ministerstvo vnutrennikh del: 1802–1902. St. Petersburg, 1902.

"Mirovoi posrednik." In Brockhaus and Efron, XIX (1896), 423–425.

Monas, S. *The Third Section.* Cambridge, Mass., 1961.

Morrison, Kerry. "Catherine II's Legislative Commission: An Administrative Interpretation." *Canadian Slavic Studies*, IV (Fall 1970), 464–484.

Muncy, L. W. *The Junker in the Prussian Administration under William II: 1888–1914.* Providence, R.I., 1944.

Muravev, N. V. *Prokurorskii nadzor v ego ustroistve i deiatelnosti.* Moscow, 1889.

Nakaz zemskim nachalnikam. St. Petersburg, 1905.

Naumov, A. N. *Iz utselevshikh vospominanii, 1868–1917.* 2 vols. New York, 1954.

Neurozhai i narodnoe bedstvie. St. Petersburg, 1892.

Nifontov, A., *et al.*, eds. *Krestianskoe dvizhenie v Rossii v 1881–1889, Sbornik dokumentov.* Moscow, 1960.

Nikolai Mikhailovich. *Le Comte Paul Stroganov.* 3 vols. Paris, 1905.

Nolde, Boris E. *Iurii Samarin i ego vremia.* Paris, 1926.

Nosov, N. E. *Ocherki po istorii mestnogo upravleniia russkogo gosudarstva pervoi poloviny XVI veka.* Moscow, 1957.

———— *et al.*, eds. *Vnutrenniaia politika tsarizma.* Leningrad, 1967.

"Novoe zemskoe polozhenie." *Iuridicheskaia letopis,* I (Oct. 1890), 299–344.

"Obozrenie prezhnego i nyneshnego sostoianiia ministerstva inostrannykh del." *SIRIO,* vol. XXXI (1880).

Obukhov, B. *Russkii administrator noveishei shkoly.* Berlin, 1868.

Okun, S. B., ed. *Krestianskoe dvizhenie v Rossii v 1857-mae 1861 gg.* Moscow, 1963.

Otchet po deloproizvodstvu Gosudarstvennogo Soveta. St. Petersburg, 1893–1906.

Otmena krepostnogo prava na Ukraine, Sbornik dokumentov i materialov. Kiev, 1961.

Padenie tsarskogo rezhima. 7 vols. Leningrad, 1924.

Paina, E. S. "Senatorskie revizii i ikh arkhivnye materialy (XIX-nachalo XX vv.)." In *Nekotorye izucheniia istoricheskikh dokumentov XIX-nachala XX veka.* Leningrad, 1967.

Pamiatniki russkogo prava. 8 vols. Moscow, 1952–1961.

Pavlenko, N. I. "Idei absoliutizma v zakondatelstve XVIII v." In Druzhinin, *Absoliutizm.*

Pavlova-Silvanskaia, M. P. "Sotsialnaia sushchnost oblastnoi reformy Ekateriny II." In Druzhinin, *Absoliutizm.*

Pazukhin, A. *Sovremennoe sostoianie Rossii i soslovnyi vopros.* Moscow, 1886.

Peretts, Egor A. *Dnevnik E. A. Perettsa.* Moscow, 1927.

Pershin, P. N. *Zemelnoe ustroistvo dorevoliutsionnoi derevni.* Moscow, 1928.

Pertsov, E. P. "Zapiski sovremennika o 1861 g." *Krasnyi Arkhiv,* XVI (1926), 126–151.

(Pervoe) polnoe sobranie zakonov Rossiiskoi Imperii. 46 vols. St. Petersburg, 1830–1839.

Pestrzhetskii, D. *O prepodavanii uzakonenii o krestianakh.* St. Petersburg, 1905.

Petrazhitskii, Lev. *Law and Morality.* Tr. Hugh W. Babb. Cambridge, Mass., 1955.

Pintner, Walter M. *Russian Economic Policy under Nicholas I.* Ithaca, N.Y., 1967.

Pipes, Richard, ed. *Karamzin's Memoir on Ancient and Modern Russia.* Cambridge, Mass., 1959.

————. *Revolutionary Russia.* Cambridge, Mass., 1968.

Plato. *Gorgias.* Tr. W. C. Helmbold. New York, 1952.

————. *Protagoras*. Tr. B. Jowett. New York, 1956.

Pobedonostsev, Konstantin. *Pisma i zapiski*. 2 vols. Moscow, 1923.

————. *Reflections of a Russian Statesman*. London, 1898.

Polanyi, Karl. *The Great Transformation*. Boston, 1957.

Polenov, D. V. "Zakonodatelnaia komissiia pri Petre II, 1728 g." *SIRIO*, vol. II (1868).

Poliakoff, I. J. *Die bäuerlichen Loskaufszahlungen in Russland mit besonderer Berücksichtigung ihrer Bedeutung innerhalb des russischen Reichsbudgets*. Munich, 1916.

Polianskii, N. N. *Tsarskie voennye sudy v borbe s revoliutsiei 1905–1907 gg.* Moscow, 1958.

"Politsiia." In Brockhaus and Efron, XXIV (1898), 320–339.

Pollard, Alan. "Consciousness and Crisis: The Self-Image of the Russian Intelligentsia, 1855–1882." Unpublished Ph.D. dissertation, University of California, 1968.

Polner, T. I. *Zhiznennyi put Kniazia Georgiia Evgenievicha Lvova*. Paris, 1932.

Polovtsov, Alexander A. *Dnevnik A. A. Polovtsova*. 2 vols. Moscow, 1966.

————. "Dnevnik A. A. Polovtseva [*sic*]." *Krasnyi Arkhiv*, IV (1923), XLVI (1931), LXVII (1934).

Portal, Roger, ed. *Le statut des paysans libérés du servage: 1861–1961*. Paris, 1963.

Poulsen, T. M. "The Provinces of Russia." Unpublished Ph.D. dissertation, University of Wisconsin, 1963.

Predtechenskii, A. V. *Ocherki obshchestvenno-politicheskoi istorii Rossii v pervoi chetverti XIX v.* Moscow, 1957.

Presniakov, A. E. *Apogei samoderzhavii*. Leningrad, 1925.

————. *The Formation of the Great Russian State*. Chicago, 1970.

Pritchard, J. B. *Ancient Near Eastern Texts*. Princeton, N.J., 1950.

Problemy arkhivovedeniia i istochnikovedeniia. Leningrad, 1964.

Prugavin, V. S. *Russkaia zemelnaia obshchina v trudakh ee mestnykh issledovatelei*. Moscow, 1888.

Raeff, Marc. "Home, School, and Service in the Life of the 18th-Century Russian Nobleman." *Slavonic and East European Review*, XL (June 1962), 295–307.

————. *Michael Speransky, Statesman of Imperial Russia*. The Hague, 1957.

————. *Origins of the Russian Intelligentsia: The Eighteenth-Century Nobility*. New York, 1966.

————. *Plans for Political Reform in Imperial Russia, 1730–1905*. Englewood Cliffs, N.J., 1966.

Rauch, G. *Russland*. Munich, 1953.

Redlich, J. *The Common Law and the Case Method in American University Law Schools*. 1914.

"Rekrutskaia povinnost." In Brockhaus and Efron, XXIV (1899), 530–532.

Repczuk, H. "Nicholas Mordvinov (1754–1845): Russia's Would-Be Reformer." Unpublished Ph.D. dissertation, Columbia University, 1962.

Rieber, A. *Politics of Autocracy.* Paris, 1966.

Rockhill, W., ed. *The Journey of William Rubruck to the Eastern Parts of the World 1253–1255, as Narrated by Himself, with Two Accounts of the Earlier Journey of John of Pian de Carpine.* London, 1900.

Rogger, Hans. *National Consciousness in Eighteenth-Century Russia.* Cambridge, Mass., 1960.

Romanovich-Slavatinskii, A. *Dvorianstvo v Rossii.* St. Petersburg, 1870.

Rossovsky, H. "The Serf Entrepreneur in Russia." In Aitken, *Explorations in Enterprise.*

Roublev, Michel. "The Periodicity of the Mongol Tribute as Paid by the Russian Princes during the Fourteenth and Fifteenth Centuries." *Forschungen zur osteuropäischen Geschichte,* vol. XV. Berlin, 1970.

Russkii biograficheskii slovar. 25 vols. St. Petersburg, 1896–1913.

Sandars, T. C., tr. *The Institutes of Justinian.* 7th ed. London, 1952.

Santoni, Wayne S. "P. N. Durnovo as Minister of Internal Affairs in the Witte Cabinet: A Study in Suppression." Unpublished Ph.D. dissertation, University of Kansas, 1968.

Sazonov, G. B. *Obzor deiatelnosti zemstv po selskomu khoziastvu, 1865–1895 g.* 4 vols. St. Petersburg, 1896.

Sbornik imperatorskogo russkogo istoricheskogo obshchestva. 148 vols. St. Petersburg, 1867–1916.

Sbornik uzakonenii o krestianskikh i sudebnykh uchrezhdeniiakh preobrazovannykh po zakonu 12-go iiuliia 1889 goda. St. Petersburg, 1895.

Sbornik zakliuchenii gubernskikh soveshchanii po proektu nakaza zemskim nachalnikam. 2 pts. St. Petersburg, 1899.

Schiemann, T. *Geschichte Russlands unter Kaiser Nikolaus I.* 4 vols. Berlin, 1908.

Schiff, W. "Die Agrargesetzgebung der europäischen Staaten vor und nach dem Kriege." *Archiv für Sozialwissenschaft und Sozialpolitik,* vol. LIV (1925).

Schmidt, W. *Lorenz von Stein.* Eckernförde, 1956.

Schurmann, H. F. "Mongolian Tributary Practices of the Thirteenth Century." *Harvard Journal of Asiatic Studies,* XIX (Dec. 1956), 304–389.

Seckendorf, Veit Ludwig von. *Teutscher Fürsten-Staat, samt des selben Herrn Autoris Zugabe sonderbarer und wichtiger Materien.* Jena, 1737.

Semevskii, V. I. *Krestiane v tsarstvovanie Imperatritsy Ekateriny II.* 2nd ed. 2 vols. St. Petersburg, 1903.

———. *Krestianskii vopros v Rossii v XVIII i pervoi polovine XIX veka.* 2 vols. St. Petersburg, 1888.

Serbina, K. N. *Ocherki iz sotsialno-ekonomicheskoi istorii russkogo goroda.* Moscow, 1951.

Sergeevich, V. I. *Lektsii i issledovaniia po drevnei istorii russkogo prava.* 4th ed. St. Petersburg, 1910.

Shcheglov, V. G. *Gosudarstvennyi Sovet v Rossii.* Iaroslavl, 1903.

Shelgunov, N. V. *Vospominaniia.* Moscow, 1923.

Shidlovskii, S. I. _Obshchii obzor trudov mestnykh komitetov._ St. Petersburg, 1905.

Shilder, N. K. _Imperator Aleksandr Pervyi._ 4 vols. St. Petersburg, 1897–1898.

———. _Imperator Nikolai Pervyi._ 2 vols. St. Petersburg, 1903.

Shingarev, A. I. _Vymiraiushchaia derevnia._ 2nd ed. St. Petersburg, 1907.

Shipov, Dmitri N. _Vospominaniia i dumy o perezhitom._ Moscow, 1918.

Shlippe, F. V. "Memoirs." Unpublished manuscript, in Russian, in the Russian Archive at Columbia University.

Shmidt, S. O. "Mestnichestvo i absoliutizm." In Druzhinin, _Absoliutizm._

Shuvaev, K. M. _Staraia i novaia derevnia._ Moscow, 1937.

Simmonds, G. "The Congress of Representatives of the Nobles' Association, 1906–1916." Unpublished Ph.D. dissertation, Columbia University, 1964.

Simmons, Edward, ed. _Continuity and Change in Russian and Soviet Thought._ Cambridge, Mass., 1955.

Sinel, A. "Educating the Russian Peasantry." _Slavic Review,_ XXVII (Mar. 1968), 49–70.

Sinton, John. "The Instructions from Kazan Gubernia at the Legislative Commission of 1767." Unpublished Ph.D. dissertation, University of Indiana, 1968.

Sirinov, M. A. _Zemskie nalogi._ Iurev, 1915.

Skerpan, A. A. "The Russian National Economy and the Emancipation." In Ferguson, _Essays._

Slany, W. "Russian Central Government Institutions: 1725–1741." Unpublished Ph.D. dissertation, Cornell University, 1958.

Small, A. W. _The Cameralists._ Chicago, 1909.

Smith, R. E. F. _The Origins of Farming in Russia._ Paris, 1959.

Solovev, Iu. B. "Pravitelstvo i politika ukrepleniia klassovykh positsii dvorianstva v kontse XIX veka." In Nosov, _Vnutrenniaia._

Solovev, S. M. _Istoriia Rossii._ 15 vols. Moscow, 1960–1966.

Sommer, Louise. "Cameralism." In _Encyclopedia of the Social Sciences._ 15 vols. New York, 1963. III, 159.

Speranskii, Mikhail. _Proekty i zapiski._ Moscow, 1961.

Sprout, Harold. _The Ecological Perspective on Human Affairs._ Princeton, N.J., 1965.

Squire, P. S. _The Third Department._ Cambridge, 1968.

Starr, S. F. "Decentralization and Self-Government in Russia, 1855–1865." Unpublished Ph.D. dissertation, Princeton University, 1968.

Statesman's Handbook for Russia. 2 vols. St. Petersburg, 1896.

Stein, Lorenz von. _Gegenwart und Zukunft der Rechts und Staatswissenschaft Deutschlands._ Stuttgart, 1876.

———. _Handbuch der Verwaltungslehre._ 2nd ed. Stuttgart, 1876.

Stepniak, S. (Kravchinskii, S. M.) _The Russian Peasant._ New York, 1888.

Stroev, V. N. _Stoletie Sobstvennoi Ego Imperatorskogo Velichestva Kantseliarii._ St. Petersburg, 1912.

Svod otzyvov gubernskikh prisutstvii po krestianskim delam i zakliuchenii *gubernatorov po proektu preobrazovaniia podushnoi sistemy sborov so-stavlennomu v ministerstve finansov.* 2 vols. St. Petersburg, 1873.

Svod vysochaishikh otmetok po vsepoddanneishim otchetam za 1895–1901. 7 vols. St. Petersburg, 1897–1904.

Svod zakonov Rossiiskoi Imperii. 16 vols. St. Petersburg, 1892.

Szeftel, M. "The Form of Government of the Russian Empire prior to the Constitutional Reforms of 1905–1906." In J. S. Curtiss, ed., *Essays in Russian and Soviet History.* New York, 1963.

———. "The Legislative Reform of August 6, 1905." In A. Marongiu, ed., *Mélanges: Études présentées à la Commission Internationale pour l'Histoire des Assemblées d'États.* Palermo, 1967.

———. "Nicholas II's Constitutional Decisions of October 17–19, 1905 and Sergius Witte's Role." In *Album J. Balon.* Namur, Belgium, 1968.

Telberg, G. *Pravitelstvuiushchii Senat i samoderzhavnaia vlast v nachale XIX veka.* Moscow, 1914.

Tenishev, V. V. *Administrativnoe polozhenie russkogo krestianina.* St. Petersburg, 1908.

———. *Pravosudie v russkom krestianskom byte.* Briansk, 1907.

Thaden, Edward. *Conservative Nationalism in Nineteenth-Century Russia.* Seattle, 1964.

Timberlake, Charles. "The Birth of Zemstvo Liberalism in Russia." Unpublished Ph.D. dissertation, University of Washington, 1968.

Tolstoi, Dmitrii N. "Zapiska Grafa Dmitrii Nikolaevicha Tolstogo." *Russkii Arkhiv,* no. 5 (1885).

Torke, H. *Das russische Beamtentum in der ersten Hälfte des 19 Jahrhunderts. Forschungen zur osteuropäischen Geschichte,* vol. XIII. Berlin, 1967.

Tourgueneff (Turgenev), Nicholas. *La russie et les russes.* 3 vols. Paris, 1847.

(Trete) polnoe sobranie zakonov Rossiiskoi Imperii. 33 vols. St. Petersburg, 1885–1916.

Troitskii, S. M. *Finansovaia politika russkogo absoliutizma v XVIII veke.* Moscow, 1966.

Troshchinskii, D. P. "Zapiska ob uchrezhdenii ministerstv." *SIRIO,* vol. III (1868).

Troyat, Henry. *Tolstoy.* New York, 1967.

Trudy komissii po preobrazovaniiu volostnykh sudov. 7 vols. St. Petersburg, 1873.

Trudy redaktsionnoi komissii po peresmotru zakonopolozhenii o krestianakh. 2 vols. St. Petersburg, 1903.

Trutovskii, V. *Sovremennoe zemstvo.* Petrograd, 1914.

Tsentralnyi gosudarstvennyi istoricheskii Arkhiv Leningrada. Fond 1149, Archive of the State Council; fond 1317, Archive of the Kakhanov Commission.

Tyme, Ronald. *The Roman Revolution.* London, 1960.

"Uezd." In Brockhaus and Efron, XXXV (1902), 134–136.

Ulam, Adam. *The Unfinished Revolution.* New York, 1960.

Ullmann, Walter. *The Growth of Papal Government in the Middle Ages.* 2nd ed. New York, 1962.

Urussov, S. D. *Memoirs of a Russian Governor.* London, 1908.

Valuev, Pavel A. *Dnevnik P. A. Valueva.* 2 vols. Moscow, 1961.

————. *Obiasnitelnaia zapiska k proektam polozheniia o zemskikh uchrezhdeniiakh i vremennykh pravil dlia ikh uchrezhdenii.* St. Petersburg, 186–.

Venturi, F. *Roots of Revolution.* New York, 1966.

Veretennikov, V. I. *Ocherki istorii general-prokurory v Rossii do ekaterinskogo vremeni.* Kharkov, 1915.

Veselovskii, B. *Istoriia zemstva za sorok let.* 4 vols. St. Petersburg, 1909–1911.

Veselovskii, S. B. *Soshnoe pismo.* 2 vols. Moscow, 1915, 1916.

Viazemskii, A. I. *Arkhiv Kniazia Viazemskogo.* St. Petersburg, 1881.

"Voennyi gubernator." In Brockhaus and Efron, VI (1892), 859–860.

Von Laue, Theodore. *Sergei Witte and the Industrialization of Russia.* New York, 1963.

Vovchik, A. F. *Politika tsarizma po rabochemu voprosu v predrevoliutsionnyi period.* Lvov, 1964.

(*Vtoroe*) *polnoe sobranie zakonov Rossiiskoi Imperii.* 55 vols. St. Petersburg, 1830–1884.

Vucinich, Wayne, ed. *The Peasant in Nineteenth-Century Russia.* Stanford, Calif., 1968.

"Vziatochnichestvo." In Brockhaus and Efron, VI (1892), 213–216.

Weber, Max. *The City.* Glencoe, Ill., 1958.

————. *Max Weber on Law in Economy and Society.* Cambridge, Mass., 1954.

————. *Theory of Social and Economic Organization.* New York, 1947.

————. "Zur Lage der bürgerlichen Demokratie in Russland." *Archiv für Sozialwissenschaft und Sozialpolitik,* vol. XXII (1906).

Witte, Sergei Iu. *Samoderzhavie i zemstvo.* Stuttgart, 1903.

————. *Vospominaniia.* 3 vols. Moscow, 1960.

Wittram, Reinhard. *Peter I, Czar und Kaiser.* 2 vols. Göttingen, 1964.

Woll, P. *Administrative Law.* Berkeley, Calif., 1963.

Wortman, R. *The Crisis of Russian Populism.* Cambridge, 1967.

Yaney, George L. "Agricultural Administration in Russia from the Stolypin Land Reform to Forced Collectivization: An Interpretive Study." In James Millar, ed., *The Soviet Rural Community.* Urbana, Ill., 1971.

————. "Bureaucracy and Freedom: N. M. Korkunov's Theory of the State." *American Historical Review,* LXXI (Jan. 1966), 468–486.

————. "Concept of the Stolypin Land Reform." *Slavic Review,* XXIII (June 1964), 275–293.

————. "The Imperial Russian Government and the Stolypin Land Reform." Unpublished Ph.D. dissertation, Princeton University, 1961.

————. "Law, Society, and the Domestic Regime in Russia in Historical

Perspective." *American Political Science Review,* LIX (June 1965), 379–390.

———. "Some Aspects of the Imperial Russian Government on the Eve of the First World War." *Slavonic and East European Review,* XLIII (Dec. 1964), 68–90.

———. "War and the Evolution of Russian Government." *South Atlantic Quarterly,* LXVI (Summer 1967), 291–306.

Zaionchkovskii, P. A. *Krizis samoderzhaviia na rubezhe 1870–1880-kh godov.* Moscow, 1964.

———. *Otmena krepostnogo prava v Rossii.* 3rd ed. Moscow, 1968.

———. *Provedenie v zhizn krestianskoi reformy 1861 g.* Moscow, 1958.

———. *Rossiiskoe samoderzhavie v kontse XIX stoletiia.* Moscow, 1970.

———. "Zakon o zemskikh nachalnikakh 12 iiuliia 1889 goda." *Nauchnye doklady vysshei shkoly,* no. 2 (1961).

Zaitsev, K. I. *Istoricheskoe mesto ukaza o volnosti dvorianstva.* Harbin, 1938.

Zapiska ot MVD k chlenam glavnogo komiteta ob ustroistve selskogo sostoianiia (27 Mar. 1873).

Zelnik, R. "The Peasant and the Factory." In Vucinich.

Zenkovsky, Serge. "The Russian Church Schism." *Russian Review,* XVI (1957), 37–58.

Zenkovsky, V. V. *A History of Russian Philosophy.* 2 vols. London, 1953.

Zimin, A. A. *I. S. Peresvetov i ego sovremenniki.* Moscow, 1958.

———. "O politicheskikh predposylkakh vozniknoveniia russkogo absoliutizma." In Druzhinin, *Absoliutizm.*

Zyzniewski, S. J. "Miljutin and the Polish Question." In H. McLean *et al.,* eds., *Harvard Slavic Studies,* vol. IV. The Hague, 1957.

Index